THE
DRAMATIC FESTIVALS
OF ATHENS

THE DRAMATIC FESTIVALS OF ATHENS

BY THE LATE

Sir Arthur Pickard-Cambridge

SECOND EDITION

REVISED BY JOHN GOULD

AND D. M. LEWIS

CLARENDON PRESS · OXFORD

OXFORD
UNIVERSITY PRESS

Great Clarendon Street, Oxford OX2 6DP

Oxford University Press is a department of the University of Oxford
It furthers the University's objective of excellence in research, scholarship,
and education by publishing worldwide in

Oxford New York

Athens Auckland Bangkok Bogotá Buenos Aires Calcutta
Cape Town Chennai Dar es Salaam Delhi Florence Hong Kong Istanbul
Karachi Kuala Lumpur Madrid Melbourne Mexico City Mumbai
Nairobi Paris São Paulo Singapore Taipei Tokyo Toronto Warsaw

and associated companies in Berlin Ibadan

Oxford is a registered trade mark of Oxford University Press
in the UK and in certain other countries

Published in the United States
by Oxford University Press Inc., New York

© Oxford University Press 1968

The moral rights of the author have been asserted
Database right Oxford University Press (maker)

Reprinted 1999

ISBN 0–19–814258–7

Printed in Great Britain
on acid-free paper by
Biddles Short Run Books
King's Lynn

NOTE

SIR ARTHUR PICKARD-CAMBRIDGE wrote to me on 27 December 1951 and asked me to see his work through the press. The preface stands as he wrote it, but pencil notes show that he would have also referred to the deaths of Edward Capps and Adolf Wilhelm and the publication of Professor W. Beare's *Roman Stage*. When he handed over to me, he had read and partially corrected the proofs of the first hundred pages and had started the index. He asked me particularly not to make 'corrections which had nothing but mere consistency to recommend them', and I have therefore made no attempt to rationalize the spelling of Greek names. Before his death on 7 February 1952 I was able to obtain his consent to various minor alterations in which I thought that the evidence could be more clearly stated, and I have added to notes and bibliography several works on which he had given me pencilled slips indicating that he proposed to refer to them. I have not availed myself of his generous suggestion that I should introduce notes or an appendix where I differed from him, because he has quoted my articles in his bibliography; I have added two which he had seen in proof, and I have discussed further some of the monuments for comedy in my *Studies in Later Greek Comedy*. For some of the illustrations he had given instructions that the 'indecencies' should be 'obliterated' and I have marked these with an asterisk in the list of illustrations and on the plates. The manuscript has now been deposited with the Clarendon Press. I am grateful to Mrs. D. J. Furley for help with the index. The compositors have had a difficult task in setting up the manuscript and the readers have saved many errors; to them above all belongs the credit of making this book, even if it lacks the author's final hand, a worthy memorial of a great scholar.

T. B. L. WEBSTER

PREFACE TO SECOND EDITION

SIR ARTHUR PICKARD-CAMBRIDGE died on 7 February 1952 while this book was in the press, and Professor T. B. L. Webster saw the work through to publication. Public demand for it was lively, and it has been out of print for some years. The Delegates to the Press asked us to prepare a second edition, and we gladly agreed. Our progress has been slower than we should have wished, but we have at any rate learnt a great deal in the process. The manuscript was essentially completed in the late summer of 1964 and we have been able to take only scattered notice of work that has appeared since then.

The subjects covered have been actively studied since 1952, but we have essentially retained the author's choice of topics and the greater part of his text and arrangement. Throughout, we have considered it more important to be faithful to his aim of setting out the primary evidence and keeping as closely as possible to it than to retain his views on particular matters at all costs. Excellent general treatments are now plentiful. This book will, we hope, continue to fulfil its function of presenting the evidence, and we offer no apology for the continued prominence of Greek text.

Our detailed editorial interventions are, we think, too numerous for constant indication of them by square brackets to be other than unsightly and disconcerting: it may therefore be helpful if we indicate here the main places where we have, in important respects, changed the views or the arrangement, as well as additions to the text. In Chapter I there is a new section on dithyramb at the Anthesteria (pp. 16 f.); the discussions of the Dionysion ἐν Λίμναις (pp. 21 ff.) and of the Lenaion (pp. 37 f.) have been modified; the treatment of the 'Lenäenvasen' (pp. 30 ff.) has been substantially altered, and a new section on the so-called 'Lenaian theatre' added (pp. 39 f.); the section on the Rural Dionysia (pp. 42 ff.) has been rearranged, and a short section added on drama at the Panathenaia (p. 56). In Chapter II we have taken different views from the author on the date and programme of the City Dionysia (pp. 63 ff.), the history of its dithyrambic contests (pp. 74 ff.), and the numbers of comic poets competing (p. 83); we have added a paragraph on the politics of choregoi (p. 90), and have revised the texts in the Appendix to Chapter II from squeezes and photographs, and amplified the notes on them. In Chapter III the treatments of the words ὑποκριτής (pp. 126 f.) and τριταγωνιστής (pp. 133 ff.) have been modified, the section on the distribution of parts (pp. 138 ff., 149 ff.) has been largely reworked; in the section on delivery (pp. 158 ff.) rather more attention has been given to the dramatic significance of changes of metre; the treatment of gesture and emotion in acting has been changed in emphasis (pp. 171 ff.). Chapter IV has been largely rewritten and the selection of illustrations to it substantially changed: teaching experience seemed to show that the large number of plates given in the first edition to South Italian vases and to Hellenistic and Roman evidence tended to neutralize the author's justified caution in his text about their relevance to the classical stage. Fresh discoveries and recent work have enabled us to do rather more about throwing the emphasis of both text and plates where it belongs. In Chapter V the late dating of Aeschylus' *Supplices* of course modifies something in the history of the chorus (pp. 232 f.), and we have restated the evidence for its numbers (pp. 234 ff.); we have changed the treatment of the parodos (pp. 242 ff.), and of the term ὑπόρχημα (pp. 255 f.), and have made a number of alterations in the account of music (pp. 257 ff.). In Chapter VI we have separated discussion of the presence of boys and women in the audience (pp. 263 ff.), rewritten the account of theoric payments (pp. 266 ff.), shortened the description of the seats in the Theatre of Dionysus (pp. 269 f.), rewritten the discussion of theatre tickets (pp. 270 ff.), and substantially changed the account of theatrical taste (pp. 274 ff.). Chapter VII has been considerably rewritten and rearranged, and the Appendix to it much expanded. An Additional Note (pp. 322 f.) prints part of an anonymous Byzantine treatment of aspects of the history of tragedy, recently published by Professor Robert Browning.

In order to lighten the revised and often expanded footnotes, we have transferred the numbers of museum objects to the List of Illustrations, and we have added a Concordance of cross-references to parallel works for the illustrations.

Our principal debt throughout has been to Professor Webster, who placed at our disposal the notes he made while preparing the first edition and has been tireless in his efforts to keep us up to date. Sir John Beazley has also provided notes, photographs, and help, and we are also grateful for help and advice to V. N. Andreyev, J. Boardman, S. Dow, H. Lloyd-Jones, C. A. P. Ruck, Miss L. Talcott, and R. E. Wycherley, and for photographs to the Ashmolean Museum, the National Museum, Warsaw, and the British Museum. We owe a special debt to the reviewers of the first edition, who did much to get us started, and to the editors and compositors of the Clarendon Press for their skill and patience in dealing with a bulky and untidy manuscript.

J. G.
D. M. L.

Christ Church, Oxford
January 1967

PREFACE TO FIRST EDITION

My first words must be an expression of deep regret at the loss to scholarship through the deaths of two most active and fruitful students of the Greek Theatre and Drama, to whom I am personally very deeply indebted. The one, Ernst Fiechter, died at St. Gallen on 19 April 1948, his invaluable work on the theatres of Greece still unfinished. We had recently entered upon what promised to be a most interesting and profitable correspondence, and I hoped great things of his future studies; but the correspondence suddenly ceased and some weeks later came the news of his death. His last published writing in his lifetime was a discriminating but most kindly review of my own *Theatre of Dionysus*, which in his posthumously published volume on the theatre in the Piraeus he treats with even greater kindness. The other, Heinrich Bulle, had escaped, carrying the manuscripts of an unfinished book, when his house in Würzburg was bombed; but the manuscripts were mostly destroyed in a later raid from the air, and he died from a heart-attack brought on by the shock. The last few years have also taken from us A. Körte, H. Schleif, and L. Deubner, all of whom are greatly missed by those who are pursuing the same studies.

The present work concludes, so far as I have been able to do it, the task which I set myself many years ago, and to the fulfilment of which the *Theatre of Dionysus* (1946) was the first instalment. I hope that the two books will be treated as, in a sense, one. I have tried so far as I could to avoid overlapping, and have referred back freely to the earlier work. On the other hand, readers of the present volume may find some small amount of repetition between the several chapters. I had to choose between this and the insertion of a number of cross-references which would have been inconvenient to readers, especially to any who might be interested in the subject of a particular chapter and might not want to turn backwards and forwards.

I have sometimes travelled away from the subject of the Athenian Dramatic Festivals, but the reader is not bound to follow; the Table of Contents will furnish him with sufficient warnings. My excuse for the last chapter is the want of any brief and satisfactory treatment known to me in English writings of a very interesting subject.

It has been my object throughout to keep as closely as possible to evidence, and to state this evidence fully enough to enable the reader to judge for himself of the value of the conclusions drawn from it. Scholarship has suffered much in the last half-century from a lack of scruple in this respect, leading, as it often has, to attractive but erroneous theories and to the suggestion of connexions and 'derivations' which cannot be substantiated. I fear that the constant reference to evidence is inconsistent with elegant essay-writing, but it seems to me to be a service that needs to be rendered, and I have tried, in a modest way, to render it—how imperfectly, I do not need to be told.

But though this attempt is based upon direct personal study of evidence, I am deeply grateful to other workers in the same field for the help which I have derived from their writings, and have tried to acknowledge it in my notes. I must express my special thanks for generous assistance in the choice and collection of illustrations to Sir John Beazley and Professor T. B. L. Webster, and to Dr. Margarete Bieber for her ready consent to my use of materials contained in her own works. I have also received welcome help from Mr. Bernard Ashmole and other members of the staff of the Department of Greek and Roman Antiquities at the British Museum. My obligations to authors and publishers for permission to reproduce illustrations and to the authorities of Museums for leave to figure objects under their care are very numerous and are acknowledged in their place. If I have accidentally failed to obtain any consent for which I should have asked, I hope that the oversight may be pardoned.

A. W. P.-C.

CONTENTS

II · THE GREAT OR CITY DIONYSIA

III · THE ACTORS

CONTENTS

IV · THE COSTUMES

V · THE CHORUS

LIST OF ILLUSTRATIONS

(*at end*)

ABBREVIATIONS

A.B.V.	J. D. Beazley, *Attic Black-figure Vase-painters*, Oxford, 1956.
A.R.V.²	J. D. Beazley, *Attic Red-figure Vase-painters*, ed. 2, 3 vols., Oxford, 1963.
A.T.L.	B. D. Meritt, H. T. Wade-Gery, M. F. McGregor, *The Athenian Tribute Lists*, Cambridge (Mass.), 1939–53.
Bekker, *Anecd.*	I. Bekker, *Anecdota Graeca*, 3 vols., Berlin, 1814–21.
Bieber, *H.T.²*	M. Bieber, *History of the Greek and Roman Theater*, ed. 2.
C.A.H.	*The Cambridge Ancient History.*
C.I.G.	*Corpus Inscriptionum Graecarum* (ed. A. Boeckh), 4 vols., Berlin, 1828–77.
Cramer, *Anecd. Par.*	J. A. Cramer, *Anecdota Graeca e codd. manuscriptis Bibliothecae Regiae Parisiensis*, 4 vols., Oxford, 1839–41.
C.V.	*Corpus Vasorum Antiquorum* (Union Académique Internationale).
D.G.E.	*Dialectorum Graecorum exempla epigraphica potiora* (ed. E. Schwyzer), Leipzig, 1923.
Dith. Trag. Com.²	A. W. Pickard-Cambridge, *Dithyramb, Tragedy and Comedy*, ed. 2.
F. Gr. Hist.	F. Jacoby, *Die Fragmente der griechischen Historiker*, Berlin and Leiden, 1923– (Erster Teil, ed. 2, 1957).
	(Note: the number key to each historian can be found at the end of Vol. IIIC.)
Furtw.-Reich.	A. Furtwängler and K. Reichold, *Griechische Vasenmalerei*, 3 vols. text, plus plates, Munich, 1904–32.
I.G.	*Inscriptiones Graecae* (ed. Kirchoff, Kaibel, *et al.*), Berlin, 1873– (i², ii², iv, ix, ed. 2 (editio minor); remaining vols. ed. 1 (editio maior)).
I.G.R.	*Inscriptiones Graecae ad res Romanas pertinentes* (ed. R. Cagnat and G. Lafaye), 4 vols., Paris, 1911–27.
Kaibel	*Comicorum Graecorum Fragmenta*, vol. i. 1 (all published), Berlin, 1899.
Kock (K)	*Comicorum Graecorum Fragmenta*, 3 vols., Leipzig, 1880–8.
Körte (Kö)	*Menander: reliquiae*, 2 vols. (revised by A. Thierfelder), Leipzig, (Teubner), 1953–5.
Le Bas	Ph. Le Bas & W. H. Waddington, *Voyage archéologique en Grèce et en Asie Mineure pendant 1834 et 1844*, Paris, 1870–6.
M.A.M.A.	*Monumenta Asiae Minoris Antiqua* (ed. W. M. Calder, *et al.*), 8 vols., London and Manchester, 1928–62.
Metzger, *Représentations*	H. Metzger, *Les Représentations dans la céramique attique du IVᵉ siècle*, Paris, 1951.

Michel	C. Michel, *Recueil d'inscriptions grecques*, 2 vols., Paris, 1900–12.
Miller, *Mélanges*	E. Miller, *Mélanges de littérature grecque*, Paris, 1868 (reprinted, Amsterdam, 1965).
M.I.N.C.	T. B. L. Webster, *Monuments illustrating New Comedy.*
M.I.T.S.	T. B. L. Webster, *Monuments illustrating Tragedy and Satyr Play.*
Nauck (N)	*Tragicorum Graecorum Fragmenta*, ed. 2, Leipzig, 1926 (reprinted, with supplement by B. Snell, 1964).
New Chapters	*New Chapters in Greek Literature* (ed. J. U. Powell and E. A. Barber), 3 series, Oxford, 1921–33.
O.G.I.S.	*Orientis Graecae Inscriptiones Selectae* (ed. W. Dittenberger), 2 vols., Leipzig, 1903–5.
O.M.C.	T. B. L. Webster, *Monuments illustrating Old and Middle Comedy.*
R.E.	*Paulys Realencyclopädie der classischen Altertumswissenschaft*, ed. G. Wissowa, W. Kroll, K. Mittelhaus, *et al.*, Stuttgart, 1894–
S.B.	*Sitzungsbericht.*
S.E.G.	*Supplementum Epigraphicum Graecum* (ed. J. J. E. Hondius and A. G. Woodhead), Leiden, 1922–
S.G.D.I.	*Sammlung der griechischen Dialekt-Inschriften*, (ed. H. Collitz, F. Bechtel, *et al.*, Göttingen, 1883–1923.
Sifakis, *Studies*	G. M. Sifakis, *Studies in the history of Hellenistic drama*, London, 1967.
*S.I.G.*³	*Sylloge Inscriptionum Graecarum* (ed. W. Dittenberger), ed. 3, 4 vols., Leipzig, 1915–24.
T.A.M.	*Tituli Asiae Minoris* (ed. E. Kalinka), Vienna, 1901–
Theatre of D.	A. W. Pickard-Cambridge, *The Theatre of Dionysus in Athens.*
Tod, *G.H.I.*	M. N. Tod, *Greek Historical Inscriptions*, vol. 1, ed. 2, Oxford, 1946.
U.D.A.	A. Wilhelm, *Urkunden dramatischer Aufführungen in Athen.*
Webster, *G.T.P.*	T. B. L. Webster, *Greek Theatre Production.*
Wehrli	*Die Schule des Aristoteles*, 10 vols., Basel, 1944–59.

I

THE LESSER FESTIVALS

A. *The Anthesteria*

THE oldest of the festivals of Dionysus at Athens was the Anthesteria, extending over the 11th, 12th, and 13th of the month Anthesterion (about the end of February), these days being known respectively as Πιθοίγια, Χόες, and Χύτροι. Each day began for religious purposes at sunset on the previous evening. Although this festival has little direct or demonstrable connexion with the history of the drama, it is necessary to study it briefly, because some elements in it have been wrongly connected with dramatic festivals—in particular, its association with the precinct of Dionysus ἐν Λίμναις, and the procession which escorted Dionysus in a car resembling a ship—and because the study will help to place the dramatic festivals in the general setting of the worship of Dionysus at Athens.

1. The following are the principal texts bearing on the Anthesteria:

(1) Thuc. ii. 15. 3–6 τὸ δὲ πρὸ τοῦ (before the ξυνοικισμός brought about by Theseus) ἡ ἀκρόπολις ἡ νῦν οὖσα πόλις ἦν, καὶ τὸ ὑπ' αὐτὴν πρὸς νότον μάλιστα τετραμμένον. τεκμήριον δέ· τὰ γὰρ ἱερὰ ἐν αὐτῇ τῇ ἀκροπόλει ⟨∗ ∗ ∗⟩ καὶ ἄλλων θεῶν ἐστι καὶ τὰ ἔξω πρὸς τοῦτο τὸ μέρος τῆς πόλεως μᾶλλον ἵδρυται, τό τε τοῦ Διὸς τοῦ Ὀλυμπίου καὶ τὸ Πύθιον καὶ τὸ τῆς Γῆς καὶ τὸ ⟨τοῦ⟩ ἐν Λίμναις Διονύσου, ᾧ τὰ ἀρχαιότερα Διονύσια τῇ δωδεκάτῃ ποιεῖται ἐν μηνὶ Ἀνθεστηριῶνι, ὥσπερ καὶ οἱ ἀπ' Ἀθηναίων Ἴωνες ἔτι καὶ νῦν νομίζουσιν. ἵδρυται δὲ καὶ ἄλλα ἱερὰ ταύτῃ ἀρχαῖα. καὶ τῇ κρήνῃ τῇ νῦν μὲν τῶν τυράννων οὕτω σκευασάντων Ἐννεακρούνῳ καλουμένῃ, τὸ δὲ πάλαι φανερῶν τῶν πηγῶν οὐσῶν Καλλιρρόῃ ὠνομασμένῃ, ἐκείνη [ἐκεῖνοί, Bekker] τε ἐγγὺς οὔσῃ τὰ πλείστου ἄξια ἐχρῶντο, καὶ νῦν ἔτι ἀπὸ τοῦ ἀρχαίου πρό τε γαμικῶν καὶ ἐς ἄλλα τῶν ἱερῶν νομίζεται τῷ ὕδατι χρῆσθαι. καλεῖται δὲ διὰ τὴν παλαιὰν ταύτῃ κατοίκησιν καὶ ἡ ἀκρόπολις μέχρι τοῦδε ἔτι ὑπ' Ἀθηναίων πόλις.

In l. 4 after θεῶν ἐστι Classen inserts καὶ τὰ τῆς Ἀθηνᾶς.

(1a) *P. Oxy.* 853, col. x. 7 ff. (commentary on Thuc. ii; second century A.D.).

τὸ ἐν Λ[ίμνα]ις Διονυσο[........
μέν φησ[ι.]ευδε Διονυ[σ.......
.]ητον[..]τ' Ἐλευθὴρ ει[. Λιμναίῳ
δὲ χ]οροστά[δ]ας ἦγον ἑ[ορτάς...
(Callimachus, fr. 305 Pf.)

10

...]ος δὲ οὔτ[ω]ς φησὶν [καλεῖσθαι
δι]ὰ τὸ ἐκλελ[ι]μνάσθαι [τὸν τόπον.
ἔσ]τι δὲ καὶ ἐν [τ]ῇ Λακωνι[κῇ τόπος
ὅπ]ου Λιμνᾶτ[ί]ς ἐστιν Ἄρτ[εμις.

ᾧ τ]ὰ ἀρχαιότατα Διονύσια τῇ ιβ′   15
ποι[εῖται·] ἐπὶ τρεῖς μέ[ν] ἐσ[τι]ν
ἑορτὴ ἡμέ[ρας] ια′ ιβ′ ιγ′, ἐπίσ[ημός
ἐσ]τι δὲ ἡ ιβ′, [ὡς] καὶ εἶπεν αὐ[τός].

For the conjectural restoration of the names in l. 7 (? Callimachus),
and l. 11 (? Philochorus or Apollodorus), see Pfeiffer on Callimachus,
fr. 305 and p. 22, n. 1 below.

(2) Eur. *Iph. Taur.* 947 ff.

       πρῶτα μέν μ᾽ οὐδεὶς ξένων
    ἑκὼν ἐδέξαθ᾽, ὡς θεοῖς στυγούμενον·
    οἱ δ᾽ ἔσχον αἰδῶ, ξένια μονοτράπεζά μοι
  950 παρέσχον, οἴκων ὄντες ἐν ταὐτῷ στέγει,
    σιγῇ δ᾽ ἐτεκτήναντ᾽ ἀπρόσφθεγκτόν μ᾽, ὅπως
    δαιτὸς γενοίμην πώματός τ᾽ αὐτοῖς δίχα,
    ἐς δ᾽ ἄγγος ἴδιον ἴσον ἅπασι βακχίου
    μέτρημα πληρώσαντες εἶχον ἡδονήν. . . .
  958 κλύω δ᾽ Ἀθηναίοισι τἀμὰ δυστυχῆ
    τελετὴν γενέσθαι, κἄτι τὸν νόμον μένειν
    χοῆρες ἄγγος Παλλάδος τιμᾶν λεών.

(3) Ar. *Ach.* 960–1.

    ἐκέλευσε Λάμαχός σε ταυτησὶ δραχμῆς
    ἐς τοὺς Χοᾶς αὑτῷ μεταδοῦναι τῶν κιχλῶν.

    Schol. εἰς τοὺς Χοᾶς· εἰς τὴν ἑορτὴν τῶν Χοῶν. ἐπετελεῖτο δὲ Πυανε-
ψιῶνος ὀγδόῃ, οἱ δὲ Ἀνθεστηριῶνος δωδεκάτῃ (δεκάτῃ MSS.). φησὶ δὲ
Ἀπολλόδωρος (244 F 133 Jac.) Ἀνθεστήρια καλεῖσθαι κοινῶς τὴν ὅλην ἑορτὴν
Διονύσῳ ἀγομένην, κατὰ μέρος δὲ Πιθοιγίαν, Χόας, Χύτρους (Χύτραν MSS.).
καὶ αὖθις, ὅτι Ὀρέστης μετὰ τὸν φόνον εἰς Ἀθήνας ἀφικόμενος, ἦν δὲ ἑορτὴ
Διονύσου Ληναίου, ὡς μὴ γένοιτό σφισιν ὁμόσπονδος ἀπεκτονὼς τὴν μητέρα,
ἐμηχανήσατο τοιόνδε τι Πανδίων· χοᾶ οἴνου τῶν δαιτυμόνων ἑκάστῳ παρα-
στήσας, ἐξ αὐτοῦ πίνειν ἐκέλευσε μηδὲν ὑπομιγνύντας ἀλλήλοις, ὡς μήτε ἀπὸ
τοῦ αὐτοῦ κρατῆρος πίοι Ὀρέστης μήτε ἐκεῖνος ἄχθοιτο καθ᾽ αὑτὸν πίνων
μόνος. καὶ ἀπ᾽ ἐκείνου Ἀθηναίοις ἑορτὴ ἐνομίσθη οἱ Χόες.
    Cf. Harpokration s.v. Χόες·....ἑορτή τις παρ᾽ Ἀθηναίοις ἀγομένη
Ἀνθεστηριῶνος δωδεκάτῃ. φησὶ δὲ Ἀπολλόδωρος (244 F 133 Jac.) Ἀνθεστήρια
μὲν καλεῖσθαι κοινῶς τὴν ὅλην ἑορτὴν Διονύσῳ ἀγομένην, κατὰ μέρος δὲ
Πιθοίγια, Χόας, Χύτρους.

(4) Ibid. 1000–2.

> ΚΗΡΥΞ. ἀκούετε λεώ· κατὰ τὰ πάτρια τοὺς Χόας
> πίνειν ὑπὸ τῆς σάλπιγγος· ὃς δ' ἂν ἐκπίῃ
> πρώτιστος, ἀσκὸν Κτησιφῶντος λήψεται.

Schol. ἐν ταῖς Χοαῖς ἀγὼν ἦν περὶ τοῦ ἐκπιεῖν τινὰ πρῶτον χοᾶ, καὶ ὁ πιὼν ἐστέφετο φυλλίνῳ στεφάνῳ καὶ ἀσκὸν οἴνου ἐλάμβανεν. πρὸς σάλπιγγος δ' ἔπινον.—ἐτίθετο δὲ ἀσκὸς πεφυσημένος ἐν τῇ τῶν Χοῶν ἑορτῇ, ἐφ' οὗ τοὺς πίνοντας πρὸς ἀγῶνα ἑστάναι, τὸν πρῶτον πιόντα δὲ ὡς νικήσαντα λαμβάνειν ἀσκόν, ἔπινον δὲ μέτρον τι οἷον χοᾶ.

(5) Ibid. 1076–7.

> ὑπὸ τοὺς Χόας γὰρ καὶ Χύτρους αὐτοῖσί τις
> ἤγγειλε λῃστὰς ἐμβαλεῖν Βοιωτίους.

Schol. Θεόπομπος (115 F 347 Jac.) τοὺς διασωθέντας ἐκ τοῦ κατακλυσμοῦ ἑψῆσαί φησι χύτραν πανσπερμίας· ὅθεν οὕτω κληθῆναι τὴν ἑορτήν. καὶ θύειν τοῖς Χουσὶν (but cf. the version of this note in pass. (8) below) Ἑρμῇ χθονίῳ, τῆς δὲ χύτρας οὐδένα γεύσασθαι. τοῦτο δὲ ποιῆσαι τοὺς περισωθέντας, ἱλασκομένους τὸν Ἑρμῆν [καὶ] περὶ τῶν ἀποθανόντων. ἤγετο δὲ ἡ ἑορτὴ Ἀνθεστηριῶνος τρίτῃ ἐπὶ δέκα, ὡς Φιλόχορος (328 F 84 Jac.). Ἄλλως· ἐν μιᾷ ἡμέρᾳ ἄγονται οἵ τε Χύτροι καὶ οἱ Χόες ἐν Ἀθήναις, ἐν ᾧ πᾶν σπέρμα εἰς χύτραν ἑψήσαντες θύουσι μόνῳ τῷ [Διονύσῳ καὶ] Ἑρμῇ. οὕτω Δίδυμος.

(Cf. Phot. s.v. Ὑδροφόρια· ἑορτὴ πένθιμος Ἀθήνησιν ἐπὶ τοῖς ἐν τῷ κατακλυσμῷ ἀπολομένοις, ὡς Ἀπολλώνιος, and Harpokration and 'Suidas' s.v. Χύτροι.)

Jacoby's note on the Philochorus fragment (from the περὶ ἑορτῶν) deals with more than the development of the tradition (*F. Gr. Hist.* iii b, Suppl. i, pp. 361–5, and Suppl. ii, pp. 265–70, 537).

(6) Ibid. 1224–5.

> ὡς τοὺς κριτάς με φέρετε· ποῦ 'στιν ὁ βασιλεύς;
> ἀπόδοτέ μοι τὸν ἀσκόν.

Schol. δηλοῖ ὡς ἄρα τὴν ἐπιμέλειαν ὁ βασιλεὺς εἶχε τῆς ἁμίλλης τοῦ χοός, καὶ τὸ ἆθλον ἐδίδου τῷ νικήσαντι, τὸν ἀσκόν.

(7) Ar. *Knights* 95.

> ἀλλ' ἐξένεγκέ μοι ταχέως οἴνου χοᾶ.

Schol. practically repeats the story of Orestes and Pandion as in Schol. Ar. *Ach.* 961.

(8) Ar. *Frogs* 211–19.

> λιμναῖα κρηνῶν τέκνα,
> ξύναυλον ὕμνων βοὰν
> φθεγξώμεθ', εὔγηρυν ἐμὰν ἀοιδάν,
>   κοὰξ κοάξ,

ἦν ἀμφὶ Νυσήιον
Διὸς Διόνυσον ἐν
Λίμναισιν ἰαχήσαμεν,
ἡνίχ' ὁ κραιπαλόκωμος
τοῖς ἱεροῖσι Χύτροισι
χωρεῖ κατ' ἐμὸν τέμενος λαῶν ὄχλος.

Schol. on l. 216. ἀπὸ τῶν ἑαυτῶν λιμνῶν μεταφέρουσιν ἐπὶ τὸν ἐν Λίμναις Διόνυσον λεγόμενον. Λίμναι δὲ χωρίον τῆς Ἀττικῆς, ἐν ᾧ Διονύσου ἱερόν. Λίμνη· τόπος ἱερὸς Διονύσου, ἐν ᾧ καὶ οἶκος καὶ νεὼς τοῦ θεοῦ. Καλλίμαχος ἐν Ἑκάλῃ (fr. 305 Pf.) "Λιμναίῳ δὲ χοροστάδας ἦγον ἑορτάς".

Schol. on l. 218. Χύτροι· ἑορτὴ παρ' Ἀθηναίοις. ἄγεται δὲ παρὰ ταύτην τὴν αἰτίαν, ἣν καὶ Θεόπομπος ἐκτίθεται γράφων οὕτως (115 F 347 Jac.)· "διασωθέντας οὖν τοὺς ἀνθρώπους, ᾗπερ ἐθάρρησαν ἡμέρᾳ, τῷ ταύτης ὀνόματι προσαγορεῦσαι καὶ τὴν ἑορτὴν ἅπασαν". ἔπειτα "θύειν αὐτοῖς ἔθος ἔχουσι, τῶν μὲν Ὀλυμπίων [θεῶν] οὐδενὶ τὸ παράπαν, Ἑρμῇ δὲ χθονίῳ, καὶ τῆς χύτρας, ἣν ἕψουσι πάντες οἱ κατὰ τὴν πόλιν, οὐδεὶς γεύεται τῶν ἱερέων. τοῦτο δὲ ποιοῦσι τῇ ⟨β'⟩ ἡμέρᾳ". καὶ "τοὺς τότε παραγενομένους ὑπὲρ τῶν ἀποθανόντων ἱλάσασθαι τὸν Ἑρμῆν". ἤγοντο δὲ ἀγῶνες αὐτόθι οἱ Χύτρινοι καλούμενοι, καθά φησι Φιλόχορος ἐν τῇ ἕκτῃ τῶν Ἀτθίδων (328 F 57 Jac.).

(9) Isaeus, Or. viii. 35. Κίρων γὰρ ἐκέκτητο οὐσίαν, ὦ ἄνδρες, ἀγρὸν μὲν Φλυῆσι . . . οἰκίας δ' ἐν ἄστει δύο, τὴν μὲν μίαν μισθοφοροῦσαν, παρὰ τὸ ἐν Λίμναις Διονύσιον, χιλίας εὑρίσκουσαν, τὴν δ' ἑτέραν κτλ.

(10) [Skylax], Peripl. 112 (Geogr. Gr. Min. i. 94). τὰ γὰρ πλάσματά (sc. κέραμος Ἀττικὸς καὶ χόες) ἐστιν ὤνια ἐν τοῖς Χουσὶ τῇ ἑορτῇ.

(11) [Dem.] in Neaeram 73–78. καὶ αὐτὴ ἡ γυνὴ ὑμῖν ἔθυε τὰ ἄρρητα ἱερὰ ὑπὲρ τῆς πόλεως, καὶ εἶδεν ἃ οὐ προσῆκεν αὐτὴν ὁρᾶν ξένην οὖσαν, καὶ τοιαύτη οὖσα εἰσῆλθεν οἷ οὐδεὶς ἄλλος Ἀθηναίων τοσούτων ὄντων εἰσέρχεται ἀλλ' ἢ ἡ τοῦ βασιλέως γυνή, ἐξώρκωσέν τε τὰς γεραρὰς τὰς ὑπηρετούσας τοῖς ἱεροῖς, ἐξεδόθη τε τῷ Διονύσῳ γυνή, ἔπραξε δὲ ὑπὲρ τῆς πόλεως τὰ πάτρια τὰ πρὸς τοὺς θεούς, πολλὰ καὶ ἅγια καὶ ἀπόρρητα. . . . (74) . . . τὸ γὰρ ἀρχαῖον, ὦ ἄνδρες Ἀθηναῖοι, δυναστεία ἐν τῇ πόλει ἦν καὶ ἡ βασιλεία τῶν ἀεὶ ὑπερεχόντων διὰ τὸ αὐτόχθονας εἶναι, τὰς δὲ θυσίας ἁπάσας ὁ βασιλεὺς ἔθυε, καὶ τὰς σεμνοτάτας καὶ ἀρρήτους ἡ γυνὴ αὐτοῦ ἐποίει, εἰκότως, βασίλιννα οὖσα. (75) ἐπειδὴ δὲ Θησεὺς συνῴκισεν αὐτοὺς καὶ δημοκρατίαν ἐποίησεν καὶ ἡ πόλις πολυάνθρωπος ἐγένετο, τὸν μὲν βασιλέα οὐδὲν ἧττον ὁ δῆμος ᾑρεῖτο . . . τὴν δὲ γυναῖκα αὐτοῦ νόμον ἔθεντο ἀστὴν εἶναι καὶ μὴ ἐπιμεμειγμένην ἑτέρῳ ἀνδρὶ ἀλλὰ παρθένον γαμεῖν, ἵνα κατὰ τὰ πάτρια θύηται τὰ ἄρρητα ἱερὰ ὑπὲρ τῆς πόλεως . . . . (76) καὶ τοῦτον τὸν νόμον γράψαντες ἐν στήλῃ λιθίνῃ ἔστησαν ἐν τῷ ἱερῷ τοῦ Διονύσου παρὰ τὸν βωμὸν ἐν Λίμναις (καὶ αὕτη ἡ στήλη ἔτι καὶ νῦν ἕστηκεν, ἀμυδροῖς γράμμασιν Ἀττικοῖς δηλοῦσα τὰ γεγραμμένα), μαρτυρίαν ποιούμενος ὁ δῆμος . . . ὅτι τήν γε θεῷ γυναῖκα δοθησομένην καὶ ποιήσουσαν τὰ ἱερὰ τοιαύτην ἀξιοῦμεν εἶναι. καὶ διὰ ταῦτα ἐν τῷ ἀρχαιοτάτῳ ἱερῷ τοῦ Διονύσου καὶ ἁγιωτάτῳ ἐν Λίμναις ἔστησαν, ἵνα μὴ πολλοὶ εἰδῶσιν

τὰ γεγραμμένα· ἅπαξ γὰρ τοῦ ἐνιαυτοῦ ἑκάστου ἀνοίγεται, τῇ δωδεκάτῃ
τοῦ Ἀνθεστηριῶνος μηνός. . . . (78) βούλομαι δ' ὑμῖν καὶ τὸν ἱεροκήρυκα
καλέσαι, ὃς ὑπηρετεῖ τῇ τοῦ βασιλέως γυναικί, ὅταν ἐξορκοῖ τὰς γεραρὰς
⟨τὰς⟩ ἐν κανοῖς πρὸς τῷ βωμῷ, πρὶν ἅπτεσθαι τῶν ἱερῶν, ἵνα καὶ τοῦ ὅρκου
καὶ τῶν λεγομένων ἀκούσητε . . . .

ΟΡΚΟΣ ΓΕΡΑΡΩΝ

ἁγιστεύω καὶ εἰμὶ καθαρὰ καὶ ἁγνὴ ἀπό ⟨τε⟩ τῶν ἄλλων τῶν οὐ καθα-
ρευόντων καὶ ἀπ' ἀνδρὸς συνουσίας, καὶ τὰ Θεοίνια καὶ τὰ Ἰοβάκχεια γεραρῶ
(Dobree for MSS. γεραίρω) τῷ Διονύσῳ κατὰ τὰ πάτρια καὶ ἐν τοῖς καθή-
κουσι χρόνοις.

Cf. Hesych. s.v. Διονύσου γάμος· τῆς τοῦ βασιλέως καὶ θεοῦ γίνεται γάμος.
Bekk. *Anecd.* i. 231. 32. γεραιραί· ἱέρειαι κοινῶς, ἰδίως δὲ παρὰ Ἀθηναίοις
αἱ τῷ Διονύσῳ τῷ ἐν Λίμναις τὰ ἱερὰ ἐπιτελοῦσαι, ἀριθμῷ δεκατέσσαρες.
(So also Hesych. s.v. γεραραί.)
Etym. Magn. 227. 35. γεραῖραι· παρὰ Ἀθηναίοις γυναῖκές τινες ἱεραί,
ἃς ὁ βασιλεὺς καθίστησιν ἰσαρίθμους τοῖς βωμοῖς τοῦ Διονύσου, διὰ τὸ
γεραίρειν τὸν θεόν. οὕτω Διονύσιος ὁ Ἁλικαρνασεύς.

(12) Aristotle, Ἀθ. Πολ. iii. 5. ἦσαν δὲ οὐχ ἅμα πάντες οἱ ἐννέα ἄρχοντες, ἀλλ' ὁ
μὲν βασιλεὺς εἶχε τὸ νῦν καλούμενον Βουκολεῖον, πλησίον τοῦ Πρυτανείου
(σημεῖον δέ· ἔτι καὶ νῦν γὰρ τῆς τοῦ βασιλέως γυναικὸς ἡ σύμμιξις ἐνταῦθα
γίνεται τῷ Διονύσῳ καὶ ὁ γάμος), ὁ δὲ ἄρχων τὸ Πρυτανεῖον, ὁ δὲ πολέμαρχος
τὸ Ἐπιλυκεῖον.

(13) Callimachus, *Aitia*, fr. 178 Pf., 1–5.

ἠὼς οὐδὲ πιθοιγὶς ἐλάνθανεν οὐδ' ὅτε δούλοις
ἦμαρ Ὀρέστειοι λευκὸν ἄγουσι Χόες·
Ἰκαρίου καὶ παιδὸς ἄγων ἐπέτειον ἁγιστύν,
Ἀτθίσιν οἰκίστη, σὸν φάος, Ἠριγόνη,
ἐς δαίτην ἐκάλεσσεν ὁμηθέας.

(14) Dion. Hal. *Antiq.* vii. 72. 11. ἐφεῖται γὰρ τοῖς κατάγουσι τὰς νίκας ἰαμβίζειν
τε καὶ κατασκώπτειν τοὺς ἐπιφανεστάτους ἄνδρας αὐτοῖς στρατηλάταις, ὡς
Ἀθήνησι τοῖς πομπευταῖς τοῖς ἐπὶ τῶν ἁμαξῶν πρότερον ἅμα σκώμμασι
παροχουμένοις, νῦν δὲ ποιήματα ᾄδουσιν αὐτοσχέδια.
Cf. Harpokr. s.v. πομπείας καὶ πομπεύειν· ἀντὶ τοῦ λοιδορίας καὶ λοιδορεῖν.
Δημοσθένης δὲ ἐν τῷ ὑπὲρ Κτησιφῶντος (11, 124). μεταφέρει δὲ ἀπὸ τῶν
ἐν ταῖς Διονυσιακαῖς πομπαῖς ἐπὶ τῶν ἁμαξῶν λοιδορουμένων ἀλλήλοις.

(15) Plutarch, *Quaest. Conv.* i. 613 b. εἰ μὲν οὖν, ὥσπερ οἱ τὸν Ὀρέστην ἑστιῶντες,
ἐν Θεσμοθετείῳ σιωπῇ τρώγειν καὶ πίνειν ἐμέλλομεν, ἦν τι τοῦτο τῆς ἀμαθίας
οὐκ ἀτυχὲς παραμύθιον.

(16) Ibid. ii. 643 a. καίτοι τίν' ἔχει διαφορὰν [ἢ] κύλικα καταθέντα τῶν κεκλημένων

ἑκάστῳ καὶ χοῦν, ἐμπλησάμενον οἴνου, καὶ τράπεζαν ἰδίαν ὥσπερ οἱ Δημοφων-
τίδαι τῷ Ὀρέστῃ λέγονται, πίνειν κελεῦσαι μὴ προσέχοντα τοῖς ἄλλοις κτλ.;

(17) Ibid. iii. 655 e. τοῦ νέου οἴνου Ἀθήνησι μὲν ἑνδεκάτῃ μηνὸς ⟨Ἀνθεστηριῶνος⟩
κατάρχονται, Πιθοίγια τὴν ἡμέραν καλοῦντες· καὶ πάλαι γ᾽ ὡς ἔοικεν εὔχοντο,
τοῦ οἴνου πρὶν ἢ πιεῖν ἀποσπένδοντες, ἀβλαβῆ καὶ σωτήριον αὐτοῖς τοῦ φαρ-
μάκου τὴν χρῆσιν γενέσθαι.

(18) Athen. iv. 130 d. σὺ δὲ μόνον ἐν Ἀθήναις μένων εὐδαιμονίζεις τὰς Θεοφράστου
θέσεις ἀκούων, θύμα καὶ εὔζωμα καὶ τοὺς καλοὺς ἐσθίων στρεπτούς, Λήναια
καὶ Χύτρους θεωρῶν. (Part of a letter of Hippolochos, addressed to Lyn-
keus, a disciple of Theophrastus.)

(19) Ibid. x. 437 b–e. Τίμαιος δέ (566 F 158 Jac.) φησιν ὡς Διονύσιος ὁ τύραννος
τῇ τῶν Χοῶν ἑορτῇ τῷ πρώτῳ ἐκπιόντι χοᾶ ἆθλον ἔθηκε στέφανον χρυσοῦν·
καὶ ὅτι πρῶτος ἐξέπιε Ξενοκράτης ὁ φιλόσοφος καὶ λαβὼν τὸν χρυσοῦν
στέφανον καὶ ἀναλύων τῷ Ἑρμῇ τῷ ἱδρυμένῳ ἐπὶ τῆς αὐλῆς ἐπέθηκεν,
ᾧπερ εἰώθει καὶ τοὺς ἀνθινοὺς ἑκάστοτε ἐπιτιθέναι στεφάνους ἑσπέρας ἀπαλ-
λασσόμενος ὡς αὐτόν· καὶ ἐπὶ τούτῳ ἐθαυμάσθη. τὴν δὲ τῶν Χοῶν ἑορτὴν
τὴν Ἀθήνησιν ἐπιτελουμένην Φανόδημός (325 F 11 Jac.) φησι Δημοφῶντα
τὸν βασιλέα ⟨***⟩ βουλόμενον ὑποδέξασθαι παραγενόμενον τὸν Ὀρέστην
Ἀθήναζε. πρὸς δὲ τὰ ἱερὰ οὐ θέλων αὐτὸν προσιέναι οὐδ᾽ ὁμόσπονδον γενέσθαι
μήπω δικασθέντα ἐκέλευσε συγκλεισθῆναί τε τὰ ἱερὰ καὶ χοᾶ οἴνου ἑκάστῳ
παρατεθῆναι, τῷ πρώτῳ ἐκπιόντι εἰπὼν ἆθλον δοθήσεσθαι πλακοῦντα. παρήγ-
γειλέ τε καὶ τοῦ πότου παυσαμένους τοὺς μὲν στεφάνους οἷς ἐστεφάνωντο πρὸς
τὰ ἱερὰ μὴ τιθέναι διὰ τὸ ὁμορόφους γενέσθαι τῷ Ὀρέστῃ, περὶ δὲ τὸν χοᾶ
τὸν ἑαυτοῦ ἕκαστον περιθεῖναι καὶ τῇ ἱερείᾳ ἀποφέρειν [τοὺς στεφάνους] πρὸς
τὸ ἐν Λίμναις τέμενος, ἔπειτα θύειν ἐν τῷ ἱερῷ τὰ ἐπίλοιπα. καὶ ἔκτοτε τὴν
ἑορτὴν κληθῆναι Χοᾶς. τῇ δὲ ἑορτῇ τῶν Χοῶν ἔθος ἐστὶν Ἀθήνησι πέμπεσθαι
δῶρά τε καὶ τοὺς μισθοὺς τοῖς σοφισταῖς, οἵπερ καὶ αὐτοὶ συνεκάλουν ἐπὶ ξένια
τοὺς γνωρίμους, ὥς φησιν Εὐβουλίδης ὁ διαλεκτικὸς ἐν δράματι Κωμασταῖς
(fr. 1 K) οὕτως

> σοφιστιᾷς, κάκιστε, καὶ Χοῶν δέῃ
> τῶν μισθοδώρων, οὐκ ἀδείπνων ἐν τρυφῇ.

Ἀντίγονος δ᾽ ὁ Καρύστιος ἐν τῷ περὶ τοῦ Διονυσίου βίου τοῦ Ἡρακλεώτου
τοῦ ἐπικληθέντος Μεταθεμένου φησὶ τὸν Διονύσιον τοῖς οἰκέταις συνεορ-
τάζοντα ἐν τῇ τῶν Χοῶν ἑορτῇ κτλ. (Cf. Philodemus, Acad. Ind. Herc. 8, p. 43.)

(20) Athen. xi. 465 a. Φανόδημος δὲ (325 F 12 Jac.) πρὸς τῷ ἱερῷ (πρὸς τὸ ἱερόν
Jacoby) φησι τοῦ ἐν Λίμναις Διονύσου τὸ γλεῦκος φέροντας τοὺς Ἀθηναίους ἐκ
τῶν πίθων τῷ θεῷ κιρνάναι, εἶτ᾽ αὐτοὺς προσφέρεσθαι· ὅθεν καὶ Λιμναῖον
κληθῆναι τὸν Διόνυσον ὅτι μιχθὲν τὸ γλεῦκος τῷ ὕδατι τότε πρῶτον ἐπόθη
κεκραμένον. διόπερ ὀνομασθῆναι τὰς [πηγὰς] Νύμφας καὶ τιθήνας τοῦ Διονύσου,
ὅτι τὸν οἶνον αὐξάνει τὸ ὕδωρ κιρνάμενον. ἡσθέντες οὖν τῇ κράσει ἐν ᾠδαῖς
ἔμελπον τὸν Διόνυσον, χορεύοντες καὶ ἀνακαλοῦντες Εὔαν τε (Εὐάνθη MS.,

defended by Deubner, *Jahrb. Arch.* 42 (1927), p. 191) καὶ Διθύραμβον καὶ Βακχευτὰν καὶ Βρόμιον.

(21) Ibid. 495 a–c. *Κράτης δὲ ἐν δευτέρῳ Ἀττικῆς διαλέκτου* (362 F 8 Jac.) *γράφει οὕτως· οἱ χόες πελίκαι, καθάπερ εἴπομεν, ὠνομάζοντο· ὁ δὲ τύπος ἦν τοῦ ἀγγείου πρότερον μὲν τοῖς Παναθηναϊκοῖς ἐοικώς, ἡνίκα ἐκαλεῖτο πελίκη, ὕστερον δὲ ἔσχεν οἰνοχόης σχῆμα, οἷοί εἰσιν οἱ ἐν τῇ ἑορτῇ παρατιθέμενοι, ὁποίους δή ποτε ὄλπας ἐκάλουν, χρώμενοι πρὸς τὴν τοῦ οἴνου ἔγχυσιν, καθάπερ Ἴων ὁ Χῖος ἐν Εὐρυτίδαις* (fr. 10 N²) *φησὶν*

ἐκ ζαθέων πιθακνῶν ἀφύσσοντες ὄλπαις
οἶνον ὑπερφίαλον κελαρύζετε.

νυνὶ δὲ τὸ μὲν τοιοῦτον ἀγγεῖον καθιερωμένον τινὰ τρόπον ἐν τῇ ἑορτῇ παρατίθεται μόνον, τὸ δ' εἰς τὴν χρείαν πῖπτον μετεσχημάτισται, ἀρυταίνῃ μάλιστα ἐοικός, ὃ δὴ καλοῦμεν χοᾶ. (Crates' date is perhaps 1st cent. B.C.)

(22) Diog. Laert. iv. 8 (on Xenokrates). *καὶ χρυσῷ στεφάνῳ τιμηθέντα ἐπάθλῳ πολυποσίας τοῖς Χουσὶ παρὰ Διονυσίῳ ἐξιόντα θεῖναι πρὸς τὸν ἱδρυμένον Ἑρμῆν, ἔνθαπερ τιθέναι καὶ τοὺς ἀνθινοὺς εἰώθει.* (See no. 19 above.)

(23) Philostratus, *Heroic.* xii. 2. *(Αἴας παῖδα) τήν τε ἄλλην ἔτρεφε τροφήν, ἣν Ἀθηναῖοι ἐπαινοῦσι, καὶ ὅτε Ἀθήνησιν οἱ παῖδες ἐν μηνὶ Ἀνθεστηριῶνι στεφανοῦνται τῶν ἀνθέων τρίτῳ ἀπὸ γενέας ἔτει, κρατῆράς τε τοὺς ἐκεῖθεν ἐστήσατο καὶ ἔθυσεν ὅσα Ἀθηναίοις ἐν νόμῳ.*

(24) Schol. on Hesiod, *Op.* 368. *καὶ ἐν τοῖς πατρίοις ἐστὶν ἑορτὴ Πιθοιγία, καθ' ἣν οὔτε οἰκέτην οὔτε μισθωτὸν εἴργειν τῆς ἀπολαύσεως τοῦ οἴνου θεμιτὸν ἦν, ἀλλὰ θύσαντας πᾶσι μεταδιδόναι τοῦ δώρου τοῦ Διονύσου.*

(25) Zenobius (in Codex Athous, 14th cent.). *θύραζε Κᾶρες, οὐκ ἔτ' Ἀνθεστήρια· φασὶν ὅτι οἱ Κᾶρές ποτε μέρος τῆς Ἀττικῆς κατέσχον· καὶ εἴ ποτε τὴν ἑορτὴν τῶν Ἀνθεστηρίων ἦγον οἱ Ἀθηναῖοι, σπονδῶν αὐτοῖς μετεδίδοσαν καὶ ἐδέχοντο τῷ ἄστει καὶ τοῖς οἰκίαις, μετὰ δὲ τὴν ἑορτὴν τινῶν ὑπολελειμμένων ἐν ταῖς Ἀθήναις, οἱ ἀπαντῶντες πρὸς τοὺς Κᾶρας παίζοντες ἔλεγον· θύραζε Κᾶρες, οὐκ ἔτ' Ἀνθεστήρια.*

To this, two collections of proverbs, in a Bodleian and a Vatican MS., both of the fifteenth century, add: *τινὲς δὲ οὕτως φασί· θύραζε Κῆρες, οὐκ ἔνι Ἀνθεστήρια.*

(26) Photius. *τὰ ἐκ τῶν ἁμαξῶν. . . . Ἀθήνησι γὰρ ἐν τῇ τῶν Χοῶν ἑορτῇ οἱ κωμάζοντες ἐπὶ τῶν ἁμαξῶν τοὺς ἀπαντῶντας ἔσκωπτόν τε καὶ ἐλοιδόρουν. τὸ δ' αὐτὸ καὶ τοῖς Ληναίοις ὕστερον ἐποίουν.* (So also 'Suidas'.)

(27) Photius. *μιαρὰ ἡμέρα· ἐν τοῖς Χουσὶν Ἀνθεστηριῶνος μηνός, ἐν ᾧ δοκοῦσιν αἱ ψυχαὶ τῶν τελευτησάντων ἀνιέναι, ῥάμνον* (MSS. ῥάμνῳ) *ἔωθεν ἐμασῶντο καὶ πίττῃ τὰς θύρας ἔχριον.* (So also Hesychius.)

(28) Id. *ῥάμνος· φυτὸν ὃ ἐν τοῖς Χουσὶν ὡς ἀλεξιφάρμακον ἐμασῶντο ἔωθεν. καὶ*

πίττῃ ἐχρίοντο τὰ δώματα· ἀμίαντος γὰρ αὕτη. διὸ καὶ ἐν ταῖς γενέσεσι τῶν
παιδίων χρίουσι τὰς οἰκίας εἰς ἀπέλασιν τῶν δαιμόνων.

(29) Id. θύραζε Κᾶρες, οὐκέτ' Ἀνθεστήρια· ἦν οἱ μὲν διὰ πλῆθος οἰκετῶν Καρικῶν
εἰρῆσθαί φασιν, ὡς ἐν τοῖς Ἀνθεστηρίοις εὐωχουμένων αὐτῶν καὶ οὐκ ἐργαζο-
μένων. τῆς οὖν ἑορτῆς τελεσθείσης λέγειν ἐπὶ τὰ ἔργα ἐκπέμποντας αὐτούς·
θύραζε Κᾶρες, οὐκέτ' Ἀνθεστήρια. τινὲς δὲ οὕτως τὴν παροιμίαν φασί·
θύραζε Κῆρες, οὐκ ἔνι Ἀνθεστήρια, ὡς κατὰ τὴν πόλιν τοῖς Ἀνθεστηρίοις τῶν
ψυχῶν περιερχομένων. ('Suidas' repeats this.)

(30) 'Suidas' s.v. Χόες. Contains nothing which is not in (3) above, though in
longer or shorter form.

(31) *I.G.* ii². 1672 (l. 204) (in the accounts of the ἐπιστάται Ἐλευσινόθεν for
329/8 B.C.). εἰς Χόας δημοσίοις ἱερεῖον ΔΔΗΗ.

(32) Sokolowski, *Lois Sacrées de l'Asie Mineure*, no. 48 (Miletus), l. 21. τοῖς δὲ
Καταγωγίοις κατάγειν τὸν Διόνυσον τοὺς ἱερεῖ[ς] καὶ τὰς ἱερείας τοῦ [Διονύ]-
σου τοῦ Βακχίου μετὰ τοῦ [ἱερέως κ]αὶ τῆς ἱερείας πρ[ὸ τ]ῆ[ς] ἡμέρας μέχρι
τ[ῆς ἡλίου δύσεως...τ]ῆς πόλεως. (Date 276–275 B.C.)

(33) Ibid., no. 37 (*S.I.G.*³ 1003), l. 19. ἐχέτω δὲ καὶ στολὴν (ὁ ἱερεὺς) ἦν ἂμ
βούληται καὶ στέφανον χρυσοῦν μῆνα Ληναιῶνα καὶ Ἀνθεστηριῶνα· καὶ τοῖς
Καταγωγίοις καθηγήσεται τῶν συγκαταγόντων τὸν Διόνυσον. (2nd cent. B.C.;
Priene.)

(34) Philostratus, *Vit. Soph.* i. 25. 1. πέμπεται γάρ τις μηνὶ Ἀνθεστηριῶνι μεταρσία
τριήρης ἐς ἀγοράν, ἣν ὁ Διονύσου ἱερεὺς οἷον κυβερνήτης εὐθύνει πείσματα ἐκ
θαλάττης λύουσαν. (This was at Smyrna in the reign of Hadrian.) (Cf.
Aristides xvii. 6; xxi. 4 Keil).

(35) *I.G.* ii². 1368, ll. 111 ff. (the Iobacchoi of Athens, 2nd cent. A.D.). ὁ ἱερεὺς
δὲ ἐπιτελείτω τὰς ἐθίμους λιτουργίας Στιβάδος καὶ ἀμφιετηρίδος εὐπρεπῶς
καὶ τιθέτω τὴν τῶν Καταγωγίων σπονδὴν Στιβάδι μίαν καὶ θεολογίαν, ἢν
ἤρξατο ἐκ φιλοτειμίας ποιεῖν ὁ ἱερασάμενος Νεικόμαχος.

(36) Philostratus, *Vit. Apoll.* iii. 14. θεῶν δὲ ἀγάλμασιν ἐντυχεῖν φασιν, εἰ μὲν
Ἰνδοῖς ἢ Αἰγυπτίοις, θαῦμα οὐδέν, τὰ δέ γε ἀρχαιότατα τῶν παρ' Ἕλλησι,
τό τε τῆς Ἀθηνᾶς τῆς Πολιάδος καὶ τὸ τοῦ Ἀπόλλωνος τοῦ Δηλίου καὶ τὸ τοῦ
Διονύσου τοῦ Λιμναίου καὶ τὸ τοῦ Ἀμυκλαίου, καὶ ὁπόσα ὧδε ἀρχαῖα, ταῦτα
ἱδρύεσθαί τε τοὺς Ἰνδοὺς τούτους καὶ νομίζειν Ἑλληνικοῖς ἤθεσι, φασὶ δ' οἰκεῖν
τὰ μέσα τῆς Ἰνδικῆς.

(37) Ibid. iv. 21. ἐπιπλῆξαι δὲ λέγεται περὶ Διονυσίων Ἀθηναίοις, ἃ ποιεῖταί
σφισιν ἐν ὥρᾳ τοῦ Ἀνθεστηριῶνος· ὁ μὲν γὰρ μονῳδίας ἀκροασομένους καὶ
μελοποιίας παραβάσεών τε καὶ ῥυθμῶν, ὁπόσοι κωμῳδίας τε καὶ τραγῳδίας
εἰσίν, ἐς τὸ θέατρον ξυμφοιτᾶν ᾤετο, ἐπεὶ δὲ ἤκουσεν ὅτι αὐλοῦ ὑποσημήναντος
λυγισμοὺς ὀρχοῦνται καὶ μεταξὺ τῆς Ὀρφέως ἐποποιίας τε καὶ θεολογίας τὰ
μὲν ὡς Ὧραι, τὰ δὲ ὡς Νύμφαι, τὰ δὲ ὡς Βάκχαι πράττουσιν, ἐς ἐπίπληξιν
τούτου κατέστη.

2. The passage quoted above (no. 23) from the *Heroicus* of Philostratus suggests that the name of the Anthesteria is connected with the ritual wearing of a crown of flowers by boys and girls who were just passing out of infancy, a rite of blessing which has parallels in other Indo-European cultures.[1] A large number of vases of the characteristic *chous* shape, mostly of the fifth century, show children garlanded and dressed for the festival: one of these is figured here (fig. 1).[2] Further, an inscription[3] on a relief commemorating a boy who had died just before he could be crowned at the festival describes him as ἡλικίης Χοϊκῶν, ὁ δὲ δαίμων ἔφθασε τοὺς Χοῦς. Hesychius[4] records that at Rhodes maidens just ripe for marriage were called ἀνθεστηριάδες. Pausanias[5] mentions a Διόνυσος Ἄνθιος as worshipped at Phlya, and an Ἀνθιστήρ in an inscription[6] of the second century B.C. at Thera is conjectured to be a Bacchic hero or the god himself.[7]

3. On the first day of the festival, called Πιθοίγια, people gathered near[8] the sanctuary of Dionysus ἐν Λίμναις, opened the πίθοι—the jars containing the wine of last autumn's grapes—and drank it after pouring libations of it to Dionysus. The object of the ritual was to remove the tabu from the food and drink of the community before they enjoyed it.[9] Their slaves shared in the drinking and the merry-making of the feast.[10]

[1] Deubner, *Attische Feste*, pp. 114 ff.

[2] Deubner, op. cit., pl. 13, no. 4; van Hoorn, *Choes and Anthesteria*, no. 23; Beazley, *A.R.V.*[2] 1601, no. 1. The vase is late fifth-century: the boy depicted is also pushing a toy wagon, a recurrent feature (e.g. van Hoorn, op. cit., nos. 405, 751, 53, 970, 397, 544), which Deubner aptly compares with the ἅμαξίς presented (in Aristophanes, *Clouds* 864) by Strep-siades to Pheidippides at the Diasia. The vase evidence has now been collected by van Hoorn, op. cit.; Nilsson, *Geschichte d. gr. Religion* i[2], p. 587, n. 3, points out that too little attention has been given to the chronology of this evidence. For the part played by children in the festival, see below, pp. 10 f.

[3] *I.G.* ii[2]. 13139. Photograph: *Jahrb. Arch.* 42 (1927), p. 191.

[4] s.v. ἀνθεστηριάδες.

[5] i. 31. 4.

[6] *I.G.* xii. 3. 329; Wilamowitz, *Glaube d. Hellenen*[2] ii, p. 76, n. 2. Cf. Nilsson, *Griechische Feste*, p. 267, n. 5.

[7] Other choes are depicted here by the kindness of Sir John Beazley, Mrs. S. P. Karouzou, and Dr. H. A. Thompson (see *A.J.A.* 50 (1946), and *Hesperia* 18 (1949)).

[8] πρὸς τῷ ἱερῷ (Phanodemos 325 F 12 Jacoby = pass. 20 above), not *in* the ἱερόν, which was only open on the next day. (So Deubner, op. cit., pp. 127–9.) But Jacoby, comm. ad loc. (= *F. Gr. Hist.* iii b, Suppl. i, pp. 185 f., and Suppl. ii, pp. 160 f.) argues for the emendation πρὸς τὸ ἱερόν. There is further doubt about the day of the festival on which this ceremony of consecration took place: Nilsson, *Gesch.* i[2], pp. 586 f., followed by B. C. Dietrich, *Hermes* 89 (1961), p. 44 and n. 7, argues that the dedication of the wine, as distinct from the opening of the πίθοι, took place on the next day, Χόες.

[9] Farnell, *Cults of the Greek States* v, p. 215; Deubner, op. cit., p. 94: cf. pass. 17 above.

[10] Pass. 24 above: cf. Eur. *Bacchae* 421 ff., 430 ff. with Dodds's notes. Miss J. E. Harrison's attempt to connect the Πιθοίγια with the cult of the dead (*Prolegomena*, pp. 42 ff.) is answered by Farnell, *Cults* v, pp. 221 ff., Deubner, op. cit., pp. 95 f., and Nilsson, *Gesch.* i[2], p. 597.

4. The second day, the Χόες, was celebrated by drinking throughout the city, vessels of a peculiar shape being appropriated to the ceremony,[1] and a drinking-match, announced by sound of trumpet, was solemnly conducted by the archon basileus at the θεσμοθετεῖον.[2] The ritual was based upon that which, according to tradition, had been observed when Orestes was entertained at Athens before he had been purified of murder; to avoid pollution each drinker had a separate vessel, and all drank in silence.[3] In the contest in the θεσμοθετεῖον the prize was a skin full of wine.[4] In unofficial drinking-matches on the same day there were cakes and garlands as prizes, and the revellers generally, at the end of the day, took the garlands which they wore, wound them round their χόες, brought them to the priestess in charge of the sanctuary ἐν Λίμναις, and poured libations of the rest of the wine.[5] A vase (a χοῦς) of the early fourth century in the Louvre (fig. 6)[6] is thought to represent the priestess receiving a youth who comes to dedicate his garland.

Other vases illustrate various phases of the festival. Miss G. M. A. Richter has published[7] two in the New York Metropolitan Museum of Art (figs. 7 and 8) of about 420 B.C., each of the characteristic form of the χοῦς, depicting (as she suggests) a reveller at the Anthesteria—the one while he is dancing, with two youthful companions (one of whom holds his clothes), the other at the moment when, having well drunk, he is trying to re-enter his own house—if indeed it is not the house of a hetaira. He ought of course to have taken his χοῦς by this time to the priestess, but it is probable that the revels which succeeded the drinking-match at the Choes went on for some time after the day called Χύτροι had technically begun, at sunset.[8] (Miss Richter also noted that the museum contains a number of miniature jugs of the same type which, she conjectured, may have been used by children taking part in the festival,

---

[1] Athen. xi. 495 a–c (pass. 21 above). A. Rumpf, *Bonner Jahrbücher* 161 (1961), p. 213, points out that the size of the vessels must also have been standardized and that the chous in question is the Attic measure of about 3¼ litres.

[2] Plut. *Quaest. Conv.* i. 613 b (pass. 15 above).

[3] Passages 2, 3, 16, 19 above.

[4] Schol. Ar. *Ach.* 1000 (pass. 4 above) asserts that the festival also included ἀσκωλιασμός, leaping upon a full wine-skin, but this is probably due to confusion: see below, p. 45.

[5] Athen. x. 437 c (pass. 19 above).

[6] Compare van Hoorn, nos. 385, 174.

[7] *Bull. Metr. Mus.* 34 (1939), pp. 231–2; van Hoorn, nos. 762, 761. A pelike from Capua in Basel, *c.* 480–470 B.C., by the Geras Painter (*A.R.V.*² 285, no. 6; van Hoorn, fig. 109) also depicts a reveller at the Anthesteria: note the chous hanging by a string from the r.h. figure's lyre: van Hoorn, pp. 32 f.

[8] In the scene in Ar. *Ach.* 1071–142, Lamachus is called out for military duties, owing to warning of a raid ὑπὸ τοὺς Χοᾶς καὶ Χύτρους, while Dikaiopolis prepares for a drinking-match (with his chous; l. 1133), evidently like that of the Anthesteria. See Immerwahr, *T.A.P.A.* 77 (1946), pp. 245 ff.

and Mrs. S. P. Karouzou[1] publishes some Athenian examples of 'children's choes' (figs. 2, 4)[2] showing children playing. A stele on one of these vases perhaps indicates that one of the children thought of had died.)[3]

A delightful picture (fig. 9)[4] on a chous in the Vlasto Collection by the Eretria Painter shows a little boy garlanded and lightly held on a swing by his father, while two older garlanded children look on. Sir John Beazley, to whom we are indebted for photographs of this vase, interprets the scene as a ceremony of purification, probably by fumes from the vessel in the centre.[5]

The sanctuary ἐν Λίμναις was open on this day only in the year, and the revellers continued to frequent it until the evening, when, strictly speaking, the day called Χύτροι had already begun.[6] In the sanctuary—doubtless in an inner chamber[7]—there then took place the secret ceremonies, conducted by the fourteen γεραιραί, preparatory to the sacred marriage of the βασίλιννα, the wife of the archon βασιλεύς, to Dionysus.[8]

[1] A.J.A. 50 (1946), pp. 122–39. She makes a very interesting attempt to show that on another such vase (fig. 81 = van Hoorn, no. 117: see also Webster, Ἀρχ. Ἐφ. 1953–4, ii, p. 197) the children are performing a parody of the Orestes story which is connected with the festival, but her argument, though very ingenious, is not (to me) quite convincing, nor is her suggestion that the ἀγῶνες χύτρινοι were originally contests of children at the festival. (The latter is not consistent with the very slight literary evidence: see below, pp. 15 f.) This is not the place to discuss further the part played by children in the festival: reference may be made to Deubner, op. cit., pp. 238 ff. It has been suggested that the very small choes may have been seasonal presents for children—like Easter eggs.

[2] van Hoorn, nos. 115, 118.

[3] For the custom of burying choes with children too young to have taken part in the festival, Rumpf (Bonner Jahrb. 161 (1961), pp. 213 f.) compares the loutrophoroi buried with girls who died before marriage, and points out that the analogy suggests that scenes on the choes need not always have reference to the Anthesteria.

[4] Published by kind permission of Mrs. Jean Serpieri, the present owner of the Vlasto Collection: van Hoorn, no. 270; A.R.V.² 1249, no. 14.

[5] This interpretation of the scene and its connexion with the Anthesteria is made more likely by a comparison with two other vases, one a chous in New York by the Meidias Painter (van Hoorn, no. 744 and fig. 12; Richter-Hall, no. 159 and figs. 158, 177/159; A.R.V.² 1313, no. 11), the other a hydria in Berlin by the Washing Painter (A.R.V.² 1131, no. 172; Greifenhagen, Antike Kunstwerke² (Berlin, 1966), pl. 48, lower): the first shows preparations for the rite, the second another example of the ceremony. Add probably Deubner, op. cit., pl. 18; Nilsson, Gesch. i², pl. 37/2 = A.R.V.² 1301, no. 7, a skyphos by the Penelope Painter showing a similar scene, but with a satyr pushing the swing. See below, p. 15, n. 3.

[6] Ar. Frogs 218 (pass. 8 above).

[7] Schol. Ar. Frogs 216 (pass. 8 above) mentions that the sanctuary contained the οἶκος and νεὼς τοῦ θεοῦ.

[8] [Dem.] in Neaeram 73–78 (pass. 11 above). For the nature of these ceremonies, see Farnell, Cults v, pp. 217 ff.; Deubner, op. cit., pp. 100 ff.; Nilsson, Gesch. i², pp. 121 f. and 122, n. 1; S.B. Munich, 1930, no. 4, pp. 7 ff. = Opusc. Sel. i, pp. 419 ff. It has been conjectured that the archon βασιλεύς himself may have impersonated the god: much remains doubtful. A miniature chous from the Anthesteria in New York (fig. 10: van Hoorn, no. 757; Deubner, op. cit., pp. 104 ff. and fig. 11/3–4; Bieber, Hesperia, Suppl. 8 (1949), pl. 5, 1 and pp. 34 f.; K. Friis Johansen, Eine Dithyrambosaufführung (Arkaeol. Kunsthist. Medd. Dan. Vid. Selsk.

The marriage itself was celebrated (by what symbolism we do not know) in the Βουκολεῖον,[1] which stood near the Πρυτανεῖον; the site of this is still a matter of controversy. It was doubtless a fertility ritual, which symbolized the union of the god of fruitfulness with the community represented by the wife of its religious head.

5. Whether or not there is a connexion between these ceremonies and the procession, represented on a number of vase-paintings, in which Dionysus was escorted riding in a car shaped like a ship on wheels, has been keenly disputed.[2] What is represented is plainly the arrival of Dionysus in Athens from overseas—whether from Thrace or Lydia or Euboea—and Deubner and Nilsson have made out a strong case for the connexion with the Anthesteria, based on a comparison of a number of vases with the evidence of ancient notices (quoted above) and of ceremonies of the type called καταγώγια (the 'bringing home' of Dionysus) in a number of Ionian states, in some of which a connexion with the local Anthesteria is affirmed; these states include Smyrna, Ephesus, Miletus, and Priene.[3]

If the Attic Anthesteria included a procession of this kind, it may have escorted the god to the Βουκολεῖον, though this is no more than a conjecture. The car of Dionysus may have been followed by the wagons from which the revellers shouted their jests,[4] while the crowd retaliated

4, no. 2, 1959) pp. 16 ff.) is now widely agreed to show children imitating part of the ceremony. But Rumpf (op. cit., pp. 210 ff.) argues strongly against this interpretation: the alleged 'basilinna' is a boy, and the attributes of a wedding are all absent.

[1] Aristotle, Ἀθ. Πολ. iii. 5 (pass. 12 above): cf. 'Suidas' s.v. ἄρχων. The expression used by Aristotle, τὸ νῦν καλούμενον Βουκολεῖον, may imply that he knew an earlier name for this building. The American excavators have made a strong case for placing the Prytaneion (mentioned by Paus. i. 18. 3–4) on the NW. slope of the Acropolis, below the precinct of Aglauros. See Hesperia 4 (1935), pp. 470–2; 18 (1949), p. 129. For earlier controversy, see Judeich, Topographie v. Athen², pp. 296 ff., 304 f. On the ἱερὸς γάμος, see most recently Erika Simon, Antike Kunst 6 (1963), pp. 6 ff. Among much that is speculative, she draws attention to a Polygnotan calyx-crater in Tarquinia (A.R.V.² 1057, no. 96 = her fig. 5. 3 : c. 430), showing perhaps Dionysus arriving at the Boukoleion.

[2] Figs. 11–14. Connexion with the Anthesteria is the most likely hypothesis (cf. Deubner, op. cit., pp. 102 ff.; Nilsson, Gesch. i², pp. 582 ff., against the attempt of Frickenhaus (Jahrb. Arch. 27 (1912), pp. 61 ff.) and others to connect the procession with the City Dionysia), but it must always remain possible that the painters are representing a popular subject, without direct dependence on any festival or ritual. Deubner (op. cit., pp. 104, 149 f.) argues from the fact that the Iobaccheion at Athens (pass. 35 above) was built over part of the remains of the precinct ἐν Λίμναις that the Καταγώγια celebrated by the Iobacchoi may have been a survival of the return of Dionysus in a ship-car many centuries before.

[3] Passages 32–35 above. It is uncertain at what time of the year the καταγώγια took place at Ephesus, Miletus, and Priene. For Ephesus, see also Maass, Orpheus, pp. 56 ff. and n. 61; Deubner, op. cit., pp. 103 f. On καταγώγια generally, see Nilsson, Jahrb. Arch. 31 (1916), pp. 309 ff., esp. 315 f., 332 ff. = Opusc. Sel. i, pp. 166 ff., esp. 175–7, 203 ff.; Boardman, J.H.S. 78 (1958), pp. 4 ff.; Nilsson, Gr. Feste, p. 268, n. 4.

[4] Photius s.v. τὰ ἐκ τῶν ἁμαξῶν; Harpokr. s.v. πομπείας καὶ πομπεύειν (passages 26, 14 above): cf. Plato, Laws i, 637 b; Schol. Lucian, Iup. trag. p. 77. 28 Rabe; Eun. 202. 15.

in like manner—a form of merriment which is attested both for the Anthesteria and for the Lenaia, as well as for the procession to Eleusis before the Mysteries. (It was perhaps a common feature of popular processions at Athens, and may have been apotropaic in its original intention.)

Fig. 11. Dionysiac procession

6. The third day of the festival, called Χύτροι, began at sunset on the evening of the day called Χόες. There is consequently some confusion here and there in the attribution of particular ceremonies to one day or the other. Thus Aristophanes (*Frogs* 217–19, pass. 8 above) speaks of the revels as occurring on the Χύτροι—and this was probably correct, though they began with the drinking-match on the Χόες—and Photius and others (pass. 27 f. above) refer to the Χόες as the day on which the ghosts wandered; such confusions are not unnatural, and there may in practice have been some overlapping; but it seems probable that, speaking generally, the cheerful ceremonies connected with the Χόες came to an end about sunset, and that the Χύτροι which then began was a day of a quite different character, devoted to the cult of the dead, and that Dionysus had little or no part in it.[1] The day was named after the pots of a kind of porridge, composed of various kinds of grain, and offered, according to our sources,[2] to Hermes Χθόνιος,[3] with intercessions

---

'Suidas', s.v. τὰ ἐκ τῶν ἁμαξῶν σκώμματα, records a peculiar (and perhaps more serious) form of vituperation from a wagon at Alexandria (see Farnell, *Cults* v, p. 212).

[1] Nilsson, *Gesch.* i², p. 597 (but Nilsson goes on to suggest that the conjunction of the two *festivals* is probably very old: he compares the Roman Parentalia and the Persian Hamaspathmaedaya, as festivals of the dead occurring in the spring: ibid., pp. 597 f. and 597, n. 3). It is very doubtful whether the ἀγῶνες χύτρινοι (see below, pp. 15 f.) were an essential or original part of the festival.

[2] In fact, more probably as food for the dead: cf. Nilsson, *Gesch.* i², p. 181.

[3] That the offering was made to Dionysus as well as Hermes is stated on the authority of

for the dead—particularly, we are told, for those who perished in Deukalion's flood.¹ It was a day of gloom, a μιαρά or ἀποφρὰς ἡμέρα, on which ghosts were abroad, and cathartic measures (such as the chewing of buckthorn and the smearing of houses with pitch) were taken as a precaution against them. At the end of the day the cry was uttered, θύραζε Κᾶρες or θύραζε Κῆρες, οὐκέτ' Ἀνθεστήρια.

This cry has been the subject of much controversy. If it was originally θύραζε Κᾶρες—an order to the country slaves, who had come in to the city to share in the feast, to go back to work—it may perhaps have become a colloquial phrase for recalling idle slaves to their task; and the literary evidence has been thought to suggest that Κᾶρες was the original form of the phrase. Zenobius (second century A.D.), who got his material from Didymus' work πρὸς τοὺς περὶ παροιμιῶν συντεταχότας (Didymus' own source being possibly the collection of proverbs in several books made by Demon in the third century B.C.), seems to have included this form only, though two collections of proverbs in manuscripts slightly later than the principal manuscript of Zenobius (evidently copying Photius, as their reproduction of the misreading ἔνι for ἔτ' shows) add the other version, θύραζε Κῆρες, and explain it by the expulsion of the ghosts who wandered about the city during the festival. The evidence, however, that the word κῆρες was ever applied to the souls of the dead, apart from this passage, is slight. Hesychius has κῆρες· ψυχαί· συμφοραί· μοῖραι θανατηφόροι, and 'Suidas' κὴρ· ψυχή, καὶ θανατηφόρος μοῖρα. καὶ κῆρες, θανατηφόροι μοῖραι . . . κὴρ δὲ καὶ ἡ ψυχή, ὅτι διάπυρος ἐστι· τὸ γὰρ ἔμφυτον θερμόν, τοῦτο ψυχή. "εἰμὶ δὲ κὴρ τυμβοῦχος, ὁ δὲ κτείνας με Κόροιβος"² (but no stress can be laid on this, as the κὴρ τυμβοῦχος is the figure on the tombstone, not the deceased). Further, there is no other evidence of the expulsion of ghosts in Athens, though it was performed in other parts of Greece, as in many other European countries: it may indeed be, as M. Ganszyniec has suggested, that the Greek proverb has been misinterpreted through learned confusion with the expulsion of ghosts that took place at the Roman festival of the Lemuria. A further difficulty arises from the fact

Didymus in schol. Ar. *Ach.* 1076 (pass. 5 above), but it can hardly be doubted that the words Διονύσῳ καί are a mistaken addition: in fact μόνῳ could not make sense with τῷ Διονύσῳ καὶ Ἑρμῇ (it would have to be μόνοις). On the text of the scholia bearing on the Χύτροι, see F. J. Tausend, *Studien zu att. Festen* (Würzburg, 1920), pp. 22 ff.; Nilsson, *Gesch.* i², p. 594 and ibid., n. 7 (quoting suggestions made by A. Wifstrand), 597. For a possible connexion of certain vases with this ceremony, see Karouzou, *A.J.A.* 50 (1946), pp. 122–3.

¹ Pass. 5, 8, 27, 28 above. It is possible that the Ὑδροφορία, the pouring of libations of water to these same victims of the flood, was also a ceremony of the Χύτροι: see Deubner, op. cit., p. 113; Nilsson, *Gesch.* i², pp. 595 f.

² *Anth. Pal.* vii. 154. 3 (date and author unknown). The MSS. of 'Suidas' have τυμβοῦλος.

that the proverb forms an iambic trimeter. There is no ground for Crusius's statement that this was a traditional metre of liturgical formula, and the line as it stands—with Κᾶρες—may come from some comedy, even if something of the sort was said at the Anthesteria. No final solution seems possible.[1]

How a day of evil omen came to be attached to the cheerful Dionysiac festival we do not know. That it was probably separate at first is shown by the fact that there is no hint of anything like it in any of the parallel festivals in Ionian states of which brief records survive. The Anthesteria was otherwise plainly a cheerful feast, and there is reason to think that it dates from before the migration from Greece to Asia Minor of the Ionian tribes who all celebrated it.[2] If so, and if it was originally an Ionian festival, there is nothing surprising in the absence from it of dramatic elements, or performances which might grow into drama, since the roots of drama were for the most part in Dorian soil.[3]

7. The only direct point of contact between the Anthesteria and the Greek drama in classical times is that furnished by the so-called ἀγῶνες χύτρινοι which were restored after an unspecified period of abeyance by a law of Lycurgus in the third quarter of the fourth century B.C. The principal authority for this is found in [Plutarch], Vit. X Orat. 841 f:

εἰσήνεγκεν δὲ καὶ νόμους, τὸν μὲν περὶ τῶν κωμῳδῶν, ἀγῶνα τοῖς Χύτροις ἐπιτελεῖν ἐφάμιλλον ἐν τῷ θεάτρῳ καὶ τὸν νικήσαντα εἰς ἄστυ καταλέγεσθαι, πρότερον οὐκ ἐξόν, ἀναλαμβάνων τὸν ἀγῶνα ἐκλελοιπότα. This can hardly refer to anything but a contest of comic actors, the victor in which

---

[1] See especially O. Crusius, *Analecta critica ad paroemiographos Graecos* (1883), pp. 48 f., 146; id., *Paroemiographica* (1910), pp. 64 ff.; id., art. Keren in Roscher's *Lexicon* ii, col. 1148; Nilsson, *Eranos* 15 (1915), pp. 182 ff. = *Opusc. Sel.* i, pp. 146 ff.; Malten in *R.E.*, Suppl. iv s.v. Ker; Ganszyniec, *Eranos* 45 (1947), pp. 100–13; Rose, *Harv. Theol. Rev.* 41 (1948), pp. 217 ff.; Nilsson, *Gesch.* i², pp. 222 ff., esp. 224–5 and most recently, van der Valk, *R.E.G.* 76 (1963), pp. 418–20. Nilsson's suggestion that Κῆρες may have been *applied* to ghosts, in the sense 'ye evil things', without *meaning* 'ghosts', and Crusius's that κᾶρες may be Doric for κῆρες, are not convincing; neither is Deubner's treatment of the line as a combination of ritual phrases in other metres, accidentally forming an iambic trimeter.

[2] Pass. 32, 33, 34 above and p. 12, n. 2 above. For the Anthesteria at Teos, see Schwyzer, *D.G.E.*, no. 710 B, l. 32. The objection that this implies a worship in Greece of Dionysus earlier than is often recognized was met by Deubner, op. cit., pp. 122 f., even before the name (not necessarily the god) 'Dionysus' was apparently recognized on the Linear B tablets from Pylos (Ventris–Chadwick, *Documents*, p. 127: the name recurs on a second tablet: PY Xb 1419). On the 'double-sidedness' of the Anthesteria, see Farnell, *Cults* v, pp. 221 ff.; Nilsson, *Gesch.* i², pp. 597 f.; Jacoby, commentary on Philochorus 328 F 84 (= *F. Gr. Hist.* iii b, Suppl. i, pp. 364 f.; Suppl. ii, pp. 268 ff. and 537).

[3] We do not here discuss the possible connexion of the rite called Αἰώρα with the Anthesteria, for lack of space: see Nilsson, *Eranos* 15 (1915), pp. 181 ff. = *Opusc. Sel.* i, pp. 145 ff.; *Gesch.* i², pp. 585 f.; Deubner, op. cit., pp. 118 ff.; Karouzou, *A.J.A.* 50 (1946), p. 122 and refs. there given; Immerwahr, *T.A.P.A.* 77 (1946), pp. 245 ff.; Dietrich, *Hermes* 89 (1961) pp. 36 ff. See also above, p. 11 and n. 5, and fig. 9.

acquired the right to act at the ensuing Dionysia ἐν ἄστει.[1] For tragedy the choice of the three protagonists was the duty of the archon, but the successful protagonist of the previous year had a right to be selected; for subordinate actors practice seems to have varied.[2] Presumably the contest at the Χύτροι was limited to protagonists, though there is no definite statement to this effect. The notice of pseudo-Plutarch is confirmed by the scholiast[3] on Aristophanes *Frogs*, l. 218, with his quotation from Philochorus (328 F 57 Jac., *c.* 280 B.C.). The nature of the contests is unrecorded. It does not seem likely that these ἀγῶνες were an essential part of the Anthesteria, the nature of which has been described above. They cannot have been an original part, because the Anthesteria was a much older festival than the Dionysia ἐν ἄστει.[4] But the festival fell at a time which would be convenient for the choice of actors to perform at the Dionysia a few weeks later; a time of public holiday-making would also be suitable, and so the contests may naturally have been 'thrown in' on the third day of the festival.

8. There is a reference in Philostratus' life of Apollonius[5] to dances in costume at the Anthesteria which shocked Apollonius, who had apparently expected to hear singing and recitation of selections from tragedy and comedy. These performances occurred in the intervals of recitations of Orphic poems. If any or all of these things formed part of the Anthesteria of the first century A.D., the festival must have changed much. These performances may have replaced the ἀγῶνες χύτρινοι on the Χύτροι. It is possible that the original character of the festival had long been forgotten, and it was probably not long after this that the sanctuary ἐν Λίμναις was partly destroyed and replaced by the Iobaccheion of which some remains are still to be seen.

9. Recently, however, a case has been made out for supposing that the Anthesteria did include one type of performance in common with the other, more clearly dramatic, festivals of Dionysus. Professor K. Friis Johansen published in 1959[6] an Attic red-figure bell-krater of the late fifth century (fig. 15: his connexion of this vase with the Kleophon

---

[1] Other interpretations are shown to be impossible by O'Connor, *Chapters in the History of Actors and Acting in Ancient Greece* (1908), pp. 54 f. The conjecture that the privilege won by the victorious actor was that of producing the Old Comedy acted, as an 'extra', at each Dionysia from 339 B.C. (i.e. from the time of Lycurgus onwards) would be attractive, but the words ἀναλαμβάνων τὸν ἀγῶνα ἐκλελοιπότα seem to exclude it.

[2] 'Suidas' s.v. νεμήσεις ὑποκριτῶν, and below, pp. 93 f.

[3] Pass. 8 above.

[4] The 'theatre' in which the Dionysia ἐν ἄστει were first celebrated cannot have been there before the sixth century B.C. See *Theatre of Dionysus*, ch. 1.

[5] Pass. 37 above.

[6] *Eine Dithyrambosaufführung*; *A.R.V.*[2] 1145, no. 35.

Painter is now confirmed by Beazley's attribution), which shows a group of male figures, garlanded and wearing ceremonial dress, himation and full-length decorated chiton: they are accompanied by a flute-player, fluting, also garlanded and in ceremonial dress, including long-sleeved chiton, and are apparently depicted as singing. The 'leader' is shown full-face, his four companions in profile, facing and looking at him: two of them carry sprigs of ivy. All six figures (including the flute-player, called Amphilochos) are named: the leader is 'Phrynichos', two of the others ('Pleistias' and 'Theomedes') bear known Athenian names.[1] The six figures are grouped three on either side of a central mast-like object, depicted as considerably taller than a man's height, and with its lower part (apparently a three-legged stand) completely wreathed in ivy. Johansen draws up a telling comparison between this and the equally mysterious object being carried by three boys on the Metropolitan Museum chous depicting children perhaps imitating the preliminaries of the ἱερὸς γάμος at the Anthesteria.[2] After considering suggested identifications of the object on the chous, he adopts a discarded suggestion of Miss Richter,[3] and identifies both as a maypole. He then proceeds to infer that the bell-krater also refers to the Anthesteria, commemorating a dithyrambic performance at that festival.[4] Now the case for recognizing the Copenhagen bell-krater as a commemorative piece, recalling a dithyrambic performance (? victory), seems overwhelming. What is a good deal less certain is the identification of the occasion of that performance with the Anthesteria: this part of Johansen's argument turns largely on the rather debatable equation of the central object on the krater with that on the New York chous (assuming the latter to refer certainly to the Anthesteria), and to a lesser extent on the assignation of a Pindar fragment (fr. 75 Snell, from a dithyramb) to a performance at the Anthesteria. Both suggestions are attractive, but neither can be considered proved.[5]

[1] Johansen suggests identifications: Pleistias perhaps the ambassador of *I.G.* i². 57. 51 (426–425 B.C.), and Theomedes perhaps Kirchner, *Prosopographia Att.*, no. 6959. His identification of 'Phrynichos' with the late fifth-century comic poet (Ar. *Clouds* 555 ff., *Frogs* 13) raises problems that cannot be gone into here. Johansen points out that identifiable and politically prominent names also appear on a contemporary krater in the manner of the Kleophon Painter in Boston (*A.R.V.*² 1149, no. 9).

[2] See above, p. 11, n. 8 and fig. 10.   [3] *Bull. Metr. Mus.* 20 (1925), p. 131.

[4] Performed, Prof. Johansen suggests, in the Agora, before the altar of the Twelve Gods: the suggestion is based on arguments drawn from Pindar, fr. 75 Snell, ll. 3–5, and the probability that the fragment comes from a dithyramb written for performance at a Dionysiac festival in early spring (ll. 6, 15 ff.), that is, the Anthesteria.

[5] Johansen's arguments are accepted by Webster in *Dith. Trag. Com.*², pp. 21, 35, 37 f. Rumpf (*Bonner Jahrb.* 161 (1961), p. 212) and Greifenhagen (*Ein Satyrspiel des Aischylos?* (118th Winckelmannsprogramm, Berlin), 1963, p. 5) suggest a performance at the City Dionysia, but see *contra*, already, Johansen, op. cit., p. 16.

10. There can be no serious doubt that the Anthesteria was identical with the ἀρχαιότερα Διονύσια mentioned by Thucydides.[1] His words admit of no other interpretation. But some scholars[2] have found a difficulty in his use of the comparative, which, they think, means that Thucydides knew only *two* Dionysiac festivals, an earlier and a later, and that as the later must have been the Great Dionysia, the earlier must have been the Lenaia which must accordingly have been, wholly or in part, identical with the Anthesteria and must have taken place ἐν Λίμναις.

In reply it may be shown (1) that the inference from the use of the comparative is unwarranted, (2) that the identification of the Anthesteria and the Lenaia is contrary to the evidence.

(1) Even if the use of the comparative implied a comparison between two terms only, these two terms might be (*a*) the Anthesteria, (*b*) the rest of the Dionysiac festivals treated as a group of more recent institutions. But in fact there are other passages in classical Greek literature in which the comparative of words denoting age, etc., is used of the oldest, not of two, but of several. Nilsson[3] collects the following instances:

Lys. x. 5. ὁ γὰρ πρεσβύτερος ἀδελφὸς Πανταλέων ἅπαντα παρέλαβε καὶ ἐπιτροπεύσας ἡμᾶς τῶν πατρῴων ἀπεστέρησεν.

Id. xiii. 67. ἦσαν τοίνυν οὗτοι, ὦ ἄνδρες δικασταί, τέτταρες ἀδελφοί· τούτων εἰς μὲν ὁ πρεσβύτερος κτλ.

Xen. *Cyr.* v. i. 6. ὡς δ᾽ ἡμῶν ὁ γεραίτερος εἶπε.[4] (The context shows that a number of persons were concerned.)

Theocr. xv. 139. οὔθ᾽ Ἕκτωρ, Ἑκάβας ὁ γεραίτερος εἴκατι παίδων.

It may, however, be suggested that for some considerable period there *were* only two Dionysiac festivals, the Anthesteria and the Lenaia, and that therefore on the strictest view of the comparative, the former would be τὰ ἀρχαιότερα, and might continue to be so spoken of even after the institution of the Great Dionysia, if no one was pedantic enough to change the appellation to the superlative.[5]

(2) The Lenaia were celebrated in the month Gamelion (elsewhere

---

[1] Pass. 1 above. The lemma of the papyrus scholium on this passage (pass. 1a above) has ἀρχαιότατα, but the temptation to substitute superlative for comparative must have been considerable.

[2] Gilbert, Dörpfeld, Capps, and others. Cf. also Appendix C to Haigh's *Attic Theatre*[3].

[3] *Studia de Dionysiis Atticis*, p. 54. Homeric instances can be found in Kühner–Gerth, *Gr. Gramm.*, § 349 b, para. 3. See further Theocr. xii. 32 with Gow's note.

[4] The reading γεραίτερος is far better supported than γεραίτατος. Grammarians and editors tend to 'emend' such comparatives into the supposed orthodox superlative, as, for example, in Lys. xiii. 67, Theocr. xv. 139 (quoted above), Ael. *Var. H.* ii. 41, etc.

[5] But it is impossible to follow Capps's distinction (*Class. Philol.* 2 (1907), pp. 25 ff.) of ἀρχαιότερα ('ancient', 'primitive') from παλαιότερα (prior in time) and the conclusions which he draws from it. Aeschines, *in Ctes.* 53, uses both words in exactly the same sense.

called Lenaion), the Anthesteria in Anthesterion:[1] and in inscriptions the two festivals are plainly treated as distinct; e.g. in the accounts of money laid out on each festival in 329–328 B.C.,[2] and in an inscription of A.D. 192–3[3] which separates the Lenaia from the Χύτροι. Photius, 'Suidas', etc., in explaining the σκώμματα ἐκ τῶν ἁμαξῶν, after referring to the custom at the Χόες, add τὸ δ' αὐτὸ καὶ τοῖς Ληναίοις ὕστερον ἐποίουν. Nothing could be clearer.[4]

That the character of the two festivals may have been quite different will be seen from the account of the Lenaia to be given in the next section of this chapter, where the connected problem of the place of the Lenaian performance will also have to be discussed.

11. The remaining question in regard to the Anthesteria concerns the site of the precinct ἐν Λίμναις, and for this the only first-hand evidence is that of Thucydides.[5] He is explaining that the earliest city (before Theseus) was quite small, consisting only of what in his own day was called the Acropolis, together with the area beneath it 'in a direction more or less south'. This latter expression must refer to the area on the southern and south-western slope of the Acropolis, then included within the same city wall as the Acropolis itself. This he confirms by noting that the temples of other gods (besides Athena) all fell within this small city, being on the Acropolis, and that the oldest sanctuaries outside this original city were also close to it—πρὸς τοῦτο τὸ μέρος[6] τῆς πόλεως μᾶλλον ἵδρυται—they 'were built with reference to—or close to—this part of Athens' (τῆς πόλεως being the Athens of Thucydides' own day)—namely, the sanctuaries of Olympian Zeus, the Pythion, the sanctuary of Ge and that of Dionysus ἐν Λίμναις, and other old sanctuaries; that the fountain originally called Kallirrhoe, but now (since Peisistratus' day) called Enneakrounos, was in the same neighbourhood; and that hence the Acropolis (which with the additional area on the south was the original city) was still commonly called πόλις.

Few, if any, of these sanctuaries can be sited with certainty. The first two should refer to the famous Olympieion begun by the Peisistratids

---

[1] Nilsson, Studia, pp. 1–37, completely disproves Gilbert's attempt to prove that the names of the months were changed and the festivals transferred from one month to another.

[2] I.G. ii². 1672. ll. 182, 204.

[3] Ibid. 2130. ll. 59 f., 69; cf. Nilsson, op. cit., pp. 38–44. He quotes other equally conclusive passages (p. 143).

[4] The schol. on Ar. Ach. 961 certainly refers to the Χόες as a festival of Διόνυσος Ληναῖος, but other accounts do not; the scholiasts are far from impeccable, and (as has often been suggested) ΛΗΝΑΙΟΥ is an easy corruption of ΛΙΜΝΑΙΟΥ.

[5] ii. 15. 3–6 (pass. 1 above). Note also the papyrus scholium on this passage (1a above).

[6] πρὸς τοῦτο τὸ μέρος: not 'to the south of the original city' but 'close to this part of Athens'.

south-east of the Acropolis near the Ilissos,[1] near which was a sanctuary of Pythian Apollo (Paus. i. 19. 1: cf. Thuc. vi. 54. 6–7, *I.G.* i². 761, found near the Olympieion): the only reason for doubt is the considerable distance from the Acropolis (more than five hundred metres from the entrance). Because of this doubt, an alternative identification has been put forward:[2] it is suggested that there was another Pythion close to the spring Klepsydra, below the north-west corner of the Acropolis. The existence of this other Pythion is an inference from Euripides, *Ion* 283 ff., and a puzzling passage of Strabo (ix. 2. 11),[3] which in turn implies an Olympieion in the same vicinity. But the evidence is at least shaky: Strabo's phrase is an odd one to describe a site on the north-west cliff of the Acropolis (it would more naturally be taken to refer to the more famous Pythion and Olympieion, and to the city wall, not to the wall of the Acropolis), and there is no archaeological confirmation. The location of the sanctuary of Ge is still more problematic: it may have been that of Ge Kourotrophos,[4] somewhere on the southern side of the Acropolis, but there are other possibilities, including the sanctuary of Ge Olympia within the Peisistratid Olympieion.[5] As for the 'other old sanctuaries', a temple of Demeter and Kore is mentioned by Pausanias,[6] apparently connected with the Eleusinion, as was the statue of Triptolemus which Pausanias mentions in the same breath. The Eleusinion has now been identified with some certainty: it stood on the Panathenaic Way, between the Agora and the Acropolis, on the north-west slope of the latter.[7] The fountain Kallirrhoe or Enneakrounos was, apparently, near these—and near enough to have been the main water supply of the original city, but its siting remains an unsolved problem: thirty years ago it was believed by Judeich and others that the problem had been solved by Dörpfeld's discovery of a fountain-house with sixth-century

[1] For the legendary antiquity of this sanctuary in Attic tradition, see Paus. i. 18. 7–8.

[2] Most recently by A. W. Parsons, *Hesperia* 12 (1943), pp. 191 f., 234 ff. The original suggestion is due to Dörpfeld (*Ath. Mitt.* 20 (1895), pp. 199 ff.). On the difficulties of this theory, see Gomme, *Historical Commentary on Thucydides* ii, pp. 57 ff.; Wycherley, *A.J.A.* 63 (1959), pp. 68 ff.; ibid. 67 (1963), pp. 76 f.

[3] ἐτήρουν δ' ἐπὶ τρεῖς μῆνας, καθ' ἕκαστον μῆνα ἐπὶ τρεῖς ἡμέρας καὶ νύκτας ἀπὸ τῆς ἐσχάρας τοῦ Ἀστραπαίου Διός· ἔστι δ' αὕτη ἐν τῷ τείχει μεταξὺ τοῦ Πυθίου καὶ τοῦ Ὀλυμπίου. The identification of the cave on the north-west cliff of the Acropolis with Strabo's Pythion is due to A. Keramopoullos, Ἀρχ. Δελτ. 12 (1929), pp. 86–92.

[4] Paus. i. 22. 3; Judeich, *Topogr. Athen*², p. 285, n. 4.

[5] Paus. i. 18. 7, with Frazer's note. For a possible sanctuary of Ge on the north-west cliff of the Acropolis, see Broneer, *Hesperia* 11 (1942), p. 260.

[6] Paus. i. 14. 1.

[7] On the Eleusinion, see now *Hesperia* 29 (1960), pp. 334 ff. and n. 8 (with refs. to earlier discussion); Wycherley, *The Athenian Agora* iii (*Testimonia*), pp. 74 ff. For the Delphinion, another ancient (Paus. i. 19. 1) sanctuary in the neighbourhood of the Olympieion, see Wycherley, *A.J.A.* 67 (1963), p. 78.

conduits at the foot of the Pnyx,[1] and it was hoped that this discovery also did away with the problem raised by Pausanias' assertion[2] that Enneakrounos was in or near the Agora, combined with the evidence of others that it was near the Ilissos.[3] Since then the American excavations of the Agora have altered the picture somewhat: the excavators now incline to believe that Enneakrounos is to be identified with a late sixth-century B.C. fountain-house discovered by them at the south-east corner of the Agora, in the hollow to the north-east of the Areopagus[4]: this certainly suits the account of Pausanias, and could perhaps be accommodated to that of Thucydides, if the phrase πρὸς νότον μάλιστα τετραμμένον were translated 'facing mainly towards the south', and 'mainly' taken to allow, not so much for geographical vagueness, as for some of the sites' mentioned by Thucydides lying in a different direction from the others, though associated with them. But here too there is no certainty.

Where, then, was the Dionysion ἐν Λίμναις?[5] Three theories have been propounded:

(1) *That it was close to (or just south of) the site of the theatre of Dionysus.* Those who (like Carroll) hold this view base it mainly on a combination of the statement of Thucydides that it was in the sanctuary ἐν Λίμναις that the ἀρχαιότερα Διονύσια were celebrated and an expression in the speech against Neaera—ἐν τῷ ἀρχαιοτάτῳ ἱερῷ τοῦ Διονύσου καὶ ἁγιωτάτῳ ἐν Λίμναις—with Pausanias' statement[6] that the ἀρχαιότατον ἱερόν of Dionysus was πρὸς τῷ θεάτρῳ. But whereas down to the fourth century the original precinct ἐν Λίμναις, wherever it was, remained in being, it had certainly disappeared by the time of Pausanias, who in describing Athens as he found it would naturally give the title of ἀρχαιότατον ἱερόν to the oldest temple which he found existing, viz. the older temple of Dionysus in

---

[1] See Gräber, *Ath. Mitt.* 30 (1905), pp. 1 ff.; Judeich, *Topogr. Athen*[2], pp. 194 ff.

[2] i. 14. 1, following on from 8. 5–6.

[3] e.g. [Plato], *Axiochos* 364 a; Cratinus, fr. 186 K; *Etym. Magn.* s.v. Ἐννεάκρουνος. See also Gomme, *Historical Commentary*, pp. 53 f.

[4] See *The Athenian Agora: a guide to the excavations and museum*[2] (1962), pp. 97 f. and plans on pp. 23 and 84; *Hesperia* 22 (1953), pp. 29 ff.; ibid. 25 (1956), pp. 49 ff.; Wycherley, *The Athenian Agora* iii (*Testimonia*), pp. 137 ff. For the SW. fountain-house (also in the Agora), previously a candidate for identification as Enneakrounos, see now *Hesperia* 24 (1955), pp. 52 ff.; ibid. 25 (1956), pp. 52 f.

[5] For discussion of this subject see esp. Dörpfeld's account of his excavations in *Ath. Mitt.* 20 (1895), pp. 161 ff. (followed by J. E. Harrison, *Primitive Athens*, pp. 89–96); M. Carroll in *C.R.* 19 (1905), pp. 325–8 and Excursus III of his edition of Pausanias' *Attica*; Dörpfeld, *Ath. Mitt.* 46 (1921), pp. 81 ff.; Judeich, *Topogr. Athen*[2], pp. 291 ff.; Gomme, *Historical Commentary*, pp. 51 f., 55.

[6] i. 20. 3. The next sentence shows that he is thinking of temples in the theatre precinct only.

the theatre precinct. His expression gives no guidance as to the place of the sanctuary ἐν Λίμναις.

Carroll's further argument that Thucydides is naming the ancient sanctuaries in the order of their localities (an unproved assumption) and that the ἐν Λίμναις must therefore be further away from the Olympieion and Pythion than the sanctuary of Γῆ Κουροτρόφος, at the southwest corner of the Acropolis, is rendered very unsafe by the fact that it is

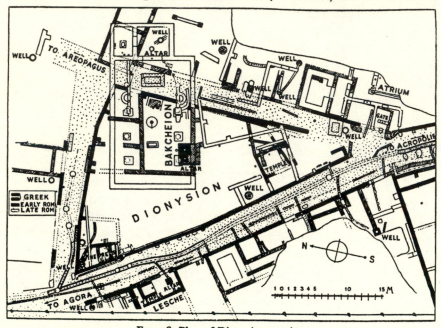

Fig. 16. Plan of Dionysian precinct

only a conjecture that this particular sanctuary of Γῆ was the one referred to by the historian.

It is also extremely doubtful whether the requisite swampy ground can be found at any period known to us in the neighbourhood of the theatre, and both the name ἐν Λίμναις and the chorus of the *Frogs* (209 ff.) demand real marshy ground.[1]

(2) *That it was in the precinct excavated by Dörpfeld* in 1894 to the west of the Acropolis in the hollow enclosed by the western slopes of the Acropolis, and the Areopagus and the Pnyx.[2] This was, as the authorities require, outside the earliest, or Thesean, city wall, but included in the

---

[1] Note too the papyrus commentary on Thuc. ii. 15. 4 (*P. Oxy.* 853 = pass. 1a above): δ]ιὰ τὸ ἐκλελ[ι]μνάσθαι [τὸν τόπον, quoting Philochorus or Apollodorus (Jacoby, *F. Gr. Hist.* 328 F 229 and commentary, iii b, Suppl. i, pp. 594 f., and Suppl. ii, p. 486; iii B, p. 744).

[2] So Deubner, *Att. Feste*, pp. 93 f.

later city, as a passage of Isaeus 'proves the sanctuary ἐν Λίμναις to have been.[1]

But the identification cannot be considered certain in the absence both of confirmation from inscriptions and of any trace of the many choes which should, according to all our evidence, have been deposited there. The case for it must be purely circumstantial. First, the question of the swamp. The area was certainly dry in the period when it was covered by the roads and buildings that Dörpfeld excavated. This argument is perhaps not decisive: a puzzling passage of Strabo,[2] in which he has been thought to be quoting the region of the Athenian Dionysion ἐν Λίμναις as a parallel to a district just outside Amyklai, which was also called Λίμναι because it had once been marshy, though it was no longer so, may imply that the Athenian sanctuary was dry in Strabo's day. But it is doubtful whether Dörpfeld's sanctuary can ever have been marshy.[3]

The authorities for the Dionysion ἐν Λίμναις state that the precinct contained a νεώς and an οἶκος,[4] and that there was a βωμός, with an inscribed στήλη close to it.[5] Dörpfeld's precinct certainly contained a temple and another building: a small temple at the south end, and at the north-west corner a building partly occupied by a winepress.[6] One of the most conspicuous objects in the precinct is the foundation of an offering table mounted on four low pillars,[7] with grooves in the foundation which may well have been intended for the reception of στῆλαι. The polygonal masonry of the lower strata of the walls,[8] and the

---

[1] viii. 35 (passage 9 above).

[2] viii. 5. 1. ὑποπέπτωκε δὲ τῷ Ταϋγέτῳ ἡ Σπάρτη ἐν μεσογαίᾳ καὶ Ἀμύκλαι, οὗ τὸ τοῦ Ἀπόλλωνος ἱερόν, καὶ ἡ Φᾶρις. ἔστι μὲν οὖν ἐν κοιλοτέρῳ χωρίῳ τὸ τῆς πόλεως ἔδαφος, καίπερ ἀπολάμβανον ὄρη μεταξύ· ἀλλ' οὐδέν γε μέρος αὐτοῦ λιμνάζει, τὸ δὲ παλαιὸν ἐλίμναζε τὸ προάστειον καὶ ἐκάλουν αὐτὸ Λίμνας· καὶ τὸ τοῦ Διονύσου ἱερὸν ἐν Λίμναις ἐφ' ὑγροῦ βεβηκὸς ἐτύγχανε, νῦν δ' ἐπὶ ξηροῦ τὴν ἵδρυσιν ἔχει. The words τὸ Δ. ἱερὸν ἐν Λίμναις seem to refer to the well-known Δ. ἐν Λίμναις, i.e. the one at Athens. Cf. passage 1a above and H. F. Tozer, Selns. from Strabo (1893), p. 212, and F. Bölte, Ath. Mitt. 34 (1909), pp. 391–2 (the latter suggests that Strabo's authority was Apollodorus); cf. also Dörpfeld, ibid. 46 (1921), pp. 82 f.

[3] G. T. W. Hooker, J.H.S. 80 (1960), p. 114.

[4] Schol. on Ar. Frogs 216 (above, p. 4); cf. Harpokr. and 'Suid'. s.v. ἐν Λίμναις Διόνυσος.

[5] [Dem.] in Neaer. 76 (above, p. 4, pass. 11).

[6] The winepress is not really relevant: it is unlikely that Λήναιον is really connected with ληνός, meaning winepress (see below, pp. 29 f.). There are other winepresses in the neighbourhood, and the fact that no other sanctuary of Dionysus contains one could be interpreted in more than one way. Furthermore, Dörpfeld's identification of the Dionysion ἐν Λίμναις with the Lenaion is fraught with difficulties (see below, pp. 39 f.).

[7] The slab of a similar altar-table, found in an Attic village in 1880 and inscribed to Dionysus Αὐλωνεύς, is described in Ath. Mitt. 5 (1880), p. 116 (I.G. ii². 4745), but as it is of imperial date, it is hardly worth mention here. Dörpfeld notes (ibid. 20 (1895), p. 168) that such altars are also found on vases, especially in connexion with Dionysus.

[8] Dörpfeld's full description in Ath. Mitt. 20 (1895), pp. 161 ff. should be consulted, or J. E. Harrison's summary in her Primitive Athens, from which Fig. 16 is borrowed by permission of the Cambridge University Press.

geometrical vases found, point to the buildings' being of the seventh or
early sixth century B.C. The Dionysiac character of the precinct is
made probable by the fact that when it was destroyed or remodelled, a
Dionysiac sanctuary—that of the Iobacchoi—was built over it in the
second century A.D.[1]

There are several difficulties in the way of acceptance of Dörpfeld's
identification.[2] The offering table is not of a type which would normally
be called a βωμός, and although the absence of inscriptions and dedications dating from pre-imperial times may be explained by the statement
that it was then open only once a year, the single small entrance to the
precinct in its earlier days, cited by Dörpfeld to support the identification,[3]
adds nothing to his case. As G. T. W. Hooker has pointed out, there is
no necessary connexion between 'open one day only in the year' and
'having only one entrance'. The major difficulty, of course, is that this
precinct is not 'more or less south' of the Acropolis: it is due west. The
case for Dörpfeld's sanctuary must, therefore, remain unproved.

(3) *That it was on the Ilissos*, near the spring Kallirrhoe said to be
there and the Olympieion of the Peisistratids. The chief obstacle to this
assumption is the considerable distance from the Acropolis (anything
from a kilometre to a kilometre and a half depending on the exact site)
and from the greater part of the original city. Its plausibility comes partly
from its position south of the Acropolis, partly from its association with
the Olympieion and Pythion of that region, though this argument might
be set aside if we assumed with Broneer[4] and others duplication of
names between the sanctuaries in this region and those about the north-
west end of the Acropolis. Once again there is doubt as to whether the
area was ever marshy,[5] though the possibility seems rather more likely
here than at either of the rival sites. Mr. Hooker has recently sought to
strengthen the case for this identification by reference to a fifth-century
inscription[6] which is evidence for a Dionysion adjoining the sanctuary of
Neleus, which Hooker would site at the spot where Kodros (who was also
associated with the sanctuary) met his death in legend[7] and where the
stone itself was found, that is on the right bank of the Ilissos, east of the

---

[1] It is here that the great inscription of this thiasos (*I.G.* ii[2]. 1368) was found. But see Nilsson,
Gesch. i[2], p. 589, n. 1.

[2] See Hooker, op. cit., pp. 113 f.; Gomme, *Historical Commentary*, pp. 55, 59.

[3] Dörpfeld, *Ath. Mitt.* 20 (1895), p. 166.

[4] *Hesperia,* Suppl. 8, pp. 47–59.

[5] Judeich, *Rh. Mus.* 47 (1892), p. 59, n. 1; Hooker, op. cit., pp. 114 f.

[6] *I.G.* i[2]. 94, esp. ll. 30 ff.; Hooker, op. cit., pp. 115 f.; Wycherley, *B.S.A.* 55 (1960),
pp. 60–66; *A.J.A.* 67 (1963), p. 78, n. 22.

[7] Lycurgus, *in Leocr.* 86–87; Paus. i. 19. 6.

Phaleron road. The point of uncertainty in this argument is, of course, the situation of the Neleion, which could on the evidence of this inscription be equally well within the city walls, between them and the Acropolis. The other difficulty is Isaeus' assertion that the sanctuary ἐν Λίμναις was ἐν ἄστει: Hooker's argument that, since Isaeus is contrasting two houses ἐν ἄστει with a country estate at Phlya, only one of them may have been literally 'in the city', will hardly do.

All things considered, then, there is no certain answer to the question: where was the sanctuary ἐν Λίμναις? The passage of Thucydides from which we began cannot, unhappily, be made to yield an unambiguous answer, and the other evidence brought forward is not yet enough to clinch any one of the possible answers. There is still less ground for proceeding, with Dörpfeld, to identify the Dionysion ἐν Λίμναις with the Lenaion. This problem will be discussed later.

B. *The Lenaia*

1. The Lenaia took place in the month which was called Gamelion in Athens, and Lenaion in Ionian states generally. It corresponded roughly to January. The following are the principal texts which bear directly or indirectly on the festival:

(1) Hesiod, *Op.* 504.

> μῆνα δὲ Ληναιῶνα, κάκ' ἤματα, βουδόρα πάντα,
> τοῦτον ἀλεύασθαι.

Schol. (*a*) μῆνα δὲ Ληναιῶνα· Πλούταρχος οὐδένα φησὶ μῆνα Ληναιῶνα καλεῖσθαι παρὰ Βοιωτοῖς· ὑποπτεύει δὲ ἢ τὸν Βουκάτιον αὐτὸν λέγειν . . . ἢ τὸν Ἑρμαῖον, ὅς ἐστι μετὰ τὸν Βουκάτιον καὶ εἰς ταὐτὸν ἐρχόμενος τῷ Γαμηλιῶνι, καθ' ὃν καὶ τὰ Λήναια παρ' Ἀθηναίοις. Ἴωνες δὲ τοῦτον οὐδ' ἄλλως, ἀλλὰ Ληναιῶνα καλοῦσι.

(*b*) . . . Ληναιὼν δὲ εἴρηται διὰ τὸ τοὺς οἴνους ἐν αὐτῷ εἰσκομίζεσθαι· οὗτος δὲ ὁ μὴν ἀρχὴ χειμῶνός ἐστιν· οἱ δὲ Ληναιῶνα φάσκουσιν αὐτὸν καλεῖσθαι διὰ τὰ Λήναια, ὅ ἐστιν ἔρια καὶ προβατοδόραν καὶ αἰγοδόραν καλοῦμεν· ἐπειδὴ Διονύσου ἐποίουν ἑορτὴν τῷ μηνὶ τούτῳ, ἣν Ἀμβροσίαν ἐκάλουν.

[This note appears here in various forms and also in Hesych. and *Etym. Magn.* s.v. Ληναιών.]

On the Ionic name Ληναιών in Hesiod, see Wackernagel, *Sprachl. Untersuchungen zu Homer,* p. 179.

(2) Schol. on Ar. *Ach.* 378. τὰ δὲ Λήναια ἐν τῷ μετοπώρῳ ἤγετο, ἐν οἷς οὐ παρῆσαν οἱ ξένοι, ὅτε τὸ δρᾶμα τοῦτο οἱ Ἀχαρνεῖς ἐδιδάσκετο.

[This is only worth quoting as showing how small may be the value of scholia.]

(3) Bekk. *Anecd.* i, p. 235. Διονύσια· ἑορτὴ Ἀθήνησι Διονύσου. ἤγετο δὲ τὰ μὲν κατ᾽ ἀγροὺς μηνὸς Ποσειδεῶνος, τὰ δὲ Λήναια Γαμηλιῶνος, τὰ δὲ ἐν ἄστει Ἐλαφηβολιῶνος.

(Hesych. s.v. Διονύσια and Schol. on Aeschin. i. 43 repeat this, but instead of Γαμηλιῶνος write μηνὸς Ληναιῶνος.. Schol. on Plato, *Rep.* 475 d (p. 234 Greene) writes μηνὸς Μαιμακτηριῶνος.)

(4) Ar. *Ach.* 202.

ἄξω τὰ κατ᾽ ἀγροὺς εἰσιὼν Διονύσια.

Schol. ἄξω τὰ κατ᾽ ἀγρούς· τὰ Λήναια λεγόμενα. ἔνθεν τὰ Λήναια καὶ ὁ ἐπιλήναιος ἀγὼν τελεῖται τῷ Διονύσῳ. Λήναιον γάρ ἐστιν ἐν ἀγροῖς ἱερὸν τοῦ Διονύσου, διὰ τὸ †πλεκτοὺς ἐνταῦθα γεγονέναι, ἢ διὰ τὸ πρῶτον ἐν τούτῳ τῷ τόπῳ ληνὸν (λήναιον codd.) τεθῆναι.

Cf. Steph. Byz. Λήναιος· ἀγὼν Διονύσου ἐν ἀγροῖς, ἀπὸ τῆς ληνοῦ. Ἀπολλόδωρος ἐν τρίτῳ Χρονικῶν (244 F 17 Jac.). καὶ ληναϊκὸς καὶ ληναιεύς. ἔστι δὲ καὶ δῆμος.

(5) Ar. *Ach.* 504–6.

αὐτοὶ γάρ ἐσμεν οὑπὶ Ληναίῳ τ᾽ ἀγών,
κοὔπω ξένοι πάρεισιν· οὔτε γὰρ φόροι
ἥκουσιν, οὔτ᾽ ἐκ τῶν πόλεων οἱ ξύμμαχοι.

Schol. (a) χειμῶνος γὰρ λοιπὸν ὄντος εἰς τὰ Λήναια καθῆκε τὸ δρᾶμα, εἰς δὲ τὰ Διονύσια ἐτέτακτο Ἀθήναζε κομίζειν τὰς πόλεις τοὺς φόρους, ὡς Εὔπολίς φησιν ἐν Πόλεσιν (fr. 240 K).

(b) ὁ τῶν Διονυσίων ἀγὼν ἐτελεῖτο δὶς τοῦ ἔτους, τὸ μὲν πρῶτον ἔαρος ἐν ἄστει, ὅτε καὶ οἱ φόροι Ἀθήνησιν ἐφέροντο, τὸ δὲ δεύτερον ἐν ἀγροῖς, ὁ ἐπὶ Ληναίῳ λεγόμενος, ὅτε ξένοι οὐ παρῆσαν Ἀθήνησι· χειμὼν γὰρ λοιπὸν ἦν.

(6) Schol. on Ar. *Ach.* 961 (relating the story of Orestes' visit, says) ἦν δὲ ἑορτὴ Διονύσου Ληναίου. [See above, p. 19 n. 4.]

(7) Ar. *Ach.* 1154 f.

ὅς γ᾽ ἐμὲ τὸν τλήμονα Λήναια χορηγῶν ἀπέλυσ᾽ ἄδειπνον.

(8) Id. *Knights* 546–8.

. . . παραπέμψατ᾽ ἐφ᾽ ἕνδεκα κώπαις
θόρυβον χρηστὸν ληναΐτην,
ἵν᾽ ὁ ποιητὴς ἀπίῃ χαίρων.

Schol. ληναΐτην· ἑορτὴ παρὰ τοῖς Ἀθηναίοις τὰ Λήναια, ἐν ᾗ μέχρι νῦν ἀγωνίζονται ποιηταὶ συγγράφοντές τινα ᾄσματα τοῦ γελασθῆναι χάριν· ὅπερ ὁ Δημοσθένης (18. 122) εἶπεν ἐξ ἁμάξης· ἐπὶ ἁμαξῶν γὰρ οἱ ᾄδοντες καθήμενοι λέγουσί τε καὶ ᾄδουσι τὰ ποιήματα.

'Suidas' s.v. ἐξ ἁμάξης repeats this schol. and adds: λέγεται καὶ ληναΐτης ὁ χορὸς ὁ τῶν Ληναίων. (See also (10) below.)

(9) Ar. *Frogs* 479

κάλει θεόν.

Schol. . . . τὸ δὲ κάλει θεόν τινες οὕτως ἀποδεδώκασιν. ἐν τοῖς Ληναϊκοῖς ἀγῶσι τοῦ Διονύσου ὁ δᾳδοῦχος κατέχων λαμπάδα λέγει 'καλεῖτε θεόν' καὶ οἱ ὑπακούοντες βοῶσι "Σεμελήϊ᾽ Ἴακχε πλουτοδότα".

(10) Photius. τὰ ἐκ τῶν ἁμαξῶν. . . . Ἀθήνησι γὰρ ἐν τῇ τῶν Χοῶν ἑορτῇ οἱ κωμάζοντες ἐπὶ τῶν ἁμαξῶν τοὺς ἀπαντῶντας ἔσκωπτόν τε καὶ ἐλοιδόρουν· τὸ δ' αὐτὸ καὶ τοῖς Ληναίοις ὕστερον ἐποίουν. (So also 'Suidas'.)

(11) *Law of Euegoros* (*ap.* Dem. *Meid.* 10).[1] Εὐήγορος εἶπεν· ὅταν ἡ πομπὴ ᾖ τῷ Διονύσῳ ἐν Πειραιεῖ καὶ οἱ κωμῳδοὶ καὶ οἱ τραγῳδοί, καὶ ἡ ἐπὶ Ληναίῳ πομπὴ καὶ οἱ τραγῳδοὶ καὶ οἱ κωμῳδοί, καὶ τοῖς ἐν ἄστει Διονυσίοις ἡ πομπὴ καὶ οἱ παῖδες καὶ ὁ κῶμος καὶ οἱ κωμῳδοὶ καὶ οἱ τραγῳδοί, καὶ Θαργηλίων τῇ πομπῇ καὶ τῷ ἀγῶνι, μὴ ἐξεῖναι μήτε ἐνεχυράσαι μήτε λαμβάνειν ἕτερον ἑτέρου μηδὲ τῶν ὑπερημέρων ἐν ταύταις ταῖς ἡμέραις.

(12) *I.G.* ii². 1496. (*a*) ll. 68 ff. [334–333 B.C.].]ἐκ τοῦ δε]ρματικοῦ. [ἐπὶ Κτησ]ι-κλέους ἄρ[χον]τος [ἐγ Διο]νυσίων τῶν [ἐμ Πει]ρα[ιεῖ παρὰ βοων]ῶν ΗΗΗΔⱵ [καὶ] τὸ περιγενόμε[νον ἀ]πὸ τῆ[ς βο]ωνίας ΗΗℙΔΔΔ [ἐγ] Διονυσίων τῶν [ἐπὶ Λ]ηναίῳ [π]αρὰ μυστηρίων [ἐπιμ]ελητῶν . . . .

(*b*) ll. 105–6 [333–332 B.C.]. [ἐγ Διονυσί]ων τῶν ἐπὶ Ληναίῳ π[αρὰ στρατηγῶν] ΗℙⱵ.

[This inscription contains the accounts of the ταμίαι τῆς θεοῦ.]

(13) Ibid. 1672. 182 ff. [329–328 B.C.]. λόγος ἐπιστατῶν Ἐλευσινόθεν καὶ ταμιῶν τοῖν θεοῖν ἐπὶ τῆς Πανδιονίδος ἕκτης πρυτανείας . . . ἐπαρχὴ Δήμητρι καὶ Κόρῃ καὶ Πλούτωνι Γ, ἐπιστάταις ἐπιλήναια εἰς Διονύσια θῦσαι ΔΔ . . . εἰς Χόας δημοσίοις ἱερεῖον ΔΔΗⱵ.

(14) Aristot. Ἀθ. Πολ. lvii. 1. ὁ δὲ βασιλεὺς πρῶτον μὲν μυστηρίων ἐπιμελεῖτ[αι μετὰ τῶν ἐπιμελητῶν ὧ]ν ὁ δῆμ[ος χ]ειροτονεῖ, δύο μὲν ἐξ Ἀθηναίων ἁπάντων, ἕνα δ' [ἐξ Εὐμολπιδῶν, ἕνα] δ' ἐκ Κηρ[ύκω]ν. ἔπειτα Διονυσίων τῶν ἐπὶ Ληναίῳ· ταῦτα δέ ἐστι [πομπή τε καὶ ἀγών τ]ὴν μὲν οὖν πομπὴν κοινῇ πέμπουσιν ὅ τε βασιλεὺς καὶ οἱ ἐπιμεληταί, τὸν δὲ ἀγῶνα διατίθησιν ὁ βασιλεύς· τίθησι δὲ καὶ τοὺς τῶν λαμπάδων ἀγῶνας ἅπαντας· ὡς δ' ἔπος εἰπεῖν καὶ τὰς πατρίους θυσίας διοικεῖ οὗτος πάσας.

(15) Pollux viii. 90. ὁ δὲ βασιλεὺς μυστηρίων προέστηκε μετὰ τῶν ἐπιμελητῶν καὶ Ληναίων καὶ ἀγώνων τῶν ἐπὶ λαμπάδι, καὶ τὰ περὶ τὰς πατρίους θυσίας διοικεῖ.

(16) *I.G.* ii². 2130. 57 ff. (*c.* A.D. 192–3). βασιλεὺς . . . ἐπετέλεσεν τὸν ἀγῶνα τῶν Ληναίων καὶ ἑστίασε τοὺς συνεφήβους καὶ τοὺς περὶ τὸ Διογένειον πάντας.

---

[1] The date of Euegoros is unknown. Stahl, *De Euegori lege disputatio* (1893), which we have been unable to obtain, places it in the fourth century B.C.

(17) Alkiphron, *Epist.* iv. 18. 10 (Schepers). ἐγὼ δὲ καὶ τὰς θηρικλείους καὶ τὰ καρχήσια καὶ τὰς χρυσίδας καὶ πάντα τὰ ἐν ταῖς αὐλαῖς ἐπίφθονα παρὰ τούτοις ἀγαθὰ φυόμενα, τῶν κατ' ἔτος Χοῶν καὶ τῶν ἐν τοῖς θεάτροις Ληναίων καὶ τῆς χθιζῆς ὁμολογίας καὶ τῶν τοῦ Λυκείου γυμνασίων καὶ τῆς ἱερᾶς Ἀκαδημείας οὐκ ἀλλάττομαι.

(18) Hippolochos (*c.* 300 b.c.) *ap.* Athen. iv. 130 d. σὺ δὲ μόνον ἐν Ἀθήναις μένων εὐδαιμονίζεις τὰς Θεοφράστου θέσεις ἀκούων, θύμα καὶ εὔζωμα καὶ τοὺς καλοὺς ἐσθίων στρεπτούς, Λήναια καὶ Χύτρους θεωρῶν.

(19) Clem. Alex. *Protrept.* i. 2 (p. 4 Stählin). ἀλλὰ γὰρ τὰ μὲν δράματα καὶ τοὺς ληναΐζοντας ποιητάς, τέλεον ἤδη παροινοῦντας, κιττῷ που ἀναδήσαντες, ἀφραίνοντας ἐκτόπως τελετῇ βακχικῇ, αὐτοῖς σατύροις καὶ θιάσῳ μαινόλῃ σὺν καὶ τῷ ἄλλῳ δαιμόνων χορῷ, Ἑλικῶνι καὶ Κιθαιρῶνι κατακλείσωμεν γεγηρακόσιν κτλ.

    Schol. ληναΐζοντας· ἀγροικικὴ ᾠδὴ ἐπὶ τῷ ληνῷ ᾀδομένη, ἢ καὶ αὐτὴ περιεῖχεν τὸν Διονύσου σπαραγμόν. πάνυ δὲ εὐφυῶς καὶ χάριτος ἐμπλέως τὸ κιττῷ ἀναδήσαντες τέθεικεν, ὁμοῦ μὲν τὸ ὅτι Διονύσῳ τὰ Λήναια ἀνάκειται ἐνδειξάμενος, ὁμοῦ δὲ καὶ ὡς παροινίᾳ ταῦτα καὶ παροινοῦσιν ἀνθρώποις καὶ μεθύουσιν συγκεκρότηται.

(20) Heraclitus, fr. B 15 (Diels–Kranz). ωὑτὸς δὲ Ἅιδης καὶ Διόνυσος, ὅτεῳ μαίνονται καὶ ληναΐζουσιν.

    Schol. ληναΐζουσιν· βακχεύουσιν· λῆναι γὰρ αἱ βάκχαι. Cf. (21) and (31) below.

(21) Hesych. λῆναι· βάκχαι. Ἀρκάδες (i.e. they were so called in Arkadia).

(22) Id. ἐπὶ Ληναίῳ ἀγών· ἔστιν ἐν τῷ ἄστει Λήναιον περίβολον ἔχον μέγαν καὶ ἐν αὐτῷ Ληναίου Διονύσου ἱερόν, ἐν ᾧ ἐπετελοῦντο οἱ ἀγῶνες Ἀθηναίων (⟨τῶν⟩ Ληναίων Wilamowitz) πρὶν τὸ θέατρον οἰκοδομηθῆναι. Cf. Bekk. *Anecd.* i, 278, 8 f.; 'Suidas' s.v. ἐπὶ Ληναίῳ; *Etym. Magn.* s.v. Ἐπιληναίῳ.

(23) Id. Λίμναι· ἐν Ἀθήναις τόπος ἀνειμένος Διονύσῳ, ὅπου τὰ †Λαια (? Λήναια) ἤγετο. Cf. id. s.v. λιμνομάχαι.

(24) Dem. *de Cor.* 129. ἢ ὡς ἡ μήτηρ τοῖς μεθημερινοῖς γάμοις ἐν τῷ κλεισίῳ τῷ πρὸς τῷ καλαμίτῃ ἥρῳ χρωμένη τὸν καλὸν ἀνδριάντα καὶ τριταγωνιστὴν ἄκρον ἐξέθρεψέ σε;

    Schol. Patm. (*a*) κλισίον· τὸ οἴκημα τὸ μεγάλας ἔχον θύρας ἐν τῇ ἀγορᾷ.

    (*b*) τὸ δὲ ἱερὸν αὐτοῦ (sc. τοῦ καλαμίτου ἥρωος) ἐστι πρὸς τῷ Ληναίῳ (*B.C.H.* i, 1877, p. 142).

(25) Photius. Λήναιον· περίβολος μέγας Ἀθήνησιν ἐν ᾧ τοὺς ἀγῶνας ἦγον πρὸ τοῦ τὸ θέατρον οἰκοδομηθῆναι ὀνομάζοντες ἐπὶ Ληναίῳ. ἔστιν δὲ ἐν αὐτῷ καὶ ἱερὸν Διονύσου Ληναίου.

(26) Id. ἴκρια· τὰ ἐν τῇ ἀγορᾷ ἀφ' ὧν ἐθεῶντο τοὺς Διονυσιακοὺς ἀγῶνας πρὶν ἢ κατασκευασθῆναι τὸ ἐν Διονύσου θέατρον.

(Cf. Pollux vii. 125. ἰκριοποιοὶ δ' εἰσὶν οἱ πηγνύντες τὰ περὶ τὴν ἀγορὰν ἴκρια, Eustathius on *Odyssey* iii. 350, Hesychius s.v. ᾠδεῖον.)

(27) Photius. ὀρχήστρα· πρῶτον ἐκλήθη ἐν τῇ ἀγορᾷ· εἶτα καὶ τοῦ θεάτρου τὸ κάτω ἡμίκυκλον, οὗ καὶ οἱ χοροὶ ᾖδον καὶ ὠρχοῦντο.

(28) Schol. on Ar. *Plut.* 954. οὐκ ἐξῆν δὲ ξένον χορεύειν ἐν τῷ ἀστικῷ χορῷ· . . . ἐν δὲ τῷ Ληναίῳ ἐξῆν· ἐπεὶ καὶ μέτοικοι ἐχορήγουν.

(29) Plato, *Protag.* 327 d. ἀλλ' εἶεν ἄγριοί τινες, οἷοί περ οὓς πέρυσι Φερεκράτης ὁ ποιητὴς ἐδίδαξεν ἐπὶ Ληναίῳ.

(30) Anon. *de Com.* 1, ll. 6 ff. (Kaibel, p. 7). τὴν αὐτὴν (sc. τὴν κωμῳδίαν) δὲ καὶ τρυγῳδίαν φασὶ διὰ τὸ τοῖς εὐδοκιμοῦσιν ἐπὶ τῷ Ληναίῳ γλεῦκος δίδοσθαι, ὅπερ ἐκάλουν τρύγα, ἢ ὅτι μήπω προσωπείων ηὑρημένων τρυγὶ διαχρίοντες τὰ πρόσωπα ὑπεκρίνοντο.

(31) *D.G.E.* 791 (Kyme). ὑπὺ τεῖ κλίνει τούτει λῆνος ὑπυ.
   (Wilam. *Glaube* ii², p. 62, n. 3, says that λῆνος here can only mean an initiated βάκχος; cf. (20) above).

2. For a long time it was assumed that the festival called Lenaia, the place of its celebration, the Lenaion, and the god worshipped, Dionysus Lenaios, were so named from a connexion with the winepress, ληνός, though the mere existence of a ληνός in one suggested location for the sanctuary ἐν Λίμναις (up to then identified with the Lenaion), and of others in the same neighbourhood, was obviously inconclusive; winepresses are common objects in a vine-growing country, and the special reference to the winepress and its god in January or February was not obviously appropriate. Consequently an alternative derivation[1] of these words, not from ληνός, but from λῆναι, known to be an appellation of bacchanals or maenads, has found more general favour. It was pointed out that the normal form of the adjective derived from ληνός would be λήνειος (cf. Καδμεῖος, οἰκεῖος, βάκχειος, ἵππειος, etc.), whereas adjectives of the -αιος form are usually connected with feminine substantives of the first declension (βίαιος, ἀγοραῖος, δίκαιος, etc.). The argument is not absolutely conclusive, because a very few feminines in -ος have corresponding adjectives in -αῖος, e.g. νῆσος (νησαῖος), ὁδός (ὁδαῖος), χέρσος (χερσαῖος), and ληνός might conceivably be one of these; but these adjectives (except χερσαῖος) are very rare, and some other feminines in -ος

[1] First suggested by Ribbeck, *Anfänge u. Entwicklung des Dionysoskultes in Attica* (1869), p. 13. Cf. Nilsson, *Studia*, pp. 109 ff.; Frickenhaus, *Lenäenvasen* (72nd Winckelmannsprogramm, Berlin, 1912), p. 27. See most recently, Nilsson, *Gesch.* i², pp. 575 f.; H. Frisk, *Gr. Etym. Wörterbuch* s.v. λῆναι.

have adjectives in -ειος, e.g. κόπρος (κόπρειος), λήκυθος (ληκύθειος, Callimachus), κέλευθος (κελεύθειος, Pausanias and Hesychius), μίλτος (μίλτειος,
Anth. Pal. vi. 103), etc. Thus the derivation from λῆναι has at least the
balance of probability; and if so, we have to do with the festival, sanctuary, and god of the maenads or women worshippers of Dionysus. The
use of the word ληναΐζουσιν by Heraclitus as the equivalent of βακχεύουσι
strongly supports this view, and Clement of Alexandria uses ληναΐζοντας
of inspired or frenzied poets, though the scholiast on his words gives the
derivation from ληνός, probably quoting it from elsewhere, as ληναΐζοντας
cannot be paraphrased as ἀγροικικὴ ᾠδή. In an inscription of the third
century B.C. from Halikarnassos (*Inscr. in Brit. Mus.* no. 902) Dionysus ·
is addressed as θοᾶν ληναγέτα Βακχᾶν.

Another line of investigation has been thought to suggest the nature of
their worship.

3. In 1912 Frickenhaus[1] described and illustrated a large number of
vases (to which others have since been added),[2] ranging over the whole
of the fifth century B.C., which, while differing in details, are almost all[3]
clearly inspired by the cult of Dionysus, who is figured in the form of a
bearded mask set upon a pole, pillar, or column,[4] often apparently of
wood; the 'pillar' is usually clothed, with varying degrees of decoration;
the mask of the god, and the 'pillar', are often crowned with ivy to which
(or to some other part of his decoration) are attached, in a number of
the vases, thin ritual cakes of the type known as πλακοῦντες, and the
adornment sometimes includes grapes. The ritual is performed invariably by women, in various stages of ecstasy, with thyrsi, torches,
flutes, and tympana. On one of the earliest of all the vases (c. 490–480 B.C.),
the work of the painter Makron and the potter Hieron (fig. 17),[5] one
carries a fawn, and an altar appears alongside the idol of Dionysus.
Towards the middle of the fifth century there is a sharp break in the

---

[1] See previous note. Frickenhaus's work is still the only comprehensive treatment.

[2] Giglioli, *Annuario* 4–5 (1921–2), pp. 131 ff.; Nilsson, *Human. Vetensk. Samf. i Lund* (Årsber. 1933), iii, pp. 44 ff. (= *Opusc. Sel.* ii, pp. 457 ff.; *A.B.V.* 560, no. 518); *S.B.* Munich, 1930, 4 (= *Opusc. Sel.* i, pp. 414 ff.; *A.B.V.* 395, no. 3); Deubner, *Jahrb. Arch.* 49 (1934), pp. 1 ff.; Haspels, *Attic Black-Figured Lekythoi*, pp. 135, n. 1; 222, no. 27; 247, no. 10; Beazley, *A.B.V.* 553, nos. 393, 394; *A.R.V.*[2] 621, nos. 38, 40, 42; 628, no. 6; 672, no. 14; 1019, no. 83; 1072; 1073, no. 11; 1249, no. 13; Shefton in Arias–Hirmer–Shefton, *A History of Gk. Vase-Painting*, p. 375. We have omitted some more speculative identifications. These additions do not materially alter the descriptive account given by Frickenhaus.

[3] On some vases (e.g. Frickenhaus, nos. 24, 25, 28) the mask-idol is not depicted.

[4] In one of the black-figure vases (Frickenhaus, no. 1 = Haspels, p. 248, no. 11 = *A.B.V.* 573, no. 2: good photograph in *B.C.H.* 87 (1963), p. 319, fig. 8), no pillar is visible, and the mask appears to be resting on the ground. That the 'pillar' is not thought of as a tree is indicated by the presence of a base in Frickenhaus, nos. 18, 19, 26, 27, 28.

[5] *A.R.V.*[2] 462, no. 48.

treatment of the scene: ecstatic maenads give way to stately aristocratic figures, and a sacred table appears in front of the idol, usually bearing two large stamnoi, out of which wine is being ladled into skyphoi which some of the women carry, and probably also into the kantharos which is depicted on some of the vases, as an offering to the god.[1] The characteristic shape used for these scenes is now the stamnos. It is not clear whether the difference in depiction implies any real change in the character of the ritual, or is rather a matter of artistic taste and fashion.[2] The maenadic character of the celebrants is not entirely lost, though much toned down;[3] in one representation (fig. 20), by the Phiale Painter[4] (440–430 B.C.), one of the celebrants carries a garlanded baby child, but the 'child' is clearly shown as a tiny satyr. Further, the painters were never tied closely to the literal fact of the ritual performed: some of the vases (e.g. fig. 21) include a naked satyr in the scene. Yet there is this striking difference between the vases painted or influenced by the Villa Giulia Painter, and those that had preceded: the ceremony of consecrating the wine (if that is what it is), which is central in the later vases and in some displaces the mask-idol altogether, is quite absent from the earlier pieces. The latest vase in the series, a stamnos in Naples by the Dinos Painter (fig. 22; c. 420 B.C.),[5] in some measure reverts to the earlier tradition: the celebrants are once again ecstatic maenads, named as such (Dione, Mainas, Thaleia, Choreia);[6] tambourines, thyrsus, and torch are once again prominent, but the centre of the chief side is still taken up with the sacred table and pair of stamnoi, and wine is being ladled into a skyphos.

[1] The presentation of the kantharos to the idol of the god (treated here almost as a statue: cf. the hairline and neck) is the moment singled out by the Eupolis Painter on two stamnoi in London and Paris (Frickenhaus, no. 26 = fig. 23 here = A.R.V.² 1073, no. 9; and Frickenhaus, no. 27 = A.R.V.² 1073, no. 10), very similar except in minor details.

[2] Shefton, op. cit., p. 374, points out the enormous influence on the vases within this sequence of the period just before and after the mid fifth century exercised by the Villa Giulia Painter. Seven of Frickenhaus's original twenty-nine vases (nos. 16–22) are by this painter (including figs. 18 and 19); two more are by his close follower the Chicago Painter, and another two by the Eupolis Painter, not far away. That fashion plays a part is clear from the appearance of torches in these scenes, in common with most other maenadic scenes of the mid fifth century and later, without the necessary implication that the scene takes place after dark (Shefton, op. cit., pp. 372 f.).

[3] Note the parasols carried by the principal figures on two stamnoi in Boston and Paris (Frickenhaus, nos. 16 and 17 = A.R.V.² 621, nos. 34, 39).

[4] Frickenhaus, no. 28 = A.R.V.² 1019, no. 82 (now Warsaw, Nat. Mus. 142465, formerly in the Czartoryski Collection, Goluchow). Beazley, Gk. Vases in Poland, pp. 52–53 is important for description and interpretation.

[5] Frickenhaus, no. 29 = A.R.V.² 1151, no. 2; good photographs in Arias–Hirmer–Shefton, op. cit., pll. 206–11; description, Shefton, ibid., p. 372.

[6] On the maenad names, cf. C. Fränkel, Satyr- u. Bakchennamen auf Vasenbildern (1912), index s.vv.

Frickenhaus's original interpretation[1] of this sequence of vases was that they represented the supposedly orgiastic rites of the Attic Lenaia, and that these rites were closely connected with, perhaps derived from, the Theban pillar-cult of Dionysus Καδμεῖος or Περικιόνιος.[2] He connected this rite with the Athenian cult of Dionysus Ὀρθός, to whom legend attributed the invention of mixing wine with water;[3] in fact it is quite uncertain whether mixing rather than consecration or some other rite connected with the wine is figured on the vases. However, the point which primarily concerns us here is Frickenhaus's ascription of the ritual depicted on the vases to the Lenaia: in this he has been followed by Deubner and a number of others.[4]

A quite different view has been taken and vigorously maintained by Nilsson,[5] who relies strongly on the passage of Phanodemos (325 F 12 Jacoby) concerning the ritual of the Anthesteria,[6] and on a striking vase by the Eretria Painter (fig. 24),[7] and ascribes all our vases to the wine-consecration ceremony of the Anthesteria. The Eretria Painter's vase (a chous) seems to show an earlier stage of the ritual depicted on the 'Lenäenvasen': the mask of the god, crowned and decorated with ivy leaves, appears cradled in a sacred basket (λίκνον) and being given offerings (including wine in a kantharos) by two women. In the absence of a pillar or column from the scene we cannot be absolutely certain that this scene *is* a forerunner of the others, but the suggestion is clearly attractive, and the shape of the vase is a point in Nilsson's favour.[8] In

---

[1] *Lenäenvasen*, pp. 20 ff. The supposition that there is any connexion between the 'Lenäen-vasen' and the alleged rousing of the infant Dionysus by the Thyiades at Delphi (Plut. *Is. et Osir.* 365 a) is ruled out both by the total lack of points of contact between the two, and by the very dubious evidence even for the existence at any early date of the latter: cf. Dietrich, *C.Q.*, N.S. 8 (1958), pp. 244 ff.; Nilsson, *Dionysiac Mysteries of the Hellenistic and Roman Age* (1957), pp. 38 ff.

[2] Wilamowitz, *Glaube* ii[2], p. 79, n. 4, notes (as had Frickenhaus, p. 20) that the περικιόνιος of Thebes was not masked, but was a simple pillar covered with ivy: cf. Eur. *Antiope*, fr. 203 N[2], εἶδον δὲ θαλάμοις βουκόλων . . . κομῶντα κισσῷ στῦλον Εὐΐου θεοῦ: the schol. on Eur. *Phoen.* 651 refers to the ivy-clad god as περικιόνιος. Wilam. suggests that the post or pillar (στῦλος) may have come from Thebes, the mask from Naxos (cf. Athen. iii. 78 c; Hesychius s.v. συκάτης). There was a mask-image of Dionysus also at Methymna: Paus. x. 19. 3. The best treatment of the mask-image itself is still W. Wrede, *Ath. Mitt.* 53 (1928), pp. 66 ff. (discussion and interpretation, pp. 81 ff.).

[3] Philochorus 328 F 5b (Jacoby).

[4] Deubner, *Att. Feste*, pp 127–32, and the article cited on p. 30, n. 2 above; Cook, *Zeus* i, p. 671; Kroll, *R.E.* xii, col. 1937 f.

[5] *Jahrb. Arch.* 31 (1916), pp. 323 ff. = *Opusc. Sel.* i, pp. 188 ff.; *Gesch.* i[2], pp. 587 f.; *Dion. Myst.*, pp. 26 ff., and the articles cited in p. 30, n. 2 above.

[6] Pass. 20 on pp. 6 f. above.

[7] *A.R.V.*[2] 1249, no. 13 = van Hoorn, no. 271 (his fig. 38); Nilsson, *Dion. Myst.*, fig. 4.

[8] Though not the conclusive proof that he would like it to be: a largish number of Attic choes depict scenes that have no special relevance to the Anthesteria: see Rumpf, *Bonner Jahrb.* 161 (1961), pp. 209 f., 212 f.; van Hoorn, p. 53.

arguing for his case, Nilsson is forced to play down the maenadic aspect of the vases, insisting that the women are priestesses, not maenads, and to stress the prominence of wine vessels in the scenes depicted: yet, as we have seen, both features are certainly present in the vases, though not (except in the Dinos Painter's stamnos) simultaneously.

The interpretation of Frickenhaus and Deubner is pressed home conversely by stressing the fact that the 'Lenäenvasen' are regularly lekythoi and stamnoi, not (except in the case of the Eretria Painter's chous) vases of the characteristic Anthesteria shape[1] (though the argument is no stronger than the converse would have been), and by emphasizing the maenadic element, at the same time connecting it with the (presumed) derivation of Lenaia from λῆναι, maenads, and asserting that this is the only ecstatic or orgiastic festival of Dionysus of which we know.[2] Both cases fall some way short of proof,[3] and the problem is complicated, as we have seen, by uncertainty as to how far artistic fashion, or the melting together of ritual and mythological elements, or even sheer fantasy, have influenced the scenes as drawn upon the vases. In the present state of the evidence, we cannot go beyond what A. D. Nock wrote in 1934, reviewing Deubner: 'the truth seems unattainable. . . . Probability appears to be on Nilsson's side, but we may be pardoned for suspending judgment.'[4] There must remain a certain doubt whether the vases do not cover two distinct rituals—the one, represented above all by Makron's kylix, being markedly ecstatic, even orgiastic in character, the other more stately and collected; and if so, it might still be possible to associate the former with the λῆναι of the Lenaia—unless

[1] Frickenhaus, pp. 18 ff., 25 and n. 16; Deubner, Jahrb. Arch. 49 (1934), p. 4; Shefton, op. cit., p. 374.

[2] Though there were private 'festivals' of a similar kind: cf. Ar. Lysistrata 1 ff. with the scholiast's comment: καὶ γὰρ πολλὰς ἑορτὰς αἱ γυναῖκες ἔξω τῶν δημοτελῶν ἦγον ἰδίᾳ συνερχόμεναι.

[3] A further argument of Nilsson's is that, though the presence of maenads is hardly more than mere 'convention' in a Dionysiac scene, the stress laid on the ladling out of wine is an unexpected, and hence significant, feature (Human. Vetensk. Samf. i Lund iii, pp. 46 f. = Opusc. Sel. ii, pp. 460 f.; Jahrb. Arch. 31 (1916), p. 329 = Opusc. Sel. i, p. 197, etc.): the point is developed from the vase evidence by Shefton, op. cit., p. 373. See further, Dodds, ed. of Eur. Bacchae², pp. xi ff. The suggestion made by C. Robert, G.G.A. 1913, p. 369, that the appearance of grapes on some of the vases (e.g. Frickenhaus, no. 11; fig. 17 here) precludes reference to a festival held in January was refuted by Deubner, Att. Feste, pp. 131 f.; cf. Nock, Gnomon 10 (1934), p. 291. Note, on the other hand, the flower (? tulip) in the hand of the r.-h. figure of Munich 1538 (= A.B.V. 395, no. 3; Nilsson, Gesch. i², pl. 36/2); another flower held by the r.-h. figure on Frickenhaus, no. 24 (= A.R.V.² 628, no. 5): but this too cannot be taken to indicate the season unequivocally: cf. the flower and the grapes (on the vine) appearing simultaneously on an amphora in Munich by the Andokides Painter (A.R.V.² 4, no. 9; Lullies–Hirmer, Gr. Vasen der reifarchaischen Zeit, pll. 1, 6).

[4] Gnomon 10 (1934), pp. 289 f.

the two sets of vases represent merely phases in the development of ceremonies of a single festival.[1]

4. If we cannot ascribe Frickenhaus's 'Lenäenvasen' with confidence to the Lenaia, then there is little enough that we do know about the ceremonies of this festival.[2] There have been several conjectures as to the meaning of a celebration conducted by maenads at a festival in January. Farnell[3] suggests that it was intended to rouse or strengthen the sleeping god, like other winter festivals known to anthropologists. There seems little direct support for this in the meagre evidence, and the ivy-clad pillar-god is hardly in keeping with this idea. Others[4] lay more stress on the fact that the archon basileus was associated in the conduct of the festival with officials of the Eleusinian Mysteries—the ἐπιμεληταί and the δᾳδοῦχος—and that according to the scholiast on Aristophanes' *Frogs* 479 (pass. (9) above) the δᾳδοῦχος, torch in hand, bade the worshippers call upon the god (καλεῖτε θεόν), and that they responded with the cry Σεμελήι᾽ ῎Ιακχε πλουτοδότα. This would not, however, justify the belief, which some hold, that it was the birth of Dionysus as son of Semele that was commemorated, because the Iakchos of the Mysteries was a young man, and πλουτοδότα is perhaps less appropriate to an infant.[5] Even if on one of the 'Lenäenvasen' (fig. 20) there is a woman holding out an infant to another, it is certain that the infant was not (as Frickenhaus thought) Dionysus or Iakchos, nor her own human infant which she had brought with her to the meeting, but rather, as Sir John Beazley has pointed out, a satyr. Nor would it be right to infer that Semele herself had any part in the celebration. It is therefore impossible

---

[1] For further discussion, see, apart from the books and articles by Nilsson, Deubner, Wrede, and Giglioli already cited, Beazley, *C.V. Oxford* i, text to pl. 28, 1–2; Buschor, *Ath. Mitt.* 53 (1928), p. 100; Willemsen, *Frühe gr. Kultbilder* (diss. Munich, 1939), pp. 35, 41 f.; Coche de la Ferté, *Rev. Arch.*, 6ᵉ série, 38 (1951), pp. 12 ff.; Dietrich, *Hermes* 89 (1961), pp. 45 ff.; Friis Johansen, *Eine Dithyrambosaufführung*, pp. 39 f.; Shefton, op. cit., pp. 372 ff. (excellent brief discussion); U. T. Bezerra de Meneses, *B.C.H.* 87 (1963), pp. 309 ff.

[2] It has been inferred from the reference to the δᾳδοῦχος in schol. Ar. *Frogs* 479 (pass. (9) on p. 27 above) and from the phrase μετὰ φωτός in two Hellenistic inscriptions (*I.G.* ii². 1006, 13; 1008, 14 (the phrase is restored in the second inscription): cf. Frickenhaus, *Jahrb. Arch.* 27 (1912), pp. 80 ff.), that the ceremonies were nocturnal: but torches could be lighted in daytime ceremonies (cf. Ar. *Thesm.* 280), and the reference of the inscriptions to the Lenaia is far from certain. Again Frickenhaus (*Lenäenvasen*, p. 29) pointed to the phrase κιττώσεις Διονύσους in an Attic festival-calendar, under the month Gamelion (*I.G.* ii². 1367), and asserted a connexion with the ivy-decorated pillar-god of the vases, but the inscription is of the first century A.D., and cannot carry much weight in regard to a time five or six centuries earlier.

[3] *Cults* v, p. 208; cf. 198 f.

[4] Deubner, *Att. Feste*, pp. 125 f.; Wilamowitz, *Glaube* ii², p. 75 with nn. 2 and 3.

[5] It would take us too far to discuss this last point in relation to the birth of Ploutos as child of Demeter.

to say with confidence what there was in common between the Lenaia and the Eleusinia.[1] If there were dances at the Lenaia, they were probably like the trieteric 'orgies' of Thyiades on Mount Parnassus and elsewhere, though annual, and probably less wild.

Another connexion with mystic rites of a different kind, the omophagy or devouring of the slain Dionysus, as in the Cretan mysteries of Zagreus, appears to be indicated by the scholiast on Clement of Alexandria, who interprets Clement's use of the word ληναΐζοντας by speaking of ἀγροικικὴ ᾠδὴ ἐπὶ τῷ ληνῷ ᾀδομένη, ἣ καὶ αὐτὴ περιεῖχεν τὸν Διονύσου σπαραγμόν. But the meaning of the note is obscure; περιεῖχεν probably only implies the mention of this σπαραγμός in the chant, and the rest of the note seems to indicate that, whatever was done, it was done by ivy-crowned *men* in a state of intoxication and has nothing to do with the women's performance. It seems doubtful whether we know enough to reconcile these isolated records, or to go beyond the comparative certainty that the Lenaia included mystical elements which were in some way the concern of the officials of Eleusis, and possibly a nocturnal worship of Dionysus by women, such as the vases depict.[2]

If the celebration came to Athens from the north—from Macedonia or Thrace—whence the worship of Dionysus by wild women came into Greece, it may well have come by way of Thebes.[3] It must have established itself at Athens before the Ionian migrations from Attica into the various Ionian towns in which (together with the name of the month Lenaion) it is recorded to have been observed.

[1] Some may infer from the juxtaposition of names in *I.G.* ii². 1672, ll. 182 ff. (see above, p. 27), that Demeter, Kore, and Pluto may have been associated with the Lenaia; but the epistatai who contributed to the Lenaia also (l. 204) contributed to the Χόες, so that the proof of a *particular* connexion with the Lenaia is not strong. The calendar of festivals at Mykonos (Dittenberger, *S.I.G.*³ 1024) shows that Demeter and Kore received sacrifices there in the month Lenaion, but this was at a late date (*c.* 200 B.C.).

[2] The treatment of words connected with the Lenaia by G. W. Elderkin (*Archaeological Papers* v, 1943) seems to rest almost entirely on false etymologies and unfounded conjectures. But as he identifies the Ἴακχος of the Lenaian chant with the dismembered Zagreus, it may be noted that there is no hint of a σπαραγμός of Iakchos before Lucian, Περὶ ὀρχήσεως 39, and that the name, so far from connoting cries of pain, is always associated with cries of joy and hope. (It is comparatively rarely that the verb ἰαχεῖν, with which he associates the name, expresses a cry of grief or fear; it is most commonly a battle-cry or shout of applause.) His interpretation of ληνός as the 'mangling-place' of grapes, with λῆναι as the 'manglers' or 'tearers of the god', identifies two very different processes. Grapes are not 'torn asunder', and ληνός seems to mean primarily a vessel of a particular shape, whether a winepress or any other (see *L.S.J.*). There is not the least reason to suppose that παλαιοῦ πένθεος in Pindar, fr. 133 relates to sufferings of Iakchos (of which nothing else is known). See Linforth, *Arts of Orpheus*, pp. 345 ff.

[3] The invocation of Iakchos as son of Semele confirms this. Farnell, op. cit., p. 213, suggests that it may have been learned by the Ionians in the Boeotian period of their history, before they came to Attica. There is much that is uncertain here. Cf. in general, Nilsson, *Jahrb. Arch.* 31 (1916), p. 327 = *Opusc. Sel.* i, pp. 194 f.

5. The passages quoted above show that the festival included a πομπή—a procession conducted by the archon basileus and the epimeletai, and that the σκώμματα ἐκ τῶν ἁμαξῶν, which were a feature of the Choes, were afterwards introduced into the Lenaia. The scholiast on Aristophanes *Knights* 546 seems to include among these σκώμματα songs of a ludicrous kind composed by poets. The wagons doubtless formed part of the πομπή. There is no evidence of any phallic elements in the procession or the festival. Inscriptions show that there was a sacrifice, but give no details. There is also no evidence of a κῶμος,[1] and if in fact the Lenaia had much in common with the Eleusinia, it can well be understood that revels and phallic ritual would be absent, though the σκώμματα with their apotropaic intention were present in both celebrations.

6. The inscriptions which are usually cited with reference to the Lenaia in places outside Athens are all of relatively late dates and throw little or no light on the Athenian festival; most merely mention the month Lenaion in dating a decree or prescribing a sacrifice or whatever it may be.[2] Two inscriptions suggest a possible connexion of the festival in these places with mystic rites—one from Mykonos[3] (dated by Dittenberger about 200 B.C.) prescribes for the 10th of Lenaion sacrifices to Demeter, Kore, and Zeus Bouleus, and for the 12th δυωδεκάτει Διονύσῳ Ληνεῖ ἐτήσιον· ὑπὲρ καρπῶν Διὶ Χθονίῳ Γῆ Χθονίη δερτὰ μέλανα ἐτήσια: the other from Magnesia on the Maeander[4] of the second century A.D., which seems to refer to a private religious society, and gives instructions to the officials ὥστε τῷ Ληνεῶνι μηνὶ τὰ εἰθισμένα αὐτοῖς προσφέρεσθαι ὑπὸ τῶν μυστῶν. It would be rash to draw any inferences from these facts to the cults of Athens many centuries earlier. The month Ληναιοβάκχιος once thought to occur at Astypalaia is now known to have been called Ἰοβάκχιος, and although festivals of Dionysus and tragic performances (not necessarily, though probably, connected with Dionysus) were certainly held during it, its position in the year is uncertain.[5] A very fragmentary record[6], once thought to commemorate victories at the

---

[1] Deubner, op. cit., p. 133, argues for a κῶμος in which men wore women's costumes and women men's; but this depends upon his false connexion with this festival of a group of vases published by Buschor (Buschor, *Jahrb. Arch.* 38–39 (1923–4), pp. 128 ff.). Buschor's original connexion of these vases with the Skirophoria is disproved by Deubner, op. cit., pp. 49 f. They have been correctly interpreted as referring to private symposia by Beazley, *Attic Vase Paintings in Boston* ii, pp. 55 ff.; cf. Nilsson, *Acta Arch.* 13 (1942), pp. 223–6 = *Opusc. Sel.* iii, pp. 81–84; Philostratus, *Imag.* i. 2; Lucian, *Calumn.* 16; Aristides, *Rhet.* 41. 9 Keil.

[2] e.g. *S.I.G.*³ 364 (Ephesus), 368 (Miletus), 799 (Cyzicus), 1014 (Erythrae), 1156 (Priene), Sokolowski, *Lois Sacrées de l'Asie Mineure* no. 8 (Lampsacus).

[3] *S.I.G.*³ 1024, see above, p. 35, n. 1.

[4] Kern, *Inschr. von Magn. am M.*, no. 117. Cf. Nilsson, *Studia*, p. 113.

[5] *I.G.* xii. 3. 169–70; xii. 7. 67A; xii, Suppl. p. 79, no. 150.   [6] *I.G.* xii. 1. 125.

Lenaia in Rhodes, probably in the first century B.C., comes from Rome and refers to the Athenian Lenaia.[1] An inscription of the second century B.C. from Priene, quoted above,[2] refers to the costume of the priest of Dionysus in the months of Lenaion and Anthesterion.

7. The Lenaian festival at Athens was held mainly in the Lenaion, ἐπὶ Ληναίῳ.[3] As to where this was, two different traditions appear in the scholia and lexicographers. According to one, the Lenaion was ἐν ἀγροῖς, outside the city walls. So says the scholiast on Aristophanes *Acharnians* 202 and 504, and also Stephanus of Byzantium s.v. Λήναιος (quoted under pass. (4) above), who claims the authority of Apollodorus (244 F 17 Jac.), though whether Apollodorus is his authority for the words ἐν ἀγροῖς or only for the words ἀπὸ τῆς ληνοῦ which follow them cannot be determined. Dramatic contests at the Lenaia were always in historical times distinguished from the Great Dionysia ἐν ἄστει. But the expression ἐν ἄστει seems to have been primarily used of the Great Dionysia in contrast to ἐν ἀγροῖς of the Rural Dionysia, and this may have been its original use, as it is not at all certain that organized dramatic contests were not held at the Rural Dionysia earlier than at the Lenaia. (This will be referred to later.) The statement that the Lenaia were held ἐν ἀγροῖς may be, as Deubner suggests,[4] due to a mistaken conflation of the fact that in the *Acharnians* Dikaiopolis refers to the Lenaia (at l. 504: οὑπὶ Ληναίῳ τ᾽ ἀγών) as the occasion of the performance, with his earlier proposal (l. 202) to enact τὰ κατ᾽ ἀγροὺς Διονύσια (of course in pretence). The rest of the evidence points to the place of the celebration's being in the market-place, which was, of course, in the city, to the north-west of the Acropolis. Hesychius[5] (repeated almost verbally by Photius) describes the Lenaion as a place ἐν ἄστει, 'having a large circumference', and having in it the ἱερόν—temple or precinct—of the Lenaian Dionysus, in which 'the contests of the Athenians' (evidently dramatic contests) were held, before the theatre was built. Photius also speaks of the ἴκρια—the wooden stands—from which the spectators watched 'the Dionysiac contests' before the theatre was built, as ἐν ἀγορᾷ—in the market-place—and the existence of a place in the Agora called ὀρχήστρα[6] squares with

---

[1] See Wilhelm, *Urkunden dram. Aufführungen in Athen*, pp. 205 ff.; below, p. 122.

[2] p. 8, no. 33.

[3] See Judeich, *Topogr. Athen*[2], pp. 293 ff.

[4] *Att. Feste*, p. 124.

[5] Hesych. s.v. ἐπὶ Ληναίῳ ἀγών (pass. (22) above): the text is uncertain.

[6] Photius s.vv. ἴκρια; ὀρχήστρα (passages (26)–(27) above); Eustathius, *Od.*, p. 1472. 5; Plato, *Apol.* 26 d–e; Tim. Soph. *Lex. Plat.* s.v. ὀρχήστρα. See also Hesychius s.vv. αἰγείρου θέα; παρ᾽ αἰγείρου θέα; Bekk. *Anecd.* i, p. 354, 25; Wycherley, *The Athenian Agora* iii (*Testimonia*), pp. 162 f., 220 f. The latter passages (quoting Cratinus and Eratosthenes), refer to a proverbial

this. Further, Demosthenes[1] associates the misbehaviour of Aeschines' mother with a κλεισίον adjoining the sanctuary of the ἥρως καλαμίτης, and the Patmos scholiast on the passage says (1) that this κλεισίον was in the Agora, and (2) that the ἱερόν of the ἥρως καλαμίτης adjoined the Lenaion. This second statement is repeated by Hesychius,[2] but the first, and crucial, one is more doubtful. The Patmos scholiast asserts that the κλεισίον had 'big doors', and other 'sheds' with 'big doors' appear in the lexicographers[3] (apparently cow-sheds or cart-sheds), without reference to the Agora or to Aeschines' mother. It is possible that the Patmos scholiast's source is such a general note, and that the specific reference given to it in his version is due to a misunderstanding.[4] No certain trace of any building that could be identified with the Lenaion has been found in the American excavations of the Agora. The possibility that the Lenaion was in the Agora must, therefore, remain open, though it may be that it, the 'orchestra', the 'ikria', and the poplar tree were all connected. At all events, in this large precinct there must have taken place the earliest dramatic performances, whatever they were like, before the later theatre of Dionysus was built, and perhaps the nocturnal celebrations (if they were nocturnal) of the λῆναι: the πομπή probably went through the streets outside also.

There is no evidence for connecting the Lenaia with the sanctuary of Dionysus ἐν Λίμναις except (1) the corrupt passage of Hesychius, s.v. Λίμναι· ἐν Ἀθήναις τόπος ἀνειμένος Διονύσῳ, ὅπου τὰ λαια ἤγετο, where most scholars accept the emendation of λαια to λήναια.[5] Such evidence is too shaky to set against that which has just been stated. (2) A scholiast on Aristophanes Acharnians 961,[6] who in describing the visit of Orestes to Athens which led to the institution of the peculiar ritual of the Choes says ἦν δὲ ἑορτὴ Διονύσου Ληναίου. But none of the other versions of the story make any allusion to Dionysus Ληναῖος, the scholiasts on Aristophanes are by no means free from mistakes, and Nilsson[7] may well be

black poplar, described as being πλησίον τοῦ ἱεροῦ (the Lenaion?) and 'near where the ἴκρια were put up for the show before the theatre was built': people apparently watched 'the show' from it. The reference would seem to be again to early performances in the Agora (though 'Suidas', s.v. ἀπ' αἰγείρου θέα, and Eustathius, Od., p. 1523. 56, refer to the same tree as being 'above the theatre'). See further Theatre of D., pp. 10 ff.

[1] de Cor. 129 (pass. 24 on p. 28).
[2] s.v. καλαμίτης ἥρως.
[3] Hesychius, s.v. †κλειόων; Pollux iv. 125; Bekk. Anecd. i, p. 272, 13; Eustathius, Od., p. 1957. 52 ff.
[4] We owe this point to Professor R. E. Wycherley.
[5] Even if there was a ληνός in the precinct ἐν Λίμναις, it would not prove anything, if (as is practically certain) the word Λήναιον has nothing to do with ληνός.
[6] Quoted above, p. 2.   [7] Studia, p. 57.

right in thinking that *Ληναίου* is a textual error for *Λιμναίου*,[1] the title
of the god as connected with the Anthesteria.

8. In 1947 Carlo Anti attempted to prove that there was a separate
'Lenaian theatre', that it was to be located in a trapezoidal area alongside Dörpfeld's 'temple *ἐν Λίμναις*', and that all Aristophanes' Lenaia
plays (*Acharnians*, *Knights*, *Wasps*, *Frogs*, and, on Anti's view, *Lysistrata*
and *Thesmophoriazousae*) were acted there, and not in the theatre of
Dionysus.[2] His thesis has been revived and modified by C. F. Russo.[3]
Anti's original argument relied heavily on shaky foundations: particularly
on Dörpfeld's location of the sanctuary *ἐν Λίμναις*, and his identification
of that sanctuary with the Lenaion, as well as on a number of dubious
topographical arguments from the text of Aristophanes' plays. These
arguments were not adequate to prove his case, and the area near
Dörpfeld's sanctuary is incredible as the site for a 'theatre', however
improvised.[4] Russo's version of the thesis is somewhat different: it rests
(*a*) on the assertion that Aristophanes' Lenaia plays (on Russo's view,
not including *Lysistrata* or *Thesmophoriazousae*, but including *Ecclesiazousae* and *Plutus*) differ markedly from those intended for the City
Dionysia in staging, use of the theatre, dramatic technique, and atmo-
sphere; (*b*) on a revised version of Anti's topographical case, insisting
that the Lenaia plays evoke particularly the area of the Pnyx and Agora,
whereas the Dionysia plays, where they are not located generally 'in
Athens' or in some fabulous setting, refer to the area of the Acropolis;
(*c*) on the proposition that the phrase *ἐπὶ Ληναίῳ ἀγών* (Ar. *Ach.* 504;
cf. Plato, *Protag.* 327 d (pass. (29) above); *I.G.* ii². 1496, 74 and 105 (pass.
(12) above); Sannyrion, fr. 2 K) means simply 'a contest in the Lenaion'
and is meant to be taken literally. Russo admits that Pollux iv. 121 (*αὐτὸ
μὲν* (sc. *τὸ θέατρον* itself as contrasted with the audience) *ἂν εἴποις* . . .
Διονυσιακὸν θέατρον καὶ Ληναϊκόν) is the only apparent reference to a
'Lenaian theatre' in antiquity, but he overstates his case: his (*a*), in almost
all points, implies no more than that the theatrical resources of the poet,
and the climate of the festival, were different at the Lenaia from those
of the City Dionysia; (*b*) still relies on two very doubtful locations, those

---

[1] This appellation of Dionysus is attested by Callimachus, Phanodemos, and Philostratus
(see above, pp. 1, 6, 8).
[2] Anti, *Teatri greci arcaici*, chs. vii and viii.
[3] *Rendiconti Accad. Lincei*, Ser. 8a. XI (1956), pp. 14–27, reprinted (with some changes)
in *Aristofane autore di teatro* (1962), pp. 3–21.
[4] See Dover, *Lustrum* 2 (1957), p. 57; Russo, *Aristofane*, pp. 5–7. Gerkan and Fensterbusch,
who originally received Anti's thesis favourably (*Deutsche Lit. Zeit.* 70 (1949), pp. 163 ff.;
Gnomon 21 (1949), pp. 303 f.), have now apparently changed their minds on the archaeological evidence (see Russo, op. cit., p. 7).

of the sanctuary ἐν Λίμναις in Dörpfeld's site, and of the Lenaion itself in the Agora; and (c) faces but cannot really overcome the probability that ἐπὶ Ληναίῳ, having *originally* meant 'in the Lenaion', came to be no more than a stereotyped formula for the festival (cf. St. Martin's in the Fields). Moreover, all our sources[1] assert that the Agora was the site of dramatic performances 'before the theatre was built': it is hard to believe, as Russo must, that this is merely a reference to the rebuilding of the theatre by Lycurgus.

9. When Aristotle[2] speaks of the ἀγών at the Lenaia as being managed by the archon basileus—apparently without the assistance of the Eleusinian officials who helped him in the conduct of the πομπή—he presumably refers to the dramatic contests of the fourth century; Aristophanes also,[3] in 425 B.C., had already, as we have seen, described the dramatic contest as ὁ ἐπὶ Ληναίῳ ἀγών, and as a domestic festival at which there were no strangers or allies present. (The seas were still too stormy, and it was not till some three months later that they were easily navigable.[4]) The evidence of inscriptions makes it practically certain that the organization of contests at the Lenaia in tragedy and comedy (parallel to those at the City Dionysia) goes back no farther than the middle of the fifth century B.C.— probably about 440 B.C.—and for what happened before that evidence is lacking. It is possible that the performances were more on the scale of those of the Dionysia ἐν ἀγροῖς of the rural demes, none of which seems to have celebrated the Lenaia,[5] and that it was comparatively late that they became more ambitious and were transferred from the market-place to the theatre of Dionysus. (The date of this transference is nowhere recorded, but possibly it may have followed the Periclean improvements in the theatre, about 445 B.C.[6]) It would be then that the inscriptional record (following the new official status of the festival) might naturally begin.[7] How the contests were organized (under the archon basileus) before this remains unknown. It may have been from the first that comic performances were more

---

[1] See passages 22, 25, 26 above and p. 37, n. 6.

[2] Ἀθ. Πολ. lvii. 1 (pass. (14) above).

[3] *Ach.* 504.

[4] Theophr. *Char.* iii τὴν θάλατταν ἐκ Διονυσίων πλόιμον εἶναι. See below, pp. 58 f.

[5] See Farnell, *Cults* v, p. 213. The dates of the Rural Dionysia may, as he suggests, have been adjusted so as to enable citizens and country-dwellers to attend both festivals. The Rural Dionysia seem to have been normally in December (see below).

[6] Dörpfeld, *Ath. Mitt.* 20 (1895), p. 183, thinks that the transference may have taken place a century later, when Lycurgus built or altered the theatre. But it seems improbable that the theatre should not have been used for the comedies of the great comic poets at the Lenaia as well as at the Dionysia.

[7] See below, pp. 72 f. and Appendix to Chapter II.

important at this festival than tragic (the reverse being the case at the City Dionysia).[1] In the fifth century only two tragic poets competed, each with two tragedies but no satyric play.[2] The great tragic poets seldom appeared at the Lenaia; Sophocles did so a few times;[3] a victory of Agathon in 416 is recorded—his first.[4] In the fourth century the tyrant Dionysius won at this festival his only success with a tragedy,[5] and victories were won by Astydamas, Achaeus,[6] and Theodektes.[7] On the other hand, the great comic poets seem to have competed indifferently at either festival, though even in comedy a special prestige attached itself to a City victory, if we may judge by Aristophanes' disappointment[8] at failing to win one with the *Clouds*, after his two Lenaian victories. As at the City Dionysia, five comic poets competed, each with one play, except during a short period in the Peloponnesian War when the number was reduced to three. That the Lenaian festival was less highly regarded than the City Dionysia is probably the reason why at the former, but not at the latter, aliens might sing in the choruses and resident aliens could be choregoi.[9]

There were contests of tragic actors and comic actors—the best in each category being awarded a prize—almost, if not quite, from the time at which the inscriptional record began;[10] but it is not certain that old plays were acted as they were at the City Dionysia,[11] and in the

---

[1] They may have developed out of dramatic elements—disguises, impersonations, etc.—in the πομπή and the σκώμματα ἐκ τῶν ἁμαξῶν. Cf. Körte, *R.E.* xi, col. 1226, 2 ff.; Kroll, *R.E.* xii, col. 1936, 34 f.; Wilamowitz, ed. of Ar. *Lysistrata*, pp. 9, 12.

[2] The chief piece of evidence is *I.G.* ii². 2319, entry for 419–418 B.C. (p. 109 below); cf. O'Connor, pp. 47 f.; Wilhelm, *Urkunden dram. Aufführungen*, p. 53.

[3] 'Suidas' s.v. Sophocles gives 24 victories; *I.G.* ii². 2325, col. i, 5 (p. 112 below: victories at the Dionysia), Diod. Sic. xiii. 103. 4 give 18: the difference between the totals of victories attributed to Sophocles is best explained by assuming that six were won at the Lenaia. So Bergk, *Rh. Mus.* 34 (1879), p. 298; Russo, *Mus. Helv.* 17 (1960), pp. 165 f.; Jacoby on Apollodorus 244 F 35. Russo, in the same article, argues that Euripides cannot have competed at the Lenaia, on arithmetical grounds: the argument is inconclusive, if only because of uncertainties about the number of plays that Euripides wrote, and about productions (e.g. of *Andromache*) which may have taken place, but did not certainly take place, outside Athens.

[4] Plato, *Sympos.* 173 a; Athen. v. 217 a.

[5] Diod. Sic. xv. 74. 1.   [6] See below, p. 114.

[7] Eight victories are attributed to Theodektes in the epitaph quoted by Stephanus of Byzantium s.v. Phaselis; seven are recorded for the Dionysia in *I.G.* ii². 2325, col. 3 (p. 112 below): the eighth was presumably at the Lenaia. Cf. Russo, op. cit., p. 165; p. 117 below.

[8] *Clouds* 520 ff.

[9] Schol. Ar. *Plut.* 953; Plutarch, *Phok.* 30. 6.   [10] See below, pp. 71–74.

[11] Meritt has argued (*Hesperia* 7 (1938), p. 117) that an inscription from the Athenian Agora (see below, pp. 123 f.) records victories at the Lenaia of various years about 255–254 B.C. in contests of old comedy, satyr play, and tragedy: but the attribution to the Lenaia is far from certain. It rests on the absence of evidence for *contests* of old plays at the Dionysia at any period, but equally there is no evidence (except this inscription) for such contests at the Lenaia.

period best known to us there was no performance of dithyrambs, and no such performance is mentioned in the Law of Euegoros;[1] but early in the third century an inscription[2] does record a dithyrambic victory at the Lenaia.

It is not certain when the contests came to an end. The monument set up by Xenokles[3] as agonothetes in 306 B.C. proves their continuance after the abolition of choregia. The list of victorious tragic poets at the Lenaia[4] goes down only to about 320 B.C., but as the victorious tragic actors' list goes down to the end of the third century (and may have gone further) the contest of poets doubtless also continued. The extant didaskalic record[5] of comedy at the Lenaia terminated soon after 284 B.C., but the list of victorious comic poets[4] continues beyond 150 B.C.

10. An inscription[6] of the middle of the third century B.C. found at Rhamnous is of interest as showing apparently that at that time there was a cult of Dionysus $\Lambda\eta\nu\alpha\hat{\iota}os$ there: $K\alpha\lambda\lambda\iota\sigma\theta\acute{\epsilon}\nu\eta s$ $K\lambda\epsilon o\beta o\acute{\upsilon}\lambda o\upsilon$ $\Pi\rho o\sigma\pi\acute{\alpha}\lambda\tau\iota os$ $\sigma\tau\rho\alpha\tau\eta\gamma\grave{o}s$ $\chi\epsilon\iota\rho o\tau o\nu\eta\theta\epsilon\grave{\iota}s$ $\dot{\epsilon}\pi\grave{\iota}$ $\tau\grave{\eta}\nu$ $\pi\alpha\rho\alpha\lambda\acute{\iota}\alpha\nu$ $\sigma\tau\epsilon\phi\alpha\nu\omega\theta\epsilon\grave{\iota}s$ $\dot{\upsilon}\pi\grave{o}$ $\tau\hat{\eta}s$ $\beta o\upsilon\lambda\hat{\eta}s$ $\kappa\alpha\grave{\iota}$ $\tauo\hat{\upsilon}$ $\delta\acute{\eta}\mu o\upsilon$ $\Delta\iota o\nu\acute{\upsilon}\sigma\omega$ $\Lambda\eta\nu\alpha\acute{\iota}\omega$ $\dot{\alpha}\nu\acute{\epsilon}\theta\eta\kappa\epsilon\nu$. But the interpretation is not perfectly clear; it at least assumes that this general had some reason for commemorating at Rhamnous a distinction conferred by the Council and People of Athens, and we do not know the history of the stone.[7]

c. *The Rural Dionysia*

1. The festivities called $\tau\grave{\alpha}$ $\kappa\alpha\tau$' $\dot{\alpha}\gamma\rho o\grave{\upsilon}s$ $\Delta\iota o\nu\acute{\upsilon}\sigma\iota\alpha$ were celebrated, at least normally,[8] in the month Poseideon, which corresponds roughly to December. The central feature was a procession escorting a phallos held aloft, and this was no doubt in origin designed to promote or encourage the fertility of the autumn-sown seed or of the earth in general, at the time when it seemed to be slumbering. When the special association with Dionysus began is not known; the rite was probably far more primitive

---

[1] See above, p. 27.

[2] *I.G.* ii². 3779 $N\iota\kappa o\kappa\lambda\hat{\eta}s$ ... $\Lambda\acute{\eta}\nu\alpha\iota\alpha$ $\delta\iota\theta\upsilon\rho\acute{\alpha}\mu\beta\omega$; but Nikokles (of Tarentum) was a citharode ($\dot{o}s$ $\dot{\epsilon}\pi\grave{\iota}$ $\mu\acute{\epsilon}\gamma\iota\sigma\tauo\nu$ $\delta\acute{o}\xi\eta$ $\sigma\kappa\iota\theta\alpha\rho\omega\delta\hat{\omega}\nu$ $\dot{\alpha}\pi\acute{\alpha}\nu\tau\omega\nu$ $\hat{\eta}\lambda\theta\epsilon\nu$, Paus. i. 37. 2), not a flute player, and this does not look like an ordinary dithyrambic contest. There was no such contest at the Lenaia in the time of Demosthenes (*Meid.* 10).

[3] *I.G.* ii². 3073. See p. 120.   [4] *I.G.* ii². 2325. See pp. 113 ff.

[5] *I.G.* ii². 2319. See below, p. 109.   [6] *I.G.* ii². 2854.

[7] Bulle, *Untersuchungen an gr. Theatern*, pp. 3–4, suggested that there was a temple on the site; Pouilloux, *La Forteresse de Rhamnonte*, p. 122, disagrees.

[8] Farnell, *Cults* v, p. 206, suggests that in Ikarion the festival may have taken place in the spring, but this seems very doubtful (Athen. ii. 40 a points to the late summer). That the usual date was in Poseideon is stated definitely by Theophrastus, *Char.* iii, and by the scholiasts to Aeschines, *in Tim.* 43, and Plato, *Rep.* v. 475 d, and this is confirmed by inscriptions (*I.G.* ii². 1183 and 1496). See below, p. 45, nn. 7 and 8.

than the worship of Dionysus in Attica, and had nothing directly to do with wine; the vintage was long past, and the new wine was not yet fit to be broached; this was left for the Πιθοίγια some two or three months later; but there need be no doubt that in the merry-making which accompanied the festival plenty of wine was drunk, and in historical times these rural festivals were regarded as being held in honour of Dionysus. Nor is it known at what date dramatic performances first came to be associated with some or all of them.

The festivals were organized by each deme for itself in historical times and at least in the early fourth century they were not held everywhere on the same date in Poseideon, since Plato[1] speaks of people going from one of the festivals to another to gratify their desire for entertainment, and at this time, when troupes of actors travelled from one to another with their repertoire of plays, time must have been allowed for their movements.

In Plutarch's day[2] slaves had their share in the enjoyment and made the most of it, as they doubtless did in Attica centuries before.

2. The only definite information about the procession at the Rural Dionysia is that which is derived from the scene in Aristophanes' *Acharnians*[3] in which Dikaiopolis carries through an imitation (on a much reduced scale) of the procession. It is headed by his daughter as κανηφόρος, carrying as an offering a cake or flat loaf on which she pours porridge with a ladle; behind her is the slave Xanthias as φαλλοφόρος (with another slave), carrying the phallos upright on a pole, and lastly Dikaiopolis himself, perhaps representing a body of revellers, singing a chant to Phales, the personified symbol of fertility, and greeted as a companion of Bacchus. The song contains what might be construed as two rude references to individuals, and it may be to songs of this kind to which Aristotle refers when he speaks of comedy as originating ἀπὸ τῶν τὰ φαλλικὰ (ἐξαρχόντων) ἃ ἔτι καὶ νῦν ἐν πολλαῖς τῶν πόλεων διαμένει νομιζόμενα.[4] An Attic black-figure cup of the mid sixth century[5] seems to portray such a procession. On one side six men carry a pole on which a phallos is mounted and a fat man rides on the pole; on the other the fat man's place has been taken by a satyr, with, on his back, a small figure with

---

[1] *Rep.* v. 475 d ὥσπερ δὲ ἀπομεμισθωκότες τὰ ὦτα ἐπακοῦσαι πάντων χορῶν περιθέουσι τοῖς Διονυσίοις οὔτε τῶν κατὰ πόλεις οὔτε τῶν κατὰ κώμας ἀπολειπόμενοι.

[2] Plut. *non posse suav. vivi sec. Epicurum* 1098 b καὶ γὰρ οἱ θεράποντες ὅταν Κρόνια δειπνῶσιν ἢ Διονύσια κατ' ἀγρὸν ἄγωσι περιιόντες, οὐκ ἂν αὐτῶν τὸν ὀλολυγμὸν ὑπομείναις καὶ τὸν θόρυβον, ὑπὸ χαρμονῆς καὶ ἀπειροκαλίας τοιαῦτα ποιούντων καὶ φθεγγομένων.

[3] ll. 241–79.   [4] *Poetics*, iv. 1449ᵃ11.

[5] Florence 3897; *Dith. Trag. Com.*², pl. IV; see in general on Phallophoria, Herter in *R.E.* xix, s.vv. Phallophorie and Phallos; Nilsson, *Gesch.* i². 590–4.

a drinking horn, the increased weight apparently necessitating two extra supporters.

Dikaiopolis' festival is private, and doubtless the processions varied greatly in elaboration from deme to deme. Our major evidence is for the Peiraeus, where the πομπή and the sacrifice are attested from the fourth century.[1] In the late second century there was an εἰσαγωγή of the god, as in Athens at the City Dionysia, and the ephebes, who took part, regularly sacrificed a bull.[2] There is also evidence for the πομπή and the sacrifice at Eleusis.[3] In smaller demes, the procession was doubtless more simple, something on the lines of Plutarch's description,[4] whether this refers to Attica or his native Boeotia—ἡ πάτριος τῶν Διονυσίων ἑορτὴ τὸ παλαιὸν ἐπέμπετο δημοτικῶς καὶ ἱλαρῶς, ἀμφορεὺς οἴνου καὶ κληματίς, εἶτα τράγον τις εἷλκεν, ἄλλος ἰσχάδων ἄρριχον ἠκολούθει κομίζων, ἐπὶ πᾶσι δ' ὁ φαλλός. There were many types of phallic procession in the Greek world, but none of those described by Athenaeus[5] are brought by him into any connexion with the Rural Dionysia.[6]

The procession is frequently said to have been accompanied by a κῶμος, but, although the word is attested for the City Dionysia,[7] it never seems to be directly associated with the Rural Dionysia. Contests of κῶμοι are attested for the τετράκωμοι, a group of four demes south-west of Athens,[8]

---

[1] The Law of Euegoros (above, p. 27, no. 11) and *I.G.* ii². 380 (320–319 B.C.), where the ἀγορανόμοι are ordered to see that the streets are in proper condition for the procession, ἐπιμεληθῆναι τοὺς ἀγορανόμους τῶν ὁδῶν τῶν πλατειῶν, ᾗ ἡ πομπὴ πορεύεται τῷ Διὶ τῷ Σωτῆρι καὶ τῷ Διονύσῳ, ὅπως ἂν ὁμαλισθῶσιν καὶ κατασκευασθῶσιν ὡς βέλτιστα. For the sacrifice, see *I.G.* ii². 1496, ll. 70, 144 (334–331 B.C.).

[2] *S.E.G.* xv. 104, ll. 24 ff. (127–126 B.C.) ἔθυσαν δὲ καὶ τοῖς [Πει]ραίοις τῷ Διονύσῳ [καὶ] εἰσήγαγον τὸν θεὸν παρακ[αθί]σαντες ἐν τῷ Πειραεῖ ἡμέρα[ς τέτταρ]ας εὐτάκτως; *Hesperia* 16 (1947), p. 171, ll. 19 f. (116–115 B.C.) εἰσήγαγον δὲ τήν τε Παλλάδα καὶ τὸν Διόνυσον ἔν τε Πειραιεῖ καὶ ἐν ἄστει καὶ ἐβουθέτησαν ἐν ἑκατέρᾳ τῶν πόλεων. In 107–106 B.C. the ephebes dedicated a φιάλη to the god costing 100 drachmae (*I.G.* ii². 1011, l. 12). See also *I.G.* ii² 1028 (101–100 B.C.), 1029 (96–95 B.C.), 1039. Compare below, pp. 60 f., for their similar activities at the City Dionysia.

[3] *I.G.* ii². 949 (165–164 B.C.) ἐπειδὴ Πάμφιλος Ἄ[ρχοντος κα]ταστασθεὶς δήμαρχος εἰς τὸν ἐπὶ Πέλοπος ἄρχοντος ἐνιαυτ[ὸν τοῖς Διονυσί]οις ἔθυσεν τῷ Διονύσῳ καὶ τὴν πομπὴν ἔπεμψεν καὶ τ[c. 18]τον, ἔθηκεν δὲ καὶ τὸν ἀγῶνα ἐν τῷ θεάτρῳ κτλ.

[4] *de cupid. divit.* 527 d. δημοτικῶς probably conveys no reference to celebration by demes. Cf. Nilsson, *Jahrb. Arch.* 31 (1916), p. 323 = *Opusc. Sel.* i, pp. 188 f. For a mysterious Attic festival called Κληματίς attested once only in 39–38 B.C. (*I.G.* ii². 1043, l. 31), see Deubner, *Att. Feste*, pp. 147 f.

[5] xiv. 621 d–622 d. The passage and the relation of comedy to the phallic κῶμος are discussed in *Dith. Trag. Com.*², pp. 134 ff. Cf. Hdt. ii. 48 f.

[6] Heraclitus, fr. B 15 may have in view some celebrations like that of the Rural Dionysia: εἰ μὴ γὰρ Διονύσῳ πομπὴν ἐποιεῦντο καὶ ὕμνεον ᾆσμα αἰδοίοισι, ἀναιδέστατα εἴργαστ' ἄν. ὡυτὸς δὲ Ἀίδης καὶ Διόνυσος, ὅτεῳ μαίνονται καὶ ληναΐζουσι.

[7] In the Law of Euegoros; see below, p. 63.

[8] *I.G.* ii². 3103 (330–329 B.C.) Ξυπεταιόνες ἐνίκων· Ἀριστοφῶν ἦρχε. κώμαρχοι (four names follow). κωμασταί (five names follow, including a pair of brothers already listed as κώμαρχοι); cf. ibid. 3102, 2830.

but their common cult was that of Herakles,[1] and there is no reason to associate the contests with Dionysus.[2] A parallel contest appears at Acharnai, with no clue to the deity honoured.[3]

3. It is commonly stated that one of the amusements of these festivals was ἀσκωλιασμός—the attempt to jump or stand on an oiled and full wineskin. Latte[4] has shown that the texts are confused, and that the word, which simply means 'hopping', has been misapplied to the game. The evidence to connect the game particularly with the Rural Dionysia consists of a passage of Virgil's second Georgic (380 ff.) which mentions it in the same breath as rural dramatic contests in Attica:

> non aliam ob culpam Baccho caper omnibus aris
> caeditur et veteres ineunt proscaenia ludi,
> praemiaque ingeniis pagos et compita circum
> Thesidae posuere, atque inter pocula laeti
> mollibus in pratis unctos saluere per utres,

and another in Cornutus,[5] εἰς τὸν ἀσκὸν ἐνάλλονται κατὰ τὰς Ἀττικὰς κώμας οἱ γεωργοὶ νεανίσκοι. Doubtless the game took place at many festivals, and it is doubtful whether it should be associated with the Rural Dionysia in particular.[6]

4. It is unlikely that all demes attached dramatic festivals to their Rural Dionysia. Conversely, it cannot be regarded as certain that all references to Dionysia or to dramatic competitions in the demes refer necessarily to the Rural Dionysia in Poseideon, which, it might be supposed, being in midwinter, might not be an appropriate time for dramatic performances in the open air. However, there is evidence for dramatic performances in Poseideon for two demes, Myrrhinous[7] and Peiraeus,[8]

---

[1] Steph. Byz. s.v. Ἐχελίδαι. Pollux iv. 105 tentatively associates a type of dance called τετράκωμος with these four demes, but cf. Hesych. τετράκωμος· μέλος τι σὺν ὀρχήσει πεποιημένον εἰς Ἡρακλέα ἐπινίκιον. See also Πολέμων 3 (1947), p. 21 for a statue of Herakles found on the same site as the inscriptions in the last note.

[2] Roussel, C.R. Acad. Inscr. 1929, pp. 195–9, Deubner, op. cit., p. 136, seem to be in error here. Wilamowitz, Glaube i², 197, n. 1 is a more balanced statement.

[3] I.G. ii². 3104 (340–339 or 313–312 B.C.) ἐπὶ Θεοφράστου ἄ[ρχοντος] Ἀντιφάνης . . . κωμαρχ[ῶ]ν ἐνίκα [τοὺς συν]άρχοντ[ας]. It is not certain whether the inscription ΚΟΜΑΡΧΟΣ attached to one of three revellers on an amphora by Euthymides (Munich 2307; A.R.V.², p. 26, no. 1: best pictures in Lullies–Hirmer, Gr. Vasen der reifarchaischen Zeit, pll. 24–31) is a name or a function.

[4] Hermes 85 (1957), pp. 385–91.

[5] 30 (p. 60, 23 Lang).

[6] The assertion of the scholiast on Ar. Plutus 1129 that there was a separate festival called the Ἀσκώλια, ἐν ᾗ ἐνήλλοντο τοῖς ἀσκοῖς εἰς τιμὴν τοῦ Διονύσου is almost certainly false.

[7] I.G. ii². 1183. 36 (second half of fourth century B.C.) τῇ δὲ ἐνάτῃ ἐπὶ δέκα τοῦ Ποσιδεῶν[ος] μην[ὸς χρηματίζε]ιν πε[ρὶ Διο]νυσίων. Wilhelm, U.D.A., p. 238, shows that this refers to an assembly after the festival.

In I.G. ii². 1496 (334–330 B.C.), in the accounts of the ταμίαι of Athena and the ἐπιμεληταί

and we can proceed to discuss the evidence for dramatic performances in the demes, without further reference to this difficulty.

5. There can be no doubt that the festival at the Peiraeus was the most important of all these. Evidence for the fifth century is confined to the story that Socrates went there to see plays by Euripides,[1] but the theatre itself is mentioned three times at the end of the century.[2] In the fourth century the interest taken in the festival by the state is clear. In the Law of Euegoros[3] it is mentioned along with the Lenaia and the City Dionysia as a period during which the exaction of debts and taking of security were forbidden. The sacrifices were on at least one occasion presided over by the strategoi, and during the administration of Lycurgus the state collected the receipts from the sale of the skins of the victims.[4] The decree already quoted about the cleaning of the streets for the πομπή is a state decree.[5] In 307–306 B.C. the state ordered that ambassadors from Kolophon be given special places at the festival.[6] The officials of the Eleusinian Mysteries seem also to have had an interest in the festival and in 329–328 B.C. contributed to the cost of a sacrifice.[7] In the second century, the importance of the festival in the calendar of the epheboi is attested by inscriptions already quoted.[8]

The management of the festival was, and this seems to be normal for all demes, in the hands of the demarch, who at the Peiraeus was, abnormally, appointed by the state; it was his duty to appoint choregoi.[9] In the early fourth century, the deme handed over the theatre to contractors, who assumed the responsibility of providing seating and appear to have collected the fees for admission,[10] though towards the end of the century we

---

established by Lycurgus, the entries are chronological, and the Dionysia in the Peiraeus fall between the Theseia (Pyanopsion 8) and the Lenaia (Gamelion). In *I.G.* ii². 456. 33 (307–306 B.C.) the Dionysia in the Peiraeus are in the near future on the last day of Maimakterion, and hence fall in Poseideon. However, in *I.G.* ii². 1672, l. 106 (329–328 B.C.) a payment by the epistatai of Eleusis [εἰς Διονύσια τ]ὰ ἐν Πειραιεῖ ἐπιστάταις εἰς θυσίαν was made during the fourth prytany, which must have ended about a week before the beginning of Poseideon. It is not clear how this is to be explained.

[1] Aelian, *Var. H.* ii. 13 καὶ Πειραιοῖ δὲ ἀγωνιζομένου τοῦ Εὐριπίδου καὶ ἐκεῖ κατῄει.

[2] Thuc. viii. 93 οἱ δὲ ἐν τῷ Πειραιεῖ ὁπλῖται τόν τε Ἀλεξικλέα ὃν ξυνέλαβον ἀφέντες καὶ τὸ τείχισμα καθελόντες εἰς τὸ πρὸς τῇ Μουνιχίᾳ Διονυσιακὸν θέατρον ἐλθόντες; Lys. xiii. 32 ἐπειδὴ ἡ ἐκκλησία Μουνιχίασιν ἐν τῷ θεάτρῳ ἐγίγνετο; Xen. *Hellen.* ii. 4. 32 ἀπέκτειναν [sc. the soldiers of Pausanias] . . . τριάκοντα τῶν ψιλῶν, τοὺς δ᾽ ἄλλους κατεδίωξαν πρὸς τὸ Πειραιοῖ θέατρον.

[3] See p. 27, no. 11.   [4] *I.G.* ii². 1496, ll. 70, 144 (334–330 B.C.).

[5] Above, p. 44, n. 1.

[6] *I.G.* ii². 456, ll. 32–33 κατανεῖμαι δ᾽ αὐτοῖς καὶ θ[έαν τὸν ἀρχιτέκτο]να εἰς τὰ Διονύσια τὰ Πειραϊκά.

[7] *I.G.* ii². 1672. 106 (see above, p. 45, n. 8).   [8] Above, p. 44, n. 2.

[9] Aristotle, Ἀθ. Πολ. liv. 8 κληροῦσι δὲ καὶ εἰς Σαλαμῖνα ἄρχοντα καὶ εἰς Πειραιέα δήμαρχον, οἳ τὰ Διονύσια ποιοῦσι ἑκατέρωθι καὶ χορηγοὺς καθιστᾶσιν· ἐν Σαλαμῖνι δὲ καὶ τὸ ὄνομα τοῦ ἄρχοντος ἀναγράφεται.

[10] *I.G.* ii². 1176 (see Wilhelm, *U.D.A.*, p. 235); a new fragment, *Hesperia* 29 (1960), p. 1.

find an ἀρχιτέκτων in charge.[1] The deme, however, retained the right to give seats to officials and anyone else whom it wished to honour,[2] a right which we find it exercising in the third century in a decree which also shows that the holders of such seats were ceremonially escorted to their places by the demarch: εἶναι δὲ αὐτῷ προεδρίαν ἐν τῷ θεάτρῳ, ὅταν ποιῶσι Πειραιεῖς τὰ Διονύσια, οὗ καὶ αὐτοῖς Πειραιεῦσι κατανέμεται, καὶ εἰσαγέτω αὐτὸν ὁ δήμαρχος εἰς τὸ θέατρον καθάπερ τοὺς ἱερεῖς καὶ τοὺς ἄλλους οἷς δέδοται ἡ προεδρία παρὰ Πειραιέων.[3]

Of the actual content of the festival we hear little. The Law of Euegoros mentions comedy and tragedy, but not dithyramb, and the inscription just quoted goes on to order the crowning of the honorand τραγωιδῶν τῷ ἀγῶνι. Beyond the fact that the ephebes of 128–127 B.C. remained in the Peiraeus for four days, we have no other information about its scope.

6. At Eleusis, the most detailed text, from the middle of the fourth century, (*I.G.* ii². 1186), is evidence for dithyramb and tragedy there.

Καλλίμαχος Καλλικράτους εἶπεν· ἐπειδὴ Δαμασίας Διονυσίου Θηβαῖος οἰκήσας Ἐλευσῖνι κόσμιός τε ὢν διατετέλεκε καὶ φιλανθρώπως ἔχει πρὸς πάντας τοὺς ἐν τῷ δήμῳ οἰκοῦντας καὶ αὐτὸς καὶ οἱ μαθηταὶ αὐτοῦ, καὶ Διονύσια ποιούντων Ἐλευσινίων ἐσπούδασεν καὶ ἐφιλοτιμήθη πρὸς τοὺς θεοὺς καὶ τὸν δῆμον τὸν Ἀθηναίων καὶ Ἐλευσινίων, ὅπως ὡς κάλλιστα γένηται τὰ Διονύσια, καὶ παρασκευάσας τοῖς αὑτοῦ τέλεσι χοροὺς δύο, τὸν μὲν παίδων, τὸν δὲ ἀνδρῶν, ἐπέδωκεν τῇ Δήμητρι καὶ τῇ Κόρῃ[4] καὶ τῷ Διονύσῳ, δεδόχθαι Ἐλευσινίοις ἐπαινέσαι Δαμασίαν Διονυσίου Θηβαῖον σωφροσύνης ἕνεκα καὶ εὐσεβείας τῆς πρὸς τὼ θεὼ καὶ στεφανῶσαι αὐτὸν χρυσῷ στεφάνῳ ἀπὸ Χ δραχμῶν. ἀνειπάτω δὲ αὐτὸν ὁ μετὰ Γνάθιν δήμαρχος Διονυσίων τῶν Ἐλευσῖνι τοῖς τραγῳδοῖς . . . . ἔστω δὲ αὐτῷ προεδρία καὶ ἀτέλεια ὧν εἰσιν κύριοι Ἐλευσίνιοι . . . . καὶ ἐπιμελέσθω αὐτοῦ ὁ δήμαρχος ὁ ἀεὶ δημαρχῶν ὅτου ἂν δέηται· ἑλέσθαι δὲ αὐτίκα μάλα ὅστις ἐπιμελήσεται ὅπως ἂν ἀναγραφῇ τόδε τὸ ψήφισμα καὶ σταθῇ ἐν τῷ Διονυσίῳ κτλ.[5]

Comedy is attested by *I.G.* ii². 3100 Ἀθηνόδωρος Γο - - - χορηγῶν κωμῳδ[οῖς ἐνίκα].

A more controversial text is *I.G.* ii². 3090. This runs

[Γ]νᾶθις Τιμοκήδους Ἀναξανδρίδης Τιμαγόρου
χορηγοῦντες κωμῳδοῖς ἐνίκων·
Ἀριστοφάνης ἐδίδασκεν.
ἑτέρα νίκη τραγῳδοῖς·
Σοφοκλῆς ἐδίδασκεν.

---

[1] Ibid. 456 (above, p. 46, n. 6). [2] As p. 46, n. 10. [3] Ibid., no. 1214.
[4] The association of Demeter and Kore in their own sacred place with Dionysus seems natural enough. Neither the Dionysion nor the theatre has been found, and the confused evidence about the place of Dionysus at Eleusis cannot be discussed here.
[5] Other inscriptions conferring προεδρία and crowns to be proclaimed at the tragic performances of the Dionysia are *I.G.* ii². 1187, 1192–4 (all fourth century B.C.). Ibid. 3107 is a choregic monument, the type of contest uncertain.

This has been generally interpreted[1] as a record, set up at home in Eleusis by two Eleusinians who had been successful in Athens during the period of synchoregia there. If this were so, the plays would almost certainly have been the *Frogs* of Aristophanes in 406–405 B.C. and the *Oedipus Coloneus* of Sophocles in 402–401 B.C. However, besides the improbability that the same pair of synchoregoi should have been victorious at Athens in two years so close to each other, it now seems most likely that synchoregia at Athens only lasted one year, 406–405 B.C.[2] It therefore seems most likely that the inscription refers to a festival or festivals at Eleusis. Since there is no reason to suppose that ἐδίδασκεν is to be taken other than literally, Sophocles and Aristophanes must both have gone to Eleusis, and the festival there will have been of importance, even if the plays were not first performances.

There is one isolated piece of evidence for the πομπή and ἀγών at Eleusis in the second century B.C.[3]

7. Ikarion[4] has a special place among Attic demes in its possession of traditions associating it with the advent of Dionysus into Attica and the beginnings of tragedy and comedy.[5] Appropriately enough, it also possesses the earliest epigraphic record of dramatic performances, a fifth-century decree,[6] very fragmentary, but showing both by its references to choregoi and otherwise that there were at the time regularly organized dramatic festivals. A fourth-century decree[7] shows the festival in the control of the demarch and two choregoi: Κάλλιππος εἶπεν· ἐψηφίσθαι Ἰκαριεῦσιν ἐπαινέσαι Νίκωνα τὸν δήμαρχον καὶ στεφανῶσαι κιττοῦ στεφάνῳ καὶ ἀνειπεῖν τὸν κηρύκα ὅτι στεφανοῦσιν Ἰκαριεῖς Νίκωνα καὶ ὁ δῆμος ὁ Ἰκαριέων τὸν δήμαρχον, ὅτι καλῶς καὶ δικαίως τῷ Διονύσῳ τὴν ἑορτὴν ἐποίησεν καὶ τὸν ἀγῶνα· ἐπαινέσαι δὲ καὶ τοὺς χορηγοὺς Ἐπικράτην καὶ Πραξίαν καὶ στεφανῶσαι κιττοῦ στεφάνῳ καὶ ἀνειπεῖν καθάπερ τὸν δήμαρχον. Ikarion was a small village, and its crowns are of ivy, not of gold, but ivy was sacred to Dionysus. Poverty is again suggested by the choregic monuments, two of which show three choregoi collaborating. In *I.G.* ii². 3095, Ἔργασος Φανομάχου | Φανόμαχος Ἐργάσου | Διόγνητος Ἐργάσου | τραγῳδοῖς χορηγήσαντες | νικῶντες ἀνέθεσαν, the victors are a father and two sons, but there is no means of tracing the relationships in *I.G.* ii². 3098 Ἀγνίας Ξάνθιππος Ξανθίδης νικήσαντες ἀνέθεσαν. There is one other tragic monument,[8] but comedy is not attested except

---

[1] See Körte, *Gnomon* 11 (1935), pp. 634–5.
[2] Capps, *Hesperia* 12 (1943), pp. 5 ff. and below, p. 102,　　　[3] See above, p. 44, n. 3.
[4] This seems the best form of the name; see *B.S.A.* 51 (1956), p. 172.
[5] *Dith. Trag. Com.*², pp. 69–89.　　　　[6] *I.G.* i². 186–7.　　　　[7] *I.G.* ii². 1178.
[8] *I.G.* ii². 3099 Μνησίλοχο[ς] Μνησιφίλου τραγῳδοῖς χορηγῶν ἐνίκα.

possibly by *I.G.* ii². 3094 [Ἄ]ρχιππος Ἀρχεδέ[κτου | ν]ικήσας ἀνέθηκε [τῷ] | Διονύσῳ. | Νικόστρατος ἐδίδασκε, where it is doubtful whether this Nikostratos is the son of Aristophanes, or the dithyrambic poet of the same name.[1]

8. At Aixone there are three decrees from the late fourth century, which also convey the thanks of the deme to the demarch and two choregoi. The most striking, illustrated here (fig. 25), is adorned with a relief of Dionysus and a satyr cup-bearer, and, above, five comic masks.[2] The date is probably 313–312 B.C. (the archonship of Theophrastus in that year being slightly more probable than the alternative date 340–339 B.C.).[3] It runs : Γλαυκίδης Σωσίππου εἶπεν· ἐπειδὴ οἱ χορηγοὶ Αὐτέας Αὐτοκλέους καὶ Φιλοξενίδης Φιλίππου καλῶς καὶ φιλοτίμως ἐχορήγησαν, δεδόχθαι τοῖς δημόταις στεφανῶσαι αὐτοὺς χρυσῷ στεφάνῳ ἑκάτερον ἀπὸ ἑκατὸν δραχμῶν ἐν τῷ θεάτρῳ τοῖς κωμῳδοῖς τοῖς μετὰ Θεόφραστον ἄρχοντα, ὅπως ἂν φιλοτιμῶνται καὶ οἱ ἄλλοι χορηγοὶ οἱ μέλλοντες χορηγεῖν, δοῦναι δὲ αὐτοῖς καὶ εἰς θυσίαν δέκα δραχμὰς τὸν δήμαρχον Ἡγησιλέων καὶ τοὺς ταμίας, ἀναγράψαι δὲ καὶ τὸ ψήφισμα τόδε τοὺς ταμίας ἐν στήλῃ λιθίνῃ καὶ στῆσαι ἐν τῷ θεάτρῳ, ὅπως ἂν Αἰξωνεῖς ἀεὶ ὡς κάλλιστα ⟨τὰ⟩ Διονύσια ποιῶσιν. One other decree[4] shows that the proclamation of crowns at the comic performances and their registration in the theatre were not confined to choregoi, and another[5] shows that this deme too conferred the honour of προεδρία. A more difficult text, often, but wrongly, attributed to Aixone, is discussed in the Appendix (below, pp. 54 ff.).

9. The evidence for other demes can be summarized more briefly. At Acharnai, besides the mysterious inscription for a κωμαρχός,[6] there is a record of a choregos who served both for comedy and dithyramb.[7] Another inscription[8] (early fourth century) probably also refers to dithyramb :

---

[1] Attested in *I.G.* i². 769.

[2] First published *Ath. Mitt.* 66 (1941), pp. 218 ff. with fig. 73. The parallel texts are *I.G.* ii². 1198 (326–325 B.C.), 1200 (317–316 B.C.). For the masks, see below, pp. 215 f.

[3] Webster, *J.H.S.* 71 (1951), p. 222, n. 7; Ἀρχ. Ἐφ. 1954, 193; *Hesperia* 29 (1960), p. 264 and n. 45, has argued for the earlier date. The date must be the same as that of *I.G.* ii². 1202, for the same archon, proposer, and demarch appear in both. In no. 1202, Aristokrates son of Aristophanes is honoured, and he is the proposer of a decree (no. 1201) in 317–316 B.C., which favours the later date, as does the lettering. Webster's arguments are less convincing for, though the choregos Auteas does appear as early as 346–345 (ibid. 2492), he is there associated with his father in a forty-year lease and may have been very young. The sister of the choregos Philoxenides married the youngest son of Lycurgus the orator ([Plut.] *Vit. X Orat.* 843 a).

[4] Ibid., no. 1202.   [5] Ibid., no. 1197.   [6] Above, p. 45, n. 3.

[7] *I.G.* ii². 3106: [– – – Δημ]οστράτου νικήσας ἀνέθηκε [κυκλίῳ] χορῷ καὶ κωμ[ῳ]ιδοῖς. Χάρης Θηβαῖος [η]ὔλει. Σπευσεάδης Ἀθηναῖος [ἐδίδασκε].

[8] Ibid. 3092. No satisfactory explanation has been given of the last line. It has been

Μνησίστρατος Μίσγωνος   Μησίμαχος Μνησιστράτο
Διοπείθης Διοδώρο ἐχορήγον   Θεότιμος Διοτίμο ἐχορήγον
[Δι]καιογένης ἐδίδασκεν.   Ἀρίφρων ἐδίδασκεν.
                                 Πολυχάρης Κώμω[ν]ος ἐ[δί]δασκεν.

But the most interesting text is a late fourth-century decree[1] which makes it clear that receipts from the theatre were here reckoned on as a part of deme revenue.

At Aigilia, we find again the pattern, already noted for Ikarion, of a father and two sons sharing the choregia.[2] An epigram,[3] probably from Anagyrus, of the second half of the fourth century, attests family pride in dramatic victories, though they may have been victories at Athens and not local.

For Kollytos, our evidence is only literary. We hear in 346–345 B.C. of comic performances at the Rural Dionysia, with the actor Parmenon performing a play which was certainly contemporary, though it may not have been a first performance.[4] It was also the scene of Aeschines' performance of the part of Oinomaos, which, according to Demosthenes,[5] he murdered. The evidence is conflicting as to whether this was in Sophocles' play or in a new play by Ischander.

Of Myrrhinous we know nothing except the institution of προεδρία[6] and the assembly after the festival.[7] Paiania has a record in the middle of the fourth century of a victory as tragic choregos by [Δη]μοσθένης Δ[ημαινέτ]ου Παιανιεύς, possibly a relation of the orator.[8] The celebration of the Rural Dionysia at Phlya with, apparently, some performance is

suggested that the reference is to a victory gained subsequently and added to the record, but the whole inscription appears to have been engraved at the same time. Others imagine that Polychares may have assisted Ariphron, but if so the record is unique. Ariphron was a well-known lyric poet, and Dikaiogenes, though primarily a tragic poet, is stated by Harpokration and 'Suidas' (s.v.) to have composed dithyrambs also.

[1] Ibid. 1206. καὶ αὐτο[ῖς δοῦναι εἰς θυσίαν] τὸν ἐνιαυτὸν ἕκα[στον τὸν ταμί]αν καὶ τὸν δήμαρχ[ον οἳ ἂν ἀεὶ ἀρ]χωσιν :ΔΔ: δραχμὰς [ἀπὸ τοῦ ἀργυ]ρίου τοῦ ἐγλεγομέ[νου ἐκ τοῦ θε]άτρου· ἐὰν δὲ τὸ θέα[τρον ἐλαττο]ν ᾖ, διδόναι αὐτοῖ[ς τὸν δήμαρχ]ον καὶ τὸν ταμίαν [οἳ ἂν ἀεὶ ἄρχω]σιν τὸ γεγραμμέν[ον ἀργύριον ε]ἰς τὴν θυσίαν ἐκ τ[ῆς κοινῆς διο]ικησέως τῆς τῶν δη[μοτῶν].

[2] Ibid. 3096: Τιμοσθένης Μειξωνίδου, Μειξωνίδης Τιμοσθένους, Κλεόστρατος Τιμοσθένους χορηγοῦντες νικήσαντες ἀνέθεσαν τῷ Διονύσῳ τἄγαλμα καὶ τὸμ [βωμον].

[3] Ibid. 3101. No. 1210 comes from the same area, and so does a new fifth-century choregic dedication, with Euripides as didaskalos, Ἀρχ. Ἐφ. 1965, pp. 163 ff.

[4] Aeschin. i. 157 πρώην ἐν τοῖς κατ᾽ ἀγροὺς Διονυσίοις κωμῳδῶν ὄντων ἐν Κολλυτῷ, καὶ Παρμένοντος τοῦ κωμικοῦ ὑποκριτοῦ εἰπόντος τι πρὸς τὸν χορὸν ἀνάπαιστον, ἐν ᾧ εἶναί τινας πόρνους μεγάλους Τιμαρχώδεις κτλ.

[5] Dem. de Cor. 180. Demochares, Demosthenes' nephew, εἰ ἄρα πιστευτέον αὐτῷ λέγοντι περὶ Αἰσχίνου, said that Aeschines was tritagonist for the τραγῳδοποιός Ischander, and fell down when, in the part of Oinomaos, he was pursuing Pelops, and had to be picked up by the chorus-trainer Sannion (*Vit. Aeschin.* ii). But Hesychius, *s.v.* ἀρουραῖος Οἰνόμαος, says that Aeschines acted Sophocles' play, and Ischander is not otherwise attested as a tragic poet.

[6] *I.G.* ii². 1182.   [7] See above, p. 45, n. 7.   [8] *I.G.* ii². 3097.

mentioned by Isaeus.[1] At Rhamnous, where the cult seems to have been specifically of Dionysus Ληναῖος,[2] we have two records of comedy.[3]

Salamis is noteworthy, since the records are spread chronologically more widely than anywhere else except the Peiraeus and Eleusis. Control was there in the hands of the archon, a state appointment, who appointed the choregoi.[4] He seems to have been assisted by ἐπιμεληταί.[5] Dithyramb is attested there in the early fourth century,[6] tragedy in the second century, though apparently not regularly.[7]

10. Deubner[8] has made a study of a sculptured frieze embodied in a wall of the little church of Hagios Eleutherios in Athens, in which the chief features or characteristic qualities or operations of the seasons are represented by symbolical figures or groups of figures, arranged in chronological order from Pyanopsion to Boedromion. In the place corresponding to Poseideon appears a group of judges sitting at a table bearing five crowns, and on the ground two fighting-cocks and a palm-branch. Deubner takes the whole to symbolize the contents of the Rural Dionysia. (Other symbols which follow are interpreted as referring to the Lenaia in Gamelion.) The frieze has been dated variously, from the second century B.C. to the imperial period. In any case, if correctly interpreted, it is a record of continued interest in the Rural Dionysia down to a comparatively late date.

11. The Rural Dionysia were closer to the earth than the great festivals of the city, and may have retained their religious content in greater strength and longer. But it is clear from the inscriptions that the festivals also afforded the demes an opportunity to mimic the city, and to assert their identities as states within the state, by proclamations of crowns for benefactors and a reflection in little of the institutions of the city. What they did will have been limited by their means. We can seldom determine how far the deme had the full range of contests. Dithyramb, tragedy, and comedy are all frequently represented, but we might argue

[1] viii. 15, cf. 35. [2] See above, p. 42.

[3] *I.G.* ii². 3108 (probably fourth century) ... 'Ραμνούσιος .... κωμῳδοῖς, 3109 (early third century, on the base of a statue of Themis) Μεγακλῆς Μεγακ[λέους 'Ραμ]νούσιος ἀνέθηκεν Θέμιδι στεφανωθεὶς ὑπὸ τῶν δημοτῶν δικαιοσύνης ἕνεκα ἐ[πὶ ἱ]ερείας Καλλιστοῦς (καὶ Φειδο-στράτης Νεμέσει ἱερείας) καὶ νικήσας παισὶ καὶ ἀνδράσι γυμνασιαρχῶν καὶ κωμῳδοῖς χορηγῶν. Χαιρέστρατος Χαιρεδήμου 'Ραμνούσιος ἐπόησε. See Pouilloux, *La Forteresse de Rhamnonte*, p. 153.

[4] See above, p. 46, n. 9.

[5] *I.G.* ii². 1227. 37, 1008. 83, 1011. 59 (131–105 B.C.).

[6] Ibid., no. 3093: Διόδωρος 'Εξηκεστίδου νικήσας χορῷ παίδων. Παιδέας ἐδίδασκε. Τηλεφάνης ηὔλει Μεγαρεύς. Φιλόμηλος ἦρχε (sc. at Salamis). For Telephanes, see *Dith. Trag. Com.²*, p. 55.

[7] *I.G.* ii². 1227. 30 (131–130) καὶ ἀνειπεῖν τὸν στέφανον τοῦτον Διονυσίων τῶν ἐν Σαλαμῖνι τραγῳδοῖς, ὅταν πρῶτον γίνηται, cf. 1008. 82, 1011. 58.

[8] *Att. Feste*, pp. 138, 248 ff. and pll. 34 ff. Deubner's study is based on earlier accounts by Robert, Svoronos, and others.

from the silence of the Law of Euegoros that there was no dithyramb at Peiraeus, and from the fact that crowns are, abnormally, proclaimed at the comic performances at Aixone that there was no tragedy there.

For the quality of the performances, there is a little information. Actors' companies, like the one to which Aeschines attached himself, toured the demes, and, though Demosthenes describes that company as βαρύστονοι and draws the blackest picture of their reception,[1] they may not have been all that bad, and they certainly performed the tragedies of the great masters.[2] In the fifth century we hear of Euripides producing at the Peiraeus, Sophocles and Aristophanes at Eleusis. The plays may have been new or already performed in the city. It is possible that the general knowledge of the subjects of tragedy, which Aristophanes seems to assume, was fostered by these festivals, though his detailed parodies perhaps most often refer to plays produced recently in Athens itself. It is uncertain how far Antiphanes[3] is to be taken seriously when, in the fourth century, he complains that everybody knows the subjects of tragedy, whereas comic poets have to invent their own stories and characters. Passages of Euripides and Aristotle point the other way,[4] but, in so far as there was a general dramatic culture, the rural festivals certainly contributed to it.

However this may be, it is interesting to note that a great part of the evidence about the Rural Dionysia comes from the fourth century B.C. This is the great era of settled, moderate prosperity in Attica, and life would never be quite so comfortable again, but it may also point to the special popularity of the drama at this period—the period in which the great work associated with the name of Lycurgus was being carried out in the theatre at Athens and theatres were springing up in many parts of Greece, while famous actors were becoming important personages and taking part in diplomatic exchanges between states.[5]

12. Few of the theatres which may have once existed in the Attic demes have left any traces. The oldest extant remains in all probability are those of Thorikos,[6] where they must be earlier than the date of any dramatic performances, and seem to go back at least to the middle of the sixth century B.C. There are remains of several lines of steps which may have served for spectators of choral dances or of any kind of festal

---

[1] de Cor. 262. [2] Ibid. 267, 180. [3] Fr. 191 (Kock).
[4] See below, pp. 275 f. [5] See below, p. 279.
[6] Dörpfeld u. Reisch, *Das griechische Theater*, pp. 109–11; Bulle, *Untersuchungen*, pp. 9 ff., 210, Taf. 1, 2; Arias, *Il Teatro greco fuori di Atene*, pp. 24 ff.; Flickinger, *Gk. Theater*, p. 227 and figs. 70, 71; Caputo in *Dioniso* 3 (1933), pp. 301 ff.; 4 (1934), p. 90; Anti, *Teatri greci arcaici*, pp. 45–48 (with criticisms in *C.R.* 62 (1948), p. 125); Dilke, *B.S.A.* 45 (1950), pp. 25 ff. (See now T. Haskens, *Ant. Class.* 34 (1965), pp. 39 ff.).

performance or for attenders at a public assembly. The form of this auditorium (Figs. 26–27) is unlike that of any other theatre, and its size was increased at some time[1] later than the original building by an addition (A) higher up on the rising ground. The area in front of the steps was terraced up to a level and no doubt in time served for dramatic

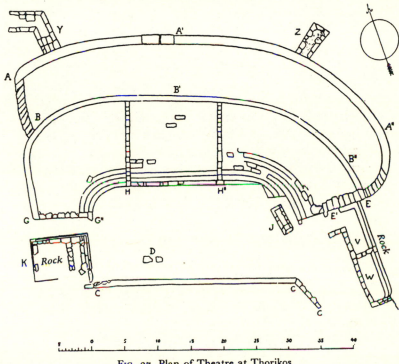

FIG. 27. Plan of Theatre at Thorikos

presentations, and it was bounded on the side furthest from the steps by a wall (D) of which some slight remains are visible. There are also the remains of a small temple (K), an altar (J), and what is sometimes regarded as a βουλευτήριον or council-chamber.

The principal remains at Rhamnous[2] (Fig. 28) are three stone seats or thrones—probably there were originally seven—dedicated to Dionysus by the priest of the Hero Archegetes;[3] they stand on a base of local marble

---

[1] Perhaps when Thorikos was fortified by the Athenians in 410–409 B.C. (Xen. *Hellen.* i. 2. 1).

[2] See Bulle, op. cit., pp. 1–4, Taf. 1; Arias, op. cit., pp. 22–24; Anti, op. cit., pp. 146–8; Dilke, *B.S.A.* 45 (1950), pp. 28 ff.; Pouilloux, pp. 73–78.

[3] *I.G.* ii². 2849 ἀνέθηκεν Διονύσῳ ἱερεὺς ἥρῳ ἀρχηγέτου . . . καὶ στεφανωθεὶς ὑπὸ τῆς βουλῆς καὶ τῶν δημοτῶν καὶ τῶν στρατιωτῶν (Pouilloux, no. 25).

and, together with what was a row of stelai in a line with them on a similar base, formed a front row behind which the crowd could stand on the rising ground, and the performances could be given on the levelled ground in front. The remains are considered to belong to the fourth century, and though the place doubtless served for the public meetings of the little village and Bulle thinks he can locate the council-chamber, it is definitely called a theatre in inscriptions.[1]

At Ikarion[2] there seems to have been a similar row of thrones, standing between the main body of spectators and the performers. Two pairs of thrones of crude workmanship are still to be seen (Fig. 29) and there are traces of an altar.

The theatre in the Peiraeus[3] in which the Dionysia were celebrated, and to which the inscriptions quoted in this chapter belong, was on the peninsula of Munychia, and has disappeared entirely. It figures occasionally in the history of the Classical period.[4] The later theatre at Zea, built probably in the second century B.C., though of some interest in the history of the development of the Greek theatre, does not come within the scope of this chapter.[5]

APPENDIX ON *I.G.* II². 3091 (AIXONE)

It is extremely doubtful whether this much-discussed inscription[6] has any reference to the Rural Dionysia at all. It was discovered near Aixone at Palaiochori, apparently on the site of Halai Aixonides, rather than that of Aixone itself,[7] inscribed on a cylindrical block of white marble which was probably the base of a statue. It runs:

'Ε[πιχάρης χορηγῶν ἐνίκα κ]ωμῳδοῖς
'Εχφαντίδης ἐδίδασκε Πείρας
Θρασύβολος χορηγῶν ἐνίκα κωμῳδοῖς
Κρατῖνος ἐδίδασκε Βουκόλους

[1] *I.G.* ii². 1311. 16 ἀναγράψαι δὲ τόδε τὸ ψήφισμα ἐν στήλῃ λιθίνῃ καὶ στῆσαι ἐν τῷ θεάτρῳ (4th cent.) (Pouilloux, no. 13).
[2] See Bulle, op. cit., pp. 4 ff., Taf. 1; Arias, op. cit., pp. 19–21; Anti, op. cit., pp. 145–6; Dilke, loc. cit., pp. 30 ff. [3] pp. 46–47. [4] See above, p. 46, n. 2.
[5] See Dörpfeld u. Reisch, pp. 97–100; Bulle, op. cit., pp. 203–4; Arias, op. cit., pp. 15–19; and *Theatre of D.*, pp. 139, 144, 181–3, 217–18. An inscription, *I.G.* ii². 2334, headed οἵδε ἐπέδωκαν εἰς τὴν κατασκευὴν τοῦ θεάτρου and containing a long list of donors, dates around the middle of the second century B.C.
[6] Published by Palaios in *Πολέμων*, I, pp. 161 ff. For discussion see *New Chapters in Gk. Lit.*, Third Series, pp. 69 ff.; Wilamowitz, *Hermes* 65 (1930), pp. 243–5; M. Guarducci, *Riv. di Fil.* 8 (1930), pp. 202 ff.; 9 (1931), pp. 243 ff.; 14 (1936), pp. 283 ff.; Mazon, *Mélanges Navarre*, (1935), pp. 297 ff.; M. Fromhold-Treu, *Hermes* 69 (1934), pp. 324 ff.; Körte, *Gnomon* 11 (1935), pp. 632 ff.; Vitucci, *Dioniso* 7 (1939), pp. 216 ff. What is said in the text is what now seems most probable in the light of the discussion, and differs in some points from my conclusions in *New Chapters*, loc. cit.
[7] See Eliot, *Coastal Demes of Attika*, pp. 29–30.

Θρασύβολος χορη[γ]ῶν ἐνίκα τραγῳδοῖς
Τιμόθεος ἐδίδασκε Ἀλκμέωνα Ἀλφεσίβο[ιαν
Ἐπιχάρης χορηγῶν ἐνίκα τραγῳδοῖ[ς
Σοφοκλῆς ἐδίδασκε Τηλέφειαν.

It is now generally agreed that the date of the inscription, as determined
by the form of the letters and the orthography, is early in the fourth century,
probably about 380 B.C.[1] At this date the monument commemorated the
choregic victories of Epichares and Thrasybulus; the victories must have
been won at different festivals, as there would not have been *two* victors either
in tragedy or in comedy at the same festival. Whether the victories are in
chronological order it is impossible to say. Inscriptions[2] make it clear that
Ekphantides' earliest victory at the City Dionysia fell between 457 and 454 B.C.,
and that he either took no part or won no victory in the Lenaian contests,
which were first state-organized about 442 B.C., so that he probably died
before this. (Geissler[3] dates his Σάτυροι between 445 and 440 B.C., but on somewhat inconclusive grounds.) The date of Cratinus' Βουκόλοι is quite uncertain.[4]
Hesychius' gloss, which is often quoted as showing that the play was refused
a chorus by the archon, does not necessarily mean this, and in its corrupt
condition affords no safe basis of argument.[5] Timotheos, otherwise unknown as
a tragic poet, may or may not have been identical with the famous lyric
poet. The Τηλέφεια of Sophocles, probably a trilogy dealing with the story
of Telephus,[6] is not recorded elsewhere.

It seems clear (despite the arguments of M. Guarducci) that the formula
ἐδίδασκε is only used in inscriptions of plays produced by the authors in
person; and though it is quite possible that greater as well as lesser poets
may occasionally have produced plays in the demes in person[7]—either for the
first time or in repetition of performances in the city—it seems more likely
that the record is that of *choregic* victories gained in Athens in the last half
of the fifth century by Epichares and Thrasybulus, demesmen of Aixone, and
commemorated either by themselves in their old age or by their family or
deme early in the fourth century, perhaps after their deaths. The victory with
the two plays of Timotheos must have been won at the Lenaia, when each
poet presented only two tragedies. The Τηλέφεια, if it was a trilogy or tetralogy,
must have been performed at the City Dionysia.

The alternative supposition—that so many famous poets of the fifth
century should all have chosen Aixone as the place for the production of their

---

[1] M. Guarducci argues for an earlier date, unconvincingly.   [2] pp. 112 f. below.
[3] *Chronologie der altatt. Komödie*, p. 16.   [4] See *New Chapters*, Third Series, p. 74.
[5] e.g. the argument that, having been refused at Athens, he may have presented it at
Aixone. Even if he were refused by the archon for the Dionysia, he may have obtained a
chorus next year—or from the βασιλεύς for the Lenaia. (See p. 84, n. 3 for this gloss.)
[6] The plays were probably the Ἀλεάδαι, Μυσοί, and Ἀχαιῶν Σύλλογος. See *New Chapters*,
Third Series, pp. 76 ff.; Fromhold-Treu, loc. cit.; and below, p. 81.
[7] Euripides certainly did (p. 46), Sophocles and Aristophanes probably (p. 47 f.). Whether
the very large numbers of plays attributed for example to Antiphanes and Menander are
to be accounted for by their following this practice remains uncertain.

plays by themselves—seems less likely; and, if so, the inscription throws no light on the Rural Dionysia at Aixone, but only on the enthusiasm of its citizens for the drama in the fourth century—a thing which is attested by other inscriptions.

D. *The Panathenaia*

Most of the musical contests at the Panathenaia fall outside the scope of this book, but two references call for notice. Thrasyllus, the astrologer friend of the Emperor Tiberius, in discussing the division of Plato's work into tetralogies, appears to have said[1] that the tragic poets competed with four plays at the Dionysia, the Lenaia, the Panathenaia, and the Chytroi. The complete silence of our sources in the Classical period makes it unlikely that tragedy at the Panathenaia started very early, but there is one clear piece of epigraphic evidence for performance of a new tragedy at it in the first century A.D.[2]

[1] Diog. Laert. iii. 56.
[2] *I.G.* ii². 3157 . . . [γωνι]σάμενος κ[υκ]λίοις χορο [ῖς]ἀνδρῶν Κεκροπίδι [φ]υ[λ]ῇ αὐτὸς χορηγῶν καὶ διδάσ[κων, κα]ὶ τραγῳδίαν Παναθήναια τ[ὰ μεγά]λα καινὴν διδ[ά]ξας . . .

II

THE CITY DIONYSIA

1. THE last of the Athenian festivals of Dionysus to be instituted was known as the 'City Dionysia'[1] by contrast with the rural festivals, and as the 'Great Dionysia'[2] on account of the importance which soon attached to it. It might also be called τὰ Διονύσια[3] without further qualification. It was instituted in honour of Dionysus Eleuthereus, whose image had been brought to Athens from Eleutherai, on the borders of Attica and Boeotia, and stood in the older temple of Dionysus within the theatre precinct.[4] The date and the circumstances of the transfer of the image to Athens are not certain, but it was said to have been brought by an otherwise unknown Pegasos, who was probably a missionary of the cult of the god. In Athens, as in some other places in Greece,[5] the god was not well received, and the men of Athens were smitten with a disease from which (it was said) they only freed themselves (on the advice of an oracle) by manufacturing φαλλοί in honour of the god.[6]

A passage of Pausanias[7] may date the mission of Pegasos in the time of the legendary Amphiktyon, King of Athens, and in another passage[8] he records that the people of Eleutherai voluntarily transferred

---

[1] Διονύσια τὰ ἀστικά, Thuc. v. 20; Διονύσια τὰ ἐν ἄστει, Law of Euegoros (Dem. Meid. 10), Aeschin. iii. 68, and, for example, I.G. ii². 851, 958. Hence also such phrases as ἐν ἄστει διδάσκειν, διδασκαλία ἀστική, εἰς ἄστυ καθιέναι, νίκη ἀστική, etc.

[2] Διονύσια τὰ μεγάλα, Aristot. Ἀθ. Πολ. lvi, and (for example) I.G. ii². 654, 682.

[3] Διονύσια, A.T.L. D 7 (447 B.C.), Thuc. v. 23. 4, Dem. Meid. 1, Aristot. Ἀθ. Πολ. lvi, and (for example) I.G. ii². 1006, 1028.

[4] See Theatre of D., pp. 3–5.

[5] Including Eleutherai itself, where the daughters of the eponymous Eleuther were driven mad by the god when he was insulted by them ('Suidas', s.v. Μελαναιγίς). Eleuther himself then organized the worship of Dionysus. (Hygin. Fab. 225 'Eleuther primus simulacrum Liberi patris constituit, et quemadmodum coli deberet ostendit.')

[6] Schol. on Ar. Ach. 243 Πήγασος ἐκ τῶν Ἐλευθερῶν (αἱ δὲ Ἐλευθεραὶ πόλις ἐστὶ Βοιωτίας) λαβὼν τοῦ Διονύσου τὸ ἄγαλμα ἧκεν εἰς τὴν Ἀττικήν· οἱ δὲ Ἀθηναῖοι οὐκ ἐδέξαντο μετὰ τιμῆς τὸν θεόν. ἀλλ' οὐκ ἀμισθί γε αὐτοῖς ταῦτα βουλευσαμένοις ἀπέβη. (The story of their punishment follows.)

[7] i. 2. 5 μετὰ δὲ τὸ τοῦ Διονύσου (i.e. Dionysus Μελπόμενος) τέμενός ἐστιν οἴκημα ἀγάλματα ἔχον ἐκ πηλοῦ, βασιλεὺς Ἀθηναίων Ἀμφικτύων ἄλλους τε θεοὺς ἑστιῶν καὶ Διόνυσον. ἐνταῦθα καὶ Πήγασός ἐστιν Ἐλευθερεύς, ὃς Ἀθηναίοις τὸν θεὸν εἰσήγαγε.

[8] i. 38. 8 πρότερον μὲν γὰρ Ἐλευθερεῦσιν ὅροι πρὸς τὴν Ἀττικὴν ἦσαν· προσχωρησάντων δὲ Ἀθηναίοις τούτων, οὕτως ἤδη Βοιωτίας ὁ Κιθαιρών ἐστιν ὅρος. προσεχώρησαν δὲ Ἐλευθερεῖς οὐ πολέμῳ βιασθέντες, ἀλλὰ πολιτείας τε ἐπιθυμήσαντες παρὰ Ἀθηναίων καὶ κατ' ἔχθος τὸ Θηβαίων. ἐν τούτῳ τῷ πεδίῳ ναός ἐστι Διονύσου, καὶ τὸ ξόανον ἐντεῦθεν Ἀθηναίοις ἐκομίσθη τὸ ἀρχαῖον. τὸ δὲ ἐν Ἐλευθεραῖς ⟨τὸ⟩ ἐφ' ἡμῶν ἐς μίμησιν ἐκείνου πεποίηται.

themselves from the Boeotian to the Athenian alliance; but there is no reason for connecting the advent of the god with this political change (of which the date is unknown). The action of Pegasos was probably an incident in the gradual spread of Dionysiac cults throughout Greece, which was unconnected with political motives.[1] What seems certain is that it was in the sixth century that the festival became important, probably through the policy of Peisistratus. That it was a relatively late institution is indicated by the fact that it was not controlled by the archon basileus, the successor of the kings as the supreme religious official of Athens,[2] but by the archon eponymos. He had charge of the procession and of the dramatic and dithyrambic contests, with the assistance of his two πάρεδροι, and (for the procession) of ten ἐπιμεληταί. The latter were originally appointed by vote of the Assembly and paid their own expenses, but in Aristotle's time[3] were chosen by lot, one from each tribe, and received 100 minae from the state for the necessary equipment. The archon and ἐπιμεληταί continued to perform their functions even when the duties of the choregoi had been handed over to an agonothetes.[4]

2. The importance of the festival was derived not only from the performances of dramatic and lyric poetry but from the fact that it was open to the whole Hellenic world and was an effective advertisement of the wealth and power and public spirit of Athens, no less than of the artistic and literary leadership of her sons. By the end of March the winter was over, the seas were navigable,[5] and strangers came to Athens from all parts for business or pleasure.[6] After the founding of the Delian League

[1] The attempt of Vollgraff (Ath. Mitt. 32 (1907), pp. 567 ff.) to prove that the statue of Eleuthereus was not brought to Athens before 420 B.C., and was then placed in the new temple of Dionysus, rests on unprovable assumptions and is sufficiently answered by Farnell, Cults v, pp. 227–9.

[2] He first appears as taking part in the festival in an inscription of the middle of the second century A.D. (I.G. ii². 2046) in which he is mentioned as offering τῷ Διονύσῳ τὴν ἐν τῇ πομπῇ θυσίαν, but he does this as gymnasiarch of the ephebes.

[3] Aristot. Ἀθ. Πολ. lvi. 4. The πάρεδροι are mentioned both by Aristotle and in a laudatory inscription in honour of the archon and πάρεδροι of the year 283–282 B.C., quoted on p. 69. The ἐπιμεληταί also are joined in such a vote of thanks in I.G. ii². 668 (266–265 B.C.). In the time of Theophrastus one of the contentions of those who favoured oligarchy was that the archon ought to manage the festival-procession without being hampered by ἐπιμεληταί responsible to the demos (Char. 26).

[4] I.G. ii². 896. See below, pp. 70, 92.

[5] One of the typical remarks of the ἀδολέσχης in Theophrastus, Char. 3, is τὴν θάλατταν ἐκ Διονυσίων πλόϊμον εἶναι. But in the time of Demetrius (Plut. Demetr. 12. 5) the procession was prevented by a snow-storm. The theatre of Dionysus was sheltered from the north wind by the Acropolis, but it can still be cold in Athens in March and April.

[6] Aeschines, in Ctes. 43, speaks of proclamations at the Dionysia as taking place ἐναντίον ἁπάντων τῶν Ἑλλήνων, and Demosthenes, Meid. 74, complains that Meidias insulted him ἐναντίον πολλῶν καὶ ξένων καὶ πολιτῶν. For the presence of strangers at the City Dionysia, in contrast with the Lenaia, see Ar. Ach. 505–6, and above, pp. 26, 40.

the allies of Athens brought their tribute at this season; Isocrates asserts that it was displayed in the theatre.[1] At the same period, before the performance of the tragedies began, the orphaned children of those who had fallen in battle for Athens, such as had reached a suitable age, were caused to parade in the theatre in full armour and receive the blessing of the People. (This practice appears to have been abolished at some time in the fourth century.[2]) The festival was also made the occasion for the proclamation of honours conferred upon citizens or strangers for conspicuous service to Athens;[3] and it was a natural time for the visits of ambassadors from other states for business requiring publicity.[4] The festival was a time of holiday; prisoners were released on bail to attend the festival and sometimes took the chance of escaping.[5] The Law of Euegoros, quoted by Demosthenes,[6] forbade legal proceedings and distraint or taking of security for debt during this and some other festivals; but the date of the law is unknown, and it is possible that in the fifth century the holding of an assembly was not excluded.[7]

3. As a rite preliminary to the festival, though perhaps not considered

[1] Eupolis, Πόλεις, fr. 240 K (with schol. on Ar. Ach. 378, 504); cf. Isocr. de Pace 82 ἐψηφίσαντο τὸ περιγιγνόμενον τῶν φόρων ἀργύριον διελόντες κατὰ τάλαντον εἰς τὴν ὀρχήστραν τοῖς Διονυσίοις εἰσφέρειν, ἐπειδὰν πλῆρες ᾖ τὸ θέατρον· καὶ τοῦτ' ἐποίουν καὶ παρεισῆγον τοὺς παῖδας τῶν ἐν τῷ πολέμῳ τετελευτηκότων, ἀμφοτέροις ἐπιδεικνύοντες, τοῖς μὲν συμμάχοις τὰς τιμὰς τῆς οὐσίας αὐτῶν ὑπὸ μισθωτῶν εἰσφερομένας, τοῖς δ' ἄλλοις Ἕλλησι τὸ πλῆθος τῶν ὀρφανῶν καὶ τὰς συμφορὰς τὰς διὰ τὴν πλεονεξίαν ταύτην γιγνομένας. (Cf. Raubitschek, T.A.P.A. 72 (1941), pp. 356–62.)

[2] Shortly after 403 B.C. Lysias attacked Theozotides for merely having proposed the exclusion of adopted and illegitimate sons from this, τὸ κάλλιστον τῶν ἐν τοῖς νόμοις κήρυγμα (P. Hib. I. 14). By 330 B.C. the practice is dead. Aeschin. in Ctes. 154 τίς γὰρ οὐκ ἂν ἀλγήσειεν ἄνθρωπος Ἕλλην ἢ καὶ παιδευθεὶς ἐλευθέρως, ἀναμνησθεὶς ἐν τῷ θεάτρῳ ἐκεῖνό γε, εἰ μηδὲν ἕτερον, ὅτι ταύτῃ ποτὲ τῇ ἡμέρᾳ μελλόντων ὥσπερ νυνὶ τῶν τραγῳδῶν γίγνεσθαι, ὅτε εὐνομεῖτο μᾶλλον ἡ πόλις καὶ βελτίοσι προστάταις ἐχρῆτο, προελθὼν ὁ κῆρυξ καὶ παραστησάμενος τοὺς ὀρφανοὺς ὧν οἱ πατέρες ἦσαν ἐν τῷ πολέμῳ τετελευτηκότες, νεανίσκους πανοπλίᾳ κεκοσμημένους, ἐκήρυττε τὸ κάλλιστον κήρυγμα καὶ προτρεπτικώτατον πρὸς ἀρετήν, ὅτι τούσδε τοὺς νεανίσκους, ὧν οἱ πατέρες ἐτελεύτησαν ἐν τῷ πολέμῳ ἄνδρες ἀγαθοὶ γενόμενοι, μέχρι μὲν ἥβης ὁ δῆμος ἔτρεφε, νυνὶ δὲ καθοπλίσας τῇδε τῇ πανοπλίᾳ, ἀφίησιν ἀγαθῇ τύχῃ τρέπεσθαι ἐπὶ τὰ ἑαυτῶν καὶ καλεῖ εἰς προεδρίαν. τότε μὲν ταῦτ' ἐκήρυττεν, ἀλλ' οὐ νῦν.

[3] This provision occurs in many inscriptions. See below, p. 82, n. 2. The proclamation was made before the tragedies began. Aeschines, in Ctes. 41, speaks as if the practice of making proclamations at the festival had sometimes been abused; cf. Dem. de Cor. 120.

[4] In Thuc. v. 23. 4 the oath of alliance between Athens and Sparta is to be renewed annually by the ambassadors of Sparta at the Dionysia. Cf. I.G. i². 57 (430 B.C.)

[5] As, according to Dem. in Androt. 68, Androtion's father did. The schol. ad loc. says ἔθος ἦν παρὰ τοῖς Ἀθηναίοις ἐν τοῖς Διονυσίοις καὶ τοῖς Παναθηναίοις τοὺς δεσμώτας ἀφίεσθαι τοῦ δεσμοῦ ἐν ἐκείναις ταῖς ἡμέραις παρασχόντας ἐγγυητάς.

[6] See above, pp. 27, 46.

[7] In Thuc. iv. 118 the Athenians are said to have ratified the truce with Sparta in 423 B.C. in the Assembly on the 14th of Elaphebolion, but it is disputed whether this date fell within the festival period at that time; see below, pp. 64, 66. In Thuc. v. 23 it is not stated· at what point in the Dionysia, or before what persons or body, the treaty with Sparta was to be renewed, but the renewal may well have required an assembly.

part of the festival itself,[1] there was a re-enactment of the original advent of Dionysus from Eleutherai. The statue of Dionysus Eleuthereus was taken to a temple in the neighbourhood of the Academy, on the road to Eleutherai, and placed by the ἐσχάρα there. There sacrifice was offered,[2] and hymns were sung,[3] and the statue was escorted back to the theatre in a torchlight procession in which the leading part was taken by the epheboi, the young men of military age. The dates of the ephebic inscriptions[4] which are the authority for these statements all fall between 127 and 106 B.C., and the εἰσαγωγή disappears from later texts; but the re-enactment of the god's advent does not look like an afterthought and probably goes back to the earliest days of the festival when, after his first cold welcome, it was desired to make amends by doing him special honour. Whether the statue thus brought to the theatre was left there till the end of the festival is not recorded. It may well have been returned to the temple in preparation for the sacrifices to which the πομπή (probably on the next day) led up, and have been brought back daily to the theatre for the performances at which it was certainly present.[5] The temple in the Academy is described by Pausanias as a small one.[6] It may have existed for this particular purpose alone. It is difficult to draw any conclusion from the fact that the altar was an ἐσχάρα (a low altar, hollowed out at the top) and not a βωμός or a θυμέλη. The uses of the several terms were not kept rigidly separate.[7]

[1] In *I.G.* ii². 1006 (122–121 B.C.) the εἰσαγωγή of the god is evidently distinguished from the Dionysia in the strict sense and from the πομπή, which was part of the festival proper. εἰσήγαγον δὲ καὶ τὸν Διόνυσον ἀπὸ τῆς ἐσχάρας εἰς τὸ θέατρον μετὰ φωτός· καὶ ἔπεμψαν τοῖς Διονυσίοις ταῦρον ἄξιον τοῦ θεοῦ, ὃν καὶ ἔθυσαν ἐν τῷ ἱερῷ τῇ πομπῇ, ἐφ' ᾧ καὶ ἐστεφανώθησαν ὑπὸ τοῦ δήμου.

[2] Perhaps not regularly: ibid. 1011 (106–105 B.C.) εἰσήγαγον δὲ καὶ τὸν Διόνυσον ἀπὸ τῆς ἐσχάρας θύσαντες τῷ θεῷ, καὶ ἀνέθηκαν φιάλην κατασκευάσαντες τῷ θεῷ ἀπὸ δραχμῶν ἑκατόν is the only evidence, and neither the sacrifice nor the phiale appears in parallel texts.

[3] Alkiphron iv. 18. 16 (Schepers), where the fictitious Menander says ἐμοὶ γένοιτο τὸν Ἀττικὸν ἀεὶ στέφεσθαι κισσὸν καὶ τὸν ἐπ' ἐσχάρας ὑμνῆσαι κατ' ἔτος Διόνυσον. Herodes Atticus (early second century A.D.) is said by Philostratus (*Vit. Soph.*, p. 549) to have given a feast of drink on a large scale to citizens and strangers at the Kerameikos, on the way to the Academy: ὁπότε δὲ ἥκοι Διονύσια καὶ κατίοι εἰς Ἀκαδημίαν τὸ τοῦ Διονύσου ἕδος ἐν Κεραμεικῷ ποτίζων ἀστοὺς ὁμοίως καὶ ξένους κατακειμένους ἐπὶ στιβάδων κιττοῦ. But this was doubtless a late perversion of a festival which had lost its meaning.

[4] Other inscriptions are *I.G.* ii². 1028 (101–100 B.C.), and 1008 (118–117 B.C.) καὶ εἰσήγαγον τὸν θεὸν ἀπὸ τῆς [ἐσχάρας εἰς τὸ θέατρον μετὰ φωτὸς κ]α[ὶ ἔπεμψαν ταῦρον τοῖς Διονυσίοις τῇ πομ]πῇ καὶ θύσαντες ἐπὶ τού[τοις ἅπασιν ἐκαλλιέρησαν]: cf. also 1030 (*post* 93 B.C.) and 1039 (83–73 B.C.). *S.E.G.* xv. 104 (127–126 B.C.) is the earliest of these texts.

[5] See Ar. *Knights* 536, *Frogs* 809, etc.; Philostr. *Vit. Apoll.* iv. 22; Dio Chrys. xxxi. 121 (p. 631 R), etc.

[6] Paus. i. 29. 2. καὶ ναὸς οὐ μέγας ἐστίν, ἐς ὃν τοῦ Διονύσου τοῦ Ἐλευθερέως τὸ ἄγαλμα ἀνὰ πᾶν ἔτος κομίζουσιν ἐν τεταγμέναις ἡμέραις.

[7] See Gow, *J.H.S.* 32 (1912), pp. 213 ff.; Nilsson, *Jahrb. Arch.* 31 (1916), p. 337, n. 4 = *Opusc. Sel.* i, p. 211, n. 124; F. Robert, *Thymélè*, pp. 260 ff.

There has been much discussion, some of it of a speculative and rambling character, of the εἰσαγωγὴ ἀπὸ τῆς ἐσχάρας.[1] The account given above attempts to keep closely to the evidence, and the same principle will be observed in regard to the πομπή, the procession with which the Dionysia in the strict sense began, and the κῶμος, which, whatever its nature, is clearly separated from the πομπή in the Law of Euegoros.

4. The πομπή was essentially a religious procession leading up to the sacrifices in the sacred precinct of Dionysus.[2] The sacrifice of a bull, which was led in the procession, by the epheboi (in the second and first centuries B.C. but probably also earlier) is well attested,[3] and no doubt many other victims were offered.[4] Many bloodless offerings were also made, and these were carried in the procession in a variety of vessels borne by men and women, both citizens and resident aliens. There was a κανηφόρος (bearer of golden baskets of offerings), a maiden of noble birth.[5] She may have led the procession, as in the 'Rural Dionysia' in the Acharnians. The ὀβελιαφόροι (carrying the loaves known as ὀβελίαι) and the σκαφηφόροι and ὑδριαφόροι and ἀσκοφόροι who are mentioned as taking part in Dionysiac functions[6] probably acted in this greatest of Dionysiac processions. Colour was lent to the procession by the scarlet of the μέτοικοι and the gorgeous robes of the choregoi of the lyric and dramatic performances which were to follow. Alcibiades on more than

[1] e.g. Nilsson, *Jahrb. Arch.* 31 (1916), pp. 309 ff. = *Opusc. Sel.* i, pp. 166 ff.; Stengel, ibid., pp. 340 ff.; Bethe, *Hermes* 61 (1926), pp. 459 ff.; Pfuhl, *de Athen. pompis sacris*, pp. 74 ff.; etc. (Frickenhaus's article in *Jahrb. Arch.* 27 (1912), pp. 80 ff., belongs to the eccentricities of scholarship.) By far the best summary is that of Deubner, *Att. Feste*, p. 139.

[2] ἐν τῷ ἱερῷ in the ephebic inscriptions quoted above.

[3] See above, p. 60, nn. 1, 4.

[4] Ferguson, *Hesperia* 17 (1948), p. 134, calculates from *I.G.* ii². 1496 that there were 240 victims in 333 B.C. An agonothetes in 250 B.C. contributed five oxen (*Hesperia* 4 (1935), p. 583).

[5] Schol. on Ar. *Ach.* 241 κατὰ τὴν τῶν Διονυσίων ἑορτὴν παρὰ τοῖς Ἀθηναίοις αἱ εὐγενεῖς παρθένοι ἐκανηφόρουν. ἦν δὲ ἐκ χρυσοῦ πεποιημένα τὰ κανᾶ, ἐφ' ὧν τὰς ἀπαρχὰς ἁπάντων ἐτίθεσαν. In *I.G.* ii². 896 (185 B.C.) a certain Zopyrus is praised for sending his daughter οἴσουσαν τὸ ἱερὸν κανοῦν τῷ θεῷ κατὰ τὰ πάτρια. That there was only one follows from the references to ὁ πατὴρ τῆς κανηφόρου in this decree and in *I.G.* ii². 668. Cf. also *I.G.* ii². 3489.

[6] Poll. vi. 75 ὀβελίαι δ' ἄρτοι οὓς εἰς Διονύσου ἔφερον οἱ καλούμενοι ὀβελιαφόροι; cf. Athen. iii. 111 b ἐκαλοῦντο δὲ καὶ ὀβελιαφόροι οἱ ἐν ταῖς πομπαῖς παραφέροντες αὐτούς (sc. τοὺς ὀβελίας) ἐπὶ τῶν ὤμων (Ephippus in the fourth century wrote a comedy called 'Ὀβελιαφόροι); 'Suid'. s.v. ἀσκοφορεῖν· ἐν ταῖς Διονυσιακοῖς πομπαῖς, τὰ μὲν ὑπὸ τῶν ἀστῶν ἐπράττετο, τὰ δὲ τοῖς μετοίκοις ποιεῖν ὑπὸ τῶν νομοθετησάντων προσετέτακτο. οἱ μὲν οὖν μέτοικοι χιτῶνας ἐνεδύοντο χρῶμα ἔχοντες φοινικοῦν καὶ σκάφας ἔφερον· ὅθεν σκαφηφόροι προσηγορεύοντο. οἱ δὲ ἀστοὶ ἐσθῆτα εἶχον ἣν ἐβούλοντο καὶ ἀσκοὺς ἐπ' ὤμων ἔφερον· ὅθεν ἀσκοφόροι ἐκαλοῦντο; 'Suid'. s.v. σκαφηφόροι (without express reference to the Dionysia)· . . . Δημήτριος γοῦν ἐν γ' Νομοθεσίας (228 F 5 Jacoby) φησίν, ὅτι προσέταττεν ὁ νόμος τοῖς μετοίκοις ἐν ταῖς πομπαῖς αὐτοὺς μὲν σκάφας φέρειν, τὰς δὲ θυγατέρας αὐτῶν ὑδρεῖα καὶ σκιάδεια; Zenob. v. 95 συντομώτερος σκάφης· παροιμία ἐπὶ τῶν τὰς σκάφας φερόντων μετοίκων . . . ἐπειδὴ οἱ μέτοικοι σκάφας ἔφερον ἐν ταῖς πομπαῖς; Poll. iii. 55 μέτοικος ὁ τὸ μετοίκιον συντελῶν· . . . σκαφηφόρος· οὕτω δὲ τοὺς μετοίκους ὠνόμαζον, καὶ τὰς γυναῖκας αὐτῶν ὑδριαφόρους, ἀπὸ τοῦ ἔργου ἑκατέρους. For citizens, apparently without official functions, see Aeschin. i. 43.

one occasion walked in a purple robe,[1] and part of Demosthenes' grievance against Meidias was that Meidias had broken into a goldsmith's shop and partly destroyed the golden crown and gold-embroidered cloak in which Demosthenes had intended to parade as choregos.[2] When Plutarch[3] spoke of the lavish display of the Dionysiac processions in his own time as compared with the original simplicity of the rustic festivals, he must have overlooked the magnificence of the Athenian processions of the fifth and fourth centuries B.C. (some 500 to 600 years earlier); but it is not in fact clear of what places or periods he is speaking. At least one of the primitive elements of Dionysiac worship which Plutarch mentions was conspicuous in the Dionysiac procession, the carrying of φαλλοί in honour of the god.

The direct evidence for this practice is indeed slight and depends upon the conjectural completion of inscriptions, but is probably sufficient. About the year 446–445 B.C. it was ordained that the new colony of Brea should annually send a phallos to the City Dionysia;[4] this is not likely to have been an isolated emblem, and the carrying of phalloi would be reminiscent of the placation of the god after his original arrival in Athens.[5]

The route taken by the procession is unknown. At some time during the festival there were dances of choruses at various altars, and especially at that of the Twelve Gods in the Agora, and these are connected by scholars either with the εἰσαγωγὴ ἀπὸ τῆς ἐσχάρας or with the πομπή. There is no evidence to show which is correct, but Xenophon mentions the dances in a passage which is primarily about πομπαί.[6]

[1] Athen. xii. 534 c ὅτε δὲ χορηγοίη πομπεύων ἐν πορφυρίδι, εἰσιὼν εἰς τὸ θέατρον ἐθαυμάζετο οὐ μόνον ὑπὸ τῶν ἀνδρῶν ἀλλὰ καὶ ὑπὸ τῶν γυναικῶν.

[2] Dem. Meid. 22 (evidence of the goldsmith Pammenes) ἐκδόντος δέ μοι Δημοσθένους, ᾧ μαρτυρῶ, στέφανον χρυσοῦν ὥστε κατασκευάσαι καὶ ἱμάτιον διάχρυσον ποιῆσαι, ὅπως πομπεύσαι ἐν αὐτοῖς τὴν τοῦ Διονύσου πομπὴν κτλ.

[3] de cupid. divit. 527 d ἡ πάτριος τῶν Διονυσίων ἑορτὴ τὸ παλαιὸν ἐπέμπετο δημοτικῶς καὶ ἱλαρῶς, ἀμφορεὺς οἴνου καὶ κληματίς, εἶτα τράγον τις εἷλκεν, ἄλλος ἰσχάδων ἄρριχον ἠκολούθει κομίζων, ἐπὶ πᾶσι δ' ὁ φαλλός· ἀλλὰ νῦν ταῦτα παρεώραται καὶ ἠφάνισται, χρυσωμάτων περιφερομένων καὶ ἱματίων πολυτελῶν καὶ ζευγῶν ἐλαυνομένων καὶ προσωπείων, οὕτω τἀναγκαῖα τοῦ πλούτου καὶ τὰ χρήσιμα τοῖς ἀχρήστοις κατακέχωσται καὶ τοῖς περίττοις. See above, p. 44.

[4] I.G. i². 46 βοῦν δὲ καὶ π[ανοπλίαν ἀπά]γειν ἐς Παναθήναια τὰ μεγάλ[α καὶ ἐς Διονύσι]α φαλλόν. A decree of 372 B.C. (Accame, Lega Ateniese, p. 230) instructs the Parians [εἰς Διονύ]σια βôν καὶ φαλλὸ[ν] ἀ[π]ά[γεν] as being Athenian colonists. Cf. also I.G. ii². 673. Phalloi were also carried at the Dionysia at Delos: see Nilsson, Gr. Feste, pp. 280–2, Gesch. i², pp. 592 f., Vallois, B.C.H. 46 (1922), pp. 94–112, and Sifakis, Studies, pp. 9 ff.

[5] See above, p. 57.

[6] Xen. Hipparch. iii. 2 τὰς μὲν οὖν πομπὰς οἶμαι ἂν καὶ τοῖς θεοῖς κεχαρισμενωτάτας καὶ τοῖς θεαταῖς εἶναι εἰ ὅσων ἱερὰ καὶ ἀγάλματα ἐν τῇ ἀγορᾷ ἐστι, ταῦτα ἀρξάμενοι ἀπὸ τῶν Ἑρμῶν κύκλῳ περὶ τὴν ἀγορὰν καὶ τὰ ἱερὰ περιελαύνοιεν τιμῶντες τοὺς θεούς, καὶ ἐν τοῖς Διονυσίοις δὲ οἱ χοροὶ προσεπιχαρίζονται ἄλλοις τε θεοῖς καὶ τοῖς δώδεκα χορεύοντες. The site of the Altar of the Twelve Gods was on the north side of the Agora; M. Crosby, Hesperia, Suppl. viii, pp. 82 ff., gives a general discussion of the site and the cult. See also R. E. Wycherley, The Athenian Agora, iii (Testimonia), nos. 363–78.

It may be assumed that the procession was enlivened by satirical songs such as were sung on all such occasions at Athens, and that these were not entirely prompted by the desire to avert the evil eye.[1] It is also related that Demetrius of Phalerum was greeted with a laudatory poem when as archon he conducted the procession.[2] Naturally the procession might also be the occasion of such encounters and love-affairs as Menander often took as the starting-point of his plots.[3]

5. Of the κῶμος nothing distinctive is known. No doubt it was a much less formal proceeding than the πομπή, and it is at least probable that the πομπή took place in the morning[4]—most likely on the 10th of Elaphebolion, before the dithyrambs were performed—and the κῶμος, if it was a revel-procession, in the evening, perhaps on the same day.[5]

6. The order of the events composing the festival cannot be determined with certainty in all respects. It is clear from the evidence that has been given that the εἰσαγωγή of the god from the temple in the Academy was a preliminary ceremony, and was distinct from the πομπή, which was an essential part of the festival itself. For the rest, the evidence is as follows:

(1) Aeschines, in Ctes. 66–68. Δημοσθένης . . . γράφει ψήφισμα . . . (67) . . . ἐκκλησίαν ποιεῖν τοὺς πρυτάνεις τῇ ὀγδόῃ ἱσταμένου τοῦ Ἐλαφηβολιῶνος μηνός, ὅτ' ἦν τῷ Ἀσκληπιῷ ἡ θυσία καὶ ὁ προαγών, ἐν τῇ ἱερᾷ ἡμέρᾳ, ὃ πρότερον οὐδεὶς μέμνηται γενόμενον . . . . (68) . . . ἐνταῦθ' ἕτερον νικᾷ ψήφισμα Δημοσθένης, ἐν ᾧ γράφει μὴ μόνον ὑπὲρ τῆς εἰρήνης ἀλλὰ καὶ συμμαχίας ὑμᾶς βουλεύσασθαι, μὴ περιμείναντας τοὺς πρέσβεις τοὺς ὑμετέρους, ἀλλ' εὐθὺς μετὰ τὰ Διονύσια τὰ ἐν ἄστει, τῇ ὀγδόῃ καὶ ἐνάτῃ ἐπὶ δέκα.

Schol. ad loc. ἐγίγνοντο πρὸ τῶν μεγάλων Διονυσίων ἡμέραις ὀλίγαις ἔμπροσθεν ἐν τῷ Ὠιδείῳ καλουμένῳ τῶν τραγῳδῶν ἀγὼν καὶ ἐπίδειξις ὧν μέλλουσι δραμάτων ἀγωνίζεσθαι ἐν τῷ θεάτρῳ· δι' ὃ ἑτοίμως προαγὼν καλεῖται. εἰσίασι δὲ δίχα προσώπων οἱ ὑποκριταὶ γυμνοί.

(The nature of the Proagon will be discussed later.)

---

[1] See Harpokr. s.v. πομπείας κτλ. (quoted above, p. 5).

[2] Athen. xii. 542 e ἐν δὲ τῇ πομπῇ τῶν Διονυσίων, ἣν ἔπεμψεν ἄρχων γενόμενος, ᾖδεν ὁ χορὸς εἰς αὐτὸν ποιήματα Σείρωνος τοῦ Σολέως, ἐν οἷς ἡλιόμορφος προσηγορεύετο, "ἐξόχως δ' εὐγενέτας ἡλιόμορφος ζαθέοις ἄρχων σε τιμαῖσι γεραίρει".

[3] Menander, fr. 382 (Körte) Διονυσίων μὲν ἦν | πομπή . . . | ὁ δέ μ' ἠκολούθησεν μέχρι τοῦ πρὸς τὴν θύραν· | ἔπειτα φοιτῶν καὶ κολακεύων ἐμέ τε καὶ | τὴν μήτερ' ἔγνω μ' . . . .

[4] See Wilamowitz, Herakl.[2] ii. 3, though Robert conjectures that it was in the evening (G.G.A. (1899), p. 543).

[5] This is suggested by the order of events as enumerated in the Law of Euegoros. But recent views on the word κῶμος in the law make it the equivalent of χοροὶ ἀνδρῶν, which were at first the only performances in the festival and are named in the law under their original name, though in the same place (after οἱ παῖδες) as in the inscriptional record, I.G. ii². 2318. This is doubtful (see pp. 27, 64, 66, 102 f.); but if it is correct, then there was no κῶμος in the sense of 'revel-procession' distinct from the πομπή.

From these passages it appears that in 346 B.C. on the 8th of Elaphebolion there were held the feast of Asklepios (introduced into Athens in 420 B.C.)[1] and the Proagon,[2] and that Demosthenes (at least according to Aeschines) wrongfully had an assembly called on a ἱερὰ ἡμέρα. The passage might equally be held to show that the day was *not* so sacred as absolutely to prohibit an assembly in case of emergency; and in fact a ἱερὰ ἡμέρα was not necessarily ἀποφράς, 'closed to civil business', and there are a number of recorded instances of assemblies held on various days during the Dionysian period of Elaphebolion.[3]

(2) Demosthenes, *Meid.* 8–10, shows that (in 348 B.C.) the law ordered that on the day following the Pandia a special assembly should be held in the theatre, to discuss the conduct of the Dionysiac festival by the archon and any alleged offences in the course of the festival—these to be the subject of προβολαί. The Law of Euegoros (quoted in § 10) speaks of the elements of the City Dionysia as ἡ πομπὴ καὶ οἱ παῖδες καὶ ὁ κῶμος καὶ οἱ κωμῳδοὶ καὶ οἱ τραγῳδοί. (The date of this law is unknown; it may not have been enacted before the fourth century: see p. 27.)

(3) Thucydides iv. 118. On the 14th of Elaphebolion in 423 B.C. the Athenians in full assembly ratified the treaty with Sparta. Allen argues that this proves that the festival must therefore have been over before the 14th. But we do not know what the law as regards assemblies during the festival may have been in 423 B.C. Even if the Law of Euegoros was already in force, it only forbids proceedings for debt, and against it are to be set the possibility (see above on Aeschin. *in Ctes.* 67) that an assembly might be held if necessary and the fact that, according to Thuc. v. 23, the annual renewal of the treaty with Sparta was fixed for the Dionysia, so that presumably not all public business was excluded.

(4) Aristophanes, *Birds* 786 ff., on any straightforward interpretation shows that in 414 B.C. comedies were acted in the afternoons of the same days as were devoted to tragedies; and as this year fell within the period when only three comedies were performed (not five),[4] we can infer that three days were taken up each with three tragedies, a satyric play, and a comedy. The passage runs:

[1] *I.G.* ii[2]. 4960. In *I.G.* ii[2]. 1496 the items referring to the Asklepieia precede those referring to the Dionysia.

[2] It is not known where the Proagon was held before Pericles built the Odeum (*c.* 444 B.C.).

[3] This is pointed out by Ferguson (*Hesperia* 17 (1948), p. 133, n. 46). See also Dinsmoor, *Hesperia* 23 (1954), p. 308.

[4] See below, p. 83. Five comedies competed in 434 B.C. when Kallias won fifth place (*I.G.* xiv. 1097 on p. 121) and again in the fourth century; but three only in 425 and during the greater part of the Peloponnesian War.

αὐτίχ' ὑμῶν τῶν θεατῶν εἴ τις ἦν ὑπόπτερος,
εἶτα πεινῶν τοῖς χοροῖσι τῶν τραγῳδῶν ἤχθετο,
ἐκπτόμενος ἂν οὗτος ἠρίστησεν ἐλθὼν οἰκάδε,
κᾆτ' ἂν ἐμπλησθεὶς ἐφ' ἡμᾶς αὖθις αὖ κατέπτετο.

(There is really no excuse for the emendation τρυγῳδῶν, nor for taking ἐφ' ἡμᾶς to refer to anything but 'comedy', as distinct from the τραγῳδοί.)

(5) The inconclusive nature of arguments from the holding of assemblies on a given day has already been noted, and most of our evidence is in any case Hellenistic. However, Ferguson[1] and Dinsmoor[2] have collected evidence to show a positive preference for holding assemblies on the 9th of Elaphebolion, and there is no clear evidence for assemblies on the 10th and 11th. Pickard-Cambridge in the first edition of this book was not entirely convinced by Ferguson's arguments that the 9th was a day of inaction in the Dionysia and that the πομπή was on the 10th, and retained the πομπή on the 9th. However, a new inscription of 271 B.C. published by Dinsmoor[3] is dated to Ἐλαφηβολιῶνος ἐνάτει ἱσταμένου τετάρτει ἐμβολίμωι, that is to say, the calendar had been stopped on the 9th of Elaphebolion for five days. This procedure is unintelligible except as a means for gaining time to complete the preparations for the Dionysia.[4] Therefore, the 9th was not part of the Dionysia, and the 10th was probably the day of the πομπή. This is confirmed by an inscription of the second century A.D.,[5] where the head of the Iobacchoi is instructed θυέτω τὴν θυσίαν τῷ θεῷ καὶ τὴν σπονδὴν τιθέτω κατὰ δεκάτην τοῦ Ἐλαφηβολιῶνος μηνός, and helps to explain the assertion of the scholiast on Aeschines that the Proagon was a few days before the main festival.

The conclusions to which the evidence seems to point[6] are:

(a) That the εἰσαγωγὴ ἀπὸ τῆς ἐσχάρας cannot be certainly dated. It was not part of the main festival, but could have been as late as the evening of the 8th or 9th of Elaphebolion.

(b) That during the whole Classical period there was a preparatory day (in the fourth century at least, the 8th of Elaphebolion) on which the Proagon was held. The Asklepieia, after their creation, were also celebrated on this day.

[1] *Hesperia* 17 (1948), p. 133, n. 46.   [2] Ibid. 23 (1954), p. 308.
[3] Loc. cit. (*S.E.G.* xiv. 65).
[4] Other instances of this practice are collected by Meritt, *The Athenian Year*, pp. 161–5.
[5] *I.G.* ii². 1368. 118–21.
[6] The earlier conflicts of opinion are best collected and discussed by J. T. Allen, *On the Program of the City Dionysia during the Peloponnesian War* (California, 1938). Besides the notes of Ferguson and Dinsmoor already referred to, see Pélékidis, *Histoire de l'Éphébie attique* (1962), pp. 301–6.

(c) That the first day of the festival proper began on the 10th with the πομπή, which may have occupied several hours early in the day.

(d) That during the Peloponnesian War the succeeding three days, the 11th, 12th, and 13th, would each be given to three tragedies, a satyr play, and a comedy.

(e) That before and after the Peloponnesian War, when there were five comedies, four days would be required (the 11th to the 14th).

Beyond this, the arrangement cannot be fixed. Pickard-Cambridge, believing that there were only five dithyrambic choruses of men and five of boys, placed all these and the κῶμος (assuming that this was a special event and not another name for the men's choruses) on the first day. This view is untenable; there were certainly ten of each,[1] and the first day would be unduly crowded, unless we assume the identity of the men's choruses and the κῶμος. With twenty dithyrambic choruses to account for, it is probable that we should return to Pickard-Cambridge's earlier view[2] of what happened when there were five comedies, that each had one day, three of them being preceded by tragedies and a satyr play and two by dithyrambic contests. Whenever the Pandia was (Wilamowitz's view that it was a full-moon festival[3] can neither be affirmed nor rejected), it is unlikely that it moved. It therefore seems most likely that an assembly was held on the 14th of Elaphebolion in 423 B.C. because the Dionysia was over (on the curtailed programme) and the Pandia not yet begun. In the fourth century, with a longer programme, the Pandia will have followed the Dionysia immediately, and the special assembly in the theatre was deferred until after the Pandia. We cannot be precise to the day, but it seems that in 346 B.C. the whole festival group and the special assembly in the theatre were over before the 18th of Elaphebolion.[4]

When the acting of old plays singly, or of one satyr play for the whole festival, was introduced, or the number of plays was varied (as happened at some periods), the calendar was naturally modified. There is ample Hellenistic evidence to show that in that period the special assembly in the theatre normally fell as late as the 21st of Elaphebolion.[5]

The shortening of the programme during the Peloponnesian War may have been intended to save both time (one day less being required) and expense, at a time when military operations and the building of ships would necessarily be the first considerations.[6]

---

[1] See below, p. 75.   [2] *Dith. Trag. Com.*[1], p. 218.   [3] *Glaube* i[2], p. 253, n. 1.
[4] See *B.S.A.* 50 (1955), p. 25.   [5] See Pélékidis, op. cit., p. 304.
[6] So J. T. Allen, op. cit., pp. 40–41. Ferguson (*Hesperia* 17 (1948), pp. 131 ff.) discusses the

To complete this sketch of the order of proceedings at the Dionysia it should be added (1) that the day's ceremonies began at daybreak;[1] (2) that at some point, probably very early in the proceedings, the theatre was purified by the offering of a sucking-pig[2] by persons called περιστίαρχοι or περιεστίαρχοι; (3) that libations were poured, apparently by the strategoi;[3] (4) that the proclamation of crowns bestowed on citizens, the display of tribute from subject states, and the parade and exhortation of the children of citizens who had fallen in battle took place before the performance of tragedies,[4] though of these ceremonies only the proclamation of crowns was still observed in the latter part of the fourth century; (5) that each 'event' in the competition was announced by sound of trumpet.[5]

7. It may be convenient to consider at this point the little that is known about the Proagon which preceded and the Ecclesia which followed the festival. The passage already quoted from Aeschines[6] shows that in 346 B.C. the Proagon took place on the 8th of Elaphebolion. The scholiast describes the ceremony as ἀγὼν καὶ ἐπίδειξις ὧν μέλλουσι δραμάτων ἀγωνίζεσθαι ἐν τῷ θεάτρῳ and as being held in the Odeum. (His 'ἀγών' is probably a mistake, arising from his interpreting προαγών as 'a preliminary contest', rather than as 'a ceremony preliminary to the contest'.) The scholiast on Aristophanes Wasps 1109 speaks of the Odeum as τόπος θεατροειδής, ἐν ᾧ εἰώθασι τὰ ποιήματα ἀπαγγέλλειν πρὸ τῆς εἰς τὸ θέατρον ἀπαγγελίας. Our most vivid account of a Proagon is in fact of the one before the Lenaia,[7] when Plato speaks of Agathon's brave appearance at it—Sympos. 194 a ἐπιλήσμων μεντἂν εἴην, ὦ Ἀγάθων ... εἰ ἰδὼν τὴν σὴν ἀνδρείαν καὶ μεγαλοφροσύνην ἀναβαίνοντος ἐπὶ τὸν ὀκρίβαντα μετὰ τῶν ὑποκριτῶν καὶ βλέψαντος ἐναντία τοσούτῳ θεάτρῳ, μέλλοντος ἐπιδείξεσθαι σαυτοῦ λόγους καὶ οὐδ' ὁπωστιοῦν ἐκπλαγέντος κτλ. It seems that each poet mounted a temporary platform with his actors and announced the subjects of the plays which he was about to produce.[8]

alterations in the order of the festival made by Demetrius Poliorketes in certain years, and the combination for a short time of the Dionysia and the Demetrieia; but these were violations of the normal arrangement, which was doubtless re-established later.

[1] ἅμα τῇ ἡμέρᾳ (Aeschin. in Ctes. 76); ἔωθεν (Dem. Meid. 74).
[2] 'Suid.' s.v. καθάρσιον; Pollux viii. 104.   [3] Plut. Kimon 8 (see below, pp. 95 f.).
[4] Aeschin. in Ctes. 153–4; Isocr. de Pace 82. See above, p. 59.
[5] Pollux iv. 88, where the custom is said to have been instituted by the failure of the actor Hermon to appear at the right moment. The incident mentioned in Ar. Ach. 11–13 probably refers to the Proagon, when the several competitors were summoned by the herald.
[6] in Ctes. 67.
[7] Athen. v. 217 a shows that the reference is to the Lenaia. I.G. ii². 780, l. 15 (252–251 B.C.) is also evidence for there having been at least one other Proagon besides the one before the Dionysia.
[8] As Haigh noted (Att. Th.³, p. 68), λόγος is used of the subjects or plots in Ar. Wasps 54

A moving incident occurred at the Proagon of 406 B.C. after the news of the death of Euripides had been received, when Sophocles appeared in mourning and brought in his chorus and actors without the customary garlands, and the audience burst into tears.[1] Actors who appeared in the Proagon did not wear masks or costumes.[2]

Whether there was a Proagon at all before the building of the Odeum by Pericles (about 444 B.C.) and, if so, where it was held, remains unknown. There is no evidence to support Müller's view[3] that the Proagon was held in the Odeum in the Agora, near the Enneakrounos; he argues that in the round Periclean Odeum half the spectators would only see the actors' backs; but the Periclean Odeum was not round,[4] and ὀκρίβας probably indicates a temporary platform.[5]

8. The law regarding the Ecclesia after the festival has already been mentioned. What purports to be its text is given by Demosthenes in the speech against Meidias (8): τοὺς πρυτάνεις ποιεῖν ἐκκλησίαν ἐν Διο-νύσου τῇ ὑστεραίᾳ τῶν Πανδίων, ἐν δὲ ταύτῃ χρηματίζειν πρῶτον μὲν περὶ ἱερῶν, ἔπειτα τὰς προβολὰς παραδιδότωσαν τὰς γεγενημένας ἕνεκα τῆς πομ-πῆς ἢ τῶν ἀγώνων τῶν ἐν τοῖς Διονυσίοις, ὅσαι ἂν μὴ ἐκτετισμέναι ὦσιν.[6] On this Demosthenes comments (9): ὁ μὲν νόμος οὗτός ἐστιν, ὦ ἄνδρες Ἀθηναῖοι, καθ' ὃν αἱ προβολαὶ γίγνονται, λέγων, ὥσπερ ἠκούσατε, ποιεῖν τὴν ἐκκλησίαν ἐν Διονύσου μετὰ τὰ Πάνδια, ἐν δὲ ταύτῃ ἐπειδὰν χρηματίσωσιν οἱ πρόεδροι περὶ ὧν διῴκηκεν ὁ ἄρχων, χρηματίζειν καὶ περὶ ὧν ἄν τις ἠδικηκὼς ᾖ περὶ τὴν ἑορτὴν ἢ παρανενομηκώς—καλῶς, ὦ ἄνδρες Ἀθηναῖοι, καὶ συμφερόντως ἔχων ὁ νόμος, ὡς τὸ πρᾶγμα αὐτὸ μαρτυρεῖ. The Law of Euegoros, which he next quotes, forbidding proceedings against debtors during certain festivals, concludes: ἐὰν δέ τις τούτων τι παραβαίνῃ, ὑπόδικος ἔστω τῷ παθόντι, καὶ προβολαὶ αὐτοῦ ἔστωσαν ἐν τῇ ἐκκλησίᾳ τῇ ἐν Διονύσου ὡς ἀδικοῦντος, καθὰ περὶ τῶν ἄλλων τῶν ἀδικούντων γέγραπται.

---

and Peace 50, and in Hesych. s.v. λόγος· ἡ τοῦ δράματος ὑπόθεσις. It is also so used in the Poetics of Aristotle. The schol. on Wasps 1109 is probably not strictly correct in using the phrase τὰ ποιήματα ἀπαγγέλλειν, if the verb is used in the same sense as ἀπαγγελία in πρὸ τῆς εἰς τὸ θέατρον ἀπαγγελίας.

[1] Vit. Eurip., p. 3, ll. 11 ff. Schwartz, λέγουσι δὲ καὶ Σοφοκλέα, ἀκούσαντα ὅτι ἐτελεύτησε, αὐτὸν μὲν ἱματίῳ φαιῷ [ἤτοι πορφυρῷ] προελθεῖν, τὸν δὲ χορὸν καὶ τοὺς ὑποκριτὰς ἀστεφανώτους εἰσαγαγεῖν ἐν τῷ προαγῶνι καὶ δακρῦσαι τὸν δῆμον.

[2] Schol. Aeschin. in Ctes. 67.

[3] Gr. Bühnenalt., p. 365.

[4] Cf. Theatre of D., pp. 1, 2 (and refs. there), and Dilke in B.S.A. 43 (1948), pp. 185–6.

[5] Cf. Theatre of D., pp. 72–73.

[6] It is very doubtful whether the text of the law is genuine. The prytaneis did indeed convoke the Assembly, but the business was conducted by the πρόεδροι (or their ἐπιστάτης for the day), and παραδιδότωσαν is post-classical for παραδόντων. The last words of the law can only mean 'unless the complainant has been paid his damages'; but ἐκτίνειν προβολήν is an odd expression.

The first duty of the Assembly was to scrutinize the conduct of the officials responsible for the festival. An inscription published by the American excavators of the Agora[1] shows that in 283–282 B.C. this duty was still taken seriously:

ἔδοξεν τῷ δήμῳ· Ἀγύρριος Καλλιμέδοντος Κολλυτεὺς εἶπεν· ἐπειδὴ Εὔθιος ἄρχων γενόμενος τάς τε θυσίας ἔθυσεν τοῖς θεοῖς κατὰ τὰ πάτρια καὶ τῆς πομπῆς τῷ Διονύσῳ ἐπεμελήθη φιλοτίμως καὶ τἆλλα πάντα ἔπραξεν τὰ περὶ τὴν ἀρχὴν δικαίως πειθόμενος τοῖς τε νόμοις καὶ τοῖς ψηφίσμασιν τῆς βουλῆς καὶ τοῦ δήμου καὶ διὰ ταῦτα αὐτὸν καὶ πρότερον ὁ δῆμος ἐπήνεσεν καὶ ἐστεφάνωσεν ἐν τῇ ἐκ-κλησίᾳ τῇ ἐν Διονύσου, ὅπως ἂν οὖν πᾶσιν φανερὸν ᾖ ὅτι ὁ δῆμος καὶ νῦν καὶ εἰς τὸν λοιπὸν χρόνον τιμήσει τοὺς δικαίως ἄρχοντας τὰς ἀρχὰς καὶ κατὰ τοὺς νόμους· ἀγαθῇ τύχῃ δεδόχθαι τῷ δήμῳ ἐπαινέσαι Εὔθιον κτλ.

After the scrutiny of the archon came the προβολαί—the complaints laid by individuals before the Assembly of misconduct on the part of un-official persons or of injuries received during the festival. The προβολή was not strictly a judicial proceeding but the delation of offenders to the Assembly, and if the Assembly accepted a motion that the accused had transgressed the law or the sanctity of the festivals, the complainant's hands were greatly strengthened in any judicial proceedings which he might subsequently take. Such was the προβολή which Demosthenes threatened to bring against Meidias in 348, when publicly assaulted by him and otherwise injured, while he was in office as choregos.[2] (In fact the case was settled by a compromise, and the speech was not de-livered.) Among other instances of προβολή, Demosthenes mentions one in which the charge was that the accused had used violence to prevent a man from taking his seat in the theatre,[3] and another in which a cer-tain Ktesikles, after a προβολή, was condemned to death for carrying a whip in the festal procession and striking one of his personal enemies with it while intoxicated.[4]

There are inscriptions which illustrate the nature of the resolutions (other than motions of censure) passed by the Assembly held in the theatre after the festival. In 342 B.C. there was a decree[5] in honour of the Boule for its care of the εὐκοσμία of the theatre—one of the very few

[1] *Hesperia* 7 (1938), p. 100.
[2] *Meid.* 1 προὐβαλόμην ἀδικεῖν τοῦτον περὶ τὴν ἑορτήν, οὐ μόνον πληγὰς ὑπ' αὐτοῦ λαβὼν τοῖς Διονυσίοις, ἀλλὰ καὶ ἄλλα πολλὰ καὶ βίαια παθὼν παρὰ πᾶσαν τὴν χορηγίαν.
[3] Ibid. 178; this case, though the Assembly passed a vote of censure on the man, was not brought into court.
[4] Ibid. 180.
[5] *I.G.* ii². 223 Κηφισοφῶν Καλλιβίου Παιανιεὺς εἶπεν· ἐπειδὴ ἡ βουλὴ ἡ ἐπὶ Πυθοδότου ἄρχοντος καλῶς καὶ δικαίως ἐπεμελήθη τῆς εὐκοσμίας τοῦ θεάτρου, ἐπαινέσαι αὐτὴν καὶ στεφανῶσαι χρυσῷ στεφάνῳ κτλ. Cf. *Theatre of D.*, p. 136.

indications that the Council was specially concerned with the festival, and indicating probably its responsibility for the maintenance of order. (In another inscription[1] not many years later there is a reference to οἱ λαχόντες ἐπιμεληταὶ τῆς εὐκοσμίας τῆς περὶ τὸ θέατρον.) In 251 B.C. there was a decree[2] commending and rewarding the agonothetes who had supervised the festival; and in 185 B.C. a resolution[3] commending Zopyrus for sending his daughter Timothea to officiate as kanephoros at the festival οἴσουσαν τὸ ἱερὸν κανοῦν τῷ θεῷ κατὰ τὰ πάτρια, and also honouring the ἐπιμεληταὶ τῆς πομπῆς for their conduct of the procession in conjunction with the archon.[4] Evidently their functions had not been superseded (as those of the choregoi had) by the institution of the agonothetes.

9. Apart from scattered notices, our information as regards the performances of lyric choruses and of plays at Athens depends upon two fragmentary but reliable sources—the series of inscriptions contained in the latest edition of the *Corpus* (together with one or two since discovered), and the statements of Alexandrian scholars contained in the 'Arguments' prefixed to many plays in our editions. Both these sources can be taken as reporting accurately the official records kept by the archons at Athens. A few statements are also found in the Parian Marble, an important chronological inscription of about 260 B.C., which, though not without its problems, is generally trustworthy.

It may be assumed that an official record was kept from the date when the festival was organized (or reorganized) under state management in the form in which it was celebrated throughout the fifth century; but it is doubtful whether any of the inscriptions which we possess is an exact transcript of this record, though it is the information contained in it that they all report or rearrange. In the latter half of the fourth century B.C. Aristotle busied himself, probably between 334 B.C. and his death, with the records of lyric and dramatic performances, and for the history up to about 334 or a little later all subsequent recorders doubtless depended on him, bringing his chronicle up to date for subsequent periods. The Alexandrian scholars of the third century—among them Eratosthenes and Lycophron—devoted great attention to the history of the Athenian drama, and Callimachus' πίναξ καὶ ἀναγραφὴ τῶν κατὰ χρόνους καὶ ἀπ' ἀρχῆς γενομένων διδασκάλων must have been a standard work.[5]

---

[1] *I.G.* ii². 354 (327 B.C.). 　　　[2] Ibid. 780. 　　　[3] Ibid. 896. See above, p. 61.

[4] Ξένων Ἀσκληπιάδου Φυλάσιος εἶπεν· ἐπειδὴ οἱ χειροτονηθέντες ἐπιμεληταὶ τῆς πομπῆς ἐπὶ Ζωπύρου ἄρχοντος τάς τε θυσίας ἔθυσαν τοῖς θεοῖς οἷς πάτριον ἦν, ἔπεμψαν δὲ καὶ τὴν πομπὴν μετὰ τοῦ ἄρχοντος ὡς ἠδύναντο φιλοτιμότατα, ἐπεμελήθησαν δὲ καὶ τῶν ἄλλων ὧν καθῆκεν αὐτοῖς, ἀγαθῇ τύχῃ δεδόχθαι τῷ δήμῳ ἐπαινέσαι τοὺς ἐπιμελητὰς τῆς πομπῆς καὶ στεφανῶσαι ἕκαστον αὐτῶν κτλ. This inscription was ordered to be erected ἐν τῷ τεμένει τοῦ Διονύσου.

[5] Callimachus, frr. 454–6 Pf.

Besides official records and the compilations of professional scholars, there were also many monuments erected by victorious choregoi and others, of which some few fragments have come down to us.

The main inscriptional records will be found in the Appendix to this chapter, with some necessary notes on each type of inscription, but a brief general account may be given here.

10. The work of Aristotle on the subject was contained in three books, enumerated in the catalogue of his writings given by Diogenes Laertius,[1] Νῖκαι Διονυσιακαὶ α΄, Περὶ τραγῳδιῶν α΄, Διδασκαλίαι α΄. The title of the first is given by Hesychius as Νικῶν Διονυσιακῶν καὶ Ληναίων α΄, showing that the one book covered both festivals, but otherwise there is no information about the book and no quotation from it remains. Nothing is known of the book Περὶ τραγῳδιῶν. But the Διδασκαλίαι no doubt took its title from the official language of the festival. The poet was said διδάσκειν τραγῳδίαν or κωμῳδίαν, his function as teacher of his chorus and actors was termed διδασκαλία, and at least from Alexandrian times onwards his work collectively might be called διδασκαλία, and the official records were an enumeration of the several διδασκαλίαι of each festival; the same ground was doubtless covered by Aristotle. That Aristotle's Διδασκαλίαι included the records of dithyrambs as well as of tragedy and comedy is proved by late allusions to the work.[2] One or two references suggest that its contents were not exactly identical with those of any of the extant inscriptions: e.g. he is said to have noted that there were two poets named Kinesias, and it is thought by some that, unlike the inscriptions, he referred to certain tetralogies by their collective names—Πανδιονίς or Οἰδιπόδεια—though the inference is by no means certain.[3] It is interesting that he entered a *Rhesus* as a genuine play of Euripides,[4] though it is not proved that this was the extant play.

11. Of the inscriptions the most discussed, *I.G.* ii². 2318, generally referred to by scholars as *Fasti*, unfortunately lacks two or possibly three of its opening columns, and it is uncertain with what year it began,

---

[1] Diog. Laert. v. 26; Hesych. Milesius, *Onomatologon*, ap. V. Rose, *Aristot. Fragm.*, p. 15. Aristotle also prepared a list of Pythian victors, in conjunction with Kallisthenes, for the temple of Apollo at Delphi; this was engraved at the public expense in 327 B.C. (see Tod, *Greek Historical Inscriptions* ii, no. 187; Lewis, *C.R.* N.S. 8 (1958), p. 108, gives the change in date).

[2] Harpokr. s.v. διδάσκαλος· ὅτι γὰρ ὁ Παντακλῆς ποιητής, δεδήλωκεν Ἀριστοτέλης ἐν ταῖς Διδασκαλίαις (Pantakles was a dithyrambic poet of the latter half of the fifth century B.C.); and schol. on Ar. *Birds* 1379 ὁ δὲ Ἀριστοτέλης ἐν ταῖς Διδασκαλίαις δύο (sc. Κινησίας) φησὶ γεγονέναι.

[3] Schol. ibid. 282 εἴη ἂν οὖν τὸν ἔποπα ἐσκευοποιηκὼς τῇ Πανδιονίδι τετραλογίᾳ, ἣν καὶ Ἀριστοτέλης ἐν ταῖς Διδασκαλίαις ἀναγράφει (= fr. 619 Rose); and schol. on Plato *Apol.* 18 b καὶ ὁ Μέλητος Οἰδιπόδειαν ἔθηκεν, ὡς Ἀριστοτέλης Διδασκαλίαις (fr. 628 Rose). See below, p. 80.

[4] Argt. Eur. *Rhesus*. All extant refs. to Aristotle's Διδασκαλίαι are collected by Rose, *Aristot. Fragm.*, nos. 618–30. See Jachmann, *De Aristotelis didascaliis* (Göttingen, 1908).

though it claims to go back to the beginning of the κῶμοι in honour of Dionysus,[1] whatever this expression means. It certainly would not have gone back as far as 534 B.C., in or about which year Thespis won a prize for tragedy[2]—under what kind of organization is not recorded. It may have gone back as far as 509 or 508 B.C., when Hypodikos is said to have produced the first dithyrambic chorus of men[3]—the first, perhaps, under a democratic régime, as Lasos seems to have preceded him under the tyrants—but perhaps the most probable view places the beginning of the record in or about 501 B.C. (It is possible that it was about this time that satyric plays were brought into the contests, but there is no certainty about this.) The first extant entry in the inscription refers to the year 472 B.C. (An earlier column must have recorded the beginning of the contest of comic poets with the victory of Chionides in 486 B.C.) For each year the inscription recorded (in the same order) (1) archon's name, (2) tribe victorious with boys' chorus, and choregos, (3) tribe victorious with men's chorus, and choregos, (4) victorious choregos and poet in comedy, (5) victorious choregos and poet in tragedy. In 447 B.C. the name of the tragic actor who won the prize is added, and considerations of spacing suggest that it appeared in two previous years. The entries for 386 and 339 B.C. respectively record the first occasions of the performance of an old tragedy and an old comedy, but the inscription never notices the name of a dithyrambic poet or a victorious comic actor or a satyric play performed singly. The extant portions end in the year 328 B.C.; the inscription may have been continued until some twenty years later, when the appointment of an agonothetes put an end to the choregic system, or may have ended earlier.

12. We have next a number of fragments (*I.G.* ii[2]. 2319–23) which are generally grouped under the title of Διδασκαλίαι. They were practically all found on the southern slope of the Acropolis, and formed part of a building (possibly, as Reisch conjectures, erected by an agonothetes in 278) which included both this record and the list of victors to be referred to in the next paragraph. This didaskalic record began in the fifth century and appears to have been originally compiled soon after 288 B.C.; after which it was supplemented (no. 2323) by records of comedies at the Dionysia extending over the rest of the third and most of the second century. The main inscription (nos. 2319–22) was arranged in the order (1) tragedies at the Dionysia, (2) comedies at the Dionysia, (3) comedies at the Lenaia, (4) tragedies at the Lenaia; and

---

[1] See Appendix, pp. 101 ff.　　　　　　　　　　　　[2] *Marm. Par.* ep. 43.
[3] Ibid., ep. 46, and Jacoby ad loc.; see *Dith. Trag. Com.*[2], p. 15.

in each category were entered (*a*) archon's name, (*b*) the names of the poets in order of success, and the name of each play with which each poet competed and of the protagonist who acted in it. (In the record of tragedies the satyric play with which, after a certain date, the performances opened and its poet, and for the Dionysia the old tragedy performed and its protagonist, preceded the enumeration of the competing poets and plays; and in the record of comedies the old comedy produced was similarly entered.) Each year's record in each category closed with the name of the victorious actor. The remains of these didaskaliai are very incomplete, but it happens that they attest a number of interesting facts showing, for example, that (1) at the Lenaia two tragedies only, and no satyric play, were offered by each poet; (2) in 340 B.C. the tragic poets at the Dionysia also offered only two tragedies each, instead of the usual three —it is not known why; (3) in many years of the second century B.C. the competition of comedies at the Dionysia was omitted. On the architraves of the building on which the didaskaliai were engraved there was inscribed another category of inscriptions (*I.G.* ii². 2325), lists of victorious tragic poets, tragic actors, comic poets, and comic actors at the Dionysia and the Lenaia—eight lists in all—the names being placed in order of the poet's or actor's first victory at the festival, and the number of his victories at that festival added. Before the name of Aeschylus (whose first victory was won in 484 B.C.) about ten lines are missing in the list of tragic poets at the Dionysia; the list of comic poets at the same festival doubtless began with Chionides in 486, though the first few lines of the list are missing. Other lists show that the contest of tragic actors at the Dionysia began in 449, when Herakleides was victorious; and that at the Lenaia contests of comedy, and probably contests of comic actors also, began in or about 442, and contests of tragic actors about the same date, or a little later.

13. Another kind of record, probably compiled by Alexandrian scholars, survives in some fragments of an inscription found in Rome (*I.G.* xiv. 1097, 1098). This record, taking poet by poet in order and perhaps going back to the first performances of comedy at each of the two festivals, contained lists of the comedies of each poet in order of the places (first, second, etc.) awarded to each play, Dionysian placings being entered before Lenaian. The extant fragments refer to Telekleides, Lysippos, and Anaxandrides. Other inscriptions are probably to be attributed to Rome, but are less informative (see p. 122).

14. Another fragment of an inscription discovered by the American investigators of the Agora is part of a record of the actors placed first,

second, or third in each of the contests in old comedy, old satyr plays, and old tragedy, and is interesting as proving that instead of the presentation of a single old play of each kind there was a contest between the old plays of each kind, or at least between their actors, and that at this date (254 B.C.) satyric plays were treated in the same way as tragedies and comedies—an illustration of the special interest which seems to have been taken in satyric drama in the third century.

The inscriptions on some private monuments are quoted in the Appendix to this chapter and in various notes.

15. The inscriptions we have just considered give no information about the performances of dithyrambs after 328 B.C. For this, we have to rely on dedications. But these decisively refute the view of Wilamowitz[1] that the contests for the prizes in dithyramb at the Dionysia ceased when choregoi were superseded by an agonothetes in the last decades of the fourth century. Tribal contests both for men's and boys' choruses continued in the third century long after the introduction of the agonothetes.[2] The only change is that the choregos disappears; the didaskalos and flute player continue to be recorded. Our record is fragmentary, but takes the story of dithyramb in Athens down to close on A.D. 200.[3] There were innovations; in one year, c. A.D. 80, all the choregoi, who seem to reappear in the Roman period, joined in one show and one monument,[4] and there is evidence in the second century A.D. for four or six tribes joining together.[5] The festival for which we have most evidence is that of A.D. 97, attended by Plutarch.[6] One of the tribes at this festival set up a monument[7] with a list of twenty-seven choreutai, a chorus of only half the classical κύκλιος χορός.

---

[1] *Gött. gel. Anz.* 1906, p. 614.

[2] The dates of *I.G.* ii². 3077–83 range from 306 to 270 B.C. *I.G.* ii². 3084–7 are other third-century inscriptions of this type.

[3] *I.G.* ii². 3088 and 3058 (*B.S.A.* 50 (1955), p. 24, no. 6), 175–174 B.C.) *I.G.* ii². 3113, 3157 (first century A.D.), 3120 (just before A.D. 200), 3121 (second century A.D.), 1105 (a letter of Hadrian).

[4] Ibid. 3114 ὁ δῆμος ἐνείκα. | Λούκιος Φλαούιος Φλάμμας | Κυδαθηναιεὺς ἦρχε. | πάντες χοραγοὶ πᾶς τε φυλέτας χορός | ἄγαλμα δήμῳ Κέκροπος ἐστάσαντό με | ἑκούσιοι μεθέντες ἐξ ἀγωνίας, | ὡς μὴ φέροι τις αἶσχος ἀποκισσούμενος. | ἐγὼ δ' ἑκάστῳ τόσσον εὐκλείας νέμω, | καθ' ὅσσον αὐτῷ ξυνὸς ὢν ὀφείλομαι.

[5] Ibid. 3116, 3117 (*T.A.P.A.* 68 (1937), pp. 78 ff.), 3118.

[6] *Quaest. Conv.* i. 628 a ἐν δὲ τοῖς Σαραπίωνος ἐπινικίοις, ὅτε τῇ Λεοντίδι φυλῇ τὸν χορὸν διατάξας ἐνίκησεν, ἐστιωμένοις ἡμῖν ἅτε δὴ καὶ φυλέταις οὖσι δημοποιήτοις οἰκεῖοι λόγοι τῆς ἐν χειρὶ φιλοτιμίας παρῆσαν. ἔσχε γὰρ ὁ ἀγὼν ἐντονωτάτην ἅμιλλαν, ἀγωνοθετοῦντος ἐνδόξως καὶ μεγαλοπρεπῶς Φιλοπάππου τοῦ βασιλέως ταῖς φυλαῖς ὁμοῦ πάσαις χορηγοῦντος. The quotation from Neanthes which follows (84 F 10 Jac.), to the effect that Aiantis had never been last in a dithyrambic contest, argues for very full records of these contests existing down to the third century.

[7] *I.G.* ii². 3112 ἡ Οἰνηὶς φυλὴ διὰ τῶν εὖ ἀγωνισαμένων χορῷ Διονυσιακῷ τὸν ἄρχοντα καὶ ἀγωνοθέτην Διονυσίων Γάιον Ἰούλιον Ἀντίοχον Ἐπιφανῆ Φιλόπαππον Βησαιέα τῆς εἰς ἑαυτὴν

16. The first step in the preparation for the contest of dithyrambs was the selection of two choregoi from each of the ten tribes, ten for choruses of men, ten for those of boys.[1] How the tribe selected its choregoi is not clear, but the choice was made a month after the last festival,[2] and it appears that the ἐπιμεληταὶ τῆς φυλῆς, of whose functions little is known, had some responsibility in the matter, as had also the archon in virtue of his general supremacy in all that concerned the festival, and when the arrangements broke down in 349 B.C. in the Pandionid tribe, the archon and the ἐπιμεληταί scolded each other, until the situation was saved by Demosthenes, who volunteered to serve as choregos for the tribe.[3] In the fourth century, the choregos for a chorus of boys had to be over forty years of age, but this rule did not apply in the fifth century.[4] The choregos will have first obtained his poet and his flute player; there was obviously competition for the best of these, and the choregoi

εὐεργεσίας ἕνεκα. ἐδίδασκε Μοιραγένης, ἐχορήγει Βούλων οἱ Μοιραγένους Φυλάσιοι. ἐπεστάτει Μένανδρος (Μενάνδρου) Φυλάσιος, εὔλει Φίλητος Μενίσκου Κολωνῆθεν, ἐχόρευον (26 or 27 names), ἐμελοποίει Μουσικός.

[1] Schol. on Aeschin. in Tim. 10 ἐξ ἔθους Ἀθηναῖοι κατὰ φυλὰς ἵστασαν πεντήκοντα παίδων χορὸν ἢ ἀνδρῶν, ὥστε γενέσθαι δέκα χορούς, ἐπειδὴ καὶ δέκα φυλαί. . . . λέγονται δὲ οἱ διθύραμβοι χοροὶ κύκλιοι καὶ χορὸς κύκλιος. (On the meaning of κύκλιος see Dith. Trag. Com.², p. 32.) Pickard-Cambridge concluded from this that there were only five men's and five boy's choruses, but the epigraphical evidence is decisive against this view, for I.G. ii². 2318. 320–4 (p. 106 here under 333–332) and 3061 show the same tribe winning both events (Brinck, De choregia quaestiones epigraphicae, p. 7; Lewis, B.S.A. 50 (1955), p. 23). Cf. Isaeus, Or. v .36 οὗτος γὰρ τῇ μὲν φυλῇ εἰς Διονύσια χορηγήσας τέταρτος ἐγένετο (i.e. was placed fourth in the contest); [Plut.] Vit. X Orat. 835 b ἐχορήγησε κυκλίῳ χορῷ τῇ αὑτοῦ φυλῇ ἀγωνιζομένῃ διθυράμβῳ.

[2] Argt. II to Dem. Meid. (after some very confused matter) παυομένης δὲ τῆς ἑορτῆς ἐν τῷ πρώτῳ μηνὶ προὐβάλλοντο οἱ χορηγοὶ τῆς μελλούσης ἑορτῆς. The records of a choregos serving for two tribes together probably refer to dithyrambs at the Thargelia (as certainly in Antiphon, de Chor. 11); e.g. Dem. in Lept. 28 τίνα ῥᾳστώνην τοῖς πολλοῖς ὁ σός, ὦ Λεπτίνη, ποιεῖ νόμος, εἰ μιᾶς ἢ δυοῖν φυλαῖν ἕνα χορηγὸν καθίστησιν, ὃς ἀνθ' ἑνὸς ἄλλου τοῦθ' ἅπαξ ποιήσας ἀπαλλάξεται; on which the schol. says that ἐξηγήσαντό τινες ὡς ἐν τοῖς Θαργηλίοις δυοῖν φυλαῖν εἰς μόνος καθίστατο χορηγός· τοῖς δὲ μεγάλοις Διονυσίοις πλείονος αὐτῷ γενομένης τῆς δαπάνης, εἰς χορηγὸς ἑκάστης φυλῆς καθίστατο. Cf. I.G. ii². 3063–72 (all of the fourth century B.C.).

[3] Dem. Meid. 13 ἐπειδὴ γάρ, οὗ καθεστηκότος χορηγοῦ τῇ Πανδιονίδι φυλῇ, τρίτον ἔτος τουτί, παρούσης δὲ τῆς ἐκκλησίας, ἐν ᾗ τὸν ἄρχοντ' ἐπικληροῦν ὁ νόμος τοῖς χοροῖς τοὺς αὐλητὰς κελεύει, λόγων καὶ λοιδορίας γιγνομένης, καὶ κατηγοροῦντος τοῦ μὲν ἄρχοντος τῶν ἐπιμελητῶν τῆς φυλῆς, τῶν δ' ἐπιμελητῶν τοῦ ἄρχοντος, παρελθὼν ὑπεσχόμην ἐγὼ χορηγήσειν ἐθελοντὴς καὶ κληρουμένων πρῶτος αἱρεῖσθαι τὸν αὐλητὴν ἔλαχον. Before the middle of the fifth century the flute player is said to have been engaged and paid by the poet, his part not having yet attained its later importance; cf. [Plut.] de Mus. 30. 1141 c–d ἀλλὰ γὰρ καὶ αὐλητικὴ ἀφ' ἁπλουστέρας εἰς ποικιλωτέραν μεταβέβηκε μουσικήν· τὸ γὰρ παλαιόν, ἕως εἰς Μελανιππίδην τὸν τῶν διθυράμβων ποιητήν, συμβεβήκει τοὺς αὐλητὰς παρὰ τῶν ποιητῶν λαμβάνειν τοὺς μισθούς, πρωταγωνιστούσης δηλονότι τῆς ποιήσεως, τῶν δ' αὐλητῶν ὑπηρετούντων τοῖς διδασκάλοις· ὕστερον δὲ καὶ τοῦτο διεφθάρη.

[4] Aristot. Ἀθ. Πολ. 56. 3; Aeschin. in Tim. 11; Plato, Laws vi. 764 e. But in 406–405 there was a boys' choregos in his early twenties (Lysias xxi. 1–5). Cf. B.S.A. 50 (1955), p. 24, and the case recorded by [And.] iv. 20–21, Dem. Meid. 117, Plut. Alc. 16; Alcibiades was certainly under forty at the time.

drew lots for the order of choice between those available.[1] It was obviously a disadvantage to be drawn last, when only one poet or flute player was left. It is very remarkable that the public inscriptions make no mention of the poet, though among the poets who competed at Athens were Pindar, Simonides, and Bacchylides, and it is also noteworthy that a large proportion of the dithyrambic poets at the Athenian Dionysia, whose names are known to us in the fifth and fourth centuries, were not of Athenian birth. Nor in fact were most of the famous flute players; but the advantage of a good flute player was rated very highly.

Having got his poet and his flute player, the choregos had to select his chorus from among the members of his tribe.[2] That the selection rested with himself is nowhere expressly stated with reference to the Dionysia, but it may be inferred from the fact that it was certainly so at the Thargelia;[3] and an inscription[4] referring to the choregos for tragedy at Ikarion may be tentatively reconstructed so as to imply that the choregos chose his singers there. There seem to have been regular officials in the tribes to give him skilled assistance in this.[5] He had also to provide them with a room for training and rehearsals,[6] and above all he had to secure a good chorus-trainer (χοροδιδάσκαλος). No small part of Demosthenes' grievance against Meidias lay in Meidias' attempt to corrupt his chorus-trainer.[7]

Xenophon[8] testifies to the importance of a skilled choice of singers

---

[1] Ar. *Birds* 1403–4 ταυτὶ πεποίηκας ἐμὲ τὸν κυκλιοδιδάσκαλον | ὃς ταῖσι φυλαῖς περιμάχητός εἰμ' ἀεί; cf. Antiphon, *Or.* vi. 11 (choice of dithyrambic poets by lot for the Thargelia); Dem. *Meid.* 13 (above, p. 75, n. 3).

[2] The restriction to members of the tribe held good only for dithyramb, not for tragedy and comedy, which were not tribally organized.

[3] The speaker in Antiphon, loc. cit., speaks of the pains which he took in collecting his dithyrambic chorus of boys for the Thargelia: τὸν χορὸν συνέλεξα, ὡς ἠδυνάμην ἄριστα, οὔτε ζημιώσας οὐδένα οὔτε ἐνέχυρα βίᾳ φέρων οὔτε ἀπεχθανόμενος οὐδενί. This suggests that pressure might sometimes be brought to bear.

[4] *I.G.* i². 186–7. The words τραγῳδοὺς κατέλεγεν ('enrolled') are certain.

[5] Antiphon, *Or.* vi. 13. δύο ἄνδρας, τὸν μὲν Ἐρεχθηίδος Ἀμεινίαν, ὃν αὐτοὶ οἱ φυλέται ἐψηφίσαντο συλλέγειν καὶ ἐπιμελεῖσθαι τῆς φυλῆς ἑκάστοτε, δοκοῦντα χρηστὸν εἶναι, τὸν δ' ἕτερον . . . τῆς Κεκροπίδος, ὅσπερ ἑκάστοτε εἴωθεν ταύτην τὴν φυλὴν συλλέγειν. Haigh, *Att. Th.*³, p. 60, says that an agent so employed was called χορολέκτης; but the word, when it actually occurs, seems to mean the leader of the chorus, who gave them the ἐνδόσιμον or starting-note (Hecataeus *ap.* Aelian, *N.A.* xi. 1, cf. xv. 5), and the word may well mean the conductor or assembler of the chorus, without implying that he had selected them. Pollux, iv. 106, mentions but does not define the word. See below, p. 262.

[6] διδασκαλεῖον (Antiphon, loc. cit., where it was in his own house); also called χορηγεῖον (Dem. *de F.L.* 200, Poll. ix. 1. 2, Bekk. *Anecd.* 72. 17.)

[7] *Meid.* 17. We hear of one choregos who φιλονικῶν engaged a chorus-trainer who was technically ineligible (Dem. *Meid.* 58–59).

[8] *Memor.* iii. 4, 3–4 καὶ ὁ Σωκράτης ἔφη· "Ἀλλὰ καὶ φιλόνικος Ἀντισθένης ἐστίν, ὃ στρατηγῷ προσεῖναι ἐπιτήδειόν ἐστιν· οὐχ ὁρᾷς ὅτι καὶ ὁσάκις κεχορήγηκε πᾶσι τοῖς χοροῖς νενίκηκε;" "Μὰ Δί'," ἔφη ὁ Νικομαχίδης, "ἀλλ' οὐδὲν ὅμοιόν ἐστι χοροῦ τε καὶ στρατεύματος προεστάναι."

and trainer, when he mentions the victorious career of Antisthenes as choregos, despite his lack of all personal knowledge of music and of training. The members of the dithyrambic chorus had to be citizens by birth, and might be challenged, though not during the actual performance, which was sacred.[1] Apparently members of a men's chorus were exempt from military service.[2] The chorus, whether of men or boys, received not only musical training but also physical, in a care for their diet which might result in excess.[3] Success naturally depended largely upon the leader of the chorus,[4] but much depended also on the readiness of the choregos to spend his money lavishly. A stingy choregos (like Dikaiogenes who is pilloried by Isaeus[5]) might disgrace himself and his tribe, while magnificence in the costumes of himself and his chorus evidently helped towards victory. Demosthenes boasts[6] of the gold-embroidered robe and golden crown which he had had made for himself, and the golden crowns intended for his chorus—all damaged by Meidias, who broke into the goldsmith's house. Other passages in the orators[7] estimate the cost of a men's chorus at 50 minae and of a boys' chorus at 15, as against 30 minae for a tragic chorus (which was much smaller than a dithyrambic) and 16 for a comic.[8]

The dithyrambic chorus, who did not wear masks, danced in circular formation in the orchestra, doubtless with the altar as their centre.

17. The successful choregos received, as the representative of his tribe,[9] a tripod which he erected at his own expense upon a monument, with an appropriate inscription. Such tripods were carried by the well-known

"Καὶ μήν," ἔφη ὁ Σωκράτης ,"οὐδὲ ᾠδῆς γε ὁ Ἀντισθένης οὐδὲ χορῶν διδασκαλίας ἔμπειρος ὢν ὅμως ἐγένετο ἱκανὸς εὑρεῖν τοὺς κρατίστους ταῦτα."

[1] Meid. 56; cf. [Andok.] in Alcib. 20 κελεύοντος δὲ τοῦ νόμου τῶν χορευτῶν ἐξάγειν ὃν ἄν τις βούληται ξένον ἀγωνιζόμενον. The speaker narrates an assault by Alcibiades on one of the choreutai of Taureas, ὃς ἀντιχόρηγος ἦν Ἀλκιβιάδῃ παισί.

[2] Dem. Meid. 15.

[3] Plut. de glor. Ath. 349 a; cf. 'Suid.' s.v. φαρυγγίνδην· ὡς ἀριστίνδην· σκώπτοντες γὰρ τὴν γαστριμαργίαν τῶν χορευτῶν Ἀττικοὶ οὕτω λέγουσι. (Neither passage seems to refer to dithyrambic choruses as distinct from tragic and comic.)

[4] Dem. Meid. 60 ἴστε δὲ δήπου τοῦθ', ὅτι τὸν ἡγεμόν' ἂν ἀφέλῃ τις οἴχεται ὁ λοιπὸς χορός.

[5] Isaeus, Or. v. 36; cf. Plut. Dem. 29. 2 ἐδόκει γὰρ ἀνταγωνίζεσθαι τῷ Ἀρχίᾳ τραγῳδίαν ὑποκρινόμενος, εὐημερῶν δὲ καὶ κατέχων τὸ θέατρον ἐνδείᾳ παρασκευῆς καὶ χορηγίας κρατεῖσθαι.

[6] Dem. Meid. 16, 22, etc.; cf. Antiphanes, fr. 204 (K), which alleges that a choregos inevitably ruined himself by his expenditure on his chorus (χορηγὸς αἱρεθεὶς | ἱμάτια χρυσᾶ παρασχὼν τῷ χορῷ ῥάκος φορεῖ); cf. Plut. in n. 7.

[7] Lysias, Or. xxi. 1, 2; the fifty included the cost of the tripod. Cf. Dem. Meid. 156, and Plut. de glor. Ath. 349 b (speaking of choregoi) καὶ τούτων τοῖς μὲν ἡττηθεῖσι περιῆν προσυβρίσθαι καὶ γεγονέναι καταγελάστους· τοῖς δὲ νικήσασιν ὁ τρίπους ὑπῆρχεν, οὐκ ἀνάθημα τῆς νίκης, ὡς Δημήτριός φησιν, ἀλλ' ἐπίσπεισμα τῶν ἐκκεχυμένων βίων καὶ τῶν ἐκλελοιπότων κενοτάφιον οἴκων. [8] For choregia in general see also below, pp. 86 ff.

[9] Lysias, Or. xxi. 5; Dem. Meid. 5; cf. schol. on Aeschin. in Tim. 10.

monuments of Lysikrates (334 B.C.)[1] and Thrasyllus (319 B.C.),[2] and the course of a 'Street of the Tripods' is described by Pausanias,[3] leading in all probability to the Propylaeum which gave entrance to the theatre.[4] Long before this a tripod dedicated by the Antiochid tribe in 476 B.C. bore an epigram[5] of Simonides, who had composed the victorious dithyramb when he was eighty years old, and other epigrams of the same period suggest that the victorious poet may have been escorted home in procession, crowned with flowers and gay ribbons;[6] but the evidence that the prize for dithyramb was a bull never refers directly to Athens.[7] In the time of Demosthenes the victorious choregos was crowned in the theatre.[8] It should be added that it does not appear to have been necessary in the Classical period that each tripod should be mounted on a separate monument; Nikias (the statesman) is said by Plutarch[9] to have erected the monument described as ὁ τοῖς χορηγικοῖς τρίποσιν ὑποκείμενος ἐν Διονύσου νεώς, and whether these tripods were all won by himself on different occasions or not, they must have been grouped on the roof of the temple.

18. It seems that there were two great periods in the history of dithyramb at Athens. The first was in the early part of the fifth century—the time of Simonides, Pindar, and Bacchylides. Some remains of the poems written by the two latter for Athens have survived. At this time the poetry was of the highest literary merit and the music subordinated to it; but already, if the fragment of Pratinas is rightly interpreted,[10] the flute was striving to gain the mastery, and with Melanippides, probably about the

---

[1] The inscription (I.G. ii². 3042) runs: Λυσικράτης Λυσιθείδου Κικυννεὺς ἐχορήγει. Ἀκαμαντὶς παίδων ἐνίκα. Θέων ηὔλει. Λυσιάδης Ἀθηναῖος ἐδίδασκε. Εὐαίνετος ἦρχε. For the monument see E. A. Gardner, Ancient Athens, pp. 399–405, Bieber, H.T.², fig. 18, and fig. 30 here.

[2] I.G. ii². 3056 Θράσυλλος Θρασύλλου Δεκελεεὺς ἀνέθηκεν χορηγῶν νικήσας ἀνδράσιν Ἱπποθωντίδι φυλῇ. Εὔιος Χαλκιδεὺς ηὔλει. Νέαιχμος ἦρχεν. Καρκίδαμος Σώτιος ἐδίδασκεν; cf. Theatre of D., pp. 138, 169. For a dedication in the same year by Nikias (I.G. ii². 3055), see below, p. 79, n. 2.

[3] Paus. i. 20. 1 ἔστι δὲ ὁδὸς ἀπὸ τοῦ πρυτανείου καλουμένη Τρίποδες, ἀφ' οὗ καλοῦσι τὸ χωρίον. ναοὶ θεῶν εἰς τοῦτο (i.e. for such a purpose) μεγάλοι, καί σφισι ἐφεστήκασι τρίποδες, χαλκοῖ μέν, μνήμης δὲ ἄξια μάλιστα περιέχοντες εἰργασμένα; cf. Judeich, Topogr. Athen², pp. 183, 305. (The monument of Thrasyllus stands, not in this street, but in the κατατομή above the theatre.)

[4] See Theatre of D., p. 2, and refs. there. We illustrate (fig. 31) a neck-amphora (A.R.V.² 1581, no. 20) commemorating a victory of Glaukon, the Periclean general, c. 460 B.C.

[5] Epigr. 147 (Bergk).

[6] Especially ibid. 148 (not in fact by Simonides himself). See Dith. Trag. Com.², p. 36.

[7] Simon. Epigr. 145, 172; Pind. Olymp. xiii. 18; schol. on Plat. Rep. iii. 394 c. See Dith. Trag. Com.², pp. 2, 15, 36.

[8] This is implied in Dem. Meid. 63 ἀλλὰ τοῖς νόμοις καὶ τῇ τῶν ἄλλων βουλήσει συγχωρῶν ἠνείχετο καὶ νικῶντα καὶ στεφανούμενον τὸν ἐχθρὸν ὁρῶν. (The reference is to two rival choregoi.)

[9] Plut. Nik. 3. 3. The identification of this monument has given rise to much controversy. See Theatre of D., p. 29 and refs. there.

[10] Fr. 1 (Page), Dith. Trag. Com.², pp. 17–20, and see Athen. xiv. 617 b and pp. 256 f. below.

middle of the century, succeeded in achieving this despite strong criticism from persons of conservative taste. This predominance of the flute and of highly elaborate music, to the detriment of the words, was characteristic of the second period of famous dithyrambic writers[1]—Melanippides, Phrynis, Kinesias, Timotheos, Philoxenos, and others, down to the middle of the fourth century, after which no names of distinguished poets are recorded, though famous flute players are often mentioned. It appears that a flute player might perform for competition an old dithyramb, as the *Elpenor* and the *Αἴας ἐμμανής* of Timotheos of Miletus were performed after his death by Pantaleon of Sikyon and Timotheos of Thebes respectively.[2] Of Hellenistic dithyramb we know little, but it has already been indicated[3] that the tribes retained their interest in dithyramb as late as the first or second century A.D.

19. Throughout the fifth century B.C. and probably, apart from a few exceptional years, through the earlier part of the fourth century also, three tragic poets entered the contest for the prize in tragedy, and each presented four plays, of which the fourth was normally a satyric play, until at some date before 341 B.C. a single satyric play came to be presented at the beginning of the programme and each tragic poet offered at most three plays only. The didaskalic inscription records three plays apiece in 341, but only two in 340; the reason for this exception is unknown. By this time the acting of an old tragedy, presented by an actor before the competition of new tragedies, was already regular, and various experiments may have been tried with a view to controlling the total length of the day's performances.

The rule by which during the fifth century and for some time afterwards each poet offered four plays was probably due to the same need; and it was necessary in the interests of fair competition, as well as for the sake of the time-table, that each poet should know what was expected of him and that the programme should be constructed on a well-understood plan. The two alleged exceptions in the fifth century were probably not such. (1) In 467 B.C.—the year when Aeschylus was victorious with *Laius*, *Oedipus*, *Seven against Thebes*, and *Sphinx*—the second place was taken by Aristias, who (according to the Hypothesis of *Seven against*

---

[1] *Dith. Trag. Com.*[2], pp. 18, 35, 55–56 (for importance of the flute player at different periods).

[2] *I.G.* ii[2]. 3055 Νικίας Νικοδήμου Ξυπεταίων ἀνέθηκε νικήσας χορηγῶν Κεκροπίδι παίδων· Πανταλέων Σικυώνιος ηὔλει· ᾆσμα Ἐλπήνωρ Τιμοθέου· Νέαιχμος ἦρχεν (i.e. 319 B.C.); and Lucian, *Harmonides* 1 ὥσπερ ὅτε καὶ σύ, ὦ Τιμόθεε, τὸ πρῶτον ἐλθὼν οἴκοθεν ἐκ Βοιωτίας ὑπηύλησας τῇ Πανδιονίδι καὶ ἐνίκησας ἐν τῷ Αἴαντι τῷ ἐμμανεῖ, τοῦ ὁμωνύμου σοι ποιήσαντος τὸ μέλος, οὐδεὶς ἦν ὃς ἠγνόει τοὔνομα, Τιμόθεον ἐκ Θηβῶν.

[3] p. 74 above. The history of dithyramb is much more fully treated in *Dith. Trag. Com.*[2], pp. 1–59.

Thebes) competed Περσεῖ, Ταντάλῳ, Παλαισταῖς σατύροις τοῖς Πρατίνου (τοῦ) πατρός; but Professor Garrod[1] is convincing when he suggests that there has been an omission here (through haplography) of Ἀνταίῳ after Ταντάλῳ. (Aristias is known otherwise to have written an *Antaios*.[2]) (2) The scholiast on Aristophanes *Frogs* 67[3] says that the son of Euripides presented three of his father's plays after his father's death, but the fact that the scholiast does not mention the satyric play does not necessarily mean that the official records did not, or that none was offered.

How long before Aeschylus the rule of four plays may have been in force there is no evidence to show. There is no certain explanation of 'Suidas'' statement that Pratinas exhibited 50 plays of which 32 were satyric;[4] 'Suidas'' numbers are never very reliable and we do not know whence he derived them; they may often depend on the number of titles known to the Alexandrian scholars or preserved in the Alexandrian library. But there is no reason to doubt that Aeschylus regularly followed the rule.

20. It is usual also to speak of Aeschylus not simply as presenting four plays but as a writer of tetralogies or (if the satyric play is disregarded) of trilogies. The name τετραλογία probably originated in reference to oratory and denoted a group of four λόγοι (speeches) concerned with the same case, like those of Antiphon, and it is not known to have been applied to tragedy before the time of the Alexandrian scholars Aristarchus and Apollonius, who also were apparently the first to use τριλογία in this application.[5] The words are very rarely found, but they seem to have been used only of groups of plays connected in subject, such as the *Oresteia*, the *Lycurgeia* of Aeschylus[6] and of Polyphrasmon,[7] the *Pandionis* of Philokles, and the *Oedipodeia* of Meletos. Aeschylus' *Suppliants*, *Seven against Thebes*, and *Prometheus Vinctus* are also each part of such tetralogies, and Wecklein and others have collected some of the titles

---

[1] *C.R.* 34 (1920), p. 130. (See also *P.Oxy.* 2256, fr. 2.)   [2] Aristias, fr. 1 (N).

[3] οὕτω γὰρ καὶ αἱ διδασκαλίαι φέρουσι τελευτήσαντος Εὐριπίδου τὸν υἱὸν αὐτοῦ δεδιδαχέναι ὁμώνυμον ἐν ἄστει Ἰφιγένειαν τὴν ἐν Αὐλίδι, Ἀλκμέωνα, Βάκχας.

[4] See *Dith. Trag. Com.*[2], pp. 65–66.

[5] Schol. on Ar. *Frogs* 1124 τετραλογίαν φέρουσι τὴν Ὀρέστειαν αἱ διδασκαλίαι Ἀγαμέμνονα Χοηφόρους Εὐμενίδας Πρωτέα σατυρικόν. Ἀρίσταρχος καὶ Ἀπολλώνιος τριλογίαν λέγουσι χωρὶς τῶν σατυρικῶν. This does not of course imply that the word τετραλογία was found in the διδασκαλίαι, any more than does the schol. on *Birds* 281 οὗτος ὁ Φιλοκλῆς ἔποπα ἐσκεύασεν ἐν τῇ Πανδιονίδι τετραλογίᾳ . . . εἴη ἂν οὖν τὸν ἔποπα ἐσκευοποιηκὼς τῇ Πανδιονίδι τετραλογίᾳ ἣν καὶ Ἀριστοτέλης ἐν ταῖς Διδασκαλίαις ἀναγράφει, or schol. on Plato, *Apol.* 18 b καὶ ὁ Μέλητος Οἰδιπόδειαν ἔθηκεν, ὡς Ἀριστοτέλης Διδασκαλίαις. Whether Aristotle (and the διδασκαλίαι) used the collective titles *Oresteia, Pandionis, Oedipodeia*, etc., remains uncertain (see above, p. 71).

[6] Schol. on Ar. *Thesm.* 135 τὴν τετραλογίαν λέγει Λυκούργειαν, Ἠδωνοὺς Βασσαρίδας Νεανίσκους Λυκοῦργον τὸν σατυρικόν.

[7] Argt. to Aesch. *Septem* (partly quoted above) . . . γ΄ Πολυφράσμων Λυκουργείᾳ.

of lost plays of Aeschylus into similar groups with more or less probability, such as Μυρμίδονες, Νηρηίδες, and Φρύγες ἢ Ἕκτορος Λύτρα (with choruses of attendants on Achilles, Thetis, and Priam) ; Ὅπλων Κρίσις, Θρῆσσαι, and Σαλαμίνιαι (presenting the story of Ajax) ; Ἀργεῖοι, Ἐλευσίνιοι, and Ἐπίγονοι (the story of the Argive attack on Thebes) ; Κάβειροι, Ὑψιπύλη, Ἀργώ (the Argonautic expedition). Μέμνων and Ψυχοστασία may have belonged to one trilogy, Τήλεφος and Μυσοί to another, and so on. But Aeschylus also at times presented four independent plays. It is, for instance, impossible to regard Φινεύς, Πέρσαι, Γλαῦκος Ποτνιεύς, and the satyric Προμηθεύς as a tetralogy,[1] and the satyric play was probably often independent of the trilogy to which it was attached.

Whether Sophocles ever composed a connected tetralogy or trilogy is uncertain. Some think that the Τηλέφεια ascribed to him in an inscription from Aixone may have been a trilogy including Ἀλεάδαι, Μυσοί, and Ἀχαιῶν Σύλλογος,[2] but it is evident that what was characteristic of him was the development of the independent single play, and this must be the meaning of the confused remark of 'Suidas' on him: καὶ αὐτὸς ἦρξεν τοῦ δρᾶμα πρὸς δρᾶμα ἀγωνίζεσθαι ἀλλὰ μὴ τετραλογίαν.[3] He certainly presented, as a rule, four independent plays. So, as a rule, did Euripides, but there seems to have been sometimes a connexion of subject between his three tragedies, e.g. in 415 B.C. between Alexandros, Palamedes, and Troades,[4] and in 410 B.C. between Oinomaos, Chrysippos, and Phoenissae.[5] Aelian[6] tells a story of Plato the philosopher that he composed a 'tetralogy', which he was on the point of getting acted at the Dionysia, when Socrates persuaded him to burn it. It is not worth while to discuss whether 'Suidas'' confused notice[7] of Nikomachos of Alexandreia Troas ascribes a trilogy to him.

21. It has already been noted that the number of the plays sometimes varies in the fourth century, and the recorded numbers of plays by Theodektes,[8] Aphareus, and others is not exactly divisible by three or four;

---

[1] Despite the attempt of Donaldson, *Gk. Theatre*, pp. 118–19, to find connexions.

[2] Above, p. 55, and *New Chapters* iii, pp. 76 ff. (But see Handley-Rea, *Telephus of Euripides* (1957).)

[3] τετραλογίαν is Meursius's emendation for στρατολογεῖσθαι or στρατολογίαν. 'Suidas' (or his authority) cannot have meant that Sophocles exhibited only one play at each festival, or that on each day of the festival each poet produced one play only. (See Haigh, *Att. Th.*³, p. 17 n.)   [4] Cf. B. Snell, 'Euripides' *Alexandros*' (*Hermes*, Einzelschr. 1937).

[5] See C. Robert, *Oidipus*, pp. 396 ff.

[6] *Var. H.* ii. 30; cf. Diog. Laert. iii. 5. According to ibid. 56 Plato was said by Thrasyllus κατὰ τὴν τραγικὴν τετραλογίαν ἐκδοῦναι τοὺς διαλόγους ... τὰ δὲ τέτταρα δράματα ἐκαλεῖτο τετραλογία. (The intervening words are probably interpolated and in any case are nonsense.)

[7] See P. Wiesmann, *Das Problem der tragischen Tetralogie*, p. 32.

[8] Theodektes is said to have written 50 tragedies and competed 13 times, Aphareus to have composed 35 tragedies (besides others of disputed genuineness) and competed 8 times ('Suid.' s.v. Θεοδέκτης, Steph. Byz. s.v. Φάσηλις; [Plut.] *Vit. X Orat.* 839 d).

but the value of these records is uncertain, and some poets, such as Chairemon, composed plays for reading, not for performance.[1] The competitions went on, and proclamations of honours were made and crowns bestowed καινοῖς τραγῳδοῖς or τραγῳδῶν ἐν τῷ ἀγῶνι at the Dionysia down to the first century B.C.,[2] but the history of the regulations for the production of plays is no longer traceable. By the time of Dio Chrysostom[3] (about A.D. 100) most, though apparently not all, of the plays performed were old, but in Lucian's day (late in the second century) the composition of new plays had ceased.[4]

22. Comedy was later than tragedy in obtaining recognition by the state, though plays had been given earlier by performers at their own charges[5]—whether at one of the regular Dionysiac festivals or not we are not told. The first victory in a state-recognized contest was won by Chionides in 486 B.C.,[6] and it must have been at the Dionysia, because Lenaian contests in comedy were only introduced in or about 442 B.C. The first victory mentioned in the extant portion of the inscription I.G. ii². 2318 is that of Magnes in 472.

Each poet offered one play only at each festival (whether Dionysia or Lenaia), at least during the fifth and probably the fourth century. The statement that Aristophanes offered two plays at the Lenaia in 422 B.C.—*Proagon* and *Wasps*—depends upon a passage[7] in the Argument

---

[1] Aristot. *Rhet.* iii. 12. 1413ᵇ12 f.

[2] See *I.G.* ii². 555 (*c.* 305 B.C.), 646 (295–294 B.C.), 682 (*c.* 274 B.C.), 851 (before 224–223 B.C.), 956 (161–160 B.C.), 957 (157–156 B.C.), 958 (152 B.C.); and many of the series of ephebic inscriptions, ibid. 1006 (122–121 B.C.) to 1043 (38–37 B.C.), e.g. nos. 1006, 1009, 1011, 1028, 1029, 1030, 1039, 1042, 1043.

[3] *Or.* xix. 4 ἥ τε φωνὴ (of the actors) μείζων . . . ἥ τε λέξις οὐκ αὐτοσχέδιος . . . ἀλλὰ ποιητῶν ἐπιμελῶς καὶ κατὰ σχολὴν πεποιηκότων. καὶ τά γε πολλὰ αὐτῶν ἀρχαῖά ἐστι, καὶ πολὺ σοφωτέρων ἀνδρῶν ἢ τῶν νῦν. (Cf. *Or.* lvii. 11.)

[4] Lucian, *Demosth. encomium* 27 καὶ τῷ Διονύσῳ τὸ μὲν ποίησιν καινὴν ποιεῖν ἐκλέλειπται, τὰ δὲ προτέροις συντεθέντα τοῖς νῦν εἰς μέσον ἐν καιρῷ κομίζουσι χάριν οὐκ ἐλάττω φέρει; and *de salt.* 27 (the actor) μονῆς τῆς φωνῆς ὑπεύθυνον παρέχων ἑαυτόν· τὰ γὰρ ἄλλα τοῖς ποιηταῖς ἐμέλησε πρὸ πολλοῦ ποτε γενομένοις.

[5] Aristot. *Poet.* v. 1449ᵇ1 f. καὶ γὰρ χορὸν κωμῳδῶν ὀψέ ποτε ὁ ἄρχων ἔδωκεν, ἀλλ' ἐθελονταὶ ἦσαν.

[6] 'Suidas' s.v. Χιωνίδης· Ἀθηναῖος, κωμικὸς τῆς ἀρχαίας κωμῳδίας, ὃν καὶ λέγουσι πρωταγωνιστὴν γενέσθαι τῆς ἀρχαίας κωμῳδίας, διδάσκειν δὲ ἔτεσιν ὀκτὼ πρὸ τῶν Περσικῶν (i.e., if the reckoning is inclusive, 486 B.C.: see Capps, *Introd. of Comedy into the City Dionysia*, p. 9, and *Hesperia* 12 (1943), p. 10; and *Dith. Trag. Com.²*, p. 189). If contests in tragedy began in 502 B.C. (or earlier) Aristotle's ὀψέ ποτε would be sufficiently justified. (See above, p. 72.) Chionides and Magnes are coupled together by Aristotle, *Poet.* iii, in a context which implies that they were the first recognized Athenian comic poets. For πρωταγωνιστήν see Rees, *The Rule of Three Actors in the Classical Drama* (Chicago, 1908), pp. 31 ff., and below, pp. 132 ff.

[7] ἐδιδάχθη ἐπὶ ἄρχοντος Ἀμεινίου διὰ Φιλωνίδου ἐν τῇ πόλει ὀλυμπιάδι. β' ἦν. εἰς Λήναια. καὶ ἐνίκα πρῶτος Φιλωνίδης Προάγωνι. Λεύκων Πρέσβεσι τρίτος. Kanngiesser's emendation ἐν τῇ πθ' ὀλυμπιάδι ἔτει β' is highly probable; but if he is right in continuing καὶ ἐνίκα πρῶτος· Φιλωνίδης Προάγωνι δεύτερος (i.e. δεύ· omitted by haplography before Λεύκων), the case

to *Wasps* which is certainly corrupt and has never been emended in any way which commands agreement, but the possibility of such an exceptional occurrence cannot be absolutely ruled out. In 284 B.C. the didaskalic inscription (*I.G.* ii². 2319) records the obtaining of the second and third places, also at the Lenaia, by Diodorus, though some scholars prefer to suppose that there were two comic poets of that name.

The normal number of comic poets competing at both the Dionysia and the Lenaia during the Classical period appears to have been five,[1] except that, during part of the Peloponnesian War, it was reduced to three,[2] probably owing to financial depression in Athens and possibly also to save a day.[3] We have no evidence for the Lenaia after 284 B.C. when the number was still five,[4] but at the Dionysia in the late third century and in the second century six appears to have been the regular number.[5] The first performance of an old comedy, produced by an actor outside the competition, is recorded for the Dionysia in 339 B.C.,[6] and in 311[7] an old comedy appears as a regular part of the programme and so it continued through most of the second century B.C.[8] The extant inscriptional record comes to an end about 143 B.C., but new comedies (and old) doubtless continued to be produced at Athens, as they were elsewhere, to at least the first century of the Christian era.[9] In the second century B.C., however, the didaskalic inscription shows that the performance of comedies became irregular. There are several occasions on which the comic performance missed one year or two, and even one gap, 163–161 B.C., when there was no comic performance in three successive years.

for the production of two plays by Aristophanes (through Philonides) goes. But there are many other emendations, which are conveniently summarized in Starkie's edition of the *Wasps*, pp. 391–2. See most recently, Russo, *Aristofane*, pp. 191–5.

[1] This is proved for 434 B.C. by *I.G.* xiv. 1097, for 388 B.C. by the Argt. to Ar. *Plutus* (in neither case is the festival known), for the fourth century Dionysia by Aristot. *Ἀθ. Πολ.* lvi. 3, and for 311 B.C. by *I.G.* ii². 2323 a (probably Dionysia). Cf. also Hesychius s.v. μισθός (p. 90, n. 1).

[2] See Argts. to Ar. *Clouds*, *Peace*, and *Birds* for the Dionysia (423–414 B.C.), and to *Acharnians*, *Knights*, *Wasps*, and *Frogs* for the Lenaia (425–405 B.C.).

[3] See above, p. 66.   [4] *I.G.* ii². 2319 (p. 109).

[5] This fact is generally overlooked, but the year recorded at the end of column iii of *I.G.* ii². 2323 (p. 111) had six poets, the year in column i and the year 184–183 at least six. The current restorations which confine the years 170–169, 168–167, and 156–155 to five poets are not compulsory. (See now Snell, *Gött. Nachr.* 1966, p. 29, n. 6.)

[6] *I.G.* ii². 2318 ἐπὶ Θεοφράστου παλαιὸν δρᾶμα πρῶτον παρεδίδαξαν οἱ κωμῳδοί.

[7] Ibid. 2323a (the play was the Θησαυρός of Anaxandrides).

[8] Ibid. 2323. There was no old comedy at the Lenaia in 284 B.C. (ibid. 2319). An inscription of 254 B.C. (p. 123) records a contest of three old comedies in that year, but it is not certain to which festival it refers.

[9] A brief sketch of theatrical performances outside Athens from the third century onwards is given in *Theatre of D.* pp. 240–6. See also below, Chapter VII.

23. The choice of the poets to be allowed to compete at the Dionysia and Lenaia rested with the relevant archon.[1] To him the poets 'applied for a chorus' (χορὸν αἰτεῖν); on what principles or evidence he made his choice and assigned the chorus (χορὸν διδόναι) we are never told; but Cratinus[2] (who had himself been refused a comic chorus[3]) attacks an archon for preferring the dissolute poet Gnesippos to Sophocles. A passage of Plato's *Laws* (vii. 817 d) suggests that each poet read specimens of his work to the archon (νῦν οὖν, ὦ παῖδες . . . ἐπιδείξαντες τοῖς ἄρχουσι πρῶτον τὰς ὑμετέρας παρὰ τὰς ἡμετέρας ᾠδάς, ἂν μὲν τὰ αὐτά γε ἦ καὶ βελτίω τὰ παρ' ὑμῶν φαίνηται λεγόμενα, δώσομεν ὑμῖν χορόν, εἰ δὲ μή, ὦ φίλοι, οὐκ ἄν ποτε δυναίμεθα). There appears to have been no limit of age for tragic or comic poets.[4] Sophocles first produced a play when he was twenty-eight, Euripides when he was twenty-six, and Aristophanes first produced a comedy in his own name (*Knights*) when he was only about twenty and had already had three other plays produced in the name of Kallistratos. Much later, Menander put on a comedy while still an ἔφηβος,[5] and perhaps was the first to do so.

24. It was usual for a poet to produce his own plays, and there are very few exceptions among tragic poets. Aristophanes hints that Iophon was helped in his plays by his father Sophocles, but that is not quite the same thing.[6] In the fourth century, however, Aphareus won two Dionysiac victories with plays produced in the name of Dionysius and two Lenaian victories in other names.[7] But in comedy the practice was not infrequent. Aristophanes' *Banqueters*, *Babylonians*, *Acharnians*, and *Lysistrata* were produced by Kallistratos, his *Wasps* and *Frogs* by Philonides, his *Birds* by

---

[1] The phrase χορὸν ἔδωκεν is found in Aristot. *Poet.* v (see above, p. 82, n. 5). 'Suidas' gloss s.v. χορὸν δίδωμι is unintelligible. χορὸν αἰτεῖν occurs in Ar. *Knights* 513.

[2] Cratinus, Βουκόλοι, fr. 15 (K) ὃς οὐκ ἔδωκ' αἰτοῦντι Σοφοκλέει χορόν, | τῷ Κλεομάχου δ', ὃν οὐκ ἂν ἠξίουν ἐγὼ | ἐμοὶ διδάσκειν οὐδ' ἂν εἰς Ἀδώνια. (Κλεομάχου is Dobree's emendation for Κλεομάχῳ; cf. Cratinus, Ὧραι, fr. 256 ἴτω δὲ καὶ τραγῳδίας | ὁ Κλεομάχου διδάσκαλος | μετ' αὐτόν, ὁ παρατιλτριῶν | ἔχων χορὸν Λυδιστὶ τιλλουσῶν μέλη | πονηρά. Athen. xiv. 638 d shows that both fragments refer to Gnesippos.)

[3] Hesych. πυρπερέγχει· Κρατῖνος ἀπὸ διθυράμβου ἐν Βουκόλοις ἀρξάμενος, ἐπειδὴ χορὸν οὐκ ἔλαβε παρὰ τοῦ ἄρχοντος †ἔστιν οὗ ἠτήρειτ†. Emendations are uncertain.

[4] The statement of schol. on Ar. *Clouds* 510 (that a man under thirty was allowed μήτε δρᾶμα ἀναγινώσκειν ἐν θεάτρῳ μήτε δημηγορεῖν) is perhaps a reminiscence of the fourth-century rule that the choregos to a chorus of boys must be over forty. Anyhow the poet did not 'read his play in the theatre'.

[5] Anon. *de Com.* (Kaibel, p. 9) ἐδίδαξε δὲ πρῶτος ἔφηβος ὢν ἐπὶ †Διοκλέους ἄρχοντος. The emendation πρῶτον seems hardly necessary, though commonly accepted. *I.G.* ii². 2323 a records that a poet (probably Ameinias) ἔφηβος ὢν ἐνεμήθη in 311 B.C.

[6] Ar. *Frogs* 73–79; with schol. which at most records a suspicion.

[7] [Plut.] *Vit. X Orat.* 839 d ἀρξάμενος δ' ἀπὸ Λυσιστράτου διδάσκειν ἄχρι Σωσιγένους ἐν ἔτεσιν εἰκοσιοκτὼ διδασκαλίας ἀστικὰς καθῆκεν ἓξ καὶ δὶς ἐνίκησε διὰ Διονυσίου, καθεὶς καὶ δι' ἑτέρων ἑτέρας δύο Ληναϊκάς. (369–368 to 342–341.)

one or other of these two friends, and his last two plays, Κώκαλος and
Αἰολοσίκων, by his son Araros, whom he desired to commend to the spectators.[1] The *Autolycus* of Eupolis was produced by Demostratos,[2] and in
the fourth century Philippus, son of Aristophanes, brought out plays for
Eubulus.[3] There is no reason to suppose that there was any concealment in
these cases, except possibly in that of Araros, and even the sale of plays to
others by Plato (the comic poet) to relieve his poverty was admitted by
himself in his *Peisandros*.[4] *Wasps*, though produced by Philonides, contains
words (1016 ff.) which are obviously spoken by Aristophanes on his own
behalf.

A poet's reason for employing someone else to produce his plays may
have been (as with Aristophanes) the natural diffidence of a young man,[5]
or the realization that composition and production may well require
different qualifications. Kallistratos may have had special experience,
and a good poet may often have been glad to escape the labour of teaching his performers and rehearsing his play, with all the attendant business.

Where, as in the case of plays brought out for Aristophanes by Kallistratos and Philonides, there was no concealment, it is natural that the
prize should go to the real composer of the play and that he should be
recorded as the victor, and (after long and keen controversy on the subject) it now seems clear that it is the real poet, not his deputy, whose
name appears in extant inscriptions. For the fourth century this is certain;
Aphareus, whose only two victories were won in the name of Dionysius,
is himself credited with these in the list of poets victorious at the Dionysia,[6]
and the inscription recording the places taken by Anaxandrides' plays[7]
mentions one produced for him by Anaxippus.[8] For the fifth century,
the name of Aristophanes is restored with practical certainty in the list
of victors at the Dionysia between those of Hermippus and Eupolis,[9] it

---

[1] Argt. iv to Ar. *Plut.* καὶ τὸν υἱὸν αὑτοῦ συστῆσαι Ἀραρότα δι' αὑτῆς τοῖς θεαταῖς βουλόμενος,
τὰ ὑπόλοιπα δύο δι' ἐκείνου καθῆκε, Κώκαλον καὶ Αἰολοσίκωνα.

[2] Athen. v. 216 d.   [3] *Vit. Aristoph.* (*Proleg.*, xiii, ed. Dindorf).

[4] Fr. 99 (K); see 'Suid.' s.v. Ἀρκάδας μιμούμενοι, and other refs. given by Kock. (The
Arkadians were proverbially said to have won military victories for others but never for
themselves.)   [5] See Ar. *Knights* 512–14; *Clouds* 528–31.

[6] *I.G.* ii². 2325.   [7] *I.G.* xiv. 1098.   [8] Or possibly Dioxippus.

[9] *I.G.* ii². 2325. Hermippus' first Dionysiac victory was won in 435 (ibid. 2318) and that
of Eupolis in 424, and Aristophanes' first victory (on which his place in the list depends)
was doubtless with the *Babylonians* produced by Kallistratos in 426. These instances seem
sufficient for the lists of victorious poets, where the interests of the compilers may be supposed
to have been purely literary; no such conclusion is possible for the didaskaliai, which may
have followed the official record more closely. For the controversy see especially Capps, *Am.
J. Phil.* 28 (1907), pp. 89 ff., and *Hesperia* 12 (1943), p. 3; W. A. Dittmer, *Fragments of Athenian
Comic Didaskaliae found in Rome*, pp. 44–46, 51–53; Geissler, *Chronologie*, pp. 2 ff.; Oellacher in
Wiener Stud. 38 (1916), pp. 101 ff.; Wilhelm, *U.D.A.*, pp. 107, etc.; Jachmann, *de Aristotelis
didascaliis*, pp. 8 ff.

being now proved that the first victory of Aristomenes, the other candidate for the place, fell much later.

It still, of course, remains possible that the official record of the archon may have entered the name of the producer, and that the producer may have formally received the prize (though it may be doubted whether he would have been allowed to retain it); and in that case the compilers of the records for our inscriptions, at a later date, may have corrected the archon's entries by substituting the names of the actual poets; but there is no evidence that it was so. After the death of Aeschylus the Athenian people gave permission for the continued production of his plays, and this may have been the point of his claim in Aristophanes' *Frogs* (866 ff.) that his poetry had not died with him like that of Euripides. Late writers imply that such productions were in competition with those of living poets,[1] but there is no trace of this in the extant records. If in some lists, Athenian or Alexandrian, such victories were entered in his own name, and in others in that of the producer, this might account for the fact that while his *Vita* says that he won thirteen victories (all Dionysiac, since tragic contests at the Lenaia had not begun in his lifetime) 'Suidas' says that some credited him with twenty-eight.

25. The appointment of the choregoi, upon whom the success of the poets' work in the competition might largely depend,[2] was one of the first duties of the archon eponymos on entering upon office.[3] At some date in the fourth century (before the composition of Aristotle's *Constitution of Athens* in 325 B.C. or thereabouts) the appointment of choregoi for comedy was transferred to the tribes. The expense of the choregia, as will be explained shortly, might be very heavy, and the duty was a λητουργία laid upon the richest citizens in turn. Any citizen so called upon might demand that another whom he considered better able to discharge the duty should do so, or else exchange property with himself; or he might claim to be excused, e.g. on the ground that he was already discharging another λητουργία or for some other sufficient reason. Such questions were settled by the archon. But it was not always easy to find

---

[1] Philostr. *Vit. Apoll.* vi. 11 ὅθεν Ἀθηναῖοι πατέρα μὲν αὐτὸν τῆς τραγῳδίας ἡγοῦντο, ἐκάλουν δὲ καὶ τεθνεῶτα ἐς Διονύσια, τὰ γὰρ τοῦ Αἰσχύλου ψηφισαμένων ἀνεδιδάσκετο καὶ ἐνίκα ἐκ καινῆς; cf. *Vit. Aesch.* 12 Ἀθηναῖοι δὲ τοσοῦτον ἠγάπησαν Αἰσχύλον ὡς ψηφίσασθαι μετὰ θάνατον αὐτοῦ τὸν βουλόμενον διδάσκειν τὰ Αἰσχύλου χορὸν λαμβάνειν. So in Ar. *Ach.* 9–12 (over thirty years after Aeschylus' death) Dikaiopolis (probably at the Proagon) is expecting the name of Aeschylus to be called, and is annoyed at being put off with Theognis.

[2] See above, pp. 75 ff., where this is emphasized in relation to dithyramb. (Choregoi for dithyramb were appointed by the tribes.)

[3] Aristot. *Ἀθ. Πολ.* lvi. 3 ἔπειτα χορηγοὺς τραγῳδοῖς καθίστησι τρεῖς ἐξ ἁπάντων Ἀθηναίων τοὺς πλουσιωτάτους· πρότερον δὲ καὶ κωμῳδοῖς καθίστη πέντε, νῦν δὲ τούτοις αἱ φυλαὶ φέρουσι. The archon then τὰς ἀντιδόσεις ποιεῖ καὶ τὰς σκήψεις εἰσ⟨άγει?⟩.

a sufficient number of choregoi,[1] and at one moment of financial stress, in the year 406–405 B.C., the duties of each choregos, both in tragedy and comedy, were divided between two synchoregoi[2]—an arrangement of which we have already noticed instances in the records of Rural Dionysia. This expedient was probably confined to the one year—at least there is no hint of anything further—and to the Dionysia, and Capps has made it clear that the inscription *I.G.* ii[2]. 2318 can best be reconstructed, as regards the relevant columns, on this supposition.[3] Lysias' client in his 21st oration was choregos, not synchoregos, for comedy in 402 B.C., and the inscription just quoted attests the existence of choregia, not synchoregia, from 398 to 329 B.C.[4]

26. It might happen that a public-spirited citizen volunteered to bear the expense of a tragic or comic chorus (as Demosthenes undertook that of a dithyramb).[5] The client of Lysias, who has just been mentioned, undertook eight choruses in nine years, and his speech[6] gives some valuable information as to the expense involved—30 minae for choregia in tragedy and 20 minae for a men's chorus at the Thargelia in 410, 50 minae for a dithyrambic chorus of men (and the erection of the tripod)

---

[1] See above (in reference to dithyramb), p. 75.

[2] Schol. on Ar. *Frogs* 404 ἔοικε δὲ παρεμφαίνειν ὅτι λιτῶς ἤδη ἐχορηγεῖτο τοῖς ποιηταῖς. ἐπὶ γοῦν τοῦ Καλλίου τούτου φησὶν Ἀριστοτέλης ὅτι σύνδυο ἔδοξε χορηγεῖν τὰ Διονύσια τοῖς τραγῳδοῖς καὶ κωμῳδοῖς· ὥστε ἴσως ἦν τις καὶ περὶ τὸν Ληναϊκὸν ἀγῶνα συστολή. (It should be noticed that this is only a conjecture by the scholiast, and that there is no other evidence to support it.) χρόνῳ δ' ὕστερον οὐ πολλῷ τινι καὶ καθάπαξ περιεῖλε Κινησίας τὰς χορηγίας· ἐξ οὗ καὶ Στράττις ἐν τῷ εἰς αὐτὸν δράματι ἔφη "σκηνὴ μὲν τοῦ χοροκτόνου Κινησίου". What Kinesias is supposed to have done does not appear, but the epithet 'murderer of choruses' probably refers to the badness of his poetry, not to any action connected with choregia, and that he took any such action may easily be a false inference by the scholiast or his authority. Certainly Kinesias did not 'abolish' choregia for good, as Aristotle's Ἀθ. Πολ. lvi. 3 proves, but he may have initiated some hostile action—cf. schol. on *Frogs* 153 ὁ Κινησίας ἐπραγματεύσατο κατὰ τῶν κωμικῶν ὡς εἶεν ἀχορήγητοι.

[3] *Hesperia* 12 (1943), pp. 5–8. It has commonly been stated that synchoregia must have continued until 401 B.C. at least, on the strength of an inscription from Eleusis (*I.G.* ii[2]. 3090; see above, pp. 47 f.) which runs: [Γ]νᾶθις Τιμοκήδους Ἀναξανδρίδης Τιμαγόρου | χορηγοῦντες κωμῳδοῖς ἐνίκων | Ἀριστοφάνης ἐδίδασκεν | ἑτέρα νίκη τραγῳδοῖς | Σοφοκλῆς ἐδίδασκεν. Jachmann, Körte, Kirchner, and others have assumed that the inscription refers to the City Dionysia and to the younger Sophocles, who produced his father's *Oedipus Coloneus* in 401 B.C. (Argt. Oed. Col.). But the inscription seems obviously to be one of a number of records of Rural Dionysia, at which synchoregia seems not to have been uncommon (e.g. *I.G.* ii[2]. 1198, 1200, 3092, 3095, 3096—of which the last two record *three* synchoregoi at Rural Dionysia; see above, pp. 48 ff.). Further, Wilhelm is certain that this inscription is shown by the script to be earlier than 406–405 B.C. Accordingly there is no obstacle to Capps's view (op. cit., p. 8) that synchoregia was only in force for the one year 406–405 B.C.

[4] So do *I.G.* ii[2]. 3042 (334 B.C.), 3055, and 3056 (319 B.C.). The explanation of the dropping of the chorus in Aristophanes' later days by the unwillingness of choregoi to come forward, as given by Platonius and in the *Life* of Aristophanes, is probably not more than guess-work. (Kaibel, p. 5, and Dübner, *Proleg. de Com.*, pp. xiii, xxviii.) Cf. *Theatre of D.*, pp. 160–7, and Maidment's discussion in *C.Q.* 29 (1935), pp. 1 ff.

[5] See above, p. 75.   [6] Lysias xxi. 1–5.

in 409, more than 15 minae for a boys' chorus in 404, 16 minae for a
comedy in 402, besides expenditure at other festivals. Another client of
Lysias[1] gives the cost of two tragic choregiai about 392 B.C. as 50 minae.
At a later date Demosthenes[2] says that it was common knowledge that
a men's chorus was much more expensive than a tragic; this may have
been mainly because of the larger number of singers,[3] and also, perhaps,
because of the temptation to extravagant ostentation which dithyramb
seems to have offered.[4] But a good deal evidently depended upon the
ambition or generosity of the choregos himself, who might be either liberal
or mean in the matter of costumes, or in supplying many or few mute
characters to form a retinue for the chief persons in the play, and so on.
Nikias is said by Plutarch[5] to have won popularity by his lavish expenditure as choregos, and never to have failed to win the prize. It was possible
to hire second-hand costumes,[6] but there were apparently limits to extravagance set by good taste. Aristotle treats an over-showy treatment
of a comic chorus as characteristic of the βάναυσος.[7] Plutarch[8] tells a story
of an actor who refused to appear unless the choregos gave him the
retinue befitting the part of a queen; Melanthios the choregos shouted
to him that a single maidservant was retinue enough for the wife of
Phokion, and that he should not give himself airs.

The chief expense which fell upon the choregos was that of the training
of the chorus, including the provision of costumes and the payment of
salaries to the singers in the chorus and to their trainer, and probably
(for tragedy and comedy, though not for dithyramb)[9] to the flute player
also; and he doubtless had the deciding voice in the provision of any
special effects which might be required.[10] It is probable that the choregos
was also responsible for such additional choruses as that of the huntsmen
in the prologue of *Hippolytus*, the προπομποί in *Eumenides*, and the shepherds in Euripides' *Alexandros*, and in comedy the chorus of frogs in

---

[1] Lysias xix. 29, 42.   [2] *Meid.* 156.
[3] Though each tragic chorus (and choregos) had to serve for a whole tetralogy (see Argt.
to Aesch. *Agam.*).   [4] See above, p. 77.   [5] *Nik.* 3. 2–3.
[6] Pollux vii. 78 τοὺς δὲ τὰς ἐσθῆτας ἀπομισθοῦντας τοῖς χορηγοῖς οἱ μὲν νέοι ἱματιομίσθας
ἐκάλουν, οἱ δὲ παλαιοὶ ἱματιομισθωτάς.
[7] *Eth. Nic.* 1123ᵃ20 ἐν γὰρ τοῖς μικροῖς τῶν δαπανημάτων πολλὰ ἀναλίσκει καὶ λαμπρύνεται
παρὰ μέλος, οἷον ἐρανιστὰς γαμικῶς ἑστιῶν, καὶ κωμῳδοῖς χορηγῶν ἐν τῇ παρόδῳ πορφύραν εἰσφέρων, ὥσπερ οἱ Μεγαρεῖς. (It is not quite clear to what Aristotle refers.) Cf. Antiphanes, fr. 204.
5 (K).   [8] Plut. *Phok.* 19. 2–3.
[9] In dithyramb also the flute player was paid by the poet until about the middle of the
fifth century ([id.] *de Mus.* xxx. 1141 d, and see above, pp. 75 f.). Athen. xiv. 617 b records that
both singers and flute players were μισθοφόροι in the time of Pratinas (αὐλητῶν καὶ χορευτῶν
μισθοφόρων κατεχόντων τὰς ὀρχήστρας), though it is not stated who paid them.
[10] Demosthenes' feigned dream (Plut. *Dem.* 29. 2, quoted above, p. 77, n. 5) illustrates the
possibility of the failure of an actor through want of χορηγία.

Aristophanes' play, though—as Haigh suggests—the latter, and the huntsmen's chorus in the *Hippolytus*, may have been sung behind the scenes by members of the regular chorus, while mute figures appeared before the spectators.[1] But in fact we hear less of any meanness on the part of choregoi than of pride in the generous carrying out of an important public service, and the sanctity attached to the holder of the office, even though in some cases there seems to have been some thought of solidifying political and personal positions by conspicuous expenditure.[2] Inefficiency may, however, be inferred from a fragment of Eupolis,[3] εἶδες χορηγὸν πώποτε ῥυπαρώτερον τοῦδε; The thorough training of a dramatic chorus was evidently regarded as a matter of some public importance, apart from its artistic attraction. Athenaeus,[4] speaking of the latter half of the fifth century B.C., says:

ἦν γὰρ τὸ τῆς ὀρχήσεως γένος τῆς ἐν τοῖς χοροῖς εὔσχημον τότε καὶ μεγαλοπρεπὲς καὶ ὡσανεὶ τὰς ἐν τοῖς ὅπλοις κινήσεις ἀπομιμούμενον. ὅθεν καὶ Σωκράτης ἐν τοῖς ποιήμασιν τοὺς κάλλιστα χορεύοντας ἀρίστους φησὶν εἶναι τὰ πολέμια, λέγων οὕτως·

οἳ δὲ χοροῖς κάλλιστα θεοὺς τιμῶσιν, ἄριστοι
ἐν πολέμῳ.

σχεδὸν γὰρ ὥσπερ ἐξοπλισία τις ἦν ἡ χορεία καὶ ἐπίδειξις οὐ μόνον τῆς λοιπῆς εὐταξίας ἀλλὰ καὶ τῆς τῶν σωμάτων ἐπιμελείας.

The scholiast on Aristophanes' *Clouds* (l. 339) says that the description of a huge feast in that passage τείνει πρός τε τοὺς παρὰ τοῖς χορηγοῖς ἐστιωμένους καὶ πρὸς τοὺς ἐν πρυτανείῳ ἀεὶ δειπνοῦντας, and this may refer to the good living of a chorus in training.[5] There is, however, a reference in Aristophanes' *Acharnians*[6] to the failure of Antimachus to feast his chorus at the end of the Lenaia. There was probably a customary banquet given by the choregos to his chorus after the Dionysia, though the only banquet recorded is that given by Agathon after the Lenaia as a successful poet, and that was probably quite unofficial.

---

[1] It is sometimes stated by modern writers that any additional provision made by a choregos over and above what was normally expected of him was termed παραχορήγημα. The meaning of this word is discussed below (p. 137); in its few occurrences it seems to mean simply a special or additional provision (χορηγεῖν in its secondary sense of 'supply') without any necessary reference to a χορηγός in the technical sense.

[2] Lysias xxv. 13 καίτοι διὰ τοῦτο πλείω τῶν ὑπὸ τῆς πόλεως προσταττομένων ἐδαπανώμην, ἵνα καὶ βελτίων ὑφ' ὑμῶν νομιζοίμην, καὶ εἴ πού μοί τις συμφορὰ γένοιτο, ἄμεινον ἀγωνιζοίμην. Cf. Lysias xxi. 11–12, Dem. *de F.L.* 282.

[3] Fr. 306 (K) And for meanness in the case of dithyramb see Isaeus, *Or.* v. 36 (and above, p. 77).   [4] xiv. 628 e–f.

[5] For the luxury of a dithyrambic chorus, see above, p. 77.

[6] 1153–5 ὅς γ' ἐμὲ τὸν τλήμονα Λήναια χορηγῶν ἀπέλυσ' ἄδειπνον. See on this, Dover, *Maia* N.S. 15 (1963), p. 23.

It does not appear that the choregos had any expense in connexion with the actors proper, nor is there any indication that he was responsible for their costumes, as he was for those of the chorus. The honorarium paid to each poet, whether successful or not, as well as the prize given to the victorious poet, was also the affair of the state. (The amounts of these are unknown, but the allusions[1] to the cutting down of the payments to comic poets seem to imply that such payments were made, and could be altered, by the Assembly. What prizes were given for the victors besides the ivy crown is unknown.)

Little material exists for investigating the problem of how far the choregos actually concerned himself with the content of the play, but this is an aspect which should not be overlooked. The thesis of Couat[2] that poets of Old Comedy wrote to suit the wishes of rich and anti-democratic archons or choregoi is too simple-minded to be true, and is more or less directly confuted by the attitude of the Old Oligarch.[3] Nevertheless, there is evidence to suggest that at least Phrynichos and Aeschylus were from time to time associated with choregoi, Themistocles and Pericles, with whom they may have been in political sympathy, and whose political aims their plays may have been partly designed to serve.[4] But we have no name of a choregos for Euripides, one fragmentary name for Sophocles, and in 458 B.C., when Aeschylus produced the Oresteia, which certainly has political implications, we have the name of the choregos, Xenokles of Aphidna,[5] but know nothing of him.

27. By the middle of the fourth century, if not before, there was probably a class of professional singers from whom the choregos chose; Aristotle notes that tragic and comic choruses might consist of the same persons.[6] But once selected, they had to be trained. The trainer (χοροδιδάσκαλος) had to be a citizen, though there were exceptions such as that of Sannio, who had been disfranchised but evidently continued his

---

[1] Ar. *Frogs* 367 ἢ τοὺς μισθοὺς τῶν ποιητῶν ῥήτωρ ὢν εἶτ' ἀποτρώγει. (The schol. says that the reference is to the reduction of the poets' payments by Archinus and Agyrrhius.) Cf. Hesych. s.v. μισθός· τὸ ἔπαθλον τῶν κωμικῶν . . . ἔμμισθοι δὲ πέντε ἦσαν. In the dithyrambic contests instituted by Lycurgus in honour of Poseidon in the Peiraeus, the prizes for the choruses placed first, second, and third were to be 10, 8, and 6 minae. (Plut. *Mor.* 842 a.)

[2] *Aristophane et l'ancienne comédie attique*, pp. 38–43.

[3] Ps.-Xen., *Ath. Pol.* ii. 18 κωμῳδεῖν δ' αὖ καὶ κακῶς λέγειν τὸν μὲν δῆμον οὐκ ἐῶσιν, ἵνα μὴ αὐτοὶ ἀκούωσι κακῶς· ἰδίᾳ δὲ κελεύουσιν, εἴ τίς τινα βούλεται, εὖ εἰδότες ὅτι οὐχὶ τοῦ δήμου ἔσται οὐδὲ τοῦ πλήθους ὁ κωμῳδούμενος ὡς ἐπὶ τὸ πολύ, ἀλλ' ἢ πλούσιος ἢ γενναῖος ἢ δυνάμενος. ὀλίγοι δέ τινες τῶν πενήτων καὶ τῶν δημοτικῶν κωμῳδοῦνται. Cf. also Gomme, *C.R.* 52 (1938), pp. 97 ff. (*More Essays in Greek History and Literature*, pp. 70 ff.)

[4] See Forrest, *C.Q.*, n.s. 10 (1960), pp. 235–40.

[5] Below, p. 104.

[6] Aristot. *Pol.* iii. 3. 1276ᵇ. It may be assumed that the selection of the chorus rested with the choregos; see above, p. 76.

career as a trainer of choruses for tragedy.[1] The earliest generation of dramatic poets taught their own choruses, inventing the dances as they required; and both Phrynichos and Aeschylus were famous for their skill in this.[2] Aeschylus also employed the services of 'Telestes', whom Athenaeus describes both as χοροδιδάσκαλος[3] and as ὁ Αἰσχύλου ὀρχηστής,[4] and as having special skill in regard to the movements of his hands and in realistic imitation. Plutarch[5] tells how Euripides rebuked a man who showed his amusement when the poet was singing over to his chorus one of his odes written in the mixolydian mode.

A trainer employed by a poet (who was himself the διδάσκαλος in the strict sense) might be termed ὑποδιδάσκαλος.[6] But the training of choruses no doubt became a professional business in time, and the professional trainers usurped the title of διδάσκαλος with no sign of subordination, except perhaps at Athens where they may still have been called ὑποδιδάσκαλοι, even when producing an old play, out of respect for the original composer.

The disciplining of the dramatic choruses, as distinct from their training, is stated by 'Suidas'[7] to have been the task of specially elected officials. Some may be tempted to connect this with a statement of Athenaeus[8] that the chorus were given drinks both before and after their performance.

28. During the régime of Demetrius of Phalerum at Athens (317–307 B.C.), the choregia was abolished, and the Dionysian festival placed under the management of an agonothetes elected annually and provided with funds for the performance of his duties. The exact date of the change is unknown. The old belief that it occurred immediately after

---

[1] Dem. Meid. 58.

[2] Athen. i. 22 a φασὶ δὲ καὶ ὅτι οἱ ἀρχαῖοι ποιηταί, Θέσπις, Πρατίνας, [Κρατῖνος], Φρύνιχος, ὀρχησταὶ ἐκαλοῦντο διὰ τὸ μὴ μόνον τὰ ἑαυτῶν δράματα ἀναφέρειν εἰς ὄρχησιν τοῦ χοροῦ, ἀλλὰ καὶ ἔξω τῶν ἰδίων ποιημάτων διδάσκειν τοὺς βουλομένους ὀρχεῖσθαι; Athen. i. 21 d, e καὶ Αἰσχύλος δὲ ... πολλὰ σχήματα ὀρχηστικὰ αὐτὸς ἐξευρίσκων ἀνεδίδου τοῖς χορευταῖς. Χαμαιλέων γοῦν πρῶτον αὐτόν φησι σχηματίσαι τοὺς χοροὺς ὀρχηστοδιδασκάλοις οὐ χρησάμενον, ἀλλὰ καὶ αὐτὸν τοῖς χοροῖς τὰ σχήματα ποιοῦντα τῶν ὀρχήσεων. Cf. Plut. Quaest. Conv. viii. 9. 732 f καίτοι καὶ Φρύνιχος ὁ τῶν τραγῳδιῶν ποιητὴς περὶ αὐτοῦ φησιν ὅτι ''σχήματα δ' ὄρχησις τόσα μοι πόρεν, ὅσσ' ἐνὶ πόντῳ | κύματα ποιεῖται χείματι νὺξ ὀλοή''.

[3] Athen. i. 21 f.

[4] Ibid. 22 a Τελέστης ὁ Αἰσχύλου ὀρχηστὴς οὕτως ἦν τεχνίτης ὥστε ἐν τῷ ὀρχεῖσθαι τοὺς Ἑπτὰ ἐπὶ Θήβας φανερὰ ποιῆσαι τὰ πράγματα δι' ὀρχήσεως. (See below, pp. 248 f., 251.)

[5] De Audiendo 46 b.

[6] Phot. s.v. ὑποδιδάσκαλος· ὁ τῷ χορῷ καταλέγων· διδάσκαλος γὰρ ὁ ποιητής, ὡς Ἀριστοφάνης. Cf. Plato, Ion 536 a, and below, pp. 291, 303 f.

[7] 'Suid.' s.v. ἐπιμεληταί· ἐπιμεληταὶ ἐχειροτονοῦντο τῶν χορῶν ὡς μὴ ἀτακτεῖν τοὺς χοροὺς ἐν τοῖς θεάτροις. (Cf. Xen. Hiero ix. 4.)

[8] xi. 464 f. καὶ τοῖς χοροῖς εἰσιοῦσιν ἐνέχεον (sc. οἱ Ἀθηναῖοι) πίνειν, καὶ διηγωνισμένοις, ὅτε ἐξεπορεύοντο, ἐνέχεον πάλιν. (Philochorus F 171, quoted in full, p. 272, n. 4.)

the death of Antipater in 319 B.C. rests on a misinterpretation of a passage in Plutarch's life of Phokion,[1] where the title is used in a general sense and without special reference to the Dionysia. Inscriptions of 319 B.C. show that choregia was still in existence in that year,[2] and on the other hand the monument of Xenokles in 306 B.C.[3] was erected by him as agonothetes and begins with the words ὁ δῆμος ἐχορήγει. It refers to the Lenaia, but it is unlikely that the new system was not applied at the same time to the City Dionysia. Demetrius probably instituted it while nomothetes in 316–315 B.C.[4]

The reason for the change may have been simply the burdensomeness of the choregia, falling upon a smaller number of men than formerly, and those poorer than rich men had been in earlier days;[5] a similar change was probably made for other festivals, both literary and gymnastic, the supervision of the performances being for most purposes transferred to an agonothetes.[6] But that the archon and the ἐπιμεληταί retained some of their functions at the Dionysia even after the institution of the agonothetes is shown by inscriptions already quoted in another context.[7]

---

[1] 31. 3 ὁ δὲ (sc. Φωκίων) τούτων μὲν οὐκ ἐφρόντιζεν, ἐντυγχάνων δὲ τῷ Νικάνορι καὶ διαλεγόμενος εἴς τε τἆλλα τοῖς Ἀθηναίοις πρᾷον αὐτὸν καὶ κεχαρισμένον παρεῖχε, καὶ φιλοτιμίας τινὰς ἔπεισε καὶ δαπάνας ὑποστῆναι γενόμενον ἀγωνοθέτην. Nicanor undertook the expense of various festivals, but this does not mean that he was elected official ἀγωνοθέτης of the Dionysia.

[2] See above, pp. 78 f.

[3] I.G. ii². 3073; see Appendix, p. 120.

[4] Marmor Parium, B 13; Dow and Travis, Hesperia 12 (1943), pp. 144 ff. The statement of Ferguson, Hellenistic Athens, p. 57, that Demetrius transferred the contests of Homeric rhapsodists from the Panathenaia to the Dionysia goes beyond the evidence of Athen. xiv. 620 b τοὺς δὲ νῦν Ὁμηριστὰς ὀνομαζομένους πρῶτος εἰς τὰ θέατρα παρήγαγε Δημήτριος ὁ Φαληρεύς. At a later date the Διονύσου τεχνῖται included professional reciters of epic, but not necessarily at the Dionysia.

[5] As early as 356 B.C. the law of Leptines seems to have attempted some reform, since it began ὅπως ἂν οἱ πλουσιώτατοι λητουργῶσι (Dem. in Lept. 127, cf. 18), though Demosthenes treats fears of shortage as exaggerated (ibid. 22), an attitude which his own later experience rebuts (see above, p. 75). For the general political background of these changes see Ferguson, op. cit., ch. ii, and Tarn, in C.A.H. vi, pp. 495 ff. The changes were not reversed when the democracy was restored in 307 B.C. Demetrius of Phalerum as a Peripatetic may have shared Aristotle's objection to χορηγίαι and certain other liturgies (Aristot. Pol. viii (v). 1309ᵃ13 ff. and 1320ᵇ4), as tending to dissipate the funds in the hands of the rich with no corresponding benefit to the state.

[6] The documents relating to the agonothetes of the Dionysia in the third century B.C. are I.G. ii². 649 (= Dinsmoor, Archons of Athens, pp. 7 f.), 657, 682, 780, 798 (= Hesperia 4 (1935), p. 583), 834, 3073–88, 3458, and Hesperia 7 (1938), p. 116 (p. 123 here). It is clear that the agonothetes had responsibility for a number of festivals (probably at least the Dionysia, Lenaia, and Thargelia) and might be involved in considerable expense (Eurykleides spent 7 talents in the 230s; I.G. ii². 834). Ferguson, Klio 8 (1908), pp. 345 ff., argued that the Panathenaia had a separate agonothetes from the beginning, but in 240 (I.G. ii². 784) the conduct of the Panathenaia was still in the hands of athlothetai, and the separate agonothetes of the Panathenaia is not attested till (?) 228 B.C. (I.G. ii². 1705).

[7] p. 70 above.

When Hadrian was in Athens in A.D. 126 he performed the office of agonothetes with distinction.[1]

29. As regards the choice of actors in tragedy and comedy, four periods seem to be distinguishable:

(1) Originally the poet acted in his own play,[2] and this is particularly recorded of Thespis. That Aeschylus also acted in person, whether only before or also after he introduced a second actor (as he had already done in the earliest extant plays), is at least probable.[3] So too, in his early plays, did Sophocles. Cratinus may have acted in his own comedies.[4]

(2) The poet employed professional actors, selected by himself. So Aeschylus employed Kleandros and afterwards Mynniskos as second and third actors.[5] Sophocles regularly employed Tlepolemos,[6] and was said to have had the special capacities of his actors in view in composing his plays.[7] The *Life* of Euripides states that Kephisophon acted for Euripides, but only on the authority of Thomas Magister, which carries no weight.[8] In comedy Krates was said to have acted in the plays of Cratinus[9] before he composed plays on his own account, and Pherekrates in those of Krates.[10]

(3) Three protagonists for tragedy were chosen by the state—it is not known how, but presumably by the archon—and allocated by lot to the poets. It is natural to connect this change with the introduction of prizes for actors, in tragedy at the Dionysia certainly in 449 B.C. and at the Lenaia possibly about 440 B.C., though there is no direct evidence about this and the change may have come later, perhaps even in the fourth century. In tragedy at least, the actor who won the prize was entitled to be one of the three competitors in the following year.[11] There

---

[1] *I.G.* ii². 1105 Bb, l. 15, and Dio Cass. lxix. 16 τά τε Διονύσια τὴν μεγίστην παρ' αὐτοῖς ἀρχὴν ἄρξας ἐν τῇ ἐσθῆτι τῇ ἐπιχωρίῳ λαμπρῶς ἐπετέλεσε. (For the combination of archonship and agonothesia in this period, cf. above, p. 74, n. 7).

[2] Aristot. *Rhet.* iii. 1. 1403ᵇ23 f. ὑπεκρίνοντο γὰρ αὐτοὶ τὰς τραγῳδίας οἱ ποιηταὶ τὸ πρῶτον; Plut. *Solon* 29. ὁ Σόλων . . . ἐθεάσατο τὸν Θέσπιν αὐτὸν ὑποκρινόμενον, ὥσπερ ἔθος ἦν τοῖς παλαιοῖς.

[3] He must have done so, if the statement in *Vit. Soph.* 4, that Sophocles was the first to abandon the practice, is correct (πρῶτον μὲν καταλύσας τὴν ὑπόκρισιν τοῦ ποιητοῦ διὰ τὴν ἰδίαν μικροφωνίαν). For Sophocles' acting, see below, p. 130, n. 4.

[4] This may perhaps be inferred from Athen. i. 22a, if he is not a dittography here.

[5] *Vit. Aesch.* 15 ἐχρήσατο δ' ὑποκριτῇ πρώτῳ μὲν Κλεάνδρῳ, ἔπειτα καὶ τὸν δεύτερον αὐτῷ προσῆψε Μυννίσκον τὸν Χαλκιδέα· τὸν δὲ τρίτον ὑποκριτὴν αὐτὸς ἐξεῦρεν, ὡς δὲ Δικαίαρχος ὁ Μεσσήνιος, Σοφοκλῆς. See below, p. 131, and Wilamowitz, *Aesch. Trag.*, p. 5, note ad loc.

[6] Schol. Ar. *Clouds* 1267.

[7] Istros, quoted in *Vit. Soph.* 6. See A. S. Owen in *Greek Poetry and Life*, pp. 148 ff.

[8] Other references to Kephisophon say nothing of his having been an actor.

[9] Schol. Ar. *Knights* 537; Anon. *de Com.* (Kaibel), p. 7.

[10] Ibid., p. 8.

[11] Hesych., 'Suid.', and Phot. s.v. νεμήσεις ὑποκριτῶν· οἱ ποιηταὶ ἐλάμβανον τρεῖς ὑποκριτὰς

is less certainty about the method of selection of comic actors. In the third quarter of the fourth century Lycurgus is said[1] to have revived a contest of comic actors at the Χύτροι, the victor in which had the right to act at the ensuing Dionysia, but this only provided for one of the five protagonists, and when or how long this method had previously been in vogue is unknown; nor is it possible to say how comic actors were chosen for the Lenaia—where the comic actors' prize was probably instituted about 442 B.C.—or for the Dionysia generally either from the beginning or from the institution of the prize for comic actors between 329 and 312 B.C. But there is no reason to doubt that each poet received his actor by lot. Under the system in vogue for tragedy, the actor allocated to each poet probably acted in all four of his plays. The didaskalic inscription[2] shows that at the Lenaia in 418 B.C. both the tragedies presented by each of the two rival poets were acted by Lysikrates and Kallippides respectively, and the same system was probably applied to the Dionysia. But later, as the poets themselves became less famous than the great three had been and actors developed greater professional skill, it was obviously felt that it was not fair to give one poet the advantage of the best actor in all his plays, and the system was changed.

(4) Three tragic actors were chosen as before, but each acted in a single tragedy of each poet, so that in 341, when Astydamas, Euaretos, and Aphareus each competed with three tragedies at the Dionysia, each had the services of the three protagonists, Thettalos, Neoptolemos, and Athenodoros, each in one play.[3] It was shortly after this that Aristotle stated that the actors were now more important than the poets.[4]

It may be presumed that the five comic actors selected were still assigned to the poets by lot, but at a late period we occasionally find the same actor serving two poets. So in 311 B.C. Asklepiodoros acted for Philippides and Ameinias, and in 155 Damon played not only for both Chairion and Biottos but also in the old play which preceded the competition, while Kallikrates acted for both Philokles and Timoxenos. (Cf. also 284 B.C.)

It is not definitely known how the second and third actors for each group of tragedies were chosen or paid. (Presumably the protagonists

κλήρῳ νεμηθέντας ὑποκρινουμένους τὰ δράματα, ὧν ὁ νικήσας εἰς τοὐπιὸν ἀκρίτως παρελαμβάνετο. The phrase ὑποκρίνεσθαι τὸ δρᾶμα is used only of protagonists; there is no direct evidence about the selection of the second and third actors for each poet.

[1] [Plut.] *Vit. X Orat.* 841 f. See above, pp. 15 f.

[2] *I.G.* ii². 2319.

[3] Ibid. 2320. In the following year Astydamas, Timokles, and Euaretos each offered two plays only; the two protagonists were Thettalos and Neoptolemos.

[4] *Rhet.* iii. 1. 1403ᵇ33 f. μεῖζον δύνανται νῦν τῶν ποιητῶν οἱ ὑποκριταί.

were paid by the state.[1]) Demosthenes[2] taunts Aeschines with hiring himself out as 'tritagonist' to the actors Simylos and Socrates, but this was for the Rural Dionysia and probably for the acting of old plays only. It seems likely that for rural festivals the whole body of performers (who might be a troupe habitually acting together) was assembled by the protagonist.

30. But the importance of the protagonist in the Athenian festivals seems almost excessive, when we remember not only the possibility of a play's being spoiled by the bad acting of secondary characters, but the heavy demands made upon these secondary characters in a Greek play.[3] It is the protagonist alone who is said to 'act the play', both in inscriptions[4] and in literature,[5] and only the protagonist could win the prize for acting. It is, however, noteworthy that the prize did not necessarily go to the actor of the successful plays. The didaskalic inscription already quoted[6] illustrates this: in 418 B.C. the successful tragedies were acted by Lysikrates, but the prize for acting went to Kallippides, and there are other possible cases, of varying degrees of probability.

31. The public performance of lyric choruses and of drama at Athens took the form of a contest, and elaborate precautions were taken to secure fairness in the selection of the judges and in their performance of their duties. The exact methods adopted have been the subject of much controversy, but an account can be given which reconciles the few passages of ancient writers which bear on the subject. Plutarch,[7] describing how in 468 B.C. the archon by a bold stroke set aside the regular procedure, shows incidentally in part what this procedure must have been:

ἔθεντο δὲ εἰς μνήμην αὐτοῦ (Kimon) καὶ τὴν τῶν τραγῳδῶν κρίσιν ὀνομαστὴν γενομένην. πρώτην γὰρ διδασκαλίαν τοῦ Σοφοκλέους ἔτι νέου καθέντος, Ἀψεφίων ὁ ἄρχων, φιλονεικίας οὔσης καὶ παρατάξεως τῶν θεατῶν, κριτὰς μὲν οὐκ ἐκλήρωσε τοῦ ἀγῶνος, ὡς δὲ Κίμων μετὰ τῶν συστρατήγων προελθὼν εἰς τὸ θέατρον ἐποιήσατο τῷ θεῷ τὰς νενομισμένας σπονδάς, οὐκ ἀφῆκεν αὐτοὺς ἀπελθεῖν, ἀλλ' ὁρκώσας ἠνάγκασε καθίσαι καὶ κρῖναι δέκα ὄντας, ἀπὸ φυλῆς μιᾶς ἕκαστον (or, as Helbig, ἀπὸ φυλῆς ἕνα ἑκάστης). ὁ μὲν οὖν ἀγὼν καὶ διὰ τὸ τῶν κριτῶν ἀξίωμα τὴν φιλοτιμίαν (? φιλονικίαν or τῇ φιλοτιμίᾳ) ὑπερέβαλε, νικήσαντος δὲ τοῦ Σοφοκλέους κτλ.

The point in the theatrical proceedings at which the archon must have called in the generals to help must have been just before the performances

---

[1] One cannot guess to what period Lucian, *Icaromenippus* 29 (a tragic actor paid 7 drachmai ἐς τὸν ἀγῶνα), refers, but, to judge by the smallness of the sum, it should be a fairly early one.
[2] *de Cor.* 262.   [3] See pp. 138 ff.   [4] See pp. 106 ff.
[5] e.g. Dem. *de F.L.* 246.   [6] *I.G.* ii². 2319.   [7] *Kimon* 8. 7–9.

of tragedy, when the audience (who had probably seen the Proagon and formed their prejudice in favour of particular competitors) was vehemently proclaiming its preferences, and would evidently put pressure on the judges if they were drawn by lot in the regular manner from the ten urns representing each of the ten tribes (see below). Instead of drawing one name from each urn, the archon called on the ten strategoi, each of whom also represented one tribe, so that at least the tribal character of the selection was preserved—a bold expedient, but one whose felicitousness, together with the popularity of the returning generals, might well capture the goodwill of the excited crowd.[1] (The only difficulty is as to the nature of the 'accustomed libations' offered by the generals, and the point in the proceedings at which they were offered, and there is no information available for solving this.)

32. Further details of the method of selection, especially in its earlier stages, are found in passages of the orators:

Isocr. xvii. 33–34. Πυθόδωρον γὰρ τὸν σκηνίτην καλούμενον, ὃς ὑπὲρ Πασίωνος ἅπαντα καὶ λέγει καὶ πράττει, τίς οὐκ οἶδεν ὑμῶν πέρυσιν ἀνοίξαντα τὰς ὑδρίας καὶ τοὺς κριτὰς ἐξελόντα τοὺς ὑπὸ τῆς βουλῆς ἐμβληθέντας; καίτοι ὅστις μικρῶν ἕνεκεν καὶ περὶ τοῦ σώματος κινδυνεύων ταύτας ὑπανοίγειν ἐτόλμησεν, αἱ σεσημασμέναι μὲν ἦσαν ὑπὸ τῶν πρυτάνεων, κατεσφραγισμέναι δ' ὑπὸ τῶν χορηγῶν, ἐφυλάττοντο δ' ὑπὸ τῶν ταμιῶν, ἔκειντο δ' ἐν ἀκροπόλει, τί δεῖ θαυμάζειν, εἰ κτλ.

Lysias iv. 3. ἐβουλόμην δ' ἂν μὴ ἀπολαχεῖν αὐτὸν κριτὴν Διονυσίοις, ἵν' ὑμῖν φανερὸς ἐγένετο ἐμοὶ διηλλαγμένος, κρίνας τὴν ἐμὴν φυλὴν νικᾶν· νῦν δ' ἔγραψε μὲν ταῦτα εἰς τὸ γραμματεῖον, ἀπέλαχε δέ. καὶ ὅτι ἀληθῆ ταῦτα λέγω, Φιλῖνος καὶ Διοκλῆς ἴσασιν, ἀλλ' οὐκ ἔστιν αὐτοῖς μαρτυρῆσαι μὴ διομοσαμένοις περὶ τῆς αἰτίας ἧς ἐγὼ φεύγω, ἐπεὶ σαφῶς ἐγνῶτ' ἂν ὅτι ἡμεῖς ἦμεν αὐτὸν οἱ κριτὴν ἐμβαλόντες καὶ ἡμῶν ἕνεκα ἐκαθίζετο.

Dem. Meid. 17. καὶ οὐδ' ἐνταῦθα ἔστη τῆς ὕβρεως, ἀλλὰ τοσοῦτον αὐτῷ περιῆν, ὥστε τὸν ἐστεφανωμένον ἄρχοντα διέφθειρε, τοὺς χορηγοὺς συνῆγεν ἐπ' ἐμέ, βοῶν, ἀπειλῶν, ὀμνύουσι παρεστηκὼς τοῖς κριταῖς . . . . 18. . . . προδιαφθείρας τοίνυν τοὺς κριτὰς τῷ ἀγῶνι τῶν ἀνδρῶν . . . ἐμοῦ μὲν ὕβρισεν τὸ σῶμα, τῇ φυλῇ δὲ κρατούσῃ τὸν ἀγῶνα αἰτιώτατος τοῦ μὴ νικῆσαι κατέστη.

33. From these passages it appears that:

(1) Before the festival (or before the particular contest) the Council drew up a list of names selected from each of the ten tribes. What qualifications were required we are not told, but it is clear that the choregoi were present and had a voice in the selection, and that a choregos

---

[1] Though the victory awarded to Sophocles on this occasion was his first, he may already have been well known and popular in Athens, and there seems to be no sufficient reason to discredit the story. (See Forrest, C.Q., n.s. 10 (1960), 238 ff.)

could (like Lysias' client) get someone pledged to support him put on the list, and that violence (like that of Meidias) might be brought to bear to influence the selection. That there was any demand for critical capacity seems unlikely. Aristophanes (*Eccl.* 1154 ff.) divides the judges into the two classes of σοφοί and ἡδέως γελῶντες, and claims the support of both.

(2) The names were then placed in ten urns, each containing the names selected from one tribe. These urns were sealed both by the prytaneis who presided at the Council and by the choregoi, and deposited in the Acropolis in the custody of the public treasurers. It was a capital offence to tamper with them, though on the occasion described by Isocrates it appears to have been done.

(3) At the beginning of the contest for which the judges were required the ten urns were placed in the theatre, and the archon drew one name from each. The ten persons selected swore to give an impartial verdict.[1] (Here Meidias again attempted to influence them.) At the end of the contest each wrote his order of merit on a tablet; the tablets were placed in an urn, from which the archon drew five at random,[2] and on these five tablets the issue of the contest was decided.

34. It is obvious that the ten judges who heard the contest officially might be influenced by the clamour of partisans in the theatre, and Plato refers to this in the *Laws*:[3]

οὔτε γὰρ παρὰ θεάτρου δεῖ τόν γε ἀληθῆ κριτὴν κρίνειν μανθάνοντα καὶ ἐκπληττόμενον ὑπὸ θορύβου τῶν πολλῶν καὶ τῆς αὑτοῦ ἀπαιδευσίας, οὔτ' αὖ γιγνώσκοντα δι' ἀνανδρίαν καὶ δειλίαν ἐκ ταὐτοῦ στόματος οὗπερ τοὺς θεοὺς ἐπεκαλέσατο μέλλων κρίνειν, ἐκ τούτου ψευδόμενον ἀποφαίνεσθαι ῥᾳθύμως τὴν κρίσιν· οὐ γὰρ μαθητὴς ἀλλὰ διδάσκαλος, ὥς γε τὸ δίκαιον, θεατῶν μᾶλλον ὁ κριτὴς καθίζει καὶ ἐναντιωσόμενος τοῖς τὴν ἡδονὴν μὴ προσηκόντως μηδὲ ὀρθῶς ἀποδιδοῦσι θεαταῖς.[4]

A story, true or false, is told by Aelian[5] that at the first performance of *Clouds* the audience noisily demanded that the judges should place Aristophanes' name first on their lists; but the poet was unsuccessful. The influence of the audience or of powerful persons may have been all the greater because it was known how each judge voted. Thus Alcibiades

---

[1] This oath is referred to in Pherekrates, fr. 96 (K) and Ar. *Eccl.* 1160, where the judges are bidden μὴ ἐπιορκεῖν.

[2] The tablet of the friend of Lysias' client was not drawn (ἀπέλαχε), and so his promise could not be fulfilled.

[3] ii. 659 a: cf. iii. 700 c–701 b, where some of the same points are made, and particularly the protest against the ἄμουσοι βοαὶ πλήθους and the κρότοι ἐπαίνους ἀποδιδόντες which prevailed in his own day. (See below, pp. 272 f.).

[4] Cf. Lucian, *Harmon.* 2 καὶ γὰρ οὖν καὶ ἐν τοῖς ἀγῶσιν οἱ μὲν πολλοὶ θεαταὶ ἴσασι κροτῆσαί ποτε καὶ συρίσαι, κρίνουσι δὲ ἑπτὰ ἢ πέντε ἢ ὅσοι δή. The reference in ἑπτά is inexplicable.

[5] *Var. H.* ii. 13.

won the victory with a boys' chorus because (according to [Andokides[1]]
τῶν κριτῶν οἱ μὲν φοβούμενοι οἱ δὲ χαριζόμενοι νικᾶν ἔκριναν αὐτόν, and
Menander, frequently defeated by Philemon by unfair means, asked
Philemon if he was not ashamed of defeating him so often.[2] Aristophanes
himself shows some consciousness of the influence of the spectators, e.g.
in *Birds* (ll. 444–5):

> ὄμνυμ' ἐπὶ τούτοις πᾶσι νικᾶν τοῖς κριταῖς
> καὶ τοῖς θεαταῖς πᾶσι,

and there was even sufficient possibility of the use of bribery (as there
was with a popular jury) for Aristophanes to disown it.[3]

35. That the final verdict was that of five judges is confirmed by lexicographers and grammarians.[4] The name of the victorious poet was proclaimed by the herald,[5] and he was crowned in the theatre by the archon
with a crown of ivy.[6]

There is nothing to show whether the same ten judges acted in all
four contests at each festival, or how the prize for the best actor, when
it was introduced, was awarded. How far the judges may have been
influenced by the fear of penalties it is impossible to say: Aeschines[7]
refers to the trial of judges of cyclic choruses (καὶ τοὺς μὲν κριτὰς τοὺς
ἐκ τῶν Διονυσίων ἐὰν μὴ δικαίως τοὺς κυκλίους χοροὺς κρίνωσι ζημιοῦτε), but
says nothing of judges of tragedy or comedy. (The reference may be to
the proceedings in the Assembly held after the festival and any subsequent legal proceedings.)

The very large number of victories won by Aeschylus and Sophocles
is a testimony to the general fairness of the verdicts and the capacity of
the judges in the fifth century B.C.; each of these poets was victorious
with more than half his plays. Euripides won few victories, partly because his views and probably his technique were less popular in his lifetime than they afterwards became, partly because he had Sophocles to

---

[1] *in Alcib.* 20.   [2] Aul. Gell. *N.A.* xvii. 4 (see below, p. 278).   [3] *Ach.* 657.

[4] Zenob. iii. 64 ἐν πέντε κριτῶν γούνασι κεῖται· παροιμιῶδες οἷον ἐν ἄλλων ἐξουσίᾳ ἐστίν·
εἴρηται δὲ ἡ παροιμία, παρόσον πέντε κριταὶ τοὺς κωμικοὺς ἔκρινον, ὥς φησιν Ἐπίχαρμος;
Hesych. s.v. πέντε κριταί· τοσοῦτοι τοὺς κωμικοὺς ἔκρινον, οὐ μόνον Ἀθήνῃσιν ἀλλὰ καὶ ἐν
Σικελίᾳ; schol. Ar. *Birds* 445 ἔκριναν ε' κριταὶ τοὺς κωμικούς, οἱ δὲ λαμβάνοντες τοὺς ε' ψήφους
εὐδαιμόνουν. Lysias (quoted above) implies that the same system was in force for dithyramb.
A passage of an unknown literary critic of about the second century B.C. (*P. Oxy.* xiii, no. 1611),
though very corrupt, seems to show that Lysippus in his Βάκχαι and Cratinus in his Πλοῦτοι
spoke of five judges, though the preceding words *may* refer to some later period in which there
were *four* judges of comedies; cf. G. Capovilla, *Menandro*, p. 34.

[5] Aristid. *Rhet.*, p. 2 (Dind.), and *Vit. Soph.* 14.

[6] Aristid., loc. cit.; Plutarch, *an seni*, 785 b; Alkiphron, *Epp.* iv. 18. 16 (Schepers); Athen.
vi. 241 f., etc.

[7] *in Ctes.* 232.

compete against. Now and then, of course, things went wrong. The *Oedipus Tyrannus* of Sophocles was defeated by the plays of Philokles, and Euripides was placed below Xenokles (in 415, the year of *Troades*) and Nikomachos, who is virtually unknown.[1] But we know nothing of the other plays produced by Sophocles and Euripides on these occasions, nor about the way in which the choregos or the chorus and actors discharged their functions. Although there may have occasionally been verdicts due to intimidation by the audience or by powerful persons,[2] Plato speaks in the *Laws*[3] as if the undue influence of the crowd had only recently become serious, and the instances of corruption mentioned by the orators also belong to the fourth century. Aristophanes[4] suggests that a poet's chances were affected by the order in which competitors had to appear. This was determined by lot, and the first place was regarded as the least and the last as the most advantageous.

36. Besides the plays or groups of plays entered for competition the festival was enlarged in the fourth century B.C., as inscriptions show,[5] by the performance of an old tragedy from 386 B.C. onwards, and of an old comedy from 339 B.C. (Whether these performances took place regularly before 341 B.C. in the case of tragedy and 311 B.C. in that of comedy the evidence does not suffice to show.) In the fifth century the only performances of old plays (with an exception to be noticed) were presentations of unsuccessful plays in a revised form—of comedies perhaps more frequently than of tragedies, though Euripides certainly revised and re-produced his *Hippolytus*, and possibly other plays.[6] But the fact that two forms of a play were known does not necessarily mean that both were performed at the City Dionysia, as the programmes of the Rural Dionysia may often have included re-productions, in their original or in revised forms, of plays which had appeared at the greater festival.[7]

[1] Argt. *O.T.*; Aelian, *Var. H.* ii. 8; 'Suid.' s.v. Νικόμαχος· . . . παραδόξως Εὐριπίδην καὶ Θέογνιν ἐνίκησε. Cf. p. 258.

[2] See above, p. 97. On the taste and influence of the audience see below, ch. vi.

[3] Probably composed after 360 B.C. See 700 c–701 a (especially 700 c) and 659 a–c, and above, p. 97.   [4] *Eccl.* 1158 ff.   [5] See above, p. 72.

[6] Argt. Eur. *Hipp.* There were said to have been two editions of the *Autolycus* and the *Phrixus*—but the evidence (see Nauck, pp. 441, 627) is not perfectly satisfactory—and also of the Λημνίαι of Sophocles (ibid., p. 215). On the *Phrixus*, see now *P. Oxy.* 2245.

[7] It would not be safe to draw any inference as to competitions of actors with single plays from the dream of Thrasyllus before the battle of Arginusae (Diod. Sic. xiii. 97. 6) that he and six of his colleagues as generals were acting the *Phoenissae* of Euripides in the theatre at Athens in competition with the hostile generals, who were performing *Suppliants*. But from Athen. xiii. 584 d it seems that Andronikos (fourth century) had been successful in a contest in acting *Epigonoi* (? of Aeschylus or Sophocles), and the story of Likymnios in Alkiphron (see below), alluding to his defeat of two rivals in acting Aeschylus' Πρόπομποι, even if fictitious, implies that such a contest in acting an old play was possible. Such contests may have taken place at rural festivals.

To the memory of Aeschylus was accorded the singular honour of a decree that anyone who desired to do so should be allowed to produce his plays at the Dionysia.[1] This was apparently something different from the practice introduced in the fourth century, when it is evident that plays of Sophocles and Euripides might be and were re-produced, and that the text of them was liable to be tampered with by the actors who produced them, so that Lycurgus passed a law to check this practice.[2] In 341 B.C. the old tragedy produced (by the famous actor Neoptolemos) was Euripides' *Iphigeneia*; in the next year the same actor produced Euripides' *Orestes*. We hear also,[3] apart from inscriptions, of performances of a number of plays of Sophocles, and of the *Kresphontes*, *Hecuba*, and *Oinomaos* of Euripides. In all these records some distinguished actor— Polos or Theodoros or Aristodemos or Andronikos—is spoken of as having 'acted the play', and in some of them, as Demosthenes unkindly suggests, Aeschines failed badly. Polos seems to have distinguished himself as protagonist in plays of Sophocles, Theodoros in the *Oinomaos* and *Hecuba* of Euripides. The only actor who is recorded as having ventured upon Aeschylus at this period was Likymnios, who according to Alkiphron defeated his rivals in acting Aeschylus' Πρόπομποι,[4] but the evidence of the continued popularity of Sophocles and Euripides is very striking.

37. A revision of comedies for re-production is known to have been made in several instances in the fifth century. Aristophanes' *Clouds* is said to have been produced in two versions, and ancient critics knew of two plays produced by him called Εἰρήνη, but were uncertain whether they were the same or not.[5] There was also a second Θεσμοφοριάζουσαι;[6] but the two plays called Πλοῦτος were probably independent and separated by a long interval of time. The *Frogs* was presented a second time in response to popular demand,[7] owing to the good advice contained in the parabasis, but there is no reason to suppose that it was revised. Eupolis is said to have revised his *Autolykos*,[8] and such revision

---

[1] See above, p. 86.

[2] [Plut.] *Vit. Orat.* 841 f. See below, p. 155; Page, *Actors' Interpolations in Greek Tragedy*, pp. 2, etc., and appendix to Vürtheim's edition of Aeschylus' *Supplices*.

[3] See Plut. *Dem.* 7, *de Alex. fort.* 334 a; Dem. *de Cor.* 180, 267, *de F.L.* 246; Aelian, *Var. H.* xiv. 40; Diod. Sic. xiii. 97; Stob. *Flor.* 97. 28; Athen. xiii. 584 d; schol. on Soph. *Ajax* 865; Philostr. *Vit. Apoll.* vii. 5; Plut. *Pelop.* 29; id. *Crass.* 33; Suet. *Nero* 21. 3; Lucian, *de hist. conscr.* 1. Such performances were sometimes only in excerpt. Cf. p. 287, n. 1.

[4] Alkiphron iii. 12. He may have defeated them in competing for the privilege of producing the old play; but some scholars treat the story as fictitious (e.g. O'Connor, p. 105), and no actor named Likymnios is otherwise known.

[5] Argt. iii to Ar. *Peace*.　　　　　　　[6] Athen. i. 29 a; see Kock, *Com. Fragm.* i, pp. 472 ff.

[7] Argt. Ar. *Frogs*, quoting Dikaiarchos (fr. 84 Wehrli) as authority.

[8] Galen xv, p. 424 (Kühn); see Kock, op. cit. i, pp. 267–8.

seems to have been frequent in the time of the Middle and New Comedy, the second version being sometimes given a different name. Thus Diphilus revised his Συνωρίς[1] and Αἱρησιτείχης (perhaps renamed Εὐνοῦχος ἢ Στρατιώτης),[2] Antiphanes his Ἄγροικος (re-produced as Βουταλίων),[3] Alexis his Δημήτριος[4] and his Φρύξ or Φρύγιος,[5] and Menander his 'Ἐπίκληρος.[6] But such re-productions may have been at the Lenaia or Rural Dionysia or some other festival; they are in any case a different thing from the regular presentation of an old comedy outside the competition. In 311 B.C. the play so presented was the Θησαυρός of Anaxandrides;[7] in the late third century an inscription records the presentation of the Phocians of Philemon, in 181 B.C. of the Ἀποκλειομένη of Poseidippus, in 167 of the Φάσμα of Menander, in 154 of the Φιλαθηναῖος of Philippides.[8]

There is no evidence as to the way in which the actor and the play for re-production were selected. Some interpret the obscure references to ἀγῶνες χύτρινοι as having to do with a contest of comic actors held at the time of the Anthesteria, to determine which should produce the old comedy at the next Dionysia, but we have already seen that there are serious difficulties in the way of this interpretation.[9]

APPENDIX TO CHAPTER II

THIS appendix contains a transcript of practically all the inscriptions bearing on the Dionysia and Lenaia, with introductions and notes where necessary, and concludes with a summary of the main chronological conclusions.

Introduction to I.G. ii². 2318

Since the inscription was printed in the Corpus some changes have been necessitated or suggested by the discovery of a new fragment, published by Capps in Hesperia 12 (1943), pp. 1 ff. (with plates), and the transcription given below embodies these alterations, and a few more, taken from squeezes.

The extant remains consist of parts of thirteen columns; these were preceded by two or three others now lost (col. vi and col. x are also missing); the first extant column begins with part of the record for 473–472 B.C., and the record goes down in a fragmentary form to 329–328 B.C. (in col. xiii). Under each year were included, in an unvarying order, the archon's name; the names

---

[1] Athen. vi. 247 b–c.   [2] See Kock, op. cit. ii, p. 542.   [3] Athen. viii. 358 d.
[4] Id. xiv. 663 c. It is uncertain whether the title Δημήτριος ἢ Φιλέταιρος combines those of the two versions.   [5] Id. x. 429 e.
[6] Id. ix. 373 c; Harpokr. s.v. ὄρον. The remark of Athenaeus (374 b) that Anaxandrides destroyed his unsuccessful plays instead of revising them implies that revision was a common practice.   [7] I.G. ii². 2323a.
[8] I.G. ii². 2323. (Also Misogynes of Menander, early second century.)
[9] See above, pp. 15 f.

of the victorious tribe in the boys' dithyrambic contest and of its choregos (but not the name of the poet); next, those of the victorious tribe and choregos in the men's contest; then the names of the victorious choregos and poet in comedy; and finally the same for tragedy—11 lines for each year until 450–449 B.C., when the name of the victorious tragic actor was added, making 12 lines. Cols. i and ii each consisted of 140 lines, cols. iii to ix of 141. (Capps's calculations in *Hesperia*, loc. cit., are virtually decisive.) In the year 406–405 some disturbance was caused by the introduction of synchoregia, necessitating 2 lines extra for that year; but if Capps's calculation (ibid., p. 8) is right, as it seems to be (see above, p. 87), this expedient was not carried beyond that year. Most of the catalogue appears to have been inscribed by the same hand, very soon after 346 B.C.; on the attribution of the later fragments to the same or different hands the experts are not agreed. Col. xi seems to have contained 153 lines, by means of crowding in the lower part of the column, while in the lower part of col. xii the lines were placed at longer intervals. The record probably ended at or before the time of the institution of the agonothetes (about 316 B.C.).

The question of the date of the beginning of the record is bound up with the problem of the heading. So far as this is preserved it runs over the top of cols. i to iv, and reads (with undoubted restorations) [ΠΡΩ]ΤΟΝ ΚΩΜΟΙ ΗΣΑΝ Τ[ΩΙ ΔΙΟΝΥΣ]ΩΙ ΤΡΑΓΩΙΔΟΙ Δ[...

It seems possible that we have here part of a relative clause such as *ἀφ' οὗ* or *ἐφ' οὗ πρῶτον κῶμοι ἦσαν τῷ Διονύσῳ*, followed by the beginning of a main clause, which Capps conjectures to have run *τραγῳδοὶ δημοτελεῖς . . . ἀγωνίσαντες ἐν ἄστει οἵδε νενικήκασιν* (*δημοτελεῖς* being supported, as the appellation of the Dionysia, by the oracle in Dem. *Meid.* 53; cf. Thuc. ii. 15, etc.). The difficulty of this is that the inscription contains so much more than the names of victorious tragic poets, and Capps's solution does not seem at all certain. As regards the first part of the heading, up to about 18 letters are needed if there were two lost columns, or up to about 27 if there were three. It is possible, moreover, that the first part was not a relative clause at all, but something like *ἐπὶ . . . ἄρχοντος πρῶτον κῶμοι ἦσαν τῷ Διονύσῳ*, continuing *τραγῳδοὶ δὲ ἐπὶ . . . κωμῳδοὶ δὲ ἐπὶ Τελεσίνου* (487–6 B.C.), following a chronological order. This would be possible, whether *κῶμοι* referred to the festival as a whole (as instituted by the state), as is commonly assumed, or (as has been more recently urged) specifically to dithyrambs. Marx, Kirchner, and others believe that *κῶμος* was specially applied to the *χοροὶ ἀνδρῶν*, on the strength of (1) Pindar, *Pyth.* v. 22 *δέδεξαι τόνδε κῶμον ἀνέρων* (but *ἀνέρων* is here explicitly mentioned), and (2) the Law of Euegoros in Dem. *Meid.* 10 *τοῖς ἐν ἄστει Διονυσίοις ἡ πομπὴ καὶ οἱ παῖδες καὶ ὁ κῶμος καὶ οἱ κωμῳδοὶ καὶ οἱ τραγῳδοί*, where, if *κῶμος = χοροὶ ἀνδρῶν*, the order is that of this inscription. The contest of men's choruses may have been the only 'event' of the festival at first, and so have been called by the more general name of *κῶμος*, but when the boys' choruses were added, though they were distinctly spoken of as *οἱ παῖδες*, they may have been popularly included with the men's choruses under the name κῶμοι. (The lawgiver Euegoros is supposed to have reverted to the original use of κῶμος = χοροὶ ἀνδρῶν; but this is not very convincing, and many scholars suppose that after καὶ οἱ παῖδες in the law the words καὶ οἱ ἄνδρες may have dropped out.[1])

But if κῶμοι means dithyrambs generally, or men's choruses, then it might be argued, the record must have gone back to about 509 B.C., since the Parian Marble (ep. 46) assigns to the archonship of Lysagoras (otherwise unknown) in a year which is either 510–509 or 509–508 B.C. the first contests of χοροὶ ἀνδρῶν, in which the victor was Hypodikos of Chalkis. (Some scholars suppose that the composer or stone-mason had mistakenly written Lysagoras for Isagoras, who was archon in 508–507 B.C., the year of the reforms of Kleisthenes; there seems no justification for this. See Cadoux in *J.H.S.* 68 (1948), p. 113.) But a record going back to that time would hardly fill three columns unless it began with some preliminary matter. The column next before the extant col. i would have included 6 lines of the year 473–472 at the foot, and 2 lines of 486–485 at the head. The column before that would have contained, at the foot, 9 lines of 486–485, and 11 lines of 487–486—the year in which contests in comedy were probably introduced. Capps[2] and Wilhelm reconstruct the whole column so as to make it begin in 502–1 or thereabouts, supposing that the festival was reorganized and the choregic system introduced at that time, and it is perhaps more probable that this was the beginning of the record than that there was another column to the left, going back to about 509 and only partly filled. If so, the contests before 502–501 B.C. would have been held under some less democratic system than that initiated in 502–1. But the dates of the introduction of the boys' contest and the competition in tragedy remain unknown, and without fresh information there can be no certainty as to the date when the record began.

There is a difference of opinion as to the relation of this inscription to the work of Aristotle entitled Νῖκαι Διονυσιακαὶ ἀστικαὶ καὶ Ληναϊκαί. (So the title is given by Hesychius Milesius. In Diog. Laert. v. 26 it appears as Νῖκαι Διονυσιακαὶ α', i.e. a single book.) But as we have no knowledge of this work except the title, the problem is insoluble.[3] On the whole, the balance of probability is against connecting the two. The inscription in its original form (without the later additions) seems to have been compiled about 346 B.C. or within a few years of that date, and it must, of course, have been copied from official records in Athens; but it seems certain that Aristotle was not in Athens,

[1] Cf. *I.G.* ii². 3133, and the commentary, perhaps unduly sceptical.
[2] See especially *Hesperia* 12 (1943), p. 10.
[3] See especially on one side Reisch in *R.E.* v, cols. 398 ff., and *Zeitschr. öst. Gym.* 58 (1907), 312 ff.; against, Körte, *Class. Philol.* 1 (1906), pp. 391 ff. (with whom the view expressed in the text is most in agreement), and Oellacher, *Wiener Stud.* 38 (1916), pp. 81 ff. There is a good discussion in Flickinger, *Greek Theater*, ch. ix. There seems to be more probability that the victors' lists, *I.G.* ii². 2325, were based on Aristotle's Νῖκαι, but this also is no more than conjecture. Other important contributions to the discussion of the inscriptions are those of Wilamowitz in *Gött. gel. Anz.* 1906, pp. 617 ff.; Körte, *Rh. Mus.* 60 (1905), pp. 425–47; Jachmann, *de Aristotelis didascaliis*; and Wilhelm's masterly survey of the whole field in his *U.D.A.* is as indispensable as ever.

at least not for any length of time, in the years 348–334 B.C. (Whether or not the inscription is in any way connected with the activities of Lycurgus in regard to the drama can only be conjectured.) The inscription itself reads like a transcript of an official record. It may have been continued down to the institution of an agonothetes (about 316).

Reisch thinks that the wall or walls on which the record must have been inscribed may have been a temple-like structure in the eastern parodos of the theatre of Dionysus, erected as part of the Lycurgean reconstruction. Against this is the fact to which Kirchner calls attention in *I.G.* ii. 2², p. 659, that all the fragments, except one of the latest, were found on the *northern* slope of the Acropolis; it is unlikely that the whole structure, or all its fragments, should have been transferred from south to north, and it seems more likely that the monument was originally placed in or near the Agora, perhaps among other records compiled by order of the archons and kept in their custody.

I.G. ii². 2318 ('*Fasti*')

The heading so far as extant ran (in a larger script) over the first four extant columns: viz.]ΤΟΝ ΚΩΜΟΙ ΗΣΑΝ Τ[ΩΙ ΔΙΟΝΥΣ]ΩΙ ΤΡΑΓΩΙ-ΔΟΙ Δ[

Col. i	*Col. ii*	*Col. iii*
[473–472]	*[460–459]*	*[448–447]*
Ξε]νοκλείδης ἐχορήγε	Πανδιονὶ[ς ἀνδρῶν	ω]ν Λαμπρ: ἐχορήγε
Μάγνης ἐδίδασκεν	Κλεαίνετ[ος ἐχορήγει	Σοφο]κλῆς ἐδίδασκεν
τραγωιδῶν	κωμωιδῶ[ν	ὑποκριτὴς Ἡρ]ακλείδης
Περικλῆς Χολαρ: ἐχορή	Θαρ[ρίας ἐχορήγει	['Επὶ Τιμαρχίδου]　　*[447–446]*
Αἰσχύλος ἐ[δ]ίδασκε		
['Επὶ Χάρητος]　*[472–471]*	[τραγωιδῶν]	
	]: ἐχορή	'Ε[ρεχθηὶς ἀνδρῶν
	[....9....] ἐδίδασκεν	Βίω[ν ἐχορήγει
	['Επὶ Φιλ]οκλέους　*[459–458]*	κωμ[ωιδῶν
	[Οἰν]ηὶς παίδων	Ἀνδ[
	Δημόδοκος ἐχορήγει	Καλ[λίας ἐδίδασκεν
ἐχ]ορήγει	'Ιπποθωντὶς ἀνδρῶν	τρα[γωιδῶν
[...ca.8... ἐδίδ]ασκεν	Εὐκτήμων 'Ελευ: ἐχορή	Θαλ[
[τραγωιδῶν]	κωμωιδῶν	Κα[ρκίνος ἐδίδασκε
ἐχ]ορήγει	Εὐρυκλείδης ἐχορήγει	ὑπ[οκριτὴς
[Πολυφράσμω]ν ἐδίδασ	Εὐφρόνιος ἐδίδασκε	'Επ[ὶ Καλλιμάχου　*[446–445]*
['Επὶ Πραξιέργο]υ　*[471–470]*	τραγωιδῶν	
πα]ίδων	Ξενοκλῆς Ἀφιδνα: ἐχορή	
ἐχο]ρήγει	Αἰσχύλος ἐδίδασκεν	
ἀνδρ]ῶν	'Επὶ Ἄβρωνος　*[458–457]*	
ἐχ]ορήγ	'Ερεχθηὶς παίδων	
	Χαρίας Ἀγρυλῆ: ἐχορή	
	Λεοντὶς ἀνδρῶν	
	Δεινόστρατος ἐχορ[ήγ	
	κωμωιδῶν	
	ἐχο]ρήγ[ει	
['Επὶ Δημοτίωνος]　*[470–469]*		
		['Επὶ Λυσιμαχίδου]　*[445–444]*
	['Επὶ Μνησιθείδου]　*[457–456]*	

Col. iv　　　　　　　　*Col. v*　　　　　　　*Col. vi (missing)*

          [*436–435*]　　　　　　　　　　[*424–423*]　['Επὶ Καλλίου]　　　[*412–411*]

'Ισοκράτη[ς ἐχορήγει
Ἕρμιππος [ἐδίδασκεν
τραγωιδ[ῶν
Νίκων Ἀ[
'Ιοφῶν ἐ[δίδασκεν
ὑποκ]ρι[τὴς

['Επὶ Ἀντιοχίδου]　　[*435–434*]

            ['Επὶ Ἀμεινίου]　　[*423–422*]

                                        ['Επὶ Θεοπόμπου]　　[*411–410*]

                  Παια[νι ἐχορήγ
            Κάνθαρ]ος ἐδί[δασκεν
            τραγ]ωιδῶν

['Επὶ Κράτητος]　　[*434–433*]　　　]ν Παιανιε[ὺς : ἐχορ
            Με]νεκράτης ἐδ[ίδασκε
            ὑπ]οκριτὴς Μυνν[ίσ]κος
            'Επ]ὶ Ἀλκαίου　　[*422–421*]
            'Ιπποθωντὶς παίδων
            Ἀρίσταρχος Δεκε : ἐχορή
            Αἰαντὶς ἀνδρῶν　　　　　　['Επὶ Γλαυκίππου]　[*410–409*]
            Δημοσθένης ἐχορήγει
            κ]ωμωιδῶν
                      ἐχο]ρήγ
            [Εὔπολις ἐδίδασκεν]

['Επὶ Ἀψεύδους]　　[*433–432*]

Col. vii　　　　　　　*Col. viii*　　　　　　*Col. ix*

['Επὶ Μίκωνος]　　[*401–400*]

                                     ['Επὶ Καλλίου]　　　[*377–376*]

['Επὶ Λάχητος]　　[*400–399*]

                  ['Επὶ Πυργίωνος]　　[*388–387*]

               Ἀρα]ρὼς ἐδ[ίδασκ]εν　　['Επὶ Χαρισάνδρου] [*376–375*]
ὑποκριτὴς Νικόστρ]ατος　　τραγωιδ[ῶν　　　　　　[　　ὶς παίδων]
'Επὶ Ἀριστοκράτου]ς　[*399–398*]　Ἀριστοκράτης Φαληρ : [ἐχορ　　[　　　ἐχορήγει]
        παίδ]ων　　Σοφοκλῆς ἐδίδασκεν　　[Πανδ]ιο[νὶς ἀνδρῶν]
            ]ἐχορ　　ὑποκριτὴς Κλέανδρο[ς　　[Μό]σχος Ἀγ[γ ἐχορήγει]
     ἀνδρῶν　　　　　'Επὶ Θεοδότου　　[*387–386*]　κω]μωιδῶν
            ]ε : ἐχορή　　παλαιὸν δρᾶμα πρῶτο[ν　　...γνητος [　ἐχορήγει
[κωμωιδῶν]　　　　παρεδίδαξαν οἱ τραγ[ωιδοὶ　　Ἀνα]ξανδρί[δης ἐδίδασκεν
            ]ἐχορή　　Ἀντιοχὶς παίδων　　τρα]γωιδῶν
[...ca. 9... ἐδίδα]σκεν　　Εὐηγέτης Παλλη : ἐχο[ρήγ　　...γένης[　ἐχορήγει
             Αἰγηὶς ἀνδρῶν　　Σο]φοκλῆς [ἐδίδασκεν
             Ἴασος Κολλυ : ἐχορήγ[ει　　ὑπ]οκριτ[ὴς
                                'Επὶ 'Ι]ππο[δάμαντος　[*375–*
                                                374]

['Επὶ Εὐθυκλέους]　　[*398–397*]

I.G. ii². 2318 (cont.)

Column x is missing. The following fragments remain of cols. xi–xiii. (The lines in this transcript are not printed to correspond for these columns as they are for cols. i–ix.)

Col. xi

.....ιλ: [ἐχορήγει   [348–347]
Ἄ]λεξις ἐδ[ίδασκε
τραγωιδῶν
Κλ]εόμαχος Ἀχα[ρν: ἐχορή
Ἀ]στυδάμας ἐδίδασκε
ὑ]ποκριτὴς Θ[ετταλός
Ἐ]πὶ Θεμιστοκ[λέους   [347–346]
Ἐρεχθηὶς π[αίδων
Διονυσ[ἐχορήγει
Ἀ]κ[αμαντὶς ἀνδρῶν
       (53 lines missing)

ἐκ Κερ]αμ: ἐχορή   [343–342]
ἐ]δίδασκε
ὑποκριτὴς Ἀ]θηνόδωρος
Ἐπὶ Σωσιγένο]υς   [342–341]
Αἰγηὶς παίδ]ων
Εὐθύδημος Δι]ομε[εὺς ἐχορ]ήγει
Ἱπποθωντὶς] ἀνδρῶν
......ἐκ Κοί]λης ἐχορή
[κωμωιδῶν]
..........Εὐω]νυ: [ἐχορή
[ἐδίδασκε]
[τραγωιδῶν]
...............ἐχ]ορ[ήγει
[Ἀστυδάμας ἐδίδασκε]
[ὑποκριτὴς Νεοπτόλεμος]

Col. xii

τρ]αγωιδῶν   [341–340]
Ἀρρενείδης Παιανι: ἐχο
Ἀστυδάμας ἐδίδ[ασκεν
ὑποκριτὴς Θεττ[α]λός
Ἐ]πὶ Θεοφράστο[υ   [340–339]
[π]αλαιὸν δρᾶμ[α πρ]ῶτο[ν
π]αρεδίδαξα[ν οἱ] κωμ[ωιδοί]
Ἀ]ντιοχὶς παί[δων
       (80 lines missing)

Ἐπὶ] Νι[κοκράτους   [333–332]
Κεκροπ[ὶς παίδων
Διόφαν[τος Ἀλαιεὺς ἐχο
Κεκροπὶς [ἀνδρῶν
Ὀνήτωρ [ἐχο
κω[μ]ωιδ[ῶν
Διοπεί[θης....ἐχο
Προκλείδ[ης ἐδίδασκε]
τραγωιδ[ῶν]
Φρ[α?.....ἐχο
       (13 lines missing)
[ὑποκριτὴς] Νικ[όστρατος]   [332–331]
Ἐ]πὶ Ἀριστοφάνους   [331–330]
Οἰνη[ὶς] παί[δων
Νικόστρατος Ἀ[χ]αρν[εὺς ἐχο
Ἱπποθωντὶς ἀνδρ[ῶν
Ἄρχιππος Πειραιε[ὺς ἐχο
[κωμωιδῶν]
.......ο[ς] Κηφισ[ιεὺς ἐχο
........ἐδ]ί[δασκε

Col. xiii

[κωμωιδῶν]   [330–329]
......ἐ]κ Κε[ραμέων
ἐ[χορήγ]ει
Θεόφιλος ἐδίδ[ασκεν
τραγωιδῶν
Θ]ηραμένης Κηφισι
ἐχορ]ήγει
Τιμο]κλῆς ἐδίδα[σκεν
ὑπο]κριτὴς
Ἀθηνόδωρος
Ἐπὶ Κηφισοφῶντος   [329–328]
Ἱ]ππ[ο]θωντὶς παί[δων

Unplaced Fragments
Insignificant, except part of k.
ἀνδρῶν]
Πολυά[ρατος?...ἐχορήγει
κωμω[ιδῶν

Notes on details of I.G. ii². 2318

Col. i. Αἰσχύλος ἐδίδασκε, 473–472 B.C. Cf. Argt. Aesch. *Pers. ἐπὶ Μένωνος τραγῳδῶν Αἰσχύλος ἐνίκα Φινεῖ, Πέρσαις, Γλαύκῳ, Προμηθεῖ.*

Πολυφράσμω]ν, suggested by Lipsius to fit the space.

Col. ii. Εὐφρόνιος ἐδίδασκε, 459–458 B.C. Cf. I.G. ii². 2325.

Ξενοκλῆς Ἀφιδναῖος, 459–458 B.C. Cf. Argt. Aesch. *Agam. ἐδιδάχθη τὸ δρᾶμα ἐπὶ ἄρχοντος Φιλοκλέους Ὀλυμπιάδι πη (i.e. ὀγδοηκοστῇ) ἔτει β΄· πρῶτος Αἰσχύλος Ἀγαμέμνονι, Χοηφόροις, Εὐμενίσι, Πρωτεῖ σατυρικῷ· ἐχορήγει Ξενοκλῆς Ἀφιδναῖος.*

Col. iii. *Καλλίας ἐδίδασκεν*. Cf. *I.G.* ii². 2325, and Capps, *Am. J. Phil.* 20 (1899), p. 396.

Κα[ρκίνος. After Lipsius.

Col. iv. *Ἕρμιππος*. Cf. *I.G.* ii². 2325, and Capps, *Hesperia* 12 (1943), p. 3. This was his first victory (436–435 B.C.).

Ἰοφῶν, son of Sophocles. He was second in 429–428 B.C. (Argt. Eur. *Hippolytus*). Cf. schol. Ar. *Frogs* 73.

Col. v. *Κάνθαρ]ος*. Cf. Oellacher, op. cit., p. 116, and *I.G.* ii². 2325.

Μυνν[ίσ]κος. Cf. *I.G.* ii². 2325; O'Connor, pp. 117 f. He acted for Aeschylus.

Δημοσθένης. The general in the Peloponnesian War.

Col. vii. *Νικόστρ]ατος*. Cf. ii². 2325; O'Connor, p. 122.

Col. viii. *Ἄρα]ρώς*, son of Aristophanes, who after 388 B.C. brought out his father's *Κώκαλος* and *Αἰολοσίκων* (Argt. Ar. *Plutus*). Whether the present entry refers to one of these or a play of his own remains uncertain. See p. 85, n. 9.

Σο]φοκλῆς ἐδίδασκεν, 388–387 B.C., son of Ariston, the son of the great Sophocles; began to exhibit in 397–396 B.C. (Diod. xiv. 53. 6). Cf. also col. ix (376–375 B.C.).

Col. ix. *Ἀναξανδρίδης ἐδίδασκεν*, 376–375 B.C. His first victory at the Dionysia was in 376 B.C. (*Marm. Par.*, ep. 70).

Col. xi. *Ἀστυδάμας ἐδίδασκε*, 348–347 B.C., i.e. Astydamas the younger, whose *Parthenopaeus* and *Lycaon* were victorious in 341–340 B.C., *I.G.* ii². 2320. Cf. Capps, *Am. J. Phil.* 21 (1900), p. 41; Wilamowitz, *Aischylos: Interpretationen*, p. 238. The name is supplied below (342–341 B.C.) by Capps, *Introd. of Comedy into the City Dionysia*, p. 18, from *I.G.* ii². 2320. His plays in that year were *Achilles*, *Athamas*, and *Antigone*.

Θετταλός. Cf. O'Connor, p. 103.

Col. xii. *Νικόστρατος*, 332–331 B.C. Cf. *I.G.* ii². 2320; O'Connor, p. 123.

Col. xiii. *Τιμο]κλῆς ἐδίδασκεν*, 330–329 B.C. Name completed on suggestion of Körte. On distinctness of Timokles tragic and T. comic poet, see T. Wagner, *Symbolarum . . . capita quattuor*; Körte, *B.Ph.W.* 1906, col. 903.

Unplaced. Πολυάρατος. Name suggested by Wilhelm, *U.D.A.*, pp. 31, 33; men from Cholargos of this name are known at the end of the fifth and at the end of the fourth centuries.

Introduction to I.G. ii². 2319–23

These inscriptions all form part of a record probably engraved on the inner walls of a square building, on the Ionic epistyle or architrave of which the lists of victors (*I.G.* ii². 2325) were inscribed in columns of 17 lines each. The record was arranged in the order: (1) tragedies at Dionysia, (2) comedies at Dionysia, (3) comedies at Lenaia, (4) tragedies at Lenaia. (The allocation of nos. 2321 and 2322 to 'comedies at Lenaia' is practically certain.) The record of comedies at the Lenaia ended a very few years after 288 B.C., and it is not likely that the record of tragedies at the Lenaia continued longer; the whole quadripartite record in its original form was probably inscribed at about this date.

Reisch believes that the monument was the work of the agonothetes of 279–278 B.C., and that the dedicatory inscription survives in *I.G.* ii². 2853 as restored by Wilhelm (*U.D.A.*, p. 90):

δ]ώρου [Φ]ρεά[ρ]ριος [Διονύ]σωι ἀ[ν]έθηκεν
. . . καὶ ἀγω]νοθέτης [γενόμενος· Ἀναξ]ικράτης ἦρχεν.

But, in *I.G.* ii². 2325, the list of victorious actors in comedy at the Lenaia continues until far down in the third century B.C., and that of victorious comic poets until 150 B.C., and as there is no ground for the suggestion, made by Reisch, that their victories were won with old plays, it must be inferred that contests in comedy at the Lenaia went on for more than a century after the main didaskalic inscription was erected. The contests in comedy at the Dionysia likewise continued, and the record of these (no. 2323) seems to have been made up at intervals by different hands and with some gaps. It is generally assumed that, so far as the record refers to the time before the Διδασκαλίαι of Aristotle (Diog. Laert. v. 26), it was a copy of that work, or at least followed it closely, though omitting the part dealing with dithyramb, and that in continuing Aristotle's work it followed the same plan. It includes the names of the actors of each play and of the victorious actor, but does not mention the choregoi; the satyric play and the old plays which after certain dates the festival included are recorded.

Since, on the lost fragment *I.G.* ii². 2319, the record of comedies at the Lenaia for the 280s is followed in the next column by records of tragedies for the years 420–419 and 419–418, it follows that the list of tragic contests at the Lenaia began relatively late. The date generally given is *c.* 432, but we do not know the length of the columns or the position of this fragment in it. No sound inference can be made from the list of tragic actors at the Lenaia (p. 115), for, although we can date one of Kallippides' five Lenaian victories to 419–418, we do not know whether this is early or late in his career. Since there are some tragic actors on the list for the Dionysia (which we can infer from *I.G.* ii². 2318 to have begun in 450–449) who are not on the Lenaia list, contests at the Lenaia presumably began some time after 449. However, the prevailing assumption that tragedy at the Lenaia began *c.* 432, some ten years later than comedy at the Lenaia, is not sufficiently supported by the evidence.

I.G. ii². 2319–23 (Διδασκαλίαι)

No. 2320 (=ii. 973)

Tragedies at Dionysia

342–1 [Ἐπὶ Σωσιγένους σατυρι]
. . . .
παλαι]ᾶι Νε[οπτόλεμος
Ἰφιγε]νείαι Εὐρ[ιπ]ίδο[υ

ποη] : Ἀστυδάμας
Ἀχι]λλεῖ ὑπε : Θετταλός
Ἀθάμαντι ὑπε : Νεοπτόλ[εμος
Ἀντιγόνηι ὑπε : Ἀθηνόδω[ρος
Ε]ὐάρετος δ[εύ :] Τεύκρωι
ὑπ]ε : Ἀθηνόδωρος
Ἀχι]λλεῖ ὑ[πε] : Θετταλός
. . . ε]ι ὑπ[ε : Ν]εοπτόλεμος

No. 2320 (cont.)

Ἀφαρεὺς] τρί : Πελιάσιν
ὑπε : Νεοπτ]όλεμος
'Ορέστηι [ὑπε : Ἀθηνόδωρος
Αὔγηι ὑπε : Θετταλ[ός
ὑπο : Νεοπόλεμος ἐνίκ[α
341–0   'Επὶ Νικομάχου σατυρι
Τιμοκλῆς Λυκούργωι
παλαιᾶι : Νεοπτόλεμ[ος
'Ορέστηι Εὐριπίδο
πoη] : Ἀστυδάμας
Παρθενοπαίωι ὑπε : Θετ[ταλός
Λυκά]ονι ὑπε : Νεοπτόλε[μος
Τιμο]κλῆς δεύ : Φρίξωι
ὑπε :] Θετταλός
Οἰδί]ποδι ὑπε : Νεοπτόλ[εμος
Εὐ[άρ]ετος τρί
Ἀλκ]μέ[ω]νι ὑπε : Θετταλός
....]ηι ὑπε : Νεοπτό[λεμος
ὑπο : Θ]ετταλὸς ἐνίκα
340–39   ἐπὶ Θεο]φράστου σα[τυρι
........Φορκίσ[ι
παλαιᾶι ?Νικ]όστρ[ατος
........Εὐ]ριπί[δου
πoη :.......]o

No. 2319 (= ii. 972), Col. ii

Tragedies at Lenaia

ειρ
ὑπε
ὑπο [....ἐνίκα
420–19   'Επὶ Ἀ[στυφίλου....
Ἀγα[μέμνονι
ὑπε
'Ηρα[κλείδης ? δευ :
Θησῆ[ι
ὑπε
ὑπο
419–18   'Επὶ Ἀρχ[ίου
Τυροῖ Τι[

ὑπε : Λυσικράτ[ης
Καλλίστρατος [δευ :
Ἀμφιλόχωι 'Ιξίο[νι
ὑπε : Καλλιππίδ[ης
ὑπ]ο : Καλλιππίδ[ης ἐνίκα
418–17   'Επ' Ἀ]ντιφ[ῶ]ντος Σ...

No. 2321 (= ii. 974)

Comedies at Lenaia (? 5th cent.)

......ηταις
['Επὶ....]
...s : Ἀριστοφ[άνης
...'Οδομ]αντοπρέσ[βεσι ?
ὑπο...ἐ]νίκα
'Επὶ...ο]υ

No. 2322 (= ii. 974 b)

Comedies at Lenaia? (4th cent.)

Ἄλεξις : [δεύ :
ὑπε : Καλλ
'Ηρακλεί[δης τρί[1] ὑπε
Θεόφιλο[ς· Εὔβουλος ? τέ :
Ναυ]σι[κάαι ? ὑπε

No. 2319 (= ii. 972), Col. i

Comedies at Lenaia (3rd cent.)

..τε :   ]αστίδι ?
ὑπε : Ἀριστόμα]χος
]ης πέμ : Ἀνασωιζομέν
ὑπε : Ἀντ]ιφάνης
ὑπο : 'Ιερ]ώνυμος ἐνίκα
285–4   'Επὶ Δι]οτίμου Σίμυλος
'Εφε]σίαι : ὑπε Ἀριστόμαχος
Διόδωρος : δεύ : Νεκρῶι
ὑπε Ἀριστόμαχος
Διόδωρος τρί Μαινομένωι
ὑπε Κηφίσιος
Φο]νικ[ίδ]ης τέ : Ποητεῖ
ὑπε Ἀντιφάν]ης ?

No. 2323 a (= ii. 974 c)

Comedies at Dionysia (4th cent.)

ὑπε : Ἀσκληπιόδ]ωρο[ς
Μένανδρος] πέμ : 'Ηνιόχωι
ὑπε : Κάλ]λιππος πρεσβύτ
ὑπο : Κάλλι]ππος νεώ : ἐνικ   'Ε[πὶ.....παλαιᾶι
312–11   'Επὶ Πολέμ]ωνος παλαιᾶι
......Θ]ησαυρῶι Ἀνάξαν
πoη : Φιλιπ]πίδης Μύστιδι   ι
ὑπε : Ἀσκ]ληπιόδωρος   γ
Νικόστ]ρατος δεύ   μ
.....οσκόπωι

---

[1] Adaeus, who was mentioned in a comedy of Herakleides, died 353 B.C. A comic poet Theophilus was victor in 329 B.C. (but on this restoration Theophilus would be an actor).

No. 2323 a (cont.)

ὑπε: Κ]άλλιππος νεώτε
Ἀμεινί]ας τρι: Ἀπολειπούσει   φ
οὗτος ἔ]φηβος ὢν ἐνεμήθη[1]   τ
ὑπε: Ἀσκ]ληπιόδωρος   Στ[τέ:
Θεόφιλο]ς (?) τέ: Παγκρατιασ   ὑπ[ε
ὑπε: ...ιπ]πος   Νι[κόστρατος? πέμ
[Μένανδρος[2] πέ: Π]αιδίωι   ύ[πε
[ὑπε:]   ύ[πο: ἐνίκα
ὑπο: Ἀσκληπιόδωρο]ς ἐνίκ[α   [ἐπὶ   ]

[*Note.* Some lines which are too fragmentary to be informative are omitted.]

No. 2323 (= ii. 975)
Comedies at Dionysia

Col. i (c. 215–210 B.C.)

     Ἐρχιεῦσιν
[ὑπε Νικόδη]μος
[ἐπὶ......] οὐκ ἐγένετο
[ἐπὶ.....π]αλαιᾶι
........Φωκεῦσι Φιλή
[πoη Ἀριστο]κράτης Ἀπε
........ὑ]πε Νικόδημος
........Ἀ]νεψιοῖς
[ὑπε   ]ος
[......Πον]ήραι
[ὑπε   ]της
[Ἐμπ]όρωι
[ὑπε]ης
    ωι
[ὑπε]ης
[Ἀγν]οοῦντι

Col. ii[3] (some omissions at beginning)

[   ] Προγαμοῦντι
[ὑπε   ]ων
   π]ρεσβύτερος τεθ
[Παρακαταθ]ήκει
[ὑπε   ]μαχος
[   ]
[ὑπε   ]
[   ]εφήβοις
[ὑπε   ]
[ὑπο   ἐ]νίκα
[Ἐπὶ   οὐ]κ ἐγένετο
[Ἐπὶ   ο]υ παλαιᾶι
[Μισογ]ύνει Μενάνδρου
[πoη   ]νης Ἀδελφαῖς
[ὑπε   ]ος
[   ] Δακτυλίωι
[ὑπε   ]ων

[   ]Ἀθην[αίωι
   (some lines missing)
ὑπ[ε
Τιμόθ[εος
ὑπε Π[
Κλεο[
ὑπε[
Ὀλυ[μπ
ὑπ[ε
   (some lines missing)

Col. iii

Τ]ι[μόστρα]τος Λυ[τρουμένωι
ὑπε [Δ]ιογείτων
ὑπο Κράτης ἐνίκα
188–187
Ἐπὶ Συμμάχου οὐκ ἐγ[ένετο
187–186
Ἐπὶ Θεοξένου οὐκ [ἐγένετο]
186–185
Ἐπὶ Ζωπύρου [παλαιᾶι
Ἐράτων Μεγ[
πoη Λαί[νης...
   (some lines missing)
184–183
ὑπε Ὀνή]σιμ[ο]ς
  Κρίτων Ἐφεσίοις
ὑπε Σώφιλος
Παράμονος Ναυαγῶι
ὑπε Ὀνήσιμος
Τιμόστρατος Φιλοικείωι
ὑπε Καλλίστρατος
Σωγένης Φιλοδεσπότωι
ὑπε Ἑκαταῖος
Φιλήμων νεώ Μιλησίαι
ὑπε Κράτης
ὑπο Ὀνήσιμος ἐνί[κα
183–182
Ἐπὶ Ἑρμογένου οὐκ [ἐγέ]νετο

---

[1] Cf. p. 85, n. 5.
[2] Webster, *C.Q.*, N.S. 2 (1952), p. 20.
[3] Prof. S. Dow and Mr. C. A. P. Ruck have generously allowed us to anticipate their forthcoming new edition of col. ii. The change in the last line of col. iii is also theirs.

Col. iii (cont.)

182–181
Ἐπὶ Τιμησιάν[ακτος π]αλαιᾶι
Φιλόστρατο[ς Ἀποκλε]ιομένει Ποσει
ποη[. . . .   ]κλήρωι
            (some lines omitted)

ποη
ὑπε Πο
Ἰόλαος
ὑπε Φ
Τιμο[Εὐ]εργετοῦντι
[ὑπε   ]
      Συνε]ξαπατῶντι
[ὑπε   ]
[ω]ν Συντ[ρ
[ὑπε   ]ης
      Συναγῶνι
ὑπε   ]ίδης
ὑπο   ξ]ένος ἐνί[κα
[Ἐπι. . .7. . .ο]υ αἱ πρω[. .

Col. iv

[Ἐπὶ   παλαιᾶι]
[   ]
ποη   Μονο]τρόπωι
[ὑπε   ]
          Ἀν]ασωιζομ[έ
[ὑπε   ]
      ]υμέναι
ὑπε. . . . . . .]ος
. . . . .Ἀγνοοῦντι
ὑπε Κριτόδ]ημος
. . . . . .Ν]εμέσει
ὑπε Σώ]νικος
Παρά]μονος Χορηγοῦντι
ὑπ]ε Μόνιμος
ὑπ]ο Κριτόδημος ἐνίκα
169–168
Ἐ]πὶ Εὐνίκου οὐκ ἐγένετο
168–167
Ἐπὶ Ξενοκλέους παλαι[ᾶι
Μόνιμος Φάσματι Μεν[άνδρου
ποη Παράμονος τεθνηκὼς. . . . . .ις
ὑπε Δάμων
Κρίτων Αἰτωλῶι
ὑπε Μόνιμος
Βίοττος Ποητεῖ
ὑπε Δάμων
Λάμπυτος[
ὑπε Κα. . . .
Ἐπικρ[άτης. . . .

ὑπ[ε   ]
[ὑπο   ἐνίκα]
167–166
[Ἐπὶ   ]
                (some lines lost)
164–163
[Ἐπὶ] Εὐερ[γέτου οὐκ ἐγένετο[1]
163–162
Ἐ]πὶ Ἐράστ[ου οὐκ ἐγένετο
162–161
Ἐπὶ Ποσει[δωνίου οὐκ ἐγένετο
161–160
Ἐπὶ Ἀριστ[όλα παλαιᾶι
Ἡρακλ[
πο[η

Col. v

ὑπε Καβεί]ριχος
Ἐπ]ιγέ[ν]ης Λυτρουμένῳ
ὑπε Καβείριχος
ὑπο Νικόλαος ἐνίκα
157–156
Ἐπὶ Ἀνθεστηρίου οὐκ ἐγένε[το
156–155
Ἐπὶ Καλλιστράτου οὐκ ἐγένε[το
155–154
Ἐπὶ Μνησιθέου παλαιᾶι
Δάμων Φιλαθηναίωι Φιλιππί[δου
πο Φιλοκλῆς Τραυματίαι
ὑπε Καλλικράτης
Χαιρίων Αὑτοῦ Καταψευδομέ[νωι
ὑπε Δάμων
Βίοττος Ἀγνοοῦντι
ὑπε Δάμων
Τιμόξενος Συγκρύπτον[τι
ὑπε Καλλικράτης
Ἀγαθοκλῆς Ὁμονοία[ι
ὑπε Νι]κ[ό]λαος
ὑπο   ἐνίκα]

Col. vi

ὑπ]ε Λυσίμαχος
      ακοντα
      Σαλαμινίαις
      Ἀτ]θίσιν
Φ]ίλων ἐνίκα
143–142
Ἐπὶ   ο]ὐκ ἐγένετο
142–141
[Ἐπὶ   οὐκ ἐγένε]το
      (The record ended *c.* 120 B.C.)

[1] See Meritt, *Hesperia* 26 (1957), p. 74, for this change.

I.G. ii². 2325 = ii. 977 (*Lists of victors*)

(Some portions which are practically uninformative are omitted in this transcript.)

Tragic Poets at Dionysia

	Col. i		Col. iii
	(about 10 lines missing)		(7 lines missing)
485–484	Αἰ]σχύ[λος Δ|||		......as
	Εὐ]έτης |		Καρκί]νος Δ|
472–471	Πο]λυφράσμ[ων	373–372	Ἀστ]υδάμας Γ||[-?
	Νόθ]ιππος |		Θεο]δέκτας Γ||
469–468	Σοφ]οκλῆς ΔΓ|||		Ἀφα]ρεύς ||
	Μέσα]τος ||[-?		....ω]ν ||
c. 460	Ἀριστ]ίας		

Tragic Actors at Dionysia

	Col. i	Col. ii (early 4th cent.)
	ὑποκριτῶν τρ[αγικῶν	(4 lines missing)
450–449	Ἡρακλεί[δης	Νι[
	Νικόμαχο[ς	Θε[
	Μυννίσκος	Ἀ]σ[
	Σαώνδας [|]	Ἀθη[
	Ἄνδρων ||	Ἀρι[στ
	Χ]αι[ρ]έστρατος |	
	Μενεκ]ράτης |||	Col. iii (late 4th cent.)
	Λεπ]τίν[ης	
		Αἰσχ]ύλ[ος
		Πλ]εισθένης |
		Γο]ργοσθένης ||
		Ἐπα]μείνων ||

Comic Poets at Dionysia

	Col. i		Col. ii
	[ἀστικαὶ ποητῶν]		Τηλεκλεί]δης |||
	[κωμικῶν]		.........]s |
487–486	[Χιωνίδης]		- -
	- -		- -
	- -		
	.........]s |	438–437	Φερ[εκράτης
	- -	436–435	Ἑρμ[ιππος
c. 480	Μάγνη]ς Δ|	427–426	Ἀρι[στοφάνης
	.......]s |	425–424	Εὔπ[ολις ||||]
	Ἀλκιμέ]νη[s?]|	423–422	Κά[νθαρος
	......]s |		Φρύ[νιχος
459–458	Εὐφρόν]ιος |	415–414	Ἀμ[ειψίας
	Ἐκφαν]τίδης ||||		Πλά[των
	Κρατῖ]νος Γ|		Φιλ[ωνίδης
	Διοπ]είθης ||		Λύκ[ις
451–450	Κρά]της |||		Λεύ[κων
447–446	Καλλία]s ||		vacat

Comic Poets at Dionysia (cont.)

	Col. iii		Col. vi

Col. iii

    Νικοφῶν
    Θεόπομπ[ος
403–402 Κ[η]φισό[δωρος

Col. v

c. 290 Πο]σείδιππος ||||
    Σατυρίων |
    Ἀ]πολλόδωρος ||
c. 279–278 Φιλή]μων ⌐|
    Δαμό]ξενος |
    Φοινικ]ίδης ||

Col. vi

    (6 lines missing)
    ....ος |
    ....θ]εος |
    Ποσεί]διππος ||
    ...... |||
    - -
    - -
    Νίκαρχος |
    Νικόμαχος |
    Ἀριστοκράτης |[
186–185 Λαίνης |||
184–183 Φιλήμω[ν

Col. vii

    (6 lines missing)
155–154 Χα[ιρίων
    Δη
    (5 lines missing)
    Πο
    Ο

Comic Actors at Dionysia

Col. ii

285–284 Ἀριστόμα]χ[ος
    Δημ]έας |
    Ἐχ]ένικος |
    Δ]έρκετος |
    Ἀριστίων ||
    Φιλωνίδη[ς
    Φιλοκλῆ[ς
    Καλλίστρ[ατος
    Ἐμμενί[δης
    Πολυκ[λῆς
    (4 lines missing)

Col. iii

    (8 lines missing)
c. 255 Φιλοκ]ύδης |||
    ....ης |
    Εὐην?]ωρ |||
    ]ν |
    Κηφι]σόδωρος ||
    Ἀρισ]τομένης ||
    Διον]ύσιος |
    ]ν ||

Comic Poets at Lenaia

Col. i

    Ληναϊκ]α[ὶ ποη]τῶν
    [κωμικ]ῶν
c. 440 Ξ]ενόφιλος |
    Τηλεκλείδης ⌐
    Ἀριστομένης ||
    Κρατῖνος |||
    Φερεκράτης ||
    Ἕρμιππος ||||
429–428 Φρύνιχος ||
    Μυρτίλος |
427–426 Εὔ]πολις |||

Col. ii

c. 412–11 Πο[λίοχος] |
    Με[ταγέν]ης ||
    Θεό[πομπ]ος ||
    Πολ[ύζηλο]ς ||||
    Νικοφ[ῶν
    Ἀπολ[λοφάν]ης |
    Ἀμ[ειψίας
    Νι[κοχάρης?
    Ξενοφῶν |
    Φιλύλλιος |
    Φιλόνικος |
    ....]ς |
    [Κηφισόδωρος](?)

Comic Poets at Lenaia (cont.)

	Col. iii		*Col. iv*
c. 378–377	Φίλιπ[πος] ||		– –
	Χόρη[γος		Διο[νύσι]ος|
	Ἀναξα[νδρί]δης |||		Κλέ[αρχ]ος [
	Φιλέτα[ιρο]s ||		Ἀθηνοκλῆς[
	Εὔβουλος ⌐|		Πυρ[ρήν]|
	Ἔφιππος |[		Ἀλκήνωρ |
	Ἀ]ντιφάνη[s] ⌐|||		Τιμοκλῆς |
	Μ]νησίμα[χος] |		Προκλείδης |
	Ναυσ[ικράτ]ης |||	321 or 320	Μ[έν]ανδρος ||[
	Εὐφάνη[s -		Φ[ι]λήμων |||
	Ἄλεξις ||[		Ἀπολλόδωρο[s
	Ἀρ]ιστ[οφῶν		Δίφιλος |||
	– –		Φιλιππίδης ||[
	– –		Νικόστρατος[
	– –		Καλλιάδης |
	– –	after 311	Ἀμεινίας |
	Ἀσκληπιόδω]ρος? |		– –

	Col. vi	*Col. vii*		*Col. viii*
	(11 lines missing)	(9 lines missing)		(9 lines missing)
	– – |	Πο]λυ[		Ἐμμ]ενίδης |
	..]όδωρος |	Θεμισ[τ		Ἀρί]στων |||
	Εὐμήδη[s] ||	Θέω[ν		Νούιος |||
	Πανδαί[τ]ης |	Θεοδ[		Διονύσιος |
	Μενεσ[θ]εύς |	Διοσκο[υρίδη]s |	155–154	Ἀγαθοκλῆς |
		Εὐβου[λίδη]s |		Ἀρχικλῆς ||
		Θεόδω[ρος		Βίοττος |
		Ὀ]νησι......|||		Νικόδημος ||

Tragic Poets at Lenaia

	Col. iii		*Col. iv*
	(2 lines missing)	c. 330	Ἀχαι[ός] |
	...7...]ης ||		Φιλ[ῖ]νος |
	Ἀπολλόδω]ρος ⌐		Ἀσκληπιάδης[
	.....]as |		Καίριος |
	.....]δης |		Τι]μόστρατ[ος
	....κ]ράτης |		
c. 340	Ἀστυδ]άμας[		
	.....]δη[s		

Tragic Actors at Lenaia

Col. i

ὑποκριτῶν τραγικῶν
Χαιρέσ[τ]ρατος |
[Με]ν[εκρ]άτης |
Λεπτίν]ης |||
- -
Μυννίσκ?]ος ||
419–418 Καλλιππῖ]δης ⌐|
Νικόστρα]τος |||

Col. ii

c. 400 Χαρίδημος [
Φίλιππος [
Φύτιος ||
Εὐπόλεμο[ς
Θρασύβο[υλος] |
Ἀριστόδ[ημος] ||
Μίρων ||
Κλ]εο[δάμα]ς |
Θεόδωρος ||||
Ἵππαρχος ⌐|
Ἀμεινίας |
Ἀν]δροσθένης |
Νεο]πτόλεμος |
348–347 Θεττ]αλός ||
.....]ς ||
Ἀριστ]ίων |
.....άδης |

Col. iii

- -
- -
........]ος ||
.......]ς ||
Ε[......]ς |
Ἀρ[ιστοφ]ῶν |
Πο[
Ν[
c. 330 Ἀρχίας [
Πραξία[ς
Ἱερομν[ήμω]ν |||
Φιλ[
Νικ[
Ἀρι[

Col. iv

- -
Ἐ[
Βακχ[
Στεμφ[ύλιος
Ξένων |
Χαρίας [
Ἀντιμέ[νης
Τεισίλα[ς
Γο[ργοσθένης
Νίκων || [
Ἀριστόνι[κος
Πύρριχος [
Ἀγήτωρ |
Θηραμέν[ης
Κλεῖτος [

Col. v

- -
Τ...
279 Κλεό[δωρος
Αἰσχύ[λος
Ἀρίμνη[στος
Ἐπαμε[ίνων
Ἐροτ[ίων
Ἀ]ρισ[τ

Col. vi

Ἡράκ[λειτος
Ἀλέξανδ[ρος
Καλλικλῆς |||
Ε]ὐρήμων |
Ἰσο]κράτης |
....]υνος ||
......]ος |
........]ος |

Col. vii

Πάμφιλος [
Σωσίθεος ||
Πολύκριτος |
Ναύσων |
Ἀρίστων |

Col. viii

Ἔχετος ||||
Ἐ]πίνικος ||||

Comic Actors at Lenaia

Columns i and ii must have gone back to about 442 B.C.

Col. iii		Col. vi
c. 375	Σάτ]υρος ΓΙ	Πολυ[κλῆς?
	Φι]λήμων ΙΙ	Λυκίσ[κος
	Κα]λλίστρατ[ος	Σωσικλῆ[ς
	(8 lines missing)	Πολύζηλο[ς
	...]κων ΙΙΙΙ	Πυθάρατος Ι
	Παρμένων Ι	Καλλίας ΙΙΙ
	Λύκων ΙΙ	Μενεκ[λῆ]ς Ι
	Ν[α]υσικ[ράτης	Δ[ημήτρ]ιος ΙΙ
	Ἀμ]φιχ[άρης	Πιτθεύς Ι
	Φο]ρ[μίων	Ἡρακλείδης ΙΙ
		- -

Col. v			
before 312	Ἀρισταγόρας Ι		........]ρος ΙΙ
	Κάλλιππος ΙΙΙΙ		.....] Ι
	Ἀσκληπιόδωρος Γ		.....]ς ΙΙ
	Π]ολύευκτος Ι		Δ[ημο?]κράτης Ι
	Π]υρραλεύς Ι		Φιλ[ο]στέφανος Ι
	Μ]οσχίων ΙΙ	*c. 240*	Ἑρμόφαντος Ι
	Δη]μ[οφῶ]ν		
286–285	Ἱ]ερώνυμος ΙΙΙΙ		
	Ἀριστόμαχος ΙΙΙ		Col. vii
	Δέρκετος Ι[		Φιλ[
	- -		Φερ[
	Φιλοκ[λῆς		Δη[μ
	Ἀριστοκράτης Ι		
	Ἐμμενίδης Ι		
	Αὐτόλυκος Ι		
	Φιλωνίδης Ι		
	Σωκράτης Ι		

Notes on *I.G.* ii². 2325

This record has been pieced together out of 41 marble fragments, nearly all found on the south slope of the Acropolis, most of them written by the same hand, but with some later portions added by others. The record was inscribed on the Ionic epistyles or architraves of the same building as carried the didaskaliai, *I.G.* ii². 2319–23, with 17 lines to each column. There is some reason for thinking (with Reisch) that the building was the votive offering of an agonothetes in the year 279–278 B.C., though the record must have been continued later. The order of the names is that of the individual poet's or actor's first victory in his appropriate category. A number of dates are confirmed, or an approximate dating rendered possible, by entries in other inscriptions, particularly (for the later period) by those recording the Soteria of Delphi and performances at Delos. (References are given by Kirchner.) Most marginal dates are of this character, and should not be taken to refer to a first victory at the festival in question.

Notes on details

Tragic poets at Dionysia

Αἰσχύλος. First victory dated 485–484 B.C. by *Marm. Par.*, ep. 50.

Πολυφράσμων. Son of the tragic poet Phrynichos ('Suidas', s.v.), whose name will have appeared higher in the column. (Phrynichos' only dated victory, 476, with Themistocles as choregos, Plut. *Them.* 5.) One Dionysiac victory known in 471 (*I.G.* ii². 2318, p. 104 here), third to Aeschylus and Aristias in 467 *Λυκουργείᾳ τετραλογίᾳ* (Argt. Aesch. *Septem*).

Νόθιππος. Mentioned Athen. viii. 344 c, and identified by Wilamowitz and Wilhelm, *U.D.A.*, p. 102, with Gnesippos.

Μέσατος. This restoration was originally made by Capps (*Am. J. Phil.* 20 (1899), p. 401), on the evidence of schol. Ar. *Wasps* 1502, but was doubted by Wilhelm, *U.D.A.*, pp. 102–3. It has since been revived by Davison (*C.R.*, N.S. 3 (1953), 144), Yorke (*C.Q.*, N.S. 4 (1954), 183 f.), and Lesky (*Hermes* 82 (1954), p. 1), on the evidence of the new papyrus fragment, *P. Oxy.* 2256, fr. 3, which seems clearly to refer to a Mesatos competing with Aeschylus and Sophocles. (The date 463 seems very likely; see p. 232, n. 3 below.)

Ἀστυδάμας. The difficulties about the two fourth-century poets of this name have hardly reached a satisfactory solution. The relevant evidence is that Diodorus, xiv. 43, says that an Astydamas produced his first play in 399–398 at the age of sixty, and that *Marm. Par.*, ep. 71 gives a first victory to an Astydamas in 373–372. See, besides the references quoted on p. 107, Reisch, *Wien. Stud.* 34 (1912), p. 338, n. 1; Snell, *Gött. Nachr.* 1966, 33–37; and, for a third-century descendant, p. 282 below.

Θεοδέκτας. Not only a tragedian, but a theorist of some note. See, for example, Webster, *Art and Literature in Fourth-century Athens*, pp. 61 ff. The epigram quoted by Steph. Byz. s.v. *Φάσηλις* gives him eight victories; one of these was presumably at the Lenaia.

Ἀφαρεύς. His two victories were won with plays presented for him by Dionysius (see p. 84, n. 7).

A very fragmentary fourth column contains the beginnings of names which may have been those of Aiantides, Homeros, and Dionysios, who were tragic poets of the Alexandrian Pleiad.

Tragic actors at Dionysia

Ἡρακλείδης. A victory in 447 (*I.G.* ii². 2318). His first victory can be placed in 449 (see above, pp. 72, 102).

Μυννίσκος. A victory in 422 (*I.G.* ii². 2318).

The names in col. ii can be shown to be early fourth-century. Hence *Θε*[is more likely to be *Θε*[όδωρος] than *Θε*[τταλός]. (But see Snell, op. cit., 21–25.)

Γοργοσθένης. Painted by Apelles (Plin. *N.H.* xxxv. 93).

Comic poets at Dionysia

Μάγνης. Cf. Anon. *de Com.* α' (p. 7 Kaibel) ἀγωνισάμενος Ἀθήνησι νίκας ἔσχεν ἔνδεκα. (See also *Dith. Trag. Com.*², 190, n. 2).

Εὐφρόνιος. See *I.G.* ii². 2318, col. ii (a victory in 458).

Κρατῖνος. First victory perhaps 454, the year under which he appears as *clarus* in Jerome, but Plato *comicus* appears in the same year.

Κράτης. *Clarus* in Jerome, 451–450.

Καλλίας. Cf. *I.G.* ii². 2318, col. iii (a victory in 446).

Λύσιππος. (Cf. p. 121.) Should fill the third or fourth space in col. ii, probably the fourth, where Wilhelm, p. 110, reports suitable traces.

Φερεκράτης. The date comes from an emendation of Anon. *de Com.* α' (p. 8 Kaibel) by Dobree νικᾷ ἐπὶ Θεοδώρου (θεάτρου MS.).

Ἕρμιππος. Cf. *I.G.* ii². 2318, col. iv (a victory in 435).

Ἀριστοφάνης. Victory probably won with the *Babylonians*, 426. The long controversy as between the rival readings Ἀρ[ιστοφάνης] and Ἀρ[ιστομένης] seems to have been finally settled in favour of the former. See p. 85, n. 9.

Εὔπολις. We have restored four victories at the Dionysia, since 'Suidas' gives him seven in all and the Lenaia list has three.

Κάνθαρος. Cf. *I.G.* ii². 2318, col. v (a victory in 422).

Φρύνιχος. First victory (which must have been at the Lenaia) in 430–429, Anon. *de Com.* α' (p. 8 Kaibel).

Ἀμειψίας. A victory with Κωμασταί, 414 (Argt. Ar. *Birds*).

Νικοφῶν. His Ἀδωνίς competed against Ar. *Plutus* in 389–388 (Argt. *Plutus*).

Κηφισόδωρος. Cf. Lysias xxi. 4 ἐπὶ δὲ Εὐκλείδου ἄρχοντος (403–402) κωμῳδοῖς χορηγῶν Κηφισοδώρῳ (Κηφισοδότῳ MS.) ἐνίκων.

Ποσείδιππος. Cf. 'Suidas' s.v. τρίτῳ ἔτει μετὰ τὸ τελευτῆσαι Μένανδρον διδάξας. (Menander died in 292–291.)

Ἀπολλόδωρος. Of Carystos; he also won three Lenaian victories.

Φιλήμων. Philemon II, son of the elder Philemon; Sifakis, *Studies*, p. 29.

Φοινικίδης. Fourth at Lenaia in 285–284 (*I.G.* ii². 2319).

Φιλήμων (col. vi), Philemon III, last at Dionysia in 183 (*I.G.* ii². 2323, col. iii), where he is labelled νεώ(τερος).

The contest in comedy at the Dionysia went on till about 120 B.C., cf. *I.G.* ii². 2323, col. vi (Reisch, *Zeitschr. öst. Gym.* 58 (1907), p. 299).

Comic actors at Dionysia

Many of these names appear in the list of actors at the Lenaia and in the inscriptions from Delos and Delphi.

Comic poets at Lenaia

The beginning of the contest in comedy, both for poets and actors, is to be placed in the period 445 to 440 B.C. See Reisch, *Zeitschr. öst. Gym.* 58 (1907), p. 308; Capps, *A.J.P.* 28 (1907), pp. 186 f.

The six names lost at the end of col. i must include those of Aristophanes, Philonides, and Archippos.

Ἀναξανδρίδης. First victory at Dionysia in 376 (*Marm. Par.*, ep. 70), another there in 375 (*I.G.* ii². 2318). See pp. 105, 107.

Μένανδρος. The passage of Anon. *de Com.* (p. 9 Kaibel; p. 84, n. 5 here) which refers to Menander's first appearance is in fact corrupt, reading ἐπὶ Διοκλέους (409–408 or 286–285). Φιλοκλέους (322–321), which is generally read, is Clinton's emendation, resting on the Armenian version of Eusebius which gives *Isandrus*' first victory under that year. Jerome has *Menander primam fabulam cognomento* ὀργην *docens superat* under 321–320. Clark, *Class. Philol.* 1 (1906), pp. 313–28, argued for Ἀντικλέους (325–324), for it is only in that year, not in 322–321, that Menander could have been an ephebe. He is supported by Dinsmoor (*Archons of Athens*, pp. 41–42), whose arguments seem conclusive. But we still have to allow for Eusebius, and it seems most likely that he is referring to a Lenaian victory. We suggest the following time table:

342–341. Born (*I.G.* xiv. 1184; Dinsmoor prefers 343–342, but see Sealey, *C.R.*, N.S. 7 (1957), pp. 195–7).

325–324. First production.

322–321 or 321–320. First Lenaian victory with Ὀργή.

317–316. Lenaian victory with Δύσκολος (Hypothesis).

316–315. First City victory (*Marm. Par.*, ep. B. 14).

292–291. Death (*I.G.* xiv. 1184; Dinsmoor, op. cit., pp. 39 ff.).

He won eight victories in all, with 105 plays (Apollodorus 244 F 43).

Wilhelm's statement (*U.D.A.*, p. 131) that he won three Lenaian victories seems to be a slip. We now know of two, and this list shows that there cannot have been more than four, which leaves four to six for the Dionysia.

Φιλήμων. First victory at the Dionysia, 328–327 (*Marm. Par.*, ep. B. 7); a Lenaia victory in 307–306 (*I.G.* ii². 3073; see p. 120).

Φιλιππίδης. Cf. *I.G.* ii². 2323a for a victory at the Dionysia in 311; in the same year Νικόστρατος was second. Philippides also had an important public career, spending much of his time at the court of Lysimachus (Plut. *Demetrius* 12; *I.G.* ii². 657 (283–282)).

Tragic poets at Lenaia

Ἀπολλόδωρος. Of Tarsus, to whom 'Suidas' ascribes six tragedies.

Ἀχαιός. The younger, from Syracuse ('Suidas' s.v.).

Tragic actors at Lenaia (see also Snell, *Gött. Nachr.* 1966, 11–13)

Some of these names appear in the list of actors at the Dionysia.

Καλλιππίδης. Victorious at the Lenaia in 419–418, *I.G.* ii². 2319.

Ἀριστόδημος. Still prominent in 348, Aeschin. ii. 15.

Θεόδωρος. Gave 70 Aeginetan drachmae (= 100 Attic) to the restoration of the Delphic temple in 360 (Tod, *G.H.I.* ii. 140, wrongly dated 363).

Ἵππαρχος. Presumably the lover of Neaera (Dem. lix. 26).

Νεοπτόλεμος. A Dionysia win in 341 (*I.G.* ii². 2320).

Θετταλός. Dionysia wins in 347 and 340 (*I.G.* ii². 2318).

Ἱερομνήμων. Possibly a Lenaia win in 307–306 (*I.G.* ii². 3073; see below).

Ἡράκλειτος. Of Argos; mentioned in records of Soteria for 256 and 252.

Comic actors at Lenaia

Φιλήμων. Acted for Anaxandrides (Aristot. *Rhet.* iii. 1413ᵇ25).

Παρμένων. Cf. Aeschin. *in Tim.* 157 (345 B.C.) (p. 234, n. 1), and p. 171.

Κάλλιππος. One win in 307–306 (*I.G.* ii². 3073, see below); won at Dionysia 312, appeared there 311 (*I.G.* ii². 2323a).

Ἱερώνυμος. One win in 286–285 (*I.G.* ii². 2319).

I.G. ii². 3073 (*Monument of Xenokles*)

(Wilhelm, *U.D.A.*, pp. 209 ff.; Capps, *A.J.A.* 4 (1900), pp. 76 f.; Reisch, *de Mus. Gr. Cert.*, p. 83; *B.C.H.* 3 (1879), pl. 5 bis)

ὁ δῆμος ἐ[χορήγει ἐπ' Ἀναξι]κράτους ἄρχοντος·   307–306
ἀγωνοθέ[της Ξενοκλῆς Ξ]είνιδος Σφήττιος
ποιητὴς τραγωιδοῖς ἐνίκα [Φανόστρατο]ς Ἡρακλείδου Ἁλικαρνασσεύς
ὑποκριτὴς τραγωιδοῖς ἐνίκ[α Ἱερομνήμω]ν Εὐανορίδου Κυδαθηναιεύς
ποιητὴς κωμωι[δ]οῖς ἐνί[κα Φιλήμω]ν Δάμωνος Διομειεύς
ὑποκριτὴς κ[ωμωιδοῖς ἐνίκα Κάλλιπ]πος Καλλίου Σουνιεύς.

The monument set up by Xenokles as agonothetes was about 14 feet high, and the tablet on which the inscription was carved was enclosed in a decorative architectural setting. That the monument refers to the Lenaia, not the Dionysia, is proved by the fact that tragedy is recorded before comedy (contrast the order of *I.G.* ii². 2318). Phanostratos is praised in a Delian decree (*I.G.* xi. 4. 528): Sifakis, *Studies*, p. 29.

I.G. xiv. 1097 *and* 1098 (*Roman fragments*)

The texts here transcribed follow the restoration by Dittmer, *The Fragments of Athenian Comic Didaskaliai found in Rome*, who assumes a line of 74 letters. See also Moretti, *Athenaeum* 38 (1960), pp. 263–82 with plates.

1098 a

(The poet first referred to is Teleikleides, and the extant portion must have been preceded by an enumeration of his three Dionysiac and five Lenaian victories.)

δεύτερος] ἐν ἄ[στει
         ] Εὐμε[νίσι
'Ε]πὶ Εὐδ[
κωμωιδι]αι Λήναια [

Στ]έρρους ἀν[εδίδαξε
] τέταρτος [ἐν ἄστει
'Ησ]ιόδοις σώιω[ι
Στρατ]ιώταις [name of poet
ἐπὶ δὲ τὴν νίκη]ν καὶ ἐπὶ τὰ τρ[ίτα καὶ τὰ τέταρτα οὐκ ἦλθε
] Ξενόφιλος [
ἐπὶ τὰ τ]ρίτα καὶ ἐπὶ τὰ [τέταρτα οὐκ ἦλθε.

Notes

l. 1. Telekleides' first Lenaian victory was won about 441–440 B.C. (*I.G.*
ii². 2325). He is identified (for this inscription) by the titles Στερροί and 'Ησίοδοι.

l. 3. There is no archon in this period beginning with Εὐδ[(*l.* 3): Kört
suggests that this is a mistake for Εὐθυδήμου (432–431 B.C.): Capps proposes
an alternative restoration 'Επὶ Ἀ]ψευδ[ους (archon 433–432 B.C.).

l. 4. κωμωιδίᾳ in this and the next fragment implies that when this record
was compiled the name of the particular play (which failed to get the first
prize) was lost.

l. 7. σώιωι, if correct, probably implies that there was a copy in the
Alexandrian Library. Perhaps read σώι[ζεται?

1097

(The first poet referred to in this fragment is Kallias, one of whose two
Dionysiac victories was in 446.)

'Ε]πὶ Ἀντιοχίδου Κύ[κλωψιν		434
]ς κωμωιδίαι Δ ἐν ἄ[στει		
κω]μωιδίαι ἐπὶ Τιμοκλέ[ους		440
ἐ]πὶ Θεοδώρου Σατύροις [		437
5 'Υπέ]ροις σιδηροῖς ἐπὶ Πυ[θοδώρου		431
Βατράχ]οις Ε ἐπὶ Ἀντιοχίδου [		434
Λ]ύσιππος ἐνίκα μὲν [ἐν ἄστει ἐπὶ	c.	440
ἐπὶ Γλαυκί]ππου Καταχήναις [		409
Βάκχ]αις αὗται μόναι σώι[ζονται		
10 ___ ἐ]πὶ Διοφάντου Διονύ[σωι		394
Β ἐν ἄσ]τει ἐπὶ Νικοτέλου[ς		390
ἀνεδίδαξ]ε ἐπὶ Λυσιμάχου[		435
Γ ἐν ἄστε]ι ἐπὶ Μορυχίδου [		439
ἐπὶ Στρατοκλέο]υς Κολεοφόροις[		424

Notes

l. 9. Some fragments of Lysippos' Βάκχαι (the only play of which the Alexandrians had a copy) are preserved.

ll. 10–14. Probably (as Capps and Dittmer propose) a record of Aristomenes,
who must have had a long career; but the case is not perfectly made out.

1098

Begins with a record of the plays of Anaxandrides; the preceding portion must have recorded his seven Dionysiac victories (the first in 376 B.C. according to *Marm. Par.*) and three Lenaian. It begins with the plays placed second.

] ἐπὶ Χίωνος Μαι[νομένωι	*364*	
]ς Διονύσου γοναῖ[ς		
] Ἀμπρακιωτίδι *Γ* ἐν [ἄστει		
ἐπὶ Λυσισ]τράτου Ἐρεχθεῖ ἐ[πὶ	*368*	
5 Ἡρακ]λεῖ ἐπὶ Χαρισάνδρο[υ	*375*	(or Ἀχιλ]λεῖ)
ἐπὶ Ἱπ]ποδάμαντος Ἰοῖ ἐ[πὶ	*374*	
] Ὀδυσσεῖ ἐπὶ Κηφισοδ[ότου	*357*	(or Κηφισοδ[ώρου 365)
] ἐπὶ Ἀπολλοδώρου Ἀγ[ροίκοις	*349*	
διὰ Ἀνα]ξίππου Λήναια ἐπ[ὶ		(or διὰ Διω]ξίππου)
10 π]οίωι ἐπὶ Ναυσιγένου[ς	*367*	
Ε̄] ἐν ἄστει ἐπὶ Χίωνος [	*364*	
Φαρμακομάν]τει ἐπὶ Ἀγαθοκλ[έους	*356*	
] ἐπὶ Θουδήμου Ἀ[	*352*	
]ου Ἀντέρωτι ἐ[πὶ		
15 Ἔφιππος ἐ]νίκα Λήναι[α		
]ι ἐν ἄστ[ει		
]ι ἐπ[ὶ		
ἐπὶ] Ἀρ[ιστοδήμου	*351*	

l. 16. Dittmer (p. 9) emends the first letter to *Γ*, but the reading is clear on Moretti's plate. This may be a case where the Lenaia victories preceded those at the Dionysia.

The whole inscription from which these three fragments come contained the lists of plays produced by each poet in order of the places awarded to each play, and under each rank (firsts, seconds, etc.), giving the Dionysian placings before the Lenaian. It is conjectured that 'the record probably extended back to the introduction of Comedy into each of the two festivals, about 486 B.C. for the City Dionysia and 442 B.C. for the Lenaia' (Dittmer, p. 7). It was probably derived from Alexandrian sources, e.g. from Callimachus' πίναξ καὶ ἀναγραφὴ τῶν κατὰ χρόνους καὶ ἀπ' ἀρχῆς γενομένων διδασκάλων, and beyond that from the official Διδασκαλίαι at Athens. Körte and others think that the great size of the inscription suggests that it occupied a wall in some great library in Rome, where the fragments were found.

For a similar inscription, dealing with actors' victories, and previously assigned to Rhodes (*I.G.* xii. 1. 125), see Wilhelm, *U.D.A.*, pp. 205 ff., and Moretti, *Athenaeum* 38 (1960), pp. 263 ff., who proves its Roman origin and adds new fragments (Snell, op. cit., 13–21, has some speculative restorations). Note also *P. Tebt.* 695, part of a list of tragedians (late third century B.C.).

Inscription in Hesperia 7 (*1938*), *pp. 116–18*

Two fragments discovered in the course of the excavations of the Agora are published by B. D. Meritt.

Fragm. A. [...............*c. 14*...]s
[........*c. 8*] δ[εύτ]ε
[.....*c. 5*]όδημος τρί
[ἐπὶ Ἀλ]κιβιάδου ἄρχον *vacat*
[ἀγων]οθέτης Νικοκλῆς
[παλ]αιᾶι κωμωιδίαι
[Καλ]λίας ἐνίκα
[Μισα]νθρώποις Διφι
[Διοσκ]ουρίδης δεύ
[Φάσμ]ατι Μενάνδρ
[.....*5*]s τρί Πτωχῆ Φιλ
[σατύροι]s παλαιοῖς
[......*6*]os ἐνίκ Ἑρμεῖ
[.......*7*] δεύ Ἀτλαν[τ
[.....τρί] Μαθητ[αῖς (?)
[παλαιᾶι τρα]γ[ωιδιᾶι

Fragm. B. [........*c. 9*.τρί] Φυλ[
[.......*c. 8*Μεν]εκρ
[παλαιᾶι τρ]αγωιδιᾶι
[......*c. 7*.ἐ]νίκα
[.......*c. 8*:Σ]οφο
[........*c. 9*.δ]εύ Ἰξί[ονι
[......*s. 7*τρί Οἰ]δίπ[οδι

The inscription recorded the actors who were placed first, second, and third in each of the contests in old comedy, old satyr play, and old tragedy, and fragment A from line 4 to the end is for the year in which Alcibiades was archon, viz. 255–254 B.C. The date to which fragment B refers is undeterminable; it may be earlier or later. Meritt argues that the inscription refers to the Lenaia, but see above, p. 41, n. 11.

Notes

A, *ll.* 1–3. Why should not these refer to the old tragedies of the year 256–255 B.C.?

Καλλίας. Cf. *I.G.* ii². 2325 (p. 116 above). His first victory was about 265 B.C.

Μισανθρώποις. Capps (*Hesperia* 11 (1942), pp. 325 ff.) stoutly defends this against Körte's proposal of Φιλάνθρωποι (*Hermes* 73 (1938), pp. 123 ff.). There can be no certainty, but Capps makes out a strong case.

Πτωχέ. Probably = Πτωχεῖ = Πτωχῇ. (See Kock, *C.A.F.* ii, pp. 495 f.)

Ἑρμεῖ. The only known *Hermes* was a satyr play by Astydamas.

The interest of the fragments is that they prove that instead of a performance of a single old play of each kind, there was at this date a contest between the old plays of each kind (or their actors), and that satyric plays were treated in the same way as tragedies and comedies. Körte connects this with the collection of old plays by the Alexandrians and the love of satyric plays at Alexandria though perhaps he overstates the case.

Chronological Summary

City Dionysia

Contest of tragic poets. Thespis *c.* 534 B.C. Record of *I.G.* ii². 2318 (*Fasti*) began ? *c.* 501 B.C.

Contest of comic poets. Probably 486 B.C. ('Suid.' s.v. Chionides). Continued at least to *c.* 120 B.C. (*I.G.* ii². 2323).

Contest of tragic actors. c. 449 B.C. (*I.G.* ii². 2325; Wilhelm, *U.D.A.*, p. 9. List begins with Herakleides).

Contest of comic actors. Began between 329 and 312 B.C. (*I.G.* ii². 2318 proves that there was no contest in 329, and *I.G.* ii². 2323a that there was a contest in 312 B.C.). Continued at least to about 120 B.C. (*I.G.* ii². 2323).

Performance of old tragedies. In 386 B.C. first performance (*I.G.* ii². 2318, παρεδίδαξαν must imply that it was an 'extra'); in 341–339 B.C. (*I.G.* ii². 2320) it is introduced by παλαιᾷ in each year, as if it was part of the regular programme.

Performance of old comedies. In 339 B.C. first performance (*I.G.* ii². 2318, παρεδίδαξαν); probably regular in 311 B.C. (παλαιᾷ, *I.G.* ii². 2323 a); last record 154 B.C. (*I.G.* ii². 2323).

Note. In the victors' list *I.G.* ii². 2325 there is no mention of prizes given to tragic or comic actors who brought out old plays, nor in the *Fasti* or didaskaliai, but in the inscription published in *Hesperia* 7 (1938), pp. 116–18, there *is* a record of contests of old comedies, old satyric plays, and old tragedies with a prize for the successful actor in each kind, in the year 254 B.C., but it is not certain that the reference is to the Dionysia.

Satyric plays. Not recorded in *Fasti* (*I.G.* ii². 2318), but in the didaskaliai for 341–339 B.C. (*I.G.* ii². 2320) the list for each year begins with a single satyric play.

For competitions of old satyric plays in 254 B.C. see note above. They are evidently at this time placed on a level with tragedies and comedies.

Dithyrambs. Inscriptional record in *Fasti* begins in 473–472 B.C. Date of earliest contests uncertain. Record in *Fasti* goes down to 328 B.C. Performances probably continued to a late date (see p. 74).

Lenaia

Contest of tragic poets. c. 440–430 B.C. Proved by tragic actors' list in *I.G.* ii². 2325. List of victorious poets goes down to about 320 B.C.; but as the tragic actors' list (so far as extant) goes down to end of third century B.C., the contest of poets doubtless also continued.

Contest of comic poets. c. 442–440 B.C. (*I.G.* ii². 2325. List of poets headed by Xenophilus and Telekleides, whose first city victory was c. 445 B.C.). The extant didaskalic record (*I.G.* ii². 2319) terminated soon after 284 B.C., being immediately succeeded by a column recording tragedies at the Lenaia, but the list of victorious comic poets continues beyond 150 B.C. (*I.G.* ii². 2325).

Contest of tragic actors. Began 440–430 B.C. (*I.G.* ii². 2325). Extant victors' list goes down to end of third century B.C.

Contest of comic actors. Began c. 442 B.C. Extant victors' list in *I.G.* ii². 2325 begins about 375 B.C. but was preceded by two other columns, which would bring it up to about 442 B.C. Extant record goes down to end of third century B.C., but contests probably continued until after 150 B.C.

Note. A fifth-century date is confirmed if a statement in the Argument to Aristophanes' *Peace*, which runs ὑπεκρίνατο Ἀπολλόδωρος ἡνίκα Ἑρμῆν λοιοκρότης, is rightly emended ἐνίκα Ἕρμων ὁ ὑποκριτής, and refers (as suggested by Körte, *Rh. Mus.* 52 (1897), p. 172) not to the extant *Peace*, which was produced at the City Dionysia in 421 B.C., but to the second play of the same name composed by Aristophanes. See O'Connor, pp. 48, 95, and, against Rose's emendation, Russo, *Aristofane*, pp. 227 f.

Satyric plays. No record, and no room for satyric play in *I.G.* ii². 2319 (c. 432 B.C. onwards).

Old tragedies. No record.

Old comedies. No record. (In 284 B.C. the plays were all new.)

Dithyrambs. *I.G.* ii². 3779 records a dithyrambic victory at the Lenaia won by a citharode early in the third century B.C. (see p. 42).

III

THE ACTORS

A. *Terminology, etc.*

1. THE word regularly used to denote an actor in tragedy or comedy from the last quarter of the fifth century B.C. onwards was ὑποκριτής. It first occurs in literature in Aristophanes, *Wasps* 1279 (422 B.C.),[1] and if the inscriptional record commonly called *Fasti* (*I.G.* ii². 2318), though itself engraved in the middle of the fourth century, transcribes accurately the archons' records of the fifth, the word was used from the first of the victorious protagonist in the actors' contest in tragedy, instituted about 449 B.C.[2]

The connected verb ὑποκρίνομαι is used in epic poetry in two senses: (1) 'interpret' omens or dreams;[3] (2) 'answer' a question;[4] and both meanings are found later,[5] the second mainly in Herodotus. The meaning to 'act' a play or a particular part is first found in literature in the middle of the fourth century,[6] but no doubt went back as far as the use of ὑποκριτής for 'actor'—probably a century or more earlier. The word ὑπόκρισις, apparently in the sense 'performance', already occurs in Pindar, fr. 140 b (Snell), l. 15. It and the kindred word ὑποκριτική are also used by Aristotle of the orator's or actor's 'declamation' or 'delivery'.[7]

---

[1] τὸν δ' ὑποκριτὴν ἕτερον ἀργαλέον ὡς σοφόν.   [2] See pp. 72 f., 102.

[3] *Il.* xii. 228; *Od.* xix. 535, 555, and probably *Od.* xv. 170, though either meaning would be possible here.   [4] *Il.* vii. 407; *Od.* ii. 111; *Hymn to Apollo* 171.

[5] The first in Aristophanes, *Wasps* 53; Hippokr. *Epist.* 15; Theocr. xxiv. 67; Philostr. *Vit. Apoll.* ii. 37. The second frequently in Hdt. (30 instances in Powell's *Lexicon*) : e.g. i. 2. 3; 164. 2; and (of an oracle) 78. 3; 91. 6; in Attic only *I.G.* i². 410, and in Thuc. vii. 44. 5 (where the reading of the tradition is certain in spite of editorial 'emendation' and cannot bear the interpretation of von Blumenthal, *Gnomon* 19 (1943), p. 33, n. 2). ὑποκριτής is used of the 'interpreter' in Plato, *Tim.* 72 b (τῆς δι' αἰνιγμῶν οὗτοι φήμης καὶ φαντάσεως ὑποκριταί), and in Lucian, *Somn.* 17. The question which of the two senses provided the derivation of the nomen agentis ὑποκριτής, meaning 'actor', has been hotly debated recently, without a certain conclusion emerging. The probabilities perhaps lie with the sense 'interpret', 'expound'. For discussion, see Lesky, *Studi in onore di U. E. Paoli* (1955), pp. 469 ff.; id. *Tragische Dichtung der Hellenen*, pp. 43 f.; Page, *C.R.*, N.S. 6 (1956), pp. 191–2; H. Koller, *Mus. Helv.* 14 (1957), pp. 100–7; H. Schreckenberg, *ΔΡΑΜΑ: vom Werden d. gr. Trag. aus dem Tanz*, diss. Würzburg (1960), pp. 111 ff.; Else, *Wien. Stud.* 72 (1959), pp. 75–107; H. Patzer, *Die Anfänge der gr. Trag.* (1962), p. 127, n. 4; Schneider, *R.E.*, Suppl. VIII s.v. ὑποκριτής, largely ignores the question.

[6] Dem. *de F.L.* 246; Aristot. *Eth. Nic.* vii. 1147ᵃ23, *Rhet.* iii. 1403ᵃ23.

[7] Ibid. 1413ᵇ23, etc.

The question whether and when the word ὑποκριτής was used in a restricted sense, of actors other than the protagonist, will be considered shortly; but there seems to have been no other word at any time for 'actors' in general (including protagonists), and in Plato[1] and other writers it is used in this general sense. Once only it is used of the chorus— in the scholium on Aeschylus *Agamemnon* 1348 πεντεκαίδεκά εἰσιν οἱ τοῦ τραγικοῦ χοροῦ ὑποκριταί; but the reference here is to the passage in which the chorus break into dialogue with one another and so behave like ὑποκριταί. Aristotle's precept,[2] καὶ τὸν χορὸν δὲ ἕνα δεῖ ὑπολαβεῖν τῶν ὑποκριτῶν, shows (in the context) that it was *not* generally so regarded. Hippocrates also refers[3] to certain παρεισαγόμενα πρόσωπα ἐν τῇσι τραγῳδίῃσιν (presumably mute characters), who σχῆμα μὲν καὶ στολὴν καὶ πρόσωπον ὑποκριτοῦ ἔχουσιν, οὐκ εἰσὶ δὲ ὑποκριταί.

2. There is more difference of opinion about the terms τραγῳδός, τραγῳδοί, κωμῳδός, κωμῳδοί. The plural is regularly used of the members of the tragic or comic chorus from Aristophanes onwards. It is also used quite commonly to denote the tragic or comic performance, contest, or festival as a whole, at least from the middle of the fourth century. Aeschines uses such expressions as γιγνομένων τῶν ἐν ἄστει τραγῳδῶν, τραγῳδῶν γιγνομένων καινῶν, τοῖς τραγῳδοῖς ('at the time of the tragic contest'), μελλόντων ὥσπερ νυνὶ τῶν τραγῳδῶν γίγνεσθαι.[4] The same use is found in an inscription[5] of the middle of the century—ἀνειπάτω δὲ αὐτὸν ὁ μετὰ Γνάθιν δήμαρχος Διονυσίων τῶν Ἐλευσῖνι τοῖς τραγῳδοῖς, in the law of Euegoros quoted by Demosthenes,[6] in the inscription of Xenokles in 306 B.C. ποιητὴς τραγῳδοῖς ἐνίκα κτλ.,[7] and possibly in the heading of the *Fasti*, but in default of any certain restoration of this heading this must remain in doubt.[8]

Closely connected with the above usages is that of the plural to represent the performers of a tragedy as a whole, without any conscious differentiation of actors and chorus. This is probably the sense throughout the *Fasti*, e.g. for the year 458 B.C.: κωμῳδῶν | Εὐρυκλείδης ἐχορήγει | Εὐφρόνιος ἐδίδασκε | τραγῳδῶν | Ξενοκλῆς Ἀφίδνα: ἐχορή | Αἰσχύλος

---

[1] e.g. *Sympos.* 194 b (of Agathon ἀναβαίνοντος ἐπὶ τὸν ὀκρίβαντα μετὰ τῶν ὑποκριτῶν; cf. *Rep.* iii. 373 b, 395 a, *Charm.* 162 d, *Laws* vii. 817 c).

[2] *Poet.* xviii. 1456ᵃ25.   [3] Νόμος (Littré, iv, p. 634), §1.

[4] *In Ctes.* 41, 34, 45, 154: cf. O'Connor, p. 23. In Dem. *de Pace* 7 εἰ γὰρ ἐν Διονύσου τραγῳδοὺς ἐθεᾶσθε the meaning 'performance of tragedies' would be possible, but the rendering 'rival tragic actors' gives more point to the passage, the comparison being with Demosthenes and Aeschines as rival orators.

[5] *I.G.* ii². 1186; see above, p. 47. *I.G.* ii². 20 (393 B.C.) almost certainly has such a use.

[6] *Meid.* 10; see above, p. 27.

[7] *I.G.* ii². 3073 (I differ from O'Connor about this). See above, p. 120.

[8] See above, p. 102.

ἐδίδασκεν. (The genitives may depend on ἐχορήγει = χορηγὸς ἦν, or on one of the lost words of the heading.) Some scholars think that in the entries for 386 B.C.: ἐπὶ Θεοδότου | παλαιὸν δρᾶμα πρῶτο[ν] | παρεδίδαξαν οἱ τραγῳδοί, and for 339 B.C.: ἐπὶ Θεοφράστου | παλαιὸν δρᾶμα πρῶτον | παρεδίδαξαν οἱ κωμῳδοί, the words refer to the actors in particular, but there seems to be no reason why they should do so, and the intrusion of a second meaning into an otherwise consistent inscription seems hardly natural, even though in *I.G.* ii². 2323 the old comedy performed is placed under the name of the protagonist.

The word τραγῳδός (with the plural τραγῳδοί) is rarely applied to the poet. It is possibly so used in Aristophanes, *Wasps* 1480, 1498, 1505, though the meaning 'actor' cannot be ruled out.[1] Other possible (though not quite certain) instances are Krates, fr. 24 (K) τοῖς δὲ τραγῳδοῖς ἕτερος σεμνὸς πᾶσιν λόγος ἄλλος ὅδ' ἔστιν; and (in the transition-period between Middle and New Comedy) Diphilus, fr. 30 (K) ὡς οἱ τραγῳδοί φασιν, οἷς ἐξουσία | ἔστιν λέγειν ἅπαντα καὶ ποιεῖν μόνοις; and Timokles, fr. 6 (K) τοὺς γὰρ τραγῳδοὺς πρῶτον εἰ βούλει σκόπει | ὡς ὠφελοῦσι πάντας.[2] The use of κωμῳδοί in Plato, *Laws* xi. 935 d is equally uncertain: τί δὲ δή; τὴν τῶν κωμῳδῶν προθυμίαν τοῦ γελοῖα εἰς τοὺς ἀνθρώπους λέγειν ἢ παραδεχόμεθα; The general meaning 'comedy' is not ruled out by the mention of poets (comic, iambic, lyric) a few lines later on, though it is at least likely that κωμῳδῶν should be rendered generally 'comic writers' (as by Rees). A more certain argument is derived from such passages as Ar. *Clouds* 1091, where τραγῳδοῦσ' ἐκ τίνων; is used in a manner exactly parallel to συνηγοροῦσιν ἐκ τίνων; and δημηγοροῦσιν ἐκ τίνων; and seems to imply τραγῳδοί (meaning tragic poets) as a parallel to συνήγοροι and δημήγοροι. In a number of other passages[3] the work of the individual comic poet is described by the verb κωμῳδεῖν, and probably implies that the poet himself could be called κωμῳδός. An almost certain instance in the Classical period is in Aristotle, *Poetics*, ch. xxii. 1458ᵇ31 ff. Ἀριφράδης τοὺς τραγῳδοὺς ἐκωμῴδει ὅτι ἃ οὐδεὶς ἂν εἴποι ἐν τῇ διαλέκτῳ τούτοις χρῶνται.[4] There is no doubt of this usage in a few passages of

---

[1] See O'Connor, pp. 19, 20, for the meaning 'poet'. But the passage of Aristophanes may imply simply that Philokleon, dancing the dances employed by the oldest tragedians (Thespis and Phrynichos), challenges any contemporary actor to produce anything better. The uncertainty is caused by the fact that at least one of the sons of Karkinos, who accept the challenge, was a poet.

[2] This is followed by a number of references to tragic heroes and heroines, but there is no mention of poets, and τοὺς τραγῳδούς may be quite general (= 'tragedy').

[3] e.g. Ar. *Ach.* 631, 655, *Peace* 751, and Aristot. *Poet.* xxii (see above): cf. Ar. *Thesm.* 85 ὁτιὴ τραγῳδῶ καὶ κακῶς αὐτὰς λέγω. The word, however, may in certain contexts refer to the style of the speaker's delivery, e.g. Dem. *de Cor.* 13 ἡλίκα νῦν ἐτραγῴδει καὶ διεξῄει.

[4] Another instance would be found in ch. v. 1449ᵇ1 f.: καὶ γὰρ χορὸν κωμῳδῶν ὀψέ ποτε

late writers, such as Plutarch (τὸ τοῦ τραγῳδοῦ, followed by a quotation) and Lucian; Pollux[1] speaks of a poet (Eudoxus) τῶν νέων κωμῳδῶν, and a scholiast on Ar. *Frogs* 86 writes εἰσὶ δέ, ὥς φασι, δύο Ξενοκλεῖς τραγῳδοὶ γεγονότες.[2]

The use of τραγῳδός, κωμῳδός to denote the actor occurs in some fourth-century writers,[3] viz. Plato, *Phaedrus* 236 c ἵνα δὲ μὴ τὸ τῶν κωμῳδῶν φορτικὸν πρᾶγμα ἀναγκαζώμεθα ποιεῖν ἀνταποδιδόντες ἀλλήλοις (though even here the general sense 'comedy' is not impossible); Chares (a fourth-century historian), 125 F 4 (Jacoby) ὑπεκρίθησαν τραγῳδοὶ μὲν Θετταλός κτλ.; and Aristotle, *Oecon*. 1. iv. 1344ᵃ20 ἡ δὲ διὰ τῆς κοσμήσεως οὐδὲν διαφέρουσά ἐστι τῆς τῶν τραγῳδῶν ἐν τῇ σκευῇ πρὸς ἀλλήλους ὁμιλία.[4] The words are regularly used of the actors in the inscriptional records of festivals at Delphi, Delos, and elsewhere from about 280 B.C. onwards,[5] as well as in late writers such as Plutarch, Athenaeus, and others. In these inscriptions it is striking that τραγῳδός and κωμῳδός are normally used of the protagonists in old plays, the other actors being called either ὑποκριταί or συναγωνισταί,[6] though ὑποκριτής could be used of the protagonist as well, and if he produced an old play he was called ὑποκριτὴς παλαιᾶς κωμῳδίας or τραγῳδίας. There seems to be no instance of τραγῳδός or κωμῳδός being used of the protagonist of a new play; this is always ὑποκριτής.

This idiomatic use of τραγῳδός in later times to signify the protagonist, as distinct from the ὑποκριταί who took the lesser roles, seems to be confirmed by a scholium on Demosthenes *de Pace* 6. Demosthenes uses the words κατιδὼν Νεοπτόλεμον τὸν ὑποκριτήν, and the scholiast states that in his own time (i.e. in that of the unknown scholar whom he is probably quoting) he would have called him τραγῳδός. Some words in the scholium are out of place, but (as restored by Capps[7]) it should run: ὑποκριτὰς ἐκάλουν οἱ ἀρχαῖοι τοὺς νῦν τραγῳδοὺς λεγομένους, [τοὺς ποιητάς, οἷον τὸν Εὐριπίδην καὶ Ἀριστοφάνην] τοὺς δὲ νῦν ὑποκριτὰς (οὗτοι δὲ ἦσαν δύο) τὸν μὲν δευτεραγωνιστὴν τὸν δὲ τριταγωνιστήν, αὐτοὺς δὲ τοὺς ποιητὰς τῶν

ὁ ἄρχων ἔδωκεν, if the emendation κωμῳδῷ, which Bywater once favoured, were adopted (see Gudeman ad loc.). Note also *Poet*. 1449ᵃ5, where Aristotle uses the word τραγῳδοδιδάσκαλοι in the sense 'tragic poets'. τραγῳδοί perhaps means 'poets' in Call. *Fr*. 203. 44.

[1] vii. 201.
[2] The use of the word here may be a reminiscence of the scene in *Wasps* 1478 ff. (see above).
[3] On Dem. *de Pace* 7 εἰ γὰρ ἐν Διονύσου τραγῳδοὺς ἐθεᾶσθε, see above, p. 127, n. 4.
[4] Here the context requires that the τραγῳδοί shall be individuals, and excludes any more general meaning. (The *Oeconomicus*, however, is possibly a third-century work, and it is not Aristotelian as it stands, though much of its material may be.)
[5] See (for a brief account) *Theatre of D*., pp. 240 ff., and below, Ch. vii.
[6] It is unnecessary to discuss here whether there are any exceptions to this general rule as laid down (for example) by O'Connor, p. 15.   [7] *Am. J. Phil*. 29 (1908), pp. 206 ff.

δραμάτων τραγῳδοὺς καὶ τραγῳδοδιδασκάλους, followed by a further scholium, τραγῳδούς· τοὺς ποιητάς, οἷον τὸν Εὐριπίδην καὶ Ἀριστοφάνην. In the scholiast's time (or that of his authority, perhaps an Alexandrian of the third or second century B.C.) the tragic 'team' included a τραγῳδός and two ὑποκριταί.[1]

Professor G. F. Else has tried[2] unconvincingly to carry this distinction between τραγῳδός and ὑποκριτής back to the earliest days of tragedy. Of these early days Aristotle in the *Poetics*[3] writes: καὶ τό τε τῶν ὑποκριτῶν πλῆθος ἐξ ἑνὸς εἰς δύο πρῶτος Αἰσχύλος ἤγαγε καὶ τὰ τοῦ χοροῦ ἠλάττωσε καὶ τὸν λόγον πρωταγωνιστὴν παρεσκεύασεν· τρεῖς δὲ καὶ σκηνογραφίαν Σοφοκλῆς. (The 'two actors' of Aeschylus are generally assumed to be the poet himself and one other. In his latest plays he required three actors who are similarly assumed to be himself and two others. The three actors of Sophocles' later career did not include himself as he had ceased to act.[4]) With this passage must be connected Themistius' account[5] of Aristotle's report: καὶ οὐ προσέχομεν Ἀριστοτέλει ὅτι τὸ μὲν πρῶτον ὁ χορὸς εἰσιὼν ᾖδεν εἰς τοὺς θεούς, Θέσπις δὲ πρόλογόν τε καὶ ῥῆσιν ἐξεῦρεν, Αἰσχύλος δὲ τρίτον ὑποκριτὰς καὶ ὀκρίβαντας, τὰ δὲ πλείω τούτων Σοφοκλέους ἀπελαύσαμεν καὶ Εὐριπίδου. Assuming the text to be correct, Thespis, acting by himself, delivered a prologue and set speech—we do not know what he called himself or was called; this was the second stage in the history of tragedy—then Aeschylus (thirdly) introduced 'actors', i.e. two persons at least, not merely declaiming speeches but acting a plot and conversing with each other and probably with the chorus, and these would be called ὑποκριταί (he himself being one of them). The lost passage of Aristotle which Themistius cites was probably the basis of Diogenes Laertius:[6] τὸ

---

[1] See later (Ch. vii) on the Διονύσου τεχνῖται, of whom these teams were members.

[2] G. F. Else, *T.A.P.A.* 76 (1945), pp. 1–10. See further, *Wien. Stud.* 72 (1959), pp. 75 ff.

[3] iv. 1449ᵃ15. On the text of this passage see R. Kassel, *Rh. Mus.* 105 (1962), pp. 117 ff.

[4] We are told that he played the lyre in his *Thamyras*, and played ball in the *Nausicaa* (or *Plyntriai*), to the delight of the audience (*Vit. Soph.* 5; Athen. i. 20 f; Eustath. *Od.*, p. 1553. 63; see also p. 93, n. 3, above). This is commonly supposed to mean that Sophocles never acted, but there seems to be some misunderstanding. It is difficult to imagine who played the lyre in *Thamyras* except the hero himself, and Eustathius explicitly says that it was in the part of Nausicaa that Sophocles played ball in the *Plyntriai*. If so, these were probably early plays, and Sophocles only later gave up acting, διὰ τὴν ἰδίαν μικροφωνίαν, and perhaps also because of the rise of professional actors.

[5] *Orat.* 26, 316 d. See Lesky, *Trag. Dichtung der Hellenen*², p. 41 with n. 1.

[6] iii. 56: cf. 'Suid.' s.v. Σοφοκλῆς· οὗτος πρῶτος τρισὶν ἐχρήσατο ὑποκριταῖς καὶ τῷ καλουμένῳ τριταγωνιστῇ; and *Vit. Soph.* 4 παρ' Αἰσχύλῳ δὲ τὴν τραγῳδίαν ἔμαθε, καὶ πολλὰ ἐκαινούργησεν ἐν τοῖς ἀγῶσι. πρῶτον μὲν καταλύσας τὴν ὑπόκρισιν τοῦ ποιητοῦ διὰ τὴν ἰδίαν μικροφωνίαν (πάλαι γὰρ καὶ ὁ ποιητὴς ὑπεκρίνετο αὐτός), τοὺς δὲ χορευτὰς ποιήσας ἀντὶ ιβ' ιε', καὶ τὸν τρίτον ὑποκριτὴν ἐξεῦρεν (I follow Else's punctuation). If Aeschylus in his latest plays adopted the innovation of Sophocles, it is easy to see that the change might be attributed by some writers to himself. Cf. Cramer, *Anecd. Par.* i, p. 19; Philostr. *Vit. Apoll.* vi. 11, Horace, *A.P.* 278.

παλαιὸν ἐν τῇ τραγῳδίᾳ πρότερον μὲν μόνος ὁ χορὸς διεδραμάτιζεν, ὕστερον δὲ Θέσπις ἕνα ὑποκριτὴν¹ ἐξεῦρεν ὑπὲρ τοῦ διαναπαύεσθαι τὸν χορόν, καὶ δεύτερον Αἰσχύλος, τὸν δὲ τρίτον Σοφοκλῆς καὶ συνεπλήρωσε τὴν τραγῳδίαν. Further, the *Life* of Aeschylus states: ἐχρήσατο δὲ ὑποκριτῇ πρώτῳ μὲν Κλεάνδρῳ, ἔπειτα καὶ τὸν δεύτερον αὐτῷ προσῆψε Μυννίσκον τὸν Χαλκιδέα· τὸν δὲ τρίτον ὑποκριτὴν αὐτὸς ἐξεῦρεν, ὡς δὲ Δικαίαρχος ὁ Μεσσήνιος, Σοφοκλῆς. (πρώτῳ does not of course mean that Kleandros was the first ὑποκριτής ever so called, but that he was the first employed by Aeschylus in addition to himself. Mynniskos would only have acted in the poet's latest plays, as he was still active many years after Aeschylus' death.²) Out of these notices a very probable account can be constructed. Tragedy began with a choral performance of τραγῳδοί: to this Thespis added a prologue and set speech delivered by himself.³ The speech (which, at any rate, as Diogenes asserts, gave the chorus a breathing-space) may or may not have been an answer to questions by the chorus. If it was, and if ὑποκριτής in the meaning 'actor' derives from the sense 'answerer', the speaker could have been termed ὑποκριτής because of this; or the term may have come into use at any time when he or his successors (before the time of Aeschylus), or Aeschylus himself, began not merely to declaim but to converse with the chorus, or, at latest, when Aeschylus called in Kleandros as a second actor and conversed with him (and probably with the chorus as well). Aeschylus and Kleandros could certainly be called ὑποκριταί, 'answerers' of each other or of the chorus;⁴ so, of course, could Sophocles' three actors, and so in Aeschylus' last plays could Aeschylus, Kleandros, and Mynniskos. But it is quite uncertain whether the true derivation of ὑποκριτής is not from the sense 'interpreter, expounder' (see above, p. 126, n. 5), and more particularly there seems to be no sufficient ground for supposing (with Else⁵) that, when Themistius says that Aeschylus invented ὑποκριταί, the word excludes the part played by the poet himself as actor; or that in the *Life* of Aeschylus the writer implies

¹ i.e. himself, but the writer is concerned only with the form of the drama, not with the names of the actors. We cannot tell whether Thespis called himself ὑποκριτής.
² *I.G.* ii². 2318, col. 5 (p. 105 above), 422 B.C.)
³ Aristot. *Rhet.* iii. 1. 1403ᵇ23 ὑπεκρίνοντο γὰρ αὐτοὶ τὰς τραγῳδίας οἱ ποιηταὶ τὸ πρῶτον, and Plut. *Solon* 29. 6 ἐθεάσατο τὸν Θέσπιν αὐτὸν ὑποκρινόμενον, ὥσπερ ἔθος ἦν τοῖς παλαιοῖς. The note of Pollux, iv. 123, ἐλεὸς δ' ἦν τράπεζα ἀρχαία, ἐφ' ἧς πρὸ Θεσπίδος εἴς τις ἀναβὰς τοῖς χορευταῖς ἀπεκρίνατο may be true, and Thespis may have substituted his more dignified pro-logue and speech for this crude procedure; but the note is of very doubtful historical value (see *Dith. Trag. Com.²*, pp. 86–88).
⁴ Photius s.v. ὑποκρίνεσθαι· τὸ ἀποκρίνεσθαι οἱ παλαιοί· καὶ ὁ ὑποκριτὴς ἐντεῦθεν, ὁ ἀπο-κρινόμενος τῷ χορῷ. Cf. Hesychius, s.vv. ὑποκρίνοιτο, ὑποκριτής; Apollonius Soph. *Lex. Hom.*, p. 166 B.
⁵ *T.A.P.A.* 76 (1945), pp. 5 f.

that Kleandros was a ὑποκριτής[1] and the poet was not. In the very sentence which precedes, ὑποκριταί is used in a sense which must cover the poet's own role as actor, and in many passages of Aristotle it is equally inclusive. Else supposes that Thespis and Aeschylus called themselves τραγῳδοί, as distinct from ὑποκριταί. They may or may not have called themselves or been called τραγῳδοί; about this there is no evidence, but it is most improbable that either Aristotle or the writer of the *Life* should have introduced in a particular sentence without warning a restricted sense of ὑποκριταί, inconsistent with their use of the word elsewhere. The partial specialization and differentiation of the words τραγῳδός and ὑποκριτής—it was never complete—belongs apparently to the organization of the Διονύσου τεχνῖται in the third century. (The victorious protagonist in the fifth and fourth centuries was always recorded under the title of ὑποκριτής in the *Fasti*, as also are the actors named in the victors' lists (*I.G.* ii². 2325).)

3. The words πρωταγωνιστής, δευτεραγωνιστής, and τριταγωνιστής, with the corresponding verbs, are occasionally, though rarely in extant literature, used of actors in the theatre, and the first two of participants in other contests. πρωταγωνιστής and πρωταγωνιστεῖν could be used metaphorically of the leader or most important agent in any activity involving effort, and they are several times found in this sense in the fourth century B.C., viz. Aristotle, *Pol.* v (viii). 4. 1338ᵇ30 ὥστε τὸ καλὸν ἀλλ' οὐ τὸ θηριῶδες δεῖ πρωταγωνιστεῖν; *Poet.* iv. 1449ᵃ17 τὸν λόγον πρωταγωνιστὴν παρεσκεύασεν; Klearchos (an historian of the fourth or third century), fr. 19 (Wehrli) τῆς ὑπηρεσίας πρωταγωνιστής. It is not known to what writers 'Suidas' is indebted when he says of Chionides, ὃν καὶ λέγουσι πρωταγωνιστὴν γενέσθαι τῆς ἀρχαίας κωμῳδίας, but the word must mean 'originator', 'first *poet*', not 'first *actor*'. They are first used with reference to the theatre in extant literature by Plutarch, *Praec. ger. reip.* xxi. 816 f. ἄτοπον γάρ ἐστι τὸν μὲν ἐν τραγῳδίᾳ πρωταγωνιστὴν Θεόδωρον ἢ Πῶλον ὄντα μισθωτὸν τῷ τὰ τρίτα λέγοντι πολλάκις ἕπεσθαι καὶ προσδιαλέγεσθαι ταπεινῶς, ἂν ἐκεῖνος ἔχῃ τὸ διάδημα καὶ τὸ σκῆπτρον, ἐν δὲ πράξεσιν ἀληθιναῖς κτλ.; and *Vit. Lysandr.* 23. 6 οἷον ἐν τραγῳδίαις ἐπιεικῶς συμβαίνει περὶ τοὺς ὑποκριτάς, τὸν μὲν ἀγγέλου τινὸς ἢ θεράποντος ἐπικείμενον πρόσωπον εὐδοκιμεῖν καὶ πρωταγωνιστεῖν, τὸν δὲ διάδημα καὶ σκῆπτρον φοροῦντα μηδὲ ἀκούεσθαι φθεγγόμενον. (Plutarch also uses πρωταγωνιστεῖν in its general sense, without reference to the drama.[2]) In Lucian, *Calumn.* 7 both the technical

---

[1] Else, op. cit., pp. 5–6, misunderstands πρωτῷ (see above).
[2] *de Alex. fort.* 332 d, and *de Mus.* 1141 d (πρωταγωνιστούσης δηλονότι τῆς ποιήσεως, sc. as compared with the flute).

and the general senses are in mind : πρῶτον . . . παραγάγωμεν τὸν πρωταγωνιστὴν τοῦ δράματος, λέγω δὲ τὸν ποιητὴν τῆς διαβολῆς. The reference
to the theatre is found in a note of Pollux with regard to the use of the
stage-doors, which is certainly untrue of the Classical period :[1] τριῶν δὲ
τῶν κατὰ τὴν σκηνὴν θυρῶν ἡ μέση μὲν βασίλειον ἢ σπήλαιον ἢ οἶκος ἔνδοξος
ἢ πᾶν τοῦ πρωταγωνιστοῦντος τοῦ δράματος, ἡ δὲ δεξιὰ τοῦ δευτεραγωνι-
στοῦντος καταγώγιον. It is quite uncertain of what period or play Pollux
is speaking. It also appears in Plotinus iii. 2. 17 ὥσπερ ἐν δράματι τὰ μὲν
τάττει αὐτὸς ὁ ποιητής, τοῖς δὲ χρῆται οὖσιν ἤδη· οὐ γὰρ αὐτὸς πρωταγωνιστὴν οὐδὲ δεύτερον οὐδὲ τρίτον ποιεῖ, ἀλλὰ διδοὺς ἑκάστῳ τοὺς προσή-
κοντας λόγους ἤδη ἀπέδωκεν ἑκάστῳ, εἰς ὃ τετάχθαι δέον;[2] and in the
scholiast on Euripides Phoenissae 93 ταῦτα μηχανᾶσθαί φασι τὸν Εὐριπίδην
ἵνα τὸν πρωταγωνιστὴν ἀπὸ τοῦ τῆς Ἰοκάστης προσώπου μετασκευάσῃ.

Apart from the passage of Pollux just quoted (where it means 'second
actor'), we find δευτεραγωνιστής used in the general sense of 'seconder'
or 'supporter' in Demosthenes, de F.L. 10, ἔχων Ἴσχανδρον τὸν Νεοπτο-
λέμου δευτεραγωνιστήν (where it seems pointless to suppose a reference
to the actor's profession, even though Neoptolemos was an actor and the
scholiast took the reference to be to Ischander's position in Neoptolemos'
troupe—he was now referred to solely as a politician), and in Lucian,
Peregr. 36 ὁ ἐκ Πατρῶν δᾷδα ἔχων, οὐ φαῦλος δευτεραγωνιστής. The only
passages in which it is generally thought to be used with reference to the
drama are in the lexicon of Hesychius, where it is rendered by δεύτερος
ἀγωνιζόμενος (and even this may be quite general), and the inaccurate
scholium on Demosthenes, de Pace 6 quoted above.[3]

On the contrary τριταγωνιστής and τριταγωνιστεῖν are always used
(except in this same scholium) with reference to an actor, and this actor
is nearly always Aeschines, taunted by Demosthenes. It is, however, ex-
ceedingly unlikely that this was its sole use or that the word was coined
by Demosthenes.[4] He uses it first in de F.L. 247. The whole passage (246–7)
must be noted :

ταῦτα μὲν γὰρ τὰ ἰαμβεῖα ἐκ Φοίνικός ἐστιν Εὐριπίδου· τοῦτο δὲ τὸ δρᾶμα οὐδεπώ-
ποτ' οὔτε Θεόδωρος οὔτ' Ἀριστόδημος ὑπεκρίναντο, οἷς οὗτος τὰ τρίτα λέγων
διετέλεσεν . . . . Ἀντιγόνην δὲ Σοφοκλέους πολλάκις μὲν Θεόδωρος, πολλάκις δ'
Ἀριστόδημος ὑποκέκριται, ἐν ᾗ πεποιημένα ἰαμβεῖα καλῶς καὶ συμφερόντως ὑμῖν

---

[1] Pollux iv. 124. See Theatre of D., pp. 238 f.

[2] Apparently the poet has a protagonist, etc., assigned to him, and so χρῆται οὖσιν ἤδη
(accepts them as assigned), but he does give to each (τάττει αὐτός) the speeches adapted to
his rank. Plotinus' date was in the third century A.D.

[3] pp. 129 f. Some late instances of the metaphorical sense are found in the scholia to Demosthenes and in 'Suid.' s.v. Ἀβρογάστης (quoted by Rees, Rule of Three Actors, pp. 33–34).

[4] As suggested by Rees, op. cit., p. 34.

πολλάκις αὐτὸς εἰρηκὼς καὶ ἀκριβῶς ἐξεπιστάμενος παρέλιπεν. ἴστε γὰρ δήπου
τοῦθ' ὅτι ἐν ἅπασι τοῖς δράμασι τοῖς τραγικοῖς ἐξαίρετόν ἐστιν ὥσπερ γέρας τοῖς
τριταγωνισταῖς τὸ τοὺς τυράννους καὶ τοὺς τὰ σκῆπτρα ἔχοντας εἰσιέναι.[1]

This passage (delivered thirteen years before the speech *On the Crown*)
does not suggest that τριταγωνιστής was anything but a current and
understood equivalent for ὁ τὰ τρίτα λέγων, or that Demosthenes had
invented it *ad hoc*. Besides this, the comic poet Antiphanes wrote a play
called *Τριταγωνιστής*, which may or may not have had any reference to
Aeschines, but may have been brought out at any date after the death
in 380–379 B.C. of Philoxenos (the dithyrambic poet), who is the subject
of the only extant passage. This passage seems likely to have been written
while the memory of the poet was still fresh (and therefore before Aeschines
was well known). The date of Antiphanes' death is uncertain, but may
have been about 334–330 B.C. But in the speech *On the Crown* in 330,
Demosthenes gives Aeschines the full benefit of both words (129 τὸν καλὸν
ἀνδριάντα καὶ τριταγωνιστὴν ἄκρον ἐξέθρεψέ σε; 209 ὦ τριταγωνιστά; 267
πονηρὸν ὄντα καὶ πολίτην καὶ τριταγωνιστήν; 262 μισθώσας σαυτὸν τοῖς
βαρυστόνοις ἐπικαλουμένοις ὑποκριταῖς, Σιμύκᾳ καὶ Σωκράτει, ἐτριταγωνίστεις; 265 ἐτριταγωνίστεις, ἐγὼ δ' ἐθεώρουν); cf. [Plutarch] *Vit. X Orat.*
840 a (on Aeschines) ὡς δὲ Δημοσθένης φησίν, ὑπογραμματεύων καὶ
τριταγωνιστῶν Ἀριστοδήμῳ ἐν τοῖς Διονυσίοις διετέλει.

On the whole the probability is that πρωταγωνιστής and πρωταγωνιστεῖν were used from the first of the actor who took the principal role in
a play,[2] though it was only late, if at all, that they became officially
recognized technical terms, and they never appear in inscriptions; that
both πρωταγωνιστής and δευτεραγωνιστής were used from an early date
with the metaphorical sense of 'leader' and 'supporter', though the
latter was evidently used much more rarely; and that τριταγωνιστής,
whenever it first came into use, gained an indelible colour from its use
by Demosthenes as a weapon of derision with which to beat Aeschines.
(Thus in the *Life* of Aeschines we read τριταγωνιστὴς ἐγένετο τραγῳδιῶν,
and in Bekker's *Anecd. Gr.* 309. 32 τριταγωνιστής· ὁ Αἰσχίνης ἀδοκιμώτατος
τῶν ὑποκριτῶν ἐν τῇ τρίτῃ τάξει καταριθμούμενος; in 'Suidas', s.v. Σοφοκλῆς·
οὗτος πρῶτος τρισὶν ἐχρήσατο ὑποκριταῖς καὶ τῷ καλουμένῳ τριταγωνιστῇ:

---

[1] This (even if not simply untrue) obviously cannot apply to plays in which (as in *Oedipus
Tyrannus*) the principal part was that of a king, but only to plays in which the king or tyrant
was a tyrant in the modern sense, and all that was required was violence and declamation,
rather than subtlety or skilful display of emotion. The schol. on this passage says that, according to Iuba, the reason for assigning such parts to the tritagonist was that ἧττόν ἐστι παθητικὰ
καὶ ὑπέρογκα.

[2] The 'competitive' implications of -αγωνιστής strongly support this view.

all these, even the last (notice the participle) are indirectly influenced by Demosthenes.) The derisory sense does not attach to the word itself, which could not mean '*third-rate* agonist', but to the implication that Aeschines never rose above the lowest place in the troupes of three actors (with their choruses) who toured the country-places in which he acted.[1] It cannot be discovered when the three words acquired a semi-technical sense with reference to the stage. They are, as has already been noticed, unknown to the inscriptions of the third or second century, in which the actors other than the principal one, the τραγῳδός or κωμῳδός, are sometimes termed συναγωνισταί. But by the third century A.D. there seems to have come about a division of the profession of actor into three classes, and the three names had reference to these and not to the position of the actor in a particular play as determined by the poet.[2] Normally, at all periods, the best actor would have taken the part or parts of greatest importance in the play, but a somewhat mysterious remark of Aristotle[3] may mean that Theodoros (in the fourth century B.C.) always insisted on taking the part of the character who appeared first, thinking that the first speaker always won the sympathy of the audience.

B. *Number of Actors and Distribution of Parts*

1. The passage has already been quoted in which Aristotle traces the history of the form of tragedy, whereby it acquired first two and then (with Sophocles) three actors, and so attained its φύσις—its complete development. Apparently Aristotle (in the second half of the fourth century) knows nothing of any fourth actor, and it follows that (with some trifling exceptions to be considered shortly) every play had to be presented by three actors. It would be a necessary consequence of this that not more than three *speakers* could take part in dialogue at any one time, and it is to this artistic principle (conceived as having an aesthetic

---

[1] See esp. O. J. Todd, *C.Q.* 32 (1938), pp. 30 ff. The implication may not have been true (it should be noted that the actors with whom Aeschines is said to have worked, men like Theodoros, Aristodemos, and Thettalos, were among the most distinguished actors of the fourth century: cf. *I.G.* ii². 2318, cols. xi, xii (p. 106 above), 2325, col. ii (p. 115 above), pp. 168, 279, etc., below), but neither Demosthenes (nor his audience) is likely to have been over-sensitive about this.

[2] Plotinus iii. 2. 17. See above, p. 133.

[3] *Pol.* vii. 17. 1336ᵇ28 ἴσως γὰρ οὐ κακῶς ἔλεγε τὸ τοιοῦτον Θεόδωρος ὁ τῆς τραγῳδίας ὑποκριτής· οὐδενὶ γὰρ πώποτε παρῆκεν ἑαυτοῦ προεισάγειν, οὐδὲ τῶν εὐτελῶν ὑποκριτῶν, ὡς οἰκειουμένων τῶν θεατῶν ταῖς πρώταις ἀκοαῖς. The interpretation given above is that of Lüders, O'Connor, and others, and is obviously better than supposing that Theodoros rearranged the play or the parts so as to bring the protagonist on first. (It is probable that the prologue was often spoken by the second or third actor.)

basis) that Horace and others[1] refer, but ὑποκριταί in Aristotle and else-where—the plural of ὑποκριτής, actor—cannot possibly mean merely 'speaking persons present at one time', as Rees and others appear to assume.[2] Moreover, the phrases often used, literally and metaphorically, for first, second, and third actor's parts never hint at a fourth.[3] Nor is it likely that in a contest to which great importance was attached the State would have provided three actors for one competitor and four for another. Some tragedies in which the difficulties caused by this limitation have led certain scholars to treat them as exceptions to the rule will be considered later.

It may be assumed that in the fifth and fourth centuries satyric drama was subject to the same rule as tragedy. Three actors are required in the *Cyclops* of Euripides, the only complete satyric play extant; the *Ichneutai* of Sophocles, so far as the extant remains give any indication, could be performed with two.[4]

As regards comedy there is less certainty. A late grammarian[5] states that it was not until the time of Cratinus (i.e. about 455 B.C.) that comedy, which had hitherto been a disorderly performance, was reduced to order and the number of actors reduced to three—a statement which must be received with caution in view of Aristotle's admission of ignorance on the subject[6]—and of the impossibility of distributing the parts of some of Aristophanes' plays between three actors only. This will be considered later, but in the meantime Tzetzes may be thought to be perhaps handing down a tradition from some earlier source. The 'disorderliness' even of Aristophanic comedy was further reduced in the time of the New Comedy,

---

[1] Horace, *A.P.* 192, and the commentators thereon (Diomedes 455 (Keil), and Porphyrio), who note that a fourth person, if present, is always mute: cf. schol. on Aesch. *Choeph.* 899 μετεσκευάσται ὁ ἐξάγγελος εἰς Πυλάδην, ἵνα μὴ δ' λέγωσιν.

[2] Rees, *Rule of Three Actors*. Rees rejected the 'three-actor rule' as a misunderstanding: so too, more recently Schneider, *R.E.*, Suppl. viii. cols. 191–3. Discussions on this point have been many: e.g. O'Connor; Kaffenberger, *Das Dreischauspielergesetz in der gr. Tragödie* (diss. Giessen, 1911); O. J. Todd, loc. cit.; E. B. Ceadel, *C.Q.* 1941, pp. 139 ff.; A. C. Schlesinger, *Proc. Am. Phil. Assoc.* 1929, p. xxvi, and *Class. Philol.* 25 (1930), pp. 230 ff.; 28 (1933), pp. 176 ff.; 46 (1951), 32 f.; Flickinger, *Greek Theater*[4], ch. iii. The treatment in the text is an attempt to adhere to the evidence and the possible meaning of words, without reciting the whole history of opinion on the subject.

[3] e.g. Strattis, fr. 1 (K) μισθωσάμενος τὰ πρῶτα τῶν ἐπῶν λέγειν (of the actor Hegelochos); Dem. *de F.L.* 246 τὰ τρίτα λέγων (of Aeschines as third actor in a troupe: see above, p. 133); Menander, fr. 418 (Kö) τὰ δεύτερ' ἀεὶ τὴν γυναῖκα δεῖ λέγειν, | τὴν δ' ἡγεμονίαν τῶν ὅλων τὸν ἄνδρ' ἔχειν; Lucian, *Tyrannicid.* 22 τὰ μὲν πρῶτα ἐγὼ ὑπεκρινάμην, τὰ δεύτερα δὲ ὁ παῖς, τὰ τρίτα δὲ ὁ τύραννος αὐτός.

[4] Aesch. *Dictyulci* perhaps required three; see Lloyd-Jones, Loeb *Aeschylus*[2] ii, p. 535, n.

[5] Tzetzes (Kaibel, p. 18) ἐπιγενόμενος δὲ ὁ Κρατῖνος κατέστησε μὲν πρῶτον τὰ ἐν τῇ κωμῳδίᾳ πρόσωπα μέχρι τριῶν, στήσας τὴν ἀταξίαν. (He has just said that οἱ περὶ Σουσαρίωνα τὰ πρόσωπα ἀτάκτως εἰσῆγον.) (Quoted in full, p. 149, n. 3.)

[6] Aristot. *Poet.*, ch. v. 1449[b]4 f.

and the evidence of the extant remains of Menander will have to be considered.

2. In any case the performance of the three actors was supplemented by the employment when required of mute persons (κωφὰ πρόσωπα), or perhaps of persons who if not absolutely mute could be left out of the reckoning. (Instances will be given below.) Such additions to the cast are very often stated to be covered by the term παραχορήγημα, but this name must be used with caution.[1] The word appears only in four scholia, and in a confused and probably corrupt passage of Pollux:[2] ὁπότε μὴν ἀντὶ τετάρτου ὑποκριτοῦ δέοι τινὰ τῶν χορευτῶν εἰπεῖν ἐν ᾠδῇ, παρασκήνιον καλεῖται τὸ πρᾶγμα, ὡς ἐν Ἀγαμέμνονι Αἰσχύλου· εἰ δὲ τέταρτος ὑποκριτής τι παραφθέγξαιτο, τοῦτο παραχορήγημα ὀνομάζεται καὶ πεπρᾶχθαί φασιν αὐτὸ ἐν Μέμνονι Αἰσχύλου. The first clause gives a highly improbable sense to παρασκήνιον, and the words ἐν Ἀγαμέμνονι Αἰσχύλου are an obvious dittography from ἐν Μέμνονι Αἰσχύλου; the contingency described in it— the singing of words by a member of the chorus instead of by a fourth actor—does not appear to have occurred in any extant play. The second clause describes the addition (παρα-) to the actors' parts of something spoken by a fourth actor. *Memnon* has perished, and the scholia give only four instances of a παραχορήγημα, viz. the parts played by Βία in the prologue of *Prometheus Vinctus* and by the Areopagites in *Eumenides* (both being silent, and so not in accordance with the definition of Pollux), the children of Trygaeus weeping for their father in Aristophanes' *Peace*, and the unseen chorus of Frogs in Aristophanes' play.[3] Evidently the word could be used loosely of any special extra provision of persons. It is in any case a late technical term,[4] though the thing perhaps denoted by it occurred occasionally in the fifth century.[5]

3. The chief disadvantages of the limitation of the number of actors to three, as exemplified in the extant remains, were the occasional necessity of dividing one role between two or more actors (a division rendered possible by the use of masks), the frequent necessity of assigning two or

---

[1] See especially Rees, 'The Meaning of Parachoregema', in *Class. Philol.* 2 (1907), pp. 387 ff. [2] Poll. iv. 109 f.

[3] Schol. *Prom.* 12 ἐν παραχορηγήματι αὐτῷ εἰδωλοποιηθεῖσα Βία; schol. *Eumen.* 573 ἐν παραχορηγήματι αὐτῷ εἰσιν οἱ Ἀρεοπαγῖται μηδαμοῦ διαλεγόμενοι; schol. *Peace* 114 τὰ τοιαῦτα παραχορηγήματα καλοῦσιν, οἷα νῦν τὰ παιδία ποιεῖ καλοῦντα τὸν πατέρα· εἶτα πρὸς οὐδὲν ἔτι τούτοις χρήσεται; schol. *Frogs* 209 ταῦτα καλεῖται παραχορηγήματα, ἐπειδὴ οὐχ ὁρῶνται ἐν τῷ θεάτρῳ οἱ βάτραχοι, οὐδὲ ὁ χορός, ἀλλ' ἔσωθεν μιμοῦνται τοὺς βατράχους. ὁ δὲ ἀληθῶς χορὸς ἐκ τῶν εὐσεβῶν νεκρῶν συνέστηκεν.

[4] It has nothing to do with χορηγοί in the sense in which the word was used in the Classical period; these χορηγοί belonged to the remote past, and the significance of the word is connected with the secondary meaning of χορηγεῖν—'furnish'. The history of this and kindred words is well worked out by Rees, op. cit. [5] See below, p. 143.

more parts in succession to the same actor, and the need in a few plays of 'lightning changes' of costume, in order to enable the actor to take up a different role after a very brief interval. There were also in some plays awkward situations (particularly those involving the sudden lapse into silence of a character now played by a κωφὸν πρόσωπον) which would have been got over if a fourth actor had been available, and at times some incongruity may have been felt by unusually severe spectators when the different roles taken by one and the same performer were very unlike one another.[1] A survey of the plays will illustrate these points.

4. In *Persae*, the first surviving play of Aeschylus, there are only two actors. One plays the part of Atossa until nearly the end of the play, the other those of the Messenger and Darius. The fact that when Atossa has gone off at l. 851 to get a change of raiment for Xerxes (expected to arrive immediately) she never returns[2] evidently means that her actor had to act the part of Xerxes from l. 907 to the end of the play, perhaps because he had a better singing voice than the actor who played the Messenger and Darius. There seems never to have been any difficulty in the same actor's taking both male and female roles in the same play. Female roles were in any case taken by male actors.

The *Suppliants* again, though it requires two actors, hardly makes full use of them.[3] Danaus is present from l. 234 to l. 523 while the King of Argos is conversing with the chorus, but for most of the time does not utter a word, and only a single word of the text shows that he is there at all (l. 319 Βῆλον δίπαιδα, πατέρα τοῦδ' ἐμοῦ πατρός); he speaks only the short speech, ll. 490–9. At l. 775 he goes off to get help,[4] but does not himself come back with the rescuers. His actor returns as the Egyptian herald at l. 872, and departs just after 951, and reappears at 980 having resumed the person and costume of Danaus. The brief but animated dispute between the King and the Herald (ll. 911–65) is the only dialogue between two actors in the play. The fact that the parts of Danaus and the Herald of the enemy are played by the same actor was of course

---

[1] Cf. Lucian, *Menipp.* 16 οἶμαι δέ σε καὶ τῶν ἐπὶ τῆς σκηνῆς πολλάκις ἑωρακέναι τοὺς τραγικοὺς ὑποκριτὰς τούτους πρὸς τὰς χρείας τῶν δραμάτων ἄρτι μὲν Κρέοντας, ἐνίοτε δὲ Πριάμους γιγνομένους ἢ Ἀγαμέμνονας, καὶ ὁ αὐτός, εἰ τύχοι, μικρὸν ἔμπροσθεν μάλα σεμνῶς τὸ τοῦ Κέκροπος ἢ Ἐρεχθέως σχῆμα μιμησάμενος μετ' ὀλίγον οἰκέτης προῆλθεν ὑπὸ τοῦ ποιητοῦ κεκελευσμένος: there is no certainty that this refers to different parts *in the same play*. For lists of parts of this kind, cf. *Pisc.* 31; *Nigrin.* 11.

[2] The mysterious and corrupt line 850 was perhaps intended as preparation for the queen's failure to reappear.

[3] For the date of the *Suppliants*, see below, p. 232, n. 3.

[4] ἐγὼ δ' ἀρωγοὺς ξυνδίκους θ' ἥξω λαβών. He hints, however, that he may be delayed and instructs the chorus how to behave in that case. See below on the failure of Xouthos to reappear in the last scene of Euripides' *Ion*.

concealed by the use of masks, and if the long actor's robe enveloped most of his body this may have assisted the concealment. At l. 234 the play perhaps illustrates a consequence of the simple structure of the drama when the chorus was dominant and there was only one actor, in the fact that the King first addresses the chorus and not their father, whom he might have been expected to notice. In the same way Darius in *Persae* addresses the chorus first, and not the widowed queen-mother, and Klytaimnestra in *Agamemnon* makes an elaborate address to the Argive elders before saying a word to her husband after his ten years' absence. Dramatic convention and tradition is probably uppermost, though her so doing is a most effective stroke of characterization.

Seven against Thebes down to l. 1004 requires only two actors, of whom one takes the parts of Eteokles and Antigone, the other those of the Scout and Ismene. The final scene in our texts (ll. 1005–78) perhaps requires three actors (Herald, Antigone, and Ismene), but it is widely believed that the scene was added in some later revision of the play, and, if so, not before the latter part of the century.[1]

Prometheus Vinctus apart from the opening scene could be acted by two actors, of whom one would play Prometheus throughout, the other Okeanos, Io, and Hermes. The first scene requires actors for Hephaistos and Kratos, as well as Prometheus and the mute *Βία*, and those who[2] wish to dispense with a third actor here imagine that Prometheus was represented by a gigantic hollow puppet, and that when Hephaistos goes off at l. 81, the actor of that part goes behind the puppet and slips inside it, and thereafter speaks as Prometheus, having just time to perform the necessary manœuvre during the six lines uttered by Kratos (with a possible dramatic pause). This would not be impossible, but the improbability of Prometheus' being so represented is so great, particularly in view of his apparent freeing in the second play of the trilogy, that it is more likely that the opening scene of the play (which on other grounds is to be placed fairly late in Aeschylus' career) was one of his first ventures upon a three-actor cast.[3]

In *Agamemnon*, one actor must have played Klytaimnestra throughout, and the parts of Agamemnon and Kassandra require two further actors (it is only in ll. 782–974 that all three actors are on stage together): the parts of the Watchman, the Herald, and Aigisthos could be variously assigned

---

[1] But see Lloyd-Jones, *C.Q.*, N.S. 9 (1959), pp. 80–115, esp. 95 f.

[2] Like Wilamowitz, *Aischylos: Interpretationen*, pp. 114 f.; Flickinger, *Greek Theater*[4], p. 166 f., 174; Kaffenberger, op. cit., pp. 27 ff., and many others.

[3] See *Theatre of D.*, pp. 37–38, 42, and the references collected in *J.H.S.* 79 (1959), p. 60, and by Lesky, *Trag. Dichtung der Hellenen*[2], pp. 77–82.

to the actors of Agamemnon and Kassandra. The latter part alone involves singing: Klytaimnestra is given only recitative (ll. 1462–1576).

Apart from one short passage, *Choephoroi* could easily be played by
three actors—one as Orestes, a second as Electra and Klytaimnestra,
a third as Pylades and the Servant. The parts of Aigisthos and the Nurse
could be assigned to any one of the three actors. This scheme involves
a 'lightning change' from the costume of the Servant into that of Pylades
between ll. 886[1] and 899—not at all impossible with practice, if it may
be assumed that Pylades does not enter until a few moments after the
entry of Orestes at l. 892—where again a dramatic pause would be most
effective. But those who dislike lightning changes imagine the introduction of a fourth actor to speak the three tremendous lines assigned to
Pylades (900–2). Aeschylus may well have been bold enough to transgress
convention in this way, but it does not seem to be necessary to suppose it.[2]
In *Eumenides* each of the three principal characters—Orestes, Apollo,
Athena—requires its actor; one actor must have added the parts of the
Pythia and the ghost of Klytaimnestra to that of Athena. Hermes (ll. 89 ff.)
is a κωφὸν πρόσωπον. The most striking feature of this play is the introduction of the jury of Areopagites, and of the members of the final great
procession, who take part with the chorus in the united celebration.[3]

5. The plays of Sophocles, with the exception of the posthumously
produced *Oedipus Coloneus*, could all be acted by three actors without
serious objection, provided that no such objection were felt to the performance of male and female roles by the same actor,[4] and that reasonable
care were taken in the choice of actors physically suited to the play.
Thus in *Ajax* it seems likely that a single actor played Ajax and then
Teukros. In the opening scene, and in the last, all three actors are needed,
and the silence of Tekmessa in the latter part of the play is explained by
the necessity of having her role in the last scene played by a κωφὸν
πρόσωπον (she goes off at 989 and returns, with an 'extra' wearing her
mask and costume, at 1168). How the remaining roles (Athena, Odysseus,
Menelaus, Agamemnon, and the Messenger) were assigned to the two
other actors it is impossible to infer from the text of the play, since for
most of the action not more than two speaking figures are on stage at
a time: it is no more than a plausible guess that Agamemnon and

---

[1] Not 889, as there is no reason to suppose that the same attendant is addressed.
[2] Discussions of this scene are innumerable: see, for example, Kaffenberger, op. cit.,
pp. 17 f.; for a different view from that given in the text see Rees, op. cit., p. 43.
[3] See especially W. Headlam, *J.H.S.* 26 (1906), p. 268.
[4] The fact that female roles were in any case played by a male actor really removes the
objection.

Menelaus were played by the same actor.[1] The child Eurysakes was played by a mute throughout. In *Antigone* the part of Kreon[2] involves one actor almost throughout the play: it could be combined only with that of Eurydike. The actor of Ismene must also have played the Guard, and Antigone's part may have been combined with that of Haimon: the remaining parts (Teiresias, and the two Messengers) could be assigned to either of the two last-named actors. In *Electra* the heroine is played by one actor throughout, Orestes and Klytaimnestra by a second, and the Paidagogos and Aigisthos by a third; Chrysothemis might be taken by either the second or third. Rees[3] is not justified in saying that 'it is beyond the power of an ordinary actor to play successfully characters so widely different as those of the girl Chrysothemis and the old Pedagogue under any arrangement', especially in interlaced order. Chrysothemis was played in any case by a male actor, and if he could change from one tone to the other once in a play he could do so twice. In the *Trachiniae* a single actor is likely to have taken first the part of Deianeira and then that of Herakles. Rees considers this objectionable in every way, partly because of the difference in temperament between the two persons (a difference for which a good actor could certainly prepare himself in an interval extending over 150 lines), partly because the parts would need actors of very different physical proportions. But there is no reason to think that Herakles, though sturdy and strong, was particularly *tall*, and the rest would be a matter of mask and dress. The sequence of scenes in the play suggests that another actor combined the parts of the Nurse, the Messenger, and the Old Man, while a third played Hyllus and Lichas. The silence of Iole throughout is both inevitable and powerful. There was, of course, no actor to play her part, but Sophocles gains dramatic effect and exploits the technical limitation: her silence has something of the same emotive effect as that of Kassandra in *Agam.* 1047 ff.

Oedipus Tyrannus and *Philoctetes* present no great difficulties. In the former one actor plays Oedipus throughout, a second Kreon and the Messenger from Corinth, a third the Priest, Iokasta, and the Herdsman. The parts of Teiresias and the second Messenger could be played by either of the last two. In the latter, the principal actor will probably

---

[1] Kaffenberger, op. cit., pp. 15 f. A possible division would be (a) Odysseus, Tekmessa; (b) Athena, Messenger, Menelaus, Agamemnon.

[2] There is a puzzle here: it is a natural assumption that the part of Kreon was played by the protagonist, yet Demosthenes asserts (xix. 247) that Aeschines, as tritagonist, had frequently played the part of Kreon in *Antigone*. The likeliest explanation is that Demosthenes is lying: he has an axe to grind, in the point he can extract from Kreon's speech (*Ant.* 175 ff.) put into the mouth of Aeschines, and the bland assertion that tyrants were always played by the tritagonist is itself suspicious (cf. p. 134, n. 1, above).   [3] Op. cit., p. 57.

have played Neoptolemos and the second Philoktetes (or vice versa), the third Odysseus, the Merchant, and Herakles.

But in *Oedipus Coloneus* difficulties do arise.[1] The part of Oedipus can be combined only with that of the Messenger, and the part of Antigone appears to involve a second actor for much of the play (ll. 1–847, 1098–1555, 1670 to the end). It is clear that a third actor played the Stranger, Ismene, Theseus (550–667), Kreon (728–1043), and Polyneikes (1253–1446). But what of the role of Theseus in the latter part of the play? At his second entry (887–1043), Kreon is still on stage. The only actor available to play Theseus is now that of Antigone (who has been dragged off at 847) : it seems then that Theseus' role was divided between at least two actors. Furthermore, it has long been observed that, when Ismene, with Antigone, is brought back by Theseus (1098), she remains silent for almost five hundred lines: her actor is once again playing the part of Theseus. She must be played by a κωφὸν πρόσωπον, since she is silent not merely when there are three other persons on stage (Oedipus and Antigone with first Theseus, then Polyneikes), but even when she is left alone with her father and sister (1446–1500). The end of the play raises new problems. Both sisters leave the stage when their father goes to meet his death (1555) : they reappear as soon as the Messenger has ended his account: indeed he announces their approach (1668–9). Yet this time Ismene is not silent, although there is no time for the actor of the Messenger to take over her part. Moreover, Theseus enters for the last time (1751), and it is natural to assume that he is now played by the actor of the Messenger, i.e. the actor of Oedipus. Thus at first glance the part of Theseus is taken in turn by each of the three actors. The awkwardness of this assumption is clear. K. F. Hermann sought to mitigate the awkwardness by pointing out that the calm and majestic Theseus of the first scene demanded very different playing from the stern and angry figure of the scene with Kreon:[2] he could have added that the final scene is wholly in recitative (anapaests), while the previous scenes were in spoken dialogue. But difficulties were felt to remain, particularly over the physical problem of fitting three different actors, perhaps of quite different build, to the same mask and costume. Various allocations of the parts in the play to four, or even to six, actors have been put forward.[3] All of these founder on one fact: the complete silence of Ismene during three scenes of the play (1098–1555, and especially

---

[1] They are well analysed by Ceadel, *C.Q.* 35 (1941), pp. 139 ff.

[2] *Disputatio de distributione personarum inter histriones in trag. Graec.* (Marburg, 1840), pp. 42–44.

[3] See Ceadel, op. cit., pp. 139 f., 142.

1446–1500). At more than one moment speech or lyric utterance is expected and not forthcoming, and it must be that Ismene is here represented by a mute 'extra', just because the poet had no fourth actor.

Many proposals have also been made for the distribution of the parts between three actors,[1] but all involve the splitting of Theseus' part between two actors at least.[2] A compromise has been suggested by Ceadel, who believes that the splitting of Theseus' role (a major one in the play and one close to Athenian sensibilities) could not have been brought off without incongruity.[3] Ceadel invokes the possibility that the actor of Antigone left the stage either at 509, where Ismene goes to make offerings to the Eumenides, or in the course of the stasimon 668–719, and that an 'extra' returned immediately, wearing her mask and robe, to play her part during the scene with Kreon up to her forcible removal (847). In this scene Antigone speaks only some six or seven lines (720 f., 722 f., 828 f., 844, 845b, 846b), and Ceadel believes this to be not more than could be given to a παραχορήγημα (the same as plays the silent Ismene from 1098 to 1555, and in Ceadel's view, sings her brief part in the final scene). Thus his scheme is: (a) Oedipus, Messenger, (b) Antigone (except 509 or 720 to 847), Kreon; (c) Stranger, Ismene (324–509), Theseus, Polyneikes; (d) παραχορήγημα: Antigone (509 or 720 to 847); Ismene (1098–1555 and 1670 to end). But it is not very likely that Antigone *did* leave the stage at either of the moments suggested by Ceadel: at 509 the words of Ismene, though they *could* be addressed to Antigone as she followed her off, strongly suggest that Antigone did not move at all, and that Antigone should go off *during* a stasimon would be quite unprecedented, besides leaving no trace in the text. In any case, suggestions such as Ceadel's represent only tinkering with the conventions of Greek staging, in order to mitigate the sense of incongruity felt by a modern reader, accustomed to modern theatrical forms. It is better to go back to

[1] Ceadel, op. cit., pp. 143 f.

[2] The number of actors playing Theseus can be kept to two by assuming that the brief lyrics given to Ismene (1724 ff., perhaps 1688–92, 1715–19) are sung off-stage by the actor who is just about to appear as Theseus, and mimed on-stage by the κωφὸν πρόσωπον who has played Ismene earlier (1098–1555): cf. Kaffenberger, op. cit., pp. 23 f.; Flickinger, *Greek Theater*⁴, p. 181.

[3] Ceadel lays stress on Oedipus' words to Theseus on his entrance at l. 891, ὦ φίλτατ', ἔγνων γὰρ τὸ προσφώνημά σου, words which, he argues, would be particularly obtrusive if uttered just when Theseus was being played for the first time by a *different* actor (with presumably a different voice) from the one who had previously taken the part. But Oedipus is blind, and these words serve to concentrate our attentions once again (cf. ll. 1 ff., 21, 81 ff., 113 f., 138, 146 f., 178 ff., 192 ff., 495 ff., etc.) on this crucial dramatic fact: see John Jones, *On Aristotle and Greek Tragedy*, pp. 218 f., 224 f.

the tougher line laid down by Kaffenberger, and to accept that the
sequence of entrances and exits in the first half of the play (especially
Ismene's delayed arrival, her departure at 509, and Antigone's removal
from the stage at 847) clearly indicates the allocation of parts in the play.[1]
As Kaffenberger himself points out, the staging conventions of the Greek
theatre are irreducibly incongruous to our differently conditioned sensibilities: the use of masks, of male actors playing female roles, the scale
and layout of the theatre are all strange to us, and it is doubtful whether
our sense of the incongruous in matters of detail is a safe guide to Sopho-
clean practice.

6. There is no play of Euripides in which the parts cannot be dis-
tributed without serious difficulty between three actors, except in so far
as, in four plays, brief singing (not speaking) parts are assigned to young
children.[2] Where these appear on stage, they obviously cannot have
been played by grown-up actors, and must have been taken by a boy
as a παραχορήγημα (with one or more as mutes if required), and spoken
or sung either by the boy himself or by a singer behind the scene.[3] Such
may have been the case in *Alcestis* 393–415, and *Andromache* 494–545,
where there is a lyric dialogue between the young Molossos and his
mother, and *Suppliants* 1113–64, where there is a κομμός between the
children and the chorus. In *Medea* the children's voices are only heard
from behind the stage.

It will already be clear from the discussion of Aeschylus and Sophocles
that the assignment of parts to actors can only be attempted within
varying limits of probability. In particular, though we can hope in many
cases to divide the roles of a play into three 'sequences', we can never
say which actor took which sequence, unless on the basis of some external
evidence or on grounds of general probability (i.e. that the first actor
had to take the most rewarding). Even here the possibilities will vary:
it will seem clear to most readers that the first actor played Medea in
Medea, but may he not have played the demanding, and hence perhaps
rewarding, sequence: Aphrodite, Phaidra, Theseus in *Hippolytus*, rather
than the title role? In what follows no attempt is therefore made to
indicate the roles played by the first, second, or third actor, and uncertainties or anomalies are explicitly referred to.

[1] For Kaffenberger's discussion of *Oed. Col.*, see his *Dreischauspielergesetz*, pp. 22–26, 36,
42 ff.
[2] There are also scenes in which children appear but do not speak, e.g. Eurysakes in
Sophocles' *Ajax*, the children of Polymestor in *Hecuba* 978, and the daughter of Teiresias
(if she was a child) in *Phoenissae* 834.
[3] Cf. Devrient, *Das Kind auf der antiken Bühne*; Dale, edn. of Euripides, *Alcestis*, introd.,
pp. xix f., and note on 393–415, p. 85.

Alcestis. The play *could* be performed with two actors: see Dale, *Alcestis*, p. xix. (*a*) Apollo, Alcestis, Herakles, Pheres; (*b*) Thanatos, Servant, Admetus: this distribution would almost certainly involve a pause, with the stage empty, between ll. 746–7. The chorus departs in slow procession after Admetus, whose actor then re-enters as the Servant. If three actors were in fact used, then the likeliest distribution would be: (*a*) Apollo, Admetus; (*b*) Alcestis, Pheres, Herakles; (*c*) Thanatos, Servant. With two actors, the silence of the restored Alcestis in the final scene could be explained by the lack of an actor to play her part: he is now playing Herakles. But the dramatic and emotive effect of her silence is another example of a playwright's exploitation of his technical limitations.

Medea. (*a*) Medea; (*b*) Nurse; (*c*) Paidagogos: the remaining parts (Kreon, Jason, Aigeus, and the Messenger) could be assigned to either (*b*) or (*c*). But the play could perhaps be performed by two actors:[1] (*a*) Paidagogos (ll. 49–91), Medea; (*b*) Nurse, Kreon, Jason, Aigeus, Paidagogos (1002–20), Messenger.[2]

Heraclidae. (*a*) Iolaus, Eurystheus; (*b*) Herald, Makaria; (*c*) Demophon: the Servant and Alkmene could be either (*b*) or (*c*), and the Messenger (784–891), if he is not the same character as the Servant (see Murray, n. on Dramatis Personae), could be (*a*).[3]

Hippolytus. Perhaps (*a*) Hippolytus, Messenger; (*b*) Aphrodite, Theseus, Phaidra; (*c*) Servant, Nurse, Artemis. But the withdrawal of all three actors from the stage at more than one point (e.g. 120, 731, 1101) makes the distribution very uncertain.

Andromache. Perhaps (*a*) Andromache, Orestes, ? Messenger; (*b*) Hermione, Menelaus, ? Thetis; (*c*) Serving Woman, Peleus, Nurse. Again a very uncertain distribution: three actors are on stage together only at ll. 545 ff., and probably at 878 ff. The child of Andromache was probably sung off-stage by (*c*): for discussion, see Kaffenberger, op. cit., p. 26.

Hecuba. Perhaps (*a*) Hecuba; (*b*) Polyxena, Agamemnon; (*c*) Odysseus, Serving Woman, Polymestor: Talthybios and Polydoros could be (*b*) or (*c*). One of the few certainties is that the Serving Woman and Polymestor were taken by the same actor; therefore, at the Serving Woman's second appearance (953 ff.: for her presence, cf. 966 ff.) the part was taken by a κωφὸν πρόσωπον.

Suppliants. (*a*) Adrastus; (*b*) Theseus; (*c*) Aithra, Herald, Athena. The Messenger could be (*b*) or (*c*), and the remaining parts (Evadne, Iphis) could be played by any of the three actors: on the complex entrances and exits

---

[1] See Page, introd. to his edition, p. xxxi and n. 3, nn. on ll. 820–1, 1250; *contra*, Regenbogen, *Eranos* 48 (1950), pp. 42 f.

[2] Not, certainly, by dividing the part of Medea between two actors, as implied by Ritchie, *The Authenticity of the 'Rhesus' of Euripides*, (1964), p. 128.

[3] The children of Herakles are present throughout as κωφὰ πρόσωπα; so too Akamas in ll. 118 ff. For the non-appearance of Alkmene in the Makaria scene (474 ff.) and of Iolaus in the closing scene (cf. especially ll. 859 ff., 936 f.), see Kaffenberger, op. cit., pp. 31 f.

of the last three hundred lines, see Kaffenberger, op. cit., pp. 33 f. For the supplementary chorus of children, see above, p. 144.

Herakles. (a) Amphitryon; (b) Megara, Theseus; (c) Lykos, Herakles. The Messenger is most likely to have been played by (b), but perhaps by (a) (Amphitryon is off-stage in ll. 887 ff.): Iris and Lyssa, who appear above a deserted stage, could have been played by any of the three actors.

(For lack of a fourth actor Herakles and Lykos never meet (Kaffenberger, op. cit., pp. 38–40), but the suggestion (ibid., pp. 37 f.) that the death of Megara, which seems to have been an innovation in the legend by Euripides, was suggested by there being no actor for her in the latter part of the play is pure speculation.)

Ion. (a) Ion; (b) Kreousa; (c) Xouthos, Prophetis, Athena. The Old Man is probably (c), though he could be (a); Hermes could be (b) or (c), the Servant (a) or (c).

(Again the lack of a fourth actor explains why Xouthos never reappears, as he might be expected to do, in the last scene. But in ll. 1130–1 he hints that he may be late in returning, and so far prepares the audience for his absence.[1])

Troades. (a) Hecuba; (b) Poseidon; (c) Athena. The part of Talthybios could be combined with that of Menelaus or of Helen and played by either (b) or (c); those of Kassandra and Andromache (certainly played by the same actor) combined with the part not given to the actor of Talthybios and played by (c) or (b).

Electra. (a) Electra; (b) Orestes; (c) Peasant, Old Man, Klytaimnestra, Kastor. The Messenger, who could be played by either (b) or (c), is perhaps more likely to be (b), in order to balance the parts. For discussion, see Kaffenberger, pp. 19 f.: Pylades is a κωφὸν πρόσωπον throughout, even when addressed (e.g. ll. 82 ff., 111, 1340 f.): the absence of a fourth actor is felt. For the silent Polydeukes, Kaffenberger compares Akamas, silent but present with Demophon in *Heraclidae* 118 ff.

Iphigeneia in Tauris. The parts of Iphigeneia, Orestes, and Pylades require three separate actors; the parts of the Herdsman and Thoas could be combined with those of Orestes or Pylades; those of Athena and the Messenger could be played by any of the three actors. The Herdsman, if he re-enters with the captive Orestes and Pylades, is there (456–70) played by a κωφὸν πρόσωπον; so too probably are Orestes and Pylades in the brief scene 1222–33. (Kaffenberger, op. cit., pp. 16 f., suggests that Thoas is played by the actor of Orestes and cannot therefore address him: hence the ritual veiling ordered by Iphigeneia. He cannot address Pylades as being the secondary figure. But the Messenger, who enters at 1284, could be played by the actor of either Iphigeneia or Orestes, and Thoas could therefore be played by the actor of Pylades: the stasimon (1234–82) allows a change of costume.)

---

[1] See above (p. 138) on the similar position of Danaus in Aeschylus' *Suppliants*.

Helen. (*a*) Helen; (*b*) Menelaus; (*c*) Servant (597–757), Theonoe, Theoklymenos. Teucer could be played by (*b*) or (*c*), the Old Woman by (*a*) or (*c*),
the Messenger and Kastor by (*a*) or (*b*). If the speaker of ll. 1627 ff. is a
second Servant (as Clark suggested) and not the chorus (as in the MSS.:
on this point see, most recently, Barrett on *Hippolytus* 1102–50, p. 367 of
his edition; Dale, *Helen*, pp. 165 f.), the part could be played by (*b*) or (*a*).

Phoenissae. A very tentative distribution would be (*a*) Iokasta, Antigone (except 1270–82), Teiresias; (*b*) Paidagogos, Polyneikes, Kreon, Antigone
(1270–82); (*c*) Eteokles, Menoikeus, Messengers, Oedipus. If the scholiast
on l. 93[1] can be relied on, the appearance of the Paidagogos alone from 88
to 102 is intended to give the actor of Iokasta time to change into the
costume of Antigone, but in one later scene (1270–82) Iokasta and Antigone
appear together and must there be played by different actors. The purpose
of the manœuvre must have been to give the singing of the elaborate arias
of the two characters to the same specially qualified actor (Iokasta, ll. 301 ff.;
Antigone, 103 ff., 1485 ff., 1710 ff.). A difficulty arises in that Oedipus
also sings (1539 ff., 1714 ff.): the second Messenger and Oedipus must be
played by the same actor, but the remaining parts could be reallocated:
e.g. Teiresias/Menoikeus could be exchanged; the Paidagogos could be
either (*b*) or (*c*).[2]

Orestes. Again very uncertain. Perhaps (*a*) Orestes, Messenger; (*b*) Electra,
Menelaus, Phrygian; (*c*) Helen, Tyndareus, Pylades, Hermione, Apollo.
There is uncertainty, in particular, over Electra's final exit—probably at
l. 1352 (l. 1618 perhaps suggests that she is off the stage). Her part and that of
the Phrygian are the only ones which involve the singing of lyrics: there is
therefore a certain likelihood that they were given to the same actor (possible
with a quick change between 1352 and 1368). The roles of Menelaus and
Tyndareus could be reversed and if they are, then Apollo must be given to
(*b*); the Messenger could be played by (*c*). Hermione in the opening scene
(112–25) and Pylades in the last scene (1567 ff.) are played by κωφὰ πρόσωπα:
in both scenes there is no fourth actor available, and in the latter (1592)
Euripides resorts to the striking device of having Orestes reply to a question
addressed to Pylades: see Kaffenberger, op. cit., pp. 13–15.

Bacchae. (*a*) Dionysus, Teiresias; (*b*) Pentheus, Agaue; (*c*) Cadmus, Servant,
first Messenger. The second Messenger (1024 ff.) could be given to (*a*) or
(*c*), perhaps even to (*b*).

Iphigeneia in Aulis. (*a*) Agamemnon, Achilles; (*b*) Menelaus, Klytaimnestra;
(*c*) Old Man, first Messenger, Iphigeneia, ? second Messenger. The ending
of the play is gravely corrupt: as the text stands, it is scarcely possible for the

---

[1] ταῦτα μηχανᾶσθαί φασι τὸν Εὐριπίδην ἵνα τὸν πρωταγωνιστὴν ἀπὸ τοῦ τῆς Ἰοκάστης προσώπου μετασκευάσῃ· διὸ οὐ συνεπιφαίνεται αὐτῷ Ἀντιγόνη, ἀλλ᾽ ὕστερον.

[2] The scholium is unique and its source undiscoverable, but it deserves to be taken seriously:
it cannot be simple inference from the text. Ritchie (op. cit., p. 128) suggests that actors were
responsible for this (later) allocation of roles, in order to give Iokasta's prologue speech to
the protagonist: for this see above, p. 135.

second Messenger to be played by (*a*). Complex arias are given only to
Iphigeneia.

Hypsipyle. The remains are too fragmentary and the order of scenes too uncertain to allow of any assurance as regards the distribution of roles; but as
Hypsipyle, Amphiaraus, and Eurydike appear together in one scene, these
parts must have been taken by three separate actors: in the surviving fragments lyric utterance is given only to Hypsipyle. Both of Hypsipyle's sons
appear to have had speaking parts (fr. I. i 7 Bond = ll. 6 ff. Page; fr. 64
Bond = ll. 304–6, 336–7 Page),[1] and both appear and speak in a scene in
which Hypsipyle and Amphiaraus are also present: but there is nothing
to show that a fourth actor is required: the few words that Thoas speaks in
this scene may have been given to a παραχορήγημα or even spoken from
behind the scene while Thoas was played by a κωφὸν πρόσωπον. The play is
a late work of Euripides.[2]

In the lost *Kresphontes* of Euripides we are told that Aeschines as third
actor took the part of the tyrannical king—Kresphontes (the leading part
that of Merope, being taken by Theodoros).[3]

Rhesus. The extant *Rhesus* has frequently been thought to be a fourth-century
play, and not the work of Euripides.[4] However that may be, many scholars
have been convinced that the scene in ll. 642 ff. requires four actors, playing
Odysseus, Diomedes, Athena, and Alexandros, all present at once. But Diomedes is clearly sent off at 636 f. (before the entry of Alexandros), while
Odysseus must go off after 626, and has in fact captured the horses of Rhesus
(as l. 671 shows) before re-entering, presumably with the chorus at 674. In
the interval the actor of Odysseus, after a quick change, played Alexandros
between 642 and 665, and made a lightning change back into the costume
of Odysseus between 666 and 674—quite possible if prepared for, especially
if the interval were prolonged by the confused and excited entry of the chorus
at 674.[5] If this be allowed, the following distribution would be possible:
(*a*) Hector, Odysseus, Alexandros; (*b*) Aeneas, Rhesus, Athena, Muse;
(*c*) Dolon, Shepherd (Messenger), Diomedes, Charioteer. But all that is certain is that Hector, Aeneas, and Dolon in the opening scene, and Odysseus,
Athena, and Diomedes later require three separate actors.

The general objection made by Rees and others to the assignment of
incongruous parts to the same actor in many of the above schemes has
already been briefly dealt with. Such incongruity would be serious if

[1] On the presence of both Thoas and Euneus as speaking characters, especially in fr. 64,
see Bond, *Euripides: 'Hypsipyle'* (1963), pp. 11, 126 f.

[2] On the date of *Hypsipyle*, see most recently Bond, op. cit., p. 144.

[3] Dem. *de Cor.* 180; Aelian, *Var. H.* xiv. 40. He similarly took the part of the cruel Oinomaos,
perhaps in Sophocles' play of that name: see p. 50, n. 5 above.

[4] The case against this view, and for attributing the play to Euripides, has been argued
most recently and most effectively by Ritchie, *The Authenticity of the 'Rhesus' of Euripides*. An
important reply to Ritchie by Fraenkel, *Gnomon* 37 (1965), pp. 228–41.

[5] See Ritchie, op. cit., pp. 126–9.

there were any elaborately naturalistic acting attached to each part, and
above all if there were scope for facial expression, which is one of the chief
modern means of expressing individual character and feeling, but the
use of masks (and probably the conventionality of costume), as well as
the relatively statuesque acting,[1] left individual expression mainly to the
tone of voice, which a competent actor would have been able to adapt
as the part required, in so far as even this was possible when the voice
was masculine throughout. To judge ancient acting by the standards of
modern and Western acting is a quite mistaken proceeding.

7. It is evident that the practice as regards the number of actors was
not so strict in comedy as in tragedy, and it appears that, though there
were three principal actors, there was much more freedom to introduce
additional performers for small parts. If comedy originated in a more
or less disorderly revel, it can be understood that this did not include
regularly constructed dramatic scenes, at least until elements from the
Dorian mime were introduced into the revel,[2] and it is not impossible to
accept the tradition recorded (probably after passing through many
hands) by a late writer that Cratinus reduced the disorderliness and, in
some sense, fixed the number of regular actors at three.[3] Nor is it surprising
that Aristophanes himself should have retained some of the old freedom.[4]

The opening scene of his first extant play, *Acharnians*, involves at
one point (ll. 94–125) four, perhaps five, speaking parts.[5] Three of the

---

[1] But the statuesqueness of the acting in the fifth century is an open question; see below,
pp. 171 ff. [2] Cf. *Dith. Trag. Com.*[2], ch. iii.

[3] Tzetzes, *Prol. de Com.* 16 (Kaibel, p. 18 = Dübner, *Anon. de Com.* v) καὶ αὐτὴ δὲ ἡ παλαιὰ
ἑαυτῆς διαφέρει· καὶ γὰρ οἱ ἐν τῇ Ἀττικῇ πρῶτον συστησάμενοι τὸ ἐπιτήδευμα τῆς κωμῳδίας
(ἦσαν δὲ οἱ περὶ Σουσαρίωνα) τὰ πρόσωπα ἀτάκτως εἰσῆγον καὶ γέλως ἦν μόνος τὸ κατασκευαζό-
μενον. ἐπιγενόμενος δὲ ὁ Κρατῖνος κατέστησε μὲν πρῶτον τὰ ἐν τῇ κωμῳδίᾳ πρόσωπα μέχρι τριῶν,
στήσας τὴν ἀταξίαν, καὶ τῷ χαρίεντι τῆς κωμῳδίας τὸ ὠφέλιμον προσέθηκε, τοὺς κακῶς πράσσον-
τας διαβάλλων καὶ ὥσπερ δημοσίᾳ μάστιγι τῇ κωμῳδίᾳ κολάζων. ἀλλ᾿ ἔτι μὲν καὶ οὗτος τῆς ἀρχαιό-
τητος μετεῖχε καὶ ἠρέμα πως τῆς ἀταξίας· ὁ μέντοι γε Ἀριστοφάνης μεθοδεύσας τεχνικώτερον
τὴν κωμῳδίαν τῶν μεθ᾿ ἑαυτοῦ ἀνέλαμψεν ἐν ἅπασιν ἐπίσημος φανείς.

[4] The most recent (and important) discussion of the problem of the distribution of parts
in Aristophanes is that of C. F. Russo in *Aristofane* (1962), pp. 112–19 (*Ach.*), 139–41 (*Knights*),
149–55, 182–5 (*Clouds*), 204–5 (*Wasps*), 225–7 (*Peace*), 252–4 (*Birds*), 278–84 (*Lysistr.*),
302–3 (*Thesm.*), 332–4 (*Frogs*), 346–7 (*Eccles.*), 360–1 (*Plutus*). Russo attempts to assign parts
to protagonist, deuteragonist, and tritagonist, but admits that considerable uncertainty is
involved. He stresses (rightly) the great difficulties caused by uncertainty over the assignment
of lines to speakers in the text of Aristophanes: manuscript evidence on this point is of no
authority, and the large number of characters, many of them all but anonymous, in Aristophanes creates many problems: on this see Wilamowitz on *Lysistr.* 74, 1216–41; J. Andrieu,
Le Dialogue antique (esp. pp. 91–95, 169 f., 209–11, 214–18, 249–52, 258 ff., 275–81); Russo,
op. cit., pp. 66–74; Dover, *C.R.*, n.s. 9 (1959), pp. 196–9; Fraenkel, *Beobachtungen zu Aristophanes* (1962), pp. 61–65, 92–94, 121–3, 132–5; J. C. B. Lowe, *Bull. Inst. Class. Stud.* (London),
9 (1962), pp. 27–42; *Hermes*, 95 (1967), pp. 53–71.

[5] The ambiguity turns on whether Amphitheos leaves the stage at 55, to return just when
wanted at 129, or remains on-stage throughout: the latter is Russo's view; for the former (and
more probable), see Dover, *Lustrum* 2 (1957), pp. 58 f.; id. *Maia*, n.s. 15 (1963), pp. 8 f.

parts—those of Dikaiopolis, Amphitheos, and the Ambassador (the same actor probably played Theoros later in the scene)—were presumably taken by the three principal actors, but the Herald (present throughout ll. 43–173) calls for a fourth actor, however described, and an extra is needed for the King's Eye, Pseudartabas (who speaks only two lines of gibberish, but is on stage at least from ll. 94 to 125). The 'fourth actor' is then available to play a number of other brief parts later in the play, amounting probably to not more than 30 lines. One of these parts was probably that of the second sycophant, Nikarchos (908–58): some scholars have found a difficulty in that a joke implies that this character was a small man, and realism demands that he be not played by an actor who elsewhere plays normal full-grown persons. But a joke is a joke, and the point of this one does not require a grotesquely small figure. A possible distribution would then be: one actor (almost certainly the protagonist) Dikaiopolis; a second, Ambassador, Theoros, Euripides, Lamachus, Megarian, Theban, Farmer, Paranymphos; a third, Amphitheos, Dikaiopolis' daughter, Euripides' slave, Sycophant, Messenger from Lamachus, second Herald, Messenger from priest of Dionysus; a fourth, Herald, Megarian's daughter, Nikarchos, Messenger from the generals; extra, Pseudartabas.

In *Knights* only three actors are needed, one representing the Sausage-seller, a second the second Slave ('Nikias') and the Paphlagonian ('Kleon'), a third the first Slave ('Demosthenes') and Demos.[1]

We have *Clouds* only in a revised or partly revised form. Obviously Strepsiades is played by one actor throughout, Socrates by a second, and Pheidippides by a third; the second also plays the first Creditor ('Pasias') and Strepsiades' slave (56–58), and the third the second Creditor ('Amynias') and one or perhaps two pupils of Socrates (133–221; 1493–1505). But in the text as it stands, four actors are required in ll. 889–1104, since it seems clear that both Strepsiades and Pheidippides must have been present during the dispute of the two Λόγοι. Socrates perhaps was not,[2] but his actor cannot have taken the part of either of the Λόγοι, as he speaks at l. 1105, and even if he returns then, would have had no time at all to change his mask and costume. The scene as a whole, then, appears to call for five actors, and the fourth and fifth actors would have parts wholly in excess of what is given to such actors elsewhere in

---

[1] Droysen and others, followed by Coulon, put ll. 1254–6 into the mouth of the first Slave ('Demosthenes'), on inadequate grounds: see Russo, *Aristofane*, pp. 139 f. If they were right, a fourth actor would be required for 'Demosthenes' here, though not necessary earlier in the play.

[2] Cf. l. 887 ἐγὼ δ' ἀπέσομαι.

extant Aristophanes. But it is quite uncertain what happened in the play as originally constructed.[1]

Wasps could not be performed without four actors. Two are required for the parts of Philokleon and Bdelykleon, and the actor of Philokleon may also have played the first Slave (Sosias). A third may have played the second Slave (Xanthias), the Dog from Kydathenaion, and the Ἀρτοπωλίς; a fourth, the Reveller and the Man with a witness (ll. 1415 ff.), but other arrangements are equally possible. The Boy (ll. 230–414) and the three sons of Karkinos, who are dancers, in the last scene must have been taken by extras.

In *Peace* the parts of the first Slave (1–49) and then Trygaeus must have been taken by one actor; a second took those of the second Slave (1–113 and 824–1126), Hermes, Kydoimos, and probably the Arms-dealer; a third, those of Polemos, Hierokles, and the Δρεπανουργός. The extra performers required include the daughter of Trygaeus (114–48), and the small sons of Lamachus (1270–94) and Kleonymos (1298–1301),[2] as well as the mute figures of Peace, Opora, and Theoria. The distribution of the parts from 1210 to 1264 depends upon whether the various Armourers, who in some texts speak in succession under different names, are not rather (as some editors have suggested with probability) all one Ὅπλων Κάπηλος (l. 1209) offering different objects successively. In that case they could all be taken by the second actor and the different pieces of military equipment carried by two κωφὰ πρόσωπα, the Κρανοποιός (1255: cf. 1213) and the Δορυξόος (1213, 1260).

Birds could be performed, for all but one scene, by three actors, without involving impossibly swift changes of costume, and the sequence of entrances and exits suggests that it was so performed, in spite of involving more parts (twenty-two) than any other extant play of Aristophanes. One actor would play Peisetairos throughout; the remaining parts could be assigned as follows: a second actor, Euelpides, Poet, Meton, Decree-seller, first Messenger (1122–63), Iris, Kinesias, Prometheus, Herakles; a third, Hoopoe's servant, Hoopoe, Priest, Oracle-monger, Inspector, second Messenger (1168–84), Herald from earth (1271–1307), Parricide, Sycophant, Poseidon. The Triballian god would be an extra, speaking a few lines of nonsense. A large number of walking-on parts includes the bird-slave Manes (1311 ff.) and the figure of Basileia in the final scene. The swiftest change occurs just before the exodos, when one of the actors

[1] For some interesting suggestions, see Russo, op. cit., pp. 155–71.

[2] On children's parts in Aristophanes (always song or recitative), see Russo, op. cit., pp. 226 f.

involved in the embassy of gods must change into a Messenger during the lyrics, ll. 1694–1705: they were perhaps preceded by dumb show (cf. 1693).

Lysistrata includes a conversation of four characters very early in the play (ll. 77–244), but for the most part could be acted by three actors, with a few very minor roles, amounting to not much more than thirty lines, given to a fourth. The part of Lysistrata would occupy one actor almost throughout, and could be combined only with that of the Spartan youth (1242–1320). A second actor could play Kalonike, the Proboulos, first Woman (728 ff.), Kinesias, Athenian (Wilamowitz and Coulon's Prytanis: 1086–1188, and probably 1216–95); a third, Myrrhine, first Old Woman (439–607),[1] third Woman (742–80), the Spartan Herald, the Spartan (1076–1188) and the second Athenian (1221 ff.). This would leave to extra performers the speeches of the second Old Woman in the scene 439–607 (3 lines), the second Woman of 735–41 (3½ lines), and the fourth Woman of the same scene (760 ff.: 2 lines), plus the Woman of 830–844 (2½ lines): all or most of these could have been taken by the fourth actor who must play Lampito in ll. 77–244. The baby of Kinesias (879) could be an extra, played by a child, but the 'baby' could as well be a doll and its cry mimicked by Kinesias. A large crowd of walking-on parts includes numerous 'women', mostly anonymous, and 'men', as well as some unnamed trouble-makers (1217–40), apparently slaves.[2]

In *Thesmophoriazousae* one actor must have played Euripides' relative ('Mnesilochus'); a second, Euripides and the first Woman; a third, Agathon's slave, Agathon, the second Woman, Kleisthenes, and third Woman (759–935), and the Archer. The Archer at his first appearance (923 ff.) is played by a κωφὸν πρόσωπον, but goes off with his prisoner at 946, and returns, played by an actor, at 1001.[3] The part of the Prytanis (929–944: 8 lines) calls for a fourth actor. The 'chorus' which sings with Agathon in the rehearsal scene (101 ff.) is certainly not visible: it is either imaginary, mimed by Agathon (a suggestion already made by the scholiast on 101 f.), or sings off-stage, like the chorus of Frogs in *Frogs*.[4]

Frogs could be played almost throughout by three actors: one taking the part of Dionysus, a second those of Xanthias and Aeschylus, and a third those of Herakles, Charon, Aiakos, the servant of Persephone,[5]

---

[1] On the two anonymous speakers in this scene, see Russo, op. cit., pp. 279 f.
[2] See Wilamowitz on 1216–41; Russo, op. cit., pp. 282–4.
[3] Russo, op. cit., pp. 153 f.
[4] So Fraenkel, *Beobachtungen zu Aristophanes*, p. 112, n. 1.
[5] Probably male, not female, as the oath μὰ τὸν Ἀπόλλω (508) indicates: see J. Werres, *Die Beteuerungsformeln in d. att. Kom.* (diss. Bonn, 1936), p. 44.

the Hostess, and Euripides; a fourth would be required for the very small parts (so far as spoken lines are concerned) of the Corpse, Plathane, and Pluton. The play involves the three actors almost constantly, and gives one of them two major parts (Xanthias and Aeschylus) in succession. Greater use of a fourth actor would enable these parts to be separated, but it remains notable that Xanthias disappears from the scene once Aeschylus appears. The unseen chorus of Frogs was no doubt sung (off-stage) by the same chorus-men as formed the regular chorus of Initiated. The walking-on parts include the Girl with the castanets ('Euripides' Muse', 1305–64).

Ecclesiazousae can also be arranged for three actors with a very little help from a fourth. One actor plays Praxagora, the second Man (746 ff.), and the first and third Old Women; a second, the first Woman, the first Man (Blepyros' neighbour: 327 ff.), Chremes, and the Young Man (938 ff.); a third, the second Woman (35 ff.), Blepyros, the female Herald, the Young Girl (884 ff.), and the Maidservant. A fourth would then take the third Woman (who speaks 3 lines in a dialogue of four characters) and the second Old Woman (1049–95).

Whether or not *Plutus* was acted by three actors depends on whether the part of Plutus was divided between two actors, perhaps with different masks—the one representing him before, the other after his restoration to health. If so, one actor might take Karion, Poverty (415 ff.), the Old Woman, and Plutus from l. 771 onwards; a second, Chremylos, the Just Man, and Hermes; a third, Plutus blind (1–286), Blepsidemos, Chremylos' Wife, the Sycophant, the Young Man, and the Priest of Zeus. But a four-actor distribution remains more likely.

It seems probable, therefore, that in the Old Comedy the greater part of the work was done by three actors, but that for a particular scene, when required, or perhaps when available, or for very small parts, a fourth was employed. When four persons converse, one of them takes a very small part (though the opening scene of the *Lysistrata* is somewhat exceptional) and the chorus does not join in the dialogue. It was obviously a less serious and less expensive matter to provide an occasional or un-important fourth actor for a single comedy, which is all that each com-petitor offered, than for three tragedies, and the structure of comedy was looser from the first than that of tragedy.[1]

---

[1] Wilamowitz (on *Lysistrata* 1114) suggested that women (not men), appearing naked, took walking-on parts in several of Aristophanes' plays. His list includes Διαλλαγαί in *Lysistrata*, the girl flute-player in *Wasps*, the girl in *Thesm.* 1175 ff., the girl flute-player and Basileia in *Birds*, Dikaiopolis' girl-friends in the exodos of *Acharnians*, and Theoria in *Peace*. If the thesis is accepted, one might add Σπονδαί in *Knights* and the Muse of Euripides in *Frogs*.

8. Whether there was any fixed custom in regard to the number of actors in the New Comedy it is not possible to say. Until recently the remains of Menander's plays[1] were too fragmentary, and the assignment of lines to particular characters frequently too uncertain. It is not safe to argue from the Roman comedy to the Greek; nor do we know whether or at what time a virtual division of the play into Acts came into vogue and with it the permission of intervals during which the scene was empty and changes of costume could be made.

The discovery of *Dyskolos* has made it a good deal easier to discuss the problem, though it would still be unsafe to generalize (*Dyskolos* was a very early play of Menander). Allocations of the parts in this play to both three and four actors have already been proposed. G. P. Goold[2] decides firmly for a three-actor solution: (*a*) Chaereas, Cnemon, Daos, Sostratus (in ll. 522–73 and 611–19), Simice (except 574–96), Callippides; (*b*) Sostratus (except 522–73, 611–19), Getas, Gorgias (in 635–8); (*c*) Pan, Pyrrhias, Cnemon's daughter, Gorgias (except 635–8), Sicon, and Simice (in 574–96). J. G. Griffith[3] offers alternative allocations: with three actors: (*a*) Sostratus, Getas (in 402–80, 879–969); (*b*) Chaereas, Cnemon, Daos, Callippides; (*c*) Pan, Pyrrhias, Gorgias, Sicon, Getas (in 546–619); extra, Cnemon's daughter and Simice. This is more nearly workable than Goold's suggestion. Assuming four actors, Griffith suggests: (*a*) Sostratus; (*b*) Pan, Cnemon, Callippides, Simice (in 620–38 and 874–84); (*c*) Pyrrhias, Gorgias, Sicon, Simice (in 574–602); (*d*) Chaereas, Daos, Getas; extra, Cnemon's daughter. The extra might be dispensed with by assigning: (*a*) Cnemon, Daos, Callippides, Simice (in 620–38, 874–84); (*b*) Sostratus; (*c*) Pan, Pyrrhias, Gorgias, Getas; (*d*) Chaereas, Cnemon's daughter, Sicon, Simice (in 574–602). But the possible permutations and combinations are numerous,[4] and it may be questioned whether the problem can ever be settled from the text. We should perhaps rather note the epigraphic evidence from the Delphic

---

[1] The number of actors in Menander's plays has been frequently discussed, e.g. in Legrand's *Daos*, pp. 365 ff.; K. Rees in *Class. Philol.* 5 (1910), pp. 291 ff.; Graf, *Szenische Untersuchungen zu Menander*, pp. 29–49; Körte, *R.E.*, s.v. Menandros (9), cols. 755 f., etc., but there are still too many 'unknown quantities' to allow of any certain solution of the problems.

[2] *Phoenix* 13 (1959), pp. 144–50.

[3] *C.Q.*, N.S., 10 (1960), pp. 113–17. See also Webster, *Studies in Menander*[2], pp. 225 f.; J.-M. Jacques, *Ménandre, Le Dyscolos* (Budé), p. 76, n. 1, 80, n. 1 (both opt for three actors).

[4] Among outstanding uncertainties are the exits of Chaereas and Pyrrhias in ll. 134 ff. and the first entry of Cnemon in the same passage; the re-entry of Pyrrhias before l. 214; the speakers of ll. 300–1 (? Pyrrhias) and 515–16 (? Getas). No distribution yet takes account of Sostratus' mother, plausibly conjectured by Ritchie as the speaker of ll. 430–1, 432–4, 436–7, 440–1. Also, do we know what length of pause was either normal or tolerated when the stage was empty (for which see Griffith, op. cit., p. 113, and add l. 455)?

Soteria (see below), which shows that in the third century the comic team was normally composed of three actors. Yet it seems likely that there are extant scenes of Menander's plays which could hardly be performed without four actors, e.g. the Arbitration scene in the *Epitrepontes*, and the one which follows it immediately, as there would be no time for Daos, the defeated litigant, to change his mask and dress and reappear as Onesimos.[1] In the *Perikeiromene* there is a scene (217 ff.) in which Polemon, Sosias, Pataikos, and Habrotonon are all present at once and all appear to take some part in the conversation, and a later scene in which Glykera, Pataikos, Doris, and Moschion (at first in hiding, but interjecting 'asides') all seem to take part. (Moreover, in both these plays the employment of three actors only would certainly entail some very awkward divisions of the same role between two or even three actors.)

The evidence as regards the number of actors employed in each play, after the organization of actors' guilds in all parts of the Greek world, is confined to the series of inscriptions recording the names of all the performers at the Soteria at Delphi from about 275 B.C. onwards.[2] At each festival three (or two) troupes of performers of tragedy and four or three troupes of performers of comedy are recorded, and in each troupe are three τραγῳδοί or κωμῳδοί (with a flute player and in nearly every case a didaskalos).[3] This implies that for any one play only three actors were available—the protagonist and two others, who in some other inscriptions are referred to as συναγωνισταί. But there is reason to believe that the actors of the later period (like the fourth-century Athenian actors whom Lycurgus compelled to keep to the authorized text of the great poets) took great liberties with the text of older plays, and may have got over difficulties by this means. They would naturally select for action only such of the newer plays as their companies could conveniently

---

[1] In the *Epitrepontes* Onesimos and Smikrines would each require a single actor; a third could play Daos and Habrotonon; the fourth, Syriskos and Chairestratos; but the distribution of the parts of Simmias, Charisios, Pamphile, Sophrone, and the Cook is quite uncertain. In the *Samia* one actor would play Demeas, a second Parmenon and possibly Chrysis also, a third, Nikeratos, Moschion, and the Cook. The division of the parts in the *Perikeiromene* is (with the text as it is) very difficult to ascertain; but Polemon obviously occupies one actor entirely, and Daos, Glykera, and Habrotonon could be played by one actor, and so could Sosias and Moschion; a fourth could take Doris and Pataikos (no part of Myrrhine's role is extant). But objections to this arrangement will easily suggest themselves.

[2] See below, pp. 283 f. (and refs. there given), and Rees in *Am. J. Phil.* 31 (1910), pp. 43 ff. The latter's difficulty, that no tragic chorus is mentioned (though there were seven comic choreutai until a late date) and that nevertheless each tragic troupe had its flute player and didaskalos, may be solved if we consider that the flute player would be needed to accompany any lyrics sung by a τραγῳδός, and that there may have been enough for the didaskalos to do in connexion with these musical portions.

[3] Where no didaskalos is mentioned, the protagonist or a leading member of the chorus may have fulfilled the task.

perform (that the same actor might take two very different parts is suggested by references in Lucian and others; see p. 138, n. 1 above).

c. *Delivery, Speech, Recitative, Song*

1. The presentation[1] of a play, whether by actors or chorus, involves three elements—the utterance of the words, the use of gestures, and the movements (or absence of movement) from place to place on the scene of action, whether on the level ground or on a stage.

The practice of Greek actors included speech unaccompanied by music, speech accompanied by an instrument (or what is conventionally termed recitative), and song. The first was normally employed for the portions of a play written in iambic trimeters (the metre considered most akin to prose speech),[2] whether in dialogue or monologue, the second for the delivery of tetrameters and of iambics inserted in the midst of lyric systems, the third for lyrics. The texts which give direct evidence on this subject are few, and except as regards recitative raise no difficulties:

(1) Aristotle, *Poet.* iv. 1449ᵃ21 ff. τό τε μέτρον (of the earliest tragedy) ἐκ τετραμέτρου ἰαμβεῖον ἐγένετο. τὸ μὲν γὰρ πρῶτον τετραμέτρῳ ἐχρῶντο διὰ τὸ σατυρικὴν καὶ ὀρχηστικωτέραν εἶναι τὴν ποίησιν. λέξεως δὲ γενομένης ('when a spoken part was introduced'?) αὐτὴ ἡ φύσις τὸ οἰκεῖον μέτρον εὗρε. μάλιστα γὰρ λεκτικὸν τῶν μέτρων τὸ ἰαμβεῖόν ἐστιν. σημεῖον δὲ τούτου· πλεῖστα γὰρ ἰαμβεῖα λέγομεν ἐν τῇ διαλέκτῳ τῇ πρὸς ἀλλήλους.

(2) Aristotle, *Rhet.* iii. 8. 1408ᵇ33 ff. ὁ δ' ἴαμβος αὐτή ἐστιν ἡ λέξις ἡ τῶν πολλῶν· διὸ μάλιστα πάντων τῶν μέτρων ἰαμβεῖα φθέγγονται λέγοντες.

(3) Aristotle, *Poet.* vi. 1449ᵇ28 ff. λέγω δὲ ἡδυσμένον μὲν λόγον (as used by tragedy) τὸν ἔχοντα ῥυθμὸν καὶ ἁρμονίαν καὶ μέλος, τὸ δὲ χωρὶς τοῖς εἴδεσι τὸ διὰ μέτρων ἔνια μόνον περαίνεσθαι καὶ πάλιν ἔτερα διὰ μέλους.

(4) Xenophon, *Symp.* vi. 3. ἢ οὖν βούλεσθε, ἔφη, ὥσπερ Νικόστρατος ὁ ὑποκριτὴς τετράμετρα πρὸς τὸν αὐλὸν κατέλεγεν, οὕτω καὶ ὑπὸ τὸν αὐλὸν ὑμῖν διαλέγωμαι; (Nikostratos was a famous tragic actor of the last part of the fifth century. See O'Connor, pp. 122–3; *I.G.* ii². 2318, col. vii; 2325, col. i.)[3]

(5) [Plutarch] *de Mus.* 1140 f. ἀλλὰ μὴν καὶ Ἀρχίλοχος τὴν τῶν τριμέτρων ῥυθμοποιίαν προσεξεῦρε καὶ τὴν εἰς τοὺς οὐχ ὁμογενεῖς ῥυθμοὺς ἔντασιν[4]

---

[1] The Greek word for 'present' is διατιθέναι; e.g. Plato, *Charmid.* 162 d ἀλλά μοι ἔδοξεν ὀργισθῆναι αὐτῷ ὥσπερ ποιητῆς ὑποκριτῇ κακῶς διατιθέντι τὰ ἑαυτοῦ ποιήματα; and *Laws* ii. 658 d ῥαψῳδὸν ... καλῶς Ἰλιάδα καὶ Ὀδύσσειαν ἤ τι τῶν Ἡσιοδείων διατιθέντα.

[2] According to Aristotle, passages 1 and 2 below, but cf. Maas, *Greek Metre* (trans. Lloyd-Jones) (1962), para. 77; Dale, *C.Q.*, n.s. 13 (1963), p. 48 and n. 2.

[3] The Xenophon passage is somewhat ambiguous: it might be taken to imply that tetrameters were *not* always 'recited' to a flute accompaniment (otherwise why mention the name of the actor?), and refers perhaps rather to a 'recital' at a symposium than to a performance in the theatre.

[4] τὴν ... ἔντασιν: the combination of iambic with rhythms of another type, e.g. (as he explains later) an iambic + paeonic line.

καὶ τὴν παρακαταλογὴν καὶ τὴν περὶ ταῦτα κροῦσιν ('recitative and its accompaniment') . . . ἔτι δὲ τῶν ἰαμβείων τὸ τὰ μὲν λέγεσθαι παρὰ τὴν κροῦσιν ('uttered to an accompaniment') τὰ δ' ᾄδεσθαι, Ἀρχίλοχόν φασι καταδεῖξαι, εἶθ' οὕτω χρήσασθαι τοὺς τραγικοὺς ποιητάς, Κρέξον δὲ λαβόντα εἰς διθυράμβων χρῆσιν ἀγαγεῖν.[1] οἴονται δὲ καὶ τὴν κροῦσιν τὴν ὑπὸ τὴν ᾠδὴν[2] τοῦτον πρῶτον εὑρεῖν, τοὺς δ' ἀρχαίους πάντα πρόσχορδα κρούειν.

(6) Aristotle, *Problems* xix. 6. διὰ τί ἡ παρακαταλογὴ ἐν ταῖς ᾠδαῖς[3] τραγικόν; ἢ διὰ τὴν ἀνωμαλίαν ('the contrast involved'); παθητικὸν γὰρ τὸ ἀνωμαλὲς καὶ ἐν μεγέθει τύχης ἢ λύπης· τὸ δὲ ὁμαλὲς ἔλαττον γοῶδες.[4]

(7) Lucian, *de saltat.* 27 (speaking with contempt of the actor who 'sings' the iambic parts of a play). εἶτ' ἔνδοθεν αὐτὸς κεκραγώς, ἑαυτὸν ἀνακλῶν καὶ κατακλῶν, ἐνίοτε καὶ περιᾴδων τὰ ἰαμβεῖα.

(8) Athenaeus xiv. 636 b. ἐν οἷς γάρ, φησί (sc. Phillis of Delos), τοὺς ἰάμβους ᾖδον ἰαμβύκας ἐκάλουν· ἐν οἷς δὲ παρακατελογίζοντο τὰ ἐν τοῖς μέτροις κλεψιάμβους. [The MSS. have παρελογίζοντο.]

The term παρακαταλογή,[5] applied to the recitation of lines to the accompaniment of the flute, the instrument best suited for tragic use,[6] is found only twice (in Aristotle's *Problems* and in 'Plutarch') and the corresponding verb once (in a conjectural reading in Athenaeus). The invention of παρακαταλογή was ascribed to Archilochus, from whom the tragic poets adopted it. The word is equivalent in meaning to καταλέγειν παρὰ τὴν κροῦσιν,[7] and it would appear that the accompaniment was on a higher note or notes than those employed by the actor. Whether the actor or the flautist kept to the same note or notes, wholly or mainly, is never stated; we have in fact very little notion what this 'recitative', later accompanied by the κλεψίαμβος, was like. (It can hardly have

[1] Krexos (4th cent. B.C.) was the first to introduce recitative (as distinct from singing) into dithyramb.

[2] ὑπὸ τὴν ᾠδήν, i.e. on a higher note or notes than the utterance of the reciter. The use of ὑπό for higher and ὑπέρ for lower was derived from the position of the higher and lower strings of the harp as held by the player. (Another terminology based on the position of the notes of the flute was also in vogue. See Weil and Reinach's edition of the *de Musica*, p. 111.)

[3] Probably refers to iambic lines inserted in or between lyric strophes. See Dale, *Lyric Metres of Gk. Drama*, pp. 197 f., and below, pp. 162 ff.

[4] On this passage, see the commentary of Flashar in *Aristoteles: Werke in deutscher Übersetzung, herausg. von E. Grumach*, vol. 19 (1962), p. 602.

[5] See Maas, *R.E.*, s.v.; Christ, *Metrik d. Griechen u. Römer*², para. 744.

[6] Plut. *de E ap. Delph.* 394 b καὶ γὰρ ὁ αὐλὸς ὀψὲ καὶ πρώην ἐτόλμησε φωνὴν ἐφ' ἱμεροῖσιν ἀφιέναι· τὸν δὲ πρῶτον χρόνον εἴλκετο πρὸς τὰ πένθη καὶ τὴν περὶ ταῦτα λειτουργίαν οὐ μάλα ἔντιμον οὐδὲ φαιδρὰν εἶχεν, εἶτ' ἐμίχθη πάντα πᾶσιν.

[7] καταλέγειν = recite (generally 'recite at length' or 'in full') with no suggestion of music. In *I.G.* ix. 2. 531. 12, 46 (Larissa, about 1 B.C.) καταλογή is hardly intelligible: it occurs twice, once with the adjective παλαιά, once with νέα, in a list otherwise largely of athletic contests, though the last two items are ἐγκώμιον λογικόν and ἐγκώμιον ἐπικόν. Hesych. καταλογή· τὸ τὰ ᾄσματα μὴ ὑπὸ μέλει λέγειν is obscure, but καταλογή here is thought to = παρακαταλογή. (He also applies the term ᾄσματα to the anapaestic tetrameters of the parabasis, which were recited, not sung.) See also below, p.323.

required a special instrument in Classical times if, as is generally believed, it was employed in the iambics inserted among lyrics. There would
hardly have been time for the rapid change of instruments implied.)
The use of the flute in the parabasis of comedy seems to be proved by
Aristophanes' *Birds* 682–4 ἀλλ' ὦ καλλιβόαν κρέκουσ' | αὐλὸν φθέγμασιν
ἠρινοῖς | ἄρχου τῶν ἀναπαίστων (schol. ad loc. πολλάκις πρὸς αὐλὸν λέγουσι
τὰς παραβάσεις). The transition in Aristophanes' *Peace* 1171–2 from sung
lyrics to recited trochaic tetrameters in the same sentence would be
much more difficult unless both were accompanied by the same instrument. The scholiast[1] on Aristophanes *Clouds* 1352 (ἤδη λέγειν χρὴ πρὸς
χορόν) speaks of the chorus's dancing during the delivery by an actor of
the various tetrameter systems—trochaic, anapaestic, and iambic, and
(if this is more than mere *ad hoc* invention) as the choral dance must in
all probability have been accompanied by the flute, the same accompaniment must have served for the actor delivering his address. It is not
surprising that this intermediate kind of delivery is sometimes called
'singing', sometimes 'speaking'. Hesychius speaks of ἀνάπαιστα as τὰ ἐν
ταῖς παραβάσεσι τῶν χορῶν ᾄσματα, though Aristophanes himself describes the chorus as 'speaking' the parabasis.[2] (There is the same in-
consistency as regards the close (or exodos) of comedy, which generally
took the form of recited or sung lines,[3] but is described by a late grammarian[4] as τὸ ἐπὶ τέλει λεγόμενον τοῦ χοροῦ—where, however, λεγόμενον
may be used in the general sense of 'utterance', as λέξις often is.)

2. This account represents the general agreement of scholars based on
the scanty evidence which has come down to us. But it raises or leaves
unsolved a number of interesting questions. For instance, is it to be
assumed that whenever trochaic tetrameters occurred they were accompanied (in the Classical period) by the flute, e.g. in the dialogues of
Aeschylus' *Persae* 155–75 and 215–48 (between the Queen and the chorus,
including the description of Athens and its government, in stichomythia),
703–58 (between Darius and the Queen—in which the narrative of the
disaster is mainly drawn out in alternate question and answer) ; or in the

---

[1] οὕτως ἔλεγον πρὸς χορὸν λέγειν, ὅτε τοῦ ὑποκριτοῦ διατιθεμένου τὴν ῥῆσιν ὁ χορὸς ὠρχεῖτο
διὸ καὶ ἐκλέγονται ὡς ἐπὶ τὸ πλεῖστον ἐν τοῖς τοιούτοις τὰ τετράμετρα ἢ τὰ ἀναπαιστικὰ ἢ τὰ
ἰαμβικά, διὰ τὸ ῥᾳδίως ἐμπίπτειν ἐν τούτοις τὸν τοιοῦτον ῥυθμόν.

[2] *Knights* 507–9 εἰ μέν τις ἀνὴρ τῶν ἀρχαίων κωμῳδοδιδάσκαλος ἡμᾶς | ἠνάγκαζεν λέξοντας
ἔπη πρὸς τὸ θέατρον παραβῆναι, | οὐκ ἂν φαύλως ἔτυχεν τούτου.

[3] Poll. iv. 108 ὁ ἐξιόντες ᾖδον, and schol. on Ar. *Wasps* 270 ἅπερ ἐπὶ τῇ ἐξόδῳ τοῦ δράματος
ᾄδεται. The scholiast quotes the end of *Plutus*, where the chorus (in two concluding anapaestic
tetrameters) end with δεῖ γὰρ κατόπιν τούτων ᾄδοντας ἕπεσθαι.

[4] *Tract. Coisl.* (Kaibel, p. 53). Other late grammarians use the definition ἡ πρὸς τῷ
τέλει τοῦ χοροῦ ῥῆσις.

altercation between Aigisthos and the chorus (with a speech of 8 lines
by Klytaimnestra) in *Agamemnon* 1649–73? The matter of these dialogue scenes does not itself perhaps suggest musical accompaniment, and
we might have here simply a survival of the use of this metre in tragedy
before the iambic trimeter was introduced for the purpose of dialogue.[1] But the sharp break in tempo and the rise in tension in the
Agamemnon passage is quite palpable.[2] Similarly, in Sophocles' *Philoctetes*
1402–8, the brief dialogue between Neoptolemos and Philoctetes, as
they are starting for the ship, showing a high degree of excitement and
leading up to the anapaests of Herakles' entry, and the tetrameter entry
of Theseus in *Oedipus Coloneus* (887–90) occur at moments of great
dramatic tension, though the words of each passage hardly in themselves
suggest music or song. But it is in Euripides, and in his later period, that
the use of this metre for dialogue is most frequent.[3] (*Philoctetes* is, of course,
later than much of Euripides' work.) The first instance is in *Herakles*
(855–74), as the dialogue between Iris and Lyssa reaches its climax, and
Lyssa prepares to go to work. Again there is a sharp break and jerk into
the new metre. In *Ion* 510–65, in the excited dialogue between Ion and
Xouthos, when the latter claims Ion as his son, most of the exchange
is in half-lines, the speakers interrupting one another constantly. The
exodos of the play ends with 17 lines of dialogue in this metre, indicating
a certain intensifying of interest, but not in themselves obviously calling
for musical accompaniment. Rapid dialogue, with each line divided
between two speakers, is characteristic of many of these Euripidean
scenes in tetrameters, e.g. *Iph. Taur.* 1203–33 (between Iphigeneia and
Thoas), *Helen* 1621–41 (between Theoklymenos and the Servant), *Phoenissae* 588–637 (between Eteokles and Polyneikes), *Orestes* 729–806 (between Orestes and Pylades—rapid stichomythia followed by divided
lines), *Iph. Aul.* 1338–401 (between Iphigeneia and Klytaimnestra).[4]
Stichomythia (alternate question and answer, each taking an entire line)
is also common in these scenes, and there are a few connected speeches,
as in *Troad.* 444–61 (the highly emotional ending of Kassandra's reply
to Talthybios), *Iph. Taur.*, loc. cit. (when the dialogue is over), *Bacchae*
604–41 (mainly Dionysus' narrative of the miracle in the palace), *Iph.
Aul.* 317–401 (where 18 lines of excited dialogue are followed by long
and bitter speeches in the same metre, delivered by Menelaus and
Agamemnon), 855–916 (where 45 lines of stichomythia, in which the

---

[1] So Aristot. *Poet.* iv. 1449[a]21.
[2] See Fraenkel on *Agam.* 1649 ff., and compare Soph. *O.T.* 1515 ff.
[3] See Krieg, *Philologus* 91 (1936), pp. 42–51; Imhof, *Mus. Helv.* 13 (1956), pp. 125–43.
[4] The brief dialogue in *Rhesus* 683–91 is also mainly in broken lines.

Old Man, Achilles, and Klytaimnestra take part, are followed by a speech of Klytaimnestra), and 1338–1401 (where the excited dialogue ends with a long and dramatic speech by Iphigeneia in the same metre).[1] It is not difficult to imagine musical accompaniment associated with most of these dialogues and speeches, and it seems probable that in most of them the metre connotes excitement or tension, and that Euripides in particular developed its use in this sense.

3. It seems probable that the anapaestic dimeters used in every play of Aeschylus were generally given in recitative accompanied by the flute. This may be taken as certain where they are uttered by the chorus as they enter the orchestra, preceded by the flute player, as at the beginning of *Persae* and *Suppliants* and in *Agamemnon* 40–103, or when they form an introduction to a sung choral ode, as in *Persae* 532–47 and 623–32, and before the κομμός, 907–30, and also in *Agamemnon* 40–103, already cited, and 355–66, and *Eumenides* 307–20. It may also be assumed that these dimeters were delivered in recitative in the long dialogue between Klytaimnestra and the chorus, 1448–1577, when the utterances of the Queen in this metre contrast with the lyric strophes and antistrophes of the chorus.[2] A similar contrast with the lyrics appears in the great litany of *Choephoroi*, where it is the chorus which from time to time speaks in a more subdued emotional tone than Electra and Orestes, and concludes (476–8) with the appropriate prayer. (A similar difference of tone seems to be marked in the two couplets in this metre in *Septem* 879–80 and 886–7.) The metre is used sometimes to express the moral of what has gone before or to utter an appropriate prayer; e.g. in *Agamemnon* 1331–42,[3] and *Choephoroi* 719–29, 855–68, 1007–9, 1018–20. In *Prometheus* 93–192 we have a hint of the formal device, common later in Euripides, by which this metre is used for the whole first scene in which a principal character speaks, and the semi-musical mode of utterance may well have been employed. Aeschylus also occasionally uses the metre when the chorus first sees or greets one of the characters, as (for example) in *Septem* 861–74, where Antigone and Ismene are discerned, and *Agamemnon* 782–809, where their address of welcome to Agamemnon is couched in anapaestic dimeters. In *Prometheus* 284–97 Okeanos announces

[1] Other tetrameter passages in Euripides are *Ion* 1250–60, where Kreousa is urged by the chorus to take refuge at the altar, *Phoen.* 1335–9, where the hurrying messenger announces disaster to Kreon, and *Orest.* 1549–53, where the chorus spies Menelaus approaching.

[2] On the structure of this scene, see Fraenkel, *Agam.* iii, pp. 660 f.

[3] Cf. Kranz, *Stasimon*, pp. 162, 202. The use of a brief anapaestic sequence here, at a moment of crisis and as a cadence before the long-awaited murder, instead of a lyric stasimon, is parallel to Euripides' later device of a single astrophic stanza: cf. *Hipp.* 1268–82, *Bacchae* 1153–64 with Dodds's note. The case is somewhat similar with *Choeph.* 855 ff.

himself in the same metre. In the possibly spurious final scene of *Septem* and in *Choephoroi* the metre is employed in the exodos, and the flute may have been used, as it doubtless was when the chorus marched out.[1]

Sophocles employs anapaestic dimeters in the Aeschylean manner in *Ajax* and *Antigone*. They are also used in the preludes to the *kommoi* of *Trachiniae* and *Tyrannus*. (In the parodos of *Electra* they are sung.) In *Philoctetes* 144–200 it is the metre in which Neoptolemos expresses himself in alternation with the lyrics of the chorus, when they are looking for Philoctetes, and in *Oedipus Coloneus* 136–75 it is much used in the agitated scene when Oedipus first confronts the chorus, both in dialogue and in the last lines of strophe and antistrophe. In both scenes the matter itself seems neither to require nor to exclude recitative. In Euripides anapaestic dimeters are constantly in use. They occur in the parodos of the chorus (*Alcestis* 77–85, *Hecuba* 98–153), and in highly emotional scenes at or near the beginning of a play (*Medea* 96–203, *Hipp.* 170–266, *Hecuba* 59 ff., *Troad.* 98–121, *Iph. Taur.* 143–235, in all of which the emotional delivery of the recitative seems more natural than bare speech), and in *Ion* 82–183 it suits the liveliness of the boy's utterance. Its appropriateness to the dialogue of Agamemnon and the Old Man at the beginning of *Iphigeneia in Aulis* and to the opening dialogue of *Rhesus* is perhaps more questionable. It may be doubted whether in *Medea* 1081–1115, where a passage in this metre takes the place of a choral ode, and in *Ion* 859–922, where dimeters form a considerable part of Kreousa's monody, the anapaests may not actually have been sung rather than recited. In the funeral procession in *Alcestis* 861–934 Admetus laments in anapaestic dimeters, alternating with the lyric strophes and antistrophes of the chorus. It has been thought that this contrast is an element in the characterization of Admetus,[2] and if so, his part was perhaps recited. In *Andromache* there is a similar contrast between the anapaests (515–22, 537–44) of the brutal Menelaus and the terrified lyrics of Andromache and her child, but it is difficult to be positive whether Menelaus required a flute accompaniment, or whether the metre merely expresses the urgency of his commands. Nor is it easy to be certain whether the brief moralizing lines, *Alcestis* 238–43, are to be thought of as spoken or as recited. (On the other hand, the prayer in 741–6 is virtually lyric in tone.) There is the same doubt about *Heraclidae* 288–96 and 702–8. The chorus's brief

---

[1] Special cases are those of *Prometheus* 276–83, where the chorus changes its position, and 877–86, where the cries of Io while rushing away are in this metre.

[2] In ll. 273–9 also Admetus' distress does not go beyond anapaestic dimeters. But see Dale, *Alcestis*, n. on ll. 280 ff., and Introduction, xxii–xxix.

cry of sympathy in *Medea* 357–63 seems to call for more than mere speech. Almost all the plays of Euripides employ anapaestic dimeters to conclude the exodos, and in nearly all of these scenes recitative and the flute may be assumed; in most there are only a few formal or almost formal lines.[1] A few special cases do not fall clearly under any of the above heads: e.g. *Hippolytus* 1282–95, where Artemis begins her address to Theseus with 12 dimeters of fierce denunciation, whether accompanied or not; *Troades* 782–98, comprising the whole brief tragic episode in which Talthybios carries Astyanax away, and certainly calling for the more intensified tone; *Electra* 1292–1341, an emotional scene of parting between Orestes and Electra in the presence of the Dioskouroi, who conclude with 14 lines in the same metre; and *Iphigeneia in Aulis* 1276–82, where 7 lines of dimeters, shared between Klytaimnestra and Iphigeneia, precede the latter's lyric monody.

There may be a difference of opinion as to the employment of recitative in some of the passages mentioned. But the most difficult class of passages consists of those, very numerous in Euripides,[2] in which a few lines in the metre are used to announce the approach of some human person or a god *ex machina* or of a procession or whatever it may be. In most of these recitative to the flute seems not impossible, e.g. *Andromache* 494–500 at the end of a choral ode, or *Hippolytus* 1342–6, prelude to a long anapaestic recitative by the actor: most lead into or out of a lyric scene, but in a few it might be thought absurd. In the present state of our knowledge the test must be mainly subjective; but it is hard to believe that anapaestic dimeters were never simply spoken, the metre itself being in that case sufficient to emphasize the appropriate tone.[3]

4. It should be noted that the word παρακαταλογή is not (in the few instances of its occurrence) applied to anapaestic dimeters, and poets were probably free to employ any of the three methods of delivery. The word does appear to apply to iambics delivered to an accompaniment,

---

[1] Five plays (*Alcestis, Medea, Andromache, Helen, Bacchae*) end with the lines πολλαὶ μορφαὶ τῶν δαιμονίων (or πολλῶν ταμίας Ζεὺς ἐν ᾿Ολύμπῳ) | πολλὰ δ᾿ ἀέλπτως κραίνουσι θεοί, | καὶ τὰ δοκηθέντ᾿ οὐκ ἐτελέσθη, | τῶν δ᾿ ἀδοκήτων πόρον ηὗρε θεός· | τοιόνδ᾿ ἀπέβη τόδε πρᾶγμα; and three (*Iph. Taur., Phoen., Orestes*) with a prayer for victory—ὦ μέγα σεμνὴ Νίκη, τὸν ἐμὸν | βίοτον κατέχοις | καὶ μὴ λήγοις στεφανοῦσα—which is really extra-dramatic. The schol. on Ar. *Wasps* 582 states definitely: ἔθος δὲ ἦν ἐν ταῖς ἐξόδοις τῶν τῆς τραγῳδίας χορικῶν προσώπων προηγεῖσθαι αὐλητὴν ὥστε αὐλοῦντα προπέμπειν. See above, p. 158; Barrett on *Hippolytus* 1462–6; Dodds on *Bacchae* 1388–92. With these formulaic lines, compare the trimeter prayer to Nike which closes Mcnander's *Dyskolos* (968–9),? *Epitrepontes* (fr. 11 Körte), and *Sikyonios* 422–3 (Kassel), and also Poseidippos' *Apokleiomene* (P. Heidelb. 183).

[2] *Alc.* 28–37; *Hipp.* 1342–6; *Androm.* 494–500, 1166–72, 1226–30; *Suppl.* 794–7, 980–9, 1113–22; *Herakles* 442–50; *Troad.* 568–76, 1118–22, 1252–9; *El.* 988–97, 1233–7; *Iph. Taur.* 456–66; *Orest.* 1013–17; *Iph. Aul.* 590–606; *Phoen.* 1480–4.

[3] See further Maas, *Greek Metre*, para. 76.

but it has already been noticed that there can be no certainty what exactly were these accompanied iambics adopted by the tragic poets from Archilochus, or those described by Athenaeus (after the almost unknown Phillis of Delos) as ἐν οἷς παρακατελογίζοντο τὰ ἐν τοῖς μέτροις. In fact a large proportion of the iambic trimeters associated with lyrics form part of symmetrical epirrhematic structures in which the lyric strophe and antistrophe are each followed by the same number of iambic lines—two, three, four, or five, or more rarely by a single line; it seems at least possible that these iambics were recited, and the contrast between these recited iambics and the sung lyrics may be what is referred to as παθητικόν in the Aristotelian *Problems* xix. 6 (see above, p. 157). There are instances in all three poets, affording impressive and symmetrical structures. Thus in Aeschylus' *Suppliants* 348–406 each choral strophe and antistrophe is followed by five iambic lines in the mouth of the King; and in ll. 736–63 the dochmiac strophes of three lines alternate with four iambic lines divided between King and chorus;[1] in *Persae* 256–89 choral strophes of three or four lines alternate with the trimeter couplets of the Messenger; in *Septem* 203–44 and 683–711 Eteokles utters three-line groups of trimeters in alternation with the choral lyrics, and it must be admitted that Eteokles' sentiments seem to demand violent speech rather than musical accompaniment. In *Agamemnon* 1072–1113 also, the trimeter couplets of the chorus are in strong dramatic contrast with Kassandra's wild lyrics,[2] and may well have been spoken. Kassandra's own lyrics end first with single trimeters (1082, 1087, etc.) and later with trimeter couplets at 1138–9, 1148–9, 1160–1, and 1171–2, and as there is no break in the sense or change of tone, these may even have been sung. Conversely the trimeters of the coryphaeus give way suddenly to excited dochmiacs at 1121, in mid-stanza, and at 1140 their utterances become wholly lyric. In Sophocles' *Ajax*, ll. 348–93 are parallel in form to the first of the instances from *Agamemnon*, the lyrics of Ajax being broken by one, two, or three trimeters of the chorus. The same typical form is found in *Electra* 1232–87, where Orestes' trimeters occur between the lyric strophe, antistrophe, and epode of Electra, and in *Oedipus Coloneus* 1447–1499, except that each group of five trimeters is a dialogue, and should perhaps be thought of as spoken rather than recited. In other passages of Sophocles the symmetry is more complicated (e.g. *Ajax* 891–914 and 925–60, *Electra* 1232–87, *Oedipus Tyrannus* 649–96,

---

[1] See Kranz, *Stasimon*, p. 15.
[2] On the structure and development of this complex and brilliant scene, see Fraenkel, *Agamemnon* iii, pp. 487 f., 538–40, 623–7.

and *Antigone* 1261–76 and 1284–1300) and in some of these the use of recitative seems very doubtful. In Euripides the more typical symmetry of alternate strophes and iambics is found in *Alcestis* 244–65, *Andromache* 825–40, and *Hippolytus* 571–97; but in *Medea* 1273–81, *Heraclidae* 75–110, and *Suppliants* 1123–63, the iambic lines are included within the strophe and antistrophe,[1] and in a number of plays we find iambic lines combined or mixed with the non-antistrophic lyrics to which Euripides was prone, e.g. *Hecuba* 684–720, *Herakles* 875–905 and 1178–1213, *Iphigeneia in Tauris* 827–67, and *Phoenissae* 103–92. Whether or how in these passages the transitions between song and parakataloge were managed must be mainly a matter of conjecture. Our authorities, such as they are, do not require us to believe that *all* iambics found in combination with lyrics were delivered in parakataloge, and the poet was perhaps free to prescribe whatever delivery he required.

5. When we pass to the Old Comedy difficulties are not at an end. In the account given earlier in this chapter it has been made plain that the anapaests of the parabasis were accompanied by the flute, as also, in all probability, were any tetrameter speeches delivered by an actor while the chorus or a semichorus was dancing, and in particular the epirrhema and antepirrhema of the parabasis, which were commonly in trochaic or iambic tetrameters. This is all that is required to satisfy the statement of the scholiast on *Clouds* 1352 (see above, p. 158), from which it is certainly impossible to infer that *all* tetrameters were accompanied by the flute. (They were certainly not all accompanied by choral dancing.) The word παρακαταλογή is never applied to comedy. But the Old Comedy included as a rule a number of epirrhematic systems besides the parabasis,[2] though not so perfectly symmetrical, such as the agon, almost entirely in tetrameters, the proagon, and the 'battle-scene'. (The parodos is also often in tetrameters, and here no doubt the chorus usually marched, or entered otherwise, to music.) In all of these scenes it is hardly possible to be guided only by the character of the words in conjecturing the manner of delivery, and opinions will inevitably differ. It seems, however, at least improbable that very long passages of close argument between two or more persons were recited to the flute, still less before a dancing chorus, while on the other hand instrumental accompaniment is practically certain in the exodos of some plays; and it is unlikely that the freedom of the poet was restricted by rigid conventions.

[1] On the structure of these scenes, see V. di Benedetto, *Hermes* 89 (1961), pp. 298 ff.

[2] The analysis of the plays in *Dith. Trag. Com.*[2], pp. 213–29, with the excursus preceding it, gives details. Some difficulties as to the rendering of certain metres in comedy are discussed by White, *Verse of Gk. Comedy*, pp. 368–71, and F. Perusino, *Quaderni Urbinati*, 1 (1966), pp. 9–14.

Of the Middle and New Comedy too little has survived to allow of any profitable discussion of delivery. It is clear that scenes in trochaic tetrameters were not infrequent; there are fragments of some twenty such scenes in the Middle Comedy. Three trochaic tetrameter scenes (with indications of another) survive in the remains of Menander's *Samia* and *Perikeiromene*, and one at a moment of climax in *Dyskolos* (708–783); no more need be implied than the quickening of the pace which goes with the metre. A few other traces of such scenes in the New Comedy are found. In the fragments of the Middle Comedy, but not of the New (except in Menander, fr. 258 Kö.), we find over a dozen in anapaestic dimeters, some of considerable length,[1] and several resembling the πνῖγος of the Old Comedy. We do not know how they were spoken or sung, except that in some of them great rapidity may be assumed. There are traces of iambic tetrameters[2] (including the clowning scene which forms the exodos of *Dyskolos*) and Eupolideans.[3] The iambic tetrameters of *Dyskolos* were apparently delivered in recitative, accompanied by the flute; cf. *Dyskolos* 880, 910. Hexameters are sometimes introduced for special effects—parody, high-stilted language, riddles, prophecy; the delivery of these may have varied.

6. The instrument by which both singing and recitative were normally accompanied in tragedy and comedy was the flute.[4] In the *Problems* of Aristotle, xix. 43, it is argued that the flute gives a better accompaniment to the human voice than the lyre, because both flute and voice are wind-instruments and so blend better (and because the flute better disguises blunders in the singing!). There is no special reference to tragedy in the passage, but it appears probable that the lyre was used in the drama mainly for special effects, as when the young Sophocles played it in his *Thamyras*, and it may have been confined almost entirely to the occasional accompaniment of monodies. In his parody of the lyrics of both Aeschylus and Euripides in *Frogs*,[5] Aristophanes has the lines which he collects from various plays of each author sung to the lyre; but, taking the context as a whole, this does not imply that all these passages were from odes or solos originally accompanied by the lyre. That Euripides punctuates some of the lines of the parodos of *Agamemnon* with τοφλαττοθρατ

---

[1] e.g. Anaxandrides, fr. 41 (K) (71 lines); Mnesimachus, fr. 4 (65 lines); Epikrates, fr. 11 (38 lines). Cf. Aeschines, *in Tim.* 157 (p. 50, n. 4).
[2] e.g. Antiphanes, fr. 25; Fr. Inc. 294; Diphilus, fr. 1; *Dyskolos* 880–958.   [3] Alexis, fr. 237.
[4] Schol. on Ar. *Clouds* 313 (μοῦσα βαρύβρομος αὐλῶν) προσηύλουν γὰρ καὶ ταῖς τραγῳδίαις καὶ τοῖς κυκλίοις χοροῖς. In Ar. *Wasps* 580–2 there is a reference to the flute-player in the *Niobe* (? of Aeschylus or Sophocles), and the schol. remarks (*inter alia*) ἔθος δὲ ἦν ἐν ταῖς ἐξόδοις τῶν τῆς τραγῳδίας χορικῶν προσώπων προηγεῖσθαι αὐλητήν. For the flute in comedy cf. Ar. *Birds* 682–4 (see p. 158) and *Eccles.* 890–2, Men. *Dyskolos* 880. For flute-players on vases, see pp. 182 ff. below.   [5] See especially ll. 1286, 1304.

τοφλαττοθρατ (having said that he is making up a passage, στάσιν μελῶν | ἐκ τῶν κιθαρῳδικῶν νόμων εἰργασμένην), and that Aeschylus in putting together a nonsensical selection of lines from Euripides calls for a lyre (ἐνεγκάτω τις τὸ λύριον—doubtless the lyre which his rival had just been using), is sufficiently explained if it is remembered that neither poet could sing the other's lines *and accompany them himself* (as the travesty demanded) on anything but the lyre—certainly not on the flute. The argument of Kranz[1] that the fact that the Furies in *Eumenides* 332[2] describe their ὕμνος as ἀφόρμικτος implies that other *choral odes in tragedy* were accompanied by the φόρμιγξ is absurd; it is enough that the music of the lyre was the common accompaniment of cheerful songs in real life.[3] On the other hand, it is quite possible that, in adopting the musical style of his friend Timotheos and the new school,[4] Euripides may also have employed the lyre, the instrument whose capacity was especially developed by Timotheos. A lyre, in fact two, are portrayed on the Pronomos vase,[5] in which the central figure is the flute-player Pronomos, surrounded by satyrs and actors in the presence of Dionysus, but it would not be safe to draw any inference from this as to the extent of the use of the lyre in tragedy or satyric drama. When theatrical companies were organized in the third century, each seems to have included a single flute-player.[6]

It is probable that the flute-player in tragedy and satyric drama wore no mask. There is indeed no literary evidence; but where satyrs are depicted as dancing to the flute, as on the Pronomos vase, the krater by the Niobid Painter of about 460 B.C. in the British Museum[7] (though this may not be connected with a theatrical performance at all), and many others, as well as on the Pompeian mosaic[8] representing the

---

[1] *Stasimon*, p. 139.

[2] Cf. *Agam.* 990 τὸν δ' ἄνευ λύρας ὅμως ὑμνῳδεῖ | θρῆνον Ἐρινύος αὐτοδίδακτος ἔσωθεν | θυμός.

[3] The application of the epithets ἄχορον ἀκίθαριν to Ares in *Suppliants* 681, and the fact that the chorus (ibid. 696) in invoking blessings on Argos prays ἀγνῶν τ' ἐκ στομάτων φερέσθω φάμα φιλοφόρμιγξ, has no discernible bearing on the use of the lyre in tragedy; and Horace, *A.P.* 216, which Kranz also quotes, has no reference to tragedy at all.

[4] See below, pp. 260f.

[5] Fig. 28. See below, pp. 186f. The vase is certainly not the reproduction of a scene in a play.

[6] Cf. pp. 283f. below. It is not known to what period Sextus Empiricus refers (*adv. Math.* vi. 17) when he writes ὡσαύτως δὲ (sc. πρὸς λύραν ᾖδετο) καὶ τὰ παρὰ τοῖς τραγικοῖς μέλη καὶ στάσιμα φυσικόν τινα ἐπέχοντα λόγον (nor, it must be admitted, exactly what he means. He cites Eur., fr. 839 (from the *Chrysippos*) as an example).

[7] See *Dith. Trag. Com.*², pp. 117–18, List of Monuments, no. 100, plate XVa (*A.R.V.*², p. 601, no. 23). See also pp. 184f. below.

[8] *Theatre of D.*, fig. 98. The picture of a rehearsal of tragedy on an engraved stone in the British Museum, figured by Wieseler, *Theatergeb.*, Taf. xii. 45, is modern; see O. M. Dalton, *Cat. of the Engraved Gems of the Post-Classical Periods*, pl. 32, 894.

rehearsal of a satyric play, the flute-player is never masked. As regards comedy, it seems uncertain whether Procne in *Birds* 665 ff. is to be regarded as wearing a bird-mask or not when she comes forward to accompany the anapaests of the parabasis. On the vase-paintings representing birds and horsemen, with a flute-player, the latter seems to be wearing only the regular mouthpiece (φορβειά).[1]

We read little of instruments, other than the flute and lyre, accompanying the actor's delivery; but in *Hypsipyle*[2] the heroine accompanies her song to her infant with κρόταλα—probably a rattle—which Aristophanes parodies by castanets played (probably) by the 'Muse of Euripides' (*Frogs* 1304 ff.) :

καίτοι τί δεῖ
λύρας ἐπὶ τούτων; ποῦ 'στιν ἡ τοῖς ὀστράκοις
αὕτη κροτοῦσα; δεῦρο, Μοῦσ' Εὐριπίδου,
πρὸς ἥνπερ ἐπιτήδεια ταῦτ' ᾄδειν μέλη.

D. *Voice and Enunciation*

There is much evidence to show that Athenian audiences attached great importance to the actor's voice, though the Athenian sound-vocabulary is not always so clear as to indicate exactly the qualities looked for, and most of the evidence is comparatively late. Obviously the voice needed to be strong enough to carry throughout the vast theatre[3] without shouting as bad actors were liable to do, but this must not be over-stressed.[4] The large theatres demanded practised voice-production rather than violent effort, and in fact the acoustic properties of the theatre of Epidaurus are such that a clear but not forced delivery of the speaker's lines from the normal place is audible as far as the uppermost row of seats, a distance of some 150 feet.[5] (The remains of the theatres at Athens (where the distance is very considerably greater) and Syracuse give less good, though not bad, results; but their condition makes a satisfactory test impossible.) Thus, while μεγαλοφωνία, εὐφωνία, and λαμπρότης were

---

[1] *Dith. Trag. Com.*², pp. 152 ff., List of Monuments, nos. 23 ff., Plates VII–IX.

[2] *Hypsipyle*, fr. 1. ii. 8 ff. Bond = 22 ff. Page. Cf. *Bacchae* 123 ff., 158 f.: τύμπανα.

[3] Note the μικροφωνία which was responsible for Sophocles' giving up acting: *Vit. Soph.* 4.

[4] Cf. Zeno *ap.* Diog. Laert. vii. 20 = fr. 327 von Arnim. On the topic of the vocal demands of ancient acting, cf. esp. B. Hunningher, *Acoustics and acting in the theatre of Dion. Eleuthereus* (Mededel. Nederl. Akad. van Wet., Afd. Letterk., N.R., 19. 9), 1956, esp. pp. 26 ff. Hunningher suggests that the restriction of actors to three was largely due to the extreme vocal demands made on the actor, and compares the modern difficulty in finding an adequate *Heldentenor*.

[5] This was demonstrated when the late Mr. H. A. L. Fisher recited a passage of Homer to myself and others there many years ago. (On the supposed effect of masks in increasing the volume of sound in the actor's voice, see below, pp. 195 f.)

commended, and it was by his voice that an actor was commonly judged, great stress is also laid on beauty of tone and adaptability to the personality or mood of the character represented. Plato speaks of the actor's fine voice (*Laws* vii. 817 c), and Dionysius the tyrant of Syracuse (early in the fourth century), in choosing actors to perform his play at Olympia, chose τοὺς εὐφωνοτάτους τῶν ὑποκριτῶν . . . οὗτοι δὲ τὸ μὲν πρῶτον διὰ τὴν εὐφωνίαν ἐξέπληττον τοὺς ἀκούοντας.[1] Demosthenes, when his voice failed to produce its effect on the Assembly, is said to have exclaimed τοὺς ὑποκριτὰς δεῖν κρίνειν ἐκ τῆς φωνῆς, τοὺς δὲ ῥήτορας ἐκ τῆς γνώμης.[2] Neoptolemos, the tragic actor in the fourth century, who was also employed as an ambassador between Philip II and Athens, is described as πρωτεύων τῇ μεγαλοφωνίᾳ καὶ τῇ δόξῃ.[3] But the need of adaptability is frequently emphasized—first of all by Aristotle, who is speaking primarily of the orator but illustrates the point, and particularly the necessity of having a voice to suit the part, from the drama; e.g. (*Rhet*. iii. 1. 1403^{b}27 ff.) ἔστι δὲ αὐτὴ μὲν ἐν τῇ φωνῇ, πῶς αὐτῇ δεῖ χρῆσθαι πρὸς ἕκαστον πάθος, οἷον πότε μεγάλη καὶ πότε μικρᾷ καὶ πότε μέσῃ, καὶ πῶς τοῖς τόνοις, οἷον ὀξείᾳ καὶ βαρείᾳ καὶ μέσῃ, καὶ ῥυθμοῖς τίσι πρὸς ἕκαστον, and (*Rhet*. iii. 2. 1404^{b}18 ff.) διὸ δεῖ λανθάνειν ποιοῦντας καὶ μὴ δοκεῖν λέγειν πεπλασμένως ἀλλὰ πεφυκότως· τοῦτο γὰρ πιθανόν . . . καὶ οἷον ἡ Θεοδώρου φωνὴ πέπονθε πρὸς τὴν τῶν ἄλλων ὑποκριτῶν. ἡ μὲν γὰρ τοῦ λέγοντος ἔοικεν εἶναι, αἱ δ' ἀλλότριαι. (Theodoros' skill in drawing tears from his audience—even from so hardened a tyrant as Alexander of Pherai—may have been as much the result of his voice as of his acting.[4]) At a later date πλάσμα was used in a less unfavourable sense than πεπλασμένως (the equivalent of 'artificial') in Aristotle, and (with kindred words) signified adaptability, as in Plutarch, *Quaest. Conv.* vii. 711 c πρόσεστι δὲ ὑπόκρισις πρέπουσα τῷ ἤθει τῶν ὑποκειμένων προσώπων, καὶ φωνῆς πλάσμα καὶ σχῆμα, καὶ διαθέσεις ('delivery') ἑπόμεναι τοῖς λεγομένοις. Lucian (*Piscat.* 31) implies the same principle: καὶ τὸ πρᾶγμα ὅμοιον ἐδόκει μοι καθάπερ ἂν εἴ τις ὑποκριτὴς τραγῳδίας, μαλθακὸς αὐτὸς ὢν καὶ γυναικεῖος, Ἀχιλλέα ἢ Θησέα ἢ καὶ τὸν Ἡρακλέα ὑποκρίνοιτο αὐτόν, μήτε βαδίζων μήτε βοῶν ἡρωικόν, ἀλλὰ

---

[1] Diod. Sic. xv. 7.

[2] [Plut.] *Vit. X Orat.* 848 b. Cicero, on the other hand (*de Orat.* iii. 224), makes a good voice the first requisite for an orator also. The anecdote in Alkiphron iii. 12 (4th cent. A.D.) of an actor named Likymnios who defeated his rivals τορῷ τινι καὶ γεγωνοτέρῳ φωνήματι is probably fictitious, but illustrates the same standard of judgement some 600 years later.

[3] Diod. Sic. xvi. 92. 3.

[4] Aelian, *Var. H.* xiv. 40 (as Merope in Euripides' *Kresphontes*); Plut. *de Alex. fort.* 334 a; *de laude ipsius* 545 e; cf. Dittenberger, *Syll.*^{3} 239 B, 67 and refs. there. The same power was a boast of Kallippides (Xen. *Symp.* iii. 11 Καλλιππίδης ὁ ὑποκριτής, ὃς ὑπερσεμνύνεται ὅτι δύναται πολλοὺς κλαίοντας καθίζειν). Compare also Satyrus' ability to transform a speech: Plut. *Dem.* 7. 1–5.

θρυπτόμενος ὑπὸ τηλικούτῳ προσωπείῳ; and (Nigrin. 11) μὴ καὶ κατ' ἄλλο τι γένωμαι τοῖς ὑποκριταῖς ἐκείνοις ὅμοιος, οἳ πολλάκις ἢ Ἀγαμέμνονος ἢ Κρέοντος ἢ καὶ Ἡρακλέους αὐτοῦ πρόσωπον ἀνειληφότες χρυσίδας ἠμφιεσμένοι καὶ δεινὸν βλέποντες καὶ μέγα κεχηνότες μικρὸν φθέγγονται καὶ ἰσχνὸν καὶ γυναικῶδες καὶ τῆς Ἑκάβης ἢ Πολυξένης πολὺ ταπεινότερον.

The skill with which Polos, the famous actor of about 300 B.C., could perform the very different parts of Oedipus as king and as beggar is referred to by Epictetus (diss. fr. 11, p. 464, Schenkl, ed. minor): ἢ οὐχ ὁρᾷς ὅτι οὐκ εὐφωνότερον οὐδὲ ἥδιον ὁ Πῶλος τὸν τύραννον Οἰδιπόδα ὑπεκρίνετο ἢ τὸν ἐπὶ Κολωνῷ ἀλήτην καὶ πτωχόν;[1]

The actor naturally had not only to adapt himself generally to the character represented, but to control every inflexion of his voice so as to express exactly the mood of the text, and so Aristotle[2] treats an ability to distinguish the 'modes of speech'—question, prayer, threat, command, statement, and so on—as an essential part of ὑποκριτική. He also[3] treats as essential to the actor's art the power to repeat the same thing in a variety of tones: ἀνάγκη γὰρ μεταβάλλειν τὸ αὐτὸ λέγοντας, ὅπερ ὥσπερ ὁδοποιεῖ τῷ ὑποκρίνεσθαι . . . οἷον καὶ Φιλήμων ὁ ὑποκριτὴς ἐποίει ἔν τε τῇ Ἀναξανδρίδου Γεροντομανίᾳ, ὅτε λέγοι ''Ῥαδάμανθυς καὶ Παλαμήδης'', καὶ ἐν τῷ προλόγῳ τῶν Εὐσεβῶν τὸ ''ἐγώ'' . . . ἀνάγκη γὰρ ὑποκρίνεσθαι καὶ μὴ ὡς ἓν λέγοντα τῷ αὐτῷ ἤθει καὶ τόνῳ εἰπεῖν. (Unhappily the point of the examples of Philemon's skill is lost to us. Anaxandrides the comic poet was composing from about 380 to 345 B.C.)

But there must have been plenty of actors even in the Classical period who did not come up to the highest standard and performed at the Rural Dionysia rather than in the City. Such were Simykas and Sokrates, the βαρύστονοι—the 'roarers'—to whom, according to Demosthenes,[4] Aeschines joined himself with poor success. Pollux[5] enumerates the terms which unkind critics might apply to bad actors: εἴποις δ' ἂν βαρύστονος ὑποκριτής, βομβῶν, περιβομβῶν, ληκυθίζων, λαρυγγίζων, φαρυγγίζων· βαρύφωνος δὲ καὶ λεπτόφωνος καὶ γυναικόφωνος καὶ στρηνόφωνος καὶ ὅσα σὺν τούτοις ἄλλα ἐν τοῖς περὶ φωνῆς εἴρηται. An amusing story is told by Philostratus[6] of an actor in the time of Nero who terrified the people of Ipola in Baetica, when pretending to reproduce the melodies sung by Nero at the Pythia in a resounding voice (ἐπεὶ ἐξάρας τὴν φωνὴν γεγωνὸν ἐφθέγξατο), so that they fled from the theatre ὥσπερ ὑπὸ δαίμονος

---

[1] Compare the story of Polos playing the part of Electra in Sophocles' play: Aul. Gell. N.A. vi (vii). 5; Bieber, H.T.², pp. 157 f. For Polos' powers of endurance as an actor, even in old age, cf. Plut. an seni 785 b.

[2] Poet. xix. 1456ᵇ10.   [3] Rhet. iii. 12. 1413ᵇ21 ff.   [4] de Cor. 262.
[5] iv. 114 (referring to ii. 111 f.).   [6] Vit. Apoll. v. 9.

ἐμβοηθέντες. Another story[1] speaks of an actor called Ἠπειρώτης (either because this was his name or because he came from Epirus) who, ἄριστα φωνῆς ἔχων, εὐδοκιμῶν δ' ἐπ' αὐτῇ καὶ θαυμαζόμενος λαμπροτέρᾳ τοῦ εἰωθότος, dared to compete against Nero himself and refused to lower his tone until Nero's own actors murdered him on stage.

There are several allusions to the careful training to which actors subjected themselves, fasting and dieting themselves and using every opportunity before and in the intervals of the performances to test their voice and bring it into condition; e.g. in Aristotle,[2] διά τί τοῖς μετὰ τὰ σιτία κεκραγόσιν ἡ φωνὴ διαφθείρεται; καὶ πάντας ἂν ἴδοιμεν τοὺς φωνασκοῦντας, οἷον ὑποκριτὰς καὶ χορευτὰς καὶ τοὺς ἄλλους τοὺς τοιούτους ἕωθέν τε καὶ νήστεις ὄντας τὰς μελέτας ποιουμένους.[3] Hermon, a comic actor of the late fifth century, is said to have missed his cue while he was trying his voice outside the theatre.[4]

The keen sensitiveness of an Athenian audience to the quality—especially, perhaps, the clearness—of an actor's voice is shown by the pains taken by the actor to come up to the standard. Their appreciation of the recitatives of Nikostratos in the fifth century has already been noticed,[5] and the importance to the protagonist (to whom, if successful, the prize for acting was open) of winning their favour is quaintly illustrated at a much later date by Cicero's statement[6] that the Greek actors of his day, who played the second or third part, modified their tone, even if they had better voices than the protagonist, so as to give him his chance. The sensitiveness of the audiences required not only good voices but clearness and correctness of enunciation, and the comic poets of the fifth century were never tired of mocking the actor Hegelochus who had pronounced the line, Eur. Orestes 279, ἐκ κυμάτων γὰρ αὖθις αὖ γαλήν' ὁρῶ, as if it had ended with γαλῆν ὁρῶ.[7] They were not above being amused

---

[1] Lucian, Nero ix. [2] Probl. xi. 22.

[3] Cf. Athen. viii. 343 e, 344 d; Plato, Laws ii, 665 e; Plut. Quaest. Conv. ix. 737 a–b.

[4] Pollux iv. 88 ὁ μὲν ἀπῆν τοῦ θεάτρου τῆς φωνῆς ἀποπειρώμενος. Cicero, de Orat. i. 251, speaks of tragic actors 'qui et annos complures sedentes declamitant, et cotidie, antequam pronuntient, vocem cubantes sensim excitant eandemque cum egerunt sedentes ab acutissimo sono usque ad gravissimum sonum recipiunt et quasi quodammodo colligunt'; and Lucian (de saltat. 27) with some contempt describes the tragic actor as ἔνδοθεν αὐτὸς κεκραγώς, ἑαυτὸν ἀνακλῶν καὶ κατακλῶν, ἐνίοτε καὶ περιάδων τὰ ἰαμβεῖα, καὶ τὸ δὴ αἴσχιστον μελῳδῶν τὰς συμφορὰς καὶ μόνης τῆς φωνῆς ὑπεύθυνον παρέχων ἑαυτόν.

[5] p. 156 above. Cf. Miller, Mélanges, p. 353 ἐγὼ ποιήσω πάντα κατὰ Νικόστρατον· εἴρηται ἡ παροιμία παρ' Εὐβούλῳ τῷ τῆς μέσης κωμῳδίας ποιητῇ (fr. 136 K). ἦν δὲ ὁ Νικόστρατος ὑποκριτὴς τραγικὸς δοκῶν καλλίστους ἀγγέλους εἰρηκέναι; Corpus Paroem. Gr. i. 395; ii. 160.

[6] In Q. Caec. Divin. 48. Cicero also (Orator 25, 27) highly extols the impeccable taste of Athenian audiences as judges of oratory.

[7] Ar. Frogs 303 and schol.; schol. Eur. Orest. 279; Strattis, frs. 1, 60 (K); Sannyrion, fr. 8 (K); 'Suidas' s.v. Ἡγέλοχος writes τοῦτον δὲ καὶ ὡς ἀτερπῆ τὴν φωνὴν Πλάτων σκώπτει.

by mere tricks of voice—the imitation of animals and inanimate noises—if they 'came off', as when Parmenon imitated the squeaking of a pig or Theodoros the sound of a windlass;[1] but few audiences do not occasionally let cleverness get the better of good taste.

E. *Gesture*

The actor's qualifications included a command not only of voice but of gesture in the widest sense. It is difficult to reach any firm conclusion on the degree of statuesqueness, or alternatively of vigour, which we are to visualize in the Greek actor's playing of his role. In part a belief in a highly statuesque style of acting arose from a failure to distinguish between the earlier and the later periods in the history of Greek costume. The thick-soled κόθορνοι—raising the actor's feet several inches above the ground—and the costume of the Rieti statuette (fig. 63) imply that the actor is as far as possible stationary, and the narrow raised stage would make careless movements inadvisable. But (as will be shown below) these are not to be found in the Classical period.

On the contrary, in the fifth century the texts of the plays seem to imply, as we shall see, a high degree of mobility, even of rapid movement, kneeling, prostration, and a free play of gesture, and this is not excluded by what we know of fifth-century costume. It was only facial expression that was unalterable, owing to the use of masks.[2] But it is precisely here that our difficulties begin, for the texts of the plays imply a degree of emotional expression which, if conceived naturalistically, was impossible for a masked actor. Thus two masked actors might embrace, and this happened often,[3] but kissing was impossible, yet it is described;[4] nor could there be any display of tears, though they are often mentioned. Thus, according to the text, the eyes of the chorus in *Prometheus* fill with tears of sympathy for the sufferer;[5] Electra bursts into violent weeping at the sight of the lock of Orestes' hair,[6] and later in the play[7] the Nurse enters in tears; the chorus weeps at the sight of Antigone being led away

---

[1] Plut. *de aud. poet.* 18 c. Parmenon's rivals, resolved to defeat him, brought a real pig into the theatre, and when it squealed the audience cried εὖ μέν, ἀλλ' οὐδὲν πρὸς τὴν Παρμένοντος ὖν. The rivals then released the pig, confounding the audience, and so creating a new proverb. (Plut. *Quaest. Conv.* v. 674 b–c.)

[2] This point is discussed at length by Robert Löhrer, O.S.B., *Mienenspiel und Maske in d. gr. Tragödie* (Studien zur Geschichte u. Kultur d. Altertums, xiv. 4–5), 1927; Hunningher, op. cit., pp. 17 ff.

[3] Eur. *Hel.* 623 ff., *Hec.* 410, *Ion* 1438, *Alc.* 1133 f., *Med.* 1070 ff., *Phoen.* 306 ff., etc.

[4] Eur. *Alc.* 402, *Troad.* 762, *Phoen.* 1671, *Herakles* 486.

[5] ll. 144 ff., 399 ff.   [6] *Choeph.* 185–6. Cf. 457.

[7] l. 731. Electra is also spoken of as weeping in Soph. *El.* 829 (ὦ παῖ, τί δακρύεις;).

to death;[1] Antigone weeps at the loss of her father;[2] Admetus bursts
into tears more than once;[3] so do Medea[4] and Kreousa.[5] In other scenes
in Euripides, Andromache or Adrastus or Klytaimnestra are seen weeping.[6] Or it may be Herakles or Menelaus or Ion or a faithful servant,[7]
or the chorus.[8] In Euripides the incongruity is often concealed by the
Greek habit of covering the head and face when in tears[9] (the frequent
tears of Agamemnon in *Iphigeneia in Aulis*[10] recall the famous painting
inspired by the play in which he is seen veiled to conceal his grief),[11] or
by turning aside so that the face was invisible.[12] The head is sometimes
bowed to conceal emotion.[13] Changes of expression and signs of temper
or mood which are mentioned in the text had always to be imagined by
the audience—as, for instance, when Klytaimnestra announces to the
chorus the fall of Troy:[14]

> XO. χαρά μ' ὑφέρπει δάκρυον ἐκκαλουμένη.
> ΚΛ. εὖ γὰρ φρονοῦντος ὄμμα σοῦ κατηγορεῖ,

and now and then the impossibility of changing the expression is almost
apologized for in the text. The Eumenides became friendly, but could
not show it in their faces, and Athena has to reassure the Athenians[15]
ἐκ τῶν φοβερῶν τῶνδε προσώπων | μέγα κέρδος ὁρῶ τοῖσδε πολίταις. Electra
in Sophocles' play explains that she cannot show in her face the joy
which she feels, owing to her long association with sorrow and hatred:[16]

> OP. οὗτως δ' ὅπως μήτηρ σε μὴ 'πιγνώσεται
> φαιδρῷ προσώπῳ νῷν ἐπελθόντοιν δόμους·
> ἀλλ' ὡς ἐπ' ἄτῃ τῇ μάτην λελεγμένῃ
> στέναζ'· ὅταν γὰρ εὐτυχήσωμεν, τότε
> χαίρειν παρέσται καὶ γελᾶν ἐλευθέρως. . . .

---

[1] *Ant.* 803–4. (When Ismene enters in tears at l. 527, the tears might conceivably have
been depicted on the mask and remained there during the short scene that follows.)

[2] *Oed. Col.* 1709–10 ἀνὰ γὰρ ὄμμα σε τόδ', ὦ πάτερ, ἐμὸν | στένει δακρῦον. Cf. 1250 f. (Poly-
neikes).

[3] *Alc.* 526, 530, 1067.   [4] *Med.* 905, 922, 1012.   [5] *Ion* 241, 876.

[6] *Androm.* 532, *Suppl.* 21, *Iph. Aul.* 888, 1433.

[7] *Herakles* 1394, *Helen* 456, *Ion* 1369, *El.* 502.

[8] *Hipp.* 853, *Herakles* 1045, *Suppl.* 449, 96, 770.

[9] *Hipp.* 243 ff., *Hec.* 487, *Suppl.* 286, *Herakles* 1111, 1198 ff., *El.* 501 ff., *Ion* 967, *Orest.* 280,
Iph. Aul. 1122 f.

[10] *Iph. Aul.* 477, 496, 650, 684.

[11] Curtius, *Wandmalerei Pompejis*, pp. 290 ff., pl. v.

[12] *Med.* 922 f., *Androm.* 942 ff., *Iph. Aul.* 851 f., *Hec.* 968 ff.

[13] Soph. *O.T.* 1121, Eur. *Orest.* 957 ff., *Ion* 582 ff. Cf. Sen. *Ep.* i. 11. 7.

[14] Aesch. *Agam.* 270–1. But the chorus are here probably facing away from the audience:
cf. Löhrer, op. cit., p. 166.

[15] *Eumen.* 990–1: Löhrer, op. cit., p. 173; Hense, *Rh. Mus.* 59 (1904), pp. 174 ff.

[16] Soph. *El.* 1296 ff., 1309 ff.: Löhrer, op. cit., pp. 147 ff.

ΗΛ. μήτηρ δ' ἐν οἴκοις· ἦν σὺ μὴ δείσῃς ποθ' ὡς
γέλωτι τοὐμὸν φαιδρὸν ὄψεται κάρα.
μῖσός τε γὰρ παλαιὸν ἐντέτηκέ μοι,
κἀπεί σ' ἐσεῖδον, οὔποτ' ἐκλήξω χαρᾷ
δακρυρροοῦσα,

and in Euripides' *Orestes*[1] she retains her gloomy expression to deceive
Hermione:

πάλιν κατάστηθ' ἡσύχῳ μὲν ὄμματι
χροᾷ τ' ἀδήλῳ τῶν δεδραμένων πέρι·
κἀγὼ σκυθρωποὺς ὀμμάτων ἔξω κόρας,
ὡς δῆθεν οὐκ εἰδυῖα τἀξειργασμένα.

In the *Suppliants* of Aeschylus (ll. 70–76) and *Choephoroi* (ll. 24–25) the
gashes spoken of as torn in their cheeks by the chorus will have had
to remain visible throughout the play as blood-red marks upon the
masks—unless indeed they were left to the imagination from the first.

It is true, of course, that certain more or less mechanical devices were
available to the poet to distract his audience from any incongruity that
might be felt between the unchanging image of the mask and the momen-
tary expression of emotion implied by the actor's words. Thus a sudden
access of joy or grief could obviously be accompanied by embraces or
other movements which would, for a few moments at least, hide the mask,
and so soften any sense of incongruity which the audience might feel.
The look of astonishment or fear at the appearance by a god *ex machina*
would not be missed, as the actors would have turned their backs to the
audience. In comedy indeed the two sides of a mask might have different
expressions (e.g. the angry and the kindly father), of which the actor
turned the appropriate one to the spectators.[2] Opportunities for a change
of mask would have been not infrequent, but there is no evidence to
suggest that an actual change took place commonly, if at all. It is generally
assumed that such a change was made in the final scene of *Oedipus
Tyrannus* and in *Helen* (1186 ff.), and perhaps after the blinding of Polymestor in *Hecuba* (1049 ff.), in *Cyclops* (663 ff.) and, after the death of
Alcestis, to the mask of Admetus (*Alc.* 512 ff., cf. 425 ff.).[3] But in any

---

[1] ll. 1317 ff. Cf. Hense, *Die Modificirung der Maske in der gr. Trag.*, pp. 6 f.; Löhrer, op. cit.,
pp. 109 ff.

[2] Quint. xi. 3. 74; Bieber, in *R.E.* s.v. Maske, cols. 2075 f., gives other references. A.
Rumpf, *A.J.A.* 55 (1951), p. 8, traces this back to the 5th-cent. painter Parrhasios.

[3] See Hense, *Die Modificirung der Maske in der gr. Trag.*, where there is a minute discussion
of all possible instances, including those in lost plays. It is perhaps doubtful whether the
avoidance of scenes of death and violence was really due to the obligation to employ masks,
which could not respond to such circumstances, but it was at least convenient.

case there will have been many moments in Greek tragedy when the changes of mood and emotion within a single scene might be felt as placing a great strain on the unchanging expression of the mask: for instance, the scene of Herakles' discovery of Alcestis' death (*Alc.* 747 ff.), or of Agaue's return to sanity (*Bacch.* 1216 ff.).[1]

To return to the question of gesture. The importance which the Athenians attached to gesture is illustrated by Aristotle's precept[2] that the poet should not only keep the scene before his eyes in composing his play, but should also, if possible, include the gestures in his composition, and so make the demonstration of passion or feeling by his characters convincing (δεῖ δὲ τοὺς μύθους συνιστάναι καὶ τῇ λέξει συναπεργάζεσθαι ὅτι μάλιστα πρὸ ὀμμάτων τιθέμενον . . . ὅσα δὲ δυνατὸν καὶ τοῖς σχήμασιν συναπεργαζόμενον· πιθανώτατοι γὰρ ἀπὸ τῆς αὐτῆς φύσεως οἱ ἐν τοῖς πάθεσίν εἰσιν, καὶ χειμαίνει ὁ χειμαζόμενος καὶ χαλεπαίνει ὁ ὀργιζόμενος ἀληθινώτατα). There is no suggestion of statuesqueness here, though Aristotle does refer later[3] to the possibility of overdoing the amount of gesture (περιεργάζεσθαι τοῖς σημείοις) or using gestures inappropriate to tragedy, and records that Mynniskos (the actor of Aeschylus) nicknamed his younger contemporary Kallippides 'the monkey' from his excess of gesture—a record which is apparent disproof of any inevitable statuesqueness in the last third of the fifth century.[4] That Euripides' practice was in accordance with Aristotle's precept is shown by the frequency with which movements and gestures are precisely indicated in the text; e.g. twice in *Hecuba*, first when Hecuba appears (ll. 59 ff.):

> ἄγετ', ὦ παῖδες, τὴν γραῦν πρὸ δόμων,
> ἄγετ' ὀρθοῦσαι τὴν ὁμόδουλον,
> Τρωάδες, ὑμῖν, πρόσθε δ' ἄνασσαν·
> λάβετε φέρετε πέμπετ' ἀείρετέ μου
> γεραιᾶς χειρὸς προσλαζύμεναι·
> κἀγὼ σκολιῷ σκίπωνι[5] χερὸς
> διερειδομένα σπεύσω βραδύπουν
> ἤλυσιν ἄρθρων προτιθεῖσα,

---

[1] See Löhrer, op. cit., pp. 121 f.

[2] *Poet.* xvii. 1455ᵃ22. Cf. *Rhet.* ii. 8 ἀνάγκη συναπεργαζομένους σχήμασι καὶ φωναῖς καὶ ἐσθῆσι καὶ ὅλως ἐν ὑποκρίσει ἐλεεινοτέρους εἶναι.

[3] *Poet.* xxvi. 1462ᵃ6.

[4] Though we should remember that what is 'excessive' in gesture is very much a relative matter. Aristotle himself points out that certain reciters of Homer and singers used 'excessive gesture'. For Kallippides, see p. 119 above. An otherwise unknown Pindaros was criticized on the same ground (Ar., ibid. 1461ᵇ35).

[5] *Vita Sophoclis* 6 says that the crooked staff, according to Satyrus, was first introduced by Sophocles; cf. Plut. *de lib. educ.* 2 d τάς γε μὴν καμπύλας τῶν ὑποκριτῶν βακτηρίας ἀπευθύνειν ἀμήχανον.

and, secondly, when Polyxena describes the gestures of Odysseus (ll. 342–4):

ὁρῶ σ᾽, ᾿Οδυσσεῦ, δεξιὰν. ὑφ᾽ εἵματος
κρύπτοντα χεῖρα καὶ πρόσωπον ἔμπαλιν
στρέφοντα, μὴ σου προσθίγω γενειάδος.

The second passage is very like Andromache's words to Peleus (*Androm.* 572–5):

ἀλλ᾽ ἀντιάζω σ᾽, ὦ γέρον, τῶν σῶν πάρος
πίτνουσα γονάτων—χειρὶ δ᾽ οὐκ ἔξεστί μοι
τῆς σῆς λαβέσθαι φιλτάτης γενειάδος—
ῥῦσαί με πρὸς θεῶν.

In these and very many other passages it is right to speak of Euripides as composing τοῖς σχήμασι συναπεργαζόμενον. Moreover, it can probably be assumed that passages of lamentation are accompanied by the usual gestures of mourning or distress such as beating the head, whether these are mentioned or not.[1] The problem is to decide with what degree of naturalism the gestures and movements thus described or implied were actually executed by the actors. For example, hurried entries and exits are frequently indicated in the words of some speaker;[2] and so are many other instances of rapid or violent movement, such as the struggle of Philoctetes and Neoptolemos (*Philoct.* 816), or of Electra and Orestes in the latter's madness (*Orest.* 253 ff.), or the flight of Helen into sanctuary (*Helen* 543–4):

οὐχ ὡς δρομαία πῶλος ἢ βάκχη θεοῦ
τάφῳ ξυνάψω κῶλον;

and, most striking of all, Ajax rushing to fall on his sword (Soph. *Aj.* 865).[3] The possible range of movement described in the text includes kneeling in supplication as Andromache does (*Androm.* 572–3) and many others, falling and lying prostrate on the ground, as do Iolaos (*Heraclid.* 75, 602 ff., 633) and Hecuba (*Hec.* 438 ff., 486 ff.; *Troad.* 37, 463), and crawling on all fours as the Pythia does in *Eumenides* and Polymestor in *Hecuba* (1058).[4] (Kneeling or prostration and kissing the ground before a human

---

[1] Those who want a more minute classification of gestures and ways of expressing emotion, including the most obvious, in the dramatists may find it in F. L. Shisler's article in *A.J.P.* 66 (1945), pp. 377 ff. or in Spitzbarth, *Unters. zur Spieltechnik der gr. Tragödie* (1946).

[2] e.g. Soph. *Ant.* 766, *Electra* 871; Eur. *Androm.* 545, *Troad.* 306 f., *Orest.* 725 ff.

[3] In *Oinomaos*, Aeschines, as Oinomaos, tripped and fell when in hot pursuit of Pelops and had to be picked up by Sannio the chorus-trainer (Dem. *de Cor.* 180 and *Vit. Aeschin.*). The play was perhaps not Sophocles' play. See p. 50, n. 5. But there is no justification for laying the blame on his κόθορνοι as some scholars have done.

[4] Further references in Spitzbarth, op. cit., pp. 24 f.

being as practised by Orientals is confined, in the extant plays, to *Persae* 152 ff., *Phoenissae* 293, and *Orestes* 1507.) Scenes of active violence involving the actors—common in the Old Comedy, but rare in extant tragedy—are found near the end of Aeschylus' *Suppliants* (825 ff.), in *Oedipus Coloneus* (820 ff.), and *Heraclidae* (59 ff.).

As we read all this, what are we to visualize? If we remember the undoubted fact that facial expressions such as weeping, which were certainly not visible on stage, are frequently described in the plays, we must at least reckon with the possibility that the descriptions of striking and vigorous movement that we meet in the plays are not unequivocal evidence for the occurrence of these same movements in a naturalistic performance by the actor. We are simply ignorant of the degree of stylization that prevailed, even in gesture.[1]

It need not be doubted that the pathetic acting of Theodoros and Polos and other great actors depended upon their use of gesture as well as upon their voice. It has already been mentioned how Theodoros could move even Alexander of Pherai to tears, and how Polos gave his impressive rendering of Oedipus as a wanderer; and how before them Kallippides boasted of his power to draw tears from his audience.[2] It is obvious that the Old Comedy allowed every kind of gesture and movement to the actor, and that no inconvenience of costume nor sense of delicacy restrained him. The lack of refinement became less in the later comedy, the masks and costume of which will be discussed later.

[1] See, most recently, P. Arnott, *Greek Scenic Conventions in the Fifth Century B.C.* (1962), pp. 69 f.
[2] Above, p. 168 and n. 4.

IV

THE COSTUMES

THE general descriptions of the actor's appearance which have come down to us are all late, and their applicability to the actors of the Classical period at least very doubtful. Lucian (in passages which will be referred to later) wrote at a time when it was the custom to exaggerate the height and size of the tragic actor to the point of grotesqueness, and the compiler of the *Life* of Aeschylus which appears in the scholia to his plays ascribes to that poet quite uncritically inventions which were introduced into tragedy at any period; his sources cannot be traced.[1]

The chief written source of information is to be found in the catalogues of Julius Pollux, in the second century A.D., and these face us with considerable problems in source-criticism and evaluation. There are two main passages, separated by a long account of the theatre and theatre buildings. The first (iv. 115–20) is an account of costume, in the imperfect tense throughout. The emphasis is on clothing, masks being briefly dismissed: καὶ ἔστιν εἰπεῖν πρόσωπον προσωπεῖον προσωπίς, μορμολυκεῖον, γοργόνειον. The only literary references which are at all clear are to the rags of Telephus, presumably in Euripides, and to a comedy called the Σικυώνιος; both Alexis and Menander wrote plays of that name. The second passage (iv. 133–54) by contrast deals only with masks, and is in the present tense, except when we are given an old name for one mask.[2] The tragic list gives no indication of date, except in references to Euhippe 'in Euripides'[3] and to Sophocles' Tyro. The comic list dismisses Old Comedy very briefly, and is concentrated on what it describes as New Comedy, but refers to no play or author.

The difference of tense and the illogical separation of the two passages suggest fairly strongly that we are dealing with two sources, though

---

[1] Cf. Cramer, *Anecd. Par.* i. 19 εἰ μὲν δὴ πάντα τις Αἰσχύλῳ βούλεται τὰ περὶ τὴν σκηνὴν εὑρήματα προσνέμειν κτλ.

[2] iv. 139 ἡ μὲν πολιὰ κατάκομος . . . πάλαι δὲ παράχρωμος ἐκαλεῖτο.

[3] Pollux names no play. It is difficult to imagine where Euhippe might have appeared in Euripides except in one of his Melanippe plays, and there is no trace of her in the evidence for either. The possibility that Pollux has given a mask to a character who does not appear in any play is alarming.

most scholars have dealt with the passages together. It certainly is a question of looking for sources. The slightest familiarity with Pollux forbids the supposition that he made personal inquiry of a theatrical troupe. He was a man of books, and this makes it hard to believe that he is simply describing the theatre of his own day. His sources are in all probability Hellenistic. Beyond this we can hardly go on our scanty knowledge of Hellenistic scholarship. Various names have been suggested. Juba, king of Mauretania, writing at the end of the first century B.C., is more likely to have shared a source with Pollux than to have been his source,[1] and the same is probably true of his contemporary Tryphon.[2] The latest investigator[3] has argued that Pollux used the Σκευογραφικός of the third-century Eratosthenes, a work of which we know nothing but its title, but his arguments bear no great weight, and, although Eratosthenes' work of at least twelve books on Old Comedy was extremely influential, there is no evidence that he touched tragedy or New Comedy, which may not have been classical enough for him.[4] Interest in New Comedy appears to begin with Eratosthenes' junior, Aristophanes of Byzantium (c. 257–180 B.C.).[5] He certainly wrote a work on masks (περὶ προσώπων), but the only fragment of it which we possess seems to conflict with the account of Pollux.[6]

It would be hypercritical to make the accounts in Pollux later than Hellenistic. The first passage on dress can be taken to purport to be an

---

[1] The case for Juba's Θεατρικὴ Ἱστορία was argued by Rohde, De Julii Pollucis in apparatu scenico enarrando fontibus (1870), and disproved by Gordziejew, Quaestionum de Julii Pollucis fontibus caput (Warsaw, 1936). The one reference to Juba in Pollux (v. 88) has no reference to theatrical subjects, and is almost certainly an interpolation.

[2] Tryphon was favoured by Bapp, 'De fontibus quibus Athenaeus in rebus musicis lyricisque enarrandis usus sit' (Leipz. Stud. 8 (1885), pp. 85–160); he is never mentioned by Pollux. Their relationship is discussed by Gordziejew, op. cit.

[3] Gordziejew, op. cit., pp. 335–41.

[4] The fragments are collected by Strecker, De Lycophrone Euphronio Eratosthene comicorum interpretibus (Greifswald, 1884). Pollux cites the work on comedy at x. 60. The only possible trace of New Comedy in Eratosthenes is in Strecker, fr. 92; Athen. iii. 123 e quotes New Comedy references for the word μετάκερας and at ii. 41 d quotes Eratosthenes for a definition of the word, but Phot. s.v. shows that the word came in Philyllios, and Eratosthenes may have been commenting on him.

[5] For his interest in Menander, see Syriani comment. in Hermog. ii. 23 Rabe; Euseb. Praep. Ev. x. 3. 12; I.G. xiv. 1183 c (Testimonia 32, 51, 61 in Körte's edition of Menander).

[6] Athen. xiv. 659 a Χρύσιππος δ' ὁ φιλόσοφος τὸν μαίσωνα ἀπὸ τοῦ μασᾶσθαι οἴεται κεκλῆσθαι, οἷον τὸν ἀμαθῆ καὶ πρὸς γαστέρα νενευκότα, ἀγνοῶν ὅτι Μαίσων γέγονεν κωμῳδίας ὑποκριτὴς Μεγαρεὺς τὸ γένος, ὃς καὶ τὸ προσωπεῖον εὗρε τὸ ἀπ' αὐτοῦ καλούμενον μαίσωνα, ὡς Ἀριστοφάνης φησὶν ὁ Βυζάντιος ἐν τῷ περὶ προσώπων, εὑρεῖν αὐτὸν φάσκων καὶ τὸ τοῦ θεράποντος πρόσωπον καὶ τὸ τοῦ μαγείρου. Aristophanes evidently treated the masks of μαίσων and θεράπων as distinct, whereas Pollux speaks of the μαίσων θεράπων, οὖλος θεράπων, and θεράπων τέττιξ, and has no special cook-mask. For other discussions of Pollux's sources, see Bethe, R.E. s.v. Iulius (Pollux), and Robert, Die Masken der neueren attischen Komödie (Halle Winckelmannsprogramm, 1911), pp. 58 ff.

account of classical practice; the second passage, on the face of it, does not claim to be more than an account of contemporary third- or second-century practice. We must bear Pollux in mind when we look at the archaeological evidence, but it is dangerous to force his classification on material which it may not be intended to fit, and due caution will be needed in matching words to objects.

The evidence of the plays themselves needs no less cautious handling. Though it is not very likely that a character described as fair-haired will in fact be dressed as dark, what has always to be borne in mind is the possibility that the poet is describing something because it cannot be seen.[1] Given the general convention of masks, if the audience is told that a character is crying it will be prepared to accept the fact without demanding that the mask be obviously tear-stained.

Our chief reliance must be on the contemporary archaeological remains, and here again we are immediately faced with problems of artistic convention. We have no masks or costumes which were actually worn on the stage. The masks of terracotta or marble which have been found (many of them perhaps votive copies) differ for the most part from original masks in linen, cork, or wood, at least in not representing coverings for the whole or the greater part of the head, but only the face and part of the crown, and they may have differed in other ways.[2] The costumes of drama come to us through the eyes and hands of artists, and the artist may have several levels of reality. He may portray a scene of rehearsal or dressing-up and give us exactly what he sees, but when he passes to the portrayal of a dramatic scene, the dressed-up actor may be transformed in the artist's eye to the character he portrays. In some cases, we may only be left with an extra-dramatic flute-player to warn us that we are on the stage and not in the imagination. In extreme cases, the flute-player will also disappear and the scene become indistinguishable from a pure representation of myth. However strongly we may feel that the artist is influenced by a dramatic performance he has seen, we cannot prove it, and the scene is no longer useful evidence for the customs of the stage.

These considerations make it desirable to describe the pieces of evidence individually and as a whole before we try to extract detailed information from them. We have tried to confine ourselves to the use of originals, for

[1] This important caveat has recently been well applied to the question of stage-settings by Arnott, *Greek Scenic Conventions*, pp. 91 ff.

[2] The eyes, for instance, are sometimes painted in and not left blank. The treatment of the parts of the face round about the eyes in the theatrical masks themselves may well have varied greatly.

copies, however interesting, are liable to involve the risk of circular argument when one attempts to date the originals. After some consideration, we have, except for New Comedy, fixed a lower limit of about 300 B.C. The evidence for Hellenistic and Roman costume is on the whole better known than the classical evidence, and easily accessible.[1]

A. *Tragedy and Satyr Play*

1. There is no evidence from the monuments that the actors, except of course for Silenus, were dressed differently for the satyr play than they had been for the tragedies which preceded it. Pollux confirms this, listing no difference in dress other than those which were peculiar to satyrs[2] and, in the section on masks, listing satyr-masks only.[3] It seems probable that one of the essentials of satyr play was that characters indistinguishable from the figures of tragedy were exposed to the disruptive incursion of a satyr chorus. It is therefore justifiable to use representations of actors in a satyric context as evidence for tragic dress, and we here describe evidence relating to both tragedy and satyr play before we begin to draw detailed conclusions.

2. The earliest evidence for the dress of tragedy is given by the fragments of an oinochoe from the Athenian Agora (fig. 32)[4] of 470–460 B.C. The most economical reconstruction gives a scene of four figures. To the left (on the bottom-left fragment on the plate) we find, standing and facing left, a figure in soft pointed boots, an ankle-length chiton, and a shin-length himation, undecorated but for a simple border. To the right (on the top fragment) a figure, identically dressed except for a rather shorter himation, moves to the right. It is reasonable to assume that these are chorus-men dressed as women. The bottom-right fragment has a foot with laced boot on the ground, facing left; brush-marks on the left peak of the fragment suggest that the other foot was off the ground. It is probable, but not quite certain, that these feet belong to the left-hand figure on the top fragment. Of this we have nothing but a fragment of drapery belonging either to a short chiton (Webster) or to the end of a scarf or folded cloak thrown across the arm (Talcott); brush-marks suggesting that the leg was just off the fragment to the left make the former slightly more probable. Webster suggests that the figure is pulling

---

[1] Bieber, *H.T.*[2], has the best collection of illustrations.   [2] iv. 118.

[3] iv. 142 σατυρικὰ δὲ πρόσωπα σάτυρος πολιός, σάτυρος γενειῶν, σάτυρος ἀγένειος, Σειληνὸς πάππος. τἆλλα ὅμοια τὰ πρόσωπα, πλὴν ὅσοις ἐκ τῶν ὀνομάτων αἱ παραλλαγαὶ δηλοῦνται, ὥσπερ καὶ ὁ Παπποσείληνος τὴν ἰδέαν ἐστὶ θηριωδέστερος.

[4] *A.R.V.*[2], p. 495; Talcott, *Hesperia* 8 (1939), pp. 267 ff., fig. 1; Webster, *Hesperia* 29 (1960), pp. 254 f., pl. 65, A1.

on a boot, like the right-hand figure in fig. 34. Clearly the materials for
identifying this figure are insufficient. We can only say that it is dressed
and shod differently from the other two, and is therefore an actor rather
than a chorus-man. The right-centre figure is a boy, presumably an
attendant. He holds by strings a carefully painted mask. Its flesh is
coloured white, the details picked out in black. The short black hair is
bound low over the brows with a purple fillet. However, the artist cannot
be reproducing the mask exactly, for he has filled in the eyes, and it may
perhaps also be doubted whether the mouth, as shown, is quite wide
enough open for acting purposes. It is, however, sufficiently clear that the
intentions of the original mask-maker were naturalistic, with no attempts
at any kind of exaggeration. Miss Talcott noted that the mask corresponds
exactly with the description given by Pollux[1] of the mask of a maiden
whose hair is cut short as a sign of mourning: ἡ δὲ κούριμος παρθένος
ἀντὶ ὄγκου ἔχει τριχῶν κατεψηγμένων διάκρισιν, καὶ βραχέα ἐν κύκλῳ περι-
κέκαρται, ὕπωχρος δὲ τὴν χροιάν. This may be no more than a coincidence,
but the mask would certainly suit a young heroine. Webster, however,
believing the left-central figure to be male and observing that the fillet
is appropriate to a maenad as well as to a mourner, regards the mask as
a chorus-mask for a maenad. But considerations of composition perhaps
make it more likely that the two central figures should be connected,
and, in default of further evidence about the left-central figure, the
matter must be left open.

   Clearer evidence about a maenad chorus comes from a bell-krater in
Ferrara, of slightly later date (perhaps 460–450 B.C.) (fig. 33).[2] This has,
on the face which concerns us, two figures only. On the right, the performer is already fully dressed and in action. The mask (seen in profile)
has its mouth open and the eyes undefined. It has tight black hair and
appears to continue over the head in a sakkos, which covers its wearer's
own hair, a little of which escapes. The chiton is ankle-length and undecorated.[3] Over it is worn a fawnskin. The boot is soft and pointed.
There can be no doubt that here we have a member of a maenad chorus,
straightforwardly represented. On the left, a very young man looks on,
holding, apparently by the back of the head, a mask of which we get
a front view. Its very long curly hair is orange-brown, and does not
cover the ears. For the rest of the mask, however, we are at the mercy

---

   [1] iv. 140.
   [2] Riccioni, *Arte antica e moderna* 5 (1959), pp. 37–42, pls. 17–18; Alfieri–Arias, *Spina:
guida al Museo archeologico in Ferrara* (Florence, 1961), p. 181, pl. lxvi.
   [3] The horizontal line below the buttocks, and a vertical line on the right shoulder, may
have been intended to indicate a short himation.

of the artist's not very accomplished drawing. Eyebrows and nose are rendered in one continuous line, the eyes are filled in, an open mouth is unconvincingly drawn. Certainly a mask for a young man, and the association with the maenad has inevitably led to Dionysus' being suggested. On this vase, however, unlike the last, the mask-carrier is dressed and shod, and it seems very likely, though perhaps not quite certain, that he is to wear the mask. He also wears a full-length, undecorated chiton, but over it he has a black-bordered himation, secured on the right shoulder and leaving his left arm free. His footwear is merely sketched. It has no points, but whether the random drawing indicates soles on calf-length boots or the top of sandals seems extremely uncertain.

The third of these dressing-up vases is a pelike in Boston, of c. 430 B.C. (fig. 34),[1] and shows two chorus-men preparing for a chorus of women. They are identically dressed, this time in shorter chitons, leaving the shoulders free, and have the soft pointed boots. The one on the left, already fully dressed, holds a himation. The one on the right is still pulling on a boot. He wears a band to restrain his own hair. His mask is on the ground. It has a full head of hair with a wide band, and has an ear-ring. Otherwise, it is not unlike the last, a straightforward female face. There is no clue to the character of the chorus.

We must now leave the dressing-room for the stage, or, rather, what the artists make of the stage. Fig. 35[2] shows us the artist's view of a stage maenad c. 460 B.C. Here the chorus-man has completely melted away, leaving behind the character he portrays, with long dank hair and naked breast. Were it not for the perfectly real flute-player, in his long, highly decorated, sleeved robe, whom we shall meet again frequently, we should not know we are on the stage at all. Clearly we cannot safely use the picture of the maenad as evidence, even for dress. She wears a himation very like those on the Agora oinochoe, and nothing else. Has the chiton vanished in the melting process, or were there choruses which really did not wear it? We may be excused, too, for disbelieving in the kid's leg which she brandishes, but her sword is perhaps more credible.

The flute-player is again our main link with reality in the earliest portrayal of a tragic scene, on some hydria fragments in Corinth of the

---

[1] *A.R.V.²*, p. 1017, no. 46 (Phiale Painter); Caskey and Beazley, *Att. Vases in Boston*, i, pl. 29/63; Buschor in Furtw.–Reich., *Gr. Vasenmalerei* iii, pp. 134–5, Abb. 62. That tragedy, and not comedy, as some have supposed, is intended, is indicated by the absence of any feature suggestive of the Old Comedy. Beazley compares the Thracian women killing Orpheus (*A.R.V.²*, p. 1014, nos. 1–2).

[2] *A.R.V.²*, p. 586, no. 47; Beazley, *Hesperia* 24 (1955), pp. 312 f., pl. 87.

second quarter of the fifth century, by the Leningrad Painter (fig. 36).[1] Here he stands to the left. His robe, not certainly sleeved, is partly patterned with black circles with brown centres, partly with a large maeander. His short hair is wreathed with red leaves and has a chaplet. The scene depicted is therefore presumably theatrical. It is certainly remarkable enough. On the top-centre fragment, an Oriental, distinguished as a king by two sceptres, rises from a pyre, already in flames. At least four other Orientals show varying degrees of astonishment. One of them is holding a sickle-like object, perhaps for tidying the fire. Where there are overlaps between the Orientals, there is no difference in costume. We can describe it as a flapped head-dress (kidaris), a garment of thick material ornamented with a pattern of black circles marked with a spot, worn over an ornamented, sleeved undergarment. Only one still has his legs, and he wears trousers, patterned with rows of lozenges alternating with wavy lines. His feet are apparently bare. The central figure, the king, is only distinguished by slight additional ornament on his kidaris and a dark wrap with a light border. The faces are bearded and natural, with no suggestion of masks. Beyond this, there seems no reason to doubt the artist, who may well be giving us a relatively accurate account of theatrical Oriental costume. The lack of differentiation between actors and chorus should be noted. On present evidence, the subject cannot be identified.

The flute-player also brings into the theatre a number of scenes with satyrs, but here there is a second important indication, for, even without a flute-player, it can be regarded as certain that satyrs who are in any way dressed, notably in tights, are not real satyrs, but stage satyrs. The earliest of these is not spectacular. On a black-figure oinochoe of the last decade of the sixth century in a private collection in London (fig. 37)[2] Dionysus, accompanied by two maenads and a naked satyr, looks to the left towards another satyr, fully clothed in chiton and himation. He is dancing, but full dress is not dancing dress, and the suggestion that he is not simply a dancer, but an actor, 'a man dressed as a satyr who is at the same time impersonating some other human or heroic character', is worth attention, though his relationship to the beginnings of satyric drama and to Pratinas[3] must remain uncertain.

---

[1] *A.R.V.*[2], p. 571, no. 74; Beazley, ibid., pp. 305–19, pl. 85. Webster, *M.I.T.S.*, p. 44, suggests Aeschylus' *Persae*, Page, *Proc. Camb. Phil. Soc.*, N.S., 8 (1962), pp. 47–49, a Croesus play; neither suggestion is very convincing, since a pyre is not a tomb, and the king is rising from it, not on it.

[2] Boardman, *Bull. Inst. Class. Stud.* (London), 5 (1958), pp. 6 f., pl. I.

[3] *Dith. Trag. Com.*[2], pp. 65–68.

The characteristic tights appear first about 480 B.C. or a little earlier
on a cup by Makron in Munich (fig. 38).[1] The spotted tights represent
a hairy skin, but otherwise the chorus-man has melted into a satyr, bald
in front. Similar satyrs but with full-length tights appear at about the
same date on a stamnos by the Eucharides Painter in the Louvre (fig. 39).[2]
They are breaking up the ground with mallets. The subject appears on
five other vases,[3] one of which (fig. 43) is certainly dramatic. In the other
vases, a woman or goddess of disputed identity rises from the ground
among the satyrs. She does not survive on this vase, if she was ever there,
but there is no doubt that a scene from a satyr play is here represented.

In a hydria in Boston (fig. 40),[4] probably by the Leningrad Painter like
fig. 36, of the second quarter of the century, the dramatic nature of the
scene is indicated both by the tights and the flute-player. In fact, we are
tied even closer to the life of the stage by the appearance on the extreme
right, behind the flute-player, of an elderly man in a plain himation,
evidently an ordinary man, perhaps the choregos. The flute-player re-
sembles those in figs. 35 and 36, except for his beard. All that has melted
here are the masks. The five satyrs are again bald in front. They carry
parts of a couch and perhaps a seat, which they will set up in preparation
for some feast.

The first representation of actors in a satyr play comes with a calyx-
krater in Vienna by the Altamura Painter of 470–460 B.C. (fig. 41).[5] It is
tied to the stage by a satyr chorus-man playing the lyre, only differing
from those which we have already considered by having his tights
ornamented with a cross. Hephaistos carries the tools of his trade in
both hands and on his back. He is wreathed and wears no chiton but
a black-bordered, plain, thigh-length himation which leaves his left arm
free. He wears soft pointed boots decorated at the top with a border
and flaps. He is escorted back to Olympus by Dionysus, ivy-wreathed,
with kantharos and thyrsos. He wears a knee-length chiton decorated
with dots between groups of vertical lines and a black-bordered himation.
He is barefoot. The masks have melted, but there is no reason to doubt
that the general picture is fairly close to the stage.

A calyx-krater in London by the Niobid Painter, c. 460–450 B.C. (fig. 42),[6]

---

[1] A.R.V.², p. 475, no. 267; Brommer, Satyrspiele², no. 5, fig. 5.

[2] A.R.V.², p. 228, no. 32; Beazley, Scritti Libertini, pp. 91–95.

[3] Discussed by Buschor, Feldmäuse (S.B. Munich, 1937).

[4] A.R.V.², p. 571, no. 75; Beazley, Hesperia 24 (1955), pp. 310 f., pl. 86b; Brommer, Satyrspiele², no. 1, pp. 12–15, fig. 6; Caskey and Beazley, Att. Vase Paintings in Boston, iii, pp. 51 f.

[5] A.R.V.², p. 591, no. 20; Brommer, Satyrspiele², no. 13, fig. 20.

[6] A.R.V.², p. 601, no. 23; Beazley, Hesperia 24 (1955), pp. 316–18, pl. 88a; Webster,
M.I.T.S., p. 45; Dith. Trag. Com.², pp. 117 f. (List of Monuments, no. 100).

presents difficulties and surprises. On one side, the upper zone has an eight-figure representation of the Pandora legend; the other side again has eight figures, a flute-player in full dress, a civilian, and six women dancing in sakkos, chiton, and himation, but of varying lengths and decoration. The lower zone has on one side a flute-player in plain clothes playing for four Pans and on the other a scene of satyrs at play. This last has certainly nothing to do with the stage. The Pandora scene might be related to the stage, but only indirectly. On the face of it, however, the vase attests the possibility that a chorus of Pans might replace a satyr chorus, and it is hard to see what is represented in the upper zone if it is not a chorus of tragedy.

In a small picture on the neck of a volute-krater in Ferrara (fig. 43),[1] c. 450 B.C., we are tied to the stage only by the flute-player and a civilian. We have already come across the subject. A goddess, crowned and sceptred, with chiton and a himation which veils the back of the head, is rising out of the ground. Behind her stands a man, carrying two torches, wreathed, with a short chiton and another garment over it. Six satyrs with mallets and a small boy are seen dismayed. In the artist's eye they have become real satyrs; their tights have melted.

Satyrs in tights appear again at roughly the same date on fragments of a cup by the Sotades Painter in Boston (fig. 44).[2] They are again accompanied by a goddess, in plain chiton and himation, with hair in a sakkos, carrying a sceptre. She is either seated or, again, rising out of the ground. One of the satyrs has his tights ornamented with a cross in a circle (cf. fig. 41). These ornaments become more prominent c. 425–420 B.C. in two works by 'the Painter of the Athens Dinos'. In one of them (fig. 45),[3] a dinos in Athens, four members of a satyr chorus strike attitudes before a flute-player in full dress and four civilians; on the other, three fragments of a bell-krater in Bonn (fig. 46),[4] at least three chorusmen stand before a flute-player in full dress. In both these, we are nearer the rehearsal than the stage, and we must be very close to the actual appearance of an Athenian satyr chorus.

The value to us of flute-player and satyr-tights should now be clear. Without them, we are on dangerous ground. There are several scenes

[1] A.R.V.², pp. 612, no. 1, 1662; Beazley, ibid., pp. 311 f., pl. 88b; Brommer, Satyrspiele², no. 15, pp. 51 f., fig. 49.

[2] A.R.V.², p. 763, no. 4; Brommer, Satyrspiele², no. 14a, fig. 8.

[3] A.R.V.², p. 1180, no. 2; Brommer, ibid., no. 2, fig. 2.

[4] A.R.V.², p. 1180, no. 3; Brommer, ibid., no. 3, fig. 3. The fragments with figures of Poseidon and Amymone in decorative robes with sleeves once associated with these (Bieber, Das Dresdner Schauspielerrelief, p. 17) do not belong (Bieber, Ath. Mitt. 36 (1911), p. 273; Buschor in Furtw.-Reich. iii, p. 139).

from the late fifth century where we may be tempted to think that a stage scene has inspired the artist, though the satyrs' tights have melted, but they are not strictly evidence. We illustrate two which are not wholly improbable, one (fig. 47)[1] depicting Prometheus in a decorated robe with short sleeves, bringing fire in a reed to the satyrs, the other (fig. 48)[2] Orpheus with a short chiton and Thracian cloak with a satyr entranced by his song. The case for their dramatic nature depends on the association of satyrs with mythical figures whom one would not expect to find them accompanying. How near the theatre we are, we can only guess.

We come now to the most complete and magnificent piece of evidence for fifth-century stage costume, the volute-krater in Naples (fig. 49)[3] by the Pronomos Painter, from the last years of the fifth century or the beginning of the fourth. On the main picture Dionysus and Ariadne, certainly divine and irrelevant to our purposes, are seated on a couch. The scene is crowded. In the foreground we can pick out two ordinary Athenians, the seated poet Demetrios and the lyre-player Charinos. There sits in the centre the flute-player Pronomos in the usual full dress. Scattered over the scene are ten men, mostly labelled with ordinary Athenian names, wearing furry drawers which support the satyr's tail and phallos; one, at the top left, has smooth tights. Only one has yet put on his bearded mask and is already sketching a step, but the others have identical masks at hand. Linked to them by the mask he carries, towards the bottom right, is an eleventh, wearing a sleeveless, ornamented chiton and a himation, perhaps the leader of the chorus. On the higher level, immediately to the left of the right-hand tripod, is another satyr figure, whom we can call Papposilenos, an older man, black-bearded, though the others were clean-shaven. His costume is tight-fitting and sleeved, represented as brown with tufts of white all over. He has a leopard skin and staff, and holds up his mask, which is white-bearded and white-haired with an ornate diadem and ivy leaves. He has no label of human or stage name, but there is no reason to doubt that the artist paints what he sees. Three figures remain for consideration, one to the left of the couch, one perched

---

[1] Some, with less probability, regard the central figure as Dionysus rather than Prometheus. See Beazley, *A.J.A.* 43 (1939), p. 636, who figures other vases depicting Prometheus and satyrs; Brommer, *Satyrspiele*², nos. 187–199a, figs. 42–46. Aeschylus wrote at least one satyr play called *Prometheus*, produced with *Persae* in 472 B.C.: see Lloyd-Jones, Loeb *Aeschylus* ii², fr. 278. However, Beazley now (*A.R.V.*², p. 1104, no. 6 (Orpheus Painter)) describes the scene as 'Dionysos (or Prometheus) chastising satyrs'.

[2] *A.R.V.*², p. 574, no. 6 (Agrigento Painter); Brommer, ibid., no. 95, fig. 53.

[3] *A.R.V.*², p. 1336, no. 1. Buschor in Fürtw.–Reich. iii, pp. 132–50, pls. 143–5; Bulle, *Eine Skenographie*, pp. 27–29; Beazley, *Hesperia* 24 (1955), p. 313; Arias and Hirmer, *A History of Greek Vase-Painting*, pp. 377–80 (with additional notes by Shefton), pls. 218–19, are the most important discussions outside Bieber and Webster.

on it, and one to the right. The last does not need his label to identify
him as Herakles. The club and lionskin he bears do that, though his
sleeved, ornamented chiton, yellow-brown corslet, and high, ornamental
boots are less distinctive. When we come to his head, however, there
seems to have been some melting under the artist's hand. Though he
carries a mask, his face has already become that mask, though the mask
has a lion's head too. The same thing has happened to the left-hand
figure, who already has the same straggly hair as the mask he carries,
though that has a tiara too. His sleeved chiton, himation, and boots
are all heavily ornamented. The figure that perches on the couch is
more enigmatic. Here there seems to be a distinction between the face
and the mask. Both are beardless. That a woman is being represented is
certain; that the face is female seems less certain. The hair is done up in
a bun with a band, while the mask has long hair and a tiara. Again,
a sleeved, ornamented chiton, though the himation is plainer, but this
character is barefoot.

The melting has caused trouble in the interpretation, but the exact
metaphysical status of the 'actors' need not concern us. It is generally
agreed that the Oriental tiaras point to the unnamed figures' being
Laomedon and Hesione. It is simplest to suppose that they and Herakles
are characters in a satyr play, and the view that they are figures from
tragedy has nothing to commend it. The position of the flute-player
Pronomos and the pattern of the name-labels suggests that the vase (or
a hypothetical votive picture which it may represent) was concerned to
stress the part played by the musicians, poet, and chorus. The personalities
of the actors have been suppressed. There is no reason to doubt that we
are given here a fairly faithful picture of stage costume.

Very close to the Pronomos vase in style and date are some fragments
from Taranto in Würzburg (figs. 50, a–c)[1]. Interpretation of it is even
more difficult, but it is agreed that here again there is a group of
divinities in the upper zone, surrounded by a dramatic cast, and that
there are a number of supernumerary figures, neither divine nor dramatic.
The flute-player is clearly to be seen, but the chorus has melted in the
same way as the actors on the Pronomos vase. They carry their curly-
haired masks, which have their mouths open but the eyes painted in,
but their hair has become that of their masks. They are a female chorus,
and the artist may have felt that the contrast between male chorus-men

---

[1] *A.R.V.²*, p. 1338; Bulle, *Corolla Curtius*, pp. 151–60, pls. 54–56; Buschor, *Studies presented
to D. M. Robinson* ii, pp. 90 ff.; Arias and Hirmer, loc. cit. Beazley points out that the sleeves
given to the poet in Wirsing's reconstruction are not paralleled by the Pronomos vase.

and female characters was one which he did not wish to make. Those members of the chorus we can see all have long, sleeveless chitons, ornamented in different ways. They are all barefoot. For the actors, our evidence is more or less confined to the top fragments of fig. 50b. There is no reason to place these fragments together, as Wirsing has done on his reconstruction (fig. 50c). To the right of the seated goddess, an arm in a sleeve of lozenged pattern holds a mask with an arched hairline and short forehead hair; the impression one gets is male, but it is broken. On the top-right fragment, there is a figure with a white chiton, gathered with a belt, and an ornamented cloak holding a staff, and another with a plain chiton ornamented with circles with a fawnskin over, which suggests Artemis. We seem to have here reasonable evidence for the dress of tragedy.

Close to these two vases in date is the relief from the Peiraeus (fig. 51).[1] Dionysus is on his couch with a female figure, whose name has been mostly obliterated. He is visited by three actors in long, sleeved chitons with high belts; the middle one wears also a long overgarment. The two to the left carry tympana. The left-hand one may have been wearing a mask, now obliterated. The middle one carries an old man's mask with longish but tidy hair, high forehead, gaping mouth, and beard. The third mask is more controversial, but appears to be of an oldish man.

In the fourth century, the quantity of evidence for tragedy from Athens itself drops off sharply, and there is little worth illustrating. The most interesting pieces are a relief in Copenhagen (fig. 52),[2] dated by Webster 360–350 B.C., of an actor dressed as a woman, with the long, sleeved chiton, himation, and soft boots, holding the mask of a middle-aged woman with long hair and sloping brows, and a red-figure fragment (fig. 53)[3] from the Athenian Agora showing a long-haired, white-faced mask, 375–350 B.C. In default of good Athenian evidence, we cannot resist going outside Athens to illustrate a Gnathia fragment from Taranto in Würzburg (fig. 54)[4] from the middle of the century. On this we have

---

[1] Studniczka, *Mélanges Perrot*, pp. 307 ff.; Bieber, *Denkm.*, pp. 104–5; *H.T.*², p. 32, who thinks that the right-hand mask is feminine or at least youthful; Buschor in Furtw.-Reich. iii, pp. 134 f.; *Studies presented to D. M. Robinson* ii, pp. 93 ff.; Webster, *G.T.P.*, p. 41; *M.I.T.S.*, p. 32. Most of these are tempted to associate the relief with Euripides' *Bacchae*, very close in date. The association would be more convincing if any of the actors was more maenadic in dress.

[2] Poulsen, *Billedtavler*, pl. 17, no. 233; Webster, *G.T.P.*, p. 43, pl. 9.

[3] Webster, *Hesperia* 29 (1960), pp. 258, 278, A1a, with pl. 65.

[4] Bulle, *Festschrift für James Loeb* (1920), pp. 5 ff., pl. ii, figs. 1, 1a, 6; *Eine Skenographie*, p. 5. To Bulle the poverty of the costume suggests a king in exile, and the combination of it with a sword brings it into relation with a royal figure on an early Apulian amphora in the Vatican, bearing a sword and taking refuge at an altar. The story, he thinks, is that of Thyestes

a tragic actor, with a sword in his left hand, and in his right the mask of a bearded man, fair-haired with curly brows. The eyes are fully painted in. He wears a short, reddish-brown, sleeved, and belted chiton fringed at the bottom, with a cloak of the same colour and high, laced, and decorated boots.

None of the masks we have so far seen are particularly exaggerated or unnatural. In particular, they all lack the ὄγκος, the very high forehead, characteristic of later tragic masks. A good example of such a later mask is to be found on a wall-painting from Herculaneum (fig. 55),[1] generally agreed to be the copy of a votive tablet dedicated by a victorious tragic actor, probably towards the end of the fourth or early in the third century B.C. The principal figure is the actor, a man with a fine face, who has just taken off his mask and ruffled his hair in doing so. A kneeling female figure is writing an inscription beneath the mask, which stands in its receptacle above a low pillar. (There is a second actor in the background.) This mask is very different from those hitherto considered, with its high ὄγκος and long hair hanging on each side, its wide-open mouth, and staring eyes.

Such evidence as is available, most of it non-Athenian, suggests that the ὄγκος came in in the last third of the fourth century, and Webster has plausibly suggested that 'this change was due to the statesman Lykourgos in the sense that when the theatre was rebuilt in stone [between 338 and 330] and adorned with the statues of Aeschylus, Sophocles, and Euripides, the new masks were also introduced to match the stately new setting'.[2] The Athenian evidence for the date of the change is not as good as one could wish. We have seen the evidence for naturalistic masks down to the middle of the century,[3] but the earliest evidence for the ὄγκος-masks is derived from a copy of a statue and a broken terracotta. The Roman copy in the Vatican (fig. 56)[4] derives, it has been argued, from the Lycurgan statue of Aeschylus. The mask which the poet carries has

and Pelopia; he dates both vases early in the fourth century. Rumpf (*Phil. Woch.* 52 (1932), cols. 209–10), on the other hand, denies that the actor represents a king in exile, and thinks his costume may have been a normal one at this period, the lack of decoration being merely indicative of a difference in fashion. He dates the vase in the time of Alexander the Great. The costume could be the actor's off-stage clothes. See also Robertson, *Greek Painting*, p. 163.

[1] For a coloured reproduction, see Maiuri, *Roman Painting* (Skira), p. 92. (We now think that what is represented is a picture of a mask, not a real mask.)

[2] *G.T.P.*, p. 43; cf. *Hesperia* 29 (1960), p. 258.

[3] Webster adds the Phaidra painting from Herculaneum (Bieber, *H.T.*², fig. 591), the original of which is dated by Rumpf (*Malerei und Zeichnung*, p. 136) c. 340.

[4] The head (of Euripides) does not belong to the original, and is here omitted. The eyebrows, nose, and beard of the mask are much restored. See Studniczka, *Neue Jahrbücher* 3 (1900), p. 170; Webster, *J.H.S.* 71 (1951), p. 229; *Hermes* 82 (1954), p. 307.

a high ὄγκος. The terracotta mask from the Agora (fig. 57),[1] which has a clear archaeological context of 325–300, has lost its top and now looks unimpressive, but the nature of the break has suggested that it once had a considerable head of hair. The earliest surviving ὄγκος on an Athenian mask is perhaps that on a colossal bronze mask from the Peiraeus (fig. 58) ;[2] the ὄγκος is low, but distinctive, the hair waved, the brows sloped, the beard curly; it may go back into the fourth century.

3. We can now proceed to a discussion of the history of tragic costume, which can be conveniently divided under the heads of masks, dress, and footwear.

There is much uncertainty as regards the use of masks in the earliest period of Athenian tragedy. Aristotle probably did not regard them as having been worn from the first,[3] and the tradition followed in 'Suidas'' lexicon held that Thespis, who gave the first performances of tragedy, first disguised his face, when acting, with white lead, then hung flowers over it, and only then took to plain linen masks, and that, after Choirilos had done something unspecified to the masks and robes and Phrynichos had introduced feminine masks,[4] it was Aeschylus who first used coloured and terrifying masks,[5] contrasting apparently with the masks ἐν μόνῃ ὀθόνῃ of Thespis. A similar tradition lies behind Horace's lines[6]

> ignotum tragicae genus invenisse Camenae
> dicitur et plaustris vexisse poemata Thespis,
> quae canerent agerentque peruncti faecibus ora ;
> post hunc personae pallaeque repertor honestae
> Aeschylus et modicis instravit pulpita tignis
> et docuit magnumque loqui nitique cothurno.

That Horace's history is in part confused or wrong does not affect the probability that he is recording a tradition prevalent in his day about Aeschylus.

---

[1] Thompson, *Hesperia* 28 (1959), pp. 141–2, pl. 29, T 88; Webster, *Hesperia* 29 (1960), pp. 258, 279, A6.

[2] References in Webster, *M.I.T.S.*, p. 31, AB1. It is eighteen inches high.

[3] He says nothing about masks in tragedy ; for comedy he appears to regard them as having been 'introduced' after comedy started, though he does not know who introduced them (*Poet.* v. 1449ᵇ4).

[4] Though γυναικεῖον πρόσωπον εἰσήγαγεν ἐν τῇ σκηνῇ might mean 'introduced a female character'. For the work of these early poets, see *Dith. Trag. Com.*², pp. 63–65, 68–69.

[5] 'Suid.' s.v. Αἰσχύλος· . . . οὗτος πρῶτος εὗρε προσωπεῖα δεινὰ καὶ χρώμασι κεχρισμένα ἔχειν τοὺς τραγικούς, καὶ ταῖς ἀρβύλαις τοῖς καλουμένοις ἐμβάταις κεχρῆσθαι.

[6] *A.P.* 275–80; cf. *Dith. Trag. Com.*², pp. 69, 79–82, and on *cothurno* see below, pp. 204 ff. On the mistaken use of the words *magnumque loqui* to support the fancy that the mask was formed as a speaking trumpet, to increase the loudness of the voice, see below, pp. 195 f. On the stage, see *Theatre of D.*, pp. 69 ff., esp. 72, against which, Arnott, *Greek Scenic Conventions*, pp. 1–41.

It does not seem possible to go behind the tradition of the use of masks by Thespis and his successors, whatever may be the truth conveyed by it, to the use of masks with some special (or, as some scholars think, some magical) significance in the worship of Dionysus. The primitive use of masks in the worship of a number of deities in Greece is well attested— Artemis Orthia and Artemis Korythalia at Sparta and Demeter Kidaria in Arkadia will serve as illustrations[1]—and in some of these cults the identification of the worshipper with his god by the wearing of his likeness was certainly felt to convey some special potency. But in tragedy, comedy, and other forms of Dionysiac κῶμοι the masks were for the most part not those of the god, and in those rites in which the god is represented by a pillar surmounted by a mask the worshippers are not disguised.[2] However, it is known that masks were *de rigueur* for those who took part in Dionysiac κῶμοι,[3] in some cases perhaps because the revels were liable to become somewhat disreputable and respectable citizens preferred to conceal their identity, but in most, probably, for the strong sense of 'identification' that it gave; and it is natural to suppose that, when the particular forms of dance or revel which developed into drama crystallized into their formal shapes, the use of masks should have continued. Satyr dances must always have been performed by masked dancers; and if the innovation of Thespis was the introduction of an actor (himself) to a chorus of masked dancers (though they were probably not satyrs),[4] he may well have thought it natural to mask his own face also, and tried various experiments before settling down to linen masks, which were later improved on by Aeschylus and others by the use of colour and the adaptation of the masks to the personality of the character represented by the actor.

The archaeological evidence for the tragic mask in the fifth and fourth centuries B.C. is before the reader, and only a few general points need be made. Our evidence starts *c.* 470 B.C. There is nothing to contradict the hypothesis that linen, perhaps artificially stiffened, was the normal material: the mask could be carried by a string (fig. 32) or a strap (fig. 49). Our earliest examples seem to cover the face alone (certainly fig. 33, perhaps fig. 32), but masks incorporating full heads of hair

---

[1] See Dawkins, *Temple of Artemis Orthia*, pp. 153, 163 ff.; Hesych. s.v. κυριττοί· οἱ ἔχοντες τὰ ξύλινα πρόσωπα κατὰ Ἰταλίαν καὶ ἑορτάζοντες τῇ Κορυθαλίᾳ γελοιασταί; Paus. viii. 15. 3, and for a fuller list, Bieber, *Jahrb. Arch.* 32 (1917), pp. 69–70. The best discussion of masking in the cult of Dionysus and its significance is still perhaps Wrede, *Ath. Mitt.* 53 (1928), pp. 87 ff. See also Nilsson, *Gesch.* i², pp. 571 f.

[2] See pp. 30 ff.

[3] Cf. Dem. *de F.L.* 287.

[4] See *Dith. Trag. Com.*², pp. 88, 94 f.

start at least as early as fig. 34, and are prevalent where the evidence is strong enough. The overriding impression is one of attempted naturalism. There is very little distortion to be seen in this period, except round the mouth, where it would be necessary for practical reasons. Since vase-painters normally fill in the eyes, there is little we can usefully say about them. Editors do not always report on colours, but one gets the impression of variety here. There is certainly a good deal of variety in hair-styles, eyebrows, noses, wrinkles, and so on. Obviously, some masks resemble others. Mask-makers would have a general idea of what sort of effect they wish to produce, but traces of standardization are not strong in this period.[1] Where appropriate, the mask might incorporate hair adornments or headgear which would help to adorn or identify the characters.[2]

In general, the texts of classical tragedies corroborate this picture, though the evidence is not large in quantity. A number of instances suggest that a hero or heroine who was regarded as beautiful or admirable wore fair hair; such were Phaidra, Iphigeneia, and Helena,[3] Hippolytus and in some plays Orestes,[4] in contrast with the wicked Polyneikes,[5] but that the ξανθός was not necessarily everyone's ideal may be inferred from Pasiphae's imaginary handsome man.[6] Orestes in his distress in Euripides' play of that name may perhaps have had a special mask displaying his squalor;[7] and it seems almost certain that the feminine beauty of Dionysus in the *Bacchae* must have been shown in his mask.[8] Personages in mourning are described as shorn,[9] and the locks are said to be cut off during the play.[10] Where the complexion of foreigners was in question, the mask-maker could doubtless oblige; the chorus-masks in the *Suppliants* of Aeschylus may have presented a dark complexion—the ἁπαλὰν Νειλοθερῆ παρειάν (ll. 70 ff.) of a μελανθὲς ἡλιόκτυπον γένος (l. 154), perhaps with traces of gashes in the cheeks, self-inflicted in distress (l. 70; cf. *Choephoroi* 24–25).

[1] Webster, *M.I.T.S.*, pp. 10–13, has the closest analysis of resemblances.

[2] e.g. the kidaris in fig. 36, the tiaras and ivy leaves in fig. 49.

[3] Eur. *Hipp.* 220, *Iph. Taur.* 174, *Helen* 1224.

[4] Eur. *Hipp.* 1343, *El.* 515, *Iph. Taur.* 52.

[5] Eur. *Phoen.* 308 βοστρύχων τε κυανόχρωτα χαίτας πλόκαμον.

[6] Eur. *Cretans* 14–15 (Page) πυρσῆς δὲ χαίτης καὶ παρ' ὀμμάτων σέλας | οἰνωπὸν ἐξέλαμπε περ-[και]νων γένυν.

[7] Eur. *Or.* 223–6 ΟΡ. ὑπόβαλε πλευροῖς πλευρά, καὐχμώδη κόμην | ἄφελε προσώπου· λεπτὰ γὰρ λεύσσω κόραις. | ΗΛ. ὦ βοστρύχων πινῶδες ἄθλιον κάρα, | ὡς ἠγρίωσαι διὰ μακρᾶς ἀλουσίας.

[8] Eur. *Bacch.* 455 ff. πλόκαμός τε γάρ σου ταναός, οὐ πάλης ὑπο, | γένυν παρ' αὐτὴν κεχυμένος, πόθου πλέως· | λευκὴν δὲ χροιὰν ἐκ παρασκευῆς ἔχεις, | οὐχ ἡλίου βολαῖσιν, ἀλλ' ὑπὸ σκιᾶς, | τὴν Ἀφροδίτην καλλονῇ θηρώμενος.

[9] Eur. *Or.* 457 f. Tyndareus is μελάμπεπλος | κουρᾷ τε θυγατρὸς πενθίμῳ κεκαρμένος.

[10] Soph. *Ajax* 1173, *El.* 449; Eur. *Helen* 1087.

Archaeological and literary evidence, then, combine to suggest that the poet and his mask-maker enjoyed great freedom, and there is no hint of any unnaturalness or exaggeration.

We have seen that there is no evidence for the ὄγκος on the tragic mask before the end of the fourth century. We can dismiss out of hand the views of Robert, who attributed to the fifth century certain of the originals of various south Italian wall-paintings where the ὄγκος is to be seen.[1] We can further confirm the conclusion we had provisionally arrived at, that the list of tragic masks in Pollux (iv. 133 ff.) is not earlier than the early Hellenistic period, for in it the ὄγκος is repeatedly referred to.

This list is, however, worth a summary, since it gives a good idea of the range of masks available, even in a period of standardization. It enumerates 6 tragic masks of old men, 8 of young men, 3 of servants, and 11 of women of various ages. Miss Bieber[2] and others, notably Prof. Webster,[3] have tried with some success to find specimens corresponding to each of them among the extant archaeological remains, and we give some references to photographs for those who wish to pursue the subject further. The basic distinction between old men and young is between bearded and non-bearded. Of the old men, the oldest is the ξυρίας— white-haired, the hair attached to the ὄγκος, and the beard closely cut; he is 'long in the cheek' (ἐπιμήκης ὢν τὰς παρειάς, the meaning of which is not quite clear without a certain specimen).[4] The λευκὸς ἀνήρ is grey-haired, with a low ὄγκος and curls round his head, a stiff beard (if this is the meaning of γένειον πεπηγός), projecting eyebrows, and a rather pale complexion (παράλευκον τὸ χρῶμα).[5] The σπαρτοπόλιος is a dark-haired man, turning grey, with a somewhat pale face (ὕπωχρος). The μέλας ἀνήρ has a dark complexion, curly hair and beard, a large ὄγκος, and a cruel face.[6] The ξανθὸς ἀνήρ has fair curls, a smaller ὄγκος, and

---

[1] *Kentaurenkampf u. Tragödienszene* (22nd Halle Winckelmannsprogramm, 1898), pp. 15 f.

[2] *R.E.* s.v. Maske, cols. 2077 ff.

[3] *Festschrift Andreas Rumpf* (1952), pp. 141 ff.; *G.T.P.*, pp. 45 ff.; *M.I.T.S.*, pp. 114 f. Both Bieber and Webster make suggestions as to how these masks might be used in the presentation of fifth-century plays, but we think these suggestions more likely to mislead than to enlighten the reader about how the plays were originally presented.

[4] A puzzle is raised here by 'Suidas' s.v. πριαμωθῆναι· ξυρηθῆναι· τὸ γὰρ τοῦ Πριάμου πρόσωπον ξυρίας ἐστί (cf. Hesychius s.v. πριαμωθήσομαι). These references have suggested that Priam wore this mask. But Pollux lists a special mask for Priam, and in Pompeian wall-paintings Priam has a considerable beard (cf. Bieber, *H.T.*[2], figs. 765, 768). The lexicographers look as if they are going back to Old Comedy and an older, different, tradition.

[5] Bieber finds an example in the left-hand mask on *Denkm.*, no. 63, and it certainly corresponds fairly well with Pollux's description. Among Webster's examples are fig. 58 here and Bieber, *H.T.*[2], fig. 768.

[6] W. compares fig. 56.

a healthy complexion (εὔχρως),[1] while the ξανθότερος, though in other ways similar, was paler and the mask of a sick man.[2]

Of the beardless νεανίσκοι, the oldest is the πάγχρηστος νεανίας. He has thick dark hair and a healthy complexion inclining towards swarthiness (μελαινόμενος). Miss Bieber is probably right in attributing this mask to the noble young hero, such as Achilles or Perseus.[3] The οὖλος is fair, with his hair closely attached to a large ὄγκος; his brows are raised, and he has a grim look (βλοσυρός).[4] The πάρουλος is like him, but younger. The ἁπαλός has light-coloured curls, a pale complexion, and a bright expression (φαιδρός); the mask is πρέπων θεῷ καλῷ.[5] The πιναρός looks swollen (ὀγκώδης),[6] has downcast eyes and discoloured complexion, very dirty, with long light hair. The δεύτερος πιναρός is thinner and younger. The ὠχρός has puffy flesh (σφριγανὸς ταῖς σαρξί), with hair all round his head, and the complexion of a sick man; the mask is for a ghost or a wounded man. The πάρωχρος is like the πάγχρηστος, but pale to denote sickness or love.

Of the three male servants represented by masks, the first, perhaps the oldest,[7] is the διφθερίας, 'the leather-clad', who wears a cap (περίκρανον) instead of an ὄγκος, with white, straight-combed hair, a pale face, an unkind sneer,[8] his forehead drawn up, his eyes gloomy (σκυθρωπούς), and a jutting beard.[9] Next in age comes the σφηνοπώγων ('wedge-bearded'), who is in the prime of life, with a high ὄγκος, flat on the top and hollowed out at the sides, light hair, and a stern red face, suited to a messenger.[10] The youngest, the ἀνάσιλλος ('with brushed-up hair'),[11] has a high ὄγκος, is fair, has his hair brushed up in the middle, is beardless with a ruddy complexion, and is also a messenger.

Of the women represented, the oldest and most dignified is the πολιὰ

[1] W. groups some Herakles masks under this head.
[2] W. compares Bieber, H.T.², fig. 766; cf. G.T.P., p. 47.
[3] Cf. fig. 60 here, and Bieber, H.T.², fig. 768.
[4] W. compares Bieber, H.T.², fig. 109.
[5] A better attested reading than θεῷ ἢ καλῷ. For revivals of Bacchae?: see above, p. 192, n. 8.
[6] We do not feel certain what ὀγκώδης really means. W. thinks that it simply = ὄγκον ἔχει, though this does not quite explain the termination. The mask admittedly recalls the description of Orestes at the beginning of Euripides' play. Cf. Bieber, H.T.², fig. 574.
[7] Cf. Varro, R.R. ii. 11. 11 cuius (skin) usum aput anticos quoque Graecos fuisse apparet, quod in tragoediis senes ab hac pelle vocantur diptheriae.
[8] μυκτῆρα τραχύν, meaning perhaps not quite certain. Webster translates 'a sharp nose', and compares Bieber, H.T.², figs. 766, 769, though they have no caps.
[9] Reading προπαλέστερος with Hemsterhuis, which is hardly an emendation, since most MSS. have προπαλαίστερος. The alternative is προπαλαίτερος—'the cut of his beard long out of date'.
[10] W. compares Bieber, H.T.², figs. 294, 310, 772.
[11] Cf. Plut. Crassus 24 τῷ ἀνασίλλῳ κομᾶν of the Parthians, and L.S.J. s.v. One MS. has ἀνάσιμος 'with upturned nose', certainly wrongly.

κατάκομος, with long white hair and a moderate ὄγκος, and rather pale; one family of MSS. adds that she was once called παράχρωμος (faded). The ἐλευθερὸν γρᾴδιον has a fair complexion,[1] a small ὄγκος, and her hair falling to her shoulders; the mask signifies calamity. The οἰκετικὸν γρᾴδιον—the old slave-woman—wears a lamb's-wool cap instead of an ὄγκος, and has a wrinkled face.[2] The οἰκετικὸν μεσόκουρον (half-shorn) has moderately long hair, only partly grey, a low ὄγκος, and a pale complexion, while the διφθερῖτις (leather-clad) is younger and has no ὄγκος. The κατάκομος ὠχρά has long black hair, a pale face, and a look of pain.[3] The μεσόκουρος ὠχρά differs from the last only in having shorter hair;[4] so has the μεσόκουρος πρόσφατος (half-shorn fresh), but she is not so pale.[5] The κούριμος παρθένος[6] has no ὄγκος, but her hair parted, combed back, and cut short, and a somewhat pale complexion,[7] and the second κούριμος παρθένος is similar but without the parting and close-cut hair, ὡς ἐκ πολλοῦ δυστυχοῦσα.[8] The κόρη has a youthful face, 'such as that of Danae or some other young girl'.

Pollux also lists special masks of tragedy—ἔκσκευα πρόσωπα—such as those of Actaeon wearing horns, the blind Phineus,[9] Thamyras with one blue eye and one dark, Argos with his many eyes, Euhippe changing into a horse, Tyro with her face bruised by her stepmother Sidero, Achilles shaven in mourning for Patroklos, Amymone, Priam, ·or the masks of a Titan, a Giant, a River, a Triton, a Fury, Death, or personifications such as Λύσσα, Οἶστρος, Ὕβρις, Ἀπάτη, Μέθη, Ὄκνος, Φθόνος, Muses, Nymphs, Horai, and Pleiades. This section contains the two explicit references to fifth-century drama, Euhippe 'in Euripides', Tyro in Sophocles, whether in original or in revival, but the degree of variety he allows for, even beside his standardized masks, encourages the belief that fifth-century mask-makers had a fairly free hand, as well as the greater naturalism that emerges from observation of the monuments.

Before turning to dress, it is only necessary to refer briefly to two suggestions which have been made with regard to the peculiarities of the tragic masks: (1) that they served to make the actor's voice more resonant, so that it could carry throughout the vast theatres; (2) that the

[1] Reading ὑπόξανθον τὴν χροιάν, rather than τὴν πολιάν.
[2] Perhaps cf. Bieber, H.T.², fig. 591.
[3] Cf., for example, Bieber, H.T.², fig. 773.
[4] W. compares Bieber, H.T.², figs. 575–6.
[5] W. compares Bieber, H.T.², fig. 769.   [6] See above, p. 181.
[7] W. compares Bieber, H.T.², fig. 567; a late fourth-century example, G.T.P., pl. 11a.
[8] Perhaps cf. G.T.P., pl. 11b.
[9] W. compares the blind mask of the early third century B.C., Mon. Piot 38 (1941), p. 113, fig. 9.

grotesqueness of the later masks, and particularly the high ὄγκος, was in some way connected with the introduction of the raised stage.

The first suggestion is based on a passage of Aulus Gellius (v. vii) who is quoting the work of an earlier writer, Gavius Bassus, de Origine Vocabulorum: 'Caput' inquit 'et os coperimento personae tectum undique unaque tantum vocis emittendae via pervium, quoniam non vaga neque diffusa est, in unum tantummodo exitum collectam coactamque vocem ciet ⟨et⟩ magis claros canorosque sonitus facit. Quoniam igitur indumentum illud oris clarescere et resonare vocem facit, ob eam causam "persona" dicta est, o littera propter vocabuli formam productiore.' The suggested derivation, of course, does not bear looking into, and some modern experiments with masks manufactured so far as possible on ancient lines make it extremely doubtful whether in fact masks ever did anything to increase sound. Certainly no 'megaphone effect' could be produced by linen masks such as Thespis is said to have used, so that it cannot have been their original object; and it is doubtful whether such effects could be satisfactorily achieved without the use of metal.[1] When Roscius introduced masks into tragedy in Rome (if he did so),[2] it was not to enhance the resonance of his voice, but to conceal his squint.

The theory that the introduction of the less natural type of mask coincided with the introduction of the raised stage is supported by Bulle,[3] but he dates the latter change in the second half of the fourth century B.C. and this may be more than a century too early,[4] at least as far as Athens is concerned. It may be that when action began to be confined to the relatively narrow stage instead of the wide orchestra, it was necessarily more restrained and statuesque, and masks of the newer type, which were suited to actors facing the audience (and that from a greater distance) and seldom seen in the round, would commend themselves as suitable; but the earliest of the masks with a high ὄγκος seem to belong to the last third of the fourth century, and cannot have been suggested by the alteration in the place of action, unless indeed these masks came first into vogue in theatres away from Athens. So much is obscure with regard to the relevant dates that it would be rash to lay down any positive statement. Certainly the most repulsive forms of tragic mask, at which Lucian scoffs, were the result of the depraved taste of the imperial period.[5]

[1] Cf. Dingeldein, Haben die Theatermasken der Alten die Stimme verstärkt? (Berlin, 1890); Hunningher, Acoustics and Acting in the Theatre of Dionysus Eleuthereus, pp. 18 f.

[2] Beare, The Roman Stage³, App. I.   [3] Festschrift für James Loeb, p. 19.

[4] Theatre of D. pp. 182, etc. For the date of the introduction of the ὄγκος-mask, see pp. 189 f. above.

[5] Lucian, de salt. 27 πρόσωπον ὑπὲρ κεφαλῆς ἀνατεινόμενον ἐπικείμενος καὶ στόμα κεχηνὸς πάμμεγα ὡς καταπιόμενος τοὺς θεατάς, κτλ. (cf. Tox. 9, Gallus 26, Anachar. 23, Iup. trag. 41).

4. We can now turn to dress, and begin with the literary evidence. That the characteristic tragic costume, whatever it was, was the invention of Aeschylus[1] was a strong tradition in the Roman period, the statements to this effect being associated with the attribution to him (certainly false, as will be seen later) of the thick-soled kothornoi. The earliest of these statements is that of Horace,[2] according to whom Aeschylus was *personae pallaeque repertor honestae*. The same tradition is found in Athenaeus and Philostratus (both about A.D. 200).

Athen. i. 21d καὶ Αἰσχύλος δὲ οὐ μόνον ἐξεῦρε τὴν τῆς στολῆς εὐπρέπειαν καὶ σεμνότητα, ἣν ζηλώσαντες οἱ ἱεροφάνται καὶ δᾳδοῦχοι ἀμφιέννυνται, ἀλλὰ καὶ πολλὰ σχήματα ὀρχηστικὰ αὐτὸς ἐξευρίσκων ἀνεδίδου τοῖς χορευταῖς. Χαμαιλέων γοῦν πρῶτον αὐτόν φησι σχηματίσαι τοὺς χοροὺς ὀρχηστοδιδασκάλοις οὐ χρησάμενον, ἀλλὰ καὶ αὐτὸν τοῖς χοροῖς τὰ σχήματα ποιοῦντα τῶν ὀρχήσεων, καὶ ὅλως πᾶσαν τὴν τῆς τραγῳδίας οἰκονομίαν εἰς ἑαυτὸν περιϊστᾶν. ὑπεκρίνετο γοῦν μετὰ τοῦ εἰκότος τὰ δράματα. Ἀριστοφάνης γοῦν—παρὰ δὲ τοῖς κωμικοῖς ἡ περὶ τῶν τραγικῶν ἀπόκειται πίστις—ποιεῖ αὐτὸν Αἰσχύλον λέγοντα "τοῖσι χοροῖς αὐτὸς τὰ σχήματ' ἐποίουν".

Philostr. *Vit. Apoll.* vi. 11, p. 219 K (after enumerating many improvements of tragedy by Aeschylus) ὁ δ' ἐνθυμηθεὶς μὲν ἑαυτὸν ὡς ἐπάξιον τοῦ τραγῳδίαν ποιεῖν φθέγγοιτο, ἐνθυμηθεὶς δὲ καὶ τὴν τέχνην ὡς προσφυᾶ τῷ μεγαλείῳ μᾶλλον ἢ τῷ καταβεβλημένῳ τε καὶ ὑπὸ πόδα, σκευοποιίας μὲν ἥψατο εἰκασμένης τοῖς τῶν ἡρώων εἴδεσιν, ὀκρίβαντος δὲ τοὺς ὑποκριτὰς ἐνεβίβασεν, ὡς ἴσα ἐκείνοις βαίνοιεν, ἐσθήμασί τε πρῶτος ἐκόσμησεν, ἃ πρόσφορον ἥρωσί τε καὶ ἡρωΐσιν ἠσθῆσθαι, ὅθεν Ἀθηναῖοι πατέρα μὲν αὐτὸν τῆς τραγῳδίας ἡγοῦντο.

Philostr. *Vit. Soph.* i. 9, p. 11 K Σικελία Γοργίαν ἐν Λεοντίνοις ἤνεγκεν, ἐς ὃν ἀναφέρειν ἡγώμεθα τὴν τῶν σοφιστῶν τέχνην, ὥσπερ ἐς πατέρα· εἰ γὰρ τὸν Αἰσχύλον ἐνθυμηθείημεν, ὡς πολλὰ τῇ τραγῳδίᾳ ξυνεβάλετο ἐσθῆτί τε αὐτὴν κατασκευάσας καὶ ὀκρίβαντι ὑψηλῷ καὶ ἡρώων εἴδεσιν ἀγγέλοις τε καὶ ἐξαγγέλοις καὶ οἷς ἐπὶ σκηνῆς τε καὶ ὑπὸ σκηνῆς χρὴ πράττειν, τοῦτο ἂν εἴη καὶ ὁ Γοργίας τοῖς ὁμοτέχνοις.

A certain caution is necessary here. Athenaeus ascribes to Chamaileon (about 300 B.C.) certain statements about Aeschylus' treatment of the chorus, but he does not refer to him as his authority in regard to costume, and in his phrasing (ἀλλὰ καὶ . . .) he seems to distinguish the two statements, and to refer to Chamaileon only for what follows. Moreover, the last sentence of the passage seems to imply that, whether for himself or for Chamaileon, the recognized authority on Aeschylus was the *Frogs*

[1] There was also a tradition that Choirilos exercised some influence on the costumes of tragedy: 'Suidas' s.v. Χοιρίλος. . . . κατά τινας τοῖς προσωπείοις καὶ τῇ σκηνῇ τῶν στολῶν ἐπεχείρησε. Even the emendation σκευῇ leaves the meaning very uncertain.

[2] *A.P.* 278 (see above, p. 190). On this Porphyrion comments: 'Aeschylus primus tragoediis coturnos et syrma et personam dedit; horum enim trium auctor est.'

of Aristophanes,[1] and this also seems to be the case with Philostratus. But all Aristophanes[2] (half a century after the death of Aeschylus, and with the comic poet's aim of producing an absurd effect) says is that Aeschylus' heroes wore more dignified robes than ordinary men:

> *ΑΙ. κάλλως εἰκὸς τοὺς ἡμιθέους τοῖς ῥήμασι μείζοσι χρῆσθαι·*
> *καὶ γὰρ τοῖς ἱματίοις ἡμῶν χρῶνται πολὺ σεμνοτέροισιν,*
> *ἀμοῦ χρηστῶς καταδείξαντος διελυμήνω σύ. ΕΥ. τί δράσας;*
> *ΑΙ. πρῶτον μὲν τοὺς βασιλεύοντας ῥάκι' ἀμπισχών . . .*

Moreover, it may be of some significance that Aristotle in enumerating the innovations made by Aeschylus in tragedy never refers to costume, except that, if Themistius is right,[3] he did ascribe ὀκρίβαντας (some kind of footwear) to him.

None of these references is very specific about dress, but there is a more specific reference in the very unreliable *Life of Aeschylus*,[4] compiled from many sources and of unknown date. It evidently repeats the same tradition as the passages already quoted, but in a rather strange phrase it does allude to the sleeves and the σύρμα:[5] *πρῶτος Αἰσχύλος πάθεσι γεννικωτέροις τὴν τραγῳδίαν ηὔξησεν . . . τούς τε ὑποκριτὰς χείρισι σκεπάσας καὶ τῷ σύρματι ἐξογκώσας μείζοσί τε τοῖς κοθόρνοις μετεωρίσας.* σύρμα is a word which appears late in Greek literature; its derivation suggests that it means a robe so long that it trails.

Apart from this evidence, which is not easily assessable, it would be unwise to conclude more from the literary sources than that it was perhaps believed, fifty years after the death of Aeschylus, that he had given the kings and heroes of tragedy a more distinguished costume than they previously wore, and that writers of a much later date interpreted the authors of the fifth century to mean that he had invented the costume to which they, and probably previous generations, had become accustomed in tragedy.

We can now turn to the archaeological evidence. The main points of interest are the development of the chiton with fitted sleeves and the growth of ornamented fabrics. Outside fig. 36 with its Oriental subject, most of our earlier fifth-century evidence has nothing particularly

---

[1] All these writers must have used also some authority, now lost, for Aeschylus' supposed use of the high-soled kothornos. See below, p. 205.

[2] *Frogs* 1060 ff.

[3] See below, p. 205, n. 3. Aristotle's low rating of the art of the σκευοποιός (*Poetics* 1450[b] 15–20) is hardly sufficient explanation.

[4] 14. The paragraph is omitted by Q and Triclinius and was thought by Wilamowitz (*Aesch. Trag.*, p. 5) to be interpolated from some other 'Life'.

[5] Cf. Porphyrion, above, p. 197, n. 2.

dramatic about it. The costumes of figs. 33, 41 would not be particularly out of the way in real life, and decoration is more or less confined to the borders. To leave chorus-men out of account, sleeves are not fitted in fig. 33 or 41. Fitted sleeves in the theatre start, as far as our scanty knowledge suggests, with the flute-player. He has them at least from the late archaic period,[1] and his dress rapidly becomes heavily ornamented (figs. 36, 40). 'Sleeves, whatever their origin, must have been welcome to the flute-player, with his raised arms, in cold weather, whether the performance was indoors or out of doors.'[2]

Fitted sleeves and heavy ornamentation next appear, for us, with the actors of Oriental parts in fig. 36 . At least one of the Orientals has fitted sleeves, but we cannot be sure about the king. Then we have a longish gap filled only by the doubtfully theatrical fig. 47, where Prometheus' chiton hardly has sleeves but is heavily ornamented. That fitted sleeves to an ornamented chiton are worn, and used by artists in this period for divinities outside theatrical contexts, is attested, e.g. by the Lyssa on a bell-krater of about 440–430 B.C. (fig. 59) ;[3] her chiton is very short.

By the end of the century this style of dress is dominant in tragic contexts, if the evidence of figs. 49–50 is enough to go by, and it is this which is generally regarded by scholars as the typical tragic dress. How far it is really peculiar to tragedy is uncertain. In the fourth century, particularly on south Italian vases, it is a most frequent costume for deities, heroes, and heroines, in scenes whose connexion with the theatre is at best doubtful.[4] The temptation to associate such scenes with the theatre is, however, sometimes very strong. For example, the Andromeda krater from Capua (fig. 60)[5] is Attic and very close in date to the Pronomos vase, and has costumes of a similar style. In the centre the heroine stands with her hands fastened to the rock, clothed in a robe reaching the ground; the lower and upper parts of this robe show bands of decorative figures or patterns. It is a single garment, but here worn with a cloak. The sleeves reaching the wrist bear a conspicuous band of decoration. Cepheus, the father of Andromeda, and Perseus her deliverer are on either side of her; Hermes

---

[1] See Beazley, *Hesperia* 24 (1955), p. 308 with n. 7, and cf. fig. 61.

[2] Beazley, loc. cit.

[3] *A.R.V.*[2], p. 1045, no. 7, by the Lykaon Painter from Vico Equense.

[4] Some examples were collected in the first edition of this book, figs. 165–73, 175–91.

[5] Metzger, *Représentations*, p. 340, no. 70. In some of the many vase-paintings of the Andromeda legend (obviously a popular subject) the costumes are of a quite different type. See Metzger, op. cit.; Engelmann, *Arch. Stud.*, pp. 63 ff. and Séchan, *Études*, pp. 256 ff.; cf. also C. M. Dawson, *Romano-Campanian Landscape Painting*, p. 143. It has been suggested that the Ethiopian on our krater may have represented a member of the chorus, which would have been female and Oriental (cf. Euripides, fr. 117 N).

and Aphrodite (in a robe without sleeves, but bearing some of the same patterns as that of Andromeda) stand on a somewhat higher level; and to the left is the seated figure of an Ethiopian in a sleeved costume richly decorated in every part, and reaching to the knee; below it the legs are encased in tight and highly ornamented trousers. The scene as depicted is plainly not one that can have been represented in the theatre. The case for supposing that it was depends on the great popularity of Euripides' *Andromeda*, first produced in 412 B.C., the nearness in date of the vase to the play, and the similarity of the costumes to those of the Pronomos vase. The case is neither contemptible nor wholly cogent.

For the fourth century, as we have seen, evidence for costume in Attica is slight. We should only remember fig. 54 as a warning that, at any rate in one part of the theatrical world, greater simplicity of dress was possible.

The origins of this special form of dress have been much disputed. The view that it was taken from the regular festal robe of the Peisistratid epoch[1] seems to have little to commend it; the fashion then was for a sleeveless garment of white linen.[2] The sleeved chiton does go back into the sixth century: it appears in the second quarter of that century on a neck-amphora in the Louvre:[3] it is worn by Poseidon on a Corinthian clay tablet,[4] an ivory statuette of a priestess from Ephesus,[5] a flute-girl on an Attic oinochoe c. 530 B.C. (fig. 61),[6] and by Dionysus on an Attic black-figure amphora c. 500 B.C. (fig. 62).[7] From the last example, it has been inferred[8] that the garment was specially associated with Dionysus, and passed from him to the actors, his ministers, but the numerous later representations of Dionysus so dressed[9] prove nothing about the origins of the dress, and there is no early evidence that it was specially connected with Dionysus.[10]

The tradition[11] that the officials of Eleusis changed their dress in admiration of Aeschylus' innovations in theatrical costume has naturally raised interest in a possible Eleusinian connexion with the theatre. Both

---

[1] Pringsheim, *Arch. Beitr. zur Gesch. des Eleusinischen Kults*, p. 14; Körte, *Festschr. Deutscher Philologen u. Schulmänner in Basel*, 1907, p. 202.

[2] Rumpf, *Phil. Woch.* 52 (1932), cols. 208–10; Bieber, *Jahrb. Arch.* 32 (1917), pp. 18, 102.

[3] *Bull. Museum of Fine Arts, Boston* 47 (1949), p. 88, figs. 4–6.

[4] See also Amelung, *R.E.* iii, s.v. χειριδωτὸς χιτών.

[5] Hogarth, *Ephesus*, pl. XXII.

[6] *A.B.V.*, p. 154, no. 45; Karouzou, *The Amasis Painter*, p. 34, no. 42, pl. 42. 3; van Hoorn, *Choes and Anthesteria*, no. 768. Cf. perhaps Karouzou, op. cit., no. 48, pl. 40. 7.

[7] Bieber, *Jahrb. Arch.* 32 (1917), pp. 19 ff., Taf. i.

[8] Ibid., and Bieber, *H.T.*², pp. 25–26.

[9] e.g. Bieber, *H.T.*², figs. 81–89.

[10] Note, for example, that the Amasis Painter, who often painted Dionysus, never depicts him thus.   [11] Athen. i. 21d (see above, p. 197).

views have been held, that the tradition is true[1] and that the reverse is true, that Aeschylus borrowed his costume from Eleusis, and that it is ultimately Thracian in origin.[2] The belief in a growth of elaboration at Eleusis is, however, not justified. There is a plainly dressed daidouchos on a sixth-century loutrophoros,[3] but another sixth-century official on a pinax by Euphiletos[4] is as elaborately dressed as the fifth-century daidouchos[5] whose elaborate costume is thought to be due to Aeschylus' influence. None of these officials has fitted sleeves, which do not appear at Eleusis until the fourth century, and are far removed from theatrical costume even then.[6] The Eleusinian officials certainly had a justified reputation for magnificence,[7] and Aeschylus' Eleusinian birth may have suggested a connexion; it is doubtful whether there is more to the tradition than that.

A short $\chi\iota\tau\acute{\omega}\nu$ with sleeves, the $\kappa\alpha\nu\delta\acute{\upsilon}s$, was certainly worn by Persians, and the theory that tragic costume was influenced by Persian costume has been revived by Alföldi,[8] who thinks it likely that the costume was introduced to the stage first for barbarian kings, then for any arbitrary ruler, and finally extended to most or all of the actors, through the crowd's weakness for the spectacular. He was writing before the publication of fig. 36, and the sleeved undergarments there may be thought to strengthen his position. Yet the clear evidence of fig. 61 that a similar dress was in use by flute-players before the Persian Wars suggests that this view is perhaps too simple. The growing ornamentation of fabrics may owe as much to technological advance as to knowledge of Persian dress,[9] and there are certain clear practical advantages for flute-player and

[1] Bieber, *H.T.*[2], pp. 24–25; Mylonas, *Eleusis and the Eleusinian Mysteries*, p. 209.

[2] Lobeck, *Aglaophamos* i. 84; Müller, *Bühnenaltertümer*, p. 229.

[3] Kourouniotes, *Ἀρχ. Ἐφ.* 1937, i, pp. 240–7, with figs. 12–14, 16–18.

[4] Ibid., fig. 15 (*A.B.V.*, p. 352).   [5] Ibid., pp. 223 ff. with figs. 1–4.

[6] Bieber and others cite a late fourth-century hydria from Capua (*H.T.*[2], fig. 79; Metzger, *Représentations*, p. 243, no. 10) showing the sleeved robe worn in an Eleusinian ceremony. It is, however, so different from the 'tragic' robe that it can hardly be used for argument. She also cites a pelike (figured by Pfuhl, fig. 596), but here again, apart from the mere fact of sleeves being worn, the differences are more striking than the resemblances. Cf. also an Attic lekane in Tübingen, and a hydria in Istanbul (Nilsson, *Gesch.* i[2], pl. 45|1, 44|1; Metzger, pp. 244 f., nos. 14, 12).

[7] Cf. Plut. *Aristid.* 5. 7. Pringsheim (*Arch. Beitr. zur Gesch. des Eleusinischen Kults*, p. 7) conjectures that $\sigma\tau o\lambda\acute{\eta}$ was a technical name for both costumes on the strength of Athenaeus, loc. cit., [Lysias] vi. 51, Plut. *Alcib.* 22. 4, Pollux iv. 115. But $\sigma\tau o\lambda\acute{\eta}$ (like 'robe') is used in many non-religious applications, and neither the tragic nor the Eleusinian costume is always called by this name. See Bieber, *R.E.* s.v. Stole.

[8] *Late Classical and Medieval Studies in honor of A. M. Friend* (1955), pp. 15–55.

[9] On the technique of ornamentation, see Brooke, *Costume in Greek Classic Drama*, pp. 12–15. The sixth-century François vase (Furtw.–Reich., pls. 1–3, 11, and 12) has elaborately decorated dresses, though their cut and ornamentation are quite distinct from the 'tragic' robe.

actor in a made-up dress with fitted sleeves which they will certainly have appreciated.[1] Effective though the normal fifth-century Athenian chiton and himation might be, they were easy to disarrange and a handicap to rapid movement. A made-up garment, on the other hand, could restrict any unwanted fullness of material to what could be controlled by a belt, would be easier to move in tidily, and easier for the making of quick changes. The fitted sleeves would not only be warmer; they would be invaluable in disguising the male forearms of the actor of women's parts. We need look little further for the explanation of the garment's success, even though its origins may rest in some doubt.

For further evidence about possible variations in tragic costume, we must turn to the text of the plays. Individual characters are frequently said to appear in mourning. Electra is doubtless in black in the *Choephoroi*,[2] in Sophocles' *Electra*[3] she is described ἀεικεῖ σὺν στολᾷ, in Euripides' *Electra* she is at first mistaken for a slave[4] and wears rags.[5] Mourning is worn by Admetus in *Alcestis*,[6] by Helen in *Helen*,[7] by Iokasta in *Phoenissae*,[8] and by Tyndareus in *Orestes*.[9] The plight of Philoctetes[10] and of Oedipus at Colonus[11] in late plays of Sophocles, and of the shipwrecked Menelaus[12] and the sick Orestes[13] in Euripides, is indicated by their garments, and his introduction of Telephus and many other heroes in rags is one of the many innovations with which Euripides is taunted by Aristophanes.[14] Special functions were no doubt specially indicated; Kassandra, for example, in *Agamemnon* was dressed as a *mantis*.[15] But there is no description in any extant play of the dress in which kings and queens and their children would normally appear in the theatre, and it is therefore impossible to compare their costume with the decorative robes shown in vase-paintings. But a passing mention may be made of the special effects of which Euripides sometimes made use, such as the black and horrible Thanatos of *Alcestis*,[16] the fine clothes in which Hermione decks herself in *Andromache*,[17] and the robes, perhaps bridal garments, in which Evadne

---

[1] Brooke, op. cit., pp. 64–66, throws a strong beam of good sense and practical experience here.

[2] ll. 16–18 imply this.   [3] l. 191.   [4] ll. 107–10.

[5] l. 185 τρύχη τάδ' ἐμῶν πέπλων.

[6] At least if this is the correct interpretation of ll. 819, 923. 512, 826 only note the difference of his hair.   [7] l. 1186—note the change in clothing.

[8] ll. 324–6 ἄπεπλος φαρέων λευκῶν, ὦ τέκνον, | δυσόρφναια δ' ἀμφὶ τρύχη τάδε | σκότι' ἀμείβομαι.   [9] l. 457.   [10] *Philoct.* 39, 274.   [11] *Oed. Col.* 555, 1597.

[12] Eur. *Helen* 416, 421, 554, 1079, 1204.   [13] *Orestes* 391.

[14] *Ach.* 412 ff.; *Frogs* 1063 ff. Not wholly trustworthy, perhaps: 'rags' may be a relative term, and a joke is a joke.

[15] 1264 ff. See Fraenkel ad loc. (iii, p. 584).   [16] l. 843.

[17] ll. 147 ff. κόσμον μὲν ἀμφὶ κρατὶ χρυσέας χλιδῆς | στολμόν τε χρωτὸς τόνδε ποικίλων πέπλων | οὐ τῶν Ἀχιλλέως οὐδὲ Πηλέως ἄπο | δόμων ἀπαρχὰς δεῦρ' ἔχουσ' ἀφικόμην, | ἀλλ' ἐκ Λακαίνης Σπαρτιάτιδος χθονὸς | Μενέλαος ἡμῖν ταῦτα δωρεῖται πατήρ.

arrays herself before leaping into her husband's funeral pyre in *Suppliants*.[1] Ion also appears to have been richly clad as the minister of Apollo,[2] and in *Rhesus* Rhesus' golden armour must have made a sensation.[3] But, on the whole, the evidence from the texts is scanty, although we cannot blame the dramatists for not describing what the audience could see.[4]

We may close this section on costume with Pollux's account of the costumes of the past, whenever that past was. He writes:[5] καὶ ἐσθῆτες μὲν τραγικαὶ ποικίλον (οὕτω γὰρ ἐκαλεῖτο ὁ χιτών), τὰ δ' ἐπιβλήματα ξυστίς, βατραχίς, χλανίς, χλαμὺς διάχρυσος, χρυσόπαστος, στατός, φοινικίς, τιάρα, καλύπτρα, μίτρα, ἀγρηνόν· τὸ δ' ἦν πλέγμα ἐξ ἐρίων δικτυῶδες περὶ πᾶν τὸ σῶμα, ὃ Τειρεσίας ἐπεβάλλετο ἤ τις ἄλλος μάντις· κόλπωμα, ὃ ὑπὲρ τὰ ποικίλα ἐνεδύοντο οἱ Ἀτρεῖς καὶ οἱ Ἀγαμέμνονες καὶ ὅσοι τοιοῦτοι. ἐφαπτὶς συστρεμμάτιόν τι πορφυροῦν ἢ φοινικοῦν, ὃ περὶ τὴν χεῖρα εἶχον οἱ πολεμοῦντες ἢ οἱ θηρῶντες. ὁ δὲ κροκωτὸς ἱμάτιον· Διόνυσος δὲ αὐτῷ ἐχρῆτο καὶ μασχαλιστῆρι ἀνθίνῳ καὶ θύρσῳ. The ποικίλον is presumably the sleeved chiton with which we have been chiefly concerned.[6] The ξυστίς is an over-garment, described by the scholiast on Ar. *Clouds* 70 as τὸ κροκωτὸν ἱμάτιον ὃ οἱ ἡνίοχοι μέχρι τοῦ νῦν φοροῦσι πομπεύοντες· χρῶνται δὲ αὐτῷ καὶ οἱ τραγικοὶ βασιλεῖς; the βατραχίς (green) and φοινικίς may have been distinguished from this principally by their colour, as may also the 'golden' or 'gold-sprinkled' χλαμύς.[7] The κροκωτός (saffron-coloured) was already worn by Dionysus in Aristophanes' *Frogs*.[8] Of the κόλπωμα worn to give the importance of increased size to royalty there is no certain illustration, nor of the ἀγρηνόν, the network of woollen threads worn by seers.[9] The στατός or στατὸς χιτών seems to have been a stiff garment falling from head to foot without a girdle.[10] The 'flowery girdle' of Dionysus is not referred to elsewhere.

At a late date tragic actors used padding above and below the waist (προστερνίδια and προγαστρίδια) to increase their size, and so incurred the ridicule of Lucian.[11] The word σωμάτιον is sometimes said to

---

[1] ll. 1054–5 ΙΦ. σκευῇ δὲ τῇδε τοῦ χάριν κοσμεῖς δέμας; | ΕΥ. θέλει τι κλεινὸν οὗτος ὁ στολμός, πάτερ.

[2] ll. 326–7. [3] ll. 382–4.

[4] See in general Dierks, *De tragicorum histrionum habitu scenico apud Graecos* (Göttingen, 1883).

[5] iv. 116–17.

[6] The χιτὼν ζωτός or ζῳδιωτός, referred to by Pollux in a non-theatrical context (vii. 55), must have been much the same.

[7] Golden clothing is sometimes characteristic of the actor in Lucian (*Nekyom.* 16, *Gallus* 26).

[8] l. 46 and schol.; cf. W. Headlam's note on Herodas viii. 28.

[9] See above, p. 202, n. 15.

[10] See *L.S.J.* s.vv. στατός and στάδιος, and 'Suid.' s.v. ὀρθοστάδια· οἱ στατοὶ χιτῶνες ὀρθοστάδιοι, οἱ δὲ συρόμενοι συρτοί.

[11] Lucian, *Iup. trag.* 41 ἀνάγκη δυοῖν θάτερον ἤτοι Πῶλον καὶ Ἀριστόδημον καὶ Σάτυρον ἡγεῖσθαί σε θεοὺς εἶναι τότε ἢ τὰ πρόσωπα τῶν θεῶν αὐτὰ καὶ τοὺς ἐμβάτας καὶ τοὺς ποδήρεις χιτῶνας

be used of the actor's robe generally,[1] and sometimes to mean such padding.

5. With regard to the footwear of the principal tragic actors, the statements of the older textbooks to the effect that the actors wore shoes in which the thickness of the soles was increased to four or even eight to ten inches, as in the Rieti statuette (fig. 63),[2] are no longer supported by any scholar of reputation. They are due mainly to an indiscriminate use of evidence without any regard for chronology. The facts are really simple.[3]

There is no evidence at all of the use of such thick soles until late in the Hellenistic age, and many scenes in the extant plays would have been impossible if such shoes had been worn. Reference has already been made[4] to the frequent scenes of rapid and even violent movement which the texts of tragedy imply. Whatever the correct interpretation of these scenes, a sufficient disproof of the use of soles several inches thick is afforded by the scene[5] where Agamemnon orders an attendant to remove his shoes as he dismounts from his chariot. Can we suppose that he suddenly became several inches shorter, or that (as some have suggested) what the attendant really did was to fasten the thick-soled shoes on, and that the king trampled on the purple carpet (and probably up some steps) with these? Moreover, such shoes are not to be seen on any early monument. The earliest example is perhaps to be found in the middle of the second century B.C., on the relief of Archelaus of Priene (the so-called Apotheosis of Homer) in the British Museum (fig. 64),[6] in which the

---

καὶ χλαμύδας καὶ χειρῖδας καὶ προγαστρίδια καὶ σωμάτια καὶ τἆλλα, οἷς ἐκεῖνοι σεμνύνουσι τὴν τραγῳδίαν, ὅπερ γελοιότατον οἶμαι; de salt. 27 ἐῶ λέγειν προστερνίδια καὶ προγαστρίδια, προσθετὴν καὶ ἐπιτεχνητὴν παχύτητα προσποιούμενος. It can hardly be inferred from the former passage that the great actors of an earlier age used these devices, though Lucian uses their names to represent the profession.

[1] Poll. ii. 235, iv. 115; Phot. s.v. σωμάτια· τὰ ἀναπλάσματα οἷς οἱ ὑποκριταὶ διασάττουσιν αὑτούς. οὕτως Πλάτων (the comic poet). (The reference may be to comedy.)

[2] This work of the late second century A.D., with its very high ὄγκος, very wide-open mouth and eyes, and the stilt-like effect its combined pegs and boots convey, is a model of what the classical actor did *not* look like, has done incalculable harm to the conventional picture of the Greek stage, and still appears on the dust-jackets of books by those who should know better.

[3] The whole matter was independently (and almost simultaneously) cleared up by K. K. Smith, 'Use of the High-soled Shoe or Buskin in Greek Tragedy', Harv. Stud. Class. Phil. 16 (1905) and A. Körte, 'Der Kothurn im fünften Jahrhundert', Festschrift Deutscher Philologen in Basel. Important later discussions are by Bieber, Dresd. Schauspielerrelief, pp. 42–69; Karouzou, J.H.S. 65 (1945), pp. 38–41; Webster, G.T.P., p. 37.

[4] Above, pp. 175 f. A number of instances are collected by K. K. Smith, op. cit., pp. 135 ff.

[5] Aesch. Agam. 944 ff. ἀλλ' εἰ δοκεῖ σοι ταῦθ', ὑπαί τις ἀρβύλας | λύοι τάχος, πρόδουλον ἔμβασιν ποδός, | καὶ τοῖσδέ μ' ἐμβαίνονθ' ἀλουργέσιν θεῶν | μή τις πρόσωθεν ὄμματος βάλοι φθόνος.

[6] B.M. Cat. Sculp. iii. 2191; see Fraser–Rönne, Boeotian and West Greek Tombstones, p. 182, n. 45 for the date.

tragic Muse wears a thick-soled shoe. This is fairly closely followed by a marble base from Halikarnassos,[1] in which she is distinguished from others by ornamental shoes with soles probably somewhat less than three inches high. After this date there are many (though not many extreme) instances.

It may be doubted whether the view that the thick sole is classical would have gained any currency at all but for the existence, here again, of late passages in which dramatic practices current in the writer's own day are attributed to the old masters. Aeschylus is once again the principal victim. His very unreliable *Life*[2] speaks of him as τούς τε ὑποκριτὰς χειρῖσι σκεπάσας καὶ τῷ σύρματι ἐξογκώσας μείζοσί τε τοῖς κοθόρνοις μετεωρίσας. Horace, *Ars Poetica* 280, seems to have the same story in mind, *et docuit magnumque loqui nitique cothurno*, and so does Philostratus.[3] But there is also a story about Sophocles;[4] Istros, an Alexandrian scholar of the late third century B.C., seems to have credited him with some kind of innovation : φησὶ δὲ ῎Ιστρος καὶ τὰς λευκὰς κρηπῖδας αὐτὸν ἐξευρηκέναι, ἃς ὑποδοῦνται οἵ τε ὑποκριταὶ καὶ οἱ χορευταί. There must surely have been some differentiation according to the characters represented; it seems improbable that all should have worn white shoes; but the word κρηπῖδες does seem to imply some kind of sole,[5] though there is no further evidence for their use by Sophocles.

Attempts have been made to extract some kind of sense from these texts. Since the monuments rule out a visible sole, Miss Bieber[6] has suggested that the innovation consisted of putting a low sole inside the boot. Mme Karouzou,[7] on the other hand, relying on the monuments we are about to examine, has thought that Aeschylus' novelty had

---

[1] Trendelenburg, 'Musenchor' (*Berlin Winckelmannsprogramm* 36 (1876)).

[2] § 14; see above, p. 198.

[3] *Vit. Apoll.* vi. 11 ὀκρίβαντος δὲ τοὺς ὑποκριτὰς ἐνεβίβασεν. Themist. *Or.* 316 d also ascribes ὀκρίβαντας to Aeschylus, and ὀκρίβας is a synonym for κόθορνος in Lucian, *Nero* 9 and Philostr. *Vit. Soph.* i. 9. 1 (see above, p. 197). (In classical Greek, e.g. Plato, *Sympos.* 194 b, it denotes a platform.) Lucian, who saw their absurdity, also uses ἐμβάται as a synonym for κόθορνοι of the thick-soled shoes; cf. *de salt.* 27 εἰς μῆκος ἀρρυθμὸν ἠσκημένος ἄνθρωπος ἐμβάταις ὑψηλοῖς ἐποχούμενος, *Gallus* 26 τῶν κοθόρνων τὴν ὑπόδεσιν ἀμορφοτάτην καὶ οὐ κατὰ λόγον τοῦ ποδός— an absurdity exposed to view when an actor tumbled down. ἐμβάται also appear in 'Suidas' s.v. Αἰσχύλος . . . οὗτος πρῶτος εὗρε ταῖς ἀρβύλαις τοῖς καλουμένοις ἐμβάταις κεχρῆσθαι. Pollux, on the other hand, regards the ἐμβάτης as a distinctively comic shoe, iv. 115 καὶ τὰ ὑποδήματα κόθορνοι μὲν τὰ τραγικὰ καὶ ἐμβάδες, ἐμβάται δὲ τὰ κωμικά (cf. vii. 91). It looks here as if καὶ ἐμβάδες is a gloss intended for ἐμβάται; ἐμβάς seems to have been used in the Classical period for any ordinary shoe, such as would also be worn in comedy; it was probably never confined strictly to one type. Cf. Pollux vii. 85 ἐμβάδες· εὐτελὲς μὲν τὸ ὑπόδημα, Θράκιον δὲ τὸ εὕρημα, τὴν δὲ ἰδέαν κοθόρνοις ταπεινοῖς ἔοικεν. ἐμβάτης is found in classical literature only in some mss. of Xen. *de equit.* xii. 10, where it would mean a riding boot.

[4] *Vita Sophoclis* 6.

[5] Bekk. *Anecd.* i, p. 273. 19 κρηπὶς δὲ εἶδος ὑποδήματος ἀνδρικοῦ ὑψηλὰ ἔχοντος τὰ καττύματα.

[6] *Dresd. Schauspielerrelief*, p. 52. [7] *J.H.S.* 65 (1945), pp. 40 f.

nothing to do with the sole, but consisted of enlarging the whole shape of the boot. But this seems too far from the texts, and it is doubtful whether they are worth saving.

We must now turn to the monuments, and it will be convenient to take actors and chorus together. With the very doubtful exception of the left-hand figure in fig. 33, there is no trace of anything like a sandal. Footwear, where worn, or at least when the artist thinks it worth showing, always comes some way up the leg. Of these boots there are, on dramatic monuments, two main kinds. Firstly, there is a loose, soft, undecorated boot, often with a pointed toe. When choruses of women wear anything on their feet, they wear this (figs. 32–34), and an actor is wearing it for a woman's part in the fourth century (fig. 52). This is certainly possible wear in everyday life too, and we figure a woman pulling them on after her bath (fig. 65).[1] A variation, with a decorated band and pendent tongues at the top, is worn by Hephaistos in fig. 41. The second is a laced boot, which begins for us as early as the left-central figurei n fig. 32. There is not enough of it left to tell how decorated it was, and a laced boot need not be decorated, as pictures of Lyssa (fig. 59) and Thamyras (fig. 66)[2], both perhaps not too far from tragic costume, though not certainly tragic, and of the Periclean period, show. Decorated laced boots are prominent on the Pronomos vase (fig. 49), were perhaps to be found on the Peiraeus relief (fig. 51), though we have lost the painted decoration, and continue into the next century and further afield, even with a plain costume, with fig. 54. The laced boot can be traced back to close to 600 B.C. in all sorts of contexts.[3]

A third possible form of boot is the cuffed boot, of which the top turns over, and apparently even looser than the first. It has no certain appearance in tragedy, though it appears on an interesting red-figure lekythos with a muffled figure, 460–450 B.C., which Mme Karouzou has claimed for the stage (fig. 67),[4] and we shall find it again in comedy (figs. 83–84).

It may be thought that such boots are peculiarly characteristic of Dionysus, that the stage adopted them in his honour, and that the

---

[1] Kylix in the Torlonia Museum in Rome, *A.R.V.*[2], p. 821, no. 3 (Boot Painter). See Bieber, op. cit., p. 51 for other instances.

[2] Hydria in Oxford, *A.R.V.*[2], p. 1061, no. 152.

[3] See Webster, *G.T.P.*, p. 37.

[4] Op. cit., pp. 38 ff., fig. 1 and pl. iv a. The latter is reproduced here by her kind permission. She argues that the figure wearing the shoes is that of an actor, or of the caricature of an actor in a satyric play, not altogether convincingly, though there are some attractive arguments which deserve careful study. 'A woman running in after bathing' (Beazley, *A.R.V.*[2], p. 645, no. 7).

decorated laced boots are particularly Dionysiac. It is doubtful whether
such a view can survive the classification which, following Webster, we
have adopted here. Dionysus in art can wear all three, the loose, decorated
type on a stamnos in London, *c.* 490–480 B.C. (fig. 68),[1] the laced boot on
an amphora by the Achilles Painter, *c.* 450 B.C. (fig. 70),[2] and the cuffed
boot on a late sixth-century amphora in London (fig. 71).[3] We have
seen these boots on other figures too, and Hermes seems to have greater
uniformity of footwear, often wearing the loose boots with prominent
flaps (figs. 72–74).[4]

Nevertheless, Dionysus does often wear boots of some kind,[5] and the
connexion of the κόθορνος with him is well enough established. We can
hardly leave the subject without discussing this word and its possible
association with any or all of the types of boot we have examined. The
earliest instances are in Herodotus. In i. 155 it is clearly a woman's shoe
or at any rate, effeminate—κέλευε δέ σφεας κιθῶνάς τε ὑποδύνειν τοῖσι
εἵμασι καὶ κοθόρνους ὑποδέεσθαι.... ταχέως σφέας γυναῖκας ἀντ’ ἀνδρῶν
ὄψεαι γεγονότας. Its shape—or at least its looseness in some of its forms—
is indicated by the story in vi. 125 of Alcmeon wearing κόθορνοι (which
must have been tall and loose) when he went to collect the gold of
Croesus and filling them so full of gold that he could hardly stagger along.
Femininity is clearly characteristic of the κόθορνος in Aristophanes. It is
worn by Lysistrata's women,[6] and in *Ecclesiazousae*[7] Blepyros cannot find
his ἐμβάδες, his Λακωνικαί, and complains bitterly of having to drag on his
wife's Περσικαί, or, alternatively, insert himself into her κοθόρνω. The
oriental[8] and effeminate character of the κόθορνος, already suggested by
the first Herodotus passage, is confirmed. When Peisetairos makes fun
of Meton then,[9] or Herakles of Dionysus:[10] τίς ὁ νοῦς; τί κόθορνος καὶ
ῥόπαλον ξυνηλθέτην; it is effeminacy that they have in mind. Which of
the vase-painters who had already given Dionysus boots knew that he was

---

[1] *A.R.V.*[2], p. 292, no. 29 (Tyszkiewicz Painter). Cf. also fig. 69 (*A.R.V.*[2], p. 31, no. 6
(Dikaios Painter)). Beazley tells us that the figure is better regarded as a bald mortal than
Dionysus, but his temper is Dionysiac.

[2] *A.R.V.*[2], p. 987, no. 2. The face of Dionysus and the top of his head are 'restored'.

[3] *A.R.V.*[2], p. 154, no. 4.

[4] Satyr as Hermes on a psykter by Douris, *c.* 490–480 B.C. (*A.R.V.*[2], p. 446, no. 262);
hydria in Leningrad, *c.* 470 B.C. (*A.R.V.*[2], 555, no. 95 (Pan Painter)); stamnos in Trieste,
c. 470–460 B.C. (*A.R.V.*[2], p. 217, no. 2). Cf. also fig. 41.

[5] Perhaps curiously, not on fig.   [6] *Lysistr.* 657.   [7] ll. 313–19, 344–6.

[8] Cf. Körte, op. cit., p. 205, and Alföldi, *Studies in honor of A. M. Friend*, pp. 50–52, though
the latter certainly goes too far. There are stage boots which have Greek origins going back
beyond all possible Persian influence.

[9] *Birds* 994 τίς ἡ ’πίνοια, τίς ὁ κόθορνος τῆς ὁδοῦ; Very obscure, but perhaps an allusion to
his shirking of military service.

[10] *Frogs* 47.

giving him effeminate boots, we cannot be sure. That κόθορνοι were as loose in Athens as they had been in Alcmeon's case emerges from Theramenes' nickname. He was called κόθορνος from his adaptability to the politics of either party;[1] obviously, the boot was loose and easy and fitted either foot. Whether the κόθορνος was the loose boot or the cuffed boot or both, it clearly cannot have been the laced ornamental boot worn by the hero Herakles on the Pronomos vase, and there is no evidence that the word was specifically applied to the stage in the Classical period.

In art and literature the κόθορνος was, of course, later associated with Dionysus. Virgil[2] bids the god come to the winepress in these words:

> huc, pater o Lenaee, veni nudataque musto
> tinge novo mecum dereptis crura cothurnis.

Pausanias[3] compares the image of Zeus Philios at Megara with Dionysus: κόθορνοί τε γὰρ τὰ ὑποδήματά ἐστιν αὐτῷ καὶ ἔχει τῇ χειρὶ ἔκπωμα, τῇ δ' ἑτέρᾳ θύρσον.

For Pollux and Lucian[4] and for Latin authors[5] the κόθορνος is the characteristic footwear of tragedy, and, for the latter at any rate, there was no doubt that it applied to the high-soled boot used by actors in their day.

One final word on footwear must be that, if the artists are to be trusted, both actors and chorus might sometimes be barefoot. There is no particular reason to find this surprising.

6. Before leaving tragedy, some specific points about the chorus call for discussion. The texts assure us that it was dressed according to its supposed nationality or occupation; e.g. in the *Suppliants* of Aeschylus, the King on first meeting them cries:[6]

> ποδαπὸν ὅμιλον τόνδ' ἀνελληνόστολον
> πέπλοισι βαρβάροισι κἀμπυκώμασι
> χλίοντα προσφωνοῦμεν; οὐ γὰρ Ἀργολὶς
> ἐσθὴς γυναικῶν οὐδ' ἀφ' Ἑλλάδος τόπων.

---

[1] Xen. *Hellen.* ii. 3. 30–31; Pollux vii. 90–91.

[2] *Georg.* ii. 7. On this Probus writes: ' "cothurni" sunt calceamentorum genera venatorum quibus crura etiam muniuntur, cuius calceamenti efficies est in simulacris Liberi et Dianae.' *Cothurni* are in fact connected with Diana in *Ecl.* vii. 32 and *Aen.* i. 336. The soft boot and the hunting boot, which must have been rather tougher, come oddly under the same name, and it is clear that at some time the word came to be employed of any boot which came some way up the leg. The Greek *vox propria* for Artemis' hunting boots is ἐνδρομίδες; cf. Callim. *Hymn to Artemis* 16 and *to Delos* 238 (with schol.), *Anth. Planud.* iv. 253, Pollux vii. 93. The word is also used of a soldier's tall boot in the *Belopoeica* of Philo Mechanicus (third–second century B.C.). Mme Karouzou, op. cit., uses it of the fifth century to distinguish tight boots from loose boots, but she takes no account of lacing, and her usage is doubtfully justified.

[3] viii. 31. 4.

[4] For references, see above, p. 205, n. 3.

[5] e.g. Horace, *A.P.* 80, 280.

[6] ll. 234–7, cf. 121 (Σιδονίᾳ καλύπτρᾳ).

Probably their dress was of some rich fabric,[1] and it was held by a girdle. (In l. 719 of the same play Danaus describes the Egyptian invaders who afterwards break into the orchestra as wearing white garments over their dark skins.) The chorus of *Persae* must have worn the dress of elderly Persian nobles. Fig. 36 gives us a good idea of the possibilities; patterned cloth, trousers,[2] the kidaris. The *Phoenissae* of Euripides may also have worn an Oriental costume, but it is not definitely indicated. Choruses of Greeks have other characteristics. The chorus of *Herakles* has the sticks befitting its age.[3] So does the chorus of *Agamemnon*,[4] but whether that chorus has swords as well has been hotly disputed.[5] In *Choephoroi* the chorus wears the black robes of mourning;[6] in Euripides' *Alcestis* they change into such robes at the appropriate moment,[7] and in his *Suppliants* they wear, if not actual mourning, at least πεπλώματ' οὐ θεωρικά.[8] In *Eumenides* the chorus may be themselves black-skinned; they are dressed in black, until perhaps at the end of the play they are adorned with scarlet cloaks.[9] In Sophocles' *Ajax* and *Philoctetes* the chorus consists of seamen, who were doubtless appropriately habited, and Philoctetes notices with pleasure[10] that they are dressed as Greeks (σχῆμα μὲν γὰρ Ἑλλάδος | στολῆς ὑπάρχει προσφιλεστάτης ἐμοί). In *Rhesus* the chorus must have been in military uniform. For the maenad chorus of *Bacchae* we have adequate artistic evidence (figs. 33, 35, ? 34).[11]

On the monuments we so rarely get a full cast that it is hard to say much about distinctions between the chorus and the actors, or inside the chorus. We can say that in fig. 36 there is little distinction between Oriental actor and Oriental chorus. In fig. 50, however, it seems to be true that the actor and flute-player wear sleeves, though the chorus does not. Choruses are not invariably uniform. In fig. 34 the length of costume seems to differ; in fig. 42 differences are more marked, and even the satyr chorus of fig. 49 has two aberrant members, one much more richly dressed. The possibility that he is leader of the chorus or semi-chorus lies to hand.

---

[1] πολυμίτων πέπλων in l. 432 is generally rendered 'damask'.

[2] Trousers are also worn by the Ethiopian in fig. 60, who is conjectured by some scholars to represent the chorus. See p. 200.

[3] ll. 254 ff. (cf. 107 f.).

[4] l. 75.

[5] See ll. 1351, 1651, and Fraenkel and Denniston–Page ad locc.

[6] l. 11.

[7] They are not in mourning at ll. 215 ff. They go out with Admetus for the funeral at 740–6, and return in mourning at 861 (cf. 923).

[8] l. 97.

[9] ll. 52; 370 (cf. 352); 1028.

[10] ll. 223–4.   [11] Fawnskins seem to be implied by ll. 111 ff.

B. *Comedy*

1. The archaeological evidence for comic costume is, for the present, in a curious condition. There is sixth-century evidence, notably in the portrayal of animal choruses, which looks as if it ought to be relevant, but only the very latest of these representations, if any, can overlap with the beginnings of organized comedy in Athens. There is then a sharp gap, with virtually nothing that can be claimed as evidence for comedy before the last quarter of the fifth century. Since the earlier evidence has been illustrated and discussed in *Dithyramb, Tragedy, and Comedy*,[1] it will be convenient here to begin after the gap, with evidence which coincides in date with the career of Aristophanes.

It is further convenient, if no more, to make a division between Old and Middle Comedy on the one hand, and New Comedy on the other. On the literary side, there is the greater naturalism of New Comedy; from the archaeological point of view, there is, as will be seen, a sharp distinction in dress; for the historian, there is the convenience that Pollux has much light to throw on New Comedy, and the greater standardization of theatrical costume facilitates a classification of the archaeological material by his catalogue. Yet the division is only a convenience. The dividing line which we think we see near the beginning of Menander's career is unlikely to have seemed so obvious to contemporaries. As will become clear, many features of New Comedy were anticipated in Middle Comedy, and, on the other hand, it is not likely that the standardization of masks achieved by the Hellenistic period was completed at a blow, say, in the year 325 B.C. With these qualifications, we can proceed. For Old and Middle Comedy the more satisfactory mode of procedure is to describe the evidence and then discuss it; for New Comedy we can start from Pollux' catalogue and illustrate it.

2. We begin with a cup fragment from the Agora (fig. 75),[2] *c.* 430 B.C. The preserved figure is male, wears tights seen on his arm, and over them apparently a short chiton. He has something, perhaps a stick, in his right hand. His claims to be connected with comedy rest on his similarity to later representations.

Next in date comes a chous from Anavyssos (fig. 76),[3] *c.* 420 B.C. To

---

[1] Ed. 2, pp. 152–4, pls. 6–9.

[2] *A.R.V.*², p. 945, no. 28; *Hesperia* 29 (1960), p. 261, pl. 67, B 1.

[3] *A.R.V.*², p. 1215, no. 1; Caputo, *Dioniso* 4 (1935), pp. 273 ff, figs. 1–5; Brommer, *Satyrspiele*², figs. 21–23; van Hoorn, no. 276; Webster, Ἀρχ. Ἐφ. 1953–4, ii, p. 200, fig. 4; Trendall, *Phlyax Vases*, no. 1. Its Attic origin was wrongly doubted in *Theatre of D.*, p. 74. For its relevance to the stage, cf. ibid.; Webster, *G.T.P.*, pp. 7, 20; Arnott, *Greek Scenic Conventions*, p. 16. There is general agreement that the actor represents Perseus.

the left are two seated spectators. On a low stage reached by steps there postures a figure with tights, a twisted-up phallos, and a himation draped over his left arm, which supports a bag and carries a scimitar. The author of this book thought that this was a portrayal of mime, rather than of comedy, but there seems to be no good evidence for phallic mime or stage mime in Attica in this period,[1] and comedy seems to be most likely here, with the audience *pars pro toto*. The mask has melted into the actor's face in the familiar way.

A chous from Cyrene in the Louvre (fig. 77),[2] *c.* 410 B.C., is more elaborate, and a representation of mime even more improbable. On a chariot there rides a caricatured Herakles, distinguished by club and head-dress, wearing a long sleeveless chiton and himation. His face is mask-like rather than a mask, but we shall find the goggling eyes, short fat nose, large mouth, and shortish beard in at least one other representation of him (fig. 91). Nike holds the reins, with wings and himation; her snub nose and dark hair also recur (fig. 85). The chariot is pulled by four centaurs, very hairy about the face, with well-marked brows. Before them prances a dancer with two torches, tights, long phallos, a scarf, and a bearded face, one eyebrow up, one down.[3]

We can take next a group of four choes, all belonging to the last twenty years of the fifth century or a little later, distinguished by a strong childish influence, even if the figures may not all be children. We need not discuss here whether the fact that they are choes points to the existence of comedy at the Anthesteria,[4] though the view of Mme Karouzou[5] that there were children's comedies at the Anthesteria seems highly improbable. If they are children, they are imitating their elders, as so often on choes, but here the elders whom they are imitating are comic actors. We begin with two, whose relevance to comedy cannot be doubted. On a fragment (fig. 80)[6] a child approaches a comic mask on an inverted amphora. The mask is bearded, and has a hooked nose and raised brows.[7] On a vase in Leningrad (fig. 78)[8] we have a larger cast. To the right,

[1] Webster, Ἀρχ. Ἐφ. 1953–4, ii, pp. 194–5. The whole article, pp. 192–201, is the most useful introduction to the costume of Old Comedy.

[2] A.R.V.², p. 1335, no. 34 (Nikias Painter); best photographs in A.J.A. 55 (1951), p. 10, figs. 5–7; *Hesperia* 24 (1955), pl. 34b, Trendall, *Phlyax Vases*, no. 3.

[3] For this phenomenon, see Rumpf, A.J.A. 55 (1951), p. 10.

[4] Above, pp. 10f., 15f.; Webster, Ἀρχ. Ἐφ. 1953–4, ii, pp. 195–6.

[5] A.J.A. 50 (1946), p. 137.

[6] van Hoorn, no. 213; Webster, loc. cit., p. 196, fig. 1; Trendall, *Phlyax Vases*, no. 4.

[7] Webster compares Bieber, H.T.², figs. 176, 524.

[8] van Hoorn, no. 585; Webster, G.T.P., pp. 61 ff., Ἀρχ. Ἐφ. 1953–4, ii, p. 198; Beazley, *Hesperia* 24 (1955), p. 314; Trendall, *Phlyax Vases*, no. 6. We owe the photographs to the kindness of Prof. V. N. Andreyev.

a flute-player in his normal dress. To the left, another figure in ornamented chiton, apparently unsleeved, carrying a mask. The three central figures are in chiton and tights. Left-centre has a himation over his, draped on his left shoulder, and his right arm is supported on a stick. The central figure is seated, with long phallos. Right-centre is standing, with coiled phallos. Left-centre and right-centre have caps to protect their heads from the masks, centre has just a headband. The four left-hand figures have between them five masks. From left to right, (1) bald in front, dark hair, with a slightly lighter, long beard; (2) above, scanty white hair, hooked nose, and a beard, possibly a crown, which has suggested Zeus; (3) held by the seated actor, bald head and scrubby beard, mild in expression; (4) turned-up nose, dark shaggy hair, and scrubby beard; (5) on the ground, full head of neater hair and beard. On the whole, apparently, we have here good evidence for comic dress, c. 400 B.C., with a fair selection of male masks, only mildly caricatured in style.

Slightly earlier, perhaps c. 420–410 B.C. (fig. 79),[1] we find a child wearing tights and a short chiton, and carrying a torch. He is accompanied by a child carrying a cake, and a dog. His nose is turned up, his hair receding. More remarkable is the character with padding, tights, and long phallos in fig. 81;[2] his mask may be like that of no. 3 on the Leningrad chous. It is hard to tell what he is doing.

The next group of vases which calls for description dates from 400 B.C. or a little earlier.[3] It is unique in technique. The vases, oinochoai, are unglazed, and the various colours are applied direct to the clay, and not to any over-painted wash. It is reasonable to connect them all with comedy. They have a general air of caricature about them, and two of them supply Attic models for south Italian phlyax vases, whose connexion with comedy is undoubted.[4] The first four were found in a group in the Agora; the fifth, now in the British Museum, was bought in Athens, though the dealer said it came from Alexandria. It would, however, be unsafe to assume that the subjects of the group were connected. The first (fig. 82) is inscribed [ΠΕΛΙΑ]Σ ΤΥΡΩ ΝΗΛΕΥΣ. Below the last name is part of a pink face, with black shaggy hair, presumably Neleus. It is safe to deduce that the recognition scene from Sophocles' *Tyro*

---

[1] van Hoorn, no. 854; Webster, Ἀρχ. Ἐφ. 1953–4, ii, p. 197; Trendall, op. cit., no. 2. Compare fig. 4 here. We do not quite understand why this is not also claimed as evidence for comedy.

[2] Karouzou, *A.J.A.* 50 (1946), pp. 132 ff., figs. 9–10, who thinks it a parody of *Eumenides*; van Hoorn, no. 117; Webster, Ἀρχ. Ἐφ. 1953–4, ii, p. 197; Trendall, op. cit., no. 5.

[3] Crosby, *Hesperia* 24 (1955), pp. 76–84, pls. 34–37; Webster, *Wien. Stud.* 69 (1956), p. 112; *Hesperia* 29 (1960), pp. 261–3; Trendall, *Phlyax Vases*, nos. 9–13.

[4] For these, see below, pp. 216 ff.

is in some way represented. The scene was familiar to Athenian comic audiences in the fifth and fourth centuries[1] and may well have been parodied on the stage. On the second (fig. 83), more complete, but without inscription, we have, kneeling or dancing, a beardless figure, not phallic, with protruding belly, naked[2] save for a scarf draped round his shoulders and the soft boots with cuffs and pointed toes. His right arm holds a staff, an oinochoe hangs from his left arm; his hair has traces of a white fillet. He is some kind of reveller; his lack of beard and phallos, and his boots, suggest effeminacy. On the third (fig. 84) two bearded running figures carry on a spit a white object, identified by Miss Crosby, almost certainly correctly, as an *obelias*, a large loaf carried in Dionysiac processions.[3] The leader wears a short white chiton, slipped below his right shoulder, and probably a double fillet. His companion has a white cap and black cuffed boots, and, apparently, an even shorter chiton. Their noses and lips are much exaggerated, and are not far from mask (4) in fig. 78. A very similar picture recurs on a south Italian bell-krater.[4] The Middle Comedy poet Ephippus wrote a play whose alternative title was *Obeliaphoroi*, and, although our vase is older than Ephippus, the subject may be older too. The fourth vase (fig. 86) has a badly damaged surface, and many details are not clear. Two very fat figures in tights and short chiton, the left, at least, apparently phallic, face each other. The left figure is labelled [ΔI]ΟΝΥΣΟΣ, the right-hand one ΦΟΡ[. Dionysus and Phormion appeared together in the *Taxiarchs* of Eupolis, but the name can be completed otherwise. On the London vase (fig. 87) a pink oarsman, apparently in tights, but non-phallic, rows an enormous blue fish. The scene reappears, without the oars, on a phlyax vase.[5]

One more Attic vase demands description (fig. 85).[6] On a bell-krater in Heidelberg, 390–370 B.C., we have two female figures. The left-hand one wears a chiton, and a himation ornamented with circles; the right-hand one has only the himation. The left-hand one wears her mask, the right-hand one has it pushed back over her head, but it appears to be the same mask, and not dissimilar to the face of Nike on fig. 77. We have here, apparently, two members of a comic chorus of women.

A remarkable grave-relief in Stockport (fig. 88),[7] *c.* 380 B.C., depicts

---

[1] Ar. *Lysistr.* 139 and schol.; Menander, *Epitrepontes* 149–57; cf. Aristot. *Poetics* xvi. 1454^{b}25.
[2] Perhaps wearing tights; at least it is hard to think what else the line on the left leg above the knee represents.
[3] See above, p. 61, n. 6, and Photius s.v. ὀβελίας ἄρτος.
[4] Bieber, *H.T.*², fig. 511 (the caption giving the older, wrong, interpretation); Trendall, *Phlyax Vases*, no. 32.   [5] Bieber, *H.T.*², fig. 496; Trendall, op. cit., no. 140.
[6] Webster, *G.T.P.*, p. 61, pl. 15a; Ἀρχ. Ἐφ. 1953–4, ii, p. 201.
[7] Webster, *Studies Presented to D. M. Robinson*, i, pp. 590 ff.

a poet holding a roll. With his right hand he holds a clear comic mask, with tidy hair and beard, raised eyebrow, wide mouth; later parallels have suggested a slave mask. In the background is an old man's mask, with a good head of hair, wrinkled brows, and a short wedge-beard.

But apart from these two last examples, the evidence in the first half of the fourth century mostly comes from terracotta figurines. These require careful handling. The positive ground for linking them with comedy is the similarity of their faces to the masks on certainly comic monuments like figs. 77 and 78. The negative ground is that it is hard to imagine what other feature in Athenian life these figures, particularly the phallic ones, represent. But even when the case for taking some as representations of the comic stage is accepted, individual cases are always problematic, and such rule of thumb tests as that an open mouth ought to point to a comic mask do not always work. (The problem, of course, becomes more acute after the disappearance of the phallos from comic costume.) There are further problems of origin and date. Terracottas were dispersed widely over the Mediterranean by copies. One may suspect an Attic prototype, even when there is no example from Athens. A terracotta type may have a long history in itself, after it has become divorced from the stage which inspired it. Useful *termini ante quem* are provided for some terracottas by the finding of examples at Olynthos (destroyed in 348 B.C.) or by the reconstruction of the Pnyx at Athens, *c.* 330 B.C.; *termini post quem* are harder to come by.

The terracotta material is rich, and we must select. A good idea of the range of characters is fortunately given by two sets of seven terracottas in New York.[1] All fourteen were found in the same grave in Athens; seven are in red clay, seven in yellow. Other copies of them have been found all over the Greek world, some at Olynthos, some in a rather earlier context (*c.* 370–360 B.C.) at Taman in South Russia. The sets therefore seem to originate fairly early in the second quarter of the century, perhaps a little earlier.

The yellow set (figs. 89–95) has (1) a nurse and baby, (2) a woman with raised arm, who has been said by various scholars to be giggling, weeping, and unveiling, (3) a Herakles with club and lion's skin, and hand to mouth, wearing a short chiton and the phallos, (4) a man with conical cap, and hand to right eye, wearing a short chiton and the phallos, (5) a man carrying a basket, with tidy hair, wrinkled brow,

[1] Richter, *Bull. Metr. Mus.* 9 (1914), pp. 235 f.; best figured in Webster, *Greek Terracottas* (1950), pls. 27–33. The parallels are collected in Webster, *O.M.C.*, pp. 22–28. See also Bieber, *H.T.*[2], pp. 45–47; Thompson, *Hesperia* 21 (1952), p. 143; Webster, *Hesperia* 29 (1960), pp. 266–8.

and a longish, pointed beard, with chiton and phallos, (6) a water carrier with the same mask, and blue himation, (7) a seated slave with crossed legs and hands round knee, and the same mask as (5) and (6). If all these belong to the same play, we might think of a Herakles play, with his food and drink provided for. The red set (figs. 96–102) again has two women and five men: (8) a woman, raising her veil with her right hand, and left hand on hip, (9) an old woman, her right hand in himation over her head, left hand on hip, (10) a man standing with his legs crossed and arms folded, himation over his head, neat hair and beard, forehead very wrinkled, phallic, (11) a very fat man with wreath on forehead, himation round his shoulders, bare body, his left hand holding phallos, wearing slippers, (12) a figure holding a purse, wearing an ἐξωμίς and seated on an altar, perhaps for sanctuary, peaked hair, one eyebrow up, one down, long pointed beard, phallic, (13) another seated man with conical cap, ἐξωμίς, and skin cloak, left hand to mouth, phallic, (14) another seated man with fuzzy hair, very high brows, triangular beard coming to a point, phallic.

In both sets, the figures seem to have a good deal of padding. All four women have chiton and himation. For the men, the short chiton predominates and the phallos is visible except where the stance hides it. Differentiation of costume is more by accessories than anything else. All male figures are bearded.

The third quarter of the century is most interestingly represented by two reliefs of comic choruses from the Agora. On the first (fig. 103),[1] of which we possess four fragments, we find padded chorus-men, not phallic, wearing tights indicated by a fold over the ankles, short chitons, chlamydes, flat hats, and staffs resting on their left shoulders. They are wedge-bearded. To the right is a figure with long chiton, and one fragmentary figure has a rounded beard. These two are presumably actors. The second (fig. 104)[2] is very similar, but its chorus is in two rows. They also have the flat caps, tights, and short chitons, have very similar masks, and are not phallic, but they have no staffs or cloaks.

This chronological survey can be concluded with a reference to the masks on the inscription from Aixone discussed in Chapter I (fig. 25).[3] We argued there that the archon Theophrastus who dates the inscription was the archon of 313–312 B.C. rather than the archon of 340–339 B.C. Webster and Rumpf[4] have preferred the early date, partly because they

---

[1] Webster, *Hesperia* 29 (1960), pp. 263–5, pl. 66, B 7, maintaining his view that it is a chorus of soldiers, but considering a chorus of kings.   [2] Ibid., p. 265, pl. 66, B 33.
[3] See above, p. 49 and n. 3.   [4] Ἀρχ. Ἐφ. 1953–4, ii, p. 193.

find the masks more characteristic of Middle than of New Comedy. But the difference of date is not great, and, even though the masks may be difficult to classify as New Comedy masks, this may only reflect the fact that masks did not become standardized very quickly. From left to right we have (1) a mask with a good head of hair and a shortish square beard; (2) a female mask with a mop of hair and a straight nose; (3) a mask with fuzzy hair and a triangular beard coming to a point (cf. fig. 102); (4) a clean-shaven male mask with longish hair; (5) a girl with short, parted hair.

3. We have already referred to the series of fourth-century south Italian vases, known generally, but perhaps misleadingly, as phlyax vases.[1] The φλύακες are referred to by Athenaeus[2] as the Italian equivalent of the Spartan comic dancers, the δεικηλισταί, but without any indication of the date. They are not known to have taken literary form before Rhinthon of Taras, who lived in the time of the first Ptolemy, presumably early in the third century.[3] For the greater part of the fifth century and the whole of the fourth, in fact, from the cessation of activity of Deinolochus[4] to Rhinthon, there is no tradition about indigenous literary comedy in south Italy and Sicily. What we do have is a vital tradition of vase-painting, represented by about 150 vases of various south Italian fabrics, depicting comic performances of many kinds, the parody of heroic legends, and particularly those of Zeus, Herakles, and Odysseus, and scenes depicting revelry, the trickery and punishment of slaves, and other parts of everyday life, and covering most of the fourth century. They are in fact contemporary with Attic Middle Comedy, and parallels with most of their themes can be found without difficulty in its literary fragments.[5] How far are they under Attic influence? A good deal must certainly be allowed for in the way of a local prehistory,[6] enough, probably, to forbid the incautious use of evidence which has no Attic parallel as evidence for Athens. But there is evidence which points to Athens and which authorizes the student of Attic drama to cast a cautious eye at these lively scenes.

Two such pieces of evidence have already been noted. The Attic polychrome oinochoai in figs. 84 and 87 have been seen to have direct descendants among these vases. Two more vases are linked to Athens by

---

[1] For a full list and bibliography, see A. D. Trendall, *Phlyax Vases*. Bieber, *H.T.*², ch. x, has a good selection of illustrations.

[2] xiv. 621 f–622. See *Dith. Trag. Com.*², pp. 138–9.

[3] For the evidence for Rhinthon, see Kaibel, *Com. Gr. Fragm.*, pp. 183 ff.

[4] See *Dith. Trag. Com.*², pp. 289–90.

[5] Webster, 'South Italian Vases and Attic Drama', *C.Q.* 42 (1948), pp. 19 ff.

[6] See Webster, *G.T.P.*, pp. 98–101.

inscriptions. On a calyx-krater in New York by the Tarporley Painter
c. 400–390 B.C. (fig. 105),[1] an old man in tights and phallos, that is, we
can safely say by now, naked for stage purposes, stands on tiptoe, his arms
above his head. He speaks: κατέδησ' ἄνω τὼ χεῖρε—'he has bound my
hands aloft', in part of an iambic trimeter. He is not visibly bound, so he
is presumably under a spell. To his left, a younger man, also stage-naked,
stands holding a stick and saying νοραρεττεβλο—a stage barbarian, then,
speaking stage-barbarian, like the τοξότης in *Thesmophoriazousae*, and incidentally, perhaps completing the line. To the right, on a low stage, rest
a dead goose and a kid in a basket. Perhaps the old man is alleged to have
stolen them. In any case, also on the stage is an old woman with out-
stretched arm. She says ἐγὼ παρήξω. Whatever that means, she is not
being sympathetic. At the top of the vase is a comic mask in profile, with
straggly dark hair and beard. To the top left stands a youth, genuinely
naked, labelled ΤΡΑΓΟΙΔΟΣ. He is presumably not part of the act, but
a tragic actor waiting for his turn to perform. The dialect is apparently
Attic, and we do not seem to be far from the Aristophanic theatre. On
a mid-fourth-century bell-krater by Asteas, not yet fully published,[2] the
fifth-century lyre-player Phrynis[3] is being dragged away by Pyronides.
Much of Phrynis' activity was in Athens, and Pyronides in the *Demes* of
Eupolis is a nickname for the Athenian general Myronides; it hardly
looks likely that this subject is purely south Italian.

Fig. 105 has already made it clear that south Italian tights and phallos
are not distinguishable from those of Attica, and there is much else in
these vases to remind us of Attic comic representation. In fig. 106,[4] for
example, Hermes and Zeus plan an assault on Alkmene. Gods or no gods,
they wear the short chiton. They are only distinguished by their attributes,
and the face and crown of Zeus have a distinct resemblance to mask (2) in
fig. 78. It is not that full dress cannot be employed when a full-scale
parody of heroic scenes is in question. When comedy plays the joke of
reversal, and Kassandra pursues Ajax to sanctuary at the foot of Athene's
statue[5] (fig. 107), the costumes are tragic, though the masks are not.
Comparisons of masks on these vases with Attic vases and terracottas
have been made with some plausibility by Webster and Trendall.[6] The

---

[1] Trendall, op. cit., no. 78; the most useful discussion is by Beazley, *A.J.A.* 56 (1952),
pp. 193–5, pl. 32.
[2] Trendall, op. cit., no. 55.
[3] See *Dith. Trag. Com.²*, p. 43.
[4] Trendall, op. cit., no. 59 (by Asteas, 350–340 B.C.).
[5] Trendall, op. cit., no. 80 (by Asteas, 350–340 B.C.).
[6] Compare their Indexes of Masks; Trendall, op. cit., p. 65; Webster, *O.M.C.*, pp. 66–68.
For the key to their nomenclature, see Webster, ibid., pp. 7–12.

difficulty here is that a representation of a mask by itself or on a terracotta is necessarily static, closer to a real mask; for the south Italian
vase-painter, it is his scene which is important, and he will make the
expression of the mask conform to the needs of the comic moment.[1] Allowing for this, the influence of Attic costumes and masks on south Italy
seems secure.

4. We can now proceed to a survey of the costume of Old and Middle
Comedy, and begin with the masks.

It is clear from the literary evidence that Old Comedy enjoyed complete freedom in the production of masks to suit its characters. Pollux[2]
draws a sharp distinction between Old and New Comedy in this respect:
τὰ δὲ κωμικὰ πρόσωπα τὰ μὲν τῆς παλαιᾶς κωμῳδίας ὡς τὸ πολὺ τοῖς προσώ-
ποις ὧν ἐκωμῴδουν ἀπεικάζετο ἢ ἐπὶ τὸ γελοιότερον ἐσχημάτιστο, τὰ δὲ
τῆς νέας κτλ. It is clear also from the texts that the masks of living persons
burlesqued by the poet might be recognizable portraits, though no doubt
with some degree of caricature. The point is proved by the exception
when in Knights[3] the poet says that none of the mask-makers dared
to produce a portrait of Kleon:

> καὶ μὴ δέδιθ᾽· οὐ γάρ ἐστιν ἐξῃκασμένος·
> ὑπὸ τοῦ δέους γὰρ αὐτὸν οὐδεὶς ἤθελεν
> τῶν σκευοποιῶν εἰκάσαι. πάντως γε μὴν
> γνωσθήσεται· τὸ γὰρ θέατρον δεξιόν.

But it may be assumed that, if the two slaves were meant for Nikias
and Demosthenes,[4] they would have been recognizable by their masks.
In Cratinus (fr. 71) Pericles was similarly represented with his abnormal
head, ὁ σχινοκέφαλος Ζεὺς ὁδὶ προσέρχεται. That the mask of Socrates in
Clouds was likewise a portrait is confirmed rather than disproved by the
story,[5] true or false, that Socrates himself stood up in the theatre so that
everyone (and particularly the many strangers present) might see who
was meant. The mask of Agathon in Thesmophoriazousae[6] was probably
an effeminate-looking caricature. Other living characters introduced by
Aristophanes were Lamachus,[7] Meton, Kinesias, and Euripides; and his

---

[1] This was pointed out by Wüst in R.E. xx. 1, col. 302, s.v. Φλύακες.

[2] iv. 143.

[3] ll. 230 ff. (see Neil's note ad loc.). What truth there may be in the scholiast's statement
that Aristophanes played the part himself, it is impossible to say.

[4] This is doubted by Dover, C.R., N.S. 9 (1959), pp. 196–9. On portrait-masks in Aristophanes, see now Dover in ΚΩΜΩΙΔΟΤΡΑΓΗΜΑΤΑ (Studia Aristophanea . . . W. J. W. Kostr
in honorem, 1967), pp. 16–28.

[5] Aelian, Var. H. ii. 13.　　　　　　　　　　　　　　　　　[6] See ll. 191–2.

[7] Whether Lamachus' mask included some traditional features of the Boastful Soldier,
who seems to belong to all periods of comedy, there is no evidence to show. His bombastic
crests are certainly mentioned. See Webster, G.T.P, p. 67.

contemporary Eupolis introduced Pericles, Nikias, Alcibiades, and Kallias. All of these could have been made immediately recognizable by
their masks. The use of portrait-masks probably went out of fashion by
the end of the fifth century, and Platonios[1] makes it characteristic of the
Middle and New Comedy that they deliberately avoided such resemblances and made use of masks with features so exaggerated that they
could not possibly be like any real human being. (He ascribes the change
to the fear lest any mask should even by accident resemble some Macedonian ruler.)

Besides these portrait masks, full play for invention was no doubt
offered for special masks, like the Βασιλέως 'Οφθαλμός in *Acharnians*, consisting, according to the usual interpretation, of a huge eye and a Persian
beard,[2] and of the Servant of the Hoopoe in *Birds*.[3] Pollux, in giving his
list of special masks,[4] says that they might be comic as well as tragic.
Some of them certainly sound adapted to the special choruses of comedy
and to its abstract characters, like Μέθη, whom we know to have been
a character in the *Pytine* of Cratinus.[5] There were many animal choruses
in the comedies, and these doubtless wore appropriate masks, like their
sixth-century forerunners;[6] and when the choruses were not strictly
animal, but at the same time not human, as in Aristophanes' *Clouds*,
grotesque masks could be invented to suit the poet's fancy. Thus the
Clouds were like women, only half-disguised (ll. 340 ff.) :

ΣΤ.   λέξον δή μοι, τί παθοῦσαι,
    εἴπερ νεφέλαι γ' εἰσὶν ἀληθῶς, θνηταῖς εἴξασι γυναιξίν;
    οὐ γὰρ ἐκεῖναί γ' εἰσὶ τοιαῦται. ΣΩ. φέρε ποῖαι γάρ τινές εἰσιν;
ΣΤ. οὐκ οἶδα σαφῶς· εἴξασιν γοῦν ἐρίοισιν πεπταμένοισιν,
    κοὐχὶ γυναιξὶν μὰ Δί' οὐδ' ὁτιοῦν· αὗται δὲ ῥῖνας ἔχουσιν.

Choruses were often composed of subspecies of their title, and in plays
like Aristophanes' *Birds* or Eupolis' Πόλεις, where the text describes
members of the chorus individually, they were doubtless distinguished
by differences of accessories, even if not by different masks.

Yet, portrait-masks and special masks aside, there would remain in
Old and Middle Comedy a considerable residue of characters who needed
to be distinguished in more general terms as 'old man', 'slave', 'young

---

[1] περὶ διαφορᾶς κωμῳδιῶν (Kaibel, p. 5). He states expressly that the characters of Menander, very human though we feel them to be, wore these hideously exaggerated masks.
[2] *Ach.* 90 ff. (For details, see Starkie's note ad loc., and for a different interpretation of the
passage, see Damste, *Mnemosyne* 43 (1915), pp. 433–41. See also Morrison, *C.Q.* 41 (1947),
p. 126.)   [3] ll. 60 ff.   [4] See above, p. 195.
[5] On these special masks, see Webster, *G.T.P.*, pp. 57–59.
[6] See *Dith. Trag. Com.*², pp. 152–4, pls. 7–9.

woman', and so on. It is here that a tendency to standardization would set in, of the type which later dominated New Comedy. This tendency will have grown and worked forwards, and will have been more marked in second-rate and derivative work. It is not sound method to work as Robert did,[1] and as Webster did in his first article on this subject,[2] and take Pollux' catalogue,[3] explicitly referring to New Comedy, as a basis for classifying early material. It inevitably leads to casting Old Comedy, and then visualizing it, in terms of Hellenistic masks. Webster's later method is much sounder, to take the Old and Middle Comedy archaeological evidence by itself and classify it by the resemblances which can undoubtedly be traced between different representations.[4] His latest list[5] distinguishes forty-three masks (Pollux has forty-four for New Comedy), but it may be doubted whether even this does justice to the resourcefulness of the mask-makers and the freedom which they allowed themselves,[6] and it must be remembered that the part of the evidence attributable to Old Comedy is still very small. Changing fashion, as beardlessness, for example, became more respectable, will have played its part.

5. When we turn to costume, the main question is the prevalence of the wearing of a leather phallos attached to the tights of characters representing males. Many incautious statements have implied that it was always worn and always visible, a view attacked with some force, but some extravagance, by Prof. Beare.[7] At the centre of the literary evidence stand the lines of Aristophanes' *Clouds* (ll. 537–9), in which he says of his comedy

ὡς δὲ σώφρων ἐστὶ φύσει σκέψασθ'· ἥτις πρῶτα μὲν
οὐδὲν ἦλθε ῥαψαμένη σκύτινον καθειμένον
ἐρυθρὸν ἐξ ἄκρου παχύ, τοῖς παιδίοις ἵν' ᾖ γέλως,

and the scholiast on it, εἰσῄεσαν γὰρ οἱ κωμικοὶ διεζωσμένοι δερμάτινα αἰδοῖα γελοίου χάριν. This may be only an inference, but it is certainly a fair inference. In the words of the author of this book, the lines are

---

[1] *Die Masken der neueren attischen Komödie*, especially pp. 63 ff., 85 ff., 108 ff.
[2] *Rylands Bulletin* 32 (1949), pp. 122 ff. [3] iv. 143–54 (see below, pp. 223 ff.).
[4] *G.T.P.*, pp. 55–73; *O.M.C.*, pp. 66–68. [5] *O.M.C.*, pp. 7–12.
[6] His mask B, for example, could be considerably subdivided.
[7] Modern discussion starts with Körte, *Jahrb. Arch.* 8 (1893), pp. 69 ff., and the earliest doubts were those of Thiele, *Neue Jahrb. f. d. klass. Alt.* 9 (1902), pp. 420–2. The Beare–Webster argument on the point will be found in *C.Q.*, n.s. 4 (1954), pp. 64–75, 5 (1955), pp. 94–95, 7 (1957), pp. 184–5, 9 (1959), pp. 126–7. Beare was particularly cavalier with the archaeological evidence, ending by implying that Middle Comedy might have been less decently dressed than Old Comedy. See also Dover, *Lustrum* 2 (1957), pp. 56–57; id. *Maia*, n.s. 15 (1963), pp. 12–13.

'unintelligible unless the practice were at least common, and it is not likely to have been common unless it were quite primitive and at one time essential'.[1] But it also seems to follow that the actors in *Clouds* do not wear a visible phallos. The attempt made by Körte and supported by Webster to throw the emphasis on καθειμένον, with an implied contrast with a tucked-up phallos, comparing the two positions of the phallos in fig. 78, is not noticeably successful. There is no evidence to show that one position was regarded as more decent than the other. Attempts to show that a visible phallos was worn even in *Clouds* by the use of ll. 653 f. and 734 are not pressed, even by Webster.

There are other passages in Old Comedy[2] which have been thought to require a visible phallos, some to be a direct indication of it with a deictic pronoun. Beare rejects them all, as needing no more than gesture. Some of the cases are certainly not strong,[3] others at least indecisive,[4] but, to take the scenes with Kinesias and the Spartan herald in *Lysistrata*[5] and between Mnesilochus, Kleisthenes, and the First Woman in *Thesmophoriazousae*[6] as a minimum, we find it hard to agree with Beare that they lend no support to the phallic theory. Beare points to parallel remarks about the female αἰδοῖον as a *reductio ad absurdum*. Some of these certainly expose the weakness of some of the male evidence: some of them seem to us to be explained by the use of women in walking-on parts, which we may follow Wilamowitz in believing in,[7] though Beare and Pickard-Cambridge[8] did not.

Beare is puzzled by the cases of Mnesilochus in *Thesmophoriazousae*, inquiring whether he takes his phallos off, and Praxagora and her women in the *Ecclesiazousae*, inquiring whether they put some on. These questions are only valid against a view that a man's phallos was visible all the time. Clearly in both cases the relevant parts are covered by cloaks.

As we have already said, the basic comic costume of tights plus phallos represents stage nudity. The most common dress we have seen on the monuments is a short chiton, which leaves the phallos visible. But the exigencies of the performance may require other clothing which will cover it. One common case will be if a man dresses as a woman. Mnesilochus[9] puts on a saffron ἱμάτιον, στρόφιον, κεκρύφαλος, μίτρα,

---

[1] *Dith. Trag. Com.²*, p. 144, n. 1.

[2] Listed and discussed by Beare, *C.Q.*, N.S. 4 (1954), pp. 70–72.

[3] *Ach.* 592, *Clouds* 653, 734, *Peace* 1349, *Thesm.* 59.

[4] *Ach.* 157 f., 1216, *Wasps* 1342 ff., *Peace* 141, *Thesm.* 141 ff., 215–16, 1114.

[5] *Lysistr.* 845–957, and particularly 863, 928, 937; 980–1013 (the cloak is an ineffective disguise, and may fall aside at 989).

[6] *Thesm.* 643–8.   [7] See above, p. 153, n. 1.

[8] In Haigh, *Att. Th.³*, p. 259.   [9] *Thesm.* 253–62.

ἔγκυκλον, and shoes. One may also suspect that parodies of heroes, tragic or non-tragic, will have often involved the use of a relatively long tragic robe. Herakles has no opportunity to be phallic in fig. 77, nor Ajax in fig. 107. And if, experimentally, as apparently Aristophanes in *Clouds*, the poet wished to abandon the phallos, the cast could be dressed in longer chitons without difficulty.

The mere absence of the phallos could make a point about the actor's effeminacy. Agathon in *Thesmophoriazousae* does not have it,[1] that is, he is like the character in fig. 83.

The evidence of the monuments we have considered is clear. Figs. 25 and 78 are certainly connected with comedy; the rest of the vases and terracottas are connected to them by the masks. Tights and phallos and the short chiton are dominant, and we are justified in speaking of them as the normal costume of Old and Middle Comedy. Variations and accessories were doubtless frequent.

It is clear both from the fragments and the monuments that many themes characteristic of New Comedy were already starting well within the period of Middle Comedy. It is not unlikely that, parallel to this development and the growing standardization of masks, there was also a trend to greater decency of comic costume. Webster has produced some evidence to point this way, but it is still very scanty.[2]

Webster has argued[3] that the chorus did not wear the phallos. His evidence for this comes from fig. 87, who does not have to be a chorus-man, and figs. 103 and 104, who come late in Middle Comedy. The case does not seem to be made out. Is the dancing figure in fig. 77 really an actor and not a chorus-man?

The question of padding remains for consideration. As with the phallos, the problem of origins confuses our approach. Actors are said to be phallic because a chorus-leader was originally phallic;[4] there is some evidence for padded dancers as part of the origins of comedy,[5] but does it follow that all comic actors were padded? In the texts, the fatness of some characters is certainly mentioned,[6] but it is hard to see how one would

---

[1] *Thesm.* 141 ff. τίς δ' αὐτός, ὦ παῖ; πότερον ὡς ἀνὴρ τρέφει; καὶ ποῦ πέος;

[2] *Hesperia* 29 (1960), pp. 269f. He lays some emphasis on the terracotta, *Olynthus* XIV, no. 388 (before 348 B.C.), but we do not know why the young man is wearing a long cloak, or whether he wears it all the time. The slave statuettes he discusses are interesting, but not conclusive.   [3] Ibid., p. 262.

[4] See, for example, *Dith. Trag. Com.*[2], p. 171. There is still only Corinthian evidence (ibid., pl. X c) for this 'forerunner'.   [5] Ibid., pp. 169–71.

[6] *Clouds* 1237–8, *Frogs* 663f., where Dionysus, hit on the belly, might be hurt without his padding, for which cf. 200 and schol.; Antiphanes, fr. 19 K; Anaxandrides, fr. 69 K. See Beare, *C.Q.*, N.S. 4 (1954), pp. 68–69.

distinguish between the fat and the not-so-fat, if all were padded. However, it does seem to be the case that most representations of comic actors are padded, though not by any means all; there is, for example, no trace of padding in fig. 76 or 84. Perhaps the joke could be played both ways. Commentators have been less assiduous in collecting jokes about thinness than about fatness, but *Plutus* 558 ff.

Πενία ... οὐ γιγνώσκων ὅτι τοῦ Πλούτου παρέχω βελτίονας ἄνδρας
καὶ τὴν γνωμὴν καὶ τὴν ἰδέαν. παρὰ τῷ μὲν γὰρ ποδαγρῶντες
καὶ γαστρώδεις καὶ παχύκνημοι καὶ πίονές εἰσιν ἀσελγῶς,
παρ' ἐμοὶ δ' ἰσχνοὶ καὶ σφηκώδεις καὶ τοῖς ἐχθροῖς ἀνιαροί

indicates that, as with the phallos, there were points to be made by the absence of padding as well as by its presence.

6. We can now turn to New Comedy and the guidance of Pollux' lists. It will be recalled that there are really two lists, the list of masks (iv. 143–54), which is explicitly about New Comedy, and a description of costumes, in the present tense. We begin with the list of masks.[1] It may not be complete or completely accurate, and the artistic representations with which we illustrate it may owe something to artist's licence, but a discussion of it should give a fairly adequate idea of the resources of New Comedy.

Old Men

(1) The πρῶτος πάππος, the oldest; his head is close-shaved, but with a full beard; his eyebrows indicate gentleness (ἡμερώτατος τὰς ὀφρῦς); he has thin cheeks, a downcast expression, a pale complexion, and a cheerful forehead (τὸ μέτωπον ὑπόφαιδρος—i.e. he does not frown).

(2) The δεύτερος πάππος is thinner, with a more intense and gloomy look, a rather pale complexion, a full beard, red hair, and bruised ears.

(3) The ἡγεμὼν πρεσβύτης has his hair raised in a στεφάνη—a kind of roll or 'wreath' of hair, running round his head, a hooked nose, a flat face, and the right eyebrow raised.[2]

(4) The πρεσβύτης μακροπώγων ἢ ἐπισείων has a στεφάνη and a long beard; his eyebrows are not raised, and he looks lethargic (νωθρός).

(5) The Ἑρμώνιος is growing bald (ἀναφαλαντίας), has a long beard, raised eyebrows, and a piercing look (τὸ βλέμμα δριμύς). According to the

---

[1] The fundamental discussion is that of Robert, *Die Masken der neueren attischen Komödie.* Other important discussions are by Bieber, *R.E.* s.v. Maske; Simon, *Comicae Tabellae* (1938), particularly for the Pompeian wall-paintings we have passed over here; Webster, *G.T.P.*, pp. 73–92; *Monuments illustrating New Comedy*, pp. 5–24.

[2] For the origins of the raised eyebrows of Old Men nos. 3 and 7, see Rumpf, *A.J.A.* 55 (1951), p. 8.

Etymologicum Magnum,[1] the name is derived from Hermon, apparently a mask-maker. But a Hermon is mentioned by Pollux[2] and by schol. on Aristophanes, *Clouds* 542[3] as a comic actor. Perhaps, then, the type goes back to the fifth century.

(6) The σφηνοπώγων is growing bald, has a wedge-shaped beard, raised eyebrows, and a rather obstinate expression (ὑποδύστροπος).

(7) The Λυκομήδειος has curly hair, a long beard, one eyebrow raised, and denotes πολυπραγμοσύνη.

(8) The πορνόβοσκος is like the Λυκομήδειος, but his lips have a slight grin, his brows are contracted, and he is wholly or partly bald.[4]

(9) The δεύτερος Ἑρμώνιος has a shaven head and a pointed beard.

The following figures illustrate this group. If we follow Webster,[5] despite Pollux' explicit attribution of his list to New Comedy, masks (1), (2), (5), and (6) are really Middle Comedy masks which do not continue in New Comedy.[6] Masks (3), (4), (7), and (8), if the identifications are right, predominate.

Fig. 108. Mask from Chatby Cemetery, Alexandria, late fourth century B.C.[7] The ἡγεμὼν πρεσβύτης.

Fig. 109. The right-hand mask on the Menander relief in the Lateran Museum, first century B.C., and perhaps reflecting earlier work.[8] The πρεσβύτης μακροπώγων.

Fig. 110. Relief in Naples, first/second century A.D.[9] The ἡγεμὼν πρεσβύτης restrains the πρεσβύτης μακροπώγων.

Fig. 111. Mask from the Agora, Athens, third century B.C.[10] Perhaps the Λυκομήδειος, since he has the curly hair and long beard, but he does not have the single raised eyebrow.

Fig. 112. Statuette from Myrina in the Louvre, Hellenistic.[11] The πορνόβοσκος.

Young Men

(1) The πάγχρηστος νεανίσκος, 'the Perfect Young Man', is reddish, has the appearance of good training (γυμναστικός), a rather sunburnt

---

[1] p. 376. 48.   [2] iv. 88 (see above, p. 170).

[3] Cf. Argt. Ar. *Peace* τὸ δὲ δρᾶμα ὑπεκρίνατο Ἀπολλόδωρος· ἐνίκα Ἕρμων ὁ ὑποκρίτης—Rose's emendation for ἠνίκα ἑρμῆν λοιοκρότης. See above, p. 125.

[4] Robert compares the description of the *leno* in Plautus, *Rudens* 317–18: 'recaluom ad Silanum senem, statutum, ventriosum, tortis superciliis, contracta fronte, fraudulentum'.

[5] *G.T.P.*, p. 75; *M.I.N.C.*, p. 15.

[6] He finds masks (1) and (2) in the second and third masks in fig. 78; mask (5) in fig. 92 and mask (6) in fig. 103.   [7] Simon, p. 193, n. 45.

[8] Studniczka, *Neue Jahrb.* 21 (1918), p. 25; Robert, op. cit., pp. 77 ff.; Webster, *G.T.P.*, pp. 75 ff.; Bieber, *Festschrift Rumpf*, pp. 14 ff. (with another version in Princeton = *H.T.*[2], fig. 316, and dating the original to the 3rd cent. B.C.).

[9] Robert, op. cit., pp. 61 ff.; cf. *Theatre of D.*, 219.

[10] Webster, *Hesperia* 29 (1960), p. 276, pl. 68, C 4.   [11] Simon, p. 192, n. 4.

complexion, light hair with a στεφάνη, a few wrinkles on the forehead, eyebrows raised.[1]

(2) The μέλας νεανίσκος is younger, more like a cultured youth than an athlete, with his eyebrows lowered.

(3) The οὖλος νεανίσκος is still younger,[2] and ruddy-complexioned, with curly hair, raised eyebrows, and one wrinkle across his forehead.[3]

(4) The ἁπαλὸς νεανίσκος is the youngest of all, with hair like the πάγχρηστος, white-complexioned, as if reared in the shade (σκιατροφίας), denoting delicacy.

(5) The ἄγροικος (the Rustic) has a dark complexion, broad lips, a snub nose, and his hair arranged in a στεφάνη.

(6) The ἐπίσειστος is a soldier and a braggart, has a dark skin and hair, and is floppy-haired.

(7) The δεύτερος ἐπίσειστος is also floppy-haired, but is more delicate and has fair hair.

(8) The κόλαξ and (9) the παράσιτος, the Flatterer and the Parasite, are of dark complexion with hooked noses; they have frequented the palaestra and are of good physique. The Flatterer has his eyebrows raised more mischievously; the Parasite has his ears more battered and is more cheerful.[4] Simon takes Gnatho in Menander's Κόλαξ and Gelasimus in Plautus' *Stichus* as examples of the two types.[5] A fragment of Alexis (116 K) distinguishes between the μέλανες παράσιτοι and the 'swell' parasites of whom the speaker says:

θάτερον ζητῶ γένος
σεμνοπαράσιτον †ἐκ μέσου† καλούμενον,
σατράπας παρασίτους καὶ στρατηγοὺς ἐπιφανεῖς,
ὑποκρινόμενον εὖ τοῖς βίοις, ὀφρῦς ἔχον
χιλιοταλάντους ἀνακυλῖόν τ' οὐσίας.

(10) The εἰκονικός, apparently another parasite, has scattered grey hairs and his beard shaved off; he is richly clad and foreign.

(11) The Σικελικός is a third type of parasite—probably derived from

---

[1] Robert and Simon compare Plesidippus in Plautus, *Rudens* 314: 'adulescentem . . . vidistis ire strenua facie, rubicundum, fortem?'

[2] μᾶλλον νέος seems a better-attested reading than καλὸς καὶ νέος.

[3] Robert compares Philocrates in Plautus, *Captivi* 647–8: 'macilento ore, naso acuto, corpore albo, oculis nigris, | subrufus aliquantum, crispus, cincinnatus.'

[4] Elsewhere in Pollux (iv. 120) he is said to carry a στλεγγίς and a λήκυθος, his patron's toilet accessories.

[5] These characters are found in Epicharmus and in Old Comedy, but whether they wore the same masks as are mentioned by Pollux there is no evidence to show. See Giese, *De parasiti persona capita selecta* (Diss. Kiel, 1908), and Simon, pp. 47–48, 53.

Sicilian farces or even from Epicharmus, who has a striking picture of a parasite.[1]

The problem of distinguishing between these young men on the monuments is complex, and well discussed by Webster,[2] though it may be doubted whether all examples will ever be neatly classifiable. As far as monuments already illustrated are concerned, the left-hand mask on the Menander relief (fig. 109) seems most likely to be the μέλας νεανίσκος and the young man on fig. 110 the δεύτερος ἐπίσειστος. We illustrate a further selection:

Fig. 113. Statuette in Athens, from Myrina,[3] Hellenistic. Probably a πάγχρηστος.
Fig. 114. Statuette in Lyons,[4] Hellenistic. Wears a wreath, and probably played a tympanum. The ἁπαλός?
Fig. 115. Mask in Munich, from Amisos,[5] second century B.C. The ἁπαλός?
Fig. 116. Statuette in Mykonos, from Delos,[6] late Hellenistic. The ἐπίσειστος.
Fig. 117. Statuette in Athens, from Myrina,[7] Hellenistic. The ἐπίσειστος.
Fig. 118. Head from the Agora, Athens,[8] third–second century B.C. The κόλαξ.
Fig. 119. Statuette in Athens, from Myrina,[9] Hellenistic. The παράσιτος.
Fig. 120. Statuette in Berlin from Capua,[10] second century B.C. The Σικελικός?

Slaves

(1) The θεράπων πάππος is a freedman and is the only grey-haired servant.[11]

(2) The ἡγεμὼν θεράπων has a roll of red hair (σπεῖραν τριχῶν πυρρῶν) on his forehead, his eyebrows raised, and his brow contracted, being among slaves what the πρεσβύτης ἡγεμών is among free men.[12]

---

[1] Fr. 35 (Kaibel); *Dith. Trag. Com.*², pp. 273–4. Simon, pp. 54 f. finds a reference to the type in Diphilus, fr. 119 (K) παχὺς ὠνθυλευμένος στέατι Σικελικῷ, but Sicilian luxury was proverbial, quite apart from parasites; cf. 'Suidas' s.v. Σικελικὴ τράπεζα; Athen. xii. 518 c, 527 c–d.   [2] *M.I.N.C.*, pp. 17–21.
[3] Robert, p. 80, fig. 98; Simon, p. 184, n. 92 thinks him an εἰκονικός.
[4] Robert, p. 66, fig. 87; Simon, p. 183, n. 58. This is the Froehner replica signed *Sodamou*, often confused with the specimen Berlin 7969 (Bieber, *H.T.*², fig. 341). We owe our knowledge of its present home to Prof. Webster.
[5] Simon, p. 184, n. 80a.
[6] *Délos* xxiii, no. 1216. This and the next are still classed as tragic by Bieber, *H.T.*², p. 85, despite Simon, p. 49. Cf. Rumpf, *Mimus und Logos*, p. 164.
[7] Simon, p. 182, n. 26 c.
[8] Webster. *Hesperia* 29 (1960), p. 277, C 7 and pl. 68.
[9] Simon, p. 44, 181 n. 1.   [10] Simon, pp. 54, 183, n. 49.
[11] The fact that almost all the slave-masks in Pollux' list are red-haired must not be taken to mean that no free man's mask was ever red-haired: Beare, *C.Q.* 43 (1949), pp. 30 f., makes it clear that in Roman comedy, and therefore probably in the Greek originals, a slave might sometimes appear in the costume of a free man and be mistaken for one.
[12] Robert compares Leonidas in Plautus, *Asinaria* 400–1: 'macilentis malis, rufulus aliquantum, ventriosus, | truculentis oculis, commoda statura, tristi fronte.'

(3) The κάτω τριχίας is red-haired but going bald, with eyebrows raised.

(4) The οὖλος θεράπων has red curly hair, a red complexion, and a squint, and is going bald.

(5) The μαίσων θεράπων[1] is bald with a red complexion.

(6) The θεράπων τέττιξ is bald and dark, with two or three black curls on head and chin, and a squint.

(7) The θεράπων ἐπίσειστος ἡγεμών is like the ἡγεμὼν θεράπων, but has floppy hair.

This list gives us less than we need to know to sort out the monuments because of its lack of information about beards.[2] We figure a selection with current identifications.

Fig. 121. Figurine in Athens, from Myrina,[3] second century B.C. The πάππος.
Fig. 122. Figurine of slave with child in Bonn, from Boeotia,[4] third century B.C. The ἡγεμών.
Fig. 123. Figurine in Paris, from Myrina,[5] first century B.C. The κάτω τριχίας.
Fig. 124. Figurine in Berlin, from Vulci,[6] late second century B.C. The οὖλος.
Fig. 125. Figurine in Athens, from Myrina,[7] second century B.C. The μαίσων.
Fig. 126. Marble mask from frieze in Berlin,[8] from Pergamon, second century B.C. The τέττιξ.
Fig. 127. Mask in London, from Melos,[9] early Hellenistic. The ἡγεμὼν ἐπίσειστος.

Old Women

(1) The ἰσχνὸν ἢ λυκαίνιον ('wolfish'), withered and long-faced, with many fine wrinkles, a pale-yellowish complexion, and a squint.[10]

(2) The γραῦς παχεῖα, who has fat cheeks, wrinkles, and a narrow band round her hair.

(3) The οἰκουρὸν γρᾴδιον ἢ οἰκετικὸν ἢ ὀξύ, the housekeeper, who has about two teeth in each jaw, and a snub nose.

[1] For the early and possibly Dorian origins of this mask, see *Dith. Trag. Com.*[2], pp. 181–2, and the passage of Athenaeus quoted above, p. 178, n. 6.
[2] A thorough discussion by Webster, *M.I.N.C.*, pp. 5–14.
[3] Robert, fig. 90; Simon, p. 190, n. 51.
[4] Cf. the scene in Menander, *Epitrepontes*, where the slave carries an exposed infant.
[5] Robert, fig. 34; Simon, p. 189, n. 29.
[6] Robert, fig. 20; Simon, p. 189, n. 31. Bieber thinks him a θεράπων πάππος.
[7] Robert, fig. 27; Simon, p. 188, n. 5.
[8] Robert, fig. 28; Simon, p. 188, n. 9. The τέττιξ illustrated in the first edition, fig. 92 (Robert, fig. 29), is a forgery (Simon, p. 189, n. 15), though it still appears in Bieber, *H.T.*[2], fig. 381.
[9] Walters, *B.M. Terracottas*, C 81.
[10] For her supposed Dorian origins see *Dith. Trag. Com.*[2], pp. 163 ff. Doubtless figures from real life influenced her development from time to time.

We illustrate:

Fig. 128. Mask in Berlin,[1] second century B.C. The λυκαίνιον?
Fig. 129. Mask in Bonn,[2] third century B.C. The παχεῖα?
Fig. 130. Mask in Berlin, from Ephesus,[3] early Hellenistic. The οἰκουρόν?

Young Women

(1) The λεκτική ('chatterbox') has hair all round her head (περίκομος) smoothed back on top (παρεψησμέναι αἱ τρίχες), straight eyebrows, and a white skin.

(2) The οὔλη is like the λεκτική, but has curly hair.

(3) The κόρη has hair brushed back, with a parting, straight dark eyebrows, and a sallow complexion.

(4) The ψευδοκόρη (the wronged girl)[4] is paler and has her hair bound round her head, and 'is like a newly wedded bride'. Her hair is presumably parted, since

(5) the ἑτέρα ψευδοκόρη is distinguished from her only by not having her hair parted.

(6) The σπαρτοπόλιος λεκτική, though classed here, is presumably not very young. The chatterbox with scattered grey hair, she denotes a retired ἑταίρα.

(7) The παλλακή (concubine) is like the last, but has hair all round her head.

(8) The τέλειον ἑταιρικόν is redder than the ψευδοκόρη and has curls about her ears.

(9) The ἑταιρίδιον ὡραῖον is unadorned and has her hair bound with a ribbon.

(10) The διάχρυσος ἑταίρα has much gold ornament about her hair.

(11) The διάμιτρος ἑταίρα has her hair bound with a multicoloured band (μίτρα).

(12) The λαμπάδιον is distinguished by a coiffure rising upwards to a point.

(13) The ἄβρα περίκουρος is a little slave girl with her hair cut short, and wears only a white chiton with a girdle.

(14) The παράψηστον θεραπαινίδιον has her hair brushed back with a

---

[1] Robert, p. 46, fig. 82; Simon, p. 199, n. 6, whom we follow. We find it quite impossible to follow Webster, *G.T.P.*, p. 85, who makes the nose the decisive feature, and has fig. 129 as the λυκαίνιον and this as the παχεῖα. Cf. Luschey, *Ganymed*, p. 77.

[2] Luschey, loc. cit.

[3] Robert, p. 46, fig. 83. Simon, pp. 130, 199, n. 9b, regards this as caricature, not comedy, and Webster, *M.I.N.C.*, p. 90, ZT10, is inclined to agree, but thinks that the stylization of brows and mouth derives from dramatic masks.

[4] Simon, p. 101, has a valuable discussion of this word.

parting. She has an upturned nose and is the servant of ἑταῖραι; she wears a scarlet chiton with a girdle.

We illustrate:

Fig. 131. Statuette in Berlin, from Capua, Hellenistic. The λεκτική?

Fig. 132. Megarian bowl from the Pnyx, Athens,[1] 225–200 B.C. The κόρη?

Fig. 133. Statuette of Muse carrying mask in London, from Tanagra (?),[2] early Hellenistic. The ψευδοκόρη?

Fig. 134. Mask in Berlin, from Corneto,[3] early Hellenistic. The παλλακή?

Fig. 135. Marble mask in Naples,[4] first century A.D. The ἑταιρίδιον ὡραῖον?

Fig. 136. Marble bust in Tivoli,[5] second century A.D. The διάχρυσος ἑταίρα?

Fig. 137. Terracotta mask on disc in Berlin, from Selymbria,[6] late Hellenistic. The διάμιτρος ἑταίρα?

Fig. 138. Terracotta mask in Oxford from Smyrna,[7] third–second century B.C. The λαμπάδιον.

Fig. 139. Marble mask in Naples from Pompeii,[8] first century A.D. The ἄβρα περίκουρος?

Not many of these identifications should be considered certain. Pollux' patience is giving out towards the end of his list, and his descriptions become very sketchy.

However, the list as a whole gives valuable help in classification. In illustrating it, we have perhaps been too incautious in using material with a wide range of date. There were developments and changes, both in the Hellenistic and Roman periods,[9] but the changes are a good deal less important than the similarities, and the imprint given to theatrical design in the age of Menander had an extremely long life. Less important still is the range of origins of our monuments, since it is quite clear that the Hellenistic period moved rapidly to uniformity of stage practice under the influence of the Artists of Dionysus.[10]

These masks did not come into being all at once. There was no clear break at the beginning of New Comedy, and some of them have origins in Middle Comedy and earlier. For these connexions the reader may be

[1] *Hesperia*, Suppl. X (1956), p. 96, pl. 39, no. 24. The other mask is Old Man no. 3.

[2] Walters, *B.M. Terracottas*, C 309.

[3] Robert, fig. 99. Bieber thinks her the σπαρτοπόλιος λεκτική; Simon, p. 197, n. 51.

[4] Simon, pp. 113, n. 67, 121, 123.

[5] The interpretation is the standard one since Bieber; cf. Simon, p. 197, n. 52. But Webster, *M.I.N.C.*, pp. 24, 35, can find no Hellenistic history for her, and inclines to the view that she is an imperial version of the διάμιτρος.

[6] Simon, p. 197, n. 66. She seems to be a pair with a youth who looks like young man no. 3 (Bieber, *H.T.*[2], fig. 340). They appeared in the first edition of this book (fig. 55) as tragic.

[7] She does have the peaked coiffure, when seen in profile.

[8] Robert, fig. 63; Simon, p. 197, n. 41.

[9] See the introduction to Webster, *M.I.N.C.*   [10] See Chapter VII.

directed to the work of Professor Webster,[1] who has been surveying the whole field with rewarding patience. The field has its temptations and uncertainties. We have been more sparing than those who work most closely with the material with suggestions as to how the archaeological remains and the descriptions of Pollux may be used to cast the characters of New Comedy and of Plautus and Terence. Nor do we think the reader will be greatly assisted if we investigate the supposed relevance to the masks[2] of the pseudo-Aristotelian *Physiognomonika*—a conflation of two treatises, perhaps of the third century B.C., based on the study of the men and women of real life, without any special reference to the stock characters of the stage, such as may perhaps sometimes be detected in Theophrastus. It is with more regret that we forbear to follow up Webster's ingenious suggestion[3] that the members of different households in a play were distinguished by their different styles of hairdressing— all those of one household, for example, whether father, son, or slave, having curly hair, while all those of the other household agreed in some other style of hair-control—but it is difficult to see how the suggestion is capable of proof. If the reader has gained some idea of the different kinds of mask available and used in New Comedy, our purposes will have been amply served.

7. In his discussion of costume,[4] not specifically tied to New Comedy, Pollux says that the comic dress is the ἐξωμίς, a plain white chiton with no seam on the left side, not fulled (ἄγναπτος), whatever the precise significance of that may be. It is to be seen on the monuments in all periods, though it tends to be cut longer in the period of New Comedy. Old men wear a himation, and carry a crooked staff; younger men wear a scarlet garment (φοινικίς) or a purple himation; rustics have a wallet, a stick, and a skin. Young men, that is, normal ones, wear red clothing, but parasites wear black or grey, except that, in the Σικυώνιος,[5] the parasite about to marry wears white. Slaves wear, besides their ἐξωμίς, a short white himation called ἐγκόμβωμα or ἐπίρρημα,[6] except that the cook's clothing is double and unfulled. Old women wear green or light blue, except priestesses, who wear white. Procuresses or mothers of ἑταῖραι have a scarlet band round their heads.[7] Young women wear

---

[1] *G.T.P.*, pp. 62 ff., 75 ff.; *O.M.C.*, pp. 7–12; *M.I.N.C.*, pp. 5–24.

[2] *G.T.P.*, pp. 76 ff.

[3] *G.T.P.*, pp. 74, 93 ff.; *M.I.N.C.*, Introduction, *passim*.

[4] iv. 118–20.

[5] Menander, fr. 377 (Körte), but Alexis also wrote a play of this name.

[6] The last word is certainly corrupt. On slave costume see Beare, *C.Q.* 43 (1949), pp. 30 f.: *The Roman Stage*³, pp. 174 ff.

[7] Cf. the description of the mask of the γραῦς παχεῖα, above, p. 227.

white or linen (βυσσίνη),[1] but heiresses wear white with fringes. πορνο-
βοσκοί are distinguished by their brightly coloured chiton and flowered
scarf, and have a straight stick called an ἄρεσκος. Parasites have a στλεγγίς
and a λήκυθος, and rustics a shepherd's crook (λαγωβόλον). Another
woman's garment is the παράπηχυ or συμμετρία, a chiton reaching to
the feet, bordered in purple.

There is no mention of tights or phallos, and no archaeological evidence
for them after the fourth century. Plautus, *Rudens* 419, certainly seems
to indicate that the phallos survived into the working life of Diphilus,
who wrote the original.[2] As far as our archaeological evidence goes, and
on colour it is particularly weak, Pollux gives here a reasonable guide
to the dress of New Comedy, and outlines a system by which certain
basic facts would become clear to the least sophisticated spectator as
soon as a character appeared. Accessories, as for the parasite or rustic,
would play their part in helping identification. Costume and text could
go hand in hand in the essential task of communication, of telling the
audience what it needed to know.[3] For New Comedy, this is the essential
function of costume. The visual jokes and spectacle, to which the costume
of Old Comedy seems to have contributed a good deal, are unimportant
to it.

---

[1] The antithesis is not clear, but it is unlikely that βυσσίνη means 'purple' here (Hesych.
s.v.).

[2] Skutsch, *Rh. Mus.* 55 (1900), p. 282, n. 2, naturally rejected by Beare (*C.Q.* 43 (1949),
p. 30, n. 1).

[3] See Beare, ibid., p. 31, for some sensible remarks on identification in Roman comedy.

V

THE CHORUS

A. *Character, Function, and Movements of the Chorus*

1. A COMPLETE account of the chorus as it presented itself in the Greek theatre could hardly be given without a full history of dithyramb, tragedy, satyric drama, and comedy—a more ambitious undertaking than can be contemplated here. For the present purpose dithyramb will be left out of consideration; there is little to add to its history since the author wrote of it in 1927,[1] and a brief account of its production is given in Chapter II of this book, pp. 74–79.

The tragic chorus, from having occupied the whole performance before Thespis introduced an actor, came gradually to carry less of the dramatic weight: the spoken element began to prevail over the musical and lyrical.[2] Uncertainties of chronology, ignorance of what the earliest tragedies were like in detail and in structure, above all the fact that we possess only a small fraction of the total output of the Greek theatre, mean that we cannot hope to map out with any confidence every stage in the development of form. The regular line of development that once seemed to be traceable from the *Suppliants* of Aeschylus, in which more than half the play is sung, now seems to have vanished,[3] and no consistent pattern to have emerged in its place. Generalization about development becomes increasingly hazardous: the play of Aeschylus in which, after *Suppliants*, the chorus comes nearest to dominating the whole is *Agamemnon*, one of his latest, while in *Prometheus Vinctus* (again probably a late play)[4] the chorus is reduced in scale to the limits with which we are

---

[1] In *Dith. Trag. Com.* (A second edition, revised by Professor Webster, appeared in 1962.) A few new fragments have been found, mainly from papyri. See Page, *Greek Literary Papyri* i, nos. 87–89 = Page, *Poetae Mel. Gr.*, nos. 925–6, 929.

[2] This development is the subject of Kranz's epoch-making and still indispensable book, *Stasimon* (1933), esp. chapters 1 and 4. The table (ibid., pp. 124 f.) gives a schema of the parodos and stasima of each of the surviving plays.

[3] The date 463 B.C. seems to be implied by *P. Oxy.* 2256, fr. 3 (assuming that the fragment began ἐπὶ Ἀρ[χεδημίδου, and not ἐπὶ ἄρ[χοντος τοῦ δεῖνα): see Lesky, *Hermes* 82 (1954), pp. 1 ff.; Lloyd-Jones, Loeb *Aeschylus* ii², pp. 595 ff. (with further bibliography).

[4] See above, p. 139, n. 3 with refs. Kranz (*Stasimon*, pp. 226–8) thinks that the second and third stasima were substitutes, written about 440–430 B.C. for Aeschylus' original work, but this conclusion is not adequately proved. (See also D. S. Robertson, *Proc. Camb. Phil. Soc.* 1938, pp. 9–10.)

familiar in Sophocles and Euripides, while from the point of view of in-
volvement in the drama it figures as little more than a sympathetic
spectator. In Sophocles and Euripides the choral element is rarely more
than a quarter of the whole, and is often very much less, but whereas in
the extant plays of Sophocles the relation of the chorus to the action
seems more or less consistent (even if ambiguous) from play to play,
there is a very wide range of variation in Euripides, from *Suppliants* and
Bacchae at one extreme to *Hippolytus* or *Electra* at the other. In both poets,
above all in Euripides, there is an equal range of variation in the formal
structure of the choruses and their relation to the actors' parts. Yet
intelligent reading will indeed show that actual irrelevance is very rare
and, where it exists, has a real dramatic justification, and in two of the
latest plays of the fifth century, *Bacchae* and *Oedipus Coloneus*, the choral
odes present some very striking examples of dramatic effectiveness as well
as of poetic beauty. But the practice, said by Aristotle to have been begun
by Agathon, of writing choral interludes (ἐμβόλιμα) which could be
transferred from one play to another, like the music of a modern theatre
band, seems to have become common by the mid-fourth century, when
Aristotle deprecates it and demands that the chorus shall be treated as
one of the actors and be interwoven with the action,[1] though there
is reason to think that at least from time to time in the fourth century
choral odes, with words and not merely dances, were still composed and
indeed Aristotle's prescription implies that it must have been so. It was
perhaps natural that when full use came to be made of three actors the
dialogue should be more between them and less between actor and
chorus; and conversely the actors themselves had already come to sing
lyric monodies by the time of Euripides.

The want of all texts, except a relatively small number of fragments,
makes it impossible to trace the later history of the tragic chorus, but
it is significant that, in the records of the 'Artists of Dionysus' from the
latter part of the third century onwards, there is no certain mention of
tragic choreutai, and it is probable that, if any appeared, they in fact
contributed nothing but *entr'actes*.[2] A satyric play without a satyr chorus
is not easy to imagine, but very little is known of the satyric drama after
the fifth century, and the name may have been given to plays very different from those of the fifth century and more like comedy;[3] but, in
whatever form, satyric plays were still composed under the early

[1] *Poet.* xviii. 1456ᵃ25. Cf. *Probl.* xix. 48, where the chorus is spoken of as κηδευτὴς ἄπρακτος·
εὔβοιαν γὰρ μόνον παρέχεται οἷς πάρεστιν; cf. *Theatre of D.*, pp. 160–3.

[2] Ibid., pp. 240–6; Sifakis, *Studies*, pp. 113–26.

[3] See *Theatre of D.*, pp. 161–2, 196, 242–4; and above, p. 124.

Roman Empire and presumably as a rule with a chorus, of whatever kind.

In comedy the chorus was a very important element down to the end of the fifth century, after which the parabasis, and the epirrhematic structure generally,[1] disappears, and in many plays the chorus simply sing interludes to break up the dialogue into scenes. Such interludes already appear, for example, in Aristophanes' *Ecclesiazousae* and *Plutus*,[2] and no words are provided by the poet for them. But that some plays of the Middle and early New Comedy still included a chorus is proved by Aristotle's statement[3] that a tragic and a comic chorus might be composed of the same persons, and a few comic choreutai are mentioned[4] as members of dramatic companies down to the time of the early Roman Empire.

2. The number of the tragic chorus appears to have been twelve in the plays of Aeschylus, and fifteen in those of Sophocles[5] and Euripides. Some scholars indeed suppose that the Danaid trilogy (including *Suppliants*) of Aeschylus had choruses of fifty; this view partly depends upon the (probably mistaken) derivation of tragedy from the dithyramb with its fifty singers,[6] partly on the fact that legend gave Danaus fifty daughters,

---

[1] On these see *Dith. Trag. Com.*[2], pp. 194 ff.

[2] E.g. *Eccles*. 729, 876; *Plut*. 771, 802. In the person of the coryphaeus, the chorus can still, of course, be involved in dialogue scenes (e.g. *Plut*. 257 ff.), and even in lyric exchanges with the actors (e.g. *Plut*. 290 ff., 637, 639 f.). *Ecclesiazousae* still retains a parodos, though of unique form: the first song of the chorus (285 ff.) is sung marching *out of* the orchestra (the members of the chorus have been on stage, treated as extras, since early in the prologue), and their entrance song proper occurs when they re-enter (478 ff.). On the handling of the chorus in these two plays, see Russo, *Aristofane*, pp. 344–6, 358–60; on XOPOY in Aristophanes, Handley, *C.Q.*,N.S. 3 (1953), pp. 55–61; Beare, *C.Q.*, N.S. 5 (1955), pp. 49–52; and in general, Maidment, *C.Q.* 29 (1935), pp. 1–24. By the time of Menander the chorus has disappeared even from the cast-list: cf. that of *Dyskolos*, on which see J.-M. Jacques, *Ménandre, Le Dyskolos* (Budé), pp. 16 f.; E. W. Handley, *The Dyskolos of Menander*, pp. 171 f., 173 f.

[3] *Politics* 1276ᵇ4 ὥσπερ γε καὶ χορὸν ὁτὲ μὲν κωμικὸν ὁτὲ δὲ τραγικὸν ἕτερον εἶναί φαμεν, τῶν αὐτῶν πολλάκις ἀνθρώπων ὄντων, *Eth. Nic.* 1123ᵃ23 κωμῳδοῖς χορηγῶν ἐν τῇ παρόδῳ πορφύραν εἰσφέρων; cf. Aeschines, *in Tim.* 157 πρῴην ἐν τοῖς κατ' ἀγροὺς Διονυσίοις κωμῳδῶν ὄντων ἐν Κολλυτῷ καὶ Παρμένοντος τοῦ κωμικοῦ ὑποκριτοῦ εἰπόντος τι πρὸς τὸν χορὸν ἀνάπαιστον. Cf. *Theatre of D.*, pp. 163–5. The χοροὶ μεθυόντων who break into some plays of Menander cannot be regarded as part of the play. Cf. *Dyskolos* 230 ff., 426, 619, 783.

[4] Ibid., pp. 240 ff., and below, p. 284.

[5] *Vit. Soph.* 4, 'Suid.' s.v. Σοφοκλῆς; cf. Pollux iv. 109, and a number of scholia, esp. on Ar. *Knights* 589. (In some of these the number is given as 14, the coryphaeus being excluded.)

[6] For the arguments against the derivation, see *Theatre of D.*, pp. 31 f. The arguments for a chorus of fifty in Aeschylus' earlier plays are well presented by Lammers, *Die Doppel- und Halbchöre in der ant. Tragödie*, pp. 20f., and more recently by Fitton Brown in *C.R.*, N.S. 7 (1957), pp. 1–4. But the objections are still stronger: in particular the passage of Pollux which is the only ancient evidence for a chorus of fifty is in itself suspicious. Poll. iv. 106–9 is for the most part unexceptionable and well informed on the technical language of the chorus, its members, and its functions. Then comes the bizarre passage on the meaning of παρασκήνιον and παραχορήγημα (on which see above, p. 137), and immediately afterwards our passage:

partly on a very improbable story narrated by Pollux,[1] that there were
fifty choreutai until the irruption of the fifty *Eumenides* so scared the
Athenian audience that the chorus was henceforth reduced. It is not
generally disputed that the number was twelve in the *Persae* and *Septem*.[2]
But some suppose that in the *Oresteia* Aeschylus adopted the change introduced by Sophocles, and employed fifteen choreutai. That he did so is
stated by two scholia,[3] but one of these certainly, and the other probably,
depends on the scholium on *Agam*. 1348, which is an attempt to square
the assumption that the number of the chorus was always fifteen with
a reading of *Agam*. 1343 ff. which acknowledges that only twelve speakers
are called for there, and neither carries more weight than modern inferences from the same passage. In this passage the cry of the king is heard
at l. 1343.

> ΑΓ. ὤμοι πέπληγμαι καιρίαν πληγὴν ἔσω.
> ΧΟ. σῖγα· τίς πληγὴν ἀυτεῖ καιρίως οὐτασμένος;
> ΑΓ. ὤμοι μάλ᾽ αὖθις, δευτέραν πεπληγμένος.
> ΧΟ. τοὖργον εἰργάσθαι δοκεῖ μοι βασιλέως οἰμώγμασιν.
> ἀλλὰ κοινωσώμεθ᾽ ἤν πως ἀσφαλῆ βουλεύματ᾽ ⟨ᾖ⟩.

Then follow twelve iambic couplets each of which is plainly the utterance
of a single choreutes.[4] The last of these twelve runs (1370–1) :

> ταύτην ἐπαινεῖν πάντοθεν πληθύνομαι
> τρανῶς Ἀτρείδην †εἰδέναι κυροῦνθ᾽ ὅπως.

Some scholars suppose that the three trochaic lines 1344, 1346–7, are
uttered by three choreutai other than the twelve who deliver the iambic
couplets. It seems much more likely that they are spoken by the coryphaeus. In lines 1346–7 he asks for advice from the rest; in the eleven
following iambic couplets he gets it, and in the twelfth he sums up. There
is certainly no argument here for fifteen choreutai.

it looks as if there is a change of source and of credibility between one section and the other.
For fifty Danaids represented by twelve choreutai, compare (against Fitton Brown, p. 2 and
n. 5) the mothers of the Seven in Euripides' *Suppliants* represented by fifteen choreutai:
the number seven is repeatedly insisted on (e.g. 12, 102, 636, 755, 1207, and esp. 963), but
'hat nur die Bedeutung der konventionellen Zahl, die fast gleich einem Namen ist' (Wilamowitz, *Griech. Tragoedien* i[6], p. 221: his remark 'da haben wir zu lernen, daß der athenische
Dichter mit ein Publikum von gefügiger Phantasie rechnen durfte' makes the point that
needs to be made). (We owe this observation to Professor P. H. J. Lloyd-Jones.)

[1] iv. 110.
[2] See Muff, *De choro Persarum fabulae Aeschyleae* (1878), pp. 16 ff., and *Der Chor in den
Sieben des Aischylos* (1882), pp. 1 f.
[3] On Ar. *Knights* 589, and Aesch. *Eumen*. 585. On the former, see Fraenkel, *Agamemnon*
iii, pp. 633–5 and Addenda, p. 831. N. G. Wilson, *C.Q.*, N.S. 12 (1962), pp. 32 ff., has shown
that the 'additions' to schol. Ar. *Knights* 589 are due to Triclinius.
[4] Note ἐγὼ μέν, ἐγὼ δέ, κἀγώ at the beginning of the first three couplets.

It has been inferred from the Pronomos vase,[1] on which eleven choreutai appear in addition to Silenus, that the satyric chorus at the end of the fifth century consisted of twelve choreutai; but the inference is based on a false assumption, namely that Silenus is merely the chorus-leader, given, as he would not be in tragedy, a name. The assumption is shown to be false by the fact that Silenus can hold an iambic dialogue with the chorus-leader (Eur. *Cyclops* 82 ff.; Soph. *Ichneutai* 107 ff. Page): Silenus is an actor,[2] and the Pronomos vase gives no certain evidence on the size of the satyr chorus. Even though it is hard to see how a satyr play can have existed without a chorus, there is no clear evidence of the existence of a satyric chorus in later periods, let alone for the number of choreutai.

That the chorus of the Old Comedy consisted of twenty-four members is agreed by all authorities,[3] and that towards the end of the third century B.C. performances were given at Delphi by seven choreutai and later still by even fewer is attested by inscriptions. Of numbers in the intervening period nothing is known.

3. In some few plays of Aeschylus and Euripides the employment of a second chorus in at least one scene of the play is beyond doubt. In the final scene of Aeschylus' *Suppliants* the handmaids of the Danaid chorus appear to join in the choral ode.[4] (They had doubtless been present all the time, distinguished from the Danaids by their costume and conveniently grouped in or around the orchestra.) At the end of *Eumenides* a chorus of Πρόπομποι escorts the Eumenides themselves to their sanctuary.[5] The *Phoenissae* of Phrynichos[6] apparently had a chorus of

---

[1] Above, p. 186 and fig. 49. The only other evidence consists of statements in two passages of Tzetzes (pp. 23, 34 Kaibel), whose authority is worthless anyhow, giving the number as 16 (said to be 'the same as in tragedy').

[2] See Dale, edn. of *Alcestis*, p. xix, n. 2; Buschor, *Satyrtänze u. frühes Drama, S.B.* Munich, 1943, p. 81; Collinge, *Proc. Camb. Phil. Soc.*, N.S. 5 (1958/9), pp. 30-32.

[3] e.g. Pollux iv. 109 and a number of scholia, e.g. on Ar. *Ach.* 211, *Birds* 297. On the possible earlier history and affinities of the comic chorus see *Dith. Trag. Com.*, ch. iii.

[4] *Suppl.* 1034 ff. For their introduction, cf. 977 ff., 1022 f. For the possible (but far from certain) intervention of a chorus of the sons of Aegyptus at 836 ff., cf. Kranz, *Stasimon*, pp. 16, 272; Maas, *Gk. Metre*, para. 76.

[5] Lammers, op. cit., pp. 40-55, argues also for a second chorus in the second and third plays of the Danaid trilogy, and in Aeschylus' Κάβειροι and Ὅπλων Κρίσις and Ἡλιάδες, and the satyric Θεωροὶ ἢ Ἰσθμιασταί and Τροφοί; but I am not convinced as regards all of these. The new fragments of the Ἰσθμιασταί (P. Oxy. 2162) do not clear up this question: the whole subject and structure of this play remain something of a puzzle: see Lloyd-Jones, Loeb *Aeschylus* ii², pp. 541 ff.

[6] The date 476 B.C. first given for *Phoenissae* by Bentley and often repeated rests on a largely unsupported combination of Plut. *Themistocles* 5. 5 (which is evidence for a victory of Phrynichos in that year, but with an unnamed sequence of plays) and the Hypothesis to Aesch. *Persae*, which implies, on the evidence of Glaucus of Rhegium, that *Phoenissae* was written earlier than *Persae*. The range of date is therefore 478 (the play probably referred to the battle

councillors as well as the main chorus of Phoenician women, though whether the councillors actually spoke or sang or did more than take part in an introductory scene there is no evidence to show.[1] There is no certain instance of a second chorus in Sophocles,[2] but in the *Suppliants* of Euripides (1123 ff.: cf. 107) there is a second chorus of the sons of the Seven. In the lost *Phaethon* there were two choruses—one of maid-servants attendant upon Klymene, the other the wedding choir which enters with Merops at a later point in the play (fr. 781);[3] and in *Alexandros*[4] there was a chorus of shepherds perhaps accompanying Paris, as well as the main chorus of Trojans—whether male or female is uncertain. The shepherds when they appear (in the middle of the play) seem to have been on the scene at the same time as the Trojan chorus. The supplementary chorus of huntsmen which accompanies the hero in *Hippolytus* but disappears before the parodos cannot be made up of the regular choreutai: there is no time for a change of costume.[5] In *Antiope*, besides the chorus of Attic shepherds,[6] there was an additional chorus of Maenads who entered (and departed) with Dirke. In this play also both choruses were on the scene at once.

4. Of the costumes worn by the chorus in tragedy, comedy, and satyric play some account has already been given. For the early period of tragedy the vases provide only sparse evidence,[7] but they afford no reason to distrust, and sometimes confirm, the natural assumption that the chorus was dressed according to the character which it assumed in the play. We have considered also the slight information furnished by the Boston pelike[8] and by the krater fragments in Würzburg[9]—the former suggesting that the choreutai wore undecorated robes, the latter that they might, if desired, be decorative, that of the leader of the chorus more so than the rest. But of the costume of the chorus after the beginning of the

of Mykale: cf. *P. Oxy.* 221, col. 3; Marx, *Rh. Mus.* 77 (1928), pp. 355 ff.) to 473, and the date 476 is only certain if we assume that Phrynichos did not compete twice in the five years in question. See further, Blumenthal in *R.E.* xx. 1, s.v. Phrynichos (4), coll. 915 f.

[1] Argt. to Aesch., *Persae* . . . πλὴν ἐκεῖ (i.e. in the *Phoenissae*) εὐνοῦχός ἐστιν ἀγγέλλων ἐν ἀρχῇ τὴν Ξέρξου ἧτταν στορνύς τε θρόνους τινας τοῖς τῆς ἀρχῆς παρέδροις, ἐνταῦθα δὲ προλογίζει χορὸς πρεσβυτῶν. See Lammers, op. cit., pp. 55–63, for a full discussion.

[2] Lammers, op. cit., pp. 81 f., thinks there may have been one in the *Thamyras*, an early work of the poet, but the argument is not convincing.

[3] See *New Chapters* iii, pp. 143 ff., and Lammers, op. cit., pp. 122–5.

[4] On this play see B. Snell's edition of the fragments (*Hermes*, Einzelschriften v (1937), Page, *Greek Lit. Pap.* i, pp. 54 ff., as well as Lammers, op. cit., pp. 107–9.

[5] See Barrett on *Hipp.* 58–71 (with comments on other supplementary choruses). For Verralls (and Murray's) hypothesis of a second supplementary chorus in *Hippolytus*. see Barrett on *Hipp.* 1102–50 (pp. 368 f. of his edn.), 1142–50.

[6] This is not the place to discuss whether they were Attic or Theban. See *New Chapters* iii, p. 107; Lammers, op. cit., pp. 109 ff.; Page, op. cit., pp. 60 ff.

[7] See above, pp. 180 ff.   [8] See p. 182, fig. 34.   [9] See pp. 187 f., fig. 50.

fourth century we know really nothing. From the time when (as in
Aristotle's day) they sang mainly ἐμβόλιμα—interludes which had
nothing to do with the play—they may not have been dressed 'in character' at all.

It is not doubted that the choruses of satyr plays were distinguished
by the loin-cloth of goatskin (more rarely linen drawers) with the phallos
and the horse's tail appended. As the satyrs appear on vases they are
otherwise naked;[1] in the theatre they may have worn close-fitting flesh-
coloured skins.[2] When, however, as was frequently the case, they appeared as hunters, reapers, shepherds, or what not, they doubtless wore
some appropriate additions to the purely satyric dress.[3] In the mosaic
representing the rehearsal of a satyr play in the Hellenistic period, the
costume is no longer phallic. (Nor was it so at this period in comedy.)
The father of the satyrs, Silenus, who was not the same person as the
coryphaeus, but always appeared in close association with the chorus,
always wore, with slight modifications, a tunic resembling a fleece
(μαλλωτὸς or χορταῖος χιτών).[5] As regards comedy, reference has already
been made to the choruses partially disguised as animals, birds, or fishes,
which figured frequently in the Old Comedy,[6] and to the freedom of
the poets to clothe their dancers in any guise which suited the play, and
this freedom doubtless persisted to later periods, though in the Middle
and New Comedy the old grotesqueness was soon abandoned, and in so
far as choruses appeared they appeared as ordinary human beings. In
more than one play the purpose was served by a band of intoxicated
young men or revellers.[7] Neither in tragedy nor in comedy was the chorus
ever a mixed crowd, such as Shakespeare was apt to introduce; but in
comedy there might be, as in *Lysistrata*, a division into male and female
semi-choruses, and in *Birds* the birds composing the chorus were not
only of many species, but consisted of roughly equal numbers[8] of cock-

---

[1] See pp. 183 ff. The vases do not reproduce scenes from satyric plays exactly as staged, but
in the matter of dress there is no reason to doubt that satyrs wearing loin-cloths are depicted
as they would be seen in the theatre. See esp. Brommer, *Satyrspiele*², figs. 2–7; Beazley,
Hesperia 24 (1955), pp. 310–12; Webster, *Hesperia* 29 (1960), pp. 256 f. with n. 10.

[2] Cf. Horace, *A.P.* 221 'mox etiam agrestes satyros *nudavit*'; but this does not necessarily
exclude the close-fitting garment of skin. On the whole subject see *Dith. Trag. Com.*², pp.
114–18.

[3] The shepherd-slaves of Polyphemus in Eur. *Cyclops* probably wore a goatskin cloak:
cf. l. 80 σὺν τᾷδε τράγου χλαίνᾳ μελέᾳ. Cf. Aesch. *Prom. Pyrkaeus*, fr. 278. 2–3 (Lloyd-Jones).

[4] Bieber, *H.T.*², fig. 36.

[5] Dion. Hal. vii. 72. 10. Cf. perhaps fig. 49 and Brommer, *Satyrspiele*², figs. 47, 48.

[6] See p. 219 and *Dith. Trag. Com.*², pp. 151 ff.

[7] See pp. 87, 234.

[8] Schol. Ar., *Knights* 589 συνειστήκει δὲ ὁ χορὸς [ὁ μὲν κωμικὸς] ἐξ ἀνδρῶν ἤδη καὶ γυναικῶν,
ὁμοῦ δὲ καὶ ἐκ παίδων [κδ΄, ὡς καὶ οὗτος ἀπηρίθμησεν ἐν Ὄρνισιν ἄρρενας μὲν ὄρνεις ιβ΄, θηλείας

and hen-birds, though the division has not the same dramatic point in this play as in *Lysistrata*.

5. The characteristic which distinguished the dramatic choruses, of all three kinds, from the κύκλιος χορός of the dithyramb was that their formation was rectangular. The positive statements to this effect[1] are indeed late, but they are unanimous, and the rectangular formation is presupposed in many references to the position of particular choreutai. It is not, of course, implied that in particular circumstances, at least in comedy, the chorus might not break into a round dance, as it does in Aristophanes' *Thesmophoriazousae*, where they join hands in such a fling at ll. 953 ff. :

> ὅρμα χώρει·
> κοῦφα ποσὶν ἄγ' ἐς κύκλον,
> χειρὶ σύναπτε χεῖρα,
> ῥυθμὸν χορείας ὕπαγε πᾶσα·
> βαῖνε καρπαλίμοιν ποδοῖν.
> ἐπισκοπεῖν δὲ πανταχῇ
> κυκλοῦσαν ὄμμα χρὴ χοροῦ κατάστασιν

and again in ll. 966 ff. :

> ἀλλὰ χρῆν
> ὥσπερ ἔργον αὖ τι καινὸν
> πρῶτον εὐκύκλου χορείας εὐφυᾶ στῆσαι βάσιν.

Whether this ever occurred in tragedy seems less certain,[2] but it may have happened at times, and the invention of new dances was doubtless not confined to Phrynichos and Aeschylus. The rectangular formation consisted in tragedy of five files (ζυγά) and three ranks (στοῖχοι),[3] in comedy

δὲ τοσαύτας]. The same scholiast, however, goes on to say that when there was a division into men and women, or adults and children, the men, or the adults, were in a majority of 13 to 11. Cf. Fraenkel, *Eranos* 48 (1950), pp. 82 ff. = *Kl. Beiträge z. kl. Phil.* i, pp. 459 ff.

[1] Tzetzes, *Prol. ad Lycophr.*, p. 254 (M) = p. 33 Kaibel τραγικῶν δὲ καὶ σατυρικῶν καὶ κωμικῶν ποιητῶν κοινὸν μὲν τὸ τετραγώνως ἔχειν ἱστάμενον τὸν χορόν; Bekker, *Anecd.*, p. 746. 27 οἱ γὰρ χορευταὶ αὐτῶν ἐν τετραγώνῳ σχήματι ἱστάμενοι τὰ τῶν τραγικῶν ἐπεδείκνυντο; *Etym. Magn.* s.v. τραγῳδία· τετράγωνον εἶχον οἱ χοροὶ σχῆμα. Pollux iv. 108–9 implies the same thing (see n. 3 below).

[2] S. Ferri in *Dioniso* 3 (1931–3), pp. 336 ff., tries to prove that a number of choral odes in extant plays were danced in circular formation, but in none of these does the text give any evidence of this, and his argument is really based on the assumption that any magical or invocational dance must have been circular. In two of the passages quoted by him in which a cyclic dance is referred to, it is *not* the dance in which the chorus itself is engaged (Eur. *Herakles* 687–93, *Iph. Taur.* 1143 ff.). *Iph. Aul.* 1475 ff. is perhaps better evidence. Cf. l. 676 and Latte, *De saltationibus Graecorum*, p. 65. The likeliest place for a round dance in extant tragedy is certainly *Eum.* 307 ff. Ferri also seems to assume that *any* invocation of Apollo in particular must have been associated with a cyclic dance, but this cannot be substantiated.

[3] Pollux iv. 108–9 μέρη δὲ χοροῦ στοῖχος καὶ ζυγόν. καὶ τραγικοῦ μὲν χοροῦ ζυγὰ πέντε ἐκ τριῶν καὶ στοῖχοι τρεῖς ἐκ πέντε· πεντεκαίδεκα γὰρ ἦσαν ὁ χορός. καὶ κατὰ τρεῖς μὲν εἰσῄεσαν,

of six files and four ranks, and its movements, in tragedy, when marching and not dancing, might be κατὰ ζυγά (with a front of three members) or κατὰ στοίχους (with a front of five). Although in particular plays, and to suit particular dramatic situations, the entry (πάροδος) of the chorus might be in single file or in some less orderly manner (particularly in comedy, but probably also in *Septem* and *Eumenides*), and in some might be κατὰ στοίχους (though there is no certain extant instance of this), it is probable that the normal entry, when it was made in regular formation, was κατὰ ζυγά. In the rare instances in which the chorus left the scene for a time (μετάστασις)[1] the manner of its re-entry (ἐπιπάροδος) evidently varied. In *Eumenides* 244 ff. the text does not suggest a formal march, nor do the astrophic lyrics (254 ff.)—the chorus plainly enter σποράδην; in Sophocles' *Ajax* 866 ff. the two semi-choruses, as the scholiast states, come in from opposite directions; in Euripides' *Alcestis* 872 ff. they are following Admetus in a mourning procession—possibly κατὰ ζυγά, but the utterances are perhaps (as in *Eumenides*) those of individual choreutai; at l. 515 of *Helen* they re-enter with a short lyric ode, which was sung as they came out of the house, but they can hardly have marched out of the door in formation. (In the *Ecclesiazousae* of Aristophanes, after a μετάστασις at l. 310, the chorus returns at l. 478, and after a very brief march breaks into strophe and antistrophe.)

The following diagram will illustrate the normal arrangement of the tragic chorus:

ζυ. 5	ζυ. 4	ζυ. 3	ζυ. 2	ζυ. 1	
(5)	(4)	(3)	(2)	(1)	στοῖχος πρῶτος
(10)	(9)	(8)	(7)	(6)	στοῖχος δεύτερος
(15)	(14)	(13)	(12)	(11)	στοῖχος τρίτος

εἰ κατὰ ζυγὰ γίγνοιτο ἡ πάροδος, εἰ δὲ κατὰ στοίχους, ἀνὰ πέντε εἰσῇεσαν. ἔσθ' ὅτε δὲ καὶ καθ' ἕνα (in single file) ἐποιοῦντο τὴν πάροδον. ὁ δὲ κωμικὸς χορὸς τέτταρες καὶ εἴκοσιν ἦσαν χορευταί, ζυγὰ ἕξ, ἕκαστον δὲ ζυγὸν ἐκ τεττάρων, στοῖχοι δὲ τέτταρες, ἐξ ἄνδρας ἔχων ἕκαστος στοῖχος.

[1] Pollux iv. 108 καὶ ἡ μὲν εἴσοδος τοῦ χοροῦ πάροδος καλεῖται, ἡ δὲ κατὰ χρείαν ἔξοδος ὡς πάλιν εἰσιόντων μετάστασις, ἡ δὲ μετὰ ταύτην εἴσοδος ἐπιπάροδος, ἡ δὲ τελευταία ἔξοδος ἄφοδος. The term πάροδος is also used of the opening chant of the chorus (e.g. Aristot. *Poet.* xii 1452[b]22 f., where it is ἡ πρώτη λέξις ὅλη χοροῦ, if the almost necessary emendation of ὅλου to ὅλη is accepted), and of the passages which gave entry to the theatre. ἐπιπάροδος is also used in Cramer, *Anecd. Par.* i. 20, and by Tzetzes, *de Trag.* 109–10 (from Eukleides), of the entry of a second chorus when the original one has left the scene (ἐπιπάροδος δὲ ἔστιν, ὅταν ἕτερος χορὸς ἀφικνεῖται τοῦ προτέρου παρελθόντος). The word seems not to occur elsewhere, and there is no extant example of an ἐπιπάροδος in the second sense, unless the entry of the main chorus of *Hippolytus* at l. 121 is treated as such, the brief appearance of the χορὸς κυνηγῶν (ll. 61 ff.) being regarded as the πάροδος; cf. de Falco, *L'Epiparodos nella tragedia greca*, p. 11. (Eukleides seems to have been a grammarian known to Tzetzes, but nothing more is known of him. Perhaps (so Cramer) the author of *Anecd. Par.* i. 20.) Reference should be made to the careful analysis of the forms of parodos by Kranz in *R.E.* xviii. 4, cols. 1689–91, esp. col. 1690 (on the parodos of *Oed. Col.*).

When, as appears to have been usual in Athens, the chorus entered by the western passage, with the auditorium on its left,[1] the left-hand rank (the ἀριστεροστάται), which was nearest to the spectators, was composed of the best choreutai, the middle rank (the λαυροστάται 'men in the alley' or δευτεροστάται) of the least efficient, and the third rank (τριτοστάται or ἔσχατοι or δεξιοστάται) might be of intermediate quality. (They would confront the audience directly in those manœuvres in which the first file faced the skene instead of the audience.) The men numbered 1, 6, 11, 5, 10, 15 were sometimes spoken of as κρασπεδῖται, 'men on the fringe', or ψιλεῖς 'unprotected' (though this may only refer to nos. 5, 10, 15).[2] The leader of the chorus (the κορυφαῖος) was no. 3, τρίτος ἀριστεροῦ or πρωτοστάτης; nos. 2 and 4, on each side of him, were his παραστάται and next to him in importance.[3] A passage of Menander's Ἐπίκληρος[4] suggests that the complement of choreutai may have been made up of mutes placed in the rank farthest from the audience:

ὥσπερ τῶν χορῶν
οὐ πάντες ᾄδουσ', ἀλλ' ἄφωνοι δύο τινὲς
ἢ τρεῖς παρεστήκασι πάντων ἔσχατοι
εἰς τὸν ἀριθμόν, καὶ τοῦθ' ὁμοίως πως ἔχει·
χώραν κατέχουσι, ζῶσι δ' οἷς ἔστιν βίος.

Hesychius seems to say that the mutes were in the central rank; but it cannot be taken as certain that Menander is speaking of dramatic and

---

[1] Schol. Aristid. iii, p. 535 (Dind.) ὅτε γὰρ εἰσῄεσαν οἱ χοροὶ πλαγίως βαδίζοντες ἐποιοῦντο τοὺς ὕμνους καὶ εἶχον τοὺς θεατὰς ἐν ἀριστερᾷ αὐτῶν καὶ οἱ πρῶτοι τοῦ χοροῦ ἀριστερὸν ἐπεῖχον . . . ἐπειδὴ ἐν μὲν χοροῖς τὸ εὐώνυμον τιμιώτερον, ἐν δὲ πολέμοις τὸ δεξιόν, and p. 536 τοὺς οὖν καλοὺς τῶν χορευτῶν ἔταττον εἰσιόντες ἐν τοῖς ἑαυτῶν ἀριστέροις, ἵνα εὑρεθῶσι πρὸς τὸν δῆμον ὁρῶντες.

Pollux ii. 161 τάχα δὲ καὶ ὁ ἀριστεροστάτης ἐν χορῷ προσήκοι ἂν τῇ ἀριστερᾷ, ὡς ὁ δεξιοστάτης τῇ δεξιᾷ, and iv. 106 δεξιοστάτης, ἀριστεροστάτης, δευτεροστάτης, τριτοστάτης, Hesych. s.v. ἀριστεροστάτης· ὁ πρωτοστάτης τοῦ χοροῦ· and s.v. λαυροστάται· οἱ ἐν τοῖς μέσοις ζυγοὶ ὄντες ἔν τισι στενωποῖς μὴ θεωρούμενοι· οἱ δὲ χείρους μέσοι ἵστανται· οἱ δὲ ἐπιτεταγμένοι (i.e. those who have to fulfil the allotted task of the chorus) πρῶτοι καὶ ἔσχατοι (i.e. third); and s.v. ὑποκόλπιον τοῦ χοροῦ· τῆς στάσεως χῶραι αἱ ἄτιμοι.

[2] Plut. Quaest. Conv. v. 678 d ὥσπερ χοροῦ . . . τὸν κρασπεδίτην τῷ κορυφαίῳ συνήκοον ἔχοντος; Hesych. s.v. ψιλεῖς· οἱ ὕστατοι χορεύοντες; 'Suid.' s.v. ψιλεύς· ἐπ' ἄκρου χοροῦ ἱστάμενος.

[3] Photius s.v. τρίτος ἀριστεροῦ· ἐν τοῖς τραγικοῖς χοροῖς τριῶν ὄντων στοίχων καὶ ⟨πέντε⟩ ζυγῶν, ὁ μὲν ἀριστερὸς στοῖχος ὁ πρὸς τῷ θεάτρῳ ἦν, ὁ δὲ δεξιὸς πρὸς τῷ προσκηνίῳ. συνέβαινεν οὖν τὸν μέσον τοῦ ἀριστεροῦ στοιχοῦ τὴν ἐντιμοτάτην καὶ οἵαν τοῦ πρωτοστάτου χώραν ἐπέχειν καὶ στάσιν; cf. Aristot. Met. iv. 1018ᵇ26 ταῦτα δ' ἐστιν ὅσα πρός τι ἐν ὡρισμένον διέστηκε κατά τινα λόγον, οἷον παραστάτης τριτοστάτου πρότερον καὶ παρανήτη νήτης· ἔνθα μὲν γὰρ ὁ κορυφαῖος, ἔνθα δὲ ἡ μέση ἀρχή, and Pol. iii. 1277ᵃ10 ἀνάγκη μὴ μίαν εἶναι τὴν τῶν πολιτῶν πάντων ἀρετήν, ὥσπερ οὐδὲ τῶν χορευτῶν κορυφαίου καὶ παραστάτου. The terms χορηγός, ἡγεμών, χοροστάτης, χορολέκτης, and others are found applied to the κορυφαῖος in a few passages. (See Müller, Bühnenalt., p. 207.)

[4] Fr. 153 (Körte).

not of dithyrambic choruses. (Fifty good voices would be less easy to find than fifteen or twenty-four.)

In its entry and its departure from the scene the chorus, at least in tragedy, was normally preceded by the flute player,[1] who, if the vase paintings are good evidence, was richly dressed, but did not, to our knowledge, ever wear a mask.[2]

But the modes of entry displayed by the choruses even of extant plays are too varied to be comprised within the simple formula of a march κατὰ ζυγά.[3] This phrase primarily describes the marching entry found in several early plays in which the first lyric strophe and antistrophe are preceded by about 40 to 65 anapaestic dimeters, probably delivered in recitative by the whole chorus[4]—Persae, Suppliants, and Agamemnon, and the Ajax of Sophocles.

The long anapaestic openings of these early plays suggest an ordered march round the orchestra before taking up its position (στάσις).[5] In the Alcestis of Euripides also (where there is internal division of speakers both in the prelude and in the following song), and in the Rhesus (again in dialogue form),[6] there is a briefer anapaestic opening, and there is a variant of this form in Sophocles' Electra, where Electra utters 35 anapaestic lines, mostly dimeters, while the chorus are coming in. What follows here is not a regular strophic entrance-song, but a κομμός or lyric exchange between chorus and actor. In Hecuba, after a similar utterance by Hecuba (ll. 59–97), the chorus delivers 56 anapaestic dimeters, and there is no lyric entrance-song, properly speaking: the anapaests lead into a duet between Hecuba and Polyxena in lyric anapaests. Yet another variation on the anapaestic entry followed by strophic lyrics occurs in the Septem of Aeschylus: here a long run of astrophic lyrics (29 lines) leads into three strophic pairs. The introduction is thus sung, not recitative, but stands in the same relation to the following lyrics as

---

[1] Schol. on Ar. Wasps 582 ἔθος δὲ ἦν ἐν ταῖς ἐξόδοις τῶν τῆς τραγῳδίας χορικῶν προσώπων προηγεῖσθαι αὐλητήν, ὥστε αὐλοῦντα προπέμπειν. When two semi-choruses entered separately, as in Lysistrata, we do not know what the flute-player did, if there was one; nor what happened when a second chorus entered (see above, p. 240).

[2] See above, pp. 166, 182 ff., 199.

[3] The structure of opening scenes and of choral entries is analysed well, if at times over-schematically, by Walter Nestle, Die Struktur des Eingangs in d. att. Trag. (Tübinger Beiträge 10), 1930, esp. pp. 14 ff., 52 ff.

[4] See above, pp. 160 ff. Some scholars suppose that they were recited by the coryphaeus alone. This, to judge from some modern performances, would have been much less impressive. See Fraenkel on Agam. 40–103.

[5] Hesychius says that lines were marked in the orchestra to help them to form a straight front: s.v. γραμμαί· ἐν τῇ ὀρχήστρᾳ ἦσαν, ὡς τὸν χορὸν ἐν ϲ ·οίχῳ ἵστασθαι.

[6] On the parodos of Rhesus and its peculiarities, see Ritchie, Authenticity of the 'Rhesus' of Euripides, pp. 101–13.

the marching anapaests of *Persae* and other plays.[1] The chorus enters in great terror (hence the lyric form), and probably in disorder. The choral entry in *Medea* is more complex still: their very brief opening anapaests (3 lines) lead straight into an equally brief sequence of astrophic lyrics, and the whole utterance breaks into an anapaestic exchange between Medea (off-stage) and the Nurse. The remainder of the parodos (148 ff.) is an epirrhematic sequence in which the stanzas of the chorus are answered by anapaests from the actors, and the whole ends with another, much longer, astrophic lyric (204 ff.). There is no clue in the text to the mode of entry, and the close-knit structure of the whole makes it difficult to assume a pause during which the chorus entered silently.

Such a pause may have occurred in a number of other plays in which there is no anapaestic opening or corresponding formal prelude, and where the chorus may have marched in in silence, κατὰ ζυγά, preceded by the flute-player, and faced the audience to sing.[2] These plays are: *Antigone, Oedipus Tyrannus,*[3] *Trachiniae,* and *Philoctetes* (where the structure of the first part of the parodos is epirrhematic, Neoptolemos' anapaests answering the lyrics of the chorus), *Hippolytus,*[4] *Andromache,*[5] *Herakles, Electra, Ion,*[6] and *Iphigeneia at Aulis.*[7] In *Phoenissae* there is a variation on this form. After the epirrhematic scene of the τειχοσκοπία, in which the Paidagogos replies in spoken trimeters to the sung lyrics of Antigone, the former announces the approach of the chorus (as an ὄχλος γυναικῶν), and both withdraw. The form is close to that in which some of the choral intermezzi of New Comedy are introduced, and the entry of the chorus was perhaps more hurried than usual. In one or two plays the chorus may have been present from the first, as it is in the *Suppliants*[8] of Euripides.

[1] See Nestle, *Struktur*, pp. 53–55.

[2] As there is no help from the text, it cannot, of course, be excluded *a priori* that the chorus began to sing the strophic parodos-song while entering, though the symmetrical structure of response makes this very unlikely.

[3] In *O.T.* they may have been present from the first as part of the group of citizens addressed in l. 1 by Oedipus, but ll. 151 ff. have the look of an entrance-song.

[4] Disregarding the χορὸς κυνηγῶν (ll. 58 ff.).

[5] In *Andromache* the chorus's opening song follows immediately on Andromache's elegiac lament, unique in Greek tragedy, on which see Page, *Greek Poetry and Life (Essays presented to Gilbert Murray)*, pp. 206 ff.

[6] In *Electra*, an aria by the actor, and in *Ion*, actor anapaests followed by an even more developed aria, lead into (or up to) the parodos of the chorus. In the latter, further, the parodos-song is itself a complex lyric exchange between different subgroups in the chorus.

[7] In *Iph. Aul.* there is an anapaestic dialogue between Agamemnon and the πρεσβύτης, immediately before the parodos, though the prologue here may have suffered much from interpolation (for this view see Page, *Actors' Interpolations*, pp. 131 ff.; Fraenkel in *Studi U. E. Paoli* (1955), pp. 293 ff. (whose conclusions are rather different from Page's); against, Ritchie, op. cit., pp. 102 f.). On the parodos, see Kranz, *Stasimon*, pp. 257 f.

[8] They must have entered in silence before the play began, as presumably did the crowd of suppliants (if there was one) in *O.T.*

In *Choephoroi* they enter silently while Orestes is speaking the prologue, and in *Bacchae*, if they were not present from the first, they may also enter during the prologue, but the fact that the first choral song begins with a short astrophic sequence strongly suggests that their entry was made as they sang these lines.[1] In *Helen* the parodos takes the form of a strophic κομμός between Helen and the chorus after a very brief prelude of three dactylic lines, delivered presumably in recitative, by Helen. In *Orestes* the chorus creep in, almost whispering, for fear of disturbing the sick hero, and join in a lyric dialogue with Electra. In two extant plays, *Eumenides*[2] and *Oedipus Coloneus*, the chorus hurried in σποράδην, one by one: they are in pursuit, and in the latter the actual entrance-song is a complex sung exchange between chorus and two actors. *Heraclidae*, *Troades* (a divided entry of two semi-choruses), and *Iphigeneia in Tauris* have each peculiarities of form, and (much earlier) the entry of the Ocean-nymphs in *Prometheus Vinctus* was evidently unique.[3]

Of the movements or attitude of the chorus during the main part of the play there is little or no direct information. When the leader engaged in dialogue with the actors, he must have faced them, as did probably the whole chorus, and in the absence of the actors they are likely, when not dancing, to have faced the audience; but by what manœuvres they changed their direction is unknown. At moments of crisis they doubtless reacted as the crisis demanded.[4]

6. There is also little direct information as to the movements of the chorus in comedy, except in so far as the texts imply a great variety and freedom in the mode of entry, great liveliness during the play, and a marching departure, headed by the flute-player and varied at times (as in *Wasps* and *Ecclesiazousae*) by a vigorous dancing exit. It has been supposed that in the parabasis of the Old Comedy the two semi-choruses stood facing one another, but the evidence for this is only a confused note of Hephaestion.[5] It seems more likely that during the delivery of the

---

[1] So Dodds, edn. of *Bacchae*², p. 71. On archaic features in the parodos of *Bacchae*, see Kranz, op. cit., pp. 234 f.

[2] Cf. *Vit. Aesch.* 9. There is a different mode of entry in each play of the *Oresteia*. It is not worth while to pursue the purely academic question which is the 'real parodos' of *Eumenides*.

[3] See *Theatre of D.*, pp. 39 ff., Wilamowitz, *Aischylos: Interpretationen*, pp. 115 ff., and most recently, Fraenkel, *Annali Pisa* 23 (1954), pp. 269 ff. = *Kl. Beiträge z. kl. Phil.* i, pp. 389 ff.

[4] For their behaviour during choral odes see below, pp. 251 f.

[5] Hephaest., p. 72, l. 13 (Consbruch), καλεῖται δὲ παράβασις, ἐπειδὴ εἰσελθόντες εἰς τὸ θέατρον καὶ ἀντιπρόσωποι ἀλλήλοις στάντες οἱ χορευταὶ παρέβαινον καὶ εἰς τὸ θέατρον ἀποβλέποντες ἐλεγόν τινα. But the words εἰσελθόντες εἰς τὸ θέατρον do not really apply to the παράβασις. In Ar. *Ach.* 629, *Knights* 508, *Peace* 735 παραβαίνειν πρὸς τὸ θέατρον is plainly used of the chorus coming forward to face the spectators for the delivery of the 'anapaests'—the long formal address. See *Dith. Trag. Com.*², p. 149; Kranz, *R.E.* s.v. Parabasis. To the

epirrhematic parts of the parabasis each semi-chorus at least should have faced the audience in turn, whether the whole chorus did so at once or not. That some part of the parabasis was accompanied by lively dancing—perhaps by the semi-chorus whose leader was not addressing the audience—is suggested by their partially discarding their costume or equipment and performing ἀποδύντες, unencumbered.[1]

7. Something has already been said in regard to the manner of delivery of the choral parts of the drama.[2] Where the chorus takes part in the dialogue, speaking normally in iambic trimeters or more rarely in trochaic tetrameters, the leader doubtless spoke for the whole, as he (or the leaders of the two semi-choruses in turn) almost certainly did (in recitative) in the parabasis of the Old Comedy, and at particular moments (especially in comedy) the leader might address his fellow choreutai.[3] In tragedy the parodos and stasima (the choral odes in the body of the play, after the chorus had reached its στάσις or normal position)[4] were as a rule sung by the whole chorus in unison, and there is no evidence for the regular delivery of strophe and antistrophe by separate semi-choruses; but there were exceptional scenes in which a division into semi-choruses was made,[5] as for a brief space in *Ajax*, when they are searching for the hero, in the parodos of *Alcestis*, in *Orestes* 1246 ff., and, in comedy, throughout *Lysistrata* and probably the ode and antode of the parabasis generally;[6] and also scenes in which the lyric utterances of individual choreutai take the place of united song—as, for instance, the opening scene of *Eumenides* and the parodos of *Ion*.[7] It is fashionable with scholars at the present time to multiply instances of this by splitting up choral systems into individual ejaculations, but this may easily be overdone, and the process is anyhow guided mainly by the scholar's personal fancy.[8]

passages cited by Consbruch on Hephaestion, loc. cit., add schol. Lucian, *Conv.* 17 (p. 32 Rabe).

[1] See *Dith. Trag. Com.*[2], pp. 142 f. On the delivery of the parabasis in song and recitative see above, p. 158.   [2] pp. 156 ff.

[3] e.g. Ar. *Wasps* 1516, *Thesm.* 655, *Frogs* 382, etc.

[4] See below, p. 251.

[5] Cf. Pollux iv. 107 καὶ ἡμιχόριον δὲ καὶ διχορία καὶ ἀντιχόρια· ἔοικε δὲ ταὐτὸν εἶναι ταυτὶ τὰ τρία ὀνόματα· ὁπόταν γὰρ ὁ χορὸς εἰς δύο μέρη τμηθῇ, τὸ μὲν πρᾶγμα καλεῖται διχορία, ἑκατέρα δὲ ἡ μοῖρα ἡμιχόριον, ἃ δ' ἀντᾴδουσιν, ἀντιχόρια. The division in the final extant scene of the *Seven against Thebes*, of which the date and authorship are problematic, is a striking instance, the two halves of the chorus siding with Antigone and Ismene respectively.

[6] The evidence is that of the Ravenna and Venetian MSS. as regards several of the plays; see Arnoldt, *Die Chorpartien bei Aristophanes*, pp. 180 ff.

[7] But the schol. on Ar. *Frogs* 372 shows that there was no unanimity even among the old commentators on such suggestions: ἐντεῦθεν Ἀρίσταρχος ὑπενόησε μὴ ὅλου τοῦ χοροῦ εἶναι τὰ πρῶτα· τοῦτο δὲ οὐκ ἀξιόπιστον· πολλάκις ἀλλήλοις οὕτω παρακελεύονται οἱ περὶ τὸν χορόν.

[8] See Page, *C.Q.* 31 (1937), pp. 94–99; Dale on *Alcestis* 77–135; Barrett on *Hipp.* 362–72, 565–600.

In the κομμός, in which chorus and actors join in a lamentation or other lyric dialogue, the poet was doubtless free to employ individual or combined utterance as he chose, and the form varied greatly.[1] A division into semi-choruses may have been more frequent in satyric drama than in tragedy, to judge from *Cyclops* and *Ichneutai*. In both plays there are also passages of non-antistrophic choral lyrics, satyric drama perhaps being in this as in other respects less formal than tragedy. *Dictyulci* and *Isthmiastae* supply little or no evidence, and there is hardly sufficient basis for any general statement. It may be added that the modern literature on the subject of the methods of delivery in Greek drama is as immense as the evidence is slight and inconclusive.

B. *Dancing in Drama*

1. The place of dancing in Greek culture and its various manifestations was much more important than it is in modern life.[2] Plato regards dancing as a form, regulated and rendered orderly, of the instinctive delight in active motion[3] which characterizes all human beings, and lays great stress on the importance of developing it in conformity with the moral and artistic sense of educated men (*Laws* ii. 654 b):

ΑΘ. ὁ καλῶς ἄρα πεπαιδευμένος ᾄδειν τε καὶ ὀρχεῖσθαι δυνατὸς ἂν εἴη καλῶς. ΚΛ. ἔοικεν. ΑΘ. ἴδωμεν δὴ τί ποτ᾽ ἐστὶ τὸ νῦν αὖ λεγόμενον. ΚΛ. τὸ ποῖον δή; ΑΘ. "καλῶς ᾄδει", φαμέν, "καὶ καλῶς ὀρχεῖται"· πότερον "εἰ καὶ καλὰ ᾄδει καὶ καλὰ ὀρχεῖται" προσθῶμεν ἢ μή; ΚΛ. προσθῶμεν.

and later (vii. 798 d):

ΑΘ. τί οὖν; τοῖς ἔμπροσθεν λόγοις πιστεύομεν, οἷς ἐλέγομεν ὡς τὰ περὶ τοὺς ῥυθμοὺς καὶ πᾶσαν μουσικήν ἐστιν τρόπων μιμήματα βελτιόνων καὶ χειρόνων ἀνθρώπων; ἢ πῶς; ΚΛ. οὐδαμῶς ἄλλως κτλ.

The Greeks tended to regard all dancing as 'mimetic',[4] or expressive,

---

[1] See Haigh, *Tragic Drama*, pp. 359–61.

[2] A brief summary of the ways in which dancing entered into every phase of Greek life is conveniently given by A. Brinkmann, 'Altgr. Mädchenreigen' (in *Bonner Jahrb.* 130 (1925), pp. 118–21). The word χορός originally means a dance-floor (Hom. *Il.* 18. 590; *Od.* 8. 260, etc.), and the agora at Sparta was called the χορός (Paus. iii. 11. 9).

[3] He connects χορός with χαρά (*Laws* ii. 654 a). Lucian, *de salt.* 25, records a tradition that Socrates οὐ μόνον ἐπῄνει τὴν ὀρχηστικήν, ἀλλὰ καὶ ἐκμαθεῖν αὐτὴν ἠξίου μέγιστον ἀπονέμων εὐρυθμίᾳ καὶ εὐμουσίᾳ καὶ κινήσει ἐμμελεῖ καὶ εὐσχημοσύνῃ τοῦ κινουμένου. But Libanius in the fourth century A.D. still found it necessary (ὑπὲρ τῶν ὀρχηστῶν) to defend the practice of dancing against the censure of the Fathers of the Church.

[4] A number of attempts have been made recently to find in the close connexion between mimesis and dance the original germ from which Greek drama grew (dance and mime being seen as lying behind the linguistic and literary origins which have proved so darkly impenetrable to scholars), but the evidence (almost entirely philological) is tenuous, and the suggestion no more than a possible guess. The most important examples of this line of thought are:

especially in its employment of rhythmical gestures and motions. So Aristotle[1] can say of dancers that διὰ τῶν σχηματιζομένων ῥυθμῶν (the rhythms embodied in gesture) μιμοῦνται καὶ ἤθη καὶ πάθη καὶ πράξεις. Athenaeus[2] quotes Damon, the friend and musical adviser of Plato, as stressing the moral implications of dancing:

οὐ κακῶς δ' ἔλεγον οἱ περὶ Δάμωνα τὸν Ἀθηναῖον ὅτι καὶ τὰς ᾠδὰς καὶ τὰς ὀρχήσεις ἀνάγκη γίγνεσθαι κινουμένης πως τῆς ψυχῆς· καὶ αἱ μὲν ἐλευθέριοι καὶ καλαὶ
ποιοῦσι τοιαύτας, αἱ δ' ἐναντίαι τὰς ἐναντίας.

He illustrates this by the story of Hippokleides, who 'danced away his wedding' with the daughter of Kleisthenes of Sikyon by a clever but vulgar performance,[3] and continues:[4]

καὶ γὰρ ἐν ὀρχήσει καὶ πορείᾳ καλὸν μὲν εὐσχημοσύνη καὶ κόσμος, αἰσχρὸν δὲ
ἀταξία καὶ τὸ φορτικόν. διὰ τοῦτο γὰρ καὶ ἐξ ἀρχῆς συνέταττον οἱ ποιηταὶ τοῖς
ἐλευθέροις τὰς ὀρχήσεις καὶ ἐχρῶντο τοῖς σχήμασι σημείοις μόνον τῶν ᾀδομένων,
τηροῦντες ἀεὶ τὸ εὐγενὲς καὶ ἀνδρῶδες ἐπ' αὐτῶν, ὅθεν καὶ ὑπορχήματα τὰ τοιαῦτα
προσηγόρευον.[5] εἰ δέ τις ἀμέτρως διαθείη τὴν σχηματοποιίαν καὶ ταῖς ᾠδαῖς
ἐπιτυγχάνων μηδὲν λέγοι κατὰ τὴν ὄρχησιν (i.e. allowed his dancing to become independent of the words), οὗτος δ' ἦν ἀδόκιμος. διὸ καὶ Ἀριστοφάνης ἢ Πλάτων[6] ἐν ταῖς Σκευαῖς, ὡς Χαμαιλέων φησίν, εἴρηκεν οὕτως

ὥστ' εἴ τις ὀρχοῖτ' εὖ, θέαμ' ἦν· νῦν δὲ δρῶσιν οὐδέν,
ἀλλ' ὥσπερ ἀπόπληκτοι στάδην ἑστῶτες ὠρύονται.

He goes on to compare choral dancing with military drill, in a passage which has already been quoted,[7] and speaks, very interestingly, of the connexion between dancing (in the wide sense, including manual gestures) and the work of the ancient sculptors:

ἐστὶ δὲ καὶ τὰ τῶν ἀρχαίων δημιουργῶν ἀγάλματα τῆς παλαιᾶς ὀρχήσεως λεί-
ψανα· διὸ καὶ ξυνέστη τὰ κατὰ τὴν χειρονομίαν ἐπιμελεστέρως διὰ ταύτην τὴν αἰτίαν.
ἐζήτουν γὰρ κἂν ταύτῃ κινήσεις καλὰς καὶ ἐλευθερίους.... καὶ τὰ σχήματα μετέ-
φερον ἐντεῦθεν εἰς τοὺς χορούς, ἐκ δὲ τῶν χορῶν εἰς τὰς παλαίστρας.

In pursuance of his general doctrine, as quoted above, Plato banishes from his ideal state all orgiastic, drunken, and indecent dancing:[8] ὅση μὲν βακχεία τ' ἐστὶν καὶ τῶν ταύταις ἑπομένων, ἃς Νύμφας τε καὶ Πᾶνας

Hermann Koller, *Die Mimesis in der Antike*, Bern, 1954; *Mus. Helv.* 14 (1957), pp. 100 ff.; Schreckenberg, *ΔΡΑΜΑ*. For an energetic reply, see Else in *Class. Philol.* 53 (1958), pp. 73 ff., 245.

[1] *Poet.* i. 1447[a]27.   [2] xiv. 628 c.   [3] Hdt. vi. 129.
[4] xiv. 628 d, e.
[5] ὑπ-όρχημα being by derivation essentially a dance which accompanied or was secondary to something else—here, to the temperament expressed in the sung words. See below, p. 255.
[6] It was Plato (the comic poet), fr. 130 (K).   [7] Above, p. 89.
[8] *Laws* vii. 815 c.

καὶ Σειληνοὺς καὶ Σατύρους ἐπονομάζοντες, ὥς φασιν, μιμοῦνται κατῳνω-
μένους, περὶ καθαρμούς τε καὶ τελετάς τινας ἀποτελούντων, σύμπαν τοῦτο
τῆς ὀρχήσεως τὸ γένος οὔθ᾽ ὡς εἰρηνικὸν οὔθ᾽ ὡς πολεμικὸν οὔθ᾽ ὅτι ποτὲ
βούλεται ῥᾴδιον ἀφορίσασθαι; such dancing was certainly not πολιτικόν,
fit for citizens. Nor were the music and dances that are characteristic
of comedy; at most they must be allowed to remain so as to illustrate
the higher type by contrast, and must be left to slaves and hireling
foreigners.[1]

2. Two characteristics of ancient Greek dancing have already been
mentioned in passing—the use made of the hands (χειρονομία), and the
predominantly expressive or mimetic character of the performance. The
former, possibly with other gestures but without necessarily any motion
of the body from place to place, was enough to constitute ὄρχησις in the
Greek sense, the word covering any series of rhythmical movements.
Such manual gesticulation seems certainly to have been more elaborately
developed when pantomimic dancing, apart from drama, became the
most popular form of entertainment, so that Demetrius the Cynic after
watching a mime 'dance' the story of Ares and Aphrodite, without words
or music, cried: ἀκούω, ἄνθρωπε, ἃ ποιεῖς, οὐχ ὁρῶ μόνον, ἀλλά μοι δοκεῖς
ταῖς χερσὶν αὐταῖς λαλεῖν,[2] and Lesbonax of Mytilene (in the Augustan
age) called dancers by the name χειρόσοφοι.[3]

Plutarch[4] speaks of a well-known dancer as χειρονομῶν ἐν ταῖς παλαί-
στραις. But it is not to be doubted that in the drama itself from the first
the use of the hands was one of the most effective methods of expression.
Athenaeus[5] says that Τέλεσις ἢ Τελέστης ὁ ὀρχηστοδιδάσκαλος πολλὰ
ἐξεύρηκε σχήματα, ἄκρως ταῖς χερσὶ τὰ λεγόμενα δεικνύς,[6] and the texts of

---

[1] Laws vii. 816 d, e. Cf. Rep. iii. 396 a γνωστέον μὲν γὰρ καὶ μαινομένους καὶ πονηροὺς ἄνδρας
τε καὶ γυναῖκας, ποιητέον δὲ οὐδὲν τούτων οὐδὲ μιμητέον.   [2] Lucian, de salt. 63.
[3] Ibid. 69. It must be remembered that when Lucian writes about dancing he has in mind
primarily the pantomimic dancing of his own day, not the drama. At this time every kind of
tour de force was open to a dancer who chose to employ it. He might imitate (ibid. 19)
ὕδατος ὑγρότητα καὶ πυρὸς ὀξύτητα . . . καὶ δένδρου δόνημα. Athenaeus xiv. 629 f records
a dance entitled κόσμου ἐκπύρωσις as mentioned by the Cynic Menippus of Gadara, who perhaps invented it to travesty Stoic doctrines of the fiery consummation of all things, just as
(according to the conjecture of Latte, De Salt. Graec., p. 4) another 'comic dance' mentioned
by Athenaeus and called χρεῶν ἀποκοπή may have travestied the agitators who demanded
novae tabulae. (For the proposed emendation κρεῶν ἀποκλοπή cf. Pollux iv. 105 and Dith.
Trag. Com.², pp. 136, 293.) Athenaeus' list includes also ἀλφίτων ἔκχυσις, θερμαυστρίς (a
μανιώδης ὄρχησις), and ἀπόκινος or μακτρισμός (cf. Ar. Knights 20 ἀλλ᾽ εὑρέ τιν᾽ ἀπόκινον
ἀπὸ τοῦ δεσπότου, where the schol. describes it as εἶδος ὀρχήσεως φορτικῆς. Athen. xiv. 629 c
refers to its mention in Cratinus' Nemesis, Cephisodorus' Amazones, and Aristophanes'
Centaur).
[4] Quaest. Conv. ix. 747 b.   [5] i. 21 f.
[6] There is some uncertainty about the identity of 'Telesis or Telestes'. It is presumably
coincidence that both names appear in inscriptions as those of κωμῳδοί at the Soteria in

the great dramatists make it plain that grief and joy, welcome and horror, must have found expression by such gestures of the chorus, no less than of the actors.

3. But in spite of the importance of the dance in Greek drama, most of such sketchy evidence as we possess is couched in highly abstract and uninformative language. Plutarch,[1] analysing the elements of ὄρχησις, distinguishes motions (φοραί), postures or attitudes (σχήματα), and indications (δείξεις). The latter, the mere pointing to objects or persons, need no further elucidation. 'Postures', σχήματα, he describes merely as the attitudes in which each motion terminated—suggesting, it might be, Apollo or Pan or a Bacchant. Like Plato and Aristotle he lays stress on the mimetic character of dancing (οὕτως ἐν ὀρχήσει τὸ μὲν σχῆμα μιμητικόν ἐστι μορφῆς καὶ ἰδέας, καὶ πάλιν ἡ φορὰ πάθους τινὸς ἐμφαντικὸν ἢ πράξεως ἢ δυνάμεως), and on the gestures being intimately associated with the words from moment to moment (ὀρχηστικῇ δὲ καὶ ποιητικῇ κοινωνία πᾶσα καὶ μέθεξις ἀλλήλων ἐστί—especially in the ὑπορχηματικὸν γένος, of which something will be said below—as if the words and the parts of the body were connected by strings which the former pulled).[2] Plutarch offers nothing more precise by way of description. The lists given by Pollux[3] and others show that in time the σχήματα of the dance—the postures or attitudes—had come to be standardized and named, but how far those which Pollux enumerates were Hellenistic in origin or were employed by choruses as well as by individual actors is a matter of conjecture. As regards tragedy he writes: καὶ μὴν τραγικῆς ὀρχήσεως σχήματα σιμὴ χείρ,[4] καλαθίσκος, χεὶρ καταπρανής, ξύλου παράληψις, διπλῆ, θερμαυστρίς, κυβίστησις, παραβῆναι τέτταρα.[5] A somewhat similar list is

the third century B.C., since Telestes is described by Athenaeus a few lines later as ὁ Αἰσχύλου ὀρχηστής. The only fifth-century figure who might conceivably be relevant is Telestes of Selinus, the dithyrambic poet, who won his first victory at Athens in 402–401 B.C. (Marm. Par. 65; Dith. Trag. Com.², pp. 52 f.). But Wilamowitz (Aesch. Trag., p. 13) suggests an identification with a Cretan dancer Telesis, mentioned elsewhere by Athenaeus (xiv. 630 a) and by Pollux (iv. 99), the inventor of a sword dance called after him (cf. Hesychius s.v. Τελεσιάς).

[1] Quaest. Conv. ix. 747 b ff.   [2] Ibid. 748 a–c.

[3] iv. 103–5. Latte (De Salt. Graec., pp. 7 ff.) argues that the chief authority on which both Athenaeus and Pollux drew was Tryphon (see above, p. 178), though they also used Didymus.

[4] σιμή and καταπρανής = 'upturned' and 'downturned'. τραγικῆς probably covers satyric drama, and σιμὴ χείρ is abundantly illustrated in the posture of satyrs on vases. (See Latte, op. cit., pp. 19, 20.) καλαθίσκος may indicate holding the hands above the head, basket-wise, like a caryatid; cf. Séchan, La Danse grecque antique (1930), pp. 135–6. θερμαυστρίς means 'a pair of tongs', and may indicate the position of the legs; it is given as the name of a dance, as well as of a σχῆμα. But some of the names are unintelligible. We can only guess how the chorus in Eur. Electra 859 ff. may have behaved when it danced ὡς νεβρὸς οὐράνιον πήδημα κουφίζουσα σὺν ἀγλαΐᾳ. See also E. Roos, Tragische Orchestik, Lund, 1951, pp. 82 ff.

[5] Possibly a movement by which a dancer or a file took up a position by passing the other four files in a chorus of five ζυγά.

given by Athenaeus,[1] who seems to enumerate tragic and comic postures together.[2] Again the names, by themselves, are not very informative. The interest of the passage lies in the quotations, which show that some of these names go back to the fifth century B.C.:

σχήματα δέ ἐστιν ὀρχήσεως ξιφισμός,[3] καλαθίσκος, καλλαβίδες,[4] σκώψ, σκώπευμα. ἦν δὲ ὁ σκὼψ τῶν ἀποσκοπούντων τι σχῆμα ἄκραν τὴν χεῖρα ὑπὲρ τοῦ μετώπου κεκυρτωκότων. μνημονεύει Αἰσχύλος ἐν Θεωροῖς (fr. 79 N²)

κ.αὶ μὴν παλαιῶν τῶνδέ σοι σκωπευμάτων,

καλλαβίδων δ᾽ Εὔπολις ἐν Κόλαξιν (fr. 304 K)

καλλαβίδας δὲ βαίνει
σησαμίδας δὲ χέζει,

θερμαυστρίς, ἑκατερίδες, σκοπός, χεὶρ καταπρηνής, χεὶρ σιμή, διποδισμός, ξύλου παράληψις, ἐπαγκωνισμός, καλαθίσκος, στρόβιλος.

4. Little is known of the history of dancing in the drama after the earliest period, when Phrynichos and Aeschylus invented many dances and σχήματα ὀρχήσεως. Phrynichos boasted, or was made to boast:[5]

σχήματα δ᾽ ὄρχησις τόσα μοι πόρεν, ὅσσ᾽ ἐνὶ πόντῳ
κύματα ποιεῖται χείματι νὺξ ὀλοή

and it is natural to connect this with Aristophanes' praise[6] of the beauty of Phrynichos' lyrics. Another passage of Aristophanes, quoted by Athenaeus,[7] records the claim of Aeschylus:

καὶ Αἰσχύλος δὲ οὐ μόνον ἐξεῦρε τὴν τῆς στολῆς εὐπρέπειαν καὶ σεμνότητα, ἣν ζηλώσαντες οἱ ἱεροφάνται καὶ δᾳδοῦχοι ἀμφιέννυνται (see above, p. 200), ἀλλὰ καὶ πολλὰ σχήματα ὀρχηστικὰ αὐτὸς ἐξευρίσκων ἀνεδίδου τοῖς χορευταῖς. Χαμαιλέων γοῦν πρῶτον αὐτόν φησι σχηματίσαι τοὺς χοροὺς ὀρχηστοδιδασκάλοις οὐ χρησά- μενον, ἀλλὰ καὶ αὐτὸν τοῖς χοροῖς τὰ σχήματα ποιοῦντα τῶν ὀρχήσεων, καὶ ὅλως πᾶσαν τὴν τῆς τραγῳδίας οἰκονομίαν εἰς ἑαυτὸν περιιστᾶν. ὑπεκρίνετο γοῦν μετὰ τοῦ εἰκότος τὰ δράματα. Ἀριστοφάνης γοῦν (παρὰ δὲ τοῖς κωμικοῖς ἡ περὶ τῶν τραγικῶν ἀπόκειται πίστις) ποιεῖ αὐτὸν Αἰσχύλον λέγοντα

τοῖσι χοροῖς αὐτὸς τὰ σχήματ᾽ ἐποίουν,

---

[1] xiv. 629 f.

[2] It is not certain how far Athenaeus' list of 'comic' σχήματα and dances included those practised in mimes, which were for centuries the most popular forms of entertainment, and were not primarily theatrical or Dionysiac, nor confined to festivals, but were the favourite amusement of the common people and provided by travelling actors (see Reich, *Mimus*, p. 320 and *passim*).

[3] ξιφισμός, the attitude of a sword-thrust. This was employed in tragedy (Hesych. s.v. σχῆμα ὀρχηστικὸν τῆς λεγομένης ἐμμελείας ὀρχήσεως. So also Phot. and 'Suid.').

[4] Phot. s.v. καλλαβίδες· τὸ διαβαίνειν ἀσχημόνως καὶ διελκεῖν τὰ ἰσχία ταῖς χερσίν.

[5] Plut. *Quaest. Conv.* viii. 732 f. (Wilamowitz, *Gr. Verskunst*, p. 465, n. 1.)

[6] *Birds* 748 ff.　　　　　　　　　　[7] i. 21 d–f. The quotations are frs. 677–8 (K).

καὶ πάλιν

τοὺς Φρύγας οἶδα θεωρῶν
ὅτε τῷ Πριάμῳ συλλυσόμενοι τὸν παῖδ᾿ ἦλθον τεθνεῶτα
πολλὰ τοιαυτὶ καὶ τοιαυτὶ καὶ δεῦρο σχηματίσαντας.

Athenaeus[1] continues (after a few lines):

Ἀριστοκλῆς[2] οὖν φησιν ὅτι Τελέστης ὁ Αἰσχύλου ὀρχηστὴς οὕτως ἦν τεχνίτης
ὥστε ἐν τῷ ὀρχεῖσθαι τοὺς Ἑπτὰ ἐπὶ Θήβας φανερὰ ποιῆσαι τὰ πράγματα δι᾿
ὀρχήσεως.[3] φασὶ δὲ καὶ ὅτι οἱ ἀρχαῖοι ποιηταὶ Θέσπις Πρατίνας [Κρατῖνος]
Φρύνιχος ὀρχησταὶ ἐκαλοῦντο διὰ τὸ μὴ μόνον τὰ ἑαυτῶν δράματα ἀναφέρειν εἰς
ὄρχησιν τοῦ χοροῦ, ἀλλὰ καὶ ἔξω τῶν ἰδίων ποιημάτων διδάσκειν τοὺς βουλομένους ὀρχεῖσθαι.

Sophocles was himself an accomplished dancer, who 'danced with
a lyre' round the trophy erected after the battle of Salamis and, while
acting the name part, joined in the game of ball in his own tragedy of
Nausicaa,[4] but nothing is known of the dancing of his choruses, nor of
those of Euripides. The falling off in dancing lamented by Plato the
comic poet (probably about the turn of the century) has already been
mentioned.[5]

5. To the most interesting problem—the action of the chorus while
delivering the strophe and antistrophe of the stasimon (and of the lyric
portion of the parodos)—there is unfortunately no answer. That they
remained absolutely immobile, as some scholiasts[6] assert, is impossible,
and the idea is generally recognized as due to a misinterpretation of the
word στάσιμον, which means not that they were standing but that they
had reached their station (στάσις) in the orchestra (they had not yet
done this in the parodos; in the exodos they were leaving it). In a few

---

[1] i. 22 a.

[2] Aristocles of Rhodes perhaps lived about the beginning of the Christian era.

[3] It is difficult to know exactly how (in *Seven against Thebes* as we know it) a single actor
could 'dance the play'. Haigh (*Att. Th.*[3], p. 317) interprets the phrase of 'dumb show'
accompanying the long descriptive speeches. But dumb show by whom? Not Eteokles or
the Messenger surely, and there was no one else. On the identity of 'Telestes', see above,
p. 248, n. 6.

[4] Athenaeus i. 20 e, f Σοφοκλῆς δὲ πρὸς τῷ καλὸς γεγενῆσθαι τὴν ὥραν ἦν καὶ ὀρχηστικὴν
δεδιδαγμένος καὶ μουσικὴν ἔτι παῖς ὢν παρὰ Λάμπρῳ. μετὰ γοῦν τὴν ἐν Σαλαμῖνι ναυμαχίαν περὶ
τρόπαιον γυμνὸς ἀληλιμμένος ἐχόρευσε μετὰ λύρας· οἱ δὲ ἐν ἱματίῳ φασί. καὶ τὸν Θάμυριν διδάσκων
αὐτὸς ἐκιθάρισεν· ἄκρως δὲ ἐσφαίρισεν, ὅτε τὴν Ναυσικάαν ἔθηκε. Cf. *Vit. Soph.* 3, 5; Eustathius,
Od., p. 1553, 64 ff.; p. 130, n. 4, above.

[5] Above, p. 247.

[6] e.g. schol. on Eur. *Phoen.* 202; Soph. *Trach.* 216; Ar. *Wasps* 270; *Frogs* 1281; 'Suid.'
s.v. στάσιμον; *Etym. Magn.* 725, etc. Aristotle (*Poet.* xii. 1452[b]23) evidently regards the characteristic of the stasimon as the absence of recitative and *marching* (not *dancing*) rhythms:
στάσιμον δὲ μέλος χοροῦ τὸ ἄνευ ἀναπαίστου καὶ τροχαίου, though the phrase is not quite correct
as regards fifth-century tragedy. To the attempt of Kranz (*De Forma Stasimi*, diss. Berlin,
1910, pp. 5 ff.; *Stasimon*, p. 114) to give stasimon the sense of 'a restrained song in tempo
moderato' Miss Dale replies conclusively (*Eranos* 48 (1950), pp. 14–18).

plays the texts[1] imply that they danced, and it can scarcely be doubted that as a rule they went through suitable, probably not as a rule violent, motions and gestures, while themselves singing the choral odes.

It is sometimes asserted that the chorus broke into gesture and movement also as they followed the action of the play and reacted to the speech and behaviour of the actors, and it may be with such movements in mind that a scholiast[2] speaks of ἡ πρὸς τὰς ῥήσεις ὑπόρχησις. But such scholiasts' notes are unlikely to be more than guesswork, and there is no adequate evidence for the assumption. There is no certainty that the movements executed by the chorus were precisely the same in the antistrophe as in the strophe of the chorus. The music was probably repeated,[3] but the gestures made while they were singing may have been accommodated rather to the words, which were on occasion quite different in tone in the two positions—violent, for instance, in one and reflective in the other. It has been pointed out[4] that in *Bacchae*, ll. 977 ff., the lines ἴτε θοαὶ Λύσσας κύνες, ἴτ' εἰς ὄρος and ὃς ἀδίκῳ γνώμᾳ παρανόμῳ τ' ὀργᾷ suggest very different movements or gestures; as do the strophe and antistrophe of *Hecuba* 923 ff., the one calling for the sudden alarm of invasion, the other for a last gaze by the women on their city. In comedy the dances both in singing choral odes and during the action must often have been much livelier, as the texts suggest,[5] though it can hardly be doubted that (for example) the incomparable lyrics of the Mystai in *Frogs* were wedded to equally lovely movement.[6]

6. Certain difficulties attach to some of the technical terms traditionally applied to the Greek dramatic dances. These are enumerated by Aristoxenus:[7] Ἀριστόξενος δὲ ἐν τῷ περὶ τραγικῆς ὀρχήσεως δηλοῖ οὕτως· ἦν δὲ τὸ μὲν εἶδος τῆς τραγικῆς ὀρχήσεως ἡ καλουμένη ἐμμέλεια, καθάπερ τῆς σατυρικῆς ἡ καλουμένη σίκιννις, τῆς δὲ κωμικῆς ὁ καλούμενος κόρδαξ, and almost in the same words by Pollux.[8] The same list is assumed by Athenaeus.[9]

---

[1] e.g. Aesch. *Eumen.* 307, Soph. *Ajax* 693 ff., *Trach.* 205 ff., Eur. *El.* 859 ff.

[2] On Ar. *Frogs* 896. Cf. schol. on *Clouds* 1352. (But see A. M. Dale, *Lyric Metres of Greek Drama*, p. 203.) The words are given as one of the current interpretations of ἐμμέλεια, but this must be a mere confusion.

[3] Dale, *Lyric Metres*, pp. 194–6. Winnington-Ingram, *Lustrum* 3 (1958), pp. 42 f. (with further refs.) is more doubtful.   [4] Dale, ibid., pp. 203–4.   [5] See above, pp. 244 f.

[6] See, for example, on the variety of dance movements in tragedy, L. B. Lawler, 'The Maenads' (*Mem. of American Acad. in Rome* 6, pp. 69–112), especially p. 109: 'The variety of metres seems to bear out the evidence of the monuments that the Maenad dance could be calm, restrained, spirited or ecstatic; rapid, medium fast or slow; furthermore, that it could be measured and dignified, or a wild, almost rhythmless rout, each dancer keeping his own rhythm.'

[7] Bekker, *Anecd.* i, p. 101, 16 = fr. 104 (Wehrli. See his note, p. 82).   [8] iv. 99.

[9] Athen. i. 20 d–e; xiv. 630 b–e, etc.; Lucian, *de salt.* 22, who describes these three as the γενικώταται ὀρχήσεις, and 26; schol. Ar. *Clouds* 540.

Besides these the term ὑπόρχημα is frequently used, in meanings which will be discussed presently.

The word ἐμμέλεια seems to be originally an abstract term, indicative of the quality of harmonious or graceful modulation of words; as such it is sometimes used of an orator's style or delivery,[1] and it may well mean this in Aristophanes' *Frogs* 895–8

καὶ μὴν ἡμεῖς ἐπιθυμοῦμεν
παρὰ σοφοῖν ἀνδροῖν ἀκοῦσαι
τίνα λόγων ἐμμέλειαν
ἔπιτε δαΐαν ὁδόν.

(The reference here must be to style rather than to music and dancing.)[2] The transition from the abstract meaning to the concrete name for a type of dance is explained in Plato's *Laws* :[3]

διὸ μίμησις τῶν λεγομένων σχήμασι γενομένη τὴν ὀρχηστικὴν ἐξηργάσατο τέχνην σύμπασαν. ὁ μὲν οὖν ἐμμελῶς ἡμῶν, ὁ δὲ πλημμελῶς ἐν τούτοις πᾶσι κινεῖται. πολλὰ μὲν δὴ τοίνυν ἄλλα ἡμῖν τῶν παλαιῶν ὀνομάτων ὡς εὖ καὶ κατὰ φύσιν κείμενα δεῖ διανοούμενον ἐπαινεῖν, τούτων δὲ ἓν καὶ τὸ περὶ τὰς ὀρχήσεις τὰς τῶν εὖ πρατ-τόντων, ὄντων δὲ μετρίων αὐτῶν πρὸς τὰς ἡδονάς, ὡς ὀρθῶς ἅμα καὶ μουσικῶς ὠνόμασεν ὅστις ποτ' ἦν, καὶ κατὰ λόγον αὐταῖς θέμενος ὄνομα συμπάσαις ἐμμελείας ἐπωνόμασε, καὶ δύο δὴ τῶν ὀρχήσεων τῶν καλῶν εἴδη κατεστήσατο, τὸ μὲν πολε-μικὸν πυρρίχην, τὸ δὲ εἰρηνικὸν ἐμμέλειαν, ἑκατέρῳ τὸ πρέπον τε καὶ ἁρμόττον ἐπιθεὶς ὄνομα.

That the concrete use was early in vogue is indicated by the story of Hippokleides (already referred to)[4] who ἐκέλευσέ οἱ τὸν αὐλητὴν αὐλῆσαι ἐμμέλειαν, πειθομένου δὲ τοῦ αὐλητέω ὠρχήσατο, as well as by the threat (referring to a tragic actor) in Aristophanes' *Wasps*,[5] ἀπολῶ γὰρ αὐτὸν ἐμμελείᾳ κονδύλου.

It is consistent with Plato's account that Athenaeus characterizes the ἐμμέλεια as marked by τὸ βαρὺ καὶ σεμνόν, 'gravity and dignity', and calls it σπουδαία as compared with the vulgar κόρδαξ,[6] but the nature of its movements is not further explained. Triclinius,[7] on Euripides' *Hecuba*, l. 647 says: ἰστέον δὲ ὅτι τὴν μὲν στροφὴν κινούμενοι πρὸς τὰ δεξιὰ οἱ χορευταὶ ᾖδον, τὴν δὲ ἀντιστροφὴν πρὸς τὰ ἀριστερά, τὴν δὲ ἐπῳδὸν ἱστάμενοι

---

[1] e.g. in Dion. Hal. *Dem.* 50, where ἐμμέλεια is a characteristic of Demosthenes, and Plutarch, *de aud.* 41d τὴν φωνὴν ἐμμελείαις τισὶ καὶ μαλακότησι καὶ παρισώσεσιν ἐφηδύνοντες ἐκβακχεύουσι καὶ παραφέρουσι τοὺς ἀκροωμένους.

[2] See Denniston, *C.Q.* 21 (1927), pp. 115 f. A scholiast on this passage evidently regarded Aristophanes' use as a solecism, ὅτι καταχρηστικῶς νῦν τὴν εὐρυθμίαν. κυρίως γὰρ ἡ μετὰ μέλους τραγικὴ ὄρχησις, οἱ δέ, ἡ πρὸς τὰς ῥήσεις ὑπόρχησις. (See also p. 252 above, n. 2.)

[3] vii. 816 a, b (cf. Lucian, *de salt.* 25, quoted above, p. 246, n. 3).

[4] Hdt. vi. 129.   [5] l. 1503.

[6] Athen. xiv. 630 e, 631 d.   [7] Dindorf, *Scholia Gr. in Eur. Trag.* i, p. 211.

ἦδον. But what was the nature of this κίνησις to right and left does not appear. (Epodes are relatively rare in tragedy, and some suppose that Triclinius is thinking of dithyramb, with a circular chorus revolving as required.) However this may be and whenever the word came to be applied to the dances of tragedy, to judge from the texts the name ἐμμέλεια has to cover a considerable variety of dances (in some of which the σχήματα enumerated were perhaps introduced), ranging from the fine serenity of the Colonus ode to the raging of the Furies and the ecstatic devotions of the Bacchae, adapting itself to every kind and degree of emotion, and presenting every form of lyric beauty.[1]

7. The name σίκιννις, denoting the satyric dance, is variously derived[2] from an eponymous Sikinnos—a barbarian or a Cretan—or from σείεσθαι, or from σείεσθαι καὶ κινεῖσθαι, or (as Athenaeus puts it) ἀπὸ τῆς κινήσεως, ἣν καὶ οἱ σάτυροι ὀρχοῦνται ταχυτάτην οὖσαν· οὐ γὰρ ἔχει πάθος αὕτη ἡ ὄρχησις, διὸ οὐδὲ βραδύνει. (The meaning of the last sentence is not very clear, and some editors emend πάθος to ἦθος.) Some said that the dance originated in Crete, others that it came from the Phrygian worship of Dionysus Sabazios,[3] and modern scholars offer a number of unprovable suggestions.[4] It is natural to conjecture that it is the dance which is being executed by a satyr on the Pronomos vase, though this gives no idea of the *pace* of the σίκιννις. It may have included a good deal of leaping; at least the Cyclops in Euripides' play[5] says to the satyrs:

ἐπεί μ' ἂν ἐν μέσῃ τῇ γαστέρι
πηδῶντες ἀπολέσαιτ' ἂν ὑπὸ τῶν σχημάτων,

which may have been the σχήματα of the σίκιννις. The mention[6] of a tune called σικιννοτύρβη and the figure on a vase of a satyr called Τυρβάς are hardly enough to relate the σίκιννις to the τυρβασία, which was the characteristic dance of the dithyramb.[7] The name Σίκινος or Σίκιννος, attached to a satyr, occurs on several vases, Attic and Italian, from about 510 B.C. onwards, with or without καλός[8].

[1] Plutarch, *Quaest. Conv.* ix. 747 b has never been satisfactorily explained: ὀρχουμένων δὲ πολλῶν προθυμότερον ἢ μουσικώτερον, δύο τοὺς εὐδοκίμους καὶ βουλομένους ἀνασῴζειν τὴν ἐμμέλειαν ἠξίουν τινὲς ὀρχεῖσθαι φορὰν παρὰ φοράν. On the whole subject see C. Kirchhoff, *Dramatische Orchestik der Hellenen* (Leipzig, 1898, Teil II), and on the ἐμμέλεια in particular, pp. 242 ff.　　　　[2] Athen. xiv. 630 b, c ; *Etym. Magn.* s.v., etc.

[3] Eustath. *Il.*, p. 1078. 20 ἦν δὲ καὶ σίκιννις κωμικωτέρα, ἣν πρῶτοί φασιν ὠρχήσαντο Φρύγες ἐπὶ Σαβαζίῳ Διονύσῳ, ὀνομασθεῖσαν κατὰ τὸν Ἀρριανὸν ἐπὶ μιᾷ τῶν ὀπαδῶν τῆς Κυβέλης νυμφῶν, ᾗ ὄνομα ἦν Σίκιννις.

[4] Some of these are collected by Latte, op. cit., p. 89, and Séchan, *La Danse grecque antique*, p. 213. G. Herbig (*S.B.* Munich, 1914, 2 Abh., p. 10) compares the Etruscan termination -*enna*. Cf. also E. Roos, *Tragische Orchestik*, pp. 166 f.　　　　[5] ll. 220–1 (cf. 37 ff.).

[6] Athen. xiv. 618 c.　　　　[7] See *Dith. Trag. Com.*², p. 33.

[8] A list is given in *R.E.* s.v. Σίκινος (3).

8. The term ὑπόρχημα is used without any real consistency during the long course of Greek literary history. In one sense it seems to denote a performance in which dancers (not themselves singing) accompany one or more singers, the dance being closely related to and illustrating the words. It was said to have originated in Crete, where Thaletas was the first to compose the πυρρίχη or armed dance in this form,[1] but Athenaeus (rightly) traces the type back to Homer.[2] In Sparta Xenodamos of Kythera was an early composer of hyporchemes (whether music, poetry, or both, we are not told), and we hear of a ὑπορχηματικὴ ὄρχησις in which men and women joined. Such dances, in which the dancers accompanied singers who did not dance, apparently continued outside the drama down to a late date and are often mentioned. Pindar composed two books in a lyric genre which the Alexandrians took to be hyporchemes (Clement of Alexandria[3] even makes him the inventor of the hyporcheme), and one or two fragments of Bacchylides are ascribed to this species. Aeschylus makes a fine use of a metaphor from the hyporcheme which implies the division of the performers into two groups—*Choeph.* 1024–5 πρὸς δὲ καρδίᾳ φόβος | ᾄδειν ἕτοιμος, ἡ δ' (ἠδ' MSS.) ὑπορχεῖσθαι κότῳ—and six hundred years later Lucian[4] describes dances at certain sacrifices in Delos (without mentioning a date): παίδων χοροὶ συνελθόντες ὑπ' αὐλῷ καὶ κιθάρᾳ οἱ μὲν ἐχόρευον, ὑπωρχοῦντο δὲ οἱ ἄριστοι προκριθέντες ἐξ αὐτῶν. τὰ γοῦν τοῖς χοροῖς γραφόμενα τούτοις ᾄσματα ὑπορχήματα ἐκαλεῖτο. Elsewhere he contrasts[5] the elegance of the dancer's facial appearance (since he could keep his mouth shut) with the gaping lips of the actor's mask, and adds: πάλαι μὲν γὰρ οἱ αὐτοὶ καὶ ᾖδον καὶ ὠρχοῦντο· εἶτ' ἐπειδὴ κινουμένων τὸ ἄσθμα τὴν ᾠδὴν ἐπετάραττεν ἄμεινον ἔδοξεν ἄλλους αὐτοῖς ὑπᾴδειν. (He is probably thinking of the development

---

[1] Sosibius (595 F 23 Jacoby) *ap.* schol. Pind. *Pyth.* ii. 127.

[2] *Il.* xviii. 569 ff.; *Od.* viii. 262 ff.; *Hymn to Apollo* 188 ff.; Ath. i. 15 d οἶδε δὲ ὁ ποιητὴς καὶ τὴν πρὸς ᾠδὴν ὄρχησιν· Δημοδόκου γοῦν ᾄδοντος κοῦροι πρωθῆβαι ὠρχοῦντο· καὶ ἐν τῇ Ὁπλοποιΐᾳ δὲ παιδὸς κιθαρίζοντος ἄλλοι ἐναντίοι μολπῇ τε ὀρχηθμῷ τε ἔσκαιρον, ὑποσημαίνεται δὲ ἐν τούτοις ὁ ὑπορχηματικὸς τρόπος, ὃς ἤνθησεν ἐπὶ Ξενοδήμου καὶ Πινδάρου. καὶ ἔστιν ἡ τοιαύτη ὄρχησις μίμησις τῶν ὑπὸ τῆς λέξεως ἑρμηνευομένων πραγμάτων; and xiv. 628 d διὰ τοῦτο γὰρ καὶ ἐξ ἀρχῆς συνέταττον οἱ ποιηταὶ τοῖς ἐλευθέροις τὰς ὀρχήσεις καὶ ἐχρῶντο τοῖς σχήμασι σημείοις μόνον τῶν ᾀδομένων, τηροῦντες ἀεὶ τὸ εὐγενὲς καὶ ἀνδρῶδες ἐπ' αὐτῶν, ὅθεν καὶ ὑπορχήματα τὰ τοιαῦτα προσηγόρευον. (Cf. also Plut. *Quaest. Conv.* ix. 748 a, b, and for Xenodamos [Plut.] *de Mus.* 1134 c.) Athenaeus quotes (from Polycrates (588 F 1 Jacoby), an historian quoted by Didymus) a description of the dances at the Spartan Hyacinthia: iv. 139 e χοροί τε νεανίσκων παμπληθεῖς εἰσέρχονται καὶ τῶν ἐπιχωρίων τινὰ ποιημάτων ᾄδουσιν ὀρχησταί τε [ἐν] τούτοις ἀναμεμιγμένοι τὴν κίνησιν ἀρχαϊκὴν ὑπὸ τὸν αὐλὸν καὶ τὴν ᾠδὴν ποιοῦνται. But note the doubts recorded by [Plut.] *de Mus.*, loc. cit., and on the confusion in the use of terms in general, see A. E. Harvey, *C.Q.*, N.S. 5 (1955), pp. 157 ff.

[3] *Stromat.* i. xvi. 78, 5 (Stählin).

[4] *de salt.* 16 (on which see Wilamowitz, *Pindaros*, p. 108; Latte, *De Salt. Gr.*, pp. 14 ff.): cf. Callimachus, *Hymn to Delos* 304 ff.   [5] *de salt.* 29, 30.

of pantomime, which was very popular in his day—often with only a single dancer.)[1]

But it is already clear that there was considerable confusion over the application of the word hyporcheme even in antiquity (the accounts of Athenaeus, Lucian, and Plutarch are not really reconcilable), and because the song and dance of this type were apparently of a very lively kind,[2] the word came to be used more or less loosely of a joyful choral song generally.[3] It can only be in this sense that modern scholars, following the example of one or two scholiasts, meaninglessly debate whether to apply the name to a number of choral odes occurring at moments of sudden joy or expectation in plays of Sophocles,[4] and allegedly distinct in character from normal tragic stasima. The distinction is expressed by the scholiast on Sophocles, *Trachiniae* 205 ff., who writes τὸ γὰρ μελιδάριον οὔκ ἐστι στάσιμον ἀλλ' ὑπὸ τῆς ἡδονῆς ὀρχοῦνται and contrasts this ode with *Hipp.* 122 ff. (which he regards as a stasimon). Similar odes are found in *Ajax* 693 ff., *Antigone* 1115 ff., *Oedipus Tyrannus* 1086 ff.; and in all these cases the excited joy of relief or anticipation darkens by contrast the calamity which falls or becomes known immediately afterwards. But the reasoning of the scholiasts is not based on this, but rather on a desire to distinguish these songs from normal stasima, which they took (incorrectly) to be sung by a static chorus: these songs demanded energetic dance. If we wish to be more exact than the evidence allows, the language of the ode in *Trachiniae* (which unlike the others, is astrophic) suggests rather that it would have been termed a paean. But the categories of ancient lyric cannot any longer be determined with any precision: indeed it is doubtful whether even Alexandria was altogether clear what they stood for.[5]

The long astrophic fragment of Pratinas, in which he protests against the threatened predominance of the flute over the words in choral poetry

[1] Lucian, *de salt.* 63.

[2] So lively that Athenaeus, xiv. 630 e, compares it with the kordax.

[3] Ibid. 631 c ἡ δ' ὑπορχηματική ἐστιν ἐν ᾗ ᾄδων ὁ χορὸς ὀρχεῖται. (This is quite inconsistent with what he says earlier, unless ὁ χορός includes both singers and dancers as in the Delian hyporchemes described by Lucian.) Cf. Cramer, *Anecd. Par.* i. 20 ὑπόρχημα δ' ἂν εἴη μᾶλλον τῶν σατύρων· ἐκεῖνοι γὰρ ᾄδοντες ἅμα καὶ ὀρχοῦνται (so also Tzetzes, *de Trag.* 114 ff., from Eukleides. See above, p. 240, n. 2), and Proclus, *Chrestom.*, § 55 ὑπόρχημα τὸ μετ' ὀρχήσεως ᾀδόμενον μέλος, and Severyns *ad loc.*

[4] The absence of all mention of hyporchemata by Aristotle in the *Poetics* (especially ch. xii) probably means that he regarded ὑπόρχημα in the strict sense as a species of poetry no less distinct from drama than (for example) the paean or the hymn. The application of the word and its derivatives to choral odes in tragedy and satyric drama is much later than Aristotle, and is almost certainly due to misunderstanding. See Dale, *Lyric Metres*, pp. 199 ff., and *Eranos* 48 (1950), pp. 18–20.

[5] See Harvey, op. cit.

is called a hyporcheme by Athenaeus,[1] and while it is possible that this came in a satyric play, this is not universally accepted,[2] and it may well have been an independent poem.[3]

In the ancient lists of dances characteristic of the several kinds of dramatic performance the κόρδαξ is always mentioned as the special dance of comedy; but as it was evidently a solo dance, it falls outside the scope of this chapter.[4] (The movements of the comic chorus have already been briefly considered.[5])

c. *Music in Drama*

1. The use of speech, recitative, and song by actors and chorus has been briefly discussed earlier in this volume, with special reference to παρακαταλογή or recitative and its uses by actors and chorus; but the greater part of the choral odes in Greek drama was sung, and there is no subject on which it is more difficult—if it is not virtually impossible—to reach a clear understanding, not to speak of appreciation, than that of the music to which the words were set and the character of the instrumental accompaniment.[6] In the first place the structure of ancient Greek music was itself extremely complicated; and in the second, our knowledge of it begins (except for one slight fragment) at a period which was perhaps two hundred years later than that at which choral odes were a regular part of the structure of a Greek play, and it cannot be assumed that it had not changed considerably in that long interval, so that as regards the Classical period—from Aeschylus to Menander—we are virtually without any direct evidence, and are dependent upon a few passages in writers who refer to the subject.

2. Greek music, no less than modern, consisted of a succession of notes separated from one another by intervals, but the intervals might be not only tones and semitones as in modern music, but fractions of a semitone, and the succession was not divided into lengths of approximately similar

---

[1] xiv. 617 b–f.

[2] See *Dith. Trag. Com.*², pp. 17 ff. and references there; also Pohlenz, *Gött. Nachr.* 1927, pp. 298 ff., and Kranz, *Stasimon*, pp. 11, 13, 270 f. On the hyporcheme generally see Deubner in *Neue Jahrbücher* 43 (1919), pp. 396 f.; Diehl s.v. in *R.E.* ix, cols. 338 ff., and T. Reinach s.v. in Daremberg–Saglio, *Dict. des antiq.*

[3] So A. M. Dale, in *Eranos* 48 (1950), p. 19. Cf. her *Words, Music and Dance*, (inaugural lecture, London), pp. 11 f. See also the important suggestion by Hugh Lloyd-Jones, *Estudios sobre la trag. griega*, Cuaderno de la Fundación Pastor, no. 13 (1966), p. 18.

[4] See *Dith. Trag. Com.*², pp. 164, 167 ff., and references there given, and Warnecke in *R.E.* xxii, cols. 1382 ff.

[5] pp. 244 f.; cf. also *Theatre of D.*, pp. 163 ff.

[6] On the significance of music in drama, especially in Aeschylus, see Kranz, *Stasimon*, pp. 137 ff.

structure, as modern music is by bars. Further, 'A Greek musician, as we learn from theoretical treatises, had at his disposal a number of modes (ἁρμονίαι or εἴδη τοῦ διὰ πασῶν) which differed from one another in the order of the larger and smaller intervals of which they were composed; each mode, within limits, might be modified by decreasing the size of the smaller intervals and increasing the size of the larger, and so have a diatonic, or a chromatic, or an enharmonic form; furthermore, these modes could be sung or played in any one of a number of keys (τόνοι)— that is to say, their absolute pitch might be varied.'[1]

Aristoxenus (who as a pupil of Aristotle may be assumed to be trust-worthy in regard to tragedy) recorded that the modes proper to the music of tragedy were the emotional Mixolydian[2] and the stately and majestic Dorian; but that these were not exclusively used is shown by Aristoxenus' own statement recorded in the *Life of Sophocles* that Sophocles had introduced the Phrygian mode (which was the special mode of dithyramb),[3] and by a passage in the Aristotelian *Problems* which justifies the use of the Hypodorian and Hypophrygian modes for the lyrics sung by actors, from whom heroic action was called for, but not for those of the chorus. It will be convenient to set out these passages at length:

(1) [Plut.] *de Mus.* 1136 d. καὶ ἡ Μιξολύδιος δὲ παθητική τίς ἐστι, τραγῳδίαις ἁρμόζουσα. Ἀριστόξενος δέ φησι (fr. 81 Wehrli) Σαπφὼ πρώτην εὑρασθαι τὴν Μιξολυδιστί, παρ' ἧς τοὺς τραγῳδοποιοὺς μαθεῖν· λαβόντας γοῦν αὐτοὺς συζεῦξαι τῇ Δωριστί, ἐπεὶ ἡ μὲν τὸ μεγαλοπρεπὲς καὶ ἀξιωματικὸν ἀποδίδωσιν, ἡ δὲ τὸ παθητικόν, μέμικται δὲ διὰ τούτων τραγῳδία.

(2) *Vit. Soph.* (§ 23). φησὶ δὲ Ἀριστόξενος (fr. 79 Wehrli) ὡς πρῶτος τῶν Ἀθήνηθεν ποιητῶν τὴν Φρυγίαν μελοποιίαν εἰς τὰ ἴδια ᾄσματα παρέλαβε καὶ τοῦ διθυραμβικοῦ τρόπου κατέμιξεν.

(3) Aristot. *Probl.* xix. 48. διὰ τί οἱ ἐν τραγῳδίᾳ χοροὶ οὔθ' ὑποδωριστὶ οὔθ' ὑποφρυγιστὶ ᾄδουσιν; ἢ ὅτι μέλος ἥκιστα ἔχουσιν αὗται αἱ ἁρμονίαι, οὗ δεῖ μάλιστα τῷ χορῷ; ἦθος δὲ ἔχει ἡ μὲν ὑποφρυγιστὶ πρακτικόν, διὸ καὶ ἐν [τε] τῷ Γηρυόνῃ[4] ἡ ἔξοδος καὶ ἡ ἐξόπλισις ἐν ταύτῃ πεποίηται, ἡ δὲ ὑποδωριστὶ

---

[1] J. F. Mountford, 'Greek Music in the Papyri and Inscriptions', in *New Chapters* ii (1929), pp. 146–83—a brief and most valuable summary of the subject. See also the article on music in the *Oxford Classical Dictionary*, a very clear (and concise) account of Greek music, with a useful bibliography. For later work, see Winnington-Ingram in *Lustrum* 3 (1958), pp. 5–57. As is clear from a reading of, for example pp. 32–37, the nature of *harmoniai* and *tonoi*, and their relation to pitch-keys, is still quite uncertain. The statement in the text is not more than a possible account.

[2] For the character of the Mixolydian, cf. the story told by Plutarch (*de audiendo* 15, 46 b) of Euripides' anger at a chorus-man who laughed when he was rehearsing a choral song composed in this mode.

[3] Cf. *Dith. Trag. Com²*., pp. 31 f., 47, 53.

[4] The reference appears to be to an otherwise unknown tragedy of Nikomachos, a con-temporary of Euripides.

μεγαλοπρεπὲς καὶ στάσιμον, διὸ καὶ κιθαρῳδικωτάτη ἐστὶ τῶν ἁρμονιῶν.
ταῦτα δ' ἄμφω χορῷ μὲν ἀνάρμοστα, τοῖς δὲ ἀπὸ σκηνῆς (lyrics sung by actors)
οἰκειότερα. ἐκεῖνοι μὲν γὰρ ἡρώων μιμηταί· οἱ δὲ ἡγεμόνες τῶν ἀρχαίων μόνοι
ἦσαν ἥρωες, οἱ δὲ λαοὶ ἄνθρωποι, ὧν ἐστὶν ὁ χορός. διὸ καὶ ἁρμόζει αὐτῷ
τὸ γοερὸν καὶ ἡσύχιον ἦθος καὶ μέλος· ἀνθρωπικὰ γάρ. ταῦτα δ' ἔχουσιν αἱ
ἄλλαι ἁρμονίαι, ἥκιστα δ' αὐτῶν ἡ [ὑπο]φρυγιστί· ἐνθουσιαστικὴ γὰρ καὶ
βακχική. κατὰ μὲν οὖν ταύτην πάσχομέν τι· παθητικοὶ δὲ οἱ ἀσθενεῖς μᾶλλον
τῶν δυνατῶν εἰσί, διὸ καὶ αὕτη ἁρμόττει τοῖς χοροῖς· κατὰ δὲ τὴν ὑποδωριστὶ
καὶ ὑποφρυγιστὶ πράττομεν, ὃ οὐκ οἰκεῖόν ἐστι χορῷ· ἔστι γὰρ χορὸς κηδευτὴς
ἄπρακτος· εὔνοιαν γὰρ μόνον παρέχεται οἷς πάρεστιν.[1]

3. It will be seen that the appropriateness of certain modes to tragedy
and to the several lyric elements in tragedy depends upon an assumed
natural association (which we cannot, with our limited information,
appreciate) of the several modes with a special range of feeling or action.
It was because they were θρηνώδεις that Plato[2] had excluded the Mixolydian, Syntonolydian, and similar harmonies from his ideal state, as
well as the Ionian and Lydian which were μαλακαὶ καὶ συμποτικαί, and
had retained only the Dorian and Phrygian, believing, as he did, that the
ἁρμονίαι had in themselves the power to influence men's characters and
emotions.[3] Aristotle is even more emphatic than Plato as to this influence,
and writes:

Politics v (viii). 1340ᵃ38. ἐν δὲ τοῖς μέλεσιν αὐτοῖς ἔστι μιμήματα τῶν ἠθῶν.
καὶ τοῦτ' ἐστι φανερόν· εὐθὺς γὰρ ἡ τῶν ἁρμονιῶν διέστηκε φύσις ὥστε ἀκούοντας
ἄλλως διατίθεσθαι καὶ μὴ τὸν αὐτὸν ἔχειν τρόπον πρὸς ἑκάστην αὐτῶν, ἀλλὰ πρὸς
μὲν ἐνίας ὀδυρτικωτέρως καὶ συνεστηκότως μᾶλλον, οἷον πρὸς τὴν μιξολυδιστὶ
καλουμένην, πρὸς δὲ τὰς μαλακωτέρως τὴν διάνοιαν, οἷον πρὸς τὰς ἀνειμένας·
μέσως δὲ καὶ καθεστηκότως μάλιστα πρὸς ἑτέραν, οἷον δοκεῖ ποιεῖν ἡ δωριστὶ
μόνη τῶν ἁρμονιῶν, ἐνθουσιαστικοὺς δ' ἡ φρυγιστί.[4]

With regard to the Phrygian mode he differs from Plato, whom he regards
as inconsistent in accepting it, while rejecting the flute as over-emotional :[5]

Politics v (viii). 1342ᵇ1. ἔχει γὰρ τὴν αὐτὴν δύναμιν ἡ φρυγιστὶ τῶν ἁρμονιῶν
ἥνπερ αὐλὸς ἐν τοῖς ὀργάνοις· ἄμφω γὰρ ὀργιαστικὰ καὶ παθητικά. δηλοῖ δ' ἡ

[1] On the text of this difficult passage, see the Teubner apparatus criticus of Ruelle–
Knoellinger–Klek, and the commentary of Flashar in *Aristoteles: Werke in deutscher Übersetzung herausg. von E. Grumach*, vol. 19 (1962), pp. 625 f. Cf. also *Probl.* xix. 30.

[2] *Rep.* iii. 398 e, 399 a.

[3] In *Laws* ii. 669 d–e he somewhat modifies this view, since he admits that in purely instrumental music (flute and lyre solos) it is very difficult to know 'what they [ρυθμός and
ἁρμονία] mean and what worth-while model is being represented'.

[4] The whole passage which intervenes between this quotation and the next should be
carefully studied.

[5] Plato's special objection to the flute is based on the great multiplicity of notes possible
in it, as compared with the kithara (*Rep.* iii. 399 c–d).

ποίησις· πᾶσα γὰρ βακχεία καὶ πᾶσα ἡ τοιαύτη κίνησις μάλιστα τῶν ὀργάνων
ἐστὶν ἐν τοῖς αὐλοῖς, τῶν δ' ἁρμονιῶν ἐν τοῖς φρυγιστὶ μέλεσι λαμβάνει ταῦτα τὸ
πρέπον, οἷον ὁ διθύραμβος ὁμολογουμένως εἶναι δοκεῖ Φρύγιον ... περὶ δὲ τῆς
δωριστὶ πάντες ὁμολογοῦσιν ὡς στασιμωτάτης οὔσης καὶ μάλιστα ἦθος ἐχούσης
ἀνδρεῖον.

In confirmation of Aristotle's opinion of the Phrygian mode it is remarkable that the one scrap of music set to fifth-century drama which
survives—a passage of Euripides, *Orestes* 338–44—appears to be in this
mode,[1] though it is too fragmentary to be wholly enlightening, both text
and notation being uncertain.

The view that different types of music influenced character—that, for
instance, enharmonic melodies (which were normal in tragedy) made
men brave— was older than Plato and did not go altogether uncontested.
An anonymous writer, probably of the fifth century B.C., possibly
Hippias,[2] attacks the view strongly, and shows the greatest contempt
for musical theoreticians whose technical skill is in inverse proportion
to their readiness to discourse on the subtleties of musical ethos. But the
views of Plato, Aristotle, and Aristoxenus had great influence, and it is
indeed possible that the music employed helped to give a certain emotional colour to the performances with which it was associated,[3] though
with music, as with metre, it is impossible to trace these effects in detail.

4. At first there can be no doubt that the music, or at least the musical
accompaniment, was strictly subordinate to the words. Pratinas' protest
against the attempt to give predominance to the flute implies this,
though the reference may well not be to theatrical performance.[4] Certainly it was essential that the words should be heard clearly throughout
the vast theatre, as words seldom are even indoors when set to modern
music and sung in parts, and it must have been necessary even for singers
in unison (as ancient Greek singers always sang) to spend infinite pains
on the enunciation of the words.[5] But what seemed to the orthodox to

---

[1] Mountford, op. cit., p. 168; *Rainer Papyri* v (1892), pp. 65–73. The papyrus in fact dates,
as Turner (*J.H.S.* 76 (1956), p. 95) has shown, from the Ptolemaic period, prob. *c.* 200 B.C.
On the text and its musical implications, see also G. A. Longman, *C.Q.*, N.S. 12 (1962),
pp. 61–66; Dale, *Lyric Metres*, pp. 197 f.

[2] *Hibeh Papyri*, vol. i, no. 13 (discussed by Mountford, op. cit., pp. 181 f.).

[3] Even today there are types of music which would be felt by some to be inappropriate in
church, and the inspiriting effect of a great march-tune is quite different from the emotions
commonly associated with a waltz, though different sorts of people experience such effects
in very different degrees, as Aristotle himself pointed out (*Pol.* v. (viii). 1340[a]31).

[4] Athen. xiv. 617 b. See above, p. 256.

[5] When Plutarch, *Quaest. Conv.* vii. 713 c, says τὸ δὲ μέλος καὶ τὸν ῥυθμὸν ὥσπερ ὄψον ἐπὶ
τῷ λόγῳ καὶ μὴ καθ' αὑτὰ προσφέρεσθαι, the context shows that he is thinking mainly of singing
at a symposium, and that λόγος means 'conversation'.

be corruption set in when a new school of poets,[1] and above all Timotheos, introduced, first into dithyrambs and νόμοι, music of a much more elaborate and florid type, abandoning strophic responsion (as Melanippides had done) and producing long and complex stanzas, with constantly shifting metre, and presumably, therefore, music. This style was adopted in tragedy by Agathon and Euripides, who are mocked by Aristophanes for their innovations[2] —their notes running hither and thither, compared with the tiny, tortuous galleries of an ant-hill, and probably also the setting of a single syllable to several notes. (This actually occurs once in the fragment of Euripides' *Orestes* already referred to.) Such things could hardly fail to rob the words of the required precision in utterance. Timotheos was kindly encouraged by Euripides when the theatre hissed him, and was assured that before long he would have the applause of every audience;[3] but it may be that the obscurity imparted to the words of the tragic chorus was one, among others, of the causes of its rapid decline in the fourth century. Audiences might not care to listen to words which they could not follow.

The problem of the relation between the music and the accentuation, and between the music and the quantities and scansion of the words sung, at present admits of no certain solution, and the evidence is conflicting. The statements of Dionysius of Halikarnassos[4] on both points appear to

---

[1] *Dith. Trag. Com.*², pp. 39 ff. The guilty poets are enumerated in Pherekrates, fr. 145 (K), and include Melanippides, Phrynis, Kinesias, and Philoxenos as well as Timotheos. On Melanippides and Philoxenos, see Maas, *R.E.* xv. i, coll. 422 f.; xx. i, coll. 192 ff.; on Pherekrates, fr. 145, see Düring, *Eranos* 43 (1945), pp. 176 ff.

[2] Ar. *Thesm.* 100 μύρμηκος ἀτραπούς, ἢ τί διαμινύρεται (sc. Ἀγάθων); cf. *Frogs* 1301 ff. See especially l. 1314, εἰειειειλίσσετε. Kranz (*Stasimon*, pp. 228 ff.) dates Euripides' adoption of the new style from the *Troades* in 415 B.C. (cf. *Troad.* 511 ἀμφί μοι Ἴλιον, ὦ Μοῦσα, καινῶν ὕμνων ἄεισον ... ᾠδάν), and notices that from this time Euripides' choruses were all feminine, and therefore, he supposes, especially suited to the new style. In fact the influence of Timotheos is perhaps most noticeable in the actor-arias of late Euripides, e.g. those of Ion (*Ion* 112 ff.— still strophic) and the Phrygian (*Orest.* 1369 ff.). On Timotheos and his relation to Euripides, see also Maas, *R.E.* s.v. Timotheos (9); Bassett, *Class. Philol.* 26 (1931), pp. 153 ff. (an important article). For Agathon's musical innovations, see below, pp. 322 f.

[3] Plutarch, *an seni* 795 d. Satyrus (*Vit. Eur.*, fr. 39, col. 22) reports that Euripides composed the prelude for Timotheos' νόμος, *The Persians*, and the story is not impossible: see Maas, loc. cit.

[4] *de Comp. Verb.* xi τάς τε λέξεις τοῖς μέλεσιν ὑποτάττειν ἀξιοῖ (sc. ἡ ὀργανικὴ καὶ ᾠδικὴ μοῦσα) καὶ οὐ τὰ μέλη ταῖς λέξεσιν, ὡς ἐξ ἄλλων τε πολλῶν δῆλον καὶ μάλιστα ἐκ τῶν Εὐριπίδου μελῶν, ἃ πεποίηκεν τὴν Ἠλέκτραν λέγουσαν ἐν Ὀρέστῃ πρὸς τὸν χορόν (*Orest.* 140-2) ... τὸ δ' αὐτὸ γίγνεται καὶ περὶ τοὺς ῥυθμούς. ἡ μὲν γὰρ πεζὴ λέξις οὐδενὸς οὔτε ὀνόματος οὔτε ῥήματος βιάζεται τοὺς χρόνους οὐδὲ μετατίθησιν, ἀλλ' οἵας παρείληφεν τῇ φύσει τὰς συλλαβὰς τάς τε μακρὰς καὶ τὰς βραχείας, τοιαύτας φυλάττει· ἡ δὲ μουσική τε καὶ ῥυθμικὴ μεταβάλλουσιν αὐτὰς μειοῦσαι καὶ παραύξουσαι, ὥστε πολλάκις εἰς τἀναντία μεταχωρεῖν· οὐ γὰρ ταῖς συλλαβαῖς ἀπευθύνουσι τοὺς χρόνους, ἀλλὰ τοῖς χρόνοις τὰς συλλαβάς. Cf. Mountford, op. cit., pp. 164 ff.; Dale, op. cit., pp. 194–6; Winnington-Ingram, *Symbolae Osloenses* 31 (1955), pp. 64 ff.; *Lustrum* 3 (1958), pp. 41–43.

contradict such evidence as the musical fragments afford, with the important exception of the *Orestes* musical papyrus and one or two other relatively early pieces; but the reader who desires to pursue the matter further may be referred to more specialist treatises, with only this caution, that we do not know how or to what music lyric excerpts (or lyric passages in reproductions of classical plays) may have been sung in the time of Dionysius some three hundred years later.

5. Little use seems to have been made in the classical drama of instrumental music apart from words; but a few notes are sometimes interjected in comedy for special purposes—the song of the nightingale imitated on the flute in *Birds*,[1] or the twanging of the lyre between the lines of Aeschylus travestied by Euripides in *Frogs* (τοφλαττοθρατ τοφλαττοθρατ). Such effects were termed διαύλιον[2] or μεσαύλιον.[3]

To lead the singing, the first note (ἐνδόσιμον) was given not by an instrument but by the coryphaeus, though it is to be feared that the start was sometimes assisted by the flute-player, not with his instrument only but with a wooden shoe (κρούπεζα) which he wore for the purpose. (Photius also speaks of a rattle.[4])

---

[1] l. 222, where the text contains the παρεπιγραφή "αὐλεῖ" and the schol. explains ὅτι μιμεῖταί τις τὴν ἀηδόνα ὡς ἔτι ἔνδον οὖσαν ἐν τῇ λόχμῃ. Cf. Menander, *Dyskolos* 880 αὐλεῖ.

[2] Schol. Ar. *Frogs* 1264, and Hesych. s.v. διαύλιον· ὁπόταν ἐν τοῖς μέλεσι μεταξὺ παραβάλλῃ μέλος τι ὁ ποιητὴς παρασιωπήσαντος τοῦ χοροῦ· παρὰ δὲ τοῖς μουσικοῖς τὰ τοιαῦτα μεσαύλια.

[3] Eustath. *ad Il.* xi. 547, p. 862, 19 μεσαύλιον, κροῦμά τι μεταξὺ τῆς ᾠδῆς αὐλούμενον.

[4] [Aristot.] *de Mundo* vi. 399ᵃ14 καθάπερ δὲ ἐν χορῷ κορυφαίου κατάρξαντος συνεπηχεῖ πᾶς ὁ χορός . . . οὕτως ἔχει καὶ ἐπὶ τοῦ τὸ σύμπαν διέποντος θεοῦ· κατὰ γὰρ τὸ ἄνωθεν ἐνδόσιμον ὑπὸ τοῦ φερωνύμως ἂν κορυφαίου προσαγορευθέντος κινεῖται μὲν τὰ ἄστρα ἀεὶ καὶ ὁ σύμπας οὐρανός; Aelian, *N.A.* xv. 5 δίδωσιν ὡσπεροῦν . . . χορολέκτης τὸ ἐνδόσιμον; cf. Poll. vii. 87 ἡ δὲ κρούπεζα ξύλινον ὑπόδημα, πεποιημένον εἰς ἐνδόσιμον χοροῦ; Phot. κρουπέζαι· . . . οἱ δὲ κρόταλον ὃ ἐπιψοφοῦσιν οἱ αὐληταί.

VI

THE AUDIENCE

1. In the description of the general character of the festival of the City
Dionysia which has already been given[1] mention has been made of
the presence in the theatre of an immense audience of citizens, increased
by the attendance of a great number of visitors from abroad, some of them
being persons of distinction specially invited to seats of honour. (At the
Lenaia only citizens and metics were present.[2]) The size of the audience
at different periods cannot be precisely determined. As reconstructed
by Lycurgus, the theatre can have held 14,000–17,000 spectators.[3] The
statement of Plato, writing in the *Symposium*[4] of Agathon's victory at the
Lenaia in 417–416 b.c., that it was gained ἐν μάρτυσι τῶν Ἑλλήνων
πλέον ἢ τρισμυρίοις cannot be accepted. Even though it refers to the
theatre as it was before Lycurgus, even assuming that there were many
spectators standing—for instance, in the roadway which ran above and
afterwards across the auditorium—there can never have been 30,000
spectators, and it is best to assume that Plato is influenced by the frequent
use of 30,000 as a conventional figure for the population of Athens.[5]
Whatever the precise size of the audience, it should not be forgotten that
it was, by modern standards for dramatic performances, very large.
However good the acoustics of the theatre, the spectacular side of production and the broader and clearer dramatic effects were always more
likely to be important.

2. Discussions as to whether women and boys were in the audience
as spectators of tragedy and comedy have been confused and protracted.
That there were boys, there can be no doubt at all,[6] and there is no
trace of worry about the propriety of allowing boys to witness comedy
before Aristotle, who would forbid young men to be spectators of comedy

---

[1] Above, pp. 58 f.   [2] Ar. *Ach.* 504–8.

[3] See *Theatre of D.*, pp. 140–1, Fiechter, *Das Dionysos-Theater in Athen* i, p. 73. Epidaurus
and Megalopolis were both slightly larger, but it is doubtful whether either of them can
have held 20,000. For Epidaurus, see now von Gerkan and Müller-Wiener, *Das Theater von
Epidauros* (1961), p. 10 and n. 10 (on p. 37): they calculate an audience of 13,000–14,000.

[4] 175 e.

[5] See Gomme, *Population of Athens*, p. 3 with n. 1, Labarbe, *La Loi navale de Thémistocle*,
pp. 157–9.

[6] See, for example, Ar. *Clouds* 537–9, *Peace* 50–53, 765–6, Eupolis, fr. 244 (K), and some
of the passages quoted later for women.

until they were of an age to take part in wine-parties and had been protected against harm by good education.[1]

About the presence of women, there is more scope for doubt.[2] Neither of the two strongest pieces of comic evidence for their presence is quite decisive. *Peace* 962–7,

> ΤΡ. καὶ τοῖς θεαταῖς ῥῖπτε τῶν κριθῶν. ΟΙ. ἰδού.
>
> ΤΡ. ἔδωκας ἤδη; ΟΙ. νὴ τὸν Ἑρμῆν, ὥστε γε
> τούτων ὅσοιπέρ εἰσι τῶν θεωμένων
> οὐκ ἔστιν οὐδεὶς ὅστις οὐ κριθὴν ἔχει.
>
> ΤΡ. οὐχ αἱ γυναῖκές γ' ἔλαβον. ΟΙ. ἀλλ' εἰς ἑσπέραν
> δώσουσιν αὐταῖς ἄνδρες

may imply that the women were seated at the back of the theatre, so that the barley-corns could not reach them, or there may be, on the surface, concern that the women have not shared in the peace-celebrations, with the pun on κριθαί running through underneath. In *Frogs* 1050–1 the noble women who have committed suicide out of shame for Euripides' attacks on their sex may have seen the plays in the theatre or may merely have heard of them. These passages are at least counterbalanced by *Peace* 50–53,

> ἐγὼ δὲ τὸν λόγον γε τοῖσι παιδίοις
> καὶ τοῖσιν ἀνδρίοισι καὶ τοῖς ἀνδράσιν
> καὶ τοῖς ὑπερτάτοισιν ἀνδράσιν φράσω
> καὶ τοῖς ὑπερηνορέουσιν ἔτι τούτοις μάλα

which has no mention of women, and, even if we argue that the whole point of the joke is in the enumeration of men in an ascending order of manliness, and that the mention of women, even if they were present, would have spoiled it, it is a little difficult to see why Menander,[3] in inviting the applause of the audience at the Lenaia,

> εἶέν· συνησθέντες κατηγωνισμένοις
> ἡμῖν τὸν ἐργώδη γέροντα, φιλοφρόνως
> μειράκια, παῖδες, ἄνδρες ἐπικροτήσατε

should so pointedly have excluded his female audience, if it existed. Perhaps clapping was just something that no lady would do.

Later anecdote about the fifth century, for what it is worth, does support the presence of women. There is the story that Aeschylus'

---

[1] *Pol.* vii. 1336^b20.

[2] Most of the passages are discussed by Haigh, *Att. Th.*[3], pp. 325 ff. (for their presence, but without distinguishing the evidence for boys), and Rogers, Introduction to *Ecclesiazousae*, pp. xxix ff. (against their presence, and certainly overstating his case).

[3] *Dyskolos* 965–7.

Eumenides horrified the women into miscarriages,[1] and Athenaeus[2] records that Alcibiades, entering the theatre as choregos dressed in a purple robe, was admired not only by the men but by the women.[3] Much importance has been attached to a decree by a certain Sphyromachos or Phyromachos, which, according to a scholiast on Aristophanes *Eccles.* 22, provided that there should be separate seats for men and women, and for free women and courtesans. Even if such a decree ever existed, Praxagora, whose women are about to pose as men in the Assembly, should not be referring to it here, and it is not impossible that the scholiast has no independent information and is merely making a bad guess at the meaning of a corrupt passage.

For the fourth century, there are passages of Plato which appear more decisive. In one passage of the *Laws*[4] tragedy is said δημηγορεῖν πρὸς παῖδάς τε καὶ γυναῖκας καὶ τὸν πάντα ὄχλον; in another[5] the Athenian speaker declares that, if all forms of public entertainment were passed in review, to be judged by the pleasure they gave, little boys would put the conjurer first, older boys the comic poet, while young men, educated women, and the public generally would prefer tragedy. (Old men would prefer the rhapsode.) Earlier, in *Gorgias*,[6] the drama is condemned as a form of rhetoric aiming solely at pleasure and addressed to children, women, and men alike, both slave and free, and the reference is explicitly to theatrical performance, not to reading.

For the Roman period, the evidence of the seats in the theatre leaves no doubt, for many of them are explicitly inscribed with the names and offices of priestesses and other ladies of distinction.[7]

The only evidence bearing on the presence of slaves is the passage of *Gorgias* just quoted and the behaviour of Theophrastus' Ἀναίσχυντος, who takes his sons and their παιδαγωγός to the theatre with tickets he has bought for someone else.[8] It is unlikely that there were ever very many.

3. The only explicit evidence about the cost of a seat is that Demosthenes[9] protests that if, in 346 B.C., he had not provided that Philip's

---

[1] *Vit. Aesch.* 9, Pollux iv. 110.

[2] xii. 534 c (p. 62 above, n. 1), probably quoting Satyrus (third century B.C.).

[3] Cf. the early third-century scrap of a work recording sayings of Socrates (*P. Hibeh* 182, col. ii. 15) ἡ δὲ Ξανθίππη βουλομ[έ]νη εἰς Διονύσια ἐξελθεῖν . . . .

[4] vii. 817 c.   [5] ii. 658 a–d.

[6] 502 b–d; see especially 502 d ΣΩ. ἦ οὐ ῥητορεύειν δοκοῦσί σοι οἱ ποιηταὶ ἐν τοῖς θεάτροις; ΚΑΛ. ἔμοιγε. ΣΩ. νῦν ἄρα ἡμεῖς ηὑρήκαμεν ῥητορικήν τινα πρὸς δῆμον τοιοῦτον οἷον παίδων τε ὁμοῦ καὶ γυναικῶν καὶ ἀνδρῶν, καὶ δούλων καὶ ἐλευθέρων, ἣν οὐ πόλυ ἀγάμεθα.

[7] *I.G.* ii², 5063 A, 5093–164.   [8] *Char.* ix. 5 (p. 266 below, n. 8).

[9] *de Cor.* 28. The comment of the scholiast—δύο γὰρ ὄντων πρέσβεων δύο ἦσαν οἱ ὀβολοί— is impossible as an interpretation of the text, but there was in later times a belief that of

ambassadors should be given seats of honour, ἐν τοῖν δυοῖν ὀβολοῖν
ἐθεώρουν ἄν, they would have watched the play from the two-obol seats,
and it is generally assumed that this implies a uniform price throughout
the theatre. Some scholiasts and lexicographers[1] support this by treating
two obols as the unit of the theorikon, and there is one other classical
text[2] which points the same way.

The price of the seat will have gone to the lessee to whom the state
granted the contract for the care of the theatre. Three names are found,
ἀρχιτέκτων,[3] θεατρώνης,[4] and θεατροπώλης.[5] The evidence is clearest for
the Peiraeus, where in the early fourth century four lessees undertook
to provide seating and appear to have been paid in cash.[6] If Ulpian is to
be believed,[7] the ἀρχιτέκτων at Athens was also paid cash, but he gives
the fee as one obol. Theophrastus attests the buying of seats[8] and also
the possibility that the θεατρῶναι might make some seats free.[9] The lessee
was responsible for the seating of those to whom the state assigned places
of honour;[10] it is not known whether he was paid for these seats.

The history of the theorikon is confused. Plutarch[11] attributes the introduction of θεωρικά to Pericles, as one of his devices for bribing the people,
and Ulpian[12] agrees with this, adding the further reason (repeated in the

the two obols only one was paid to the lessee of the theatre, and the other was for refreshments; see the quotation from Ulpian, below, n. 7.

[1] Schol. on Ar. *Wasps* 1189; *Etym. Magn.* p. 448, 47 ff.; 'Suidas' s.v. θεωρικόν; Ulpian, below,
n. 7.

[2] Dem. περὶ συντάξεως 10 (*c.* 352 B.C.) πολλῶν καὶ μεγάλων καὶ καλῶν ὄντων τούτων ἁπάντων,
τῶν μὲν ἄλλων οὐδενὸς οὐδεὶς μέμνηται, τοῖν δυοῖν δ' ὀβολοῖν ἅπαντες.

[3] *I.G.* ii². 466, 500, 512 (late fourth century), *S.E.G.* xiv. 65 (271–270 B.C.), *I.G.* ii². 792
(252–251 B.C.), all Athens; *I.G.* ii². 456 (307–306 B.C.), Peiraeus; Ulpian, below, n. 7.

[4] Theophr. *Char.* xxx. 6 καὶ ἐπὶ θέαν τηνικαῦτα πορεύεσθαι ἄγων τοὺς υἱεῖς, ἡνίκα προῖκα
ἀφιᾶσιν οἱ θεατρῶναι (certainly the best reading; see Dilke, *B.S.A.* 43 (1948), p. 130).

[5] Pollux vii. 199 θεατροπώλης ὁ θέαν ἀπομισθῶν.   [6] *I.G.* ii². 1176.

[7] On Dem. *Olynth.* I. i, p. 32 Dindorf, ἐπειδήπερ χρήματα ἔχοντες στρατιωτικὰ οἱ Ἀθηναῖοι
ἔναγχος αὐτὰ πεποιήκασι θεωρικά, ὥστε λαμβάνειν ἐν τῷ θεωρεῖν ἕκαστον τῶν ἐν τῇ πόλει δύο
ὀβολούς, ἵνα τὸν μὲν ἕνα κατασχῇ εἰς ἰδίαν τροφήν, τὸν δὲ ἄλλον παρέχειν ἔχωσι τῷ ἀρχιτέκτονι
τοῦ θεάτρου· οὐδὲ γὰρ εἶχον τότε θέατρον διὰ λίθων κατεσκευασμένον, which implies, as at the
Peiraeus, the lessee's responsibility for providing seating.

[8] *Char.* ix. 5 καὶ ξένοις δὲ αὐτοῦ θέαν ἀγοράσας μὴ δοὺς τὸ μέρος θεωρεῖν, ἄγειν δὲ καὶ τοὺς
υἱεῖς εἰς τὴν ὑστεραίαν καὶ τὸν παιδαγωγόν, generally thought to imply that foreigners could
not buy seats, but this does not seem a safe deduction.   [9] Above, n. 4.

[10] Dem. *de Cor.* 28 and the epigraphical references in n. 3 above.

[11] *Per.* 9. 2–3 τούτοις (sc. Kimon's lavishness) ὁ Περικλῆς καταδημαγωγούμενος τρέπεται
πρὸς τὴν τῶν δημοσίων διανομήν, συμβουλεύσαντος αὐτῷ Δαμωνίδου τοῦ Ὄαθεν, ὡς Ἀριστοτέλης
ἱστόρηκε· καὶ ταχὺ θεωρικοῖς καὶ δικαστικοῖς λήμμασιν ἄλλαις τε μισθοφοραῖς καὶ χορηγίαις
συνδεκάσας τὸ πλῆθος ἐχρῆτο κατὰ τῆς ἐξ Ἀρείου πάγου βουλῆς. The source is Theopompus
(Wade-Gery, *Essays in Greek History*, pp. 236–8); Aristotle (Ἀθ. Πολ. xxvii. 3–4) is only
quoted for the part of Damonides, and does not mention the θεωρικά.

[12] On Dem. *Olynth.* I. i, p. 33 Dindorf, ἰστέον δὲ ὅτι τὰ χρήματα ταῦτα τὰ δημόσια θεωρικὰ
ἐποίησεν ἐξ ἀρχῆς ὁ Περικλῆς δι' αἰτίαν τοιαύτην· ἐπειδὴ πολλῶν θεωμένων καὶ στασιαζόντων
διὰ τὸν τόπον, καὶ ξένων καὶ πολιτῶν, καὶ λοιπὸν τῶν πλουσίων ἀγοραζόντων τοὺς τόπους,

lexicographers) that the struggle of both citizens and foreigners for seats in the theatre had become so violent and the buying up of seats such an abuse that to give the poor their chance Pericles instituted a theoric fund from which they were given money to buy seats. The figure is given both as two obols and as one drachma; perhaps the latter figure represents the three days of tragedies. Something also happened to the institution in the first decade of the fourth century, to judge from Harpokration's assertion that Agyrrhios founded it, which may be a confusion with his institution of assembly-pay[1] or merely concern the source of the money, and the statement of 'Suidas'[2] that ἐπὶ Διοφάντου (395–394 B.C.) τὸ θεωρητικὸν ἐγένετο δραχμή.

The problem is made more difficult by references to a διωβελία founded by Kleophon.[3] This is probably a special measure of poor-relief started in the closing stages of the Peloponnesian War. There is no reason to connect the word with the theatre.[4]

How far the scale of theoric distributions had risen by the time of Demosthenes and how many festivals it covered (we hear at least of the Dionysia and Panathenaia)[5] we cannot say. The highest figure we hear of is five drachmae, drawn by a certain Konon on behalf of his son.[6]

βουλόμενος ἀρέσαι τῷ δήμῳ καὶ τοῖς πένησιν, ἵνα ἔχωσι καὶ αὐτοὶ πόθεν ὠνεῖσθαι τόπους, ἔγραψε τὰ προσοδευόμενα χρήματα τῇ πόλει γενέσθαι πᾶσι θεωρικὰ τοῖς πολίταις. Cf. Harpokr. s.v. θεωρικά· . . . θεωρικὰ ἦν τινὰ ἐν κοινῷ χρήματα ἀπὸ τῶν τῆς πόλεως προσόδων συναγόμενα, ταῦτα δὲ πρότερον μὲν εἰς τὰς τοῦ πολέμου χρείας ἐφυλάττετο, καὶ ἐκαλεῖτο στρατιωτικά, ὕστερον δὲ κατετίθετο εἴς τε τὰς δημοσίας κατασκευὰς καὶ διανομάς, ὧν πρῶτος ἤρξατο Ἀγύρριος ὁ δημαγωγός. Φιλόχορος δὲ ἐν τῇ τρίτῃ τῆς Ἀτθίδος (F 33) φησί "τὸ δὲ θεωρικὸν ἦν τὸ πρῶτον νομισθὲν δραχμὴ τῆς θέας, ὅθεν καὶ τοὔνομα ἔλαβε"; and 'Suidas' s.v. θεωρικά (and also Photius) πλεονεκτουμένων δὲ τῶν πενήτων διὰ τὸ ῥαδίως τοῖς πλουσίοις πλείονος τιμῆς τοῦτο γίνεσθαι, ἐψηφίσαντο ἐπὶ δραχμῇ καὶ μόνον εἶναι τὸ τίμημα; cf. schol. on Lucian, Tim. 49 (Jacobitz iv, p. 50, not accepted by Rabe) δραχμὴ δὲ ἦν τὸ διδόμενον καὶ οὔτε πλέον ἐξῆν δοῦναι δραχμῆς οὔτε ἔλαττον.

[1] Aristot. Ἀθ. Πολ. xli. 3.

[2] s.v. δραχμὴ χαλαζῶσα. For a different interpretation, see Cawkwell, J.H.S. 83 (1963), p. 55, n. 53.

[3] Aristot. Ἀθ. Πολ. xxviii. 3 τοῦ δὲ δήμου (προειστήκει) Κλεοφῶν ὁ λυροποιός, ὃς καὶ τὴν διωβελίαν ἐπόρισε πρῶτος· καὶ χρόνον μέν τινα διεδίδου, μετὰ δὲ ταῦτα κατέλυσε Καλλικράτης Παιανιεὺς πρῶτος ὑποσχόμενος ἐπιθήσειν πρὸς τοῖν δυοῖν ὀβολοῖν ἄλλον ὀβολόν. Sandys (ad. loc.) thinks that this refers to the θεωρικά, but see Tod, G.H.I. i, p. 206. The accounts of the Treasurers of Athena for 410–409 and 407–406 B.C. (Tod, nos. 83, 92) mention a number of payments by them to the Hellenotamiai ἐς τὴν διωβελίαν and Xenophon, Hellen. i. vii. 2, speaks of Ἀρχέδημος ὁ τοῦ δήμου τότε (406 B.C.) προεστηκὼς ἐν Ἀθήναις καὶ τῆς διωβελίας ἐπιμελόμενος.

[4] It is probably therefore to this institution and not to the θεωρικά which Aristot. Pol. ii. 1267[b]1 refers: ἔτι δ' ἡ πονηρία τῶν ἀνθρώπων ἄπληστον, καὶ τὸ πρῶτον μὲν ἱκανὸν διωβολία μόνον, ὅταν δ' ἤδη τοῦτ' ᾖ πάτριον, ἀεὶ δέονται τοῦ πλείονος.

[5] Hesych. s.v. θεωρικὰ χρήματα, Dem. in Leocharem 37.

[6] Hypereid. in Dem., col. 26 καὶ Κόν[ων] μὲν ὁ Παιανιεύς, [ὃς] ὑπὲρ τοῦ υἱοῦ ἔλαβ[εν] τὸ θεωρικὸν ἀπ[οδη]μοῦντος, πέντ[ε δρα]χμῶν ἕνεκεν [ἱκε]τεύων ὑμᾶς τάλαντον ὤφλεν ἐν τῷ δικαστηρίῳ, τούτων κατηγορούντων; Deinarch. in Dem. 56 πάλιν τὸν τὴν πεντεδραχμίαν ἐπὶ τῷ τοῦ μὴ παρόντος ὀνόματι λαβεῖν ἀξιώσαντα καὶ τοῦτον ὑμῖν ἀπέφηνε (sc. the Areopagus).

He was fined a talent for so doing, but inferences from the figure are uncertain, for he may have claimed for more than one festival. At any rate, the situation was such that Demosthenes felt justified in making a political issue of the matter, though ft is unlikely that the cost of the institution was ever a significant part of public expenditure.[1] As Demosthenes says himself,[2] 'the sum of money about which you are debating is small, but the habit of mind which goes with it is important'.

The θεωρικόν was paid by deme officials to full citizens on the deme register.[3] There is no reason to doubt that it was paid in cash. It seems to have covered more than the price of the ticket and contributed to a citizen's festival expenses.[4] Even the rich are said to have drawn it.[5]

4. The right to a seat of honour (προεδρία)[6] was given by the State, and was probably enjoyed *ex officio* by certain priests, of whom the priest of Dionysus always held the seat in the centre of the front row,[7] by the archons, and (at least in the course of time) by the generals; but at the time of Aristophanes' *Knights*[8] the generals seem not to have received it as a matter of course, since they can be thought of as threatening to go on strike if they did not get it:

> καὶ στρατηγὸς οὐδ' ἂν εἷς
> τῶν πρὸ τοῦ σίτησιν ᾔτησ' ἐρόμενος Κλεαίνετον·
> νῦν δ' ἐὰν μὴ προεδρίαν φέρωσι καὶ τὰ σιτία,
> οὐ μαχεῖσθαί φασιν.

The orphan sons of those who had fallen in battle received the privilege on becoming ἔφηβοι,[9] and it could be conferred on great public benefactors, such as Kleon[10] and Demosthenes,[11] and (on a vote of the Council) on ambassadors from foreign states.[12] Persons so privileged might be honourably escorted to their seats—in the Peiraeus by the demarch;[13]

---

[1] See A. H. M. Jones, *Athenian Democracy*, pp. 33–35.

[2] περὶ συντάξεως 2.   [3] Dem. *in Leocharem* 37.   [4] Ulpian, above, p. 266, n. 7.

[5] Dem. *Philippic* iv. 38.

[6] Schol. Ar. *Knights* 575 ἐξῆν δὲ τοῖς τῆς τιμῆς ταύτης τυχοῦσι καὶ ἐν βουλευτηρίῳ καὶ ἐν ἐκκλησίᾳ καὶ ἐν θεάτροις καὶ ἐν ἄλλῳ παντὶ συλλόγῳ τοὺς προλαμβάνοντας, οἵτινες ἦσαν, ἐξεγείραντας αὐτοὺς εἰς τὸν ἐκείνων τόπον καθίσαι.

[7] For the existing seat, see *Theatre of D.*, p. 143 and figs. 39–41; cf. Ar. *Frogs* 297 and scholia.

[8] ll. 573 ff. Kleainetos was the father of Kleon. The μικροφιλότιμος (Theophr. *Char.* xxi) tries to sit near the generals, for whose seats see *I.G.* ii². 500. 35–36.

[9] Aeschin. *in Ctes.* 154 (see above, p. 59, n. 2).   [10] Ar. *Knights* 702.

[11] The decree quoted in [Plut.] *Vit. X Orat.* 850 f extends the privilege to Demosthenes' descendants.

[12] Dem. *de Cor.* 28, Aeschin. *in Ctes.* 76; cf. *I.G.* ii². 456 (ambassadors from Kolophon given προεδρία in the Peiraeus, 307 B.C.).

[13] *I.G.* ii². 1214. 22 καὶ εἰσαγέτω αὐτὸν ὁ δήμαρχος εἰς τὸ θέατρον καθάπερ τοὺς ἱερεῖς καὶ τοὺς ἄλλους οἷς δέδοται ἡ προεδρία παρὰ Πειραιέων.

and Aeschines taunts Demosthenes with his undue servility towards the ambassadors of Philip in performing this duty and providing them with cushions and purple rugs or carpets (φοινικίδες) with his own hand.[1]

There are fifth-century blocks with fragmentary inscriptions which have been plausibly referred to permanent places of προεδρία,[2] but the bulk of our evidence relates to the imperial period. In the front row of the theatre of Dionysus as it is are sixty seats inscribed[3] with the names of persons and officials (mainly priests) for whom places were thus reserved; in the row behind and in other suitable places other reservations are similarly marked. A few of these seats are no longer in their original positions, and a few which were in the front row are now missing. Most of the extant inscriptions date from the time of Hadrian, and all but about a dozen are carved over earlier inscriptions wholly or partially erased. They throw a flood of light on the religious institutions of Athens in this period, but they have little to tell us about the classical theatre, coming as they do from a period when the seats of honour might be spattered with the blood of gladiators.[4]

Besides the seats assigned for προεδρία there were special parts of the theatre reserved for the Council, apparently in the middle, and for the epheboi;[5] the decree of Phyromachos, if genuine, assigned women separate places from men and courtesans from other women,[6] and it has been inferred from Aristophanes[7] that women were seated at a distance from the skene. Whether it can be inferred from a fragment of Alexis' Γυναικοκρατία that foreigners (or foreign women) were placed in one of the extreme left or right blocks is not quite certain without the context:[8]

> ἐνταῦθα περὶ τὴν ἐσχάτην δεῖ κερκίδα
> ὑμᾶς καθιζούσας θεωρεῖν ὡς ξένας.

A fifth-century inscription appears to have marked the place of the Council's attendants, but another, thought to have reserved a place for the heralds (or the γένος of the Kerykes), was not found in the theatre

---

[1] Aeschin. in Ctes. 76. Demosthenes was booed for it.

[2] See Dilke, B.S.A. 43 (1948), pp. 165–6.

[3] I.G. ii². 5021–5164. (A few minor corrections have been made in Hesperia, 16 (1947), pp. 76–77, and by Dilke, op. cit., p. 178.)

[4] Dio. Chrys. xxxi. 121 . . . Ἀθηναῖοι δὲ ἐν τῷ θεάτρῳ θεῶνται τὴν καλὴν ταύτην θέαν ὑπ' αὐτὴν τὴν ἀκρόπολιν, οὗ τὸν Διόνυσον ἐπὶ τὴν ὀρχήστραν τιθέασιν· ὥστε πολλάκις ἐν αὐτοῖς τινα σφάττεσθαι τοῖς θρόνοις, οὗ τὸν ἱεροφάντην καὶ τοὺς ἄλλους ἱερεῖς ἀνάγκη καθίζειν.

[5] Ar. Birds 794 ἐν βουλευτικῷ; schol. ad loc. οὗτος τόπος τοῦ θεάτρου ὁ ἀνειμένος τοῖς βουλευ-ταῖς, ὡς καὶ ὁ τοῖς ἐφήβοις ἐφηβικός; Peace 878–87, where the scholiast glosses ἐς μέσους as τοὺς θεατὰς ἢ τὸ βουλευτήριον; Poll. iv. 122 ἐκαλεῖτο δέ τι καὶ βουλευτικὸν μέρος τοῦ θεάτρου καὶ ἐφηβικόν.

[6] See above, p. 265.   [7] See above, p. 264.

[8] Fr. 41 (K). See Rogers, Introduction to Ecclesiazousae, pp. xxxiii f.

and may have nothing to do with it.[1] It has been thought that each of the tribes (φυλαί) had its own block of seats out of the thirteen wedge-shaped blocks (κερκίδες) into which the theatre was divided. In the time of Hadrian, a statue of the emperor, of which the base is preserved, stood at the foot of the central block, erected by the Areopagus, the Council, and the people of Athens in A.D. 112;[2] the bases of three statues of Hadrian are also preserved, erected respectively by the tribes Erechtheis, Akamantis, and Oineis, at the foot of the first and sixth blocks from the east and the sixth block from the west.[3] On the assumption that the central block was the βουλευτικόν or official quarter, the positions of these bases correspond with the order of the tribes on the official list; it is therefore probable that the series of statues was once complete, and that each stood at the foot of a block appropriated wholly or in part to the tribe which dedicated it. That seating may have been by tribes in some periods is partly confirmed by the appearance of tribe names on some of the 'theatre-tickets' shortly to be discussed. Since the Lycurgan theatre was built with thirteen blocks at a time when there were only ten tribes, its original seating arrangements cannot be certainly inferred, let alone the arrangements before it.

5. The question of the existence and use of theatre tickets in Athens needs a re-examination which it cannot be given here. There is no reference to them in the literary evidence, though a passage of Theophrastus[4] indicates the use of σύμβολα as giving a right to a free seat at a conjurer's show. As has been seen, there is no evidence that the θεωρικόν was paid other than in cash. Nevertheless, we can imagine uses for such tickets, either because seats were paid for in advance, or to indicate the right of the holder to a special and perhaps free seat.

Many surviving objects have been claimed to have been theatre tickets,[5] but their right to the title is in most cases very doubtful. Svoronos[6] collected and attributed to the theatre a series of bronze tokens, stamped on one side with the head of Athena or a lion's head or some other emblem, on the other with a letter of the alphabet.[7] Some have letters on both sides. Svoronos argued that the letters referred to blocks of seats

---

[1] Theatre of D., p. 20. [2] I.G. ii². 3286. [3] Ibid., no. 3287.

[4] Char. vi. 4 καὶ ἐν θαύμασι δὲ τοὺς χαλκοῦς ἐκλέγειν καθ᾽ ἕκαστον παριὼν καὶ μάχεσθαι τούτοις τοῖς τὸ σύμβολον φέρουσι καὶ προῖκα θεωρεῖν ἀξιοῦσι.

[5] Most of the material can be found in Benndorf, Zeitschr. öst. Gym. 26 (1875), 1 ff., 83 ff., 579 ff., and Svoronos, Journ. internat. d'archéologie numismatique, 1 (1898), pp. 37–120; 3 (1900), pp. 319–43; 8 (1905), pp. 323–38.

[6] Op. cit. 1 (1898), pp. 37–120, Trésor des monnaies d'Athènes, pls. 101–2.

[7] Specimens are illustrated in the first edition of this book, fig. 205, and in Bieber, H.T.², fig. 270.

in the theatre, but he leant very heavily on the appearance of mysterious letters on the water-channel of the theatre of Dionysus.[1] These letters have been given a different and more plausible interpretation by Broneer,[2] and the last blow to Svoronos' theory has been given by the discovery in the Agora excavations of identical tokens in buildings used as law-courts.[3] Whatever these bronze tokens were, they were not theatre tickets. A series of ivory and bone tokens of the Roman period, bearing Greek and Latin numerals up to fifteen, one of which bore a picture of stage buildings and the name of Aeschylus, used to be thought to represent theatre tickets of a superior kind;[4] Rostovtzeff[5] has shown that they are counters in a game.

The only objects with a good claim to be Athenian theatre tickets are of lead, and mostly have types on one side only.[6] Their claim derives from the appearance on some of them of tragic and comic masks, tripods, and other agonistic symbols. Their lettering assigns them to various officials, and the names of tribes also appear. Their chronology needs investigation, but the spelling βολή and the letter-forms of one reading ΠΕΝ (for the Council of the πεν(τακόσιοι)) suggests that the tickets for the Council start not later than the first half of the fourth century. Some tickets of the tribe Aiantis at least appear to be of the fourth century, but the tribal tickets continue at least until after the foundation of Attalis in 200 B.C., and many of the tickets are obviously much later.[7] That lead was a convenient material for tickets is obvious, as leaden

---

[1] *Theatre of D.*, pp. 145 f.

[2] *Classical Studies presented to Edward Capps*, pp. 29–34.

[3] Boegehold, *Hesperia* 29 (1960), pp. 397–8.

[4] First edition of this book, fig. 206, nos. 9–10; Bieber, *H.T.*[2], fig. 813.

[5] *Rev. Arch.*, 4e série, 5 (1905), pp. 110 ff.

[6] The Athens specimens were collected by Svoronos, op. cit., 3 (1900), pp. 319–43 without commentary. The difficulty, even with the lead tokens, of determining whether they were used for theatrical purposes or other official business is well brought out by M. Crosby, *The Athenian Agora* x, pp. 76–82. We illustrate (fig. 140) a token stamped on one side only with a mask, inscribed ƎΠ (Crosby, L 209), which will go back to the fourth century B.C. and be an admission ticket for a member of the Council, if the conventional expansion πε(ντακόσιοι) is to be accepted, a Hellenistic double-sided token (Crosby, L 79), with, on one side, two bearded masks back to back and the inscription ΕΡΑΤΟ, and, on the other side, a kithara, which ought to be a token of admission to a musical performance, whether the inscription be expanded to ΕΡΑΤΟ(ΥΣ) or to a personal name, and, from the mid-third century A.D., a token with three masks and the inscription ΘΕΟΦΟΡΟΥ ΜΕΝΗ in two lines (Crosby, L 329). The vulgate reading Θεοφορου(μένη) Μενά(νδρου) is certainly wrong (so, already, Mylonas, *Ἀρχ. Ἐφ.* 1901, p. 120), but no other play of the name but Menander's is known. As many as twelve examples of this last are now known, which suggests strongly that the performance of the play for which this token was a ticket or souvenir was not long before the Herulian sack of Athens in A.D. 267.

[7] Other tickets thought by Svoronos to refer to plays (loc. cit., pp. 342–3) are all more or less doubtful. Αἴας, Αἰγεύς, and Οἰνεύς will all be tribal eponyms.

tokens could easily be melted down after they had been surrendered, and then re-stamped and used again.

6. With performances going on continuously from dawn to evening,[1] the audience naturally provided itself with refreshments. Some may have left the theatre for a time and gone home for a meal—as Aristophanes suggests in *Birds*,[2] it would be easy to do if they had wings; but there was also some circulation of provisions in the theatre itself, which were consumed, as Aristotle tells us, when the acting was bad,[3] and perhaps not only then. Philochorus[4] (half a century after Aristotle) gives a picture of the habits of the Athenian spectators in the past, who had a good meal before they came to the theatre, wearing garlands on their heads,[5] and kept themselves refreshed throughout the performances with wine and dried fruits and confectionery, which might also be used to pelt actors whom they did not like.[6] There is also more than one allusion to the scattering of such things among the audience by comic actors.[7] The discomfort of the hard seats was mitigated by the use of cushions, but the ostentatious placing of cushions for guests or patrons was a form of compliment which might suggest interested motives.[8] In the time of Hadrian there seem to have been awnings to shelter the two front rows in the Athenian theatre from sun and rain.[9]

There is plenty of evidence of the noisiness of Athenian audiences, both in their approval and their disapproval of a performance. Plato[10] speaks of the σύριγξ (hissing or whistling) and ἄμουσοι βοαὶ πλήθους and the κρότοι ἐπαίνους ἀποδιδόντες which had been carried so far as to establish a kind of θεατροκρατία over the poets; Demosthenes[11] asserts that

---

[1] See above, pp. 66 f. The early start is referred to in Xen. *Oecon.* iii. 7, but perhaps with reference to the Rural Dionysia.

[2] 786–9 αὐτίχ' ὑμῶν τῶν θεατῶν εἴ τις ἦν ὑπόπτερος | εἶτα πεινῶν τοῖς χοροῖσι τῶν τραγῳδῶν ἤχθετο, | ἐκπτόμενος ἂν οὗτος ἠρίστησεν ἐλθὼν οἰκάδε, | κᾆτ' ἂν ἐμπλησθεὶς ἐφ' ἡμᾶς αὖθις αὖ κατέπτατο.

[3] *Eth. Nic.* x. 1175ᵇ12 καὶ ἐν τοῖς θεάτροις οἱ τραγηματίζοντες, ὅταν φαῦλοι οἱ ἀγωνιζόμενοι ὦσι, τότε μάλιστα αὐτὸ δρῶσιν.

[4] 328 F 171 Jacoby *apud* Athen. xi. 464 f λέγει δὲ περὶ τούτων ὁ Φιλόχορος οὑτωσί· "Ἀθηναῖοι τοῖς Διονυσιακοῖς ἀγῶσι τὸ μὲν πρῶτον ἠριστηκότες καὶ πεπωκότες ἐβάδιζον ἐπὶ τὴν θέαν καὶ ἐστεφανωμένοι ἐθεώρουν, παρὰ δὲ τὸν ἀγῶνα πάντα οἶνος αὐτοῖς ᾠνοχοεῖτο καὶ τραγήματα παρεφέρετο, καὶ τοῖς χοροῖς εἰσιοῦσιν ἐνέχεον πίνειν καὶ διηγωνισμένοις, ὅτ' ἐξεπορεύοντο, ἐνέχεον πάλιν· μαρτυρεῖν δὲ τούτοις καὶ Φερεκράτη τὸν κωμικόν (fr. 194 K), ὅτι μεχρὶ τῆς καθ' ἑαυτὸν ἡλικίας οὐκ ἀσίτους εἶναι τοὺς θεωροῦντας."

[5] Cf. the oracles in Dem. *Meid.* 52–53.

[6] Dem. *de Cor.* 262—who, however, is speaking of the Rural Dionysia. Whether he is to be taken seriously when he speaks (*de F.L.* 337) of Aeschines' having been almost stoned to death may be doubted.

[7] Ar. *Wasps* 58 and schol.; *Peace* 962; *Plutus* 797–9.

[8] Aeschin. *in Ctes.* 76, *de F.L.* 111; Theophr. *Char.* ii. 11 (the κόλαξ takes the cushion from the slave and lays it for his patron himself).   [9] See *Theatre of D.*, p. 263.

[10] *Laws* iii. 700 c ff.; cf. *Rep.* vi. 492 b.   [11] *Meid.* 226.

the spectators hissed and hooted at Meidias when he entered the theatre, and if an actor or a poet was forced to retire (ἐκπίπτειν, with the active form ἐκβάλλειν), the hissing might be accompanied by the noise of heels kicking against the seats.[1] Pollux[2] speaks of a day on which the audience (evidently in a bad mood) hissed off one comic actor (and his play) after another, and Athenaeus[3] has a story of the comic poet Diphilus being violently ejected from the theatre. But physical violence in the theatre was legally an offence, which might in aggravated circumstances be punished by death. Even an official could not employ it,[4] but had to use beadles (ὑπηρέται, ῥαβδοῦχοι, or ῥαβδοφόροι)[5] to keep order. These were apparently distinct from the special officials who had to curb disorder among the singers.[6] The fight in the theatre between Alcibiades and Taureas, when they were rivals as choregoi in a dithyrambic contest and Alcibiades drove Taureas away with blows, was doubtless exceptional,[7] but the story, which narrates that, despite his conduct, the judges were intimidated into awarding the victory to Alcibiades, although the spectators were in favour of Taureas, at least illustrates the uncertainty of decisions in the theatre. At a much later date Plutarch[8] speaks of tragic actors needing the support of a claque in the theatre. The theatre beadles are not recorded to have dealt with such bad manners as those of Theophrastus' βδελυρός and ἀναίσθητος, of whom the former[9] deliberately hissed when others applauded, and applauded when the rest of the audience was silent, apart from his habit of belching in quiet moments, and the latter[10] slept soundly throughout the performances and was left sleeping when the theatre had emptied, but there is enough evidence to show that officials praised after the festival for their care for the εὐκοσμία τοῦ θεάτρου[11] had had no easy task.

---

[1] Pollux iv. 122 τὸ μέντοι τὰ ἑδώλια ταῖς πτέρναις κατακρούειν πτερνοκοπεῖν ἔλεγον· ἐποίουν δὲ τοῦτο ὁπότε τινὰ ἐκβάλοιεν. The practice is thought by some to imply wooden seats (as well as wooden shoes); see *Theatre of D.*, p. 19, and Dilke, *B.S.A.* 43, p. 148. For hissing, cf. Dem. *de Cor.* 265 ἐξέπιπτες, ἐγὼ δ' ἐσύριττον and many passages of Lucian (see, for example, below, p. 305, n. 3). The hissing might be reinforced by the peculiar sound denoted by κλώζειν; cf. Dem. *Meid.* 226 and Harpokr. s.v. ἐκλώζετε· κλωσμὸν ἔλεγον τὸν γιγνόμενον ἐν τοῖς στόμασι ψόφον, ᾧ πρὸς τὰς ἐκβολὰς ἐχρῶντο τῶν ἀκροαμάτων, ὧν οὐχ ἡδέως ἤκουον.

[2] iv. 88.   [3] xiii. 583 f.

[4] Dem. *Meid.* 178–80; cf. above, p. 69.

[5] Dem. *Meid.* 179; Ar. *Peace* 734 and schol.; Plato, *Laws* iii. 700 c.

[6] See above, p. 91.

[7] [Andoc.] *in Alc.* 20–21. Compare the uproar on the occasion of Sophocles' first competition (p. 95 above).

[8] *quomodo adulator* 63 a ἀλλ' ὥσπερ οἱ τραγῳδοὶ χοροῦ δέονται φίλων συνᾳδόντων ἢ θεάτρου συνεπικροτοῦντος. Cf. Alkiphron, *Epp.* iii. 35. 3 (Schepers) σὺ δὲ ἡμῖν μετὰ τῶν συνηθῶν ἐπίσειε τοὺς κρότους, ἵνα κἄν τι λάθωμεν ἀποσφαλέντες, μὴ λάβῃ χώραν τὰ ἀστικὰ μειράκια κλώζειν ἢ συρίττειν, ἀλλ' ὁ τῶν ἐπαίνων κρότος τὸν θροῦν τῶν σκωμμάτων παραλύσῃ.

[9] *Char.* xi. 3.   [10] *Char.* xiv. 4.   [11] See above, pp. 69f.

7. There is no reason to doubt, however, that most of the audience took its playgoing seriously. We hear of tears from the audience as early as Phrynichos' *Capture of Miletus*.[1] The reason on that occasion was extra-dramatic; at other times the credit might be divided between the actor[2] and the situation.[3] We hear remarkably little of the response to a scene as a whole and the nature of the response. If there is anything in the anecdote about the first performance of *Eumenides*,[4] spectacle was the operating feature. Plutarch[5] gives a vivid account of an audience's dread lest, in Euripides' *Kresphontes*, the old man who was to arrest Merope's blow, when she was about to murder her son, should not arrive in time, but he is not speaking of Athens.

The bulk of our evidence is of a different character, a series of anecdotes about the response of the audience to individual lines or passages, mainly prompted by moral reasons. The interests of our sources partly, but not completely, explain this preponderance. For Aeschylus, there is the line οὐ γὰρ δοκεῖν ἄριστος ἀλλ' εἶναι θέλει and its supposed reference to Aristides,[6] and the alleged attack on the playwright when he was supposed to be 'revealing the mysteries'.[7] Euripides is rich in sentiments which might be tumultuously applauded, like a line from *Aeolus*,[8] or equally tumultuously hissed, if the audience disapproved, as they did when in *Danae* they heard an eloquent passage in praise of money, and were only quieted when the poet sprang forward and advised them to wait and see what happened to the character who uttered the sentiment,[9] or when *Wise Melanippe* opened with the line, Ζεύς, ὅστις ὁ Ζεύς, οὐ γὰρ οἶδα πλὴν λόγῳ.[10] Socrates himself is said to have called for a repetition of the first three lines of *Orestes*, which contain a not very profound observation, but Cicero, who tells the story, does not say what happened.[11] To this

---

[1] Hdt. vi. 21. 2.   [2] Xen. *Symp*. iii. 11 (see p. 168, n. 4, above).

[3] Isocr. *Paneg*. 168 ἐπὶ μὲν ταῖς συμφοραῖς ταῖς ὑπὸ τῶν ποιητῶν συγκειμέναις δακρύειν ἀξιοῦσιν, ἀληθινὰ δὲ πάθη κτλ.   [4] *Vit. Aeschyli* 9, Pollux iv. 110: see above, p. 265.

[5] *De esu carn*. ii 998 e σκόπει δὲ καὶ τὴν ἐν τῇ τραγῳδίᾳ Μερόπην, ἐπὶ τὸν υἱὸν αὐτὸν ὡς φονέα τοῦ υἱοῦ πέλεκυν ἀραμένην καὶ λέγουσαν "ὠνητέραν δὴ τήνδ' ἐγὼ δίδωμί σοι | πληγήν", ὅσον ἐν τῷ θεάτρῳ κίνημα ποιεῖ, συνεξορθιάζουσα φόβῳ, καὶ δέος μὴ φθάσῃ τὸν ἐπιλαμβανόμενον γέροντα καὶ τρώσῃ τὸ μειράκιον (Eur., fr. 456, from the *Kresphontes*).

[6] Aesch. *Septem* 592, Plut. *Aristid*. 3. 5.

[7] Aristot. *Eth. Nic*. 1111ᵃ9; *Anon. in Eth. Arist*., p. 145 (Heylbut); Wilamowitz, *Aesch. Trag*., p. 15.

[8] τί δ' αἰσχρὸν ἦν μὴ τοῖσι χρωμένοις δοκῇ; (Plut. *de aud. poet*. 33 c; Stobaeus iii. 5. 36 (Hense); Nauck², fr. 19). For *Aeolus*, see now *P. Oxy*. xxvii. 2457.

[9] Seneca, *Ep*. 115. 14–15 (Nauck², fr. 324).

[10] Plut. *Amator*. 756 b. See *New Chapters* iii, p. 115 for this line and the substitute which he is said to have provided later, Ζεὺς ὡς λέλεκται τῆς ἀληθείας ὕπο. *P. Oxy*. xxvii. 2455, fr. 1 appears to have had a third version.

[11] *Tusc. Disp*. iv. 63. The lines run οὐκ ἔστιν οὐδὲν δεινὸν ὧδ' εἰπεῖν ἔπος | οὐδὲ πάθος οὐδὲ ξυμφορὰ θεήλατος | ἧς οὐκ ἂν ἄραιτ' ἄχθος ἀνθρώπου φύσις.

evidence of sensitivity in regard to anything which appealed to or con-
flicted with the Athenians' moral and political sentiments, we can add
the popular demand for the repetition of *Frogs* on account of the political
wisdom contained in the parabasis.[1] In *Frogs* itself most of the tests by
which the rival poets are tried, so far as they are serious, have a moral
or utilitarian background. To explore in detail the general question of
the relation between the political views of the audience and the political
content of Old Comedy is beyond the scope of this chapter. To put the
question in a concrete form, how could *Knights* win first prize without,
apparently, Kleon's political position being affected in the least? Part of
the answer certainly lies in the festival nature of comedy; it belongs to an
occasion where everything might reasonably be expected to be topsy-
turvy. But it is hard to steer a line between extreme views which, on the
one side, see political propaganda as Aristophanes' principal interest[2]
and, on the other, view him as a pure dramatist with no ascertainable
political views at all.[3] A modern reader is probably best advised to think
of this aspect of Aristophanes as analogous to the political cartoon, in
which the artist is compelled by his nature and vocation to criticize the
prominent and influential, though his own convictions may vary in
depth from case to case, and in which the response of the audience to good
work may not be substantially affected by its own political views.

Other special tastes are hard to define. The Athenians liked stock
jokes[4] and disliked monotony.[5] What audience does not? Agathon is said
to have failed through crowding too many events into a single plot,[6] and
the word used ($\dot{\epsilon}\xi\dot{\epsilon}\pi\epsilon\sigma\epsilon\nu$) implies that the audience as well as the judges
showed their disapproval.

Such forms of appreciation need little critical equipment, and the
general level of education among the audience should not be too highly
rated. A previous knowledge of the plot is something which a modern
audience generally manages to do without, but it is perhaps worth noting
that the Athenian audience could not, as a whole, be expected to be
familiar with the background of heroic legend on which the tragedians
drew. The clearest evidence comes from *Hippolytus*,[7]

---

[1] First hypothesis to *Frogs* (Dikaiarchos fr. 84 Wehrli).

[2] e.g. the books of Couat and Croiset.

[3] Gomme, *C.R.* 52 (1938), pp. 97–109 (= *More Essays in Greek History and Literature*, pp. 70–91).

[4] Ar. *Frogs* 1 εἴπω τι τῶν εἰωθότων, ὦ δέσποτα, | ἐφ' οἷς ἀεὶ γελῶσιν οἱ θεώμενοι;

[5] Aristot. *Poet.* xxiv. 1459ᵇ30 τὸ γὰρ ὅμοιον ταχὺ πληροῦν ἐκπίπτειν ποιεῖ τὰς τραγῳδίας.

[6] Ibid. xviii. 1456ᵃ17, where Aristotle says that poets who do this ἢ ἐκπίπτουσιν ἢ κακῶς ἀγωνίζονται, ἐπεὶ καὶ Ἀγάθων ἐξέπεσεν ἐν τούτῳ μόνῳ.

[7] 451–6: but see also Barrett's notes on ll. 41–50, 42.

ὅσοι μὲν οὖν γραφάς τε τῶν παλαιτέρων
ἔχουσιν, αὐτοί τ' εἰσὶν ἐν μούσαις ἀεί,
ἴσασι μὲν Ζεὺς ὥς ποτ' ἠράσθη γάμων
Σεμέλης, ἴσασι δ' ὡς ἀνήρπασέν ποτε
ἡ καλλιφεγγὴς Κέφαλον ἐς θεοὺς Ἕως
ἔρωτος οὕνεκ',

and this is supported by Aristotle's quite casual statement, as if of an obvious fact, in the *Poetics*[1] that even the well-known stories are well known only to a few. The comic poet Antiphanes, in contrast, complains of the advantage possessed by tragedy, as against comedy, in being able to count on a general knowledge of its themes,[2] but there can be little doubt, even without the context, that he is making an easy and obvious joke rather than giving a balanced account of the audience's education.

There were books,[3] but probably not more than a tiny fraction of the audience possessed them. Dionysus may embody one kind of Athenian when he tells of his enjoyment in reading Euripides' *Andromeda*,[4] and it must not be forgotten that after the disaster in Sicily some of the Athenian expedition secured food and water, and some even their freedom, by repeating passages of Euripides which they knew by heart.[5] In the time of Theophrastus an ability to recite ῥήσεις, presumably tragic, appears to be a social accomplishment.[6] But to generalize from such evidence would be dangerous, and the evidence from Aristophanes' literary allusions is equally difficult to assess. Some knowledge of literature is certainly pre-supposed by the abundance of parodies and allusions in his plays, but many of these are allusions to plays very recently produced or consist of parodies of the tragic style or of an author's manner rather than of particular passages. Even though some allusions may seem very recondite, an author may at times be aiming at a very small part of his audience,[7] and the same may be true of subtleties in tragedy. A readiness to admit

---

[1] ix. 1451ᵇ25 ἐπεὶ καὶ τὰ γνώριμα ὀλίγοις γνώριμά ἐστιν, ἀλλ' ὅμως εὐφραίνει πάντας.

[2] Fr. 191 K μακάριον ἐστὶν ἡ τραγῳδία | ποίημα κατὰ πάντ', εἴ γε πρῶτον οἱ λόγοι | ὑπὸ τῶν θεατῶν εἰσὶν ἐγνωρισμένοι, | πρὶν καί τιν' εἰπεῖν· ὥσθ' ὑπομνῆσαι μόνον | δεῖ τὸν ποιητήν· Οἰδίπουν γὰρ ἂν μόνον | φῶ, τἄλλα πάντ' ἴσασιν· ὁ πατὴρ Λάϊος, | μητὴρ Ἰοκάστη, θυγατέρες, παῖδες τίνες, | τί πείσεθ' οὗτος, τί πεποίηκεν. ἂν πάλιν | εἴπῃ τις Ἀλκμέωνα, καὶ τὰ παιδία | πάντ' εὐθὺς εἴρηχ', ὅτι μανεὶς ἀπέκτονεν | τὴν μητέρ', ἀγανακτῶν δ' Ἄδραστος εὐθέως | ἥξει πάλιν τ' ἄπεισι.

[3] Cf. E. G. Turner, *Athenian Books in the Fifth and Fourth Centuries B.C.*, especially pp. 16 ff.; Denniston, *C.Q.* 21 (1927), pp. 117–18; Meineke, *Com. Gr. Fr.*, Index s.vv. βιβλίον, βιβλιοπώλης.

[4] Ar. *Frogs* 52.

[5] Plut. *Nikias* 29. 3; Satyrus in *P. Oxy.* ix, no. 1176, fr. 39, col. xix. No doubt some of them had been members of dramatic choruses. That Pheidippides in *Clouds* 1371 'sang' an unedifying passage of Euripides of course proves nothing about the average Athenian.

[6] *Char.* xv. 10, xxvii. 2. See also Aeschin. i. 168, Men. *Epitr.* 767 f.

[7] See in general, on Aristophanes' literary allusions, K. J. Dover in *Fifty Years of Classical Scholarship*, p. 101.

this is compatible with a rejection of, say, Verrall's theory that many Euripidean plays were meant to be received on two levels. Aristophanes may for his own purposes flatter the audience with an allusion, it might be not without a touch of irony, to their literary sense.[1] He puts in the mouth of Aeschylus[2] the sentiment that there were no judges of poets in the world like the Athenians, but this is counterbalanced by the appeal of Euripides in Hades to the baser elements in the crowd,[3] and when Aristophanes flatters he is hardly to be taken more seriously than Demosthenes, who half a century later told the Assembly that no one was more acute than they.[4] The philosophers are more critical. Both Plato[5] and Aristotle[6] speak of poets and actors as lowering themselves to suit the depraved taste of a public dominated by the less cultivated elements in it. This view cannot be dismissed out of hand.

But there is another side, which also appears in Aristotle[7] when he says that the opinion of the multitude on literary works (not necessarily on particular performances) is worth more than that of the single critic, which may be one-sided. The roots of drama are in the theatre, not in the study, and throughout European literary history most plays of importance have been originally successful in the theatre for which they were written. Parts of them may not be to our taste, and we blame them on the conditions of their time. But their time and their audience must also be given credit for their good points. By this standard, the Athenian audience comes off triumphantly. If it could follow devotedly the three great tragedians day after day and could enjoy the wit of Aristophanes, it must have possessed on the whole a high degree of both seriousness and intelligence. It knew who its great men were, and their plays were regularly

---

[1] e.g. *Knights* 233 τὸ γὰρ θέατρον δεξιόν, *Frogs* 1109 ff. εἰ δὲ τοῦτο καταφοβεῖσθον, μή τις ἀμαθία προσῇ | τοῖς θεωμένοισιν, ὡς τὰ | λεπτὰ μὴ γνῶναι λεγόντοιν, | μηδὲν ὀρρωδεῖτε τοῦθ'· ὡς οὐκέθ' οὕτω ταῦτ' ἔχει. | ἐστρατευμένοι γάρ εἰσι, | βιβλίον τ' ἔχων ἕκαστος μανθάνει τὰ δεξιά: on the latter, see Fraenkel, *Beobachtungen zu Aristophanes*, pp. 177 ff.

[2] *Frogs* 809–10 λῆρόν τε τἄλλ' ἡγεῖτο τοῦ γνῶναι πέρι | φύσεις ποιητῶν.

[3] Ibid. 771 ff.   [4] *Olynth.* iii. 15 καὶ γνῶναι πάντων ὑμεῖς ὀξύτατοι τὰ ῥηθέντα.

[5] *Laws* ii. 659 b–c, iii. 700 c–701 a.

[6] Aristot. *Pol.* viii. 1341ᵇ15 ὁ γὰρ θεατὴς φορτικὸς ὢν μεταβάλλειν εἴωθε τὴν μουσικήν, ὥστε καὶ τοὺς τεχνίτας τοὺς πρὸς αὐτὸν μελετῶντας αὐτούς τε ποιούς τινας ποιεῖ καὶ τὰ σώματα διὰ τὰς κινήσεις, and 1342ᵃ18 ἐπεὶ δ' ὁ θεατὴς διττός, ὁ μὲν ἐλεύθερος καὶ πεπαιδευμένος, ὁ δὲ φορτικὸς ἐκ βαναύσων καὶ θητῶν καὶ ἄλλων τοιούτων συγκείμενος, ἀποδοτέον ἀγῶνας καὶ θεωρίας καὶ τοῖς τοιούτοις πρὸς ἀνάπαυσιν . . . ποιεῖ δὲ τὴν ἡδονὴν ἑκάστοις τὸ κατὰ φύσιν οἰκεῖον. διόπερ ἀποδοτέον ἐξουσίαν τοῖς ἀγωνιζομένοις πρὸς τὸν θεατὴν τὸν τοιοῦτον τοιούτῳ τινὶ χρῆσθαι τῷ γένει τῆς μουσικῆς. In the *Poetics* xiii. 1453ᵃ34, he speaks of the love of 'poetic justice'—of the play which ends well for the good and badly for the bad—as due to the ἀσθένεια of the spectators, ἀκολουθοῦσι γὰρ οἱ ποιηταὶ κατ' εὐχὴν ποιοῦντες τοῖς θεαταῖς.

[7] *Pol.* iii. 1281ᵇ7 διὸ καὶ κρίνουσιν ἄμεινον οἱ πολλοὶ καὶ τὰ τῆς μουσικῆς ἔργα καὶ τὰ τῶν ποιητῶν· ἄλλοι γὰρ ἄλλο τι μόριον, πάντα δὲ πάντες; cf. 1286ᵃ30 (without special reference to poetry) διὰ τοῦτο κρίνει ἄμεινον ὄχλος πολλὰ ἢ εἰς ὁστισοῦν.

performed. In the long run, the chances of the system of judging were of little importance. Sophocles won the first prize seventeen times against Euripides' five, but Euripides was played and recognized in his own time, though his greatest popularity came later.[1] In the one case where posterity decidedly came down against the Athenian audience, in its preference for Philemon over Menander, we have no means of judging the truth.[2]

[1] On the general question of Euripides' relations with the Athenian public, and for a modification of some extreme views, see Stevens, *J.H.S.* 76 (1956), pp. 87 ff.

[2] Quintil. x. i. 72: 'Philemon, qui ut pravis sui temporis iudiciis Menandro saepe praelatus est, ita consensu tamen omnium meruit credi secundus.' Compare the anecdote in Aulus Gellius, *N.A.* xvii. 4, where Philemon's success is attributed to *ambitus, gratia*, and *factiones*.

VII

THE ARTISTS OF DIONYSUS

1. THE organization of dramatic and musical performers into guilds or colleges at Athens and elsewhere is first definitely recorded about the end of the first quarter of the third century B.C., but it had been rendered almost inevitable by the growing importance of such performers during the fourth century, in the second half of which not only did small groups of actors go from deme to deme of Attica, but more famous actors toured the Greek world, visited the courts of Macedonian kings, and became persons of such significance that they were employed as accredited diplomatists both by Athens and by Philip. Demosthenes might ridicule Aeschines for his association with groups of inferior actors in performances in the demes,[1] but he himself more than once refers (with an obvious sense of their importance) to the diplomatic activities of such famous actors as Neoptolemos and Aristodemos in the negotiations between Athens and Philip.[2] The fact that the profession of these actors conferred upon them[3] freedom of travel and immunity from hostile action indicates that they had a recognized status. Immunity from military and naval service may also have been commonly conceded, but that it cannot have been claimed as a right is shown by the cases of Sannio, a chorus-trainer of repute, and Aristeides, a choreutes, whom Demosthenes mentions as having been punished for evading service; and the attempts of Meidias to prevent the chorus to which Demosthenes was choregos from obtaining exemption imply that it was not given as a matter of course.[4] Passages in Demosthenes imply that there must have been a large number of such professionals available, when called upon, to meet at Philip's court or camp, as, for instance, after the fall of Olynthos in 348, when he held

[1] See above, pp. 52, 169.

[2] For the public activities of these, Ktesiphon, and others, see Dem. *de Pace* 6 πάλιν τοίνυν, ὧ ἄνδρες Ἀθηναῖοι, κατιδὼν Νεοπτόλεμον τὸν ὑποκριτὴν τῷ μὲν τῆς τέχνης προσχήματι τυγχάνοντ' ἀδείας, κακὰ δ' ἐργαζόμενον τὰ μέγιστα τὴν πόλιν καὶ τὰ παρ' ὑμῶν διοικοῦντα Φιλίππῳ καὶ πρυτανεύοντα . . . , also *de F.L.* 12, 18, 94, 315; *de Cor.* 21; Aeschin. *de F.L.* 15, 16, 52, and passages in the 'Arguments' to the speeches of both orators *de F.L.*

[3] Under what kind of international law actors and musicians at this date obtained and enjoyed these immunities remains very obscure. About 279 B.C. they are guaranteed by a decree of the Amphiktyonic Council; see below, p. 282.

[4] Dem. *Meid.* 15, 58–60.

an 'Olympian festival' there, with competitions, prizes, and presents for
the performers.[1] But there is no indication that the actors of this time
formed an organized body, nor can this be inferred from the references to
them in Aristotle,[2] who says that, while they called themselves τεχνῖται,
others termed them Διονυσοκόλακες and in the *Problems* (if it be his work)
asks the reasons for their general depravity and attributes it to their
having to spend most of their time in making a living and to their habitual
intemperance.[3] (There were doubtless persons of all kinds in the profession then as now.)

2. Alexander showed an even greater passion for musicians and actors
than his father.[4] After the capture of Thebes in 335 B.C. he held a nine-
day festival at Dion, devoted mainly to dramatic contests,[5] and another
such festival in 332 at Tyre,[6] where he is said to have been distressed at
the defeat of Thettalos by Athenodoros in the competition for the actors'
prize.[7] An account given by Chares in his *History of Alexander* of the great
wedding-feast celebrated at Susa is preserved by Athenaeus.[8] The performers included, besides conjurers, a rhapsode, solo performers on the
harp and flute, singers accompanied by each instrument, tragedians,
and comedians, and the rewards given were enormous. There are also
accounts[9] of an even more extravagant festival at Ecbatana, where three
thousand Greek 'Artists' had assembled.

The example of Alexander was followed by his successors. Antipater
made the actor Archias his agent in the pursuit of Demosthenes and other
Athenian orators;[10] and Antigonus held a festival in 302 B.C. on a great
scale, gathering the most famous performers from the whole of Greece,

---

[1] Dem. *de F.L.* 192–3 ἐπειδὴ γὰρ εἷλεν Ὄλυνθον Φίλιππος, Ὀλύμπι' ἐποίει, εἰς δὲ τὴν θυσίαν
ταύτην καὶ τὴν πανήγυριν πάντας τοὺς τεχνίτας συνήγαγεν. ἑστιῶν δ' αὐτοὺς καὶ στεφανῶν τοὺς
νενικηκότας ἤρετο Σάτυρον τουτονὶ τὸν κωμικὸν ὑποκριτήν, τί δὴ μόνος οὐδὲν ἐπαγγέλλεται.

[2] *Rhet.* iii. 2. 1405ᵃ23 f.

[3] *Probl.* xxx. 10 διὰ τί οἱ Διονυσιακοὶ τεχνῖται ὡς ἐπὶ τὸ πολὺ πονηροί εἰσιν; ἢ ὅτι ἥκιστα λόγου
σοφίας κοινωνοῦσι διὰ τὸ περὶ τὰς ἀναγκαίας τέχνας τὸ πολὺ μέρος τοῦ βίου εἶναι, καὶ ὅτι ἐν
ἀκρασίαις τὸ πολὺ τοῦ βίου εἰσίν, τὰ δὲ καὶ ἐν ἀπορίαις; ἀμφότερα δὲ φαυλότητος παρασκευαστικά.

[4] Plut. *Alex.* 4. 11.

[5] Diod. xvii. 16 (Arrian i. 11. 1 says it was at Aigai). Similar festivals had been held earlier
by Archelaus.

[6] Plut. *Alex.* 29; *de Alex. fortuna* ii. 2.

[7] Athenodorus was fined by the Athenians for his failure to appear at the Dionysia, and the
fine was paid by Alexander. The liability of artists to fines of this kind is laid down in the
Euboean Law, *c.* 290 B.C. (Appendix, no. 1), and elaborate provisions are made. See below,
p. 282 and also p. 300.

[8] xii. 538 c–539 a. See especially 538 f καὶ ἔκτοτε οἱ πρότερον καλούμενοι Διονυσοκόλακες
Ἀλεξανδροκόλακες ἐκλήθησαν διὰ τὰς τῶν δώρων ὑπερβολάς, ἐφ' οἷς καὶ ἥσθη ὁ Ἀλέξανδρος.
ὑπεκρίθησαν δὲ τραγῳδοὶ μὲν Θεσσαλὸς καὶ Ἀθηνόδωρος καὶ Ἀριστόκριτος, κωμῳδοὶ δὲ Λύκων
καὶ Φορμίων καὶ Ἀρίστων. παρῆν δὲ καὶ Φρασίμηλος ὁ ψάλτης. οἱ δὲ πεμφθέντες, φησί, στέφανοι
ὑπὸ τῶν πρεσβευτῶν καὶ τῶν λοιπῶν ταλάντων ἦσαν μυρίων πεντακισχιλίων.

[9] Plut. *Alex.* 72; Arrian vii. 14.   [10] Plut. *Demosth.* 28.

at Antigoneia.[1] But there is still no suggestion of organized guilds,[2] such as are spoken of a quarter of a century later (and from then onwards) in connexion with festivals regularly celebrated at Delphi or organized by great patrons, and we can only conjecture the reasons which led to the almost sudden springing into existence of guilds, κοινά or σύνοδοι,[3] of Dionysiac artists, including musicians (both soloists and accompanists) and actors. Those who joined in them may have been impelled by their own interest and convenience; theatres were being built everywhere, to which they travelled to earn their livelihood, and some degree of organization would be almost necessary; while, on the other hand, local associations may have been encouraged by the authorities of the more important towns, so as to secure performers for their own festivals. The records show that dramatic and musical contests were far from being confined to festivals of Dionysus, and it is evident that the drama and music thus circulating throughout the Greek world were the most popular and influential form of culture for several hundred years. New festivals[4] were instituted from time to time in honour of kings and princes, and of Rome also, when Rome acquired the empire of Greece and Asia Minor. Local 'Olympian' and 'Pythian' festivals sprang up in many places. At all of these the services of the Artists of Dionysus might be demanded, and this required that there should be a recognized organization of the artists, and some regular connexion between their guilds and the cities and courts at which they appeared.

3. The birth of the guilds can be approximately dated. The remarkable law or agreement[5] between the cities of Euboea, which was passed in a year falling between 294 and 288 B.C., shows no knowledge of them, and assumes that arrangements were made by the cities for their several festivals with individual artists.[6] The law makes elaborate regulations for the Dionysia at Karystos, Eretria, Chalkis, and Oreos,[7] the Demetrieia

---

[1] Diod. xx. 108.

[2] It is probable that Chamaileon (quoted by Athen. ix. 407 b) was guilty of an anachronism when he said of Hegemon, the parodist of the fifth century, ὁ δὲ παραγενόμενος καὶ συναγαγὼν τοὺς περὶ τὸν Διόνυσον τεχνίτας προσῆλθε μετ' αὐτῶν Ἀλκιβιάδῃ βοηθεῖν ἀξιῶν, but in any case his language does not necessarily imply a κοινόν or σύνοδος.

[3] On the slight distinction sometimes implied between κοινόν and σύνοδος, and the history of the two terms in application to the artists' guilds, see Poland, R.E., zweite Reihe, v. 2480. The distinction is generally almost imperceptible, but σύνοδος seems gradually to have prevailed over κοινόν as the name of a guild.

[4] For lists and accounts of these see Ferguson, Hellenistic Athens, pp. 295 ff.; Tarn–Griffith, Hellenistic Civilisation, pp. 113–14.

[5] Appendix, no. 1.

[6] Compare S.E.G. i. 362, where, c. 306, Samos sends ambassadors to the tragic actor Polos to fix the terms on which he will appear. He settles for the takings at the theatre and no fixed fee.

[7] The Dionysia at Eretria and Oreos were in the month Lenaion.

at Oreos, and the Aristonikeia[1] at Karystos. It appoints agents or contractors (ἐργολάβοι), who are put on oath and required to engage performers and take guarantees from them and to provide for them during
the festivals; each of the four cities of Euboea is required to send θεωροί
to each festival at its own expense, and is to give 600 drachmae of
Demetrian currency (the coinage of Demetrius I of Macedonia, c. 294–
288 B.C.) to each flute-player, 400 to a κωμῳδός, 300 to a costumier
(ἱματιομίσθης)—the figure for a τραγῳδός is lost—and daily rations to
all, including trainers (διδάσκαλοι) and members of cyclic choruses.
ἐργολάβοι, τεχνῖται, and their guarantors are subjected to fines and other
penalties for default, though excuses on oath (ἐξωμοσίαι) are allowed
under very elaborate provisions.

But shortly afterwards two decrees from Delphi attest the existence
of organized guilds of the artists. The first[2] is of uncertain date, but
certainly precedes the Gallic invasion of 279, and runs Δελφοὶ ἔδωκαν τῷ
κοινῷ τῶν τεχνιτᾶν τοῖς ἐς Ἰσθμὸν καὶ Νεμέαν συμπορευομένοις προμαντείαν,
προεδρίαν, προδικίαν, ἄρχοντος Αἰνησίλα. The second,[3] more informative,
is almost certainly to be dated precisely to 279–278, after the repulse of
that invasion. We possess two copies of it, one from Athens and one
from Delphi, both made one hundred and fifty years or so later, but
there is no reason to doubt its authenticity. In it the Amphiktyons
guarantee to οἱ ἐν Ἀθήναις τεχνῖται freedom from arrest in war and peace,
exemption from military and naval service, and, generally, safety of
person and property, any offender against them, and even the city in
which the offence was committed, being made responsible to the Amphiktyons. This immunity is regarded as previously existing, συγκεχωρη-
μένη ὑπὸ πάντων τῶν Ἑλλήνων. But this is the first appearance of the
organized Athenian guild, which seems to be represented by its own
ambassadors, Astydamas the tragic poet and Neoptolemos the tragic
actor, clearly descendants of the fourth-century figures of the same names
and professions.

These two major guilds, the Isthmian–Nemean and the Athenian,
seem then to have come into existence at roughly the same time. It is
true that an Amphiktyonic decree of the late second century[4] asserts
the priority of the Athenian guild, but, as will be seen, it was passed at
a time when the Athenian guild was in the ascendant and the Isthmian–
Nemean guild in disgrace, and it may simply have in mind the acknowledged fact that Athens was the first home of plays and actors.

---

[1] Aristonikos was a companion of Alexander and a distinguished ball-player (Athen. i. 19 a).
[2] S.I.G.³ 460 (wrongly dated).　　　[3] Appendix, no. 2.　　　[4] S.I.G.³ 704E.

4. It has been suggested[1] that this Amphiktyonic support for the Artists of Dionysus reflects a wish to enlist their help for the festival of the Soteria, newly founded to commemorate the repulse of the Gauls. The problems connected with the Soteria are extremely complex and deeply involved with wider problems concerning the chronology of the third century.[2] It must suffice here to say that it seems most probable that we have to deal with two series of festivals, one organized by the Amphiktyons and most probably annual, starting shortly after the Gallic invasion, and a second, celebrated probably every four years and starting possibly in 248, under the direct patronage of the Aetolian League, which had come to control Delphi. It is with the first group that we have direct evidence of the participation of the guilds. Its earliest inscriptions[3] begin with a prescript, which, after the names of the Delphic archon and the Amphiktyonic *hieromnemones*, continues ἐπὶ ἱερέως δὲ Πυθοκλέους τοῦ Ἀριστάρχου Ἑρμιονέος ἐκ τῶν τεχνιτῶν, τὸ κοινὸν τῶν τεχνιτῶν ἐπέδωκε τῶι θεῶι καὶ τοῖς Ἀμφικτύοσιν εἰς τὰ Σωτήρια τὸν ἀγῶνα παντελῆ. They continue ἠγωνίσαντο οἵδε, giving a full list of those taking part. The later inscriptions of this group[4] retain the reference to the priest, but omit the statement that the guild, which is never directly named, but which appears to be the Isthmian–Nemean, contributed its services with all the expenses to the god and to the Amphiktyons. Whether the guild thought it had done enough for prestige or whether the Amphiktyons became more solvent is doubtful, but henceforth the waiving of his fee by an individual competitor becomes a matter for special thanks by the Amphiktyons, as we see from the case of Menalkes, an Athenian citharode, who παραγενόμενος εἰς Δελφοὺς εἰς τὰ Σωτήρια τόν τε ἄλλον ἀγῶνα καλῶς καὶ φιλοτίμως ἠγωνίσατο καὶ προσεπέδωκε τῶι θεῶι καὶ τοῖς Ἀμφικτύοσι τὸν ἀγῶνα and was rewarded with a crown of the god's own bay.[5]

These Soteria inscriptions throw valuable light on the membership of the guild in the third century and on the production of drama. In a typical year[6] these competing include 2 rhapsodes, 2 κιθαρισταί, 2 κιθαρωιδοί, 5 παῖδες χορευταί, and 5 ἄνδρες χορευταί (these ten probably being only the leaders of their dithyrambic choruses), 2 αὐληταί each with a διδάσκαλος, three tragic teams, each consisting of 3 τραγωιδοί, an

---

[1] Flacelière, *Les Aitoliens à Delphes*, pp. 121–2.

[2] Ibid., pp. 134–77; Dinsmoor, *The Athenian Archon List*, pp. 109–40. These provide the best general introduction. That we are in any way near a solution is due to Roussel, *R.E.A.* 26 (1924), pp. 97–111. See, most recently, Sifakis, *Studies*, pp. 63–71.

[3] *S.E.G.* i. 187B with *Fouilles de Delphes*, iii. 1. 563; *S.E.G.* i. 187A; *S.I.G.*³ 489 with *B.C.H.* 83 (1959), pp. 167 ff.

[4] The most complete are *S.G.D.I.* 2563–6 (single specimens in *S.I.G.*³ 424 and Michel 895).

[5] *S.I.G.*³ 431 (same year as *S.G.D.I.* 2564).   [6] *S.G.D.I.* 2563 = *S.I.G.*³ 424.

αὐλητής, and a διδάσκαλος, four comic teams, each consisting of 3 κωμωιδοί, an αὐλητής, and a διδάσκαλος, 7 χορευταὶ κωμικοί, and 3 ἱματιομίσθαι. Of a tragic chorus there is no trace. This is impressive variety, and equally impressive is the wide area from which the competitors are drawn. The inscriptions of the Amphiktyonic Soteria list some 251 different artists, 41 from Arkadia, 40 from Corinth, Megara, and Sikyon, 24 from the rest of the Peloponnese, 29 from Athens, 57 from Boeotia, 12 from west-central Greece, 10 from north Greece, 4 western Greeks, 13 islanders, 11 from Asia Minor and the East, and 10 from the Black Sea area.[1]

The two known priests of the guild, who seem to serve for several years each, call for some comment. The earlier, Pythokles of Hermione, appears also in the inscriptions as leader of a men's chorus, together with his brother Pantakles. He seems to have been one of the most famous artists of his day. The epitaph which Pantakles raised for him at Hermione is now lost, but even the imperfect copy[2] shows us that he had thirteen victories at the Nemea, Isthmia, and Pythia together, perhaps three at Olympia, and numerous others up and down Greece. Reference is made to the Muses of Helicon and Dionysos Kadmeios, and the triumphant conclusion is

[κ]αὶ [β]ασιλεῖς δώροισιν ἐτίμησαν τὸν ἀοιδόν,
[υ]ἱὸν Ἀριστάρχου θεοῖς φίλον Ἑρμιονῆ.

Which kings these were, we do not know, but he received the proxeny of Delphi,[3] as much, no doubt, for his services as priest of the technitai as for his prowess as a citharode. The later priest, Philonides of Zakynthos, was a comic actor, appearing as such in one of the years in which he acts as priest, and we have records of his appearances at Delos and at Athens.[4]

The records of the Aetolian Soteria hardly throw any light on the guilds. The priest disappears and the guilds are not mentioned. Even our knowledge of the competition is sadly cut down since only the victors' names are inscribed.[5]

5. Elsewhere in this century, however, the help of the guilds was clearly regarded as essential in the establishment or enlargement of a festival. Two of these 'new' festivals, that for the Muses of Helicon and

---

[1] The figures are from Kahrstedt, *Hermes* 72 (1937), p. 380, and could now be slightly modified. Sifakis, *C.Q.* 15 (1965), 206–14 = *Studies*, pp. 136–46, argues that the festival was not confined to one guild.   [2] *I.G.* iv. 682.

[3] *S.G.D.I.* 2602.   [4] *I.G.* xi. 2. 113, l. 25; above, pp. 113, 116.

[5] *S.I.G.*³ 509 is a convenient example.

that for Dionysos Kadmeios at Thebes, have already been referred to in the epitaph of Pythokles, but they have considerable epigraphic documentation besides.

The Mouseia of Thespiae clearly have a long history, but the documents which concern us here come from a group which belongs to a reorganization between 211 and 208 B.C.,[1] as a result of which the θυμελικὸς ἀγών, that is, the competitions for a ποιητὴς ἐπῶν, an αὐλητής, an αὐλῳδός, a καθαριστής, and a κιθαρῳδός, first became στεφανίτης. We possess a well-preserved decree of the Isthmian–Nemean guild[2] in response to the invitation to attend, dilating on the close links which have always existed between it, the city of Thespiae and the Boeotian League, and the Mouseia, recalling how they have joined in the sacrifice, chosen their own priest, proposed decrees, and joined in embassies about the festival. There is also a decree of the Athenian guild, badly preserved, by the side of similar acceptances of the improved status of the festival by the reigning Ptolemy, and at least one city.[3] The association of the technitai with the Mouseia continued for well over a century, and they are regularly represented in the prescripts of the victor-lists[4] by a priest and sometimes also by a πυρφόρος. During the second century their representative is sometimes described as ἀπὸ τῶν τεχνιτῶν τῶν συντελούντων εἰς Ἑλικῶνα, and this seems to be a branch of the wider Isthmian–Nemean guild.

Similar collaboration between the Isthmian–Nemean guild and a city is attested by Amphiktyonic decrees acknowledging the enlargement, perhaps c. 228 B.C., of the festival of the Agrionia, dedicated to Dionysos Kadmeios at Thebes.[5] Here it is clear that the city of Thebes and the guild made a joint approach to the Amphiktyons, asking for a guarantee of the safety of person and property of those who attend the festival. This the Amphiktyons grant; it is noteworthy that they specifically exclude from the privilege any flautist, dancer, or actor who has been nominated for the festival by the technitai and who does not perform according to the Theban city-law. Here we see the actual procedure by which performers were provided by the guild. Here again we find the technitai providing their own priest, who appears in the prescript of an Agrionia victor-list,[6] and here again there seems to be a local branch in Thebes of the wider guild.[7]

---

[1] Feyel, *Contribution à l'épigraphie béotienne*, pp. 116–17, established the limits 215–208 B.C. Schachter, *Num. Chr.* 1961, pp. 67–69, argues for a date after 211 B.C.

[2] Appendix, no. 3.   [3] Feyel, op. cit., pp. 90–115.

[4] e.g. Michel 891–2; Feyel, op. cit., pp. 117–23. See Sifakis, *Studies*, pp. 145 f.

[5] Appendix, no. 4.   [6] *I.G.* vii. 2447.   [7] *I.G.* vii. 2484–5.

Elsewhere in Greece in the third century our information about the guilds is limited. Our extensive records of dramatic festivals from Athens and Delos do not mention the guilds, but, besides the references to the Athenian guild at Delphi and Thespiae, it has left two documents in Athens, the base of the statue of the tragic poet Xenokrates which it had erected,[1] and a decree from near the end of the century,[2] apparently from a sanctuary of the technitai near the Dipylon, honouring two of their officials, a tragic actor and a singer. The decree was set up in 'the dedication of Poseidippos', and it is a fair presumption that this poet of the New Comedy was prominent in the affairs of the guild in its first years. On the whole, it is likely that the Athenian guild was not prominent internationally in the third century, particularly during the period of Macedonian domination. We have already seen the pre-eminence of the Isthmian–Nemean guild in central Greece, and it has also left two decrees at Delos, one honouring a Delian, one of unknown purport.[3] It was the Isthmian–Nemean guild which was taken as a model, when *c.* 235 B.C. the Aetolian League, which was now in full control of Delphi, granted privileges to another guild of which we now hear for the first time, the Ionia–Hellespont guild.[4]

Late in the third century—in 226 or 225 B.C.—we hear of Artists of Dionysus in the Peloponnese being caused to perform for the pleasure of Cleomenes III after his conquest of Megalopolis,[5] and (probably about the same time) of artists travelling to Kythera.[6] Plutarch[7] also speaks of the participation of the Dionysiac artists in the festival founded in commemoration of Aratos after his death at Sikyon in 213 B.C. A monument erected by a travelling actor at Tegea,[8] of which he was a native, in commemoration of his victories away from home, probably belongs to the same period; the festival of the Naia at Dodona, where one of his successes was won, is not likely to have outlasted the destruction of Dodona by the Aetolians in 219 B.C.[9] He was victorious at the Dionysia at Athens in Euripides' *Orestes*, at the Soteria in Euripides'

---

[1] *I.G.* ii². 3211 τὸ κοινὸν τῶν τεχνιτῶν Ξενοκράτην Κυδαντίδην ποιητὴν τραγῳδιῶν.

[2] *I.G.* ii². 1320.   [3] *I.G.* xi. 4. 1059–60.

[4] *S.I.G.*³ 507 (see p. 291).

[5] Plut. *Cleom.* 12 ἐμβαλὼν οὖν εἰς τὴν Μεγαλοπολιτικὴν ὠφελείας τε μεγάλας ἤθροισε . . . τέλος δὲ τοὺς περὶ τὸν Διόνυσον τεχνίτας ἐκ Μεσσήνης διαπορευομένους λαβὼν καὶ πηξάμενος θέατρον ἐν τῇ πολεμίᾳ καὶ προθεὶς ἀπὸ τεσσαράκοντα μνῶν ἀγῶνα μίαν ἡμέραν ἐθεᾶτο καθήμενος, οὐ δεόμενος θέας ἀλλ' οἷον ἐντρυφῶν.

[6] Aelian, *N.H.* xi. 19 Παντακλῆς ὁ Λακεδαιμόνιος ἀναστείλας διὰ τῆς Σπάρτης ἐλθεῖν τοὺς ἐς Κύθηρα ἀπιόντας τῶν περὶ τὸν Διόνυσον τεχνιτῶν, εἶτα καθήμενος ἐν τῷ ἐφορείῳ ὑπὸ κυνῶν διεσπάσθη.

[7] *Arat.* 53. 6 μέλη δὲ ᾔδετο πρὸς κιθάραν ὑπὸ τῶν περὶ τὸν Διόνυσον τεχνιτῶν.

[8] *S.I.G.*³ 1080.   [9] *I.G.* ii². 3150, 3152, however, point to a later revival.

Herakles and Archestratos' *Antaios*, at the Heraia at Argos in Euripides' *Herakles* and *Archelaos*, and at the Naia in Euripides' *Archelaos* and Chaeremon's *Achilles*. The list is interesting as illustrating the continued popularity of Euripides.[1]

6. Meanwhile in Egypt matters seem to have run on similar lines. An account by the historian Kallixenos, preserved by Athenaeus,[2] of a great procession at Alexandria in the reign of Ptolemy Philadelphus (282–246 B.C.) mentions the part taken by the τεχνῖται there, led by the poet Philiskos, who was 'priest of Dionysos'—an expression which probably implies that he was president of the local guild. We should probably not be far wrong in placing the organization of the Egyptian guild about this time, but our main information comes from early in the next reign. Two decrees[3] of the local branch at Ptolemais, technically an independent Greek city, honour a local magistrate and a royal official. Much light is thrown on the inner workings of the guild, which describes itself as τεχνῖται οἱ περὶ τὸν Διόνυσον καὶ Θεοὺς Ἀδελφούς, particularly through the list of members arranged by categories which follows one decree. The inscriptions present much which later becomes familiar in the guild of Pergamon—the close association of the cult of Dionysus with a royal house, the proclamation in honour of a benefactor at the Dionysia, the statue and inscription, the mention of priest, secretary, and accountant, and the long and varied list of members, including poets, instrumental soloists and accompanists, principal actors, and συναγωνισταί, with trumpeter, costumier, πρόξενοι, and patrons. The πρόξενοι are particularly striking. They and the word τεχνίτευμα, modelled on the familiar Ptolemaic πολίτευμα, indicate that the guild is itself almost a city.

It is convenient to notice, along with these Egyptian records,[4] some second-century references to the activities of a Dionysiac guild in Cyprus, where, as in Egypt, the guild was dedicated to the reigning princes as well as to Dionysus.[5] The guild, sometimes referred to as τὸ κοινὸν τῶν ἐν τῷ κατὰ Κύπρον γραμματείῳ περὶ τὸν Διόνυσον τεχνιτῶν, sometimes as οἱ περὶ τὸν Διόνυσον καὶ Θεοὺς Εὐεργέτας τεχνῖται, seems to have been governed by a board of three ἄρχοντες, on one occasion a citharode, a tragic poet, and a satyric poet, assisted by an οἰκονόμος, a tragic

---

[1] That this period did not always take its Euripides neat is shown by *S.I.G.*[3] 648, where a recital includes ᾆσμα μετὰ χοροῦ Διόνυσον καὶ κιθάρισμα ἐκ Βακχῶν Εὐριπίδου.   [2] v. 198 c.

[3] Appendix, no. 5. *O.G.I.S.* 50–51; Michel 1017–18. See San Nicolò, *Aegyptisches Vereinswesen*, i, pp. 46–61 (also interesting for later developments); Plaumann, *Ptolemais in Oberaegypten*, pp. 60–65.   [4] See also Polybius xvi. 21. 8, xv. 30. 4.

[5] The references are best collected by Mitford, *Opuscula Atheniensia* i, p. 136 n. 14 (add *J.H.S.* 79 (1959), pp. 100–1, 121, n. 93). The most important document is no. 6 in the Appendix.

συναγωνιστής, and a secretary, a comic poet. The prominent part played by the officials of the guild in general public life is noteworthy.[1]

7. In the second century the greater part of our information deals with the increasing rivalry of the Athenian and Isthmian guilds and the activities of the Ionian–Hellespontine guild, whose centre was at Teos.

For the greater part of the second century, our information about the Athenian guild remains small, though we possess an elaborate decree[2] from soon after the middle of the century paying honour to Ariarathes, king of Cappadocia. As with other guilds and cities, the patronage and benefactions of princes were important. The Isthmian–Nemean guild remained prominent and extended its activities widely over the Greek mainland. The branches of Thebes and Helicon have already been noticed, and it seems likely that the guild extended its activities into Thessaly[3] and Macedonia.[4] A branch at Chalkis in Euboea is attested by an inscription of the early part of the century,[5] and a decree of the branch at Opous[6] honours its munificent benefactors, Soteles and his wife Xenola. But the most striking evidence of a certain independence enjoyed by the branches of the guild is to be found in a long decree[7] (probably 114–113 B.C.) in honour of Zenon, who was treasurer and also a conspicuous benefactor of the branch at Argos; among other things he had superintended extensive repairs to the buildings belonging to the branch and the erection of a statue to Nikomedes, king of Bithynia, who had given assistance to the branch. A statue is voted to Zenon, with a crown and a proclamation to be made at the next Nemean games.

The exact causes of the dispute between the two mainland guilds, which came to a head in the latter part of the century, are nowhere quite clearly stated, but it may have turned in part on an attempt of the Isthmian artists to prevent the Athenians from performing at festivals at which they themselves claimed prescriptive rights, or to interfere in other ways with their free pursuit of their profession; and, perhaps because

---

[1] e.g. O.G.I.S. 166 Ἀφροδίτηι Παφίαι ἡ πόλις ἡ Παφίων Κάλλιππον Καλλίππου, δὶς γραμματεύ-σαντα τῆς βουλῆς καὶ τοῦ δήμου καὶ ἠρχευκότα τῆς πόλεως καὶ τῶν περὶ τὸν Διόνυσον καὶ Θεοὺς Εὐεργέτας τεχνιτῶν, τὸν γραμματέα τῆς πόλε[ω]ς, γυ[μνα]σιαρχήσαντα καλῶς τὸ ιβ' ἔτος. (Shortly after 106–105 B.C. See J.H.S. 79 (1959), p. 125, n. 108.)

[2] Appendix, no. 7. See also I.G. ii². 1331 (as revised in I.G. ii². i. ii, p. 673). For what looks like an inventory of the guild's sanctuary, see Hesperia 32 (1963), pp. 33–36.

[3] Mélanges Navarre, pp. 8 ff.

[4] I.G. vii. 2486 [τὸ κοινὸν τῶν περὶ τὸν Διόνυσον τεχνιτῶ]ν τῶν εἰς Ἰσθ[μὸν καὶ εἰς] Πιερίαν συντελούν[των . . . . . .] Ζευ[ξ]ίππου τὸμ πρόξενο[ν τὸν] ἑαυτῶν Διονύσῳ ἀρετῆς ἕνεκεν καὶ εὐνοίας ἣν ἔχων διατελεῖ εἴς τε τοὺς τεχνίτας καὶ τῆς εἰς τὸν θεὸν εὐσεβείας. There does not appear to be room to restore a reference to Nemea.

[5] I.G. xii. 9. 910 τὸ κοινὸν τῶν περὶ τὸν Διόνυσον τεχνιτῶν τῶν [ἐ]ξ Ἰσθμοῦ καὶ Νεμέας [σ]υντελού[ντων δὲ ἐν] Χαλκίδι.

[6] I.G. ix. 1. 278 (Michel 1013).

[7] Appendix, no. 8.

the Athenian people seems to have been solidly behind its guild, the matter was not without its political importance. An inscription[1] is thought to record a letter from the proconsul Mummius in 146 B.C. after the destruction of Corinth, giving or confirming to the artists of the Isthmian guild freedom from taxation and from other public services.[2] However this may be—and the matter is not certain—about the year 130 B.C. the Athenian guild sent a deputation to request the Amphiktyons to renew the privileges which had been conferred on them by the decree of 279–278 B.C., and these were now revived by a formal decree[3] which concludes significantly : εἶναι δὲ ταῦτα τοῖς ἐν Ἀθήναις τεχνίταις, ἐὰν μή τι Ῥωμαίοις ὑπεναντίον ᾖ. A decree of a few years later[4] shows that the Athenian guild was in high favour with the Amphiktyons for its participation in 128–127 B.C. in the Pythais, a sacred mission from Athens to Apollo,[5] and confirms and augments the privileges of the Athenian guild. To this Pythais Daux attributes the two hymns with musical notation discovered at Delphi and sung by the Athenian guild.[6] Both are paeans addressed to Apollo. In the first the dedication runs ὁ δὲ [τεχνι|τ]ῶν πρόπας ἑσμὸς Ἀτθίδα λαχ[ὼν | τὸν κιθαρί]σει κλυτὸν παῖδα μεγάλου [Διὸς ὑ|μνοῦσί σε πα]ρ' ἀκρονιφῆ τόνδε πάγον; in the second ἀνθ' ὧν | ἐκείνας ἀπ' ἀρχᾶς Παιήονα κικλήσκ[ομεν ἅπας λ]αὸς α[ὐ|το]χθόνων ἠδὲ Βάκχου μέγας θυρσό-πλη[ξ ἑσμὸς ἱ]ερὸς τεχνι|τῶν ἔνοικος πόλει Κεκροπίᾳ. Unfortunately, our knowledge of relations between the Amphiktyons and the Isthmian guild is imperfect, for there is as yet no means of dating the interesting docu-ment[7] of the period in which that guild sent representatives to the otherwise unknown 'Winter Soteria', and in which relations between the guild and Delphi are still cordial.

The first Roman intervention between the two guilds was a *senatus consultum*, passed in the praetorship of P. Cornelius Lentulus,[8] which seems to have imposed terms on them, perhaps requiring the Athenian guild to become part of the Isthmian, and the Isthmian guild erected

---

[1] *I.G.* vii. 2413–14. See Klaffenbach, *Symbolae ad hist. colleg. artif. Bacchiorum*, pp. 24 ff.

[2] Among other privileges the technitai are to be ἀνεπιστάθμευτοι, free from liability to have soldiers quartered on them. On privileges of technitai, see in general Sifakis, *Studies*, pp. 99–105.

[3] *I.G.* ii². 1132 (latter part). Attic epigraphists date this in 130 B.C., Daux in 134 B.C.

[4] *S.I.G.*³ 698. A decree of the same year (ibid. 699) honours the σύνοδος τῶν ἐν Ἀθήναις ἐποποιῶν for their part in the same festival. Whether these were distinct from the τεχνῖται or a subdivision of them is uncertain. There is a record of a Pythais in 138–137 B.C., but no express mention of the guild.

[5] See Daux, *Delphes au II* et au I*er siècle*, p. 525. The festival had probably lapsed, and was revived by Athens in the latter half of the second century.

[6] *Fouilles de Delphes* iii. 2, nos. 137–8; see Daux, op. cit., pp. 724–5.

[7] *S.I.G.*³ 690. See Daux, op. cit., p. 357; it must fall between 145 and 125 B.C.

[8] This is often dated to 128 B.C., on Pomtow's illegitimate restoration of *S.I.G.*³ 704c.

a statue to Lentulus at Delphi. But the quarrel was only quiescent for a time, and (after various moves on which only the most fragmentary information exists) in 118 B.C. the Athenian guild carried its grievances to Sisenna, proconsul of Macedonia, who summoned both parties to a hearing at Pella; he imposed an agreement on them and required the Isthmian guild to pay 10 talents to the Athenian; the agreement as a whole was plainly favourable to Athens. The Isthmian guild repudiated the signature of its delegates, and a schism followed, the authorities of the guild calling an assembly of its members at Sikyon, while the dissentients, supported by the Athenian artists, established themselves at Thebes. The Athenians then appealed to the Roman Senate, alleging that the Isthmians had contravened the agreement made before Sisenna, and had appropriated funds belonging in part to themselves. The Isthmians in reply disowned the agreement made πρὸς τοὺς ἐν Ἀθήναις φάσκοντας εἶναι τεχνίτας, and accused the Athenians of conspiring with 'some of the τεχνῖται in Thebes and Boeotia' to cause a schism and appropriate records, funds, and offerings. A remarkable *senatus consultum* in 112 B.C., in response to an appeal from the people of Athens, determined the dispute in a way generally favourable to the Athenian guild, confirming the order of Sisenna and sending the allegations about the theft of funds to an arbitrator.[1]

As the Athenian position with the Romans improved, the Amphiktyons followed suit. In about 125 B.C. a much warmer decree than that of 130 B.C. began with fulsome praise of the services of Athens to culture and religion and compliments to its τεχνῖται, and gave the priests chosen by the τεχνῖται the right to wear crowns of gold and purple robes in all cities, an honour about which difficulties might have been made in places where their Isthmian rivals were at home.[2] In autumn 112 B.C., after the final settlement by the Senate, they confirmed the privileges of the Athenian guild in strong terms:

ἐκρίναμε[ν τὰ κεχρημα]τισμένα ἐν τῇ μεθοπ[ωρινῇ πυλαίᾳ ἐπ]ὶ ἄρχοντος ἐν Δελφοῖς Ε[ὐκλείδου] κύρια εἶναι καὶ βέβαια εἰς [τὸν ἄπαντα χρό]νον καὶ μηθὲν ὑπεναν-
τίον αὐ[τοῖς] ἐπιχρηματίζειν δίκαιον ἡγ[εῖσθαι καὶ] διαφυλάσσειν τὰς δεδομένας ὑφ'
ἡμῶν τῷ δήμῳ τιμάς, ὁμοίως δὲ κα[ὶ τοῖς] παρ' ὑμῖν τεχνίταις τὰ ὑπάρχοντα
φιλάνθρωπα περί τε τῆς ἀσυλίας καὶ ἀσ[φα]λείας καὶ χρυσοφορίας, ἔτι δὲ καὶ τῆς

---

[1] The details of the story are uncertain at various points. The documents are collected in *S.I.G.*³ 704, 705, and discussed by Klaffenbach, op. cit., pp. 29 ff., and Daux, who is followed here, op. cit., pp. 356–72.

[2] *I.G.* ii². 1134 (*Fouilles de Delphes* iii. 2, no. 69). For the reading χρυσοφορεῖν ... καὶ [πορφυρο]-φορεῖν (rather than [στεφανη]φορεῖν) see Daux, op. cit., p. 367.

συνεργασίας, θεωροῦντες καὶ τοὺς κοινοὺ[ς ἐ]υεργέτας 'Ρωμαίους ἐπὶ τῆς αὐτῆς
γεγονότας γνώμης.[1]

After this there are further decrees of the Amphiktyons paying honour
in extravagant terms to the Athenian guild for its help in the Pythais
in 105 B.C.[2] and again in 97 B.C.[3] In 105 the Athenians had sent ἐπιμελητὰν
μὲν καὶ ἀρχιθέωρον (the comic poet Alexander), 7 θεωροί (consisting of
a tragic ὑποδιδάσκαλος, 2 κωμῳδοί, 2 tragic poets, and 2 tragic συναγωνισταί), a διδάσκαλος τοῦ μεγάλου χοροῦ, singers of paeans, and instrumentalists; ἐξαπέστειλαν δὲ καὶ τοὺς συναγωνιξαμένους τὸν θυμελικὸν ἀγῶνα καὶ
τὸν σκανικόν—3 epic poets, 3 rhapsodes, 4 κωμῳδοί with 6 συναγωνισταί,
2 τραγῳδοί with 7 συναγωνισταί, 2 tragic poets, and 5 satyric poets.[4] The
same Alexander is again ἐπιμελητής in the later inscription.

8. The fourth of the guilds which divided the Greek world between
them makes its appearance first in an Aetolian decree of about 235 B.C.,[5]
which has already been noticed, conferring ἀσφάλεια and ἀσυλία on the
registered members of the guild, and next in records which date from
just before the beginning of the second century. It was known as the
κοινὸν τῶν περὶ τὸν Διόνυσον τεχνιτῶν ἐπ' Ἰωνίας καὶ 'Ελλησπόντου. Its
centre was at Teos, and we possess a decree of Teos, joining the Artists
in the state prayers and buying land for the Artists, to be free of the taxes
imposed by the city.[6] When the people of Teos, on the strength of their
legendary connexion with Dionysus, sought and obtained special privileges for themselves and their territory from Delphi and the Aetolians
in power there, as well as from many other Greek states and finally from
Rome, these privileges were modelled upon those already given to the
Artists of Dionysus. The decree of the Amphiktyons[7] may be quoted as
typical:

ἔδοξε τοῖς Ἀμφικτιόνοις, τὰμ π[όλιν καὶ τὰν] χώραν τῶν Τηίων ἱερὰν εἶμεν καὶ
ἄσυλον Δι[ονύσου ἀπὸ] πάντων, καὶ ὑπάρχειν τοῖς Τηίοις καὶ τοῖς ἐν Τέω[ι κατ-
οικ]εόντοις παρ' Ἀμφικτιόνων τὰ φιλάνθρωπα καὶ τίμια [πάν]τα ὅσα καὶ τοῖς
Διονυσιακοῖς τεχνίταις δέδοται [παρὰ] τῶν Ἀμφικτιόνων.

The dates of these decrees seem to fall between 205 and 201 B.C., and
in 193 B.C. the Roman Senate sent a dispatch acknowledging the sanctity

---

[1] S.I.G.[3] 704 H; I.G. ii[2]. 1134.

[2] S.I.G.[3] 711 L.   [3] S.I.G.[3] 728 K (see Daux, op. cit., pp. 564 ff.).

[4] There is a similar list in S.I.G.[3] 698 for 128–127 B.C., but with no mention of satyric
poets. On these lists see Daux, op. cit., pp. 725 ff.

[5] S.I.G.[3] 507; see above, p. 286. See further Hahland in W. Jahreshefte 38 (1950), pp. 66 ff.;
Ruge in R.E. s.v. Teos.   [6] Appendix, no. 9.

[7] S.I.G.[3] 564. The decrees of the Aetolians (ibid. 563) and the Delphians use very similar
language. The decrees of a number of Cretan townships, passed after the visit of the ambassadors of Teos, are to be found in Michel, nos. 52–66; their dates are discussed by Holleaux,
Études iv, p. 178.

of Teos and ordering that it should be ἄσυλον καὶ ἀφορολόγητον ἀπὸ τοῦ δήμου τοῦ 'Ρωμαίων.[1]

About the same time the guild—on this occasion termed simply τὸ κοινὸν τῶν περὶ τὸν Διόνυσον τεχνιτῶν—accepted[2] an invitation to a musical and gymnastic festival at Magnesia on the Maeander in honour of Artemis Leukophryene, the great goddess of Magnesia, and conferred on the people of Magnesia a crown, the award of which was to be proclaimed both ἐν τῇ πανηγύρει τῶν τεχνιτῶν and in Magnesia. An inscription[3] very shortly afterwards recorded a complimentary vote by the guild of crowns for the people of Magnesia and the representatives sent by it to Teos, as well as a stele to be erected in the temple of Artemis Leukophryene, and the same inscription records the acceptance of these compliments by the Magnesian people.

In the reign of Eumenes II of Pergamon (205–159 B.C.) Teos, and with it the guild, fell under the domination of the Pergamene king, and this is reflected in an interesting series of inscriptions, dating probably from shortly before the middle of the century, in which the guild appears under the title τὸ κοινὸν τῶν περὶ τὸν Διόνυσον τεχνιτῶν τῶν ἐπ' Ἰωνίας καὶ Ἑλλησπόντου καὶ τῶν περὶ τὸν καθηγεμόνα Διόνυσον. The original guild had become fused or allied with the society of worshippers of Διόνυσος καθηγέμων, who was a special object of worship to the Attalid house,[4] and was also the god to whom the theatre at Pergamon,[5] which must have been one of the chief scenes of the guild's performances, was consecrated. The guild retained its attachment to him even after the extinction of the Attalid dynasty, as we shall see.

Most of these inscriptions have to do with honours paid to the flute-player Kraton of Chalkedon, who had held high office in the guild and had been a munificent benefactor to it. He had brought distinction to it by his performance at many Greek festivals,[6] and had performed the offices of priest and agonothetes with special distinction. His personal character also is warmly praised, and he was in high favour at Pergamon, where he had been given citizenship. The longest of the decrees of the guild[7] orders that he shall be crowned annually 'on the day of the

---

[1] S.I.G.[3] 601. [2] Kern, Inschr. von Magn. 54. [3] Ibid. 89.
[4] See von Prott, Ath. Mitt. 27 (1902), pp. 161 ff.; Hansen, The Attalids of Pergamon, pp. 409 f., 418.
[5] This fine theatre (fig. 141), whether or not it had a more modest predecessor, was built in the reign of Eumenes II. See Dörpfeld and Reisch, pp. 150 f.; von Gerkan, Das Theater von Priene, p. 101; Bulle, Untersuchungen, p. 256.
[6] e.g. at Iasos, where the guarantors of a festival had engaged him to play (Michel 909). On Kraton in general, see Daux, B.C.H. 59 (1935), pp. 210 ff.
[7] Appendix, no. 10a. The date is before 167 B.C., but not by much.

procession' and that a statue of him shall be erected in the theatre at Teos,[1] where it is to be crowned at the Dionysia and on other occasions, and a second at Delos, to be crowned by the τεχνῖται there, and a third wherever he pleases. The guild is to send special representatives to the peoples of Delos and Teos to secure the appropriate sites. In the second of the longer decrees of the guild[2] it is not only ordered that the proclamation of the crown awarded to Kraton shall be made annually by the agonothetes and priest of Eumenes[3] ἐν τῇ βασιλέως Εὐμένου ἡμέρᾳ ὅταν ἥ τε πομπὴ διέλθῃ καὶ αἱ στεφανώσεις συντελῶνται, but also (somewhat amusingly) ὁμοίως δὲ καὶ παρὰ τὸν πότον γινέσθω τῇ αὐτῇ ἡμέρᾳ μετὰ τὰς σπονδὰς ὑπὸ τῶν ἀρχόντων ἡ ἀναγγελία τοῦ στεφάνου. A tripod and altar of incense (which is to be offered annually) is to be placed by his statue in the theatre.

Somewhat earlier a special decree[4] in his honour was passed by the κοινὸν τῶν συναγωνιστῶν, which is now generally agreed to have been a subordinate guild or club within the general guild, and to have included, in all probability, members other than the leading tragic and comic actors.[5] Kraton had been a member of this. The honours voted to him are somewhat less resplendent than those in the decrees of the general guild, but include a stele to be set up by the Dionysion in the most conspicuous situation, and a painted portrait.

Another inscription[6] records the gratitude of the Ἀτταλισταί, a thiasos attached to the cult of the Attalid house, which Kraton had founded and provided with an Ἀτταλεῖον close to the theatre at Teos. This tribute was paid after his death and mentions his bequests to the thiasos. Apart from this striking personality, the chief interest of the inscriptions of this group relates to the courtesy and generosity of the guild in sending a group of performers to Iasos to enable the people of Iasos to maintain their festivals at a time (about the middle of the second century B.C.) when they had fallen on evil days.[7] Two flute-players are sent, two tragic

[1] On this theatre and the Dionysion connected with it (the masterpiece of Hermogenes) see Vitruvius iii. 3. 8; vii, praef. 12.   [2] Michel 1016A.

[3] This double function of the presiding officer corresponds to the double title of the guild.

[4] Michel 1016B.

[5] The fact that a συναγωνιστὴς τραγικός was sent as the envoy of the guild to Iasos (Appendix, no. 11) seems to prove that they were recognized members of the guild. But it cannot be assumed that the title συναγωνιστής was always used in precisely the same sense.

[6] Appendix, no. 10b. The date is certainly later than 152 B.C., when Kraton was certainly still alive (O.G.I.S. 325). If Klaffenbach's restorations of I.G. vii. 2414 are right (see above, p. 281, n. 1), it is later than 146. Some details of Kraton's bequests are recorded in C.I.G. 3071.

[7] A series of 47 inscriptions from Iasos (Le Bas 252 ff.; Brinck, Inscriptiones, pp. 216–44; specimens in Michel 508–12) gives lists of those who undertook to be responsible for engaging and paying for each festival (see above, p. 292, n. 6, on the engagement of Kraton). This payment of individual performers was evidently preferred, though with the alternative of a lump sum paid down, as a method of financing the festivals. See also Annuario, N.S. 23–24 (1961–2), 582 ff.

and two comic actors, a κιθαρῳδός, and a κιθαριστής, with the necessary
supporting cast; and it was expressly provided that the performances
should be in accordance with the customs of the people of Iasos, and that
the artists selected by the assembly of the guild should be bound to serve,
on pain of a heavy fine. A friendly delegation is to carry this decree to
Iasos.[1]

Unhappily, the prosperity of the guild did not continue. Even in the
reign of Eumenes II there had been disputes between the guild and the
people of Teos, which had been settled by the king;[2] and at some time
late in the reign of Attalus II or during that of his successor Attalus III
(138–133 B.C.) the quarrel was renewed. According to Strabo,[3] the guild
first migrated to Ephesus, but was then settled in Myonnesos by Attalus.
When the people of Teos protested to the Roman authorities that this
was dangerously near Teos, the Romans moved the guild to Lebedos,
where it was welcomed as increasing the population of that desolate town,
and where it remained in the time of Strabo. We have no other evidence
to support this account, however, and some scattered evidence pointing
to other places. An inscription of 129 B.C.[4] attests a continued close connexion with Pergamon; a passage of Plutarch[5] suggests a connexion with
Priene in the time of Antony; evidence shortly to be considered shows
strong links with Cos.[6]

---

[1] Appendix, no. 11.

[2] Fränkel, *Inschr. von Pergamon*, no. 163; Welles, *Royal Correspondence*, no. 53; cf. Hansen,
op. cit., p. 158; Sifakis, *Studies*, pp. 139 f.

[3] Strabo xiv. 1. 29 εἶτα Λέβεδος ... ἐνταῦθα τῶν περὶ τὸν Διόνυσον τεχνιτῶν ἡ σύνοδος καὶ
κατοικία τῶν ἐν Ἰωνίᾳ μέχρι Ἑλλησπόντου, ἐν ᾗ πανήγυρίς τε καὶ ἀγῶνες κατ᾿ ἔτος συντελοῦνται τῷ
Διονύσῳ. ἐν Τέῳ δὲ ᾤκουν πρότερον τῇ ἐφεξῆς πόλει τῶν Ἰώνων, ἐμπεσούσης δὲ στάσεως εἰς
Ἔφεσον κατέφυγον· Ἀττάλου δ᾿ εἰς Μυόννησον αὐτοὺς καταστήσαντος μεταξὺ Τέω καὶ Λεβέδου,
πρεσβεύονται Τήιοι δεόμενοι Ῥωμαίων μὴ περιδεῖν ἐπιτειχιζομένην σφίσι τὴν Μυόννησον, οἱ δὲ
μετέστησαν εἰς Λέβεδον δεξαμένων τῶν Λεβεδίων ἀσμένως διὰ τὴν κατέχουσαν αὐτοὺς ὀλιγανδρίαν.
For the unattractiveness of Lebedos in the time of Horace, cf. *Epp.* i. 11. 7 'scis Lebedus
quid sit, Gabiis desertior atque | Fidenis vicus'.

[4] *S.I.G.*[3] 694. 46.

[5] *Antony* 57. It is not at all certain that those whom Antony settled at Priene belonged to
the group associated with Teos a century earlier; and some think that they were the world-wide
group in its early stages; see Klaffenbach, op. cit., p. 8. A Samothracian *theorodokoi*-list
(*I.G.* xii. 8. 163) of the first century or a little earlier lists the representatives τοῦ κοινοῦ τῶν
πε[ρὶ τὸν Διόνυσον] τεχνειτῶν τῶν [ἀπὸ Ἰωνίας] καὶ Ἑλλησπόντο[υ] immediately after that of
Priene, but there is no rigid geographical order, and the inscription can only be considered
evidence for the assimilation of the guild to an independent state.

[6] We take Paton and Hicks, *Inscriptions of Cos*, no. 24, a decree of an unidentified guild of
technitai for a citizen of Cos, to be rather earlier than this period. It certainly gives no ground
for believing in a base of the technitai on Cos. The Dodecanese are in general badly docu-
mented. Rhodes in the third century seems to have had at least three independent companies. *Annuario* 2 (1916), p. 139, no. 10 has an individual crowned [ὑπ]ὸ τεχνιτᾶν τῶν π[ερὶ
τ]ὰς Διονύσ[ου] Μούσας, ὑπὸ τῶν· περὶ τὸν Διόνυσον τὸν Μουσαγέταν τεχνιτᾶν Εὐδαμείων, and
ὑπὸ Ἀγητορείων Πολυστρατείων τῶν [π]ερ[ὶ] Διόνυσον καὶ τὰς Μούσας τεχνιτᾶν. Eudamos,
Hagetor, and Polystratos are presumably leaders or former leaders of these groups.

9. Tempting though it may be to believe that the guilds played a part in the transmission of the Greek theatre to the Roman stage, there is very little evidence in regard to activities of the guilds in the West at this period, unless the long Corcyrean inscription[1] relating to a benefaction of Aristomenes and Psylla can be treated as such. The benefaction was an endowment for the hiring of τεχνῖται annually to perform at the Dionysia in Corcyra, and the deed contained elaborate provisions for its administration, but there is no actual mention of the guilds. There are also inscriptions dedicating rewards voted by the κοινὸν τῶν περὶ τὸν Διόνυσον τεχνιτῶν to benefactors at Syracuse[2] and at Rhegium,[3] but the dates are unknown.

10. From the first century B.C., as from the second, there are records which may imply the use of the services of the guilds, but do not actually mention them. Such are the well-known inscription of 92–91 B.C. regulating the mysteries of Andania in Messenia,[4] and various victor-lists, mostly Boeotian, of which the most remarkable, relating to the Sarapieia of Tanagra,[5] has appended to it the fullest set of accounts of the financing of a Greek dramatic festival. The importance of the Athenian guild in the life of the time is indicated by the part which it played in the extravagant welcome given by Athens to Athenion, the envoy of Mithradates, in 88 B.C.[6] The envoy was greeted as the 'messenger of the new Dionysus'[7] and made an honoured guest at the ceremonies of the guild, which offered sacrifices in his honour in its τέμενος.[8] The action of the guild obviously indicated hostility towards Rome, and after the ruin inflicted by Sulla on Athens the Athenian guild seems to have sunk to only local importance. Its local activities are, however, well illustrated by

---

[1] *I.G.* ix. 1. 694 (second century B.C.) ; cf. Lüders, *Die dionysischen Künstler*, pp. 121–4.

[2] *I.G.* xiv. 12, 13.

[3] Ibid. 615 ἀρχόντων δὲ (four names) τὸ κοινὸν τῶν περὶ τὸν Διόνυσον τεχνιτῶν καὶ προ[ξ]ένων Αἰνησοῦν Νίκ[ω]νος κτλ.

[4] *S.I.G.*[3] 736. The relevant passage runs (73–75) τεχνιτᾶν εἰς τὰς χοριτείας. οἱ ἱεροὶ προγραφόντω κατ᾽ ἐνιαυτὸν τοὺς λειτουργήσοντας ἔν τε ταῖς θυσίαις καὶ μυστηρίοις αὐλητὰς καὶ κιθαριστάς, ὅσους κα εὑρίσκωντι εὐθέτους ὑπάρχοντας, καὶ οἱ προγραφέντες λειτουργούντω τοῖς θεοῖς.

[5] Ἀρχ. Ἐφ. 1956, pp. 34 ff. Some of the figures must be wrongly read; otherwise we should have reproduced it here.

[6] Athenaeus v. 212 d–e (from Poseidonius) συνήντησαν δ᾽ αὐτῷ καὶ οἱ περὶ τὸν Διόνυσον τεχνῖται τὸν ἄγγελον τοῦ νέου Διονύσου καλοῦντες ἐπὶ τὴν κοινὴν ἑστίαν καὶ τὰς περὶ ταύτην εὐχάς τε καὶ σπονδάς. . . . ἐν δὲ τῷ τεμένει τῶν τεχνιτῶν θυσίαι τε ἐπετελοῦντο ἐπὶ τῇ Ἀθηνίωνος παρουσίᾳ καὶ μετὰ κήρυκος προαναφωνήσεως σπονδαί.

[7] The title of νέος Διόνυσος here given to Mithradates Eupator was frequently accorded to his contemporary Ptolemy Philopator (*O.G.I.S.* 186–93) and much later to Hadrian and Antoninus Pius (see below, pp. 298, 300).

[8] For the evidence bearing on the site of this τέμενος, see R. E. Wycherley, *The Athenian Agora*. III (*Testimonia*), pp. 20–21; *Hesperia* 32 (1963), pp. 33–36.

a remarkable inscription from Eleusis[1] from the years between 80 and
70 B.C., recording how the σύνοδος τῶν περὶ τὸν Διόνυσον τεχνιτῶν had always
done its best to promote the worship of the gods, and particularly of
Demeter and Kore, and had provided an altar and a τέμενος where they
offered libations and sang paeans at the time of the Mysteries; and how
the altar and τέμενος had been destroyed during the disturbances of the
time, but the traditional sacrifices and the expenses of the σύνοδος had
been provided by Philemon, their ἐπιμελητής, at his own cost, and the
sanctuary and altar had been rebuilt and all the costs connected with
the services had been given freely by him, when he had accepted office
for the fourth time on the urgent request of the guild—all of which is
set out in language of enthusiastic approval.

Sulla, however, was no enemy to τεχνῖται in general. He was entertained by some at Aedepsus in Euboea in 84,[2] and an inscription of
Cos[3] gives parts of a letter from him as dictator and of a *senatus consultum*
confirming, at the request of a lyre-player from Laodicea, all privileges
given by the Senate, magistrates, or promagistrates to the Ionia–Hellespont guild. As usual, these concern taxation, burdensome offices, and
billeting.

The continued life of the Isthmian–Nemean guild in the first century,
with a centre at Elis (among other places), is attested by the dedication
of a statue to a benefactor at Olympia,[4] and the Asiatic artists are mentioned by Plutarch[5] as having been collected by Tigranes in great numbers
at Tigranocerta and used by Lucullus to entertain his victorious army
when he captured the city in 69 B.C.

In the last half of the century Naples seems to have been a resort of
the Artists. According to Plutarch,[6] Brutus found many there in 44 B.C.,
and arranged for the collection of famous performers for his purposes. (He
was collecting wild beasts for shows at the same time.) In 32 B.C. the
Διονύσου τεχνῖται from the whole of the eastern Greek world were obliged
to assemble at Samos for the delectation of Antony and Cleopatra, and,
as Plutarch remarks somewhat bitterly,[7] τῆς ἐν κύκλῳ σχεδὸν ἁπάσης
οἰκουμένης περιθρηνουμένης καὶ περιστεναζομένης μία νῆσος ἐφ᾽ ἡμέρας πολλὰς
κατηυλεῖτο καὶ κατεψάλλετο, πληρουμένων θεάτρων καὶ χορῶν ἀγωνιζομένων.

Antony's gift of Priene to the artists has already been noted.[8] Besides

[1] Appendix, no. 12. For the date, see Dow, *Hesperia*, Suppl. viii. 125. [2] Plut. *Sulla* 26. 5.
[3] Appendix, no. 13. For another inscription of Cos which may indicate that the Artists
were at home there at this time, see *B.C.H.* 59 (1935), p. 199. Sherk, *Historia* 15 (1966), pp.
211–16, argues against the view that Sulla's letter indicates that the guild had a base on Cos.
[4] *Inschriften von Olympia*, no. 405 τεχνῖται περὶ τὸν Διόνυσ[ον ἐξ Ἰσθμοῦ κ]αὶ Νεμέας οἱ
εἰς Ἦλιν συμπορευόμενοι . . . a Μεσσήνιο[ν] τὸν αὐτῶν πρόξενον καὶ ε[ὐεργέτην] Διὶ Ὀλυμπίῳ.
[5] *Lucull.* 29. 4.   [6] *Brutus* 21. 5.   [7] *Ant.* 56. 7–8.   [8] Above, p. 294.

this there exists a letter written by him as triumvir in 33–32 B.C. to the assembly of Asiatic Greeks, which had sent him a petition on behalf of ἡ σύνοδος τῶν ἀπὸ τῆς οἰκουμένης ἱερονικῶν καὶ στεφανειτῶν, whose privileges he confirms.[1] This letter is generally thought to refer to a combined world organization of athletes and artists, but there is no reference to τεχνῖται or to Dionysus, the intermediary Artemidorus is referred to as an ἀλείπτης, and this body only appears elsewhere[2] as organizing an athletic festival. It does not therefore seem justifiable to use this letter as evidence for a combined world organization, which, as we shall see, would have rapidly split.

11. It is in any case clear that a world-wide organization of Dionysiac artists was organized at about this time. The earliest certain reference is in a letter addressed to it by Claudius in A.D. 43.[3] He writes τοῖς ἀπὸ τῆς οἰκουμένης περὶ τὸν Διόνυσον τεχνείταις ἱερονείκαις στεφανείταις καὶ τοῖς τούτων συναγωνισταῖς, allows them to set up statues for his worship, and ends τὰ δὲ ὑπὸ τοῦ θεοῦ Σεβαστοῦ δεδομένα ὑμῖν νόμιμα καὶ φιλάνθρωπα συντηρῶ. Very similar language is found in an inscription from Miletus[4] containing a letter of the same emperor τοῖς περὶ τὸν Διόνυσον ἱερονείκαις καὶ τεχνείταις, again confirming τὰ ὑπὸ τῶν πρὸ ἐμοῦ Σεβαστῶν καὶ τῆς συγκλήτου δεδομένα δίκαια. From these two sources it would appear that the grant of privileges to a world-wide organization by emperors and Senate goes back to Augustus.

The full flood of our evidence on the world-wide guild, however, begins in the second century, and it is an interesting sign of the spread of Greek culture that the Trajanic inscriptions come from Jerash (Gerasa) and Nîmes (Nemausus). At Gerasa[5] we have a decree in honour of T. Flavius Gerrenus, who had served as agonothetes on a great occasion:

ψήφισμα τῆς ἱερᾶς συνόδου τῶν ἀ[πὸ τ]ῆς [οἰκο]υμέν[ης περὶ τὸν Διόνυσον καὶ τὸν κύριον ἡμῶν Αὐτοκράτορα] Νέρουαν Τραιανὸν Καίσαρα Σεβαστὸν Γερμανικὸν Δακικ[ὸν τεχνιτῶν ἱερονικῶν στεφανιτῶν] καὶ τῶν τούτων συναγωνιστῶν.

The same titulature is found at Nîmes.[6] The relation of these συναγωνισταί to the world-wide society is not definitely ascertainable; but from these

---

[1] In a papyrus published by Kenyon, C.R. 7 (1893), p. 477; see also Brandis, Hermes 32 (1897), pp. 509 ff.; Poland, R.E., zweite Reihe, v A 2515; Magie, Roman Rule in Asia Minor, p. 1279.   [2] Didyma, die Inschriften, no. 201.

[3] In the dossier B.G.U. 1074, reprinted and fully discussed by Viereck, Klio 8 (1908), pp. 413 ff., and its twins P. Oxy. 2476, 2610.   [4] Rehm, Milet i. 3, no. 156.

[5] Kraeling, Gerasa, pp. 442 ff. (cf. S.E.G. vii. 825, Phil. Woch. 55 (1935), pp. 141 ff., Mélanges Dussaud, pp. 735 ff.).

[6] I.G.R. i. 18. Other inscriptions of Nemausus are ibid. 19, 20, and 17 (to which add Espérandieu, Inscriptions latines de Gaule, no. 427).

and other inscriptions, as has already been suggested,[1] the subordinate
performers appear to have formed a special society within the larger
whole. In the same way, the local guilds may have retained a separate,
though subordinate, existence, or may only gradually have been merged
in the world-wide guild. Thus a stele erected at Ephesus in the second
century[2] by Ulpia to her two sons describes one of them as (*inter alia*)
ἀγωνοθετήσαντα τῶν μεγάλων Πυθίων καὶ ἀρχιερατεύσαντα τῶν ἐπ' Ἰωνίας καὶ
Ἑλλησπόντου καὶ ἀγωνοθετήσαντα τῶν χρυσοφόρων and even in the third
century an inscription of Tralles[3] refers to ἡ σύνοδος τῶν ἀπὸ Ἰωνίας
καὶ Ἑλλησπόντου. Smyrna appears to have kept its own guild in some
special connexion with the mystic cult of Dionysus Briseus. Under
Hadrian we find it called οἱ τοῦ μεγάλου πρὸ πόλεως Βρεισέως Διονύσου
μύσται.[4] Under Antoninus Pius they are the σύνοδος τῶν περὶ τὸν Βρεισέα
Διόνυσον[5] or the σύνοδος τῶν ἐν Σμύρνῃ μυστῶν,[6] but we find them describing themselves at about the same time as the ἱερὰ σύνοδος τῶν περὶ
τὸν Βρεισέα Διόνυσον τεχνειτῶν καὶ μυστῶν.[7]

From the rich second-century evidence, three inscriptions are particularly worthy of attention, two illustrating the guild as an independent
corporation, one its connexions with artistic activity.

In Ancyra in A.D. 128[8] a ψήφισμα τῶν ἀπὸ τῆς οἰκουμένης περὶ τὸν
Διόνυσον καὶ Αὐτοκράτορα Τραιανὸν Ἀδριανὸν Σεβαστὸν Καίσαρα νέον
Διόνυσον τεχνειτῶν ἱερονεικῶν στεφανειτῶν καὶ τῶν τούτων συναγωνιστῶν
καὶ τῶν νεμόντων τὴν ἱερὰν θυμελικὴν σύνοδον (perhaps a local organization)
honours a local agonothetes who had carried out a festival presented by
the emperor with particular extravagance and consideration for the Artists.
The Artists set up a statue for him at Ancyra, which shall be wreathed by
all future contestants, under pain of exclusion from the contests for ingrati-
tude and disobedience to the decrees of the guild. A statue will also be set
up in Naples, and the decrees of the guild will be communicated to the
emperor and the governor. This decree is proposed by a κωμῳδὸς ὀλυμπι-
ονείκης, and put to the vote by a κωμῳδὸς (?) παράδοξος, and other officers
of the guild named are the ἄρχων, the γραμματεύς, and the νομοδείκτης.

A little later in the century an imperial secretary T. Aelius Alcibiades

---

[1] Above, p. 293.
[2] *Ancient Gk. Inscr. in Brit. Mus.* iii, no. 618.
[3] *O.G.I.S.* 501. It is to be doubted whether we should assume that the stone-cutter missed
out τῶν περὶ τὸν Διόνυσον τεχνιτῶν accidentally, simply to gain conformity with the old title.
It is even more unlikely that *C.I.G.* 3082 (*I.G.R.* iv. 1568), sometimes quoted in this context,
ever had any reference to the Ionia–Hellespont guild.
[4] *B.C.H.* 57 (1933), p. 308.
[5] *S.I.G.*³ 851, a letter from M. Aurelius (147 A.D.).
[6] Ibid., a letter from Antoninus Pius (158 A.D.).   [7] *C.I.G.* 3190.
[8] Appendix, no. 14.

showed particular favour to the guild.[1] More particularly, he adorned the τέμενος at Rome belonging to the world organization with βιβλία θαυμαστά,[2] and presented it with stables, the income from which would provide for an annual distribution on Hadrian's birthday. In gratitude, οἱ ἐπὶ ῾Ρώμης τεχνεῖται made him high priest of the guild for life. There were evidently several of these honorary posts, but it was specifically provided that Alcibiades should rank first. Note was taken of this decree of the Roman branch by the guild meeting at Ephesus for the Great ᾿Εφέσηα, and this meeting voted gilded statues of Alcibiades to be set up in the temples of the emperors in Asia and in Alcibiades' home town of Nysa; also that there should be general publication of a decree expressing their gratitude and a special embassy to Nysa. The titles of the proposer, the chairman, and the ambassadors are not without interest.

Perhaps the most interesting of these second-century documents is a dossier from early in the reign of Commodus.[3] M. Ulpius Appuleius Eurykles, already experienced in the finances of the cities of Asia Minor, has been made λογιστής of Aphrodisias. A local benefactor, Flavius Lysimachus, has provided by will for a new festival, but there has been some doubt as to the capacity of the endowment to meet the demands on it. Eurykles has investigated the matter, out of piety to the emperor and regard for the wishes of the deceased and the glory of the city, and under constant pressure from the σύνοδος (ἤδη καὶ τῶν ἀπὸ τῆς συνόδου πολλάκις ἐντυχόντων μοι), and now finds that there will be enough funds to provide a festival, whose place in the cycle of Asiatic festivals he fixes. The power of the guild as a pressure-group in its own interests is nowhere better illustrated.[4] We possess the list of prizes for these games. They range from 2,500 denarii for the victorious tragic actor to 150 for the second prize in old comedy. New comedy and a new tragedy are also represented, but there is no clear reference to an old tragedy.

The scattered and fragmentary references may be passed over here, with a few important exceptions. Athens continued to be a centre. The Artists there had a council chamber in the Kerameikos,[5] and it was probably they who in the latter half of the second century set up a

[1] Appendix, no. 15.
[2] Robert suggests that these were the works of Phlegon of Tralles, a friend of Alcibiades' father.
[3] Appendix, no. 16a.
[4] Another side of their activities might be more clearly shown, if we possessed more of Sardis vii. 1, no. 13, which seems to be an offer to provide a free festival for Sardis.
[5] Philostratus, Vit. Soph. ii. 8. 2; see also above, p. 295, n. 8.

monument[1] to a famous comic actor and περιοδονείκης named Strato, who had been honoured with an ivy crown:

τῆδε Μενανδρείων ἐπέων δεδαηκότα πάσας
τύξιας εὐιέροις ἀγλαὸν ἐν θυμέλαις
ἐκτέριϑαν θεράποντες ἀερσίφρονος Διονύσου
αὐτῷ κισσοφόρῳ τοῦτο χαριζόμενοι.

An inscription from Rhodiapolis[2] records that, along with others, Ἀθηναῖοι καὶ ἡ ἱερωτάτη Ἀρεοπαγειτῶν βουλὴ καὶ οἱ Ἀθήνησιν Ἐπικούρειοι φιλόσοφοι καὶ ἡ ἱερὰ θυμελικὴ σύνοδος paid honour to the physician Herakleitos. An inscription[3] of the time of Antoninus Pius is probably Athenian in origin—it was brought to London with the Elgin Marbles—and describes itself as ψήφισμα τῆς ἱερᾶς Ἀδριανῆς Ἀντωνείνης θυμελικῆς περιπολιστικῆς μεγάλης συνόδου τῶν ἀπὸ τῆς οἰκουμένης περὶ τὸν Διόνυσον καὶ Αὐτοκράτορα Καίσαρα Τίτον Αἴλιον Ἀδριανὸν Ἀντωνεῖνον Σεβαστὸν Εὐσεβῆ νέον Διόνυσον [τεχνιτῶν]. The importance of the guild at Athens in this period is illustrated by the appropriation of two front seats in the theatre of Dionysus to members of it holding certain priesthoods. The seats are inscribed ἱερέως Διονύσου Μελπομένου ἐκ τεχνειτῶν and ἱερέως Ἀντινόου χορείου ἐκ τεχνειτῶν (of the time of Hadrian, whose visit is also commemorated otherwise in the theatre).[4]

There is little other information from mainland Greece, except from Epidaurus, where two inscriptions[5] from the early Christian era, tabulating fines inflicted on artists who had failed to keep their engagements, may or may not imply the action of a guild:

ἐπὶ ἀγωνοθέτα τῶν Ἀσκλαπιείων καὶ Ἀπολλωνίων Σωστράτου τοῦ Πατροκλείδα
κατάδικοι οἱ γενόμενοι τῶν τεχνιτᾶν διὰ τὸ μὴ ἀγωνίξασθαι κεκομισμένοι τὸν μισθόν
(two lines missing) κωμῳδὸς Διονύσιος Διονυσίου Ῥόδιος μνᾶν τεσσάρων.

The Artists are still attested at Teos[6] and Pergamon,[7] and in Egypt the references are copious, but fragmentary.[8]

---

[1] I.G. ii². 12664. For τύξιας cf. Hesych. τύξιν· τεῦξιν, παρασκευήν ('device'). For περιοδονείκης see below, p. 305. Strato's brother seems also to have been commemorated here.

[2] I.G.R. iii. 733 (T.A.M. ii. 910). See Ziebarth, Das gr. Vereinswesen, p. 88, n. 1.

[3] I.G. ii². 1350. Another inscription (ibid. 1348) contains fragments of a letter of the Artists to Hadrian or Antoninus Pius and his reply. Another (ibid. 1105, with S.E.G. xxi. 507) seems to have had a whole dossier of imperial letters.

[4] I.G. ii², nos. 5060, 5062. The importance of Διόνυσος Μελπόμενος in connexion with theatrical performances is illustrated by S.I.G.³ 1003 (Priene; second century B.C.), where public sacrifices and prayers to him in the theatre are prescribed.

[5] I.G. iv². 99–100.

[6] C.I.G. 3082 (I.G.R. iv. 1568), probably early third century A.D.; see p. 298, n. 3.

[7] I.G.R. iv. 468.　　　　　　　　[8] e.g. P. Oxy. 171 (in ii, p. 208), 908, 1691, 2476.

In the West the headquarters of the world organization was naturally in Rome, where we have already seen it in action. Its title there is normally, in the time of Antoninus Pius, ἡ ἱερὰ Ἁδριανὴ Ἀντωνεινὴ περιπολιστικὴ θυμελικὴ μεγάλη νεωκόρος ἐπὶ ʻΡώμῃ σύνοδος. The epithet περιπολιστική which occurs frequently from the time of Antoninus or a little earlier indicates that the members of the guild travelled from place to place. There was a great multiplication of festivals, many of them connected with the cult of the emperor, during this century, and the services of the Artists were constantly in demand in places far apart. The title νεωκόρος connotes the guardianship of a cult-sanctuary, usually relating to the Divine Emperor, and here especially of the central sanctuary in Rome. Philostratus[1] describes the control exercised over the Dionysiac artists by Euodianus of Smyrna, whose task appears to have been none too easy. In a Neapolitan inscription of the time of Antoninus[2] the ἱερὰ σύνοδος commemorates the series of victories won by Aelius Antigenidas, a flute-player, including a victory at the Eusebeia instituted by Antoninus in honour of his appellation Pius. The fragmentary inscriptions which attest a centre of the Artists at Nîmes have already been noticed.[3]

There is little need to follow the story into the third century. The athletic guild, already referred to, had followed similar lines of development, and one interesting development is a tendency of the two great guilds to combine. An inscription of the early part of the third century from Prusias[4] shows them acting in concert, and in Alexandria[5] they seem to be joined. To modern readers this may suggest a fusion of the Old Vic with the Football League, but the two guilds had important common interests, notably the desire to ensure exemption from taxation and liturgies. These privileges they seem certainly to have misused. Two important dossiers[6] recounting imperial grants, from which we have already quoted the letter of Claudius, date from A.D. 275 and 289. It would appear that wealthy men were buying from the guild purely honorary positions as secretary or high-priest and then applying as Artists to their cities for exemption from taxation. It is hardly surprising that our story ends with an edict of Diocletian and his colleagues[7] *ad synodum xysticorum*

---

[1] *Vit. Soph.* ii. 16 ἐπιταχθεὶς δὲ καὶ τοῖς ἀμφὶ τὸν Διόνυσον τεχνίταις, τὸ δὲ ἔθνος τοῦτο ἀγέρωχοι καὶ χαλεποὶ ἀρχθῆναι, ἐπιτηδειότατος τὴν ἀρχὴν ἔδοξεν καὶ κρείττων ἢ λαβεῖν αἰτίαν.

[2] *I.G.R.* i. 442.   [3] p. 297, n. 6.

[4] *I.G.R.* iii. 61 τῶν ἱε[ρῶν] συνόδ[ων] οἰκο[υμ]ενικῶν πε[ρι]πολισ[τικ]ῶν τῆς [τε] ξυστικῆς καὶ τῆς θυμελι[κῆς].

[5] *O.G.I.S.* 713 ἀπὸ τῆς ἱερᾶς θυμελικῆς καὶ ξυστικῆς συνόδου.

[6] See p. 297, n. 3. *P. Oxy.* 2610 is not precisely dated.   [7] Appendix, no. 17.

et thymelicorum. They maintain the general principle of confirming privileges conferred by their divine predecessors, but tighten the rules, so that immunity from *munera civilia* shall be confined to professional competitors who have won at least three crowns of a certain standing.

12. The inscriptions and passages of various authors selected for quotation in this account of the Artists of Dionysus will have given some idea of the character and importance of the guilds. The Artists stood on a higher plane in public regard than the actors of mimes and similar performers; these were never admitted to the guilds. The fact that each artist is named in inscriptions—there are at least very few exceptions—with his country's name virtually proves that they were citizens with full rights, however widely they may have been scattered and mingled in the guilds with the citizens of strange towns and countries.[1] The guilds were evidently organized with some thoroughness,[2] and their corporate existence and independence were recognized not only in the grants of special privileges which have been noticed, but in the reception of envoys from them by cities almost as if they were independent states, in the appointment and recognition of their πρόξενοι both by states and by other guilds, and in the sending of θεωροί by the guilds, in addition to those of the cities, to great festivals. Their officers were annually appointed; all appointments, whether of officers, envoys, or πρόξενοι, were normally made by the κοινόν—the whole body of each guild—and it was the whole κοινόν that voted statues and crowns to famous actors and to kings and benefactors. The whole body was probably the authority which inflicted and adjudicated upon the fines which actors might have to pay, particularly for failing to appear at festivals to which they were sent.[3] As we have seen, it is not always clear whether the assembly or authorities of the guild nominated the performers who were to appear at a festival. At Athens and Delos, for example, where our lists of performers are among the fullest, there is no clear evidence at all of the participation of the guilds. But it was doubtless always the guild as a corporate body which (as at Eleusis and Magnesia) determined the

---

[1] It would be rash to infer from the language of Appendix, no. 11 that there was a general distinction between ἐγγεγραμμένοι—registered members—and μετέχοντες.

[2] Each had its own νόμοι (e.g. Appendix, no. 11) and some at least their common seal (e.g. *S.E.G.* vi. 58).

[3] The Euboean Law provided for various fines even before the institution of the guilds, and the fining of actors for non-appearance was evidently a legal proceeding in the time of Demosthenes and Alexander (see above, p. 280, n. 7). The Corcyrean decree (see p. 295) regulating the newly endowed Dionysia also inflicts fines. In all these cases the authority must have been that of the state, but the guilds may have assumed the right of fine as they became constituted.

part which it should play in the worship and festivals of gods other than Dionysus.[1]

The officers of the guilds seem to have varied from time to time and place to place. In the Hellenistic period, the chief official of the Isthmian–Nemean and of the Hellespontine guilds seems to have been the ἱερεύς, the priest of Dionysus, of whom most is to be learnt from the inscriptions of Teos. He was elected annually and was re-eligible, and seems generally to have been a performing artist. Our earliest Athenian record,[2] however, seems to show that guild under the control of two ἱεροποιοί with ἐπιμεληταί to assist them, but by 133 B.C.[3] the chief administrative officer is an ἐπιμελητής and remains so. The Cypriote guild, as we have seen,[4] was at one time governed by three ἄρχοντες, assisted by an οἰκονόμος and a γραμματεύς. These two minor officials recur at Ptolemais, but there will always have been a good deal of variety. At Argos, for example,[5] we have a ταμίας, a γραμματεύς, and an ἐπιστάτης. In the imperial period, a good deal is heard of ἀρχιερεῖς, but their functions seem to be purely honorary. There is no reason to doubt that the normal officers were an ἄρχων, a γραμματεύς, and a νομοδείκτης. We hear also[6] of a λογιστής, not an officer of the guild, but an external commissioner, appointed by the emperor to keep an eye on its affairs, as happened so frequently with cities.

The members of the guild included poets of various kinds (dramatic, epic, and lyric), actors of tragedy, comedy, and satyric plays, singers in the choruses, instrumentalists, rhapsodes, and before long reciters of encomia and similar compositions, and διδάσκαλοι—trainers of choruses—who might themselves be actors or singers; the names of some occur from time to time both as διδάσκαλοι and as choreutae. ὑποδιδάσκαλοι are also mentioned. These were probably at first professional trainers employed by the poets who were the διδάσκαλοι proper,[7] but

---

[1] It is incorrect to speak of the guilds as θίασοι of Dionysus. They formed a professional body who worked under the patronage of Dionysus, but not a body consisting of voluntary devotees of a particular cult.

[2] *I.G.* ii². 1320 (see above, p. 286).   [3] Appendix, no. 7.

[4] Appendix, no. 6 (see above, p. 287).   [5] Appendix, no. 8 (see above, p. 288).

[6] *Annuario* 2 (1916), pp. 146–7, no. 19 ὁ δᾶμος ὁ Ῥοδίων καὶ ἁ βουλὰ Τίτον Αὐρηλιανὸν Νε[ικ]όστρατον Νεικοστράτου Ἄμιον τὸν σοφιστάν, τετειμαμένον καὶ ὑπὸ τοῦ μεγίστου Αὐτοκράτορος καθέδρᾳ καὶ λογιστείᾳ τᾶς ἱερᾶς συνόδου θυμελικᾶς, πολλά[ς] τε πρεσβείας πρεσβεύσαντα ὑπὲρ πατρίδος κτλ. This Nikostratos appears in 'Suidas', and the inscription is Antonine in date. Earlier texts (*C.I.G.* 2529; *I.G.* xii. 1. 83; *I.G.R.* iv. 1134) have been responsible for some curious speculation. We also hear of a προήγορος, apparently an honorary position (*M.A.M.A.* viii, no. 418 c).

[7] Phot. s.v. ὑποδιδάσκαλος· ὁ τῷ χορῷ καταλέγων· διδάσκαλος γὰρ αὐτὸς ὁ ποιητής, ὡς Ἀριστοφάνης. This is implied also in the list in Plato, *Ion* 536 a ὁρμαθὸς πάμπολυς ἐξήρτηται χορευτῶν τε καὶ διδασκάλων καὶ ὑποδιδασκάλων. See also Sifakis, *Studies*, pp. 80 f., 119 f.

later the title may have been applied at Athens to the producers of old plays, the original poet being still regarded as the true διδάσκαλος. The costumiers (ἱματιομίσθαι) were doubtless also members of the guild. Their importance is attested, even before the existence of guilds, in the Euboean inscription.[1] In the Ptolemais inscription[2] the term used is σκευοποιός, as in Aristotle's *Poetics*.[3] Whether the σαλπιγκτής, the trumpeter who announced the beginning of each event in the contests,[4] and the κῆρυξ were members or servants of the guild is not quite certain.[5] It has already been noted that within the guild the actors of secondary rank, the συναγωνισταί, might form a special society of their own. In the time of Plato tragic and comic actors appear to have been rigidly separate;[6] in Cicero's day exceptional performers might excel in both kinds,[7] but the inscriptional records show that this must have been very rare.[8]

There is little satisfactory evidence of the payments made to artists.[9] Such evidence as we have for prizes is difficult to evaluate, since we can never be sure of the relative importance of any particular festival. Festivals seem to have been distinguished as στεφανῖται (though the crown may have had a large cash value), θεματικοί, ἡμιταλαντιαῖοι, and ταλαντιαῖοι. The sums prescribed in the Euboean decree are not likely to have been exceptional for the early part of the third century B.C.; the Corcyrean inscription of the second century B.C.[10] gave each tragic or comic troupe and its flute-player 8⅓ Corinthian minae in addition to rations, and we have elaborate lists of prizes from Tanagra[11] in about 100 B.C. and from Aphrodisias in imperial times.[12] Curiously enough, at Tanagra the actors, except for the actor of old tragedy, fare less well than the poets, and at Aphrodisias the contrary is true.

In any case, the members of the guild certainly had a rich social life. Inscriptions show the annual πανήγυρις, the monthly feasts, celebrations of the birthdays of princes and benefactors, common dinners, and wine-parties. They took a conspicuous part in the public sacrifices of sanctuaries and towns, and might march in processions clad in purple and gold.

---

[1] Appendix, no. 1.   [2] Appendix, no. 5.
[3] 1450[b]20.   [4] Cf. Pollux iv. 87, 91.
[5] The crowns that they receive in the Sarapieia inscription (see p. 295) are of the middle range of value, and argue fairly strongly for their high status.
[6] *Rep.* iii. 395 a οὐδὲ μὴν ῥαψῳδοί γε καὶ ὑποκριταὶ ἅμα· . . . ἀλλ' οὐδέ τοι ὑποκριταὶ κωμῳδοῖς τε καὶ τραγῳδοῖς οἱ αὐτοί.   [7] Cic. *Orat.* 109.
[8] *Didyma, die Inschriften*, no. 183 provides a stray exception.
[9] A story is told in various forms that Polos or Aristodemos (second half of the fourth century) boasted that he had made a talent in two days ([Plut.] *Vit. X Orat.* 848 b; Gell. *N.A.* xi. 9).   [10] Above, p. 295. For Delos, see Sifakis, *Studies*, p. 38.
[11] Above, p. 295.   [12] Appendix, no. 16b, and Le Bas 1620 c (tragic prizes only).

The flattery of successful actors and instrumentalists in the imperial age seems to have reached the same height of absurdity as that of film stars in the present day. In addition to the title ἱερονείκης which could be used of any victor in sacred games or belonging to a ἱερὰ σύνοδος, we find περιοδονείκης used to indicate a victor in all the four great festivals of Greece, and πλειστονείκης of one who broke the record in the number of his victories; παράδοξος is constantly used of the victor and παραδοξονείκης is found. Successful performers accumulated the citizenships of many cities, and cities erected their statues.

But in spite of all this flattery it is not easy to get a clear general idea of the social position and reputation of the actor at different periods. The depreciatory estimate of Aristotle has already been quoted,[1] but the language used of Kraton by his guild at Teos is that of warm personal regard, and there are similar expressions in inscriptions of later periods. Yet Philostratus[2] speaks of actors as haughty and undisciplined, and Lucian has little good to say of them. But the actors of whom Lucian[3] speaks as being whipped, at the pleasure of the audience, if they acted badly, or at best as being hissed off the stage, and as wandering about in beggary and starvation when they had put off the fine stage robes which they wore as gods and kings and heroes, seem to belong to a different world from Kraton and from others mentioned in inscriptions of Lucian's own time. Probably most of the actors whose names appear in the inscriptions are those who were specially selected to perform at great or special festivals, while Lucian is thinking of theatrical performances which were commonly held in all towns, large or small, and at many seasons.

[1] Above, p. 280. [2] Above, p. 301, n. 1.

[3] e.g. *Piscator* 33 ἐπεὶ καὶ οἱ ἀθλοθέται μαστιγοῦν εἰώθασιν, ἤν τις ὑποκριτὴς Ἀθηνᾶν ἢ Ποσειδῶνα ἢ τὸν Δία ὑποδεδυκὼς μὴ καλῶς ὑποκρίνοιτο μηδὲ κατ' ἀξίαν τῶν θεῶν, καὶ οὐ δή που ὀργίζονται αὐτοῖς ἐκεῖνοι (sc. οἱ θεοί), ὅτι τὸν περικείμενον αὐτῶν τὰ προσωπεῖα καὶ τὸ σχῆμα ἐνδεδυκότα ἐπέτρεψαν παίειν τοῖς μαστιγοφόροις, ἀλλὰ καὶ ἥδοιντ' ἄν, οἶμαι, μαστιγουμένων· οἰκέτην μὲν γὰρ ἢ ἄγγελόν τινα μὴ δεξιῶς ὑποκρίνασθαι μικρὸν τὸ πταῖσμα, τὸν Δία δὲ ἢ τὸν Ἡρακλέα μὴ κατ' ἀξίαν ἐπιδείξασθαι τοῖς θεαταῖς ἀποτρόπαιον ὡς καὶ αἰσχρόν; *Apol. de mercede cond.* 5 (ὑποκριταὶ) οἱ ἐπὶ μὲν τῆς σκηνῆς Ἀγαμέμνων ἕκαστος αὐτῶν ἢ Κρέων ἢ αὐτὸς Ἡρακλῆς εἰσιν, ἔξω δὲ Πῶλος ἢ Ἀριστόδημος ἀποθέμενοι τὰ προσωπεῖα γίγνονται ὑπόμισθοι τραγῳδοῦντες, ἐκπίπτοντες καὶ συριττόμενοι, ἐνίοτε δὲ καὶ μαστιγούμενοί τινες αὐτῶν, ὡς ἂν τῷ θεάτρῳ δοκῇ; *Nigrin.* 8 ἤδη τραγικοὺς ἢ καὶ νὴ Δία κωμικοὺς φαύλους ἑώρακας ὑποκριτάς, τῶν συριττομένων λέγω τούτων καὶ διαφθειρόντων τὰ ποιήματα καὶ τὸ τελευταῖον ἐκβαλλομένων; *Menipp.* 16; *Navig.* 46.

APPENDIX

INSCRIPTIONS RELATING TO THE ARTISTS OF DIONYSUS

1. The Euboean Law on engaging Artists (294–288 B.C.). *I.G.* xii. 9. 207 and p. 176; *I.G.* xii, Suppl., p. 178; Wilhelm, *Griechische Inschriften rechtlichen Inhalts*, pp. 79–83.

[- - - - - - -]ν Δαμασίας Παράμονο[ς - - - - - - - - - - - - - -]φαντος Ἀπολλωνίδης
Ἀριστίων· αἱρεῖσ[θαι ἄνδρας - - - οἵτινες παραγενήσονται εἰ]ς Χαλκίδα διαδώ-
σοντες τὰ ἔργα τοῖς τεχνίτα[ις μηνὸς Ἀπατουριῶνος ὡς Χαλκιδεῖς] ἄγουσι, ὡς δὲ
Ἰστιαιεῖς Ἀρείου, ὡς δὲ Ἐρετριεῖς [- - - - - - -]ορκος· ὀμόσαι δὲ τοὺς αἱρεθέντας
ἔν τε τῆι ἰδίαι πό[λει - - - καὶ ὅταν π]αραγένωνται εἰς Χαλκίδα τὸν αὐτὸν ὅρκον
ἐπὶ τ[- - - - - - τῶν τε]χνιτῶν τῶν ἐπαγγελλομένων τοῖς ἀρίστοις κατ[ὰ - - - - οὔτε
χ]άριτος ἕνεκα οὔτε ἔχθρας οὐδεμιᾶς, καὶ δῶρα οὐ [δέξομαι - - - - - -]λη τέχνηι
οὐδὲ παρευρέσει οὐδεμιᾶι ἕξιν τῆ[ς - - - - - - κ]αὶ τὸν Ἀπόλλω καὶ τὴν Δ[ή]μητρα
καὶ τὸν Διόνυσον· [καὶ εὐορκοῦντι μέν μοι εἴη τἀγαθά], ἐπιορκοῦντι δὲ τἀναντία.
ὑπὲρ ἐργολαβι[ῶ]ν. ἐπειδὰν δὲ [ὀμόσωσι, διδόντων τὰ ἔργα κηρ]ύξαντες καὶ
ἐπαγγείλαντες τοῖς τεχνίταις ἀπὸ τῆς εἰκάδος [τοῦ Ἀπατουριῶνος μηνός· πεμπ]όντων
δὲ αὐλητὰς τρεῖς, τραγωιδοὺς τρεῖς, εἰς δὲ Κάρυσ[τ]ον δύο [- - - - - - -]τέτταρας
καὶ χοροὺς παίδων τρεῖς καὶ ἀνδρῶν τρεῖς πλὴν εἰς τὸν χ[ορὸν τῶν - - - - - -]ργον
ὅστις παρέξει ἱμάτια τοῖς τραγωιδοῖς καὶ κωμωιδοῖς πάντα ὅσων [ἂν προσδέωνται·
καὶ ἐγγύους π]αρ' ἑκάστου τῶν τεχνιτῶν δεχέσθων ἀξιοχρέους πλὴν μὴ Εὐβοέας.
[ὑπὲρ θεωρῶν· πέμπειν δὲ τ]ὰς πόλεις εἰς τοὺς ἀγῶνας τῶν Διονυσίων καὶ
Δημητρείων ἑλομένους θε[ωροὺς κομίζοντας τὸ κατὰ τ]ὸ ψήφισμα καλλιστεῖον,
λαμβάνοντας ἀργύριον παρὰ τῆς ἰδίας πόλε[ως δραχμὰς - - - - κον]τα καὶ συμπον-
πεύειν καὶ τἆλλα πάντα πράττειν κατὰ τὸν Εὐβοϊκὸν νόμο[ν. ὑπὲρ μισθοῦ·
διδόναι δὲ πόλι]ν ἑκάστην νομίσματος Δημητρείου αὐλητεῖ δραχμὰς ἑξακοσίας,
τραγωιδῶ[ι Διονυσίων - -, Δημητρεί]ων ἀγῶνι Η, κω[μ]οιδοῖς ΗΗΗΗ, ἱματιομίσθει
ΗΗΗ. ὑπὲρ σιτηρεσίων· διδότω δὲ καὶ σιτη[ρέσιον ἑκάστη πόλις τοῖς τεχ]νίταις
ἡμερῶν πέντε τῆς ἡμέρας ἑκάστης ἐννέ' ὀβολοὺς καὶ τῶν ἐμβολίμων [ἡμερῶν - - -,
τοῖς δὲ διδασ]κάλοις τῶν τραγωιδῶν καὶ κωμωιδῶν ἡμερῶν δέκα, τοῖς δὲ τῶν κυκλίων
χορ[ῶν - - - - - - δρα]χμὰς εἴκοσι. ὑπὲρ τῶν ἀγώνων· γίνεσθαι δὲ τοὺς ἀγῶνας
τῶν Διονυσίων ἐν Καρ[ύστωι μηνὸς - - - ὡς Κα]ρύστιοι ἄγουσι ἀπὸ τῆς δωδεκάτης,
ἔπειτα ἐν Ἐρετρίαι μηνὸς Ληναιῶνος ὡς Ἐρετ[ριεῖς ἄγουσι ἀπὸ τῆς - - - -],
ἔπειτα ἐν Χαλκίδι μηνὸς Ληναιῶνος ὡς Χαλκιδεῖς ἄγουσι ἀπὸ τῆς εἰκάδος, ἔπειτ[α
ἐν Ὠρεῶι - - ὡς Ἰστιαιε]ῖς ἄγουσι ἀπὸ τῆς ὀγδόης ἀπιόντος. ὑπὲρ ἐμβολίμων
ἡμερῶν· ἐάν που προδέωνται [- - - - -] ἐ[μβ]ολίμων ἡμερῶν, ἐ[ξε]ῖν αὐτοῖς ἐν-
βαλέσθαι μέχρι ἡμερῶν τριῶν· ἄρχειν δὲ τοὺς αὐλητὰς α[- - - - - - τὸ]ν χορὸν
εἰσάγειν, τοὺς δὲ τραγωιδοὺς τοὺς ἐργολαβήσαντας καταλ[είπ]ειν τοῖς α[ὐ]λη[ταῖς - -
ἐπὶ τὴν - -]ιαν καὶ τοὺς χοροὺς τῶν ἀνδρῶν τραγωιδῶν τοῖς ὑποκριταῖς τὰ ἱμάτια
νέα πα[ρέχειν - - - - εἰσ]άγει· τοὺς δὲ χορηγοὺς τοὺς ἀποδεδειγμένους ἐν ταῖς πόλεσι
δέχε[σ]θαί τε τοὺς τ[εχνίτας - - - - -] κατὰ τοὺς νόμους. [ὑ]πὲρ τῆς κρίσεως·
ἐπειδὰν δὲ ὁ ἀγὼν γένηται, κρινόντων [οἱ κ]ριταὶ [- - - - - -]ους γράψαντες εἰς

γρ[αμμ]ατεῖον καὶ θέντες εἰς τὸ φανερὸν πρ[ὸ]ς τὸν ἀρ[χαῖον ν]α[ὸ]ν ο[ὗ - - - -
κηρ[υσσέ]τω [τὰ ὀ]νόματα τῶν χορηγῶν ἐπὶ τοὺς τεχνίτας, ὁ δὲ [ἄ]ρχων [τοὺς]
κεκριμένους [- - -, καὶ ὁ ποιητὴς τοῦ δράμ]ατος νικάτω. ὑπὲρ Δημητριέων·
εἰς δὲ τὰ Δημήτρεια τὰς ἐργολαβίας γίν[εσ]θαι ἐν [Χαλκίδι - - - - -]νεσθειαν ἀπὸ
τῶν πόλεων, τὸν δὲ ἀγῶνα ποιούντων πρῶτον ἐν Ὠρεῶι τοῦ Δημητριῶνος μη[νὸς
ὡς Ἱστιαιεῖς ἄγουσι ἀπὸ τῆς - -]της ἱσταμένου, εἶτα ἐν Χαλκίδι το[ῦ Ἱπ]πιῶνος
μηνὸς ὡς Χαλκιδεῖς ἄγουσι ἀπὸ τῆς [δωδ]εκάτης, [εἶτα ἐν Ἐρετρίαι τοῦ . . . . . .ῶ]νος
μηνὸς ὡς Ἐρετριεῖς [ἄγ]ουσιν ἀπ[ὸ] τῆς δεκάτης μετ' εἰκάδας, ἔπειτα ἐν Καρύστωι
τοῦ Βουφον[ιῶνος μηνὸς ὡς Καρύστιοι ἄ]γουσι ἀπὸ τῆς ὀγδόης ἀπιόντος· εἶναι δὲ καὶ
τῶν Δημητριείων τὰς κρίσεις τῶν τεχνιτῶν ἐν ταῖς πόλεσιν ο[- - - - - - -] καθάπερ
καὶ τοῖς Διονυσίοις [γέ]γραπται· Καρυστίους δὲ χρῆσθαι τοῖς τεχνίταις εἰς τὰ Ἀρι-
στονίκ[ει]α. [ὑπὲρ ζημιῶν· ἐὰν δέ τ]ινες τῶν τεχνιτῶν λίπωσι τῶν ἔργων τι τῶν
ἐγδοθέντων, ἀποτινόντων ζημίαν τὸ διπλάσιον οὗ ἂν [λάβωσι τὸ ἔργον, ἡ δὲ π]ρᾶξις
ἔστω τοῦ τεχνίτου καὶ τοῦ ἐργολάβ[ου καὶ] τοῦ ἐγγύου καθ' ἑκάστην πόλιν ἐν αἷς
ἂν λίπωσιν, κ[αὶ ἔστωσαν ἐντὸς] τῆς Εὐβοίας ἀγώγιμοι καὶ αὐτοὶ καὶ ὅσ' ἂν ἔχοντες
δια[πορε]ύωνται δι' Εὐβοίας στερέσθων πάντων, ἕως ἂν [ἐκτείσωσι τ]ὴν ζημίαν
καθὰ γέ[γ]ραπται· τὸ δ' εἰσπραττόμενον ἀργύριον ἀ[πὸ ⟨τῶν⟩ λι]πόντων ἔστω ἱερὸν
τοῦ Διονύσου ἐν τεῖ πόλει, εἰ ἂν τ[ὸ ἔργον ἦι], ὅσα δ' ἂν ἔχοντες διαπορεύωνται, τὰ
μὲν ἡμίσεα τοῦ ἀ[φ]ελό[ντος] ἔστω, τὰ δὲ ἡμίσεα τῆς πόλεως, ἐξ ἧς ἂν ὁ ἀφελόμε[νος
ἦι·] ἐὰν δέ τις ἐν ταῖς πόλεσι γράψηι ἢ ἐπιψηφίσει ὡς δεῖ ἀφεῖσθαί [τινος] τῶν τὸ
ἔργον λιπόντων τὴν ζημίαν, ἔνοχος [βι]αί[ω]ν ἔσται ὅ τε γράψας καὶ ὁ ἐπιψηφίσας,
ἐὰμ μὴ ὁ βασιλε[ὺς ἄ]λλο περ[ὶ α]ὐτῶν ἐπιστείληι· τῶι δὲ ἀπὸ τού[τ]ων γιν[ομέν]ωι
[ἀ]ργυρίωι ἐν ταῖς πόλεσιν καταχρῆσθων εἰς τὸ ἱερὸν τοῦ [Δι]ονύσου, εἰς ἄλλο δὲ
μηθέν. περὶ ἐμβολίμων μην[ῶν· π]ερὶ δὲ τῶν ἐμβολαίων μηνῶν ἐπιμελεῖσθαι τοὺς
ἄρχοντας ἐν ταῖς πόλε[σι μ]ετὰ τῶν ἡιρημένων ὅταν καθήκει, ὅπως ἂν ἅμα ἐν [τ]ῆι
Εὐβοίαι γίνωνται. ὑπὲρ ἐξω[μ]οσιῶν· ἐξωμοσίαν δὲ εἶναι τοῖς τεχνίτα[ις] τοῖς
λιποῦσί τι τῶν ἔργων αὐτοῖς παραγενομέν[οις ε]ἰς τὴν πόλιν οὗ ἂν λίπωσι τὸ ἔργον
ἐντὸς τοῦ χειμῶνος ἐν ἐγμήνω[ι· πρ]ότερον δὲ μὴ εἶναι ἐξηιρῆσθαι· παρόντων τ[ῶν]
διδόντων τὰ ἔργα· ἐὰν δέ τις τῶν τεχνιτῶν τῶν λαβόντων τὰ ἔργα ἐ[ν Ε]ὐβοίαι ἀγωνίζηται ἔν τινι πόλει ἐξ ἧς μὴ [ἔστιν αὐτῶι] παραγενέσθαι εἰς τοὺς χρόνους ἐν οἷς οἱ
ἀγῶνές εἰσιν ἐν [Εὐ]βοίαι, γινέσθω αὐτῶι ἡ ἐξωμοσία. τὰ δ[ὲ δόξαντ]α ἀναγράψαι τοὺς
ἄρχοντας ἐν ἑκάστ[ηι] τῶν πόλεων ἐν στ[ή]ληι λιθίνηι καὶ ἀν[α]θεῖναι εἰς τὴν πάρ[ο-
δον τοῦ] θεάτρου· τὸ δὲ ἀνάλωμα τὸ εἰς τὴν στήλην ὑποθεῖναι ἑκάστ[ου]ς παρ' ἑαυ-
[το]⟨ῖ⟩ς τῶι θεάτρωι, ὅταν ποιή[σωντ]αι τὴν μίσθω]σιν κατὰ τὰ ἐπιόντα Διονύσια. ὅπως
ἂν γίνωνται ⟨αἱ ἐργολαβίαι⟩, τὰς πόλεις ἑλομένας τοὺς ἄνδρας κατὰ τὴν διαγρα[φὴν
πέμψαι] εἰς Χαλκίδα πρὸ τῆς εἰκάδος τοῦ Ἀπατουριῶνος μηνός, ὡς Χαλκιδεῖς
ἄγουσιν, ὅπως ἂν ἐγδῶσιν τὰ ἔ[ργα τοῖς τεχ]νίταις· τοὺς δὲ προβού[λου]ς καὶ
στρατηγοὺς τοὺς Χαλκιδέων ἀποστεῖλαί τινα πρὸς τοὺς τεχνίτας ἐπαγγε[λοῦντα τὰς]
ἐργολαβίας καὶ ὅπως ἂν παρῶσιν οἱ βουλόμενοι ἐργολαβεῖν τοῦ [Ἀπατ]ουριῶνος
μηνός, ὡς Χαλκιδεῖς ἄγουσιν, π[ρὸ εἰκάδων τ]ῶν κατὰ θεόν· ἐὰν δέ τινες τῶν
[πρό]τερον ἐζημιωμένων ἐν ταῖς πόλεσιν τεχνιτῶν πρὸ τοῦ τὸν νόμον κυρω[θῆναι
βούλ]ωνται ἐργολαβεῖν τὸ Εὐβοϊκὸν ἔργον, εἶναι αὐτοῖς ὅταν παραγένωνται ἐξομοσα-
μένοις ἀφεῖσθαι τῶν προτέρων ζημ[ιῶν. ἀσφ]άλειαν εἶναι τοῖς ἐργολαβήσασιν τεχνίταις
τὸ Εὐβοϊκὸν ἔργον ἐν [ταῖς] πόλεσι ταῖς ἐν Εὐβοίαι πάσαις κατὰ τὸν καιρ[ό]ν, [ἐὰ]ν
τῶν [ἀγ]ώνων ἕνεκεν ἐνδημῶσι, ἀπὸ τῶν πολιτικῶν ἐγκλημάτων· ἐπιμελεῖσθαι δὲ

τῆς ἀσφαλείας τοὺς στρατη[γοὺς καὶ] τοὺς ἄρχοντας τοὺς κατὰ πόλ[ιν]. ἐὰν δέ τινες τῶν
τεχνιτῶν λίπωσι τῶν ἔργων τι, ἀν[α]β[άλλε]σθαι τὰς ἐγδόσεις τῶν ἔργ[ω]ν [ἁ]πάν
των, εἰ μὴ ἀπε[ίρη]ται, ⟨καὶ⟩ μισ[θ]ῶσαί [πο]θεν τεχνίτας ἀντὶ τῶν λειπόντων, ἐὰν
ὦσι δυνατοί· οἱ δὲ μισθωθέντες ὑπαρχόντω[ν καὶ] εἰς τὰς ἄλλας πόλεις, ἐν αἷς ἂν λείπη
ται τὰ ἔργα· ἐὰν δὲ οἱ τεχνῖται ἢ τῶν ἐργολάβων τινὲς δυνατοὶ ὄντες ἐργολ[α]βεῖν
καὶ βουλομένων αὐτοῖ[ς τῶν ἀρχόν]των τὰ ἔργα διδόναι μὴ ἐργολαβῶσι ἀλλ' ἐγ......
ωνται παρὰ τοὺς κειμένου[ς] τοῖς Εὐβοιεῦσι περὶ τούτων νόμους, ὑποτελεῖς αὐτοὺς
εἶναι πάντων ὧν ἂν ἔχοντες ἐπιβαίνωσι τῆς Εὐβοίας καὶ εἰσάγον[τας] καὶ ἐξάγοντας·
τοὺς δὲ διδόντας τὰ ἔργα οὓς ἂν κρίνωσιν τῶν τεχνιτῶν ἢ τῶν ἐργολάβων ἀδικεῖν
περὶ ταῦτα ἀ[πογ]ράψαι ταῖς ἰδίαις πόλεσιν· ἐπιμελεῖσθαι δὲ μετὰ τῶν ἀρχόντων καὶ
στρατηγῶν τοὺς ἡιρημένους πρὸς τὰς ἐργολαβὰς τρόπωι ὅτωι ἂν ἐπίστωνται, ὅπως
οἱ ἀπογραφέντες τὰ τέλη τιθῶσι κατὰ τὰ δόξαντα τοῖς Εὐβοιεῦσιν· ἐὰν δέ τινες
τῶν τεχνιτῶν ἀτακτοῦντές τι περὶ τοὺς ἀγῶνας ζημιωθῶσιν ὑπὸ τῶν ἀγωνοθετῶν,
ὑπολογεῖν αὐτοῖς τὰς ζημίας ἐκ τῶν μισθῶν ὅταν κομίσωνται παραχρῆμα.

2. The Amphiktyons recognize the Athenian guild, 278 B.C. *I.G.* ii². 1132, ll. 1–
39, restored with the help of the Delphic copy, *Fouilles de Delphes* iii. 2, no. 68, ll.
61–94. Cf. *S.I.G.*³ 399. We have only bracketed words preserved in neither copy.

ἐκ τοῦ μητρώιου· ἐπὶ Ἱέρωνος ἄρχοντος ἐν Δελφοῖς, πυλαίας ἐαρινᾶς, ἱερομνα
μονούντων Θεσσαλῶν Ἱπποδάμα, Λέοντος· Αἰτώλων Λυκέα, Δωριμάχου· Βοιωτῶν
Ἀσώπωνος, Διονυσίδου· Φωκέων Εὐφρέα, Χαρέα· ἔδοξεν τοῖς Ἀμφικτίοσιν καὶ τοῖς
ἱερομνάμοσιν καὶ τοῖς ἀγορατροῖς· ὅπω[ς] ἦι εἰς πάντα χρόνον ἀσυλία καὶ ἀτέλεια
τοῖς τεχνίταις τοῖς ἐν Ἀθήναις καὶ μὴ ἦι ἀγώγιμος μηθεὶς μηθαμόθεν μήτε πολέμου
μήτε εἰρήνης μήτε τὰ χρήματα αὐτῶν, ἀλλ' ἦι αὐτοῖς ἀτέλεια καὶ ἀσφάλεια εἰς
πάντα χρό[ν]ον ἡ συνκεχωρημένη ὑπὸ πάντων τῶν Ἑλλήνων βεβαία, εἶ[ν]αι δὲ τοὺς
τεχνίτας ἀτελεῖς στρατείας πεζικᾶς καὶ ναυτικᾶς καὶ εἰσφορᾶς πάσας, ὅπως
τοῖς θεοῖς αἱ τιμαὶ καὶ αἱ θυ[σίαι ἐ]φ' ἃς εἰσι τεταγμένοι οἱ τεχνῖται συντελῶνται ἐν
τοῖς καθήκουσιν χρόνοις ὄντων αὐτῶ[ν ἀπολυπραγ]μονήτων καὶ ἱερῶν πρὸς ταῖς
τῶν θεῶ[ν λειτουργί]αις· μὴ ἐξέστω δὲ μηδενὶ ἄγειν τὸν τ[εχνίταν, μήτε] πολέμου
μήτε εἰρήνας μηδὲ συλᾶν εἴ κα [μὴ χρέ]ος ἔχων πόλει ἦι ὑπόχρεως, καὶ ἐὰν ἰδίου ἦι
συν[βολαί]ου ὑπόχρεος ὁ τεχνίτας· ἐὰν δέ τις παρὰ ταῦτα ποιῆι, ὑπόδικος ἔστω ἐν
Ἀμφικτίοσιν αὐτός τε καὶ ἁ πόλις ἐν ἇι τὸ ἀδίκημα κατὰ τοῦ τεχνίτα συντελεσθῆι.
εἶμεν δὲ τὰν ἀτέλειαν καὶ τὰ[ν ἀσ]φάλειαν τὰν δεδομέναν ὑπὸ Ἀμφικτιόνων τοῖς ἐν
[Ἀθήναις τ]εχνίταις εἰς τὸν ἀεὶ χρόνον οὖσιν ἀπολυπραγμον[ή]τοις· τοὺς δὲ γραμμα
τεῖς ἀναγράψαι τὸ δόγμα εἰστήλαν λιθίναν καὶ στῆσαι ἐν Δελφοῖς· πέμψαι δὲ καὶ ποτὶ
Ἀθηναίους τοῦ δόγματος τοῦδε ἀντίγραφον ἐσφραγισμένον, ἵνα εἰδῶντι οἱ τεχνῖται
ὅτι οἱ Ἀμφικτίονες πλείσταν ἔχοντι πρόνοια[ν] ὑπὲρ τᾶς πρὸς τοὺς θεοὺς εὐσεβείας
καὶ κατακολουθήκα[ν]τι τοῖς παρακαλουμένοις ὑπὸ τῶν τεχνιτᾶν, πειράσονται δὲ
καὶ εἰς τὸ λοιπὸν ταῦτά τε φυλάσσειν εἰς τὸν ἅπαντα χρόνον καὶ ἄλλο ὅ τι ἂν ἔχωντι
ἀγαθὸν προσαύξειν ὑπὲρ τῶν περὶ τὸν Διόνυσον τεχνιτᾶν. πρέσσβεις· Ἀστυδάμας
ποιητὴς τραγωιδιῶν, Νεοπτόλεμος τραγωιδός.

3. The Isthmian–Nemean guild accept an invitation to the Mouseia, *c.* 211 B.C.
*S.I.G.*³ 457; Feyel, *Contribution à l'épigraphie béotienne*, pp. 89–90.

ὁ θυμελικὸς ἀγὼν στεφανίτης πρῶτον ἐγένετο ἀγωνοθετοῦντος Ἱεροκλέος, ἱερέως

δὲ τῶν Μουσῶν Μνασίωνος, ἀπὸ δὲ τῶν τεχνιτῶν Αἰσχύλου, καὶ δόγματα περὶ τοῦ
ἀγῶνος τῶν Μουσείων·

τεχνιτῶν· ἔδοξε τοῖς τεχνίταις τοῖς ἐξ Ἰσθμοῦ καὶ Νεμέας· ἐπειδὴ παραγενόμενος πρεσβευτὴς Ἱεροκλῆς παρὰ τῆς πόλεως Θεσπιέων καὶ τοῦ κοινοῦ τῶν
Βοιωτῶν ψηφίσματά τε ἀπέδωκεν καὶ ἐπιστολήν, ἐν ἧι παρεκάλει τοὺς τεχνίτας,
τῆς πόλεως τῶν Θεσπιέων προκεχειρισμένης τὸν ἀγῶνα τὸν ἐν τῶι Ἑλικῶνι
γινόμενον ταῖς Μούσαις στεφανίτην εἶναι τὸν θυμελικὸν τόν τε τῶν αὐλητῶν καὶ
αὐλωιδῶν καὶ κιθαριστῶν καὶ κιθαρωιδῶν καὶ ἐπῶν ποιητῆι, καὶ ὅπως ἂν ὁ ἐνιαυτὸς
μετατεθῆι, ἐν ὧι ὁ ἀγὼν γίνεται, καὶ συνπρεσβεύσωσιν περὶ τούτων οὗ ἂν παρα-
καλῆι ἡ πόλις ἡ τῶν Θεσπιέων, καθὼς καὶ ἐν τοῖς ἔμπροσ[θ]εν χρόνοις, πράττωσι δὲ
οἱ τε[χνῖ]ται καὶ ἐὰν ἄλλο [τ]ι χρήσιμον [ἢ ἔνδ]οξον ε[ἶ]ναι δόξηι] ἢ [- - - - - καὶ
ἐπειδὴ Ἱεροκλῆς λόγους ἐποιήσατο ἀκολούθως] τοῖς ἐν τοῖς ψηφίσμασι γεγραμ-
μένοις, ἐπέδειξε δὲ καὶ τὰ ἐξ ἀρχῆς προγεγονότα φιλάνθρωπα τῆι πόλει τῶν
Θεσπιέων πρὸς τοὺς τεχνίτας καὶ τοῖς τεχνίταις πρὸς τὴν πόλιν τῶν Θεσπιέων·
περὶ δὴ τούτων πάντων ἀγαθῆι τύ[χ]ηι δεδόχθαι τοῖς τεχνίταις, ἐπαινέσαι μὲν τὴν
πόλιν τῶν Θεσπιέων καὶ τὸ κοινὸν τῶν Βοιωτῶν ἐπὶ τῆι φιλοτιμίαι, ἧι ἔχουσιν εἰς
τε τὸ ἱερὸν τῶν Μουσῶν καὶ τὸ κοινὸν τῶν τεχνιτῶν· ἀποκρίνασθαι δὲ αὐτοῖς, ὅτι
καὶ πρότερον οἱ τεχνῖται, κοινὸν ὑπολαμβάνοντες εἶναι τὸν ἀγῶνα τῶν Μουσῶν τῆι
τε πόλει Θεσπιέων καὶ αὐτοῖς, τὴν πᾶσαν προθυμίαν ἐνεδείξαντο καὶ συνθύοντες καὶ
ἱερέα ἐξ αὐτῶν αἱρούμενοι καὶ θεωροὺς ἀποστέλλοντες καὶ ψηφίσματα γράφοντες
καὶ συμπρεσβεύοντες περὶ τοῦ ἀγῶνος καὶ πρὸς τοὺς λοιποὺς Ἕλληνας, καθὼς ἂν
ἡ πόλις παρ[α]καλῆι τῶν Θεσπιέων· ἐμφανίζειν δὲ αὐτοῖς ὅτι καὶ νῦν πρῶτοι τὸν
ἀγῶνα ταῖς Μούσαις στεφα[νί]την ἀποδέχοντ[αι - - - -]

4. The Amphiktyons reply to the Artists and to Thebes about the Agrionia,
between 228 and 215 B.C. *Fouilles de Delphes* iii. 1, no. 351 and p. 402 (Nikit-
sky, *J. Min. Publ. Instr.*, March 1912, pp. 130 ff.) ; Robert, *B.C.H.* 59 (1935)
pp. 196–7; Feyel, *Contribution à l'épigraphie béotienne*, pp. 140–7; Bousquet,
B.C.H. 85 (1961), pp. 78–85. We omit the fragmentary lines 1–10, which
order the publication of the two following decrees.

[ἐπὶ Νικάρχου ἄρχοντος ἐν Δε]λφοῖς, π[υλαίας ὀπωρινῆς, ἔδοξεν τοῖς Ἀμφι]κτίοσιν·
ὅπως ἂν ἡ θυσία τῶι Διονύσωι [ἡ τῶν τριετηρίδων καὶ οἱ] ἀγῶνες οὓς σ[υντελεῖ ἡ
πόλις τῶν Θηβαίων καὶ τὸ κ]οινὸν τῶν τεχνιτῶν τῶν εἰς Ἰσθμὸν [καὶ Νεμέαν συμ-
πορευο]μένων γίνητ[αι ὡς κάλλιστα, ἐπιμελεῖσθαι] τοὺς ἱερομνήμονας οἳ ἂν ὦσιν ἐν
τῶι [συνεδρίωι ὅπαν αἱ τ]ριετηρίδες κα[ὶ οἱ ἀγῶνες συντελῶνται ἐν τῶι Κα]δμείωι
ἐν Θήβαις ὑπὲρ τοῦ[των ὅπως ἕκαστα γίνηται] ἐν τῆι ἡμέρα[ι ἧι ἂν ἡ πόλις τῶν
Θηβαίων καὶ τὸ κ]οινὸν τῶν τεχνιτῶ[ν ἐ]θελ[ήσω]σιν - - - - - - - άναι ἐν τῶι
ἱερῶι παρὰ τὸν ση[κὸν τῆς Σεμέλης - - - - - · εἶ]ναι δὲ καὶ ἀσφάλειαν καὶ ἀσυλίαν
πᾶσι το[ῖς τεχνίταις τοῖς νεμηθεῖσιν εἰς τὰν θυσία]ν τῶν τριετηρίδων, πένθ' ἡμέρας
πορευ[ομένοις, καὶ ἀπερχομένοις ἄλλας τοσαύτας, κ]αὶ ἕως ἂν ἡ πανήγυρις γίνηται,
καὶ αὐτοῖς κ[αὶ τοῖς συνεργαζομένοις αὐτοῖς πα]νταχοῦ· ἐὰν δέ τις παρὰ ταῦτα
ἄγηι τινὰ ἢ ῥυσιάζηι, ὑ[πόδικος ἔστω ἐν Ἀμφικτίο]σιν· εἶναι δὲ καὶ τὸ ἱερὸν τοῦ
Διονύσου τοῦ Καδμείου [τὸ ἐν Θήβαις ἀπὸ πάντων ἄ]συλον καθάπερ καὶ τὸ ἐν
Δελφοῖς· τὴν δὲ θυσίαν καὶ ἐκεχε[ιρίαν ἐπαγγέλλειν] ἐπὶ τὰς πόλεις τήν τε τῶν
Θηβαίων πόλιν καὶ τοὺς τεχνίτας· κ[υρίους δ' εἶναι οἰκονο]μοῦντας τὰ κατὰ τὸ ἱερὸν

τόν τε ἱερέα τοῦ Διονύσου καὶ τοὺς ἐπιμελ[ητὰς τοὺς ὑπὸ τῶ]ν τεχνιτῶν εἰρημένους
καὶ τὸν ἀγωνοθέτην Θηβαίων· ἀναγράψαι δὲ τὸν [γραμματέα τόδ]ε τὸ ψήφισμα
ἐν στήλαις δυσὶν καὶ ἀναθεῖναι τὴν μὲν ἐν Δελφοῖς ἐν τῶ[ι ἱερῶι τοῦ Ἀπόλλωνο]ς
ὅπου ἂν δοκῆι ἐγ καλλίστωι εἶναι, τὴν δὲ ἐν Θήβαις παρὰ τὸν σηκὸ[ν τῆς Σεμέλης,
ἀν]αθεῖναι δὲ καὶ τῶν ἄλλων ἱερῶν ὅπου ἂν δοκῆι ἐν καλλίστωι εἶναι. ἐπὶ Νικάρχου ἄρχοντος ἐ[ν Δελφοῖς, πυλαία]ς ὀπωρινῆς, ἔδοξεν τοῖς Ἀμφικτίοσιν· ἐπειδὴ
ἁ πόλις τῶν Θηβαίων κα[ὶ οἱ τεχνῖται οἱ εἰς] Ἰσθμὸν καὶ Νεμέαν συντελοῦντες
παρεκάλεσαν τοὺς Ἀμφικτίονας τό τε [ἱε]ρὸν [τοῦ Διονύσου] ἄσυλον ποιῆσαι καὶ
ἐπιμέλειαν ποιήσασθαι τᾶς ἀ[σ]φαλείας καὶ τοῦ ἀγῶ[ν]ος· ὅπω[ς ἂν οὖν ἁ θυσία ἁ]
τῶν τριετηρίδων ὡς κάλλιστα συντελῆται τῶι Διονύσωι τῶι Καδμε[ίω]ι, δεδόχ[θαι
τοῖς Ἀμφικτ]ιόνεσσι· αἴ τίς κα τῶν αὐλητᾶν ἢ τῶν χορευτᾶν ἢ τῶν τραγωιδῶν ἢ
τῶν κω[μωιδῶν τῶν νε]μηθέντων εἰς τὰς τριετηρίδας ὑπὸ τῶν τεχνιτᾶν μὴ ἀγωνίζηται
[τ]ὰς τριετηρίδα[ς καὶ τοὺς ἀγῶ]νας κατὰ τὸν νόμον τᾶς πόλιος τῶν Θηβαίων, ἀλλὰ
ὑγιαίνων λίπη[ι τὸν] ἀγῶνα, μὴ ε[ἶμεν αὐτῶι ἀσφ]άλειαν μηδὲ τοῖς συνεργαζομένοις
αὐτῶι μήτε πολέμου μήτε εἰρά[να]ς· αἴ κα μὴ ἀγ[ωνίζηται, καὶ] κα ζαμιωθῆι ὑπὸ
τοῦ ἀγωνοθέτα, καὶ ἀγώγιμος ἔστω πανταχόθεν· [αἴ κά] τις πόλις ἢ [ἀρχεῖον ἢ
ἰδιώτ]ας [τ]ὰν ζαμίαν ἀφέληται τὸν ἐζαμι[ωμ]ένον, - - - -

5. Two decrees of the Egyptian Artists, c. 240 B.C. O.G.I.S. 50–51.

(a) The Artists honour Dionysius.

ἔδοξεν τοῖς τεχνίταις τοῖς περὶ τὸν Διόνυσον καὶ Θεοὺς Ἀδελφοὺς καὶ τοῖς τὴν
σύνοδον νέμουσιν, στεφανῶσαι Διονύσιον Μουσαίου πρύτανιν διὰ βίου κισσοῦ
στεφάνωι κατὰ τὰ πάτρια εὐνοίας ἕνεκα τῆς εἰς τὴν πόλιν τῶν Πτολεμαιέων καὶ
τοὺς τεχνίτας τοὺς [περὶ] τὸν μέγαν Διόνυσον καὶ Θεοὺς Ἀδελφούς, ἀναγ[ορε]ῦσαι
δὲ τὸν στέφανον τοῖς Διονυσίοις καὶ ἀναγραφῆναι [τὸ] ψήφισ[μα] τόδε εἰς στή[λ]ην
[καὶ] ἀναθεῖναι πρὸ τοῦ νεὼ τοῦ Διονύσου. τὸ δὲ ἀνάλωμα τὸ εἰς τὴν στήλην δοῦναι
τὸν οἰ[κον]όμο[ν] Σωσίβιον.

(b) The Artists honour Lysimachus.

ἔδοξεν τεχνίταις τοῖς περὶ τὸν Διόνυσον καὶ Θεοὺς Ἀδελφούς· ἐπειδὴ Λυσίμαχος
Πτολεμαίου Σωστρατεύς, ὁ ἱππάρχης καὶ πρύτανις διὰ βίου, τήν τε εἰς τὸν βασιλέα
καὶ τοὺς τούτου γονεῖς εὔνοιαν καὶ πρότερον μέν, ἔτι καὶ νῦν δὲ διὰ πλειόνων
ἀποδέδεικται καὶ πρὸς τὸν Διόνυσον καὶ τοὺς ἄλλους θεοὺς εὐσεβῶς καὶ ὁσίως
διακείμενος τυγχάνει τοῖς τε τεχνίταις φιλανθρώπως ἅπαντα χρῆται καὶ κατ᾽ ἰδίαν
ἑκάστου καὶ κατὰ κοινὸν πάντων ἀντιλαμβάνεται προθύμως καὶ ἐκτενῶς ἑαυτὸν
συνεπιδιδοὺς εἰς τὸ συναύξεσθαι τὸ τεχνίτευμα, καλῶς δ᾽ ἔχει τοὺς τοιούτους
τῶν ἀνδρῶν ἐπισημαινομένους τιμᾶν ταῖς πρεπούσαις τιμαῖς, δεδόχθαι τῶι κοινῶι
τῶν περὶ τὸν Διόνυσον τεχνιτῶν, ὧν καὶ τὰ ὀνόματα ὑπογέγραπται, στεφανῶσαι
Λυσίμαχον κιττοῦ στεφάνωι κατὰ τὰ πάτρια τῇ ια᾽ τοῦ Περιτίου μηνὸς τοῖς
Διονυσίοις ἀρετῆς ἕνεκα καὶ εὐσεβείας τῆς εἴς τε βασιλέα Πτολεμαῖον καὶ τὸν
Διόνυσον καὶ τοὺς ἄλλους θεοὺς καὶ εὐνοίας τῆς εἰς τὸν βασιλέα καὶ τοὺς τούτου
γονεῖς καὶ τῆς εἰς τοὺς τεχνίτας τύχηι τῆι ἀγαθῆι. ἀναθεῖναι δ᾽ αὐτ[οῦ] καὶ εἰκόνα
γραπτὴν ἐν τῇ προστάδι τοῦ πρυτανείου. ἀναγράψαι δὲ καὶ τὸν γραμματέα τοῦ
κοινοῦ Δήμαρχον τὸ ψήφισμα τόδε εἰς στήλην καὶ ἀναθεῖναι πρὸ τοῦ νεὼ τοῦ
Διονύσου· τὸ δ᾽ εἰς ταῦτ᾽ ἀνάλωμα δοῦναι τὸν οἰκονόμον Σωσίβιον.

Ζώπυρος ὁ πρὸς τοῖς ἱεροῖς τῆς τριετηρίδος καὶ ἀμφιετηρίδος καὶ τούτου ἀδελφοί

Διονύσιος	τραγῳδός	αὐλητὴς τραγικός
Ταυρῖνος	Μητρόδωρος	Θραικίδης
τραγῳδιῶν ποιηταί	κωμῳδοί	σαλπικτής
Φαίνιππος	Τελέμαχος	Θρασύμαχος
Διόγνητος	Ἀγαθόδωρος	σκευοποιός· Βάτων
κωμωιδιῶν ποιηταί	Ἀπολλώνιος	πρόξενοι
Στράταγος	Ἀσκληπιόδωρος Ἀπολλωνίου	Δημήτριος
Μουσαῖος	Ἀπολλώνιος	Φαίδιμος
ἐπῶν ποιηταί	Διόδωρος	Ἀρτεμίδωρος
Δήμαρχος	συναγωνισταὶ τραγικοί	Σπουδί[ας]
Θεογένης	Ἀπολλωνίδης Ἄρδωνος	Διονύσιος
Ἀρτεμίδωρος	Κλεῖτος	φιλοτεχνῖται
κιθαρῳδός	[Π]τολεμαῖος	Δημήτριος
Μένιππος	[Ζώ]πυρος	Στέφανος
κιθαριστής	[χορ]οδιδάσκαλ[ος]	Λέων
Ἡράκλειτος	- - - - - -	Ἀρτεμίδωρος
ὀρχηστής		Δημήτριος
Πτολεμαῖος		Ἀριστόνους
- - - - - -		- - - - - -

6. The Cypriote Artists honour the nauarch's son, 114–131 B.C. *S.E.G.* xiii. 586.

[Θεόδωρον, τῶν πρώτων φίλω]ν, τὸν [υἱὸν τὸν Σελεύκου τοῦ συγγενοῦς τοῦ βασιλέως καὶ στρατηγ]οῦ καὶ ναυάρ[χου καὶ ἀρχιερέως τῆς νήσου, τὸ κοινὸν τῶν ἐν τῶι κ]ατὰ Πάφον γραμματείωι περ[ὶ τὸν Διόνυσον καὶ Θεοὺς Ἐπιφανεῖς τεχ]νιτῶν, εὐεργεσίας ἕνεκεν τῆς εἰ[ς ἑαυτό· - - - - -.] ἀρχόντων Κρίτωνος κιθαρωι[δοῦ, - - - ποιητοῦ σατύ]ρων, Διονυσίου ποιητοῦ τραγῳ[διῶν, οἰκονομοῦντος - - -] συναγωνιστοῦ τραγικοῦ, γραμ[ματεύοντος - - - ποιητοῦ κωμ]ῳδιῶν.

7. The Athenian guild honours King Ariarathes V, shortly before 130 B.C. *I.G.* ii². 1330; Leonardos, Ἀρχ. Ἐφ. 1922, p. 109; Wilhelm, *Jahreshefte* 24 (1929), pp. 184–5; Robert, *B.C.H.* 50 (1926), pp. 497–8, 506, *Études épigraphiques et philologiques*, pp. 38 ff.

- - - - - υσαν, παρεκά[λεσαν δὲ τὸν βασιλέα ἐπιμελεῖσθαι ὅπως ἡ σύ]νοδ[ος τῶν τεχνιτῶν α]ὐξηθήσεται τ[- - - - - -] καὶ [- - - - -]ιας, ἐφ' οἷς ἀποδ[εξάμενος αὐτοὺς φιλοφρόνως ἐπηγ]γείλ[ατο ὁ βασιλεὺς π]έμψειν δωρεάς [- - - - - - - -]νηφ[- - - -]ια. καὶ ἐξαπέστ[ειλεν - - - - - -] τρι⟨π⟩ό[δα - - , ἵνα οὖν φαίνητ]αι καὶ ἡ σύνοδος [τῶν περὶ τὸν Διόνυσον τεχνιτῶν τοὺς]μεγα[λομερῶς εὐεργετοῦν]τας ἑαυτὴν ἀπο[δεχομένη καὶ μὴ λειπομένη ἐγ]χάριτ[ο]ς [ἀποδόσει], ἀλλὰ μεγάλαις καὶ [ἀξίαις τιμαῖς αὐτοὺς τιμῶσα, ἥ τε πρὸς τοὺς] εὐεργέτας [χάρις] ἅπασιν ἀνθρώποις [φανερὰ γίνηται, ἀγαθῆι τύχηι· δεδόχθαι] τοῖς περὶ τὸν Διόνυσον τεχνίταις ἐπ[αινέσαι μὲν βασιλέα Ἀριαράθην Εὐσεβῆ] καὶ Φιλοπάτορα βασιλέως Ἀριαράθου [Εὐσεβοῦς καὶ βασιλίσσης Ἀντιοχίδος] εὐσεβείας ἕνεκεν καὶ δικαιοσύνης καὶ [φιλοτιμίας τῆς εἰς τοὺς τεχνίτας·] στῆσαι

δὲ αὐτοῦ καὶ ἄγαλμα παρὰ τὸν θε[ὸν - - - - καὶ εἰκόνα χαλ]κῆν ἐν τῶι προπυλαίωι
τοῦ τεμένους καὶ [- - - - - ἀνειπεῖν δὲ] καὶ τῶν εἰκόνων τὴν ἀνάθεσιν Διονυσί[ων
τε τῶν ἐν ἄστει καινοῖς τραγωι]δοῖς καὶ Παναθηναίων καὶ Ἐλευσινίων τοῖ[ς
γυμνικοῖς ἀγῶσι· τῆς δὲ ἀναγορεύ]σεως ἐπιμεληθῆναι τὸν ἐπιμελητήν. πα[ρασκευάσαι
δὲ καὶ ἱερεῖα εἰς θυσίαν τῶι] Διονύσωι ἀπὸ τῶν προσόδων κοινῶν κ[άλλιστα τὸν
ἐπιμελητὴν καὶ Μενέλαον] ποιητὴν τραγικὸν μετὰ τοῦ ἱερέως τοῦ Δ[ιονύσου καὶ
θῦσαι ὑπὲρ σωτηρίας τῆς] συνόδου καὶ βασιλέως Ἀριαράθου καὶ βασιλ[ίσσης Νύσης
καὶ τῶν παιδίων] καὶ μερίδα νεῖμαι πᾶ[σ]ιν τοῖς μετέχουσιν [τῆς συνόδου καὶ
παισὶ καὶ γυναιξὶν αὐ[τ]ῶν. μερίσαι δὲ τὸν [ἐπ]ιμελητὴν τοῦ Μετ[αγειτνιῶνος μηνὸς
τὴν τετράδα ἐ]πὶ δέκα ὑπὲρ τοῦ βασ[ιλ]έως καὶ τὴν πέμπτ[ην ἐπὶ δέκα ὑπὲρ τῆς
βασιλίσσης καὶ τῶν] παι[δίω]ν, τὸν [δ'] ὑπηρέτην προγρ[ά]ψαι - - - - - - - ἡμερῶ[ν]
τοῦ βασιλέως Ἀριαράθου καὶ σ[τε]φα[νοῦν τὸ ἄγαλμα τὸ τοῦ βασιλέως] καὶ θυμιᾶν
κ[αὶ] δᾶιδα ἱστάνειν καὶ ἐν τ . . . σι[- - - - - - βα]σιλεῖ Ἀριαράθει Εὐσεβεῖ καὶ
Φιλοπάτορι [- - - - . ἄγεσθαι δὲ αὐτοῦ καὶ ἡμέ]ραν ἐπώνυμον κατὰ μῆνα τὴν
τετράδα ἐπὶ δ[έκα - - - - καὶ τῆι ἡμέ]ραι ταύτει μετὰ τὸ τοῦ Διον[ύ]σου καὶ ἰδία[ι
θῦ]σα[ι - - - -]μένου τὸ νικῆσαν· καταλέγειν δὲ τὸν ἐπιμελη[τὴν τοὺς - - - - -]
ἀπαρξο[μέ]νους· εἰ δὲ μή, ζημιοῦν τὸμ μὴ πε[π]οι[η]κότα· τῆι δὲ - - - τοῦ αὐ]τοῦ
μηνὸς τοῦ βασιλέως Ἀριαράθου κατ' ἐνιαυ[τὸν ἀγῶνα μουσικὸν τιθέναι τοὺς]
τεχνίτας καὶ διδόναι τῶν ὠιδῶν τῶι νικήσα[ντι - - - - - -] καὶ κωμωιδοῖς παλαιοῖς
καὶ τραγωιδοῖς, κατὰ [τὰ αὐτὰ δὲ καὶ καινοῖς κωμωι]δοῖς καὶ τραγωιδοῖς· ἑλέσθαι
δὲ ἤδη ἐξ ἑαυτ[ῶν τρεῖς ἄνδρας μετὰ τοῦ ἐπιμελη]τοῦ καὶ τοῦ ἱερέως τοὺς τεχνίτας
οἵτιν[ες τῆς τε ποιήσεως τῶν εἰκό]νων ἐπιμελήσονται καὶ ἀναθήσουσιν ὡς κ[άλλιστα
- - - -] κοινά. καὶ [ἐ]ὰν πρεσβεία τις ἔλθη παρὰ Ἀρια[ράθου - - - - - -] γίνωνται,
θεωροδόκον ἀεὶ ὑπακούειν κα[ὶ - - - - - τὸν] ἐπιμελητὴν τῶν τεχνιτῶν καὶ ἐὰν καὶ
[- - - - - - Παναθηναίοις] ἢ Ἐλευσινίοις βοῦν τε παρασκευάζε[ιν - - - - - - - ἑλέ]σθαι
ἐξ ἑαυτῶν οἵτινες ὑπὲρ βασιλέ[ως Ἀριαράθου καὶ βασιλίσσης Νύσης] θύσουσιν καὶ
τἆλλα πράξουσιν ὅσα κα[λὰ νομίζεται, ἵνα τούτων συντελου]μένων ἀ[π]ολαμβάνη τὰς
προση[κ]ούσας [χάριτας παρὰ τῶν τεχνιτῶν καὶ πολ]λοὶ [ζ]ηλωταὶ γίνωνται τῆς
ὁμοίας αἱρ[έσεως, ὁρῶντες τιμωμένους τοὺς] τοῖς περὶ τὸν Διόνυσον τεχνίταις αἴτι[ους
γιγνομένους ἀγαθῶν. ἑλέσθαι δὲ ἤ]δη τρεῖς ἄνδρας ἐξ ἑαυτῶν οἵτινες τό [τε ψήφισμα
τόδε παραδώσουσι καὶ εὐ]χαριστήσουσιν τῶι βασιλεῖ Ἀριαράθει [καὶ παρακαλέσουσι
διατελεῖν παρ]έχοντα τήν τε ἀσυλίαν καὶ ἀσφάλειαν [τοῖς τεχνίταις τοῖς ἀφικνου-
μένοις πρὸς] αὐτὸν τὴν δεδομένην ἐξ ἀρχῆς π[αρὰ] Ἀ[μφικτυόνων καὶ βασιλέων καὶ
δυναστῶν] καὶ τῶν ἄλλων ⟨Ἑλλήνων⟩ ἁπάντων καὶ ἀεί τινος [ἀγαθοῦ παραίτιον
γίγνεσθαι αὐτοῖς] καθάπερ καὶ αὐτὸς ἐπαγγέλλεται. ἀνα[γράψαι δὲ τὸν γραμματέα
τόδε τὸ] ψήφισμα εἰς στήλην λιθίνην κ[α]ὶ στῆσα[ι παρὰ τὴν εἰκόνα, εἰς δὲ τὴν
ποί]ησιν καὶ τὴν ἀναγραφὴν μερίσαι τὸν ἐπ[ιμελητὴν τὸ γενόμενον ἀνάλωμα]. πρέσβεις εἱ[ρέθησαν] Μενέλαος ποιητὴς τραγικός, Θεόδοτος κιθ[αρωιδός, - - - -]

A fragmentary decree follows for Ariarathes' queen, Nysa.

8. The Argive branch honours its treasurer, c. 115 B.C. Michel 1011; *I.G.* iv.
   558; Vollgraff, *Mnemosyne* 49 (1921), pp. 113–17; Robert, *B.C.H.* 50 (1926),
   pp. 498–501.

ἐπειδὴ Ζήνων Ἑκατοδώρο[υ Ἀργεῖος ἐν παντὶ καιρῷ διατελεῖ εὐσεβῶς καὶ ὁσίως
δια]κείμενος τὰ πρὸς τοὺς θεούς, εὐνοϊ[κῶς δὲ πρὸς τὸ κοινὸν τῶν περὶ τὸν

Διόνυσον τεχνιτῶν] τῶν ἐξ Ἰσθμοῦ τε καὶ Νεμέας τῆς ἐν Ἄργε[ι συνόδου καὶ ἐν
πᾶσι πολλὰς καὶ μεγάλας ἀποδεί]ξεις πεποιημένος τῆς ἑαυτοῦ καλοκἀγαθίας τὰς
[ἐπιμελείας τὰς κατὰ τὰς μεγίστας τῆς] συνόδου ἀρχὰς πάσας πεποίηται καλῶς καὶ
συνφερόντω[ς τοῖς κοινοῖς τῆς συνόδου πρά]γμασιν ἐν πᾶσιν ἀναστρεφόμενος ἀξίως
τῆς ἐκ παιδὸς αὐτῶι [ἀνηκούσης εὐγενείας, κατα]σταθεὶς δὲ καὶ ταμίας ὑπὸ τῆς
συνόδου εἰς τὸ δεύτερον καὶ τρια[κοστὸν ἔτος καὶ εὑρὼν] πολλὰ τῶν τῆς συνόδου
διαφόρων ἀποστατοῦντα, τῶν κεφαλαίων [καὶ τόκων πάντας τοὺς τι] ἐφηλκυσμένους
ἐξ ἐτῶν καὶ πλειόνων ἐνεφάνισέν τε τῶι πλή[θει τῶν τεχνιτῶν καὶ πα]ρακληθεὶς
ὑπὸ τῶν τεχνιτῶν ἐποιήσατο τὴν ἐπιμέλειαν τῆς ἀν[απράξεως, ἐν ἅπασιν ἀνα-]
στρεφόμενος καλῶς καὶ συμφερόντως τοῖς κοινοῖς τῆς συνόδου [πράγμασι, καὶ ἐκ
τῶν ἀνα]πραχθέντων ὑπ᾽ αὐτοῦ διαφόρων ἐπετέλεσεν κατὰ μῆνα τοῖς τε [θεοῖς
καὶ τοῖς εὐεργέταις ὑπὲρ] τῆς συνόδου τὰς κατὰ τοὺς νόμους θυσίας, διελέγη δὲ
μετὰ προ[θυμίας ὅπως κατασκευ]ωθῆι ἄγαλμα Διονύσου τῆι συνόδωι ἀκρ[ό]λιθον,
χρυσόειμον, ἐξάπε[δον, ψηφισαμένης δὲ] τῆς συνόδου ἔδωκεν τὰ διάφορα ἐκ τῶν
ἀναπ[ραχθέν]των ὑπ᾽ αὐτοῦ, δ[ιελέγη δὲ μετὰ σπουδῆς] καὶ ὑπὲρ τοῦ κατασκευωθῆναι
τ[- - - - -] ἐν τῶι τεμένε[ι - - - - -] καὶ παρακληθεὶς ὑπὸ τῶν τεχνιτῶν π[οιήσασθαι]
ἐπιμέλειαν τ[ῶν ἐντεμενίων ἱερῶν ἐποιή]σατο τὰς ἐγδόσεις τ[ῶν] ἔργων πάσας
[πρὸς τὰ ἱε]ρὰ μετὰ πάσ[η]ς [σπουδῆς αἴτιος πλείστων ἀγα]θῶν ἐπὶ τὴν σύν[οδον
γενόμενος - - - - - - - - -]ν, ἐπὶ [δὲ τούτοις διελέγη ὅπως κατα]σκευωθῶσι τῆι
συν[όδωι - - - - -] καὶ τρίπ[οδες] Βακ[χεῖοι, ἐποιήσατο δὲ τὰς ἐγδό]σεις λυσιτελῶς,
ἐν πᾶσι τούτοις ἀνα[στρεφόμε]νος ἀξίω[ς τῆς] ἐν τ[ῆι πάσηι ζωῆι ἀεὶ οἰκεί]ας αὐτοῦ
καλοκἀγαθίας ἀνέγ[κλητος ὢν] καὶ τῶν χε[ρνίβων ἔ]ν τῶι [τεμένει προὐνόει ὑπὲρ
τῆς σ]υνόδου καὶ παρασεσιωπημένα [ἐπετέλε]σε[ν ἄλλα πολλὰ] ὑπὲ[ρ τῆς συνόδου,
ἐποιήσατο δὲ τ]ὴν ἐπιμέλειαν καὶ ὑπὲρ τοῦ κατασκευωθῆναι βάθρον [τῆι] εἰκόνι
[τοῦ εὐεργέτου ἡμῶν] βασιλέως Νικομήδους καὶ τῆς ἀναθέσεως τῆς εἰκόνος,
ἄλ[λα]ς δὲ καί τι[νας ἔστησεν ἐντὸς τοῦ τεμέ]νους, διελέγη δὲ καὶ ὑπὲρ τοῦ κατασκευωθῆναι τόπον τῶι θεῶι καὶ ὑπερθυρω[θῆναι τὴν εἴσοδον καὶ]ὑπὲρ τοῦ ὀροφωθῆναι
τὸν τόπον, ἐν ὧι ἔσται θές[ις ἐλαίου τῆ συνόδωι, ἐκ τῶν ἀναπραχθέντων ὑπ᾽ αὐτοῦ]
διαφόρων· ὅπως οὖν καὶ οἱ τεχνῖται φαίνωνται [χάρισιν ἀπονέμοντες ἀξίαις τοῖς
εὐεργέταις ἔπαινον] καὶ τιμὰς καὶ πολλοὺς ἔχωσιν τῶν ὁμοίων ζηλωτάς, [τύχηι τῆι]
ἀγαθῆι δεδόχθαι τοῖς [περὶ τὸν Διόνυσον τε]χνίταις τοῖς ἐξ Ἰσθμοῦ καὶ Νεμέας τῆς
ἐν Ἄργει συνόδου ἐπαι[νέ]σαι Ζήνωνα Ἑκα[τοδώρου Ἀργεῖον ἐπὶ τῆι] εὐνοίαι τε καὶ
φιλαγαθίαι περὶ τὰ κοινὰ τῆς συνόδου πράγματα καὶ [στεφα]νῶσαι αὐ[τὸν κισσοῦ
στεφάνωι], ὧι πάτριον ἡμῖν ἐστιν, ἐν τῆι τοῦ θεοῦ ἡμέραι, στῆσαι δὲ αὐτοῦ καὶ
[εἰκ]όνα χαλκῆ[ν ἔχουσαν τήνδε τὴν ἐπι]γραφήν· τὸ κοινὸν τῶν περὶ τὸν Διόνυσον
τεχνιτῶν τῶν ἐξ Ἰσθμοῦ καὶ Νεμέ[ας τῆς ἐν Ἄργει συνόδου Ζήνωνα] Ἑκατοδώρου
Ἀργεῖον ἀρετῆς ἕνεκεν καὶ εὐεργεσίας τῆς εἰς [τὴν σύνο]δον· [τὸ δὲ γινόμενον
ἀνάλωμα εἰς τὴν εἰκό]να δότω τῶι κατασταθέντι τῆς εἰκόνος ἐπιστάτηι Ξένων
ὁ [ταμίας, τὴν] δὲ [ἐπιμέ]λε[ιαν τῆς ἀναγγελίας τοῦ στε]φάνου ποιησάσθω ὁ γραμματεὺς Ἀριστοκλῆς, καὶ οἱ ἄρχοντες [οἵ τε νῦν] κ[αὶ οἱ ἀεὶ κατασταθέντες καὶ
ὁ ἀεὶ] γραμματεὺς ποιείσθωσαν τὴν ἐπιμέλειαν ἐν τῆι τοῦ θεοῦ ἡ[μέραι ὅπως ἀναγο-
ρεύηται τὸ ψήφισμα τόδε, ποιείσθω] δὲ τὴν ἐπιμέλειαν ὁ κατασταθεὶς γραμματεὺς
ε[ἰς τὸ - - - καὶ τριακοστὸν ἔτος ὅπως τοῖς Νε]μείοις ἐν τῶι ἀγῶνι τῶι γυμνικῶι
ἀνακηρυχθῆι τὸ κήρυγμα [τόδε· τὸ κοινὸν τῶν περὶ τὸν Διόνυσον τεχνιτῶν] τῶν ἐξ
Ἰσθμοῦ καὶ Νεμέας τῆς ἐν Ἄργει συνόδου στε[φανοῖ κισσοῦ στεφάνωι Ζήνωνα

Ἑκατοδώρου Ἀργεῖον ἀρε]τῆς ἔνεκεν καὶ εὐεργεσίας, ἧς ἔχων διατελεῖ ε[ἰς τὴν σύνοδον καὶ ἔστησεν αὐτοῦ εἰκόνα χαλκὴν ἐν τῶι τε]μένει, τύχηι τῆι ἀγαθεῖ. ἀναγραψάτω δὲ καὶ ὁ καταστ[αθεὶς τῆς εἰκόνος ἐπιστάτης τὸ τῆς συνόδου ψήφισμα τόδε] εἰς τὸ βάθρον τῆς εἰκόνος.

9. The city of Teos buys land for the Artists, third century B.C. *B.C.H.* 46 (1922), p. 312, no. 2; *S.E.G.* ii. 580; Robert, *Études anatoliennes*, pp. 39 ff.

[- - - εὔχεσθαι] τὸν ἱερέα το[ῦ Διονύσου ἐν τοῖς Διονυσί]οις καὶ [τὸν πρ]ύτανιν ἐν τῶι πρυ[τανείωι καὶ τὸν ἱε]ροκήρυκα [ἐν τ]αῖς ἐκλησίαις γίνεσθαι τἀγαθὰ καὶ τῶι κοινῶι τῶ[ν περὶ τ]ὸν Διόνυσον τεχνιτῶν. ἀγοράσαι δὲ αὐτοῖς καὶ κ[τῆμα] ἔγγεον ἐν τῆι πόλει ἢ τῆι χώραι ἀπὸ δρα(χμῶν) ⊓Χ [καὶ] προσαγορεύεσθαι τὸ ἀγορασθὲν κτῆμα ἱερὸν ὃ ἀν[έθηκε] ὁ δῆμος τῶι κοινῶι τῶν περὶ τὸν Διόνυσον τ[εχ]νιτῶν, ὃν ἀτελὲς ὢν ἡ πόλις ἐπιβάλλει τελῶν· ἀ[πο]δεῖξαι δὲ καὶ ἄνδρας δύο, οἵτινες κτηματωνήσου[σιν ἐ]π' ἀναφορᾶι τῆι πρὸς τὸν δῆμον· ἵνα δὲ τὸ ἀργύριο[ν ὑπ]άρχηι εἰς τὴν κτηματωνίαν, τοὺς ταμίας τοὺς [ἐν]εστηκότας δοῦναι τοῖς ἀποδειχθησομένοις δρα(χμὰς) [Χ]ΧΧ ἐκ τοῦ μετενηνεγμένου ἐκ τοῦ λόγου τῆς ὀ[χυρ]ώσεως, ὃ δέδοται εἰς τὴν τιμὴν τοῦ σίτου· τὸ δὲ ὑπ[ολι]πὲς δρα(χμὰς) ΧΧΧ δότωσαν οἱ εἰσιόντες ταμίαι ἐκ τ[ῶν πρ]ώτων δοθησομένων αὐτοῖς ἐγ βασιλικοῦ εἰς τ[ὴν τῆ]ς πόλεως διοίκησιν· δεδόσθαι δὲ αὐτοῖς καὶ ἐπο[χὴ]ν ἔτη πέντε ἀπὸ μηνὸς Λευκαθεῶνος καὶ πρυτ[άνεως] Μητροδώρου· ὅπως δὲ καὶ τὰ δόξαντα τῶι δήμ[ωι πά]ντες εἰδῶσιν, ἀναγράψαι τόδε τὸ ψήφισμα εἰς [στήλη]ν λιθίνην καὶ τὸν στέφανον καὶ ἀναθεῖναι παρὰ [τὸ]ν νεὼ τοῦ Διονύσου. ἀναγράψαι δὲ καὶ εἰς τὴν παρ[αστά]δα τοῦ θεάτρου τὸ ψήφισμα τόδε καὶ τὸν στέφαν[ον· τῆ]ς δὲ ἀναγραφῆς τῶν στεφάνων καὶ ψηφισμάτ[ων καὶ τ]ῆς στήλης τὴν κατασκευὴν τὴν ἔγδοσιν π[οιείσθ]ωσαν οἱ ἐνεστηκότες ταμίαι καὶ τὸ ἀνάλωμ[α δότ]ωσαν οἱ ἐνεστηκότες ταμίαι· τοὺς δὲ πρεσβ[ευτὰς] τοὺς ἀποδεδειγμένους ἀποδοῦναι τὸ ψήφι[σμα τόδ]ε τοῖς περὶ τὸν Διόνυσον τεχνίταις καὶ ἐπ[αινέσαι α]ὐτοὺς ἐπὶ τῆι εὐνοίαι, ἣν ἔχοντες διατε[λοῦσι] περὶ τὸν δῆμον τὸν Τηίων. ἀπεδείχθη[σαν κτ]ηματωνήσοντες . . . . . . s Ἐπιτιμίδου, Θερσίων Φάνου.

10a. The Ionian Artists honour Kraton, shortly before 167 B.C. *C.I.G.* 3067; Michel 1015; *I.G.* xi. 4. 1136+1061; Durrbach, *Choix d'inscriptions de Délos*, no. 75; Laqueur, *Epigraphische Untersuchungen*, pp. 92–96; Wilhelm, *Jahreshefte* 24 (1929), pp. 174 ff.; Robert, *B.C.H.* 59 (1935), pp. 193–8; Daux, ibid., pp. 210–18.

τὸ κ[ο]ινὸν τῶν περὶ τὸν Διόνυσον τεχνιτῶν τῶν ἐπ' Ἰ[ωνίας] καὶ Ἑλλησπόντου καὶ τῶν περὶ τὸν καθηγεμόνα Διό[νυσον] Κράτωνα Ζωτίχου εὐεργέτην ἀρετῆς ἔνεκεν καὶ ε[ὐνοίας] ἣν ἔχων διατελεῖ εἰς τὸ κοινὸν τῶν περὶ τὸν Διόνυσον [τεχνιτῶν].

ἐδ[οξε]ν τῷ κοινῷ τῶν περὶ τὸν Διόνυσον τεχνιτῶν τῶν ἐπ' Ἰωνίας καὶ Ἑλλησ[π]ό[ντου καὶ τῶν περὶ τὸν καθη]γ[ε]μόνα Διόνυσον· ἐπειδὴ Κράτων Ζωτίχου αὐλητὴς πρότερόν τε γενόμενο[ς ἱερεὺς τοῦ Διονύσου κ]αὶ ἀγ[ων]οθέτης καλῶς καὶ ἐνδόξως προέστη τῆς τε ἱερεωσύνης καὶ τῆς ἀγων[οθεσίας καὶ νῦν δὲ κριθε]ὶς ἄξιος εἶναι ταύτης τῆς τιμῆς ὑπὸ τοῦ πλήθους τῶν τεχνιτῶν καὶ αἱρεθε[ὶς τὸ δεύτερον ἱερεὺς τ]οῦ Διονύσου καὶ ἀγωνοθέτης ἐν τῷ αὐτῷ ἔτει, ὑπερθέμενος τοὺς π[ρὸ αὐτοῦ γενομένους ἱερέας κ]αὶ ἀγωνοθέτας τῇ τε χορηγίᾳ καὶ τῇ δαπάνῃ καὶ τῇ αὐτοῦ μεγαλοψ[υχίᾳ

καὶ ἀναστραφεὶς πρεπόν]τως καὶ ἀξίως τῆς συνόδου πάντα τὰ πρὸς τιμὴν καὶ δόξαν
ἀνήκοντα [ἐπετέλεσεν τῷ τε Διονύ]σῳ καὶ ταῖς Μούσαις καὶ τῷ Ἀπόλλωνι τῷ
Πυθίῳ καὶ τοῖς ἄλλοις θεοῖς πᾶ[σι, ὁμοίως δὲ καὶ τοῖς τε βασι]λεῦσι καὶ ταῖς βασιλίσ-
σαις καὶ τοῖς ἀδελφοῖς βασιλέως Εὐμένου καὶ τῷ [κοινῷ τῶν περὶ τὸν Διόνυ]σον
τεχνιτῶν, ἀποδεικνύμενος τὴν αὐτοῦ καλοκἀγαθίαν καὶ εὐσέβε[ιαν καὶ φιλοτιμίαν
ἐν παντὶ και]ρῷ καὶ ἰδίᾳ καὶ κοινῇ ἀεί τινος ἀγαθοῦ παραίτιος γινόμενος· ὅπως δ'
ἄ[ν φανερὰ γίνηται εἰς τὸν ἀεὶ] χρόνον ἡ παρὰ τῶν τεχνιτῶν ἀθάνατος δόξα, οὓς καὶ
θεοὶ καὶ βασιλεῖς [κ]α[ὶ πάντες οἱ ἄλλοι Ἕλ]ληνες τιμῶσιν δεδωκότες τήν τε ἀσυλίαν
καὶ ἀσφάλειαν πᾶσι τ[οῖ]ς τεχν[ί]ται[ς καὶ πολέμου καὶ εἰ]ρήνης, κατακολουθοῦντες
τοῖς τοῦ Ἀπόλλωνος χρησμοῖς δι' οὓς [κ]αὶ ἀ[γωνίζονται τοὺς ἀγῶνας τοῦ] Ἀπόλλωνος τοῦ Πυθίου καὶ τῶν Μουσῶν τῶν Ἑλικωνιάδων καὶ τοῦ Διον[ύσου, ἐν Δελφοῖς
μὲν τοῖς] Πυθίοις καὶ Σωτηρίοις, ἐν Θεσπιαῖς δὲ τοῖς Μουσείοις, ἐν Θήβαις δὲ
τοῖς Ἀγρ[ιανίοις, εἶναι δοκοῦντες] ἐκ πάντων τῶν Ἑλλήνων εὐσεβέστατοι· ἀγαθῇ
τύχῃ· δεδόχθαι ὅπως [οὖν ἡ σύνοδος φαίνηται τιμῶ]σα τοὺς αὑτῆς εὐεργέτας
καταξίως τῶν εὐεργετημάτων, στεφαν[ο]ῦ[ν μὲν Κράτωνα Ζωτίχου αὐλητ]ὴν
εὐεργέτην καθ' ἕκαστον ἔτος εἰς ἀεὶ ἐν τῷ θεάτρῳ ἐν ᾗ ἡμέρᾳ ἡ π[ανήγυρις τοῦ
κοινοῦ συντελ]εῖται μετὰ τὴν στεφάνωσιν τῶν δήμων στεφάνῳ τῷ ἐκ τοῦ νόμο[υ
ἀρετῆς ἔνεκεν καὶ εὐν]οίας ἣν ἔχων διατελεῖ εἰς τὸ κοινὸν τῶν περὶ τὸν Διόνυσον
τεχνιτῶ[ν· τῆς δὲ ἀναγγελίας τοῦ στεφ]άνου ἐπιμέλειαν ποιεῖσθαι τὸν ἑκάστοτε
γινόμενον ἀγωνοθέτην· [ἀναθεῖναι δὲ αὐτοῦ εἰκόνας τ]ρεῖς, τὴν μὲν μίαν ἐν Τέῳ ἐν
τῷ θεάτρῳ, ὅπως οἱ καθ' ἕκαστον ἔτος ἀγ[ωνοθέται ἐν τῇ τοῦ κοινοῦ π]ανηγύρει
καὶ ὅταν ἡ Τηίων πόλις συντελῇ Διονύσια ἢ ἄλλον τινὰ [ἀ]γῶν[α στεφανῶσι τὴν
εἰκόνα] τὴν Κράτωνος στεφάνῳ τῷ ἐκ τοῦ νόμου ᾧ πάτριόν ἐστι τοῖς τεχν[ίταις
στεφανοῦν τοὺς αὑ]τῶν εὐεργέτας, τὴν δὲ ἄλλην ἐν Δήλῳ ὅπως καὶ ἐκεῖ στεφανῶται
ὑ[πὸ τῶν περὶ τὸν Διόνυσον τε]χνιτῶν, τὴν δὲ τρίτην οὗ ἂν ἀναθῇ Κράτων, ἵνα εἰς
ἅπαντα τὸ⟨ν⟩ χρό[νον αὐτῷ ὑπάρχῃ τῆς τε πρὸς] τὸ θεῖον εὐσεβείας καὶ τῆς εἰς
τοὺς βασιλέας καὶ βασιλίσσας φιλοδο[ξίας καὶ τῆς εἰς τοὺς ἀδελφοὺς] βασιλέως
Εὐμένου καὶ τὸ κοινὸν τῶν περὶ τὸν Διόνυσον τεχνιτῶν [εὐνοίας ὑπόμνημα, ἔτι
δὲ] καὶ τῇ συνόδῳ τῆς εὐχαριστίας διότι τὸν αὑτῆς εὐεργέτην [Κράτωνα Ζωτίχου
ἐτίμησεν ἀπο]διδοῦσα χάριτας τὰς δικαίας τῶν εὐεργετημάτων· ἀναγράψαι [δὲ τὰ
δεδομένα τίμια] εἰς στήλην λιθίνην καὶ στῆσαι παρὰ ταῖς εἰκόσι ταῖς Κράτων[ος·
ἀποστεῖλαι δὲ πρεσβευτὰς] δύο πρὸς τὸν δῆμον τὸν Τηίων οἵτινες αἰτήσονται τόπον
ἐν τῷ [θεάτρῳ ἐν ᾧ σταθήσεται] ἡ εἰκὼν Κράτωνος καὶ ἄλλους πρὸς τὸν δῆμον
τὸν Δηλίων οἵτ[ινες ἀφικόμενοι εἰς Δῆλον καὶ] ἐπελθόντες ἐπὶ τὸν δῆμον καὶ τὴν
βουλὴν ἀξιώσουσιν Δ[ηλίους φίλους ὄντας καὶ συγγε]νεῖς δοῦναι τῇ συνόδῳ τῶν
τεχνιτῶν τὸν τόπον ἐν ᾧ [σταθήσεται ἡ εἰκὼν Κράτωνος.]

10b. The Attalistai praise Kraton dead. *O.G.I.S.* 326.

ψήφισμα Ἀτταλιστῶν.

γνώμη τοῦ κοινοῦ τῶν Ἀτταλιστῶν· ἐπειδὴ ὁ ⟨ἱρ⟩εὸς τῆς συνόδου Κράτων Ζωτίχου
ἔν τε τῶι ζῆν πολλὰς καὶ μεγάλας ἀποδείξεις ἐποιεῖτο τῆς πρὸς τοὺς Ἀτταλιστὰς
εὐνοίας καὶ κατ' ἰδίαν ὑπὲρ ἑκάστου καὶ κατὰ κοινὸν τῶν ὑφ' ἑαυτοῦ συνηγμένων καὶ
κε[κρι]μένων τὴν πλείστην ποιούμενος πρόνοιαν, σπουδῆς καὶ φιλοτιμίας οὐθὲν
ἐλλείπων, καὶ πολλὰ μὲν [καλ]ὰ καὶ φιλάνθρωπα τῆι συνόδωι παρὰ τῶν βασιλέων

ἐποίησεν, ἀποδεχομένων αὐτῶν τήν τε ἐκείνου [κατ]ὰ πάντα τρόπον πρὸς ἑαυτοὺς
εὔνοιαν καὶ τὴν ἡμετέραν αἵρεσιν καὶ συναγωγὴν ἀξίαν οὖσαν τῆς ἑαυτῶν ἐπωνυμίας,
οὐκ ὀλ⟨ίγα⟩ δὲ καὶ τῶν ἰδίων ἐπιδιδοὺς καὶ χορηγῶν διετέλει, βουλόμενός τε τοῖς
προϋπηργμένοις ἀκόλουθα πράσσειν καὶ μεταλλάσσων τὸν βίον ἐν Περγάμωι
προενοήθη τῆς συνόδου καὶ γράψας ἐπιστολὴν πρὸς τοὺς Ἀτταλιστὰς καὶ νόμον
ἱερὸν ἀπολιπών, ὃν ἐξαπέστειλεν ἡμῖν βασιλεὺς Ἄτταλος, ἐπισημοτέραν ἐποίησεν
τὴν ὑπάρχουσαν ἐς τὴν σύνοδον εὔνοιαν, δι' ὃν τό τε Ἀττάλειον τὸ πρὸς τῶι θεάτρωι,
ὃ καὶ ζῶν καθιερώκει, τοῖς Ἀτταλισταῖς ἀνατίθησιν καὶ τὴν συνοικίαν τὴν πρὸς τῶι
βασιλείωι, τὴν πρότερον οὖσαν Μικ[κά]ρου· ἀνατίθησιν δὲ καὶ καθιεροῖ τῆι συνόδωι
καὶ ἀργυρίου Ἀλεξανδρείου δραχμὰς μυρίας καὶ πεντακοσίας, ἀφ' ὧν ἐκ τῆς προσόδου
θυσίας τε καὶ συνόδους [πε]ποιήμεθα, καθὼς αὐτὸς ἐν τῆι νομοθεσίαι περὶ ἑκάστων
δια[τέ]ταχεν· ἀνατίθησιν δὲ καὶ σώματα τοῖς Ἀτταλισταῖς, περὶ ὧν τὰ κατὰ μέρος
ὑπὲρ ἁπάντων ἐν τῶι καθιερωμένωι ὑφ' ἑαυτοῦ νόμωι δεδήλωκεν· ἀ[πέ]λιπεν δὲ καὶ
τὰ πρὸς εὐσχημοσύνην τῶι τεμένει χρηστήρια ἱκανά, παραλῦσαι βουλόμενος καὶ τῆς
εἰς ταῦτα δαπάνης καὶ χορηγίας τοὺς Ἀτταλιστάς· ἵνα οὖν καὶ ἡ σύνοδος τῶν Ἀτταλι-
στῶν ἀξίας φαίνηται τοῖς εὐεργέταις ἀπονέμουσα χάριτας, δεδόχθαι τοῖς Ἀτταλισταῖς,
κυρῶσαι μὲν τὸν ἱερὸν νόμον τὸν ἀπολελειμμένον ὑπὸ Κράτωνος, συν[τελεῖσθαι
δ]ὲ ἐπωνύμους ἡμέρας Κράτωνός τε καὶ - - -

11. The Ionian Artists provide performers for Iasos, second century B.C.
Michel 1014; Wilhelm, *U.D.A.*, p. 46, n. 1; Robert, *Études anatoliennes*,
pp. 446 ff.

γνώμη τοῦ κοινοῦ τῶν περὶ τὸν Διόνυ[σον τεχ]νιτῶν [τῶ]ν ἐν Ἰωνίαι [κ]α[ὶ] Ἑλλησ-
πόντωι καὶ τῶν περὶ τὸν καθηγεμόνα Δι[όνυ]σον· ἐπειδὴ Ἰασεῖς φίλοι καὶ οἰκεῖο[ι
κ]α[ὶ] εὐ[εργέ]ται ὑπάρχοντες καὶ [τὴν προϋπάρχουσαν εὔνοιαν καὶ] φιλίαν ἐ[κ παλαιῶν χρόνων τηρ]οῦντες τὴν πρὸς τοὺ[ς τεχνίτας - - - - - καὶ τὸν τῶν Τηίων (?)]
δῆμον, [διατηρ]οῦντες δὲ καὶ τὰ δεδο[μένα τίμια τῶι κ]οινῶι τῶν περὶ τὸν Διόνυσον
τεχνιτῶν ὑπὸ [τῶν Ἑλλή]νων κατὰ τὰς [μαντείας καὶ ὑπὸ Ῥωμ]αίων τῶν κοινῶν
[εὐεργετῶν καὶ] σωτήρων ἔν τε τοῖς πρότερον χρόνοις [πᾶσ]αν σπουδὴν καὶ φιλοτιμίαν
[δείξαντες] περὶ τῆς τῶν ἀγώνων ερ - - - - - - - τὴν αἵρεσιν ἔχοντες - - τ[- - - - -
- - - κ]αὶ ἐκτένειαν, ἐν δὲ τῶι ν[ῦν καιρῶι] σκ[- - - - χ]ρήματα καλ - - - - - αιρ - - ·
ἀγ[αθῆι τ]ύχηι· δεδόχθαι [τῶι] κοινῶι[τῶν περὶ τ]ὸν Διόνυσον τεχνιτῶν· ἵνα - - - -
σωτηρίας τ[- - - , νέμειν τῶι] Διονύσωι καὶ Ἰασεῦσιν εἰς τοὺς [συντελουμέν]ο[υ]ς
παρ' α[ὐ]τοῖς τῶι Διονύσωι ἀγῶν[ας ἐκ] τῶν ἐγγεγραμμένων τεχνιτῶν καὶ μετεχόν-
των τῆς [ἡμετέρας συνόδου] φιλίας ὑπαρχούσης ἡμῖν ἐκ παλαιῶν χρόνων αὐλητὰς
δύο, τραγωιδοὺς δύο, κωμωιδοὺς δύο, κιθαρωιδόν, κιθαριστήν, ὅπως ἄγωσιν τῶι
θεῶι τοὺς χοροὺς κατὰ τὰς πατρίας αὐτῶν διαγραφάς, προσνεῖμαι δὲ τούτων καὶ
τὰς ὑπηρεσίας - - - - - · τοὺς δὲ νεμηθέντας πάντας ἐπιτελέσαι τοὺς τῶν Διονυσίων ἀγῶνας ἐν τοῖς ὡρισμένοις καιροῖς πάντα παρασχόντας ἀκολούθως τοῖς
Ἰασέων νόμοις· ὃς δὲ τῶν νεμ[η]θέντων ὑπὸ τοῦ πλήθους μὴ παραγένηται εἰς Ἰασὸν
ἢ μὴ ἐπιτελ[έ]σηι τοὺς ἀγῶνας, ἀποτεισάτω τῶι κοινῶι τῶν περὶ τὸν Διόνυσον
τεχνιτῶν Ἀντιοχ[ι]κὰς δραχμὰς χιλίας ἱερὰς ἀπαραιτήτους τοῦ θεοῦ, ἐὰν μή τις δι'
ἀσθένειαν ἢ διὰ χειμῶνα ἀδύνατος γένηται· τούτωι δὲ ἔστω παραίτησις τῆς ζημίας
ἀπολογισαμένωι ἐπὶ τοῦ πλήθους καὶ ἐμφανεῖς τὰς δείξεις εἰσενεγκαμένωι καὶ
ἀπολυθέντι ψήφωι κατὰ τὸν νόμον· ἵνα δὲ καὶ Ἰασεῖς ἐπιγειν[ώ]σκωσιν τὴν τοῦ

πλήθους ἡμῶν σπουδὴν καὶ ἣν ἔχομεν πρὸς τοὺς φίλους ἐκτένειαν ἐν τοῖς ἀναγκαιοτάτοις καιροῖς, ἑλέσθαι πρεσβευτάς, οἵτινες ἀφικόμενοι εἰς Ἰασὸν καὶ ἀναδόντες τόδε τὸ ψήφισμα τοῖς προστάταις καὶ ἐπελθόντες ἐπὶ τὴν βουλὴν καὶ τὸν δῆμον καὶ ἐμφανίσαντες περὶ τῶν ἐψηφισμένων τιμῶν αὐτοῖς καὶ ἀνανεωσάμενοι τὰ διὰ προγόνων ὑπάρχοντα πρὸς ἀλλήλους φιλάνθρωπα παρακαλέσουσιν Ἰασεῖς διαφυλάσσειν τὴν πρὸς τὸ κοινὸν τῶν περὶ τὸν Διόνυσον τεχνιτῶν οἰκειότητα συναύξοντας τὴν φιλίαν ἀκολούθως τῆι διὰ προγόν[ω]ν ὑπαρχούσηι εὐνοίαι. πρεσβευταὶ [ἡ]ιρέθησαν Πλουτιάδης κιθαρωιδός, Λυσίμαχος ποιητὴς τραγωιδιῶν, Νικόστρατος συναγωνιστὴς τραγικός. οἵδε ἐνεμέθησαν σὺν ταῖς ὑπηρεσίαις·—αὐληταί, Τιμοκλῆς,—Φαΐτας·—τραγωιδοί, Ποσειδώνιος, Σωσίπατρος· κωμωιδοί,—Ἀγάθαρχος, Μοιρίας· κιθαρωιδός, Ζηνόθεος· κιθαριστής, Ἀπολλώνιος Σάμιος.—ἐπὶ στεφανηφόρου Ἀπόλλωνος τοῦ τρίτου μετὰ Μένητα Τυρταίου, Ἀπατουριῶνος ἕκτηι ἐκυρώθη.

12. The Athenian guild honours Philemon, 80–70 B.C. *I.G.* ii². 1338.

- - - - τῆι Ἀθηναίων περ[ι - - - - - - - τ]ῶν ἰδίων ἀπαλλαγέντες [- - - - - - - ἄν]θρωποι διεξαγωγὴν τῶν μ[- - - - - - - - -]σιν ἐποιήσατο, θυσίας δὲ καὶ μυστ[ήρια - - - - καὶ ἀγῶνας γυμνικοὺς καὶ μουσ]ικούς τε καὶ σκηνικοὺς αὐτὸς ἐπιτελεῖν ἐψ[ηφίσατο - - - - - καὶ ἡ σύν]οδος τῶν περὶ τὸν Διόνυσον τεχνιτῶν διὰ παντὸ[ς - - - - διατελεῖ] συναύξουσα καθ᾽ ὅσον ἐστὶ δυνατὴ τάς τε θυσίας καὶ τἄλλα πάντα τ[ὰ ἐψηφισμένα ὑ]π᾽ αὐτ[οῦ] τοῖς τε θεοῖς καὶ τοῖς εὐεργέταις τίμια ἐψηφίσατο καὶ αὐτὴ θύε[ιν καὶ σπένδ]ειν τῆι Δήμητρι καὶ τῆι Κόρηι ταῖς μυστηριώτισιν ἡμέραις καὶ βωμὸν ἱδρυσ[αμένη καὶ] τέμενος κατασκευάσασα ἐν Ἐλευσῖνι σπονδὰς καὶ παιᾶνας ἐπιτελεῖν· ὧν ἐπισχ[εθέντω]ν ἐπὶ ἔτη καὶ πλείονα καὶ τοῦ τε βωμοῦ καὶ τοῦ τεμένους ἀναιρε[θέντ]ος διὰ τὴν κοινὴν περίστασιν Φιλήμων ἐπιμελητὴς τὸ [τρ]ί[τον γενόμ]ενος ἐν τῶι ἐπὶ Αἰσχραίου ἄρχοντος ἐνιαυτῶι ἀνεκτ[ή]σα[το τὰς] πατρίους ταῖς θεαῖς θυσίας καὶ πρῶτος αὐτὸς θύσας [ἐ]ν Ἐ[λευσ]ῖνι τῆι Δήμητρι καὶ τῆι Κόρηι καὶ τὴν λοιπὴν δαπάνην καὶ χορη[γίαν] ἐπιδεξάμενος ὑπεδέξατο τὴν σύνοδον ἐκ τῶν ἰδίων, [προσ]εμέρισεν δὲ καὶ ἐκ τῶν κοινῶν εἰς ἄλλας ἡμέρας δύο καὶ ἐμ [πάσα]ις καλλιερήσας ταῖς ἡμέραις τὰς ἐψηφισμένας ὑπὸ τῶν πατέ[ρων] σπονδὰς καὶ ἐπιχύσεις καὶ παιᾶνας ταῖς θεαῖς ἐπετέλεσεν, [ὧ]ν ἀσμένως οἱ τεχνῖται λαβόντες ἀνάμνησιν παρεκάλεσαν [α]ὐτὸν καὶ προστρέψαντο μετὰ πάσης προθυμίας προνοηθῆναι καὶ τῆς τοῦ τεμένους κατασκευῆς ὅπως ἐπὶ τῆς πατρώιας ἑστίας ἀν[εμ]ποδίστως κατ᾽ ἐνιαυτὸν ἐπιτελῶσιν τὰς θυσίας, ὁ δὲ καὶ διὰ τὴ[ν] πρὸς τὰς θεὰς εὐσέβειαν καὶ διὰ τὴν πρὸς τοὺς τεχνίτας ἀνυπέρθετον εὔνοιαν διὰ τῆς ἰδίας ἐπιμελείας ἐξ ὧν ἀνεῦρεν αὐτὸς τῆι συνόδωι προσόδων τὴν κατασκευὴν τοῦ τεμένους ἐποιήσατο καὶ τὸν ἀνειρημένον ὑπὸ τῆς περιστάσεως βωμὸν αὐτὸς πάλιν καθιδρύσατο, προενοήθη δὲ ἐκτενῶς καὶ τῆς τῶν κοινῶν ἐμ πᾶσιν ἐπανορθώσεως καὶ τὸν κύκλον τῶν δανείων μεταπαρέδωκεν ἐκβαίνων, ἐκ τῶν ἐπιμελειτειῶν πολλοῖς ἐπευξημένον χρήμασιν, ὥστε μὴ μόνον εἰς [ἃ]ς ἀνενεώσατο τῆι Δήμητρι καὶ τῆι Κόρηι θυσίας, ἀλλὰ καὶ εἰς ἑτέρας πλείονας διὰ τὴν τούτου σπουδὴν γεγονέναι τῆι συνόδωι προσόδους· βιασαμένων δὲ αὐτὸν τῶν τεχνιτῶν πάλιν τὸ τέταρτον ὑπομεῖναι ἐπιμελητὴν εἰς τὸν ἐπὶ Σελεύκου ἄρχοντος ἐνιαυτὸν πρὸς ταῖς λοιπαῖς εἰσφοραῖς καὶ χορηγίαις καὶ ἐν Ἐλευσῖνι θύσας ἔν τε τῶι ἱερῶι καὶ ἐν ὧι πρῶτος αὐτὸς κατεσκευάσατο τεμένει ἐφ᾽, οὗ ἰδρύσατο βωμοῦ τά τε θύματα καὶ τὴν λοιπὴν χορηγίαν πᾶσαν ἐπιδεξάμενος ὑπεδέξατο τὴν σύνοδον ἐκ τῶν ἰδίων μεγαλομερῶς, προσεμέρισε δὲ καὶ τὰς

διατεταγμένας ἐκ τῶν κοινῶν ἡμέρας δύο καὶ ἐμ πάσαις ἐκαλλιέρησε ταῖς θεαῖς καὶ
τὰς πατρίους σπονδὰς ἐπετέλεσεν· [πολλὰ δὲ κα]ὶ ἄλλα ἐπολιτεύσατο καλὰ καὶ
συμφέροντα τῆι συνόδωι καὶ [προσεδαπάνησεν ἐκ τ]ῶν ἰδίων ἔν τε ταῖς ἐπιμελητείαις
καὶ ἱερωσύναις [- - - - - προκρίνω]ν τὴν τῶν τεχνιτῶν εὔνοιαν παντὸς χρήμα[τος
- - - - - -] οὐ μόνον δὲ πρὸς τὴν σύνοδον - - - - - - - - διακείμενος ἀποδο[χῆς
- - ἠξιώθη - - - ἐκ τῶ]ν νόμων καὶ - - - - - - - λιμεν - - - .

13. Sulla and the Senate confirm the privileges of the Ionian guild, 81–79 B.C.
  Rivista di filologia 66 (1938), pp. 253 ff.

ἀγαθᾶι τύχαι.

[Λ]εύκιος Κορνήλιος Λευκίου υἱὸς Σύλλας Ἐπαφρόδειτος δικτάτωρ Κώων ἄρχουσι
βουλῆ δήμῳ χαίρειν. ἐγὼ Ἀλεξάνδρῳ Λαοδικεῖ κιθαριστῆ, ἀνδρὶ καλῷ καὶ ἀγαθῶι
καὶ φίλῳ ἡμετέρῳ, πρεσβευτῆ παρὰ τοῦ κοινοῦ τῶν περὶ τὸν Διό[ν]υσον τεχνιτῶν
τῶν ἐπὶ Ἰωνίας καὶ Ἑλλησπόντου [καὶ τ]ῶν περὶ τὸν καθηγεμόνα Διόνυσον ἐπέ-
τ[ρεψα στήλην] παρ' ὑμεῖν ἐν τῷ ἐπισημοτάτῳ τόπωι ἀναθή[σεσθαι ἐν ᾗ] ἀναγραφή-
σεται τὰ ὑπ' ἐμοῦ δεδομένα [τοῖς τεχνίταις] φιλάνθρωπα· πρεσβεύσαντος δ[ὲ νῦν
αὐτοῦ εἰς Ῥώμην], τῆς συγκλήτου δὲ δόγμα π[ερὶ τούτων ψηφισαμένης, ὑμᾶς] οὖν
θέλω φροντίσαι ὅπως [ἀποδειχθῆ παρ' ὑμεῖν τόπος ἐπισ]ημότατος ἐν ᾧ ἀναθή[σεται
ἡ στήλη ἡ περὶ τῶν τεχνιτῶ]ν. ὑπογέγραφφα δὲ [τῆς παρ' ἐμοῦ ἐπιστολῆς τοῦ τε
δόγματος] τῆς συγκλή[του - - -]ντα - - - -
  . . . δει, σὺν δὲ καὶ ἣν ἔχετε πρὸς [ἡμ]ᾶς [εὔ]νο[ιαν], ὑμᾶς οὖν θέλω [ἐ]πεγνωκέναι
ἐμὲ ἀπὸ συμβο[υ]λίου γνώμης γνώμην ἀποπεφάνθαι, ἃ φιλάνθ[ρω]πα κα[ὶ τι]μᾶς
ἀλειτουργησίας τε ὑμεῖν καταλο[γῆς] τοῦ Διονύσου καὶ τῶν Μουσῶν καὶ τῆς
πο[λι]τείας ὑμῶν χάριτι σύνκλητος ἄρχοντές τε [ἢ ἀν]τάρχοντες ἡμέτεροι ἔδωκαν
σ[υνεχώ]ρησαν, ἵνα ταῦτα ἔχετε, καὶ κ[αθὼς καὶ πρὶν] πάσης τε λειτουργίας
ἀλε[ιτούργητοι ἦτε] στρατείας τε, μήτε τινὰ [εἰσφορὰν ἢ δαπά]νας εἰσφέρητε, μήτε
[ἐ]ν[οχλῆσθε ὑπό τινος] παροχῆς ἕνεκέν τ[ε καὶ ἐπισταθμείας, μήτε] τινὰ δέχεσθ[αι
καταλύτην ἐπαναγκάζησθε,] ἵνα δὲ καὶ [- - - -

14. The World Guild honours an agonothetes at Ancyra, A.D. 128. *S.E.G.* vi. 59.

ἀγαθῆι τύχηι.

ψήφισμα τῶν ἀπὸ τῆς οἰκουμένης περὶ τὸν Διόνυσον καὶ Αὐτοκράτορα Τραιανὸν
Ἀδριανὸν Σεβαστὸν Καίσαρα νέον Διόνυσον τεχνειτῶν ἱερονεικῶν στεφανειτῶν καὶ
τῶν τούτων συναγωνιστῶν καὶ τῶν νεμόντων τὴν ἱερὰν θυμελικὴν σύνοδον. ἐπειδὴ
προταθεὶς ὑπὸ τῆς ἱερωτάτης βουλῆς Οὔλπιος Αἴλιος Πομπειανὸς ἀγωνοθετῆσαι
τὸν ἀγῶνα τὸν μυστικὸν δοθέντα ὑπὸ τοῦ Αὐτοκράτορος ἐν ὀλίγαις τῇ πόλει, τῇ
τε χειροτονίᾳ ταχέως ὑπήκουσεν καὶ τὸν ἀγῶνα διαφανῶς ἐπετέλεσεν ἐκ τῶν ἑαυτοῦ,
μηδεμιᾶς ἀπολειφθεὶς λαμπρότητος καὶ μεγαλοψυχίας, ἀλλὰ τήν τε εὐσέβειαν τῆς
πατρίδος εἰς ἀμφοτέρους τοὺς θεοὺς ἐπεψήφισεν καὶ τὰς ἐπιδόσεις πάσας δὲ ἀφειδῶς
ἐποιήσατο, πρὸς μηδεμίαν δαπάνην ἀναδὺς καὶ τῷ τε τάχει τῆς σπουδῆς ὁδεύοντας
ἤδη τοὺς ἀγωνιστὰς ἀνεκαλέσατο καὶ παντὶ μέρει τοῦ μυστηρίου [ἐπή]ρκεσεν, τῇ μὲν
συνόδῳ τὰ ἆθλα προθείς, [τὸν δὲ μυστικ]ὸν ἀγῶνα κατασχὼν ὡς προκεκ[ριμένος
μόνος] εὖ ποιεῖν τὴν πόλιν· [δεδόχθαι οὖν] ἡμεῖν ὑπὲρ τοῦ τετηρῆσθαι μὲν [τὰς τειμὰς
τῷ τε] Αὐτοκράτορι καὶ τῷ Διονύσῳ, διασε[σαφῆσθαι δὲ εἰς] αἰῶνα τῇ πόλει, τὸν ἄνδρα

τετιμῆ[σθαι ἀνδριάντ]ι, ὃς ἀναστήσεται ἐν ἐπιφανεστά[τῳ μὲν τόπῳ τ]ῆς μητρο
πόλεως, ἰδίῳ δὲ τῶν ἀγω[νιζομένων ἐ]ν τῷ θεάτρῳ, παράδιγμα κάλλιστον [ἀρετῆς
τοῖς θε]ωμένοις, ᾧ καὶ τὸν εἰσιόντα ἀγωνι[στὴν εἰς μυστικ]ὸν ἀγῶνα ἐψηφίσθαι
στεφάνους [εἰσφέρειν], εἰ δὲ μή, εἴργεσθαι τοῦ ἀγῶνος ἀχαρι[στίας πρὸς τὸν ἄ]ριστον
ἄνδρα ἕνεκεν καὶ ἀπειθε[ίας τῶν ἐψηφι]σμένων τῇ συνόδῳ, ἀναστῆσαι [δὲ τοῦ ἀνδρὸς
ἀ]νδριάντα καὶ ἐν Νεαπόλει· τῷ [δὲ μεγίστῳ Αὐτοκρά]τορι Καίσαρι Τραιανῷ
Ἀδριανῷ Σε[βαστῷ καὶ τῷ κ]ρατίστῳ ἡγεμόνι Τρεβίῳ Σεργια[νῷ μαρτυρῆσαι]
διὰ ψηφίσματος τήν τε τοῦ ἀνδρὸς [μεγαλομέρ]ειαν καὶ τὴν τῆς συνόδου δικαίαν
[εὐχαριστίαν· ἐ]ισηγησαμένου Γαΐου Ἀντωνίου Πολ . . . . ὡς κωμῳδοῦ
ὀλυμπιονείκου, ἐ[πιψηφισαμέν]ου Γαΐου Ἰουλίου Κολλήγα Νεο[. . . . . κωμῳ]
δοῦ παραδόξου. ἐγένετο ἐν [τῇ μητροπόλει τῇ]ς Γαλατίας Ἀγκύρα ἀγῶνος τε[λου
μένου μυσ]τικοῦ ἐπὶ ἑλλαδάρχου Οὐλπί[ου Αἰλίου Πομπε]ιανοῦ καὶ ἀρχιερέως
Μεμμίου . . . . ου Διονυσίου τοῦ ἑλλαδάρχου [. . . . . . . ἐπὶ ἄρχο]ντος
Τίτου Φλαουΐου Ἰουλια[νοῦ . . . . γραμ]ματέως Ἀλεξάνδρου Σωπά[τρου . . . .
. . . . καὶ] Λαοδικέως κιθαρῳδοῦ σεβαστο[νείκου παραδόξου] τοῦ τρὶς ἀρχιερέως,
νομοδεί[κτου . . . . Ἐ]πόπτου Τρωαδέως πλειστ[ονείκου. ἐπὶ ὑπάτων
Ν]ωνίου Τορκ[ουά]του Ἀσπρή[να καὶ Μ. Ἀννίου Λίβωνο]ς, πρὸ ζʹ εἰδ(ῶν) Δεκεμ
βρίων.

15. The World Guild honours Aelius Alcibiades, c. A.D. 142. B.C.H. 9 (1885),
   pp. 124 ff.; Ἀρχ. Δελτ. 7 (1922), pp. 83 ff.; Jahreshefte 24 (1929), pp. 191 ff.;
   S.E.G. iv. 418; Robert, Études épigraphiques et philologiques, pp. 45 ff.

[ἐ]ισηγησαμένου Ποπλίου Αἰλίου Πομπη[ια]νοῦ [Π]αίονος Σιδήτου καὶ Ταρσέ[ως]
καὶ Ῥοδίο[υ ποιη]τοῦ πλειστονείκου, μελοποιοῦ καὶ ῥαψ[ῳδοῦ Θε]οῦ Ἀδριανοῦ,
θεολόγου ναῶν τῶν ἐν Π[εργάμωι, ἀγ]ωνοθέτου ἀποδεδειγμένου τῶν Σεβ[αστῶν
Πυ]θίων, ἐπιψηφισαμένου Πο. Αἰλίου [. . . . . . Κυ]ζικηνοῦ, κιθαρῳδοῦ Καπετωλιο
νείκου Ὀλυμπιονείκου παραδόξου· ἐπειδὴ Αἴλι[ος] Ἀλκιβιάδης ἀνὴρ παιδείᾳ καὶ
μεγαλοφροσ[ύνῃ δ]ιαφέρων, τοῖς τε ἄλλοις τῆς ἀ[ρ]ε[τ]ῆς καλο[ῖς] κεκοσμημένος ἐκ
πολλοῦ δια[τελεῖ] καὶ ἐ[κ] δώδεκα ἐτῶν καὶ [πρώ]ην πάντας εὖ ποιῶν το[ὺς] μουσι
κοὺς καὶ πρὸς ἀξίωμα καὶ μεγαλοπρ[έπ]ειαν τῆι συνόδωι συλλαμβάνων καὶ περ[ὶ
π]ολλῶν αὐτοφιλοτειμημάτων εἰς ἡμᾶ[ς καὶ τ]ὸ κοινόν, ἔτι βιβλίοις θαυμαστο[ῖς
ἐπεκ]ό[σ]μησεν τὸ ἱερὸν ἐπὶ Ῥώμης τέμενος [τῶν] ἀπὸ τῆς οἰκουμένης τεχνειτῶν καὶ
δῶρα μεγαλοπρεπῆ παρέ[χεται] χωρίων ἱπποσ[τάσιον ἀ]πονείμας, ἀφ' οὗ πρόσοδον
αἰώνιον δ[ιηνε]κῆ [καρπ]ωσόμεθα, νεμόμενοι τὰ[ς προσ]όδους καθ' ἑκάστην ἐτήσιον
θεοῦ Ἀδρ[ιανοῦ γ]ενέθλιον ἡμέραν, ἐφ' οἷς ἀμ[ει]βόμενοι τ[ὴν χάρι]ν οἱ ἐπὶ Ῥώμης
τεχνεῖται καὶ ἄλλας μὲν [αὐ]τῶι τειμὰς προσηκούσας ἐψηφίσαντο [καὶ ἀρχι]ερέα
τε αὐτὸν διὰ παντὸς τοῦ αἰῶνος ἀ[πέδειξα]ν προτετειμῆσθαί τε ἠξίωσαν τῆι τά[ξει]
τῶν ἄλλων ἀρχιερέων πρῶτον ταῖς διπ[τύχοις ἐ]νγραφόμεν[ον], ἀνθ' ὧν ἐπεκόσμησε
μὲ[ν τ]ὴν ἀθάνατον Ἀδριανοῦ μνήμην, ἐνδ[οξοτ]έραν δὲ τὴν σύνοδον ἀπέφηνεν ταῖς
αὐτοῦ δωρεαῖς πομπάς τε πέμπουσα[ν με]γαλοπρεπῶς καὶ πολυτελεῖς ἱερομηνία[ς
ἐπ]ιτελοῦσαν, διὰ ταῦτα καὶ νῦν τύχηι ἀγαθ[ῆι δ]εδόχθαι τοῖς ἀπὸ τῆς οἰκουμένης
περ[ὶ τὸν] Διόνυσον καὶ Αὐτοκράτορα Καίσαρα Τ. [Αἴλιον] Ἀδριανὸν Ἀντωνεῖνον
Σεβαστὸν Εὐ[σεβῆ] τεχνείταις ἱερονείκαις στεφανείτα[ις καὶ] τοῖς τούτων συναγω
νισταῖς τοῖς ἀπ[αντῶ]σιν ἐπὶ τὸν ἐν τῇ μεγίστηι καὶ πρώτηι μη[τρο]πόλει τῆς
Ἀσίας καὶ δὶς νεωκόρωι τῶν Σεβα[σ]τῶν Ἐφεσίων πόλει τῶν μεγάλων Ἐφεσίων

[πε]νταετηρικὸν ἀγῶνα, καὶ αὐτοὺς ἐπὶ ταῖς ἤ[δη] δεδογμέναις εἰς τὸν ἄνδρα τειμαῖς
προσεπινοῆσαι χάριν ἀμοιβῆς δικαίαν ψηφίσασθαί [τε εἰ]κόνας ἐπιχρύσους καὶ
ἀνδριάντας ἀναστῆ[σαι] ἔν τε τοῖς ἱεροῖς τῆς Ἀσίας τῶν αὐτοκρατόρ[ων] ναοῖς ἔν
τε τῆι φιλοσεβάστωι Νύσηι πατρίδι τ[οῦ Ἀλ]κιβιάδου στήλλην τε ἐν τῶι ἱερῶι τοῦ
Ἀπόλλων[ος] ἀναγράψαι τῶν ψηφισμάτων καὶ ἐν τοῖς λοιπ[οῖς α]ὐτοῦ ἔργοις καὶ
κατὰ πόλεις ἀπάσας ἵν' ἀ[μφο]τέρων ὑπόμνημα χρηστὸν ἦ καὶ τῆς τοῦ [Ἀλκιβ]ιάδου
μεγαλοφροσύνης καὶ τῆς τῶν εὖ πα[θόν]των χάριτος, τετειμῆσθαί τε αὐτὸν ἀναγο-
ρε[ύσει] χρυσῶι στεφάνωι ἐν ταῖς τοῦ διὰ πάντων ἀγῶ[νος] ἱερουργίαις τε καὶ
σπονδαῖς καὶ κατὰ πάντα σ[ύλ]λογον ἀναγορεύεσθαί τε καὶ προτειμᾶσθαι, ἀντ[ίγρα]φά
τε τῶν ψηφισμάτων καὶ παρ' αὐτὸν ἐκπέμψαι κα[ὶ] πρὸς τὴν λαμπροτάτην πατρίδα
αὐτοῦ Νυσαέω[ν] πόλιν διὰ πρεσβευτῶν Πο. Αἰλίου Πομπηιανο[ῦ] Παίονος Σιδήτου καὶ Ταρσέως καὶ Ῥοδίου, ποι[η]τοῦ πλειστονείκου, μελοποιοῦ καὶ ῥαψῳδο[ῦ]
Θεοῦ Ἀδριανοῦ, θεολόγου ναῶν τῶν ἐν Περγ[ά]μωι καὶ ἀγωνοθέτου ἀποδεδειγμένου τῶν Σ[ε]βαστῶν Πυθίων, καὶ Ἀριστείδου τοῦ Ἀριστείδ[ου] Γαίου Περγαμηνοῦ
ποιητοῦ παραδόξου, σ[τεῖ]λαί τε πρεσβείαν καὶ παρὰ τὸν μέγιστον Α[ὐτο]κράτορα
καὶ πρὸς τὴν ἐν Ῥώμηι σύνοδον [χάριν] ὁμολογοῦσαν ὑπὲρ τῶν πεπραγμένων [τῶι
εὐ]εργέτηι Ἀλκιβιάδηι.—ἀντίγραφον ψηφίσ[ματος] τοῦ ἀπὸ Ῥώμης κομισθέντος
διὰ Ποτάμω[νος] τοῦ Ποτάμωνος Νυσαέως κήρυκος· ψήφισμα τῆς ἱερᾶς Ἀδριανῆς
Ἀντωνείν[ης] θυμελικῆς περιπ[ο]λιστικῆς μεγάλ[ης] νε[ωκόρου] ἐπὶ Ῥώμης συνόδου
[τῶν ἀπ]ὸ τῆς οἰκ[ουμένης πε]ρὶ τὸν Διό[νυσον καὶ Αὐτοκρά]τορα Καί[σαρα Τ.
Αἴλιο]ν Ἀδρι[ανὸν Ἀντωνεῖνον Σ]εβασ[τόν . . . .]

The decree of the Roman branch is lost. The other side of the stone has a
decree of the city of Nysa.

16a. Eurykles the logistes agrees to the starting of the Lysimacheia, shortly
after A.D. 180. *O.G.I.S.* 509.

ἀγαθῆι τύχηι.

Μᾶρκος Οὔλπιος Ἀππουλήιος Εὐρυκλῆς, ἀρχιερεὺς Ἀσίας ἀποδεδειγμένο[ς] ναῶν
{καὶ} τῶν ἐν Σμύρνῃ τὸ β, Ἀφροδισιέων ἄρχουσι βουλῇ δήμῳ χαίρειν· βουληθέντων
ὑμῶν πρόνοιαν ποιήσασθαί με καὶ τῶν κατὰ τοὺς ἀγῶνας διά τε τὴν πρὸς τὸν
μέγιστον αὐτοκράτορα εὐσέβειαν Μᾶρκον Αὐρήλιον Κόμοδον Ἀντωνῖνον Σεβαστὸν
καὶ διὰ τὴν πρὸς τοὺς διαθεμένους μνήμην καὶ διὰ τὴν τῆς πόλεως δόξαν, ἤδη καὶ τῶν
ἀπὸ τῆς συνόδου π[ολ]λάκις ἐντυχόντων μοι, οὐδὲ τοῦτο τὸ μέρος κατέλιπον ἀδιάκρι-
τον, ἑπόμενος τῇ κατὰ τὴν λογιστείαν τάξε[ι] καὶ προθυμίᾳ μέχρι νῦν τῆς περὶ τοὺς
ἀγῶνας καταστάσεως ἐνλειπούσης διὰ τὴν τῶν χρημάτων παρασκευήν, ὀφειλόντων
συναυξη⟨θῆ⟩ναι κατά τε τὰς τῶν τελευτησάντων γνώμας καὶ κατὰ τὸ ἀξίωμα τοῦ
πόρου, ἀφ' οὗ χρὴ τοὺς ἀγῶνας ἐπιτελεῖσθαι. ἀγὼν μὲν δὴ ὁ ἐκ τῶν Φλαβίου Λυσιμάχου διαθηκῶν προελήλυθεν εἰς ἀρχαίου πόρου μυριάδας δώδεκα, ὡς δύνασθαι ἀπὸ
τούτων παρὰ ἔτη τέσσερα πληροῦσθαι τὸν μουσικὸν ἀγῶνα, καθὰ τῷ διαθεμένῳ ἔδοξεν.
αἱ δὲ μετὰ τὰς δώδεκα μυριάδας οὖσαι ἐν ἐκδανεισμῷ καὶ ὁ προσγεγονὼς τούτοις
τόκος μέχρι ἀρχῆς τοῦ ⟨ἔτου⟩ς ποιεῖ κεφαλαίου δηναρίων μυριάδας τρεῖς δηνάρια
χείλια ὀκτωκόσια τριάκοντα ἐννέα. δύνασθε οὖν ἀρχομένου τοῦ ἔτους τοῦτον τὸν
ἀγῶνα ἐπιτελεῖν ἀγαθῆι τύχῃ ἐπὶ ἄθλοις ταλαντιαίοις καὶ ἀγωνίσμασιν κατὰ τὰ
ἄθλα. προθεσμία δὲ εἰς τὸν ἑξῆς χρόνον καὶ τὴν ἐπιοῦσαι· τετραετηρίδα ἔστω χρό[νος]
ὁ ἀπὸ [Βαρβ]ιλλήων τῶν ἐν Ἐφέσῳ [ἀγομ]έ[νων] πρὸς [κοινὰ] Ἀσίας [ἐν Σμύρνῃ].

16*b*. The prize-list of the Lysimacheia. Le Bas 1620d; *M.A.M.A.* viii. 420.

ἀγῶνος ταλαντ⟨ι⟩αίου Φλαβίου Λυσιμάχου πενταετηρικοῦ
μουσικοῦ μόνου θέματα τὰ ὑπογεγραμμένα·

σαλπικτῇ	* φ′	χοραύλῃ	* ͺαφ′	κοινῇ κωμῳδῶν	* σ′
κήρυκι	* φ′	δευτερείου	* φ′	κοινῇ τραγῳδῶν	* συ′
ἐνκωμιογράφῳ	* ψυ′	χορῷ τραγικῷ	* φ′	καινῇ κωμῳδίᾳ	* φ′
ποιητῇ	* ψυ′	χορῷ κιθαρεῖ	* ͺαφ′		
πυθαύλῃ	* ͺα	δευτερείου	* φ′	ἀρχαίᾳ κωμῳδίᾳ	* τυ′
δευτερείου	* τυ′	κωμῳδῷ	* ͺαφ′	δευτερεῖον	* ρυ′
ψειλοκιθαρεῖ	* ͺα	δευτερείου	* φ′	καινῇ τραγῳδίᾳ	* ψυ′
δευτερείου	* τυ′	τριτείου	* τ′	πυρριχῇ	* ͺα
παιδὶ κιθαρῳδῷ	* ψυ′	τραγῳδῷ	* βφ′	δευτερεῖον	* τυ′
δευτερείου	* συ′	δευτερείου	* ω′	ἀνδρὶ κιθαρῳδῷ	* —
		τριτείου	* υ′	δευτερεῖον	* —

17. Diocletian and Maximian on actors' privileges, A.D. 286–305. Mitteis–
Wilcken, *Grundzüge und Chrestomathie der Papyruskunde*, II. ii, no. 381, with their
emendations; Cavenaile, *Corpus Pap. Lat.*, no. 241.

Impp. Diocletianus et Maximianus Augg. et Constantius et Maximianus
nobb. Caess. Ad synodum xysticorum et thymelicorum et ibidem. Familiare
nobis, praerogativas integras inlibatas servare quas divorum parentium Augg.
constitutiones in suis quibusque concedunt. Sed ne sub specie coronarum de-
clinandi munera civilia potestas omnibus detur, ideo ad praeces vestras dato
rescripto declaramus eis demum a muneribus civilibus personalibus immuni-
tatem iure competere qu[i], ⟨cum⟩ per omne te[m]pus aetatis suae certaminibus adfuisse⟨nt⟩, non nova corruptela et subscripto interveniente, non
minus quam tres coronas certaminis nobilis retulerint in quibus vel urbicae
victoriam vel antiquae Graec[ia]e vel ex n[umine n]ostro comoediae ⟨vel⟩
certaminis constituram no[. . . . .] a [. .] . necet [. . . . .] quae species
privilegii intra personam eorum quorum i . . [. . . non h]uiusm[odi] beneficio
remunerare placuit const[are] nequit ut iu[st]ius persuasum [habe]an[t]
a[. .] . . o . . [. . . . .] . . .a. [.] . . huiu[smo]di pe[rso]na - - - nisi haec persona
sub aemula consessione pa[r]entium [p]riv[i]legii speciem in se provocaverit.

[Haec] sententia ubicum[que servabitur.]

ADDITIONAL NOTE

In *ΓΕΡΑΣ: Studies presented to George Thomson* (Acta Universitatis Carolinae 1963, Philosophica et Historica 1, Graeco-latina Pragensia II), pp. 67–81, Professor Robert Browning publishes, with commentary, an anonymous text *Περὶ τραγῳδίας*, perhaps by Michael Psellos, certainly deriving in part from the same source as Tzetzes' iambic poem of the same name. This important text contains significant amounts of new information, and we print here some of the more interesting passages.

(5). Ἡ δὲ παλαιὰ τραγικὴ μελοποιία γένει μὲν τῷ ἐναρμονίῳ ἐχρήσατο ἀμιγεῖ καὶ μικτῷ γένει τῆς ἁρμονίας καὶ διατόνων, χρώματι δὲ οὐδεὶς φαίνεται κεχρημένος τῶν τραγικῶν ἄχρις Εὐριπίδου· μαλακὸν γὰρ τὸ ἦθος τοῦ γένους τούτου. τῶν δὲ τόνων πλεῖστον μὲν ἡ παλαιὰ κέχρηται τῷ τε Δωρίῳ καὶ τῷ Μιξολυδίῳ, τῷ μὲν ὡς σεμνότητος οἰκείῳ, τῷ δὲ Μιξολυδίῳ ὡς συνεργῷ πρὸς τοὺς οἴκτους. κέχρηται δὲ καὶ ταῖς ἀνειμέναις τότε καλουμέναις ἁρμονίαις, τῇ τε Ἰαστὶ καὶ ἀνειμένῃ Λυδιστί. τοῦ δὲ Φρυγίου καὶ Λυδίου Σοφοκλῆς ἥψατο πρῶτος. κέχρηται δὲ τῷ Φρυγίῳ διθυραμβικώτερον. ὁ δὲ Ὑποφρύγιος καὶ ὁ Ὑποδώριος σπάνιοι παρ' αὐτῇ εἰσιν, ὡς ... διθυράμβῳ προσήκοντες. πρῶτος δὲ Ἀγάθων τὸν Ὑποδώριον τόνον εἰς τραγῳδίαν εἰσήνεγκεν καὶ τὸν Ὑποφρύγιον. ὅ γε μὴν Λύδιος τῷ κιθαρῳδικῷ τρόπῳ οἰκειότερός ἐστι. συστήμασι δὲ οἱ μὲν παλαιοὶ μικροῖς ἐχρῶντο, Εὐριπίδης πρῶτος πολυχορδίᾳ ἐχρήσατο. ἐκαλεῖτο ὑπὸ τῶν μουσικῶν ⟨τῶν⟩ παλαιῶν ἀνάτρητος ὁ τρόπος οὗτος τῆς μελοποιίας· καὶ καθόλου εἰπεῖν Εὐριπίδης πολυειδέστερός ἐστι τῶν πρὸ αὐτοῦ καὶ πολυχρούστερος· καὶ ἐχρήσατο καὶ τοῖς προσήκουσι ῥυθμοῖς καὶ βακχείοις ἁπλοῖς τε καὶ διπλοῖς, καὶ τῷ ἀπ' ἐλάττονος ἰωνικῷ, καὶ ἐπ' ὀλίγον προκελευσματικῷ. ... (8) ... τὸ δὲ ἀναπαιστικὸν τετράμετρον παρὰ Φρυνίχῳ μόνον τῷ παλαιῷ τετύχηκε χρήσεως. (9) Ἔστι δὲ καὶ ἕτερά τινα συντάττομενα τοῖς τραγικοῖς μέλεσί τε καὶ μέτροις, οἷον μεσαύλιον, ἐπίφθεγμα, ἀναβόημα, ἀνάπαιστον ἔρρυθμον. ἔστι δὲ τὰ μεσαύλια κρούματα βραχέα μεταξὺ τῶν μελῶν ταττόμενα. τῶν δὲ ἐπιφθεγμάτων πλείω μέν ἐστιν ἡ χρῆσις ἐν τοῖς σατυρικοῖς δράμασιν· ἔστι δὲ καὶ ἐν τοῖς τραγικοῖς. τὸ δὲ ἀναβόημά ἐστι μὲν τῶν ᾀδομένων σχεδόν τι, μεταξὺ δέ ἐστιν ᾠδῆς καὶ καταλογῆς. ἔστι δὲ ὅτε οἱ τραγικοὶ ἐπίσκηνα συντιθέασιν ἀνάπαιστα, καὶ χορικὰ ἀπὸ σκηνῆς. καὶ γὰρ ἀγγέλων ὅλα πρόσωπα ἐκπληροῦσι δι' αὐτῶν καὶ ἐν ταῖς παρόδοις προτάττουσιν αὐτὰ τῶν μελῶν. ... (11) Τῶν δὲ ὑποκριτῶν οὐδεὶς οὐδέποτε ἐν τραγῳδίᾳ ὠρχήσατο (Winnington-Ingram; ἐχρήσατο MS.), ἀλλ' ἦν ἴδιος τοῦ χοροῦ ἡ τοιαύτη ἐνέργεια. ... (12) Μετὰ πλείστης δὲ σπουδῆς τὰς περιόδους πρὸς αὐλὸν ᾖδον οἱ τραγικοὶ χοροί, καὶ προσήλουν αὐταῖς οἱ κράτιστοι αὐληταί, ὁ μὲν τὴν χρωματικὴν περίοδον, ὁ δὲ τὴν ἐναρμόνιον, ὁ δὲ τὴν σύντονον. καὶ κιθάρᾳ δὲ ἐν ταῖς τραγῳδίαις ἐχρήσατο καὶ Εὐριπίδης καὶ Σοφοκλῆς, Σοφοκλῆς δὲ καὶ λύρᾳ ἐν τῷ Θαμύρᾳ.

With the statement in para. 5 on Euripides' use of the chromatic genus, compare Plutarch, *Quaest. Conv.* iii. 654 d–e: θαυμάζω δὲ καὶ ... τουτονὶ τὰς μὲν ἐν τοῖς μέλεσι παραχρώσεις βδελυττόμενον καὶ κατηγοροῦντα τοῦ καλοῦ Ἀγάθωνος, ὃν πρῶτον εἰς τραγῳδίαν φασὶν ἐμβαλεῖν καὶ ὑπομῖξαι τὸ χρωματικόν, ὅτε τοὺς Μυσοὺς ἐδίδασκεν κτλ., and contrast *de Mus.* 1137 e–f: τῷ γὰρ χρωματικῷ γένει . . . τραγῳδία μὲν οὐδέπω καὶ τήμερον κέχρηται κτλ. For the use of the Lydian and Ionian modes in tragedy, compare [Plut.] *de Mus.* 1137 a: καὶ περὶ τοῦ Λυδίου δ' οὐκ ἠγνόει [sc. Plato] καὶ περὶ τῆς Ἰάδος· ἠπίστατο γὰρ ὅτι ἡ τραγῳδία ταύτῃ τῇ μελοποιίᾳ κέχρηται, and Athen. xiv. 625 b. The assertion that Agathon used the Hypophrygian and Hypodorian in tragedy is relevant to the discussion of Aristot. *Probl.* xix. 48 (pp. 258 f. above). Para. 9 provides a slightly less dubious example of καταλογή apparently meaning 'recitative' (see p. 157, n. 7, above).

BIBLIOGRAPHY

THE following list makes no claim whatever to completeness. In particular, it cites only those histories of Greek literature and of Greek drama, and those books on the Greek dramatists, which have been extensively used, or which bear directly on the topics discussed in this book. Further bibliographical information is contained in the footnotes.

Ancient authors are in general cited from the latest relevant edition in the *Oxford Classical Texts* or *Bibliotheca Teubneriana* series. In a few cases where doubt might arise the editor's name follows after the reference. In addition, the following editions and commentaries are cited in the text:

Poetae Melici Graeci, ed. D. L. Page, Oxford, 1962.

Select Papyri: iii. Literary Papyri (Poetry), ed. D. L. Page (Loeb), London and Cambridge (Mass.), 1941 (reprinted 1950).

Aeschyli Tragoediae (Aesch. Trag.), ed. U. von Wilamowitz-Moellendorf, Berlin, 1914 (reprinted 1958).

Aeschylus, ed. H. Weir Smyth (Loeb), vol. ii, with appendix by P. H. J. Lloyd-Jones, London and Cambridge (Mass.), 1957.

Aeschylus, *Agamemnon*, ed. E. Fraenkel, 3 vols., Oxford, 1950.

Aristophanes, *Lysistrate*, ed. U. von Wilamowitz-Moellendorf, Berlin, 1927 (reprinted 1958).

Euripides, *Alcestis*, ed. A. M. Dale, Oxford, 1954.

Euripides, *Bacchae*, ed. E. R. Dodds, ed. 2, Oxford, 1960.

Euripides, *Helen*, ed. A. M. Dale, Oxford, 1967.

Euripides, *Hippolytus*, ed. W. S. Barrett, Oxford, 1964.

Euripides, *Hypsipyle*, ed. G. W. Bond (*Oxford Classical and Philosophical Monographs*), Oxford, 1963.

Euripides, *Medea*, ed. D. L. Page, Oxford, 1938.

Menander, *Dyscolos*, ed. E. W. Handley, London, 1965.

Menander, *Dyscolus*, ed. J.-M. Jacques (Budé), Paris, 1963.

Menandri Sicyonius, ed. R. Kassel (*Kleine Texte*), Berlin, 1965.

A. W. Gomme, *A historical commentary on Thucydides*, vol. ii (Books ii–iii), Oxford, 1956.

GENERAL

(i) *Greek drama and the history of the theatre*

J. T. ALLEN, *Stage antiquities of the Greeks and Romans*, New York, 1927.

J. ANDRIEU, *Le Dialogue antique: structure et présentation*, Paris, 1954.

C. ANTI, *Teatri greci arcaici da Minosse e Pericle*, Padua, 1947.

P. E. ARIAS, *Il teatro greco fuori di Atene*, Florence, 1934.

P. ARNOTT, *Greek scenic conventions in the fifth century B.C.*, Oxford, 1962.

W. BEARE, *The Roman Stage*, ed. 3, London, 1964.

E. BETHE, *Prolegomena zur Geschichte des Theaters im Alterthum*, Leipzig, 1896.

M. BIEBER, *Die Denkmäler zum Theaterwesen im Altertum*, Berlin, 1920.

—— *History of the Greek and Roman Theater*, Princeton, ed. 1, 1939; ed. 2, 1961.

W. Buchwald, *Studien zur Chronologie der attischen Tragödien 455 bis 431*, diss. Königsberg, 1939.

H. Bulle, *Eine Skenographie* (94. Berliner Winckelmannsprogramm), Berlin, 1934.

—— *Das Theater zu Sparta* (*S.B.* Munich, 1937, Heft 5).

—— *Untersuchungen an griechischen Theatern* (*Abhandlung* Munich, vol. 33), 1928.

N. E. Collinge, 'Some reflections on satyr-plays' (*Proc. Camb. Phil. Soc.* n.s. 5 (1958/9), pp. 28–35).

A. Couat, *Aristophane et l'ancienne comédie attique*, ed. 2, Paris, 1903.

M. Croiset, *Aristophane et les partis à Athènes*, Paris, 1906.

O. A. W. Dilke, 'The Greek theatre cavea' (*B.S.A.* 43 (1948), pp. 125–92).

—— 'Details and chronology of Greek theatre caveas' (*B.S.A.* 45 (1950), pp. 21–62).

W. Dörpfeld and E. Reisch, *Das griechische Theater: Beiträge zur Geschichte des Dionysos-Theater in Athen und anderer griechischer Theater*, Athens, 1896.

J. W. Donaldson, *The Theatre of the Greeks*, ed. 6, London, 1849.

G. F. Else, *The origin and early form of Greek tragedy* (Martin Classical Lectures, 20), Cambridge (Mass.), 1965.

E. Fiechter, *Das Dionysos-Theater in Athen*, i–iv (= *Antike griechische Theaterbauten*, parts 5–7, 9), (Sächsische Forschungsinstitute in Leipzig, Forschungsinstitut für klassische Philologie und Archäologie), Stuttgart, 1935–50.

R. C. Flickinger, *The Greek theater and its drama*, ed. 4, Chicago, 1936.

E. Fraenkel, *Beobachtungen zu Aristophanes*, Rome, 1962.

E. Fraenkel, 'Zum Schluß der Sieben gegen Theben' (*Mus. Helv.* 21 (1964), pp. 58–64).

P. Geissler, *Chronologie der altattischen Komödie* (Philologische Untersuchungen, 30), Berlin, 1925.

A. von Gerkan and W. Müller-Wiener, *Das Theater von Epidaurus*, Stuttgart, 1961.

A. W. Gomme, 'Aristophanes and Politics' (*C.R.* 52 (1938), pp. 97–109 = *More Essays in Greek History and Literature*, Oxford, 1962, pp. 70–91).

H. R. Graf, *Szenische Untersuchungen zu Menander*, diss. Giessen, 1914.

A. E. Haigh, *The Attic Theatre*, ed. 3, revised and in part rewritten by A. W. Pickard-Cambridge, Oxford, 1907.

N. C. Hourmouziades, *Production and imagination in Euripides*, Athens, 1965.

J. Jones, *On Aristotle and Greek tragedy*, Oxford, 1962.

H. Kenner, *Das Theater und der Realismus in der griechischen Kunst*, Vienna, 1954.

K. Latte, 'Zur Geschichte der griechischen Tragödie in der Kaiserzeit' (*Eranos* 52 (1954), pp. 125–7).

P. E. Legrand, *Daos: Tableau de la comédie grecque pendant la période dite nouvelle* (Annales de l'Université de Lyon), 1910.

A. Lesky, 'Die Datierung der Hiketiden und der Tragiker Mesatos' (*Hermes* 82 (1954), pp. 1–13 = *Gesammelte Schriften*, Bern and Munich, 1966, pp. 220–32).

—— *Geschichte der griechischen Literatur*, ed. 2, Bern and Munich, 1963.

A. Lesky, *Die tragische Dichtung der Hellenen* (Studienhefte zur Altertumswissenschaft, 2), ed. 2, Göttingen, 1964.

P. H. J. Lloyd-Jones, 'The end of the *Seven against Thebes*' (*C.Q.* n.s. 9 (1959), pp. 80–115).

—— 'Problems of early Greek tragedy: Pratinas, Phrynichus the Gyges fragment' (*Estudios sobre la tragedia griega*, Cuaderno de la Fundación Pastor, 13, Madrid, 1966, pp. 11–33).

E. Mensching, 'Zur Produktivität der alten Komödie' (*Mus. Helv.* 21 (1964), pp. 15–49).

A. Müller, *Lehrbuch der griechischen Bühnenalterthümer*, Freiburg im B., 1886.

—— *Das attische Bühnenwesen*, ed. 2, Gütersloh, 1916.

O. Navarre, *Dionysos. Étude sur l'organisation matérielle du théâtre athénien*, Paris, 1895.

—— *Le Théâtre grec*, Paris, 1925.

H. Oellacher, 'Zur Chronologie der altattischen Komödie' (*Wiener Stud.* 38 (1916), pp. 81–157).

D. L. Page, *Actors' interpolations in Greek tragedy*, Oxford, 1934.

H. Patzer, *Die Anfänge der griechischen Tragödie*, Wiesbaden, 1962.

E. Petersen, *Die attische Tragödie als Bild- und Bühnenkunst*, Bonn, 1915.

A. W. Pickard-Cambridge, *The Theatre of Dionysus at Athens*, Oxford, 1946.

—— *Dithyramb, Tragedy and Comedy*, ed. 1, Oxford, 1927; ed. 2, revised by T. B. L. Webster, Oxford, 1962.

M. Pohlenz, 'Das Satyrspiel und Pratinas von Phleius' (*Gött. Nachr.* 1927, pp. 298–321 = *Kleine Schriften*, ii, pp. 473–96).

—— *Die griechische Tragödie*, ed. 2, 2 vols., Göttingen, 1954.

W. Ritchie, *The authenticity of the 'Rhesus' of Euripides*, Cambridge, 1964 (reviewed by E. Fraenkel in *Gnomon* 37 (1965), pp. 228–41).

C. F. Russo, *Aristofane: autore di teatro*, Florence, 1962.

W. Schmid and O. Stählin, *Geschichte der griechischen Literatur*, vols. ii–v (Handbuch der Altertumswissenschaft, VII. 1. 2–5), Munich, 1929–48.

G. M. Sifakis, *Studies in the history of Hellenistic drama*, London, 1967.

F. Susemihl, *Geschichte der griechischen Literatur in der Alexandrinerzeit*, 2 vols., Leipzig, 1891–2.

E. G. Turner, 'Dramatic representations in Graeco-Roman Egypt: how long do they continue?' (*L'Antiquité Classique* 32 (1963), pp. 120–8).

T. B. L. Webster, 'Chronological notes on Middle Comedy' (*C.Q.* n.s. 2 (1952), pp. 13–26).

—— *Studies in later Greek comedy*, Manchester, 1953.

—— 'Fourth-century tragedy and the *Poetics*' (*Hermes* 82 (1954), pp. 294–308).

—— *Greek theatre production*, London, 1956.

—— *Studies in Menander*, ed. 2, Manchester, 1960.

—— *Griechische Bühnenaltertümer* (Studienhefte zur Altertumswissenschaft, 9), Göttingen, 1963.

H. Weil, *Études sur le drame antique*, Paris, 1897.

F. Wieseler, *Theatergebäude und Denkmäler des Bühnenwesens*, Göttingen, 1851.

P. Wiesmann, *Das Problem der tragischen Tetralogie*, Abhandlung, Zurich, 1929.

U. von Wilamowitz-Moellendorff, *Analecta Euripidea*, Berlin, 1875 (reprinted 1963).

—— *Einleitung in die griechische Tragödie*, Berlin, 1907 (reprinted 1959).

—— *Aischylos: Interpretationen*, Berlin, 1914 (reprinted 1966).

E. C. Yorke, 'Mesatus Tragicus' (*C.Q.* n.s. 4 (1954), pp. 183–4).

T. Zielinski, *Tragodoumenon Libri Tres*, Krakow, 1925.

(ii) *Greek religion and the cult of Dionysus*

L. Deubner, *Griechische Feste*, Berlin, 1932.

L. R. Farnell, *The Cults of the Greek States*, vol. v, Oxford, 1909.

M. P. Nilsson, *Studia de Dionysiis atticis*, Lund, 1890.

—— *Griechische Feste von religiöser Bedeutung, mit Ausschluß der attischen*, Leipzig, 1906.

—— *Opuscula Selecta* (Skrifta utgivna av Svenska Institutet i Athen), 3 vols., Lund, 1951–60.

—— *Geschichte der griechischen Religion*, vol. i, ed. 2 (Handbuch der Altertumswissenschaft, V. 2. 1), Munich, 1955.

—— *The Dionysiac Mysteries of the Hellenistic and Roman age*, Lund, 1957.

E. Pfuhl, *De Atheniensium pompis sacris*, diss. Berlin, 1900.

A. Rumpf, 'Attische Feste—attische Vasen' (*Bonner Jahrbücher* 161 (1961), pp. 208–14).

F. T. Tausend, *Studien zu attischen Festen*, diss. Würzburg, 1920.

U. von Wilamowitz-Moellendorff, *Der Glaube der Hellenen*, ed. 2, Darmstedt, 1955. (The pagination of this reprint differs from that of the first edition.)

(iii) *Dramatic festivals: the documentary evidence*

A. Brinck, *Inscriptiones graecae ad choregiam pertinentes*, Diss. Phil. Halenses 7 (1886), pp. 71–274.

—— *De choregia quaestiones epigraphicae*, Programm, Kiel, 1906.

E. Capps, 'The catalogues of victors at the Dionysia and Lenaea (*C.I.A.* ii. 977 [= *I.G.* ii². 2325])' *A.J.P.* 20 (1899), pp. 388–405).

—— 'Chronological studies in the Greek tragic and comic poets' (*A.J.P.* 21 (1900), pp. 38–61).

—— 'The dating of some didaskalic inscriptions' (*A.J.A.* 4 (1900), pp. 74–79).

—— 'Studies in Greek agonistic inscriptions' (*T.A.P.A.* 31 (1900), pp. 112–37).

—— 'The Roman fragments of Athenian comic didascaliae' (*Class. Phil.* 1 (1906), pp. 201–20).

—— 'Epigraphical problems in the history of Attic comedy' (*A.J.P.* 28 (1907), pp. 179–99).

—— '*Misanthropoi* or *Philanthropoi*' (*Hesperia* 11 (1942), pp. 325–8).

—— 'Greek inscriptions: a new fragment of the List of Victors at the City Dionysia' (*Hesperia* 12 (1943), pp. 1–11).

W. A. Dittmer, *The fragments of Athenian comic didaskaliae found in Rome*, diss. Princeton, Leiden, 1923.

G. Jachmann, *De Aristotelis didascaliis*, diss. Göttingen, 1909.

A. Körte, 'Inschriftliches zur Geschichte der attischen Komödie' (*Rhein. Mus.* 60 (1905), pp. 425–47).

—— 'Aristoteles' Νῖκαι Διονυσιακαί' (*Class. Phil.* 1 (1906), pp. 391–8).

—— 'Bruchstücke einer didaskalischen Inschrift' (*Hermes* 73 (1938), pp. 123–7).

N. Kyparissis and W. Peek, 'Griechische Urkunden' (*Ath. Mitt.* 66 (1941), pp. 218–19).

B. D. Meritt, 'Greek inscriptions' (*Hesperia* 7 (1938), pp. 116–18).

L. Moretti, 'Sulle didascalie del teatro attico rinvenute a Roma' (*Athenaeum* 38 (1960), pp. 263–82).

E. Reisch, Art. 'Didaskaliai' (*R.E.* v (1903), cols. 394–401).

—— 'Urkunden dramatischer Aufführungen in Athen' (*Zeitschr. öst. Gymnasien* 58 (1907), pp. 289–315).

—— 'Zu den Listen der Tragödiensieger *I.G.* ii. 977 [= *I.G.* ii². 2325]' *Wiener Stud.* 34 (1912), pp. 332–41).

—— 'Eine monumentale Chronik der athenischen Theateraufführungen' (*Verhandlungen der 55. Versammlung deutscher Philologen . . . in Erlangen*, Leipzig, 1926, pp. 26–27).

B. Snell, 'Zu den Urkunden dramatischer Aufführungen' (*Gött. Nachr.* 1966, pp. 11–37).

A. Wilhelm, *Urkunden dramatischer Aufführungen in Athen* (Sonderschriften des österreichischen archäologischen Institutes in Wien, 6), Vienna, 1906.

(See also the bibliographies prefixed to the items in the Appendix to Chapter VII.)

(iv) *Dramatic festivals: topography*

American School of Classical Studies at Athens, *The Athenian Agora: a guide to the excavation and Museum*, ed. 2, Athens, 1962.

M. Carroll, 'Thucydides, Pausanias, and the Dionysium in Limnis' (*C.R.* 19 (1905), pp. 325–8).

W. Dörpfeld, 'Die Ausgrabungen am Westabhänge der Akropolis: ii. Das Lenaion oder Dionysion in den Limnai' (*Ath. Mitt.* 20 (1899), pp. 161–206).

—— 'Das Dionysion in den Limnai und das Lenaion' (*Ath. Mitt.* 46 (1921), pp. 81–104).

G. T. W. Hooker, 'The topography of the *Frogs*' (*J.H.S.* 80 (1960), pp. 112–17).

W. Judeich, *Topographie von Athen* (Handbuch der Altertumswissenschaft, III. 2. 2), ed. 2, Munich, 1931.

R. E. Wycherley, *The Athenian Agora: vol. iii: Literary and epigraphical testimonia*, Princeton, 1957.

—— 'Neleion' (*B.S.A.* 55 (1960), pp. 60–66).

THE LESSER FESTIVALS

M. Bieber, 'Eros and Dionysus on Kerch Vases' (*Hesperia*, Supplement 8: Commemorative Studies in honor of T. L. Shear (1949), pp. 31–38).

J. Boardman, 'A Greek vase from Egypt' (*J.H.S.* 78 (1958), pp. 4–12).

E. Capps, 'The "more ancient Dionysia" at Athens—Thucydides ii. 15'
(*Class. Phil.* 2 (1907), pp. 25–42).

L. Deubner, 'Dionysos und die Anthesterien' (*Jahrb. Arch.* 42 (1927), pp. 172–92).

—— 'Eine neue Lenäenvase' (*Jahrb. Arch.* 49 (1934), pp. 1–5).

B. C. Dietrich, 'A rite of swinging during the Anthesteria' (*Hermes* 89 (1961), pp. 36–50).

A. Frickenhaus, 'Der Schiffskarren des Dionysos in Athen' (*Jahrb. Arch.* 27 (1912), pp. 61–79).

—— *Lenäenvasen* (72. Berliner Winckelmannsprogramm), Berlin, 1912.

G. Q. Giglioli, 'Una nuova rappresentazione del culto attico di Dionysos' (*Annuario* 4–5 (1921–2), pp. 131–45).

K. Friis Johansen, *Eine Dithyrambosaufführung* (Arkaeologisk-kunsthistoriske Meddelelser udgivet af Det Kongelige Danske Videnshabernes Selskab, Bind 4, nr. 2), Copenhagen, 1959.

H. T. Immerwahr, 'Choes and Chytroi' (*T.A.P.A.* 77 (1946), pp. 245–60).

S. P. Karouzou, 'Choes' (*A.J.A.* 50 (1946), pp. 122–39).

K. Latte, 'Ἀσκωλιασμός' (*Hermes* 85 (1957), pp. 385–91).

M. P. Nilsson, 'Die Anthesterien und die Aiora' (*Eranos* 15 (1915), pp. 181–200 = *Opusc. Sel.* i, pp. 145–65).

—— 'Die Prozessionstypen im griechischen Kult: mit einem Anhang über die dionysischen Prozessionen in Athen' (*Jahrb. Arch.* 31 (1916), pp. 309–39 = *Opusc. Sel.* i, pp. 166–214).

—— 'Eine Anthesterien-Vase in München' (*S.B.* Munich, 1930, Heft 4 = *Opusc. Sel.* i, pp. 414–28).

—— 'Eine neue schwarzfigurige Anthesterienvase' (*Human. Vetensk. Samf. i Lund, Årsber.* 1933, iii, pp. 44–48 = *Opusc. Sel.* ii, pp. 457–62).

G. M. A. Richter, 'Two Athenian jugs' (*Bull. Metropolitan Museum,* 34 (1939), pp. 231–2).

C. F. Russo, 'Euripide e i concorsi tragici lenaici' (*Mus. Helv.* 17 (1960), pp. 165–70).

E. Simon, 'Ein Anthesterien-Skyphos des Polygnotos' (*Antike Kunst* 6 (1963), pp. 6–22).

G. van Hoorn, *Choes and Anthesteria,* Leiden, 1951.

G. V. Vitucci, 'Le rappresentazioni drammatiche nei demi attici' (*Dioniso* 7 (1939), pp. 210–25, 312–25).

W. Wrede, 'Der Maskengott' (*Ath. Mitt.* 53 (1928), pp. 66–95).

THE CITY DIONYSIA

J. T. Allen, 'On the program of the City Dionysia during the Peloponnesian War' (*University of California Publications in Classical Philology,* 12, no. 3 (1938), pp. 35–42.

E. Bethe, 'Programm und Festzug der großen Dionysien' (*Hermes* 61 (1926), pp. 459–64).

E. Capps, 'The introduction of comedy into the City Dionysia' (*Decennial Publications of the University of Chicago,* 1st series, vol. 6, no. 11 (1904), pp. 259–88).

P. Stengel, 'Die εἰσαγωγὴ τοῦ Διονύσου ἀπὸ τῆς ἐσχάρας' (*Jahrb. Arch.* 31 (1916), pp. 340–4).

See also *General (iii): Dramatic festivals: the documentary evidence.*

ACTORS AND ACTING

J. T. Allen, 'Greek acting in the fifth century' (*University of California Publications in Classical Philology*, 2, no. 15 (1916), pp. 279–89).

G. Capone, *L'arte scenica degli attori tragici greci*, Padua, 1935.

E. Capps, 'ΥΠΟΚΡΙΤΗΣ and ΤΡΑΓΩΙΔΟΣ in Schol. Dem. *de Pace* 6' (*A.J.P.* 29 (1908), pp. 206–11).

E. B. Ceadel, 'The division of parts among actors in Sophocles' *Oedipus Coloneus*' (*C.Q.* 35 (1941), pp. 139–47).

H. Devrient, *Das Kind auf der antiken Bühne*, Weimar, 1904.

G. F. Else, 'The case of the third actor' (*T.A.P.A.* 76 (1945), pp. 1–10).

—— 'ΥΠΟΚΡΙΤΗΣ' (*Wien. Stud.* 72 (1959), pp. 75–107).

G. P. Goold, 'First thoughts on the *Dyscolus*' (*Phoenix* 13 (1959), pp. 139–50).

J. G. Griffith, 'The distribution of parts in Menander's *Dyskolos*' (*C.Q.* n.s. 10 (1960), pp. 113–17).

O. Hense, 'Der Costüm- und Maskenwechsel des Chors in der griechischen Tragödie' (*Rhein. Mus.* 59 (1904), pp. 170–85).

—— *Die Modificirung der Maske in der griechischen Tragödie*, ed. 2, Freiburg im Br., 1905.

K. F. Hermann, *Disputatio de distributione personarum inter histriones in tragicis graecis*, Marburg, 1840.

B. Hunningher, *Acoustics and acting in the theatre of Dionysus Eleuthereus* (Mededelingen der Koninklijke Nederlandse Akademie van Wetenschappen, n.s. 19, no. 9, Amsterdam, 1956).

H. Kaffenberger, *Das Dreischauspielergesetz in der griechischen Tragödie*, diss. Giessen, 1911.

H. Koller, 'Hypokrisis und Hypokrites' (*Mus. Helv.* 14 (1957), pp. 100–7).

A. Lesky, 'Hypokrites' (*Studi in onore di U. E. Paoli* (Florence, 1955), pp. 469–76 = *Gesammelte Schriften*, pp. 239–46).

R. Löhrer, *Mienenspiel und Maske in der griechischen Tragödie* (Studien zur Geschichte und Kultur des Altertums, 14. 4–5), Paderborn, 1927.

J. C. B. Lowe, 'The manuscript evidence for changes of speaker in Aristophanes' (*Bull. Inst. Class. Stud.* 9 (1962), pp. 27–42).

—— 'Some questions of attribution in Aristophanes' (*Hermes* 95 (1967), pp. 53–71).

J. B. O'Connor, *Chapters in the history of actors and acting in Ancient Greece, together with a Prosopographia Histrionum Graecorum* (diss. Princeton), Chicago, 1908.

D. L. Page, 'ὑποκριτής' (*C.R.* n.s. 6 (1956), pp. 191–2).

I. Parenti, 'Per una nuova edizione della "Prosopographia Histrionum Graecorum" ' (*Dioniso* 35 (1961), pp. 5–29).

K. Rees, 'The meaning of Parachoregema' (*Class. Phil.* 2 (1907), pp. 387–400).

—— *The so-called rule of three actors in the Classical Greek Drama*, Chicago, 1908.

—— 'The number of the dramatic company in the period of the Technitae' (*A.J.P.* 31 (1910), pp. 43–54).

—— 'The three-actor rule in Menander' (*Class. Phil.* 5 (1910), pp. 291–302).

F. L. SHISLER, 'The portrayal of emotion in tragedy' (*A.J.P.* 66 (1945), pp. 377–97: cf. ibid. 69 (1948), pp. 229–31).

A. SPITZBARTH, *Untersuchungen zur Spieltechnik der griechischen Tragödie*, Winterthur, 1945.

O. J. TODD, '*Τριταγωνιστής*: a reconsideration' (*C.Q.* 32 (1938), pp. 30–38).

B. ZUCCHELLI, *ΥΠΟΚΡΙΤΗΣ: origine e storia del termine*, Genoa, 1962.

COSTUME: GENERAL

A. ALFÖLDI, 'Gewaltherrscher und Theaterkönig' (*Late Classical and Mediaeval Studies in honor of A. M. Friend*, Princeton, 1955, pp. 15–55).

W. BEARE, 'Slave costume in New Comedy' (*C.Q.* 43 (1949), pp. 30–31).

—— 'The costume of the actors in Aristophanic comedy' (*C.Q.* n.s. 4 (1954), pp. 64–75).

—— 'Aristophanic costume again' (*C.Q.* n.s. 7 (1957), pp. 184–5).

—— 'Aristophanic costume: a last word' (*C.Q.* n.s. 9 (1959), pp. 126–7).

J. D. BEAZLEY, 'Prometheus fire-lighter' (*A.J.A.* 43 (1939), pp. 618–39).

—— 'The New York "Phlyax vase" ' (*A.J.A.* 65 (1952), pp. 193–5).

—— 'Hydria-fragments in Corinth' (*Hesperia* 24 (1955), pp. 305–19).

—— 'A stamnos in the Louvre' (*Scritti in onore di Guido Libertini*, Florence, 1958, pp. 91–95).

E. BETHE, Art. 'Iulius (Pollux)' (*R.E.* x (1917), cols. 773–9).

M. BIEBER, *Das Dresdener Schauspielerrelief: ein Beitrag zur Geschichte des tragischen Costüms und der griechischen Kunst*, Bonn, 1907.

—— 'Die Herkunft des tragischen Kostüms' (*Jahrb. Arch.* 32 (1917), pp. 15–104).

—— 'Das Menander-Relief der Sammlung Stroganoff' (*Festschrift für A. Rumpf*, Krefeld, 1952, pp. 14–17).

J. BOARDMAN, 'An early actor' (*Bull. Inst. Class. Stud.* 5 (1958), pp. 6–7).

L. BREITHOLTZ, *Die dorische Farce im griechischen Mutterland vor dem 5. Jahrhundert: Hypothese oder Realität?*, Göteborg and Uppsala, 1960; Appendix II: Einige Reflexionen über das Kostüm des komischen Schauspielers (pp. 188–97).

F. BROMMER, *Satyroi*, Würzburg, 1937.

—— *Satyrspiele: Bilder griechischer Vasen*, ed. 2, Berlin, 1959.

I. BROOKE, *Costume in Greek classic drama*, London, 1962.

H. BULLE, 'Von griechischen Schauspielern und Vasenmalern' (*Festschrift für James Loeb*, Munich, 1930, pp. 5–43).

—— 'Weihebild eines tragischen Dichters' (*Corolla Curtius*, Stuttgart, 1937, pp. 151–60).

E. BUSCHOR, *Feldmäuse* (*S.B.* Munich, 1937, Heft 1).

—— 'Zwei Theaterkratere' (*Studies presented to David M. Robinson*, St. Louis, Missouri, 1951–3, vol. ii, pp. 90–95).

G. CAPUTO, 'Palcoscenico su vaso attico' (*Dioniso* 4 (1935), pp. 273–80).

332   BIBLIOGRAPHY

M. Crosby, 'Five comic scenes from Athens' (*Hesperia* 24 (1955), pp. 76–84).

H. Dierks, *De tragicorum histrionum habitu scaenico apud Graecos*, diss. Göttingen, 1883.

R. Engelmann, *Archäologische Studien zu den Tragikern*, Berlin, 1900.

J. H. Huddilston, *Greek tragedy in the light of vase-paintings*, London, 1898.

A. Körte, 'Archäologische Studien zur alten Komödie' (*Jahrb. Arch.* 8 (1893), pp. 61–93).

D. L. Page, 'An early tragedy on the fall of Croesus?' (*Proc. Camb. Phil. Soc.* n.s. 8 (1962), pp. 47–49).

G. Riccioni, 'Cratere attico a figure rosse con scena di teatro'. (*Arte antica e moderna* 5 (1959), pp. 37–42).

G. Richter, 'Department of Classical Art: accessions of 1913: vases and terracottas' (*Bull. Metr. Mus.* 9 (1914), pp. 235–6).

C. Robert, *Kentaurenkampf und Tragödienszene* (22. Hallische Winckelmannsprogramm), 1898.

A. Rumpf, 'Parrhasios' (*A.J.A.* 55 (1951), pp. 1–12).

L. Séchan, *Études sur la tragédie grecque dans ses rapports avec la céramique*, Paris, 1926 (reprinted 1967) (reviewed by A. Rumpf, *Phil. Woch.* 52 (1932), cols. 208 ff.).

F. Studniczka, 'Über das Schauspielerrelief aus dem Peiraeus' (*Mélanges G. Perrot*, Paris, 1903, pp. 307–16).

L. Talcott, 'Κούριμος παρθένος' (*Hesperia* 8 (1939), pp. 267–73).

A. D. Trendall, *Phlyax Vases* (*Bull. Inst. Class. Stud.*, Supplement 8), 1959.

—— 'Addenda to "Phlyax Vases"' (*Bull. Inst. Class. Stud.* 9 (1962), pp. 21–26).

T. B. L. Webster, 'South Italian vases and Attic drama' (*C.Q.* 42 (1948), pp. 15–21: cf. A. W. Pickard-Cambridge, ibid. 43 (1949), p. 57).

—— 'Grave relief of an Athenian poet' (*Studies presented to David M. Robinson*, Saint Louis, Missouri, 1951–3, vol. i, pp. 590–3).

—— 'Attic comic costume: a re-examination' (Ἀρχ. Ἐφ. 1953–4, ii, pp. 192–201).

—— 'Greek comic costume: its history and diffusion' (*Bull. John Rylands Library* 36 (1954), pp. 563–88).

—— 'The costume of the actors in Aristophanic comedy' (*C.Q.* n.s. 5 (1955), pp. 94–95).

—— 'Scenic notes' (*Wien. Stud.* 69 (1956), pp. 107–15).

—— 'A reply on Aristophanic costume' (*C.Q.* n.s. 7 (1957), p. 185).

—— 'Greek dramatic monuments from the Athenian Agora and Pnyx' (*Hesperia* 29 (1960), pp. 254–84).

—— *Monuments illustrating Old and Middle Comedy* (*Bull. Inst. Class. Stud.*, Supplement 9), 1960.

—— *Monuments illustrating New Comedy* (*Bull. Inst. Class. Stud.*, Supplement 11), 1961.

—— *Monuments illustrating Tragedy and Satyr Play* (*Bull. Inst. Class. Stud.*, Supplement 14), 1962.

E. Wüst, Art. 'Φλύακες' (*R.E.* xx. 1 (1941), cols. 292–306).

COSTUME: MASKS

M. Bieber, Art. 'Maske' (*R.E.* xiv. 2 (1930), cols. 2070–120).

O. Dingeldein, '*Haben die Theatermasken der Alten die Stimme verstärkt?*' (Berliner Studien für classische Philologie und Archäologie, vol. 11, no. 1), Berlin, 1890.

K. J. Dover, 'Portrait-masks in Aristophanes' (*ΚΩΜΩΙΔΟΤΡΑΓΗΜΑΤΑ: Studia Aristophanea . . . W. J. W. Koster in honorem*, Amsterdam, 1967, pp. 16–28).

H. Luschey, 'Komödien-Masken' (*Ganymed: Heidelberger Beiträge zur alten Kunstgeschichte*, Heidelberg, 1949, pp. 70–84).

C. Robert, *Die Masken der neueren attischen Komödie* (25. Hallische Winckelmannsprogramm), 1911.

A. Rumpf, 'Einige komische Masken' (*Mimus und Logos: Festgabe für Carl Niessen*, Emsdetten, 1952, pp. 163–70).

A. K. H. Simon, *Comicae Tabellae: die Szenenbilder zur griechischen neuen Komödie*, Emsdetten, 1938.

T. B. L. Webster, 'The masks of Greek comedy' (*Bull. John Rylands Library* 32 (1949), pp. 97–135).

—— 'Masks on Gnathia vases' (*J.H.S.* 71 (1951), pp. 222–32).

—— 'Notes on Pollux' list of tragic masks' (*Festschrift A. Rumpf*, Krefeld, 1952, pp. 141–50).

—— 'More dramatic masks on Gnathia vases' (*Antike Kunst* 3 (1960), pp. 30–36).

—— 'Leading slaves in New Comedy: 300 B.C.–300 A.D.' (*Jahrb. Arch.* 76 (1961), pp. 100–10).

COSTUME: FOOTWEAR

M. Bieber, Art. 'Kothurn' (*R.E.* xi (1922), cols. 1520–26).

S. P. Karouzou, 'Vases from Odos Pandrosou' (*J.H.S.* 65 (1945), pp. 38–44).

A. Körte, 'Der Kothurn im fünften Jahrhundert' (*Festschrift zur 49. Versammlung deutscher Philologen . . . in Basel*, Basel, 1907, pp. 198–212).

K. K. Smith, 'The use of the high-soled shoe or buskin in Greek tragedy of the fifth and fourth centuries B.C.' (*Harvard Stud. Class. Phil.* 16 (1905), pp. 123–64).

THE CHORUS

R. Arnoldt, *Die Chorpartien bei Aristophanes*, Leipzig, 1873.

W. Beare, '*XOPOY* in the *Plutus*: a reply to Mr. Handley' (*C.Q.* n.s. 5 (1955), pp. 49–52).

E. Buschor, *Satyrtänze und frühes Drama* (*S.B.* Munich, 1943, Heft 5).

W. M. Calder III, 'The staging of the prologue of the *Oedipus Tyrannus*' (*Phoenix* 13 (1959), pp. 121–9).

E. Capps, 'The chorus in the later Greek drama with reference to the stage question' (*A.J.A.* 11 (1895), pp. 287–325).

V. de Falco, *L'epiparodos nella tragedia greca*, Naples, 1925 (= *Studi sul teatro greco*, ed. 2, Naples, 1958, pp. 1–55).

A. D. FITTON-BROWN, 'The size of the Greek tragic chorus' (*C.R.* N.S. 7 (1957), pp. 1–4).

E. FRAENKEL, 'Der Einzug des Chors im Prometheus' (*Annali della Scuola Normale Superiore di Pisa*, Serie II, 23 (1954), pp. 269–84 = *Kleine Beiträge zur klassischen Philologie*, i, pp. 389–406).

E. W. HANDLEY, '*XOPOY* in the *Plutus*' (*C.Q.* N.S. 3 (1953), pp. 55–61).

A. KÖRTE, 'Das Fortleben des Chors im griechischen Drama' (*Neue Jahrbücher* 5 (1900), pp. 81–89).

—— '*XOPOY*' (*Hermes* 43 (1908), pp. 299–306).

W. KRANZ, *Stasimon*, Berlin, 1933.

—— Art. 'Parabasis' (*R.E.* xviii. 3 (1949), cols. 1124–6).

—— Art. 'Parodos' (*R.E.* xviii. 4 (1949), cols. 1686–94).

J. LAMMERS, *Die Doppel- und Halbchöre in der antiken Tragödie* (diss. Münster), Paderborn, 1931).

F. LEO, '*XOPOY*' (*Hermes* 43 (1908), pp. 308–11).

K. J. MAIDMENT, 'The later comic chorus' (*C.Q.* 29 (1935), pp. 1–24).

C. MUFF, *De choro Persarum fabulae Aeschyleae*, 1878.

—— *Über den Vortrag der chorischen Partien bei Aristophanes*, Halle, 1872.

—— *Der Chor in den Sieben des Aischylos*, Halle, 1882.

WALTER NESTLE, *Die Struktur des Eingangs in der attischen Tragödie* (Tübinger Beiträge zur Altertumswissenschaft 10), Stuttgart, 1930 (reprinted 1967).

D. L. PAGE, 'The chorus of Alcman's Partheneion: division of speakers in strophic choruses' (*C.Q.* 31 (1937), pp. 94–99).

E. REISCH, Art. 'Chor' (*R.E.* iii (1899), cols. 2373–404).

G .M. SIFAKIS, *Studies in the history of Hellenistic drama*, London, 1967, Appendix I: 'High stage and chorus in the Hellenistic theatre' (pp. 113–35).

DANCE IN DRAMA

M. EMMANUEL, *La danse grecque antique*, Paris, 1896 (English tr., *The antique Greek dance*, ed. 2, London, 1927).

V. FESTA, 'Sikinnis' (*Mem. del R. Accademia di Archeologia, Lettere e Belle Arte di Napoli*, 2. 2 (1918), pp. 35–78).

V. FLACH, *Der Tanz bei den Griechen*, 1881.

CHR. KIRCHHOFF, *Dramatische Orchestik der Hellenen*, Leipzig, 1898).

H. D. F. KITTO, 'The dance in Greek tragedy' (*J.H.S.* 75 (1955), pp. 36–41).

M. KOKOLAKIS, 'Pantomimus and the treatise περὶ ὀρχήσεως' (*ΠΛΑΤΩΝ* 11 (1959), pp. 3–56).

H. KOLLER, *Die Mimesis in der Antike*, Bern, 1954.

K. LATTE, *De saltationibus Graecorum capita quinque* (Religiongeschichtliche Versuche und Vorarbeiten, 13. 3), Giessen, 1913.

L. M. LAWLER, 'The Maenads' (*Mem. Am. Acad. Rome* 6 (1927), pp. 69–112).

—— *The dance in Ancient Greece*, London, 1964.

—— *The dance of the ancient Greek theatre*, Iowa, 1964.

G. PRUDHOMMEAU, *La danse grecque antique*, 2 vols., Paris, 1965.

E. ROOS, *Die tragische Orchestik im Zerrbild der altattischen Komödie*, Lund, 1951.

H. SCHNABEL, *Kordax: Archäologische Studien zur Geschichte eines antiken Tanzes und zum Ursprung der griechischen Komödie*, Munich, 1910.

H. Schreckenberg, *ΔPAMA: vom Werden der griechischen Tragödie aus dem Tanz*, diss. Würzburg, 1960.

L. Séchan, *La danse grecque antique*, Paris, 1930.

F. Weege, *Der Tanz in der Antike*, Halle, 1926.

MUSIC AND METRE IN DRAMA

S. E. Bassett, 'The place and date of the first performance of the *Persians* of Timotheus' (*Class. Phil.* 26 (1931), pp. 153–65).

V. di Benedetto, 'Responsione strofica e distribuzione delle battute in Euripide' (*Hermes* 89 (1961), pp. 298–321).

E. Bethe, 'Die griechische Tragödie und die Musik' (*Neue Jahrbücher* 19 (1907), pp. 81–95).

R. Browning, 'A Byzantine treatise on tragedy' (*ΓΕΡΑΣ: Studies presented to G. Thomson*, Acta Universitatis Carolinae 1963: Graeco-latina Pragensia II, Prague, 1963, pp. 67–81).

A. M. Dale, *The lyric metres of Greek Drama*, Cambridge, 1948.

—— 'Stasimon and Hyporcheme' (*Eranos* 48 (1950), pp. 14–20).

—— 'Greek metric 1936–1957' (*Lustrum* 2 (1957), pp. 5–51).

—— *Words, Music and Dance*, inaugural lecture, London, 1960.

I. Düring, 'Studies in musical terminology in 5th century literature' (*Eranos* 43 (1945), pp. 176–97).

S. Eitrem, L. Amundsen, and R. P. Winnington-Ingram, 'Fragments of Greek tragic texts with musical notation' (*Symbolae Osloenses* 31 (1955), pp. 1–87).

O. Gombosi, *Tonarten und Stimmungen der antiken Musik*, Copenhagen, 1939 (reprinted 1950).

M. I. Henderson, 'Ancient Greek music' (*New Oxford History of Music: I. Ancient and Oriental Music*, Oxford, 1957, pp. 336–403).

M. Imhof, 'Tetrameterszenen in der Tragödie' (*Mus. Helv.* 13 (1956), pp. 125–43).

H. Koller, *Musik und Dichtung im alten Griechenland*, Bern and Munich, 1963.

W. Krieg, 'Der trochäische Tetrameter bei Euripides' (*Philologus* 91 (1936), pp. 42–51).

G. A. Longman, 'The musical papyrus: Euripides, *Orestes* 332–40' (*C.Q.* n.s. 12 (1962), pp. 61–66).

P. Maas, Art. 'Melanippides' (*R.E.* xv. 1 (1932), cols. 422–3).

—— Art. 'Timotheos (9)' (*R.E.*, zweite Reihe, vi (1937), cols. 1331–7).

—— Art. 'Philoxenos' (*R.E.* xx. 1 (1941), cols. 192–4).

—— *Greek metre* (trans. P. H. J. Lloyd-Jones), Oxford, 1962.

J. F. Mountford, 'Greek music in the papyri and inscriptions' (*New Chapters in Greek literature*, second series, Oxford, 1929, pp. 146–83).

—— and R. P. Winnington-Ingram, Art. 'Music' (*Oxford Classical Dictionary*, 1949, pp. 584–91).

F. Perusino, 'Il problema della paracataloghé nei tetrametri giambici catalettici della commedia greca' (*Quaderni Urbinati di cultura classica* 1 (1966), pp. 9–14).

E. Pöhlmann, *Griechische Musikfragmente* (Erlanger Beiträge zur Sprach- und Kunstwissenschaft, 8), Nuremberg, 1960.

K. Schlesinger, *The Greek aulos*, London, 1939.

O. Schroeder, *Aeschyli cantica*, ed. 2, Leipzig, 1916.

—— *Sophoclis cantica*, ed. 2, Leipzig, 1923.

—— *Euripidis cantica*, ed. 2, Leipzig, 1928.

—— *Aristophanis cantica*, ed. 2, Leipzig, 1930.

B. Snell, *Griechische Metrik* (Studienhefte zur Altertumswissenschaft, 1), ed. 3, Göttingen, 1962.

W. Vetter, Art. 'Musik' (*R.E.* xvi (1935), cols. 823–76).

M. Wegner, *Das Musikleben der Griechen*, Berlin, 1949.

—— *Musikgeschichte in Bildern*: Band ii, Lieferung 4: *Griechenland*, Leipzig, 1963.

J. W. White, *The verse of Greek comedy*, London, 1912.

U. von Wilamowitz-Moellendorff, *Griechische Verskunst*, Berlin, 1921 (reprinted 1958).

R. P. Winnington-Ingram, 'Ancient Greek Music, 1932–57' (*Lustrum* 3 (1968), pp. 5–57).

THE AUDIENCE

M. Lang and M. Crosby, *The Athenian Agora: vol. x: Weights, Measures and Tokens*, Princeton, 1964, pp. 76–82.

B. B. Rogers, Introduction to Aristophanes' '*Ecclesiazousae*', London, 1902, pp. xxix–xxxv.

P. T. Stevens, 'Euripides and the Athenians' (*J.H.S.* 76 (1956), pp. 87–94).

THE 'ARTISTS OF DIONYSUS'

G. Daux, *Delphes au IIe et au Ier siècle* (Bibliothèque des Écoles françaises d'Athènes et de Rome, fasc. 140), Paris, 1936.

R. Flacelière, *Les Aitoliens à Delphes* (Bibliothèque des Écoles françaises d'Athènes et de Rome, fasc. 143), Paris, 1937.

P. Foucart, *De collegiis scaenicorum artificum apud Graecos*, diss. Paris, 1873.

W. Hahland, 'Der Fries des Dionysostempels in Teos' (*Wiener Jahreshefte* 38 (1950), pp. 66–109).

U. Kahrstedt, 'Zu den delphischen Soterienurkunden' (*Hermes* 72 (1937), pp. 369–403).

G. Klaffenbach, *Symbolae ad historiam collegiorum artificum bacchiorum*, diss. Berlin, 1914.

O. Lüders, *Die dionysischen Künstler*, Berlin, 1873.

J. B. O'Connor, *Chapters in the history of actors and acting in Ancient Greece* (diss. Princeton), Chicago, 1908.

J. Oehler, *Epigraphische Beiträge zur Geschichte der dionysischen Künstler*, Programm, Vienna, 1908.

F. Poland, *De collegiis artificum dionysiacorum*, Programm, Dresden, 1895.

—— *Geschichte des griechischen Vereinswesens*, Leipzig, 1909, pp. 129–47.

—— Art. 'Technitai' (*R.E.*, zweite Reihe, v (1934), cols. 2473–558).

E. Reisch, *De musicis Graecorum certaminibus capita quattuor*, diss. Vienna, 1885.

G. M. Sifakis, *Studies in the history of Hellenistic drama*, London, 1967: Appendix II; 'Organization of festivals and the Dionysiac guilds' (pp. 136–71).

E. Ziebarth, *Das griechische Vereinswesen*, Leipzig, 1896, pp. 74–89.

CONCORDANCE

*D.F.A.*²	=	this book (references to figures)
*D.F.A.*¹	=	this book, first edition (references to figures)
B.D.	=	Bieber, *Denkmäler*
*B.H.T.*¹	=	Bieber, *History of the Greek and Roman Theater*, 1939 (references to figures)
*B.H.T.*²	=	Bieber, *History of the Greek and Roman Theater*, 1961 (references to figures)
G.T.P.	=	Webster, *Greek Theatre Production*
(W)	=	Webster
M.I.T.S.	=	*Monuments illustrating Tragedy and Satyr Play*
PH	=	Trendall, *Phlyax Vases*
O.M.C.	=	*Monuments illustrating Old and Middle Comedy*
M.I.N.C.	=	*Monuments illustrating New Comedy*

Numbers in brackets indicate other copies of the same terracotta

*D.F.A.*²	*D.F.A.*¹	*B.D.*	*B.H.T.*¹	*B.H.T.*²	*G.T.P.*	(W)
1	1a	..	..	..	..	..
2	1b	..	..	..	..	..
3	1c	..		..	..	..
4	2a	..	..	..	..	..
5	2b	..	..	..	..	..
6	2c	..	..	..	..	..
7	3	..	..	..	..	..
8	4	..	..	..	..	..
9	5	..	..	..	..	..
10	..	..	..	218	..	..
11	6	33	140	58	..	..
12	7a	33	141	..	..	..
13	7b	33	139	56	..	..
14	8	..	33	59	..	..
15	..	..	..	..	..	..
16	9	..	..	216	..	..
17	10	..	..	..	..	..
18	11b, 12	..	..	..	..	..
19	11a	..	..	..	..	..
20	14	..	..	..	..	..
21	13	..	..	..	..	..
22	16	..	17	25	..	..
23	15	..	..	..	..	..
24	17	..	..	..	..	..

D.F.A.²	D.F.A.¹	B.D.	B.H.T.¹	B.H.T.²	G.T.P.	(W) O.M.C.
25	18	..	..	215	B31	AS2
26	19	..	..	..	..	..
27	20	2	167	231	..	..
28	21	..	..	..	..	..
						M.I.T.S.
29	22	..	..	..	..	..
30	23	..	10	18	..	AS8
31	..	..	..	..	..	..
32	25	..	..	74	A4	AV9
33	..	..	..	..	..	AV10
34	39	..	108	90	A7	AV20
35	..	..	..	..	A6	AV15
36	..	..	..	..	..	AV13
37	..	..	..	..	..	..
38	..	..	..	..	A2	AV6
39	..	..	..	..	..	AV3
40	..	..	..	15	A3	AV14
41	..	..	..	..	..	AV16
42	..	39	..	16	A5	AV17
43	..	..	..	..	..	AV18
44	..	..	..	..	..	AV19
45	30	..	..	27	..	AV23
46	31	..	..	28	..	AV24
47	32	..	..	..	..	..
48	33	..	..	..	..	..
49	28	34	20	31–33	A9	AV25
50	40	..	..	34–35	A12	AV27
51	26	41	66–67	113	A11	AS1
52	..	..	..	..	A20	AS4
53	..	..	..	..	..	AV38
54	34–35	..	216	306	A34	GV3
55	43	44	217	302	A57	NP33
56	45	27	35	64	A21	AS9
57	..	..	..	..	..	AT7
58	..	..	..	301	..	AB1
59	174	..	..	..	..	..
60	164–5	40	61–64	110–11	A10	AV34
61	..	..	..	..	..	..
62	162	..	43	80	..	..
63	66	59	533	799	..	II1
64	194	..	1	1–2	A78	ES1
65	195	..	..	..	..	..
66	204	..	57	104	..	..
67	202	..	..	..	..	AV11
68	198	..	..	..	..	..

D.F.A.²	D.F.A.¹	B.D.	B.H.T.¹	B.H.T.²	G.T.P.	(W)
69	196	..	..	..	..	..
70	203	..	..	..	..	..
71	197	..	..	..	..	..
72	199	..	..	..	..	..
73	200	..	..	..	..	..
74	201	..	..	..	..	..
75	..	..	..	..	..	PH8
76	..	..	..	202	B1	PH1
77	..	..	..	..	B2	PH3
78	80	97	121	184	B4	PH6
79	..	..	..	..	B3	PH2
80	..	..	..	..	..	PH4
81	..	..	..	..	B8	PH5
82	..	..	..	..	..	PH10
83	..	..	..	..	..	PH11
84	..	..	..	209	B6	PH12
85	..	..	..	..	B9	PH7
86	..	..	..	..	B7	PH13
87	..	..	..	210	B5	PH9
						O.M.C.
88	89	..	..	201	B10	AS1
89	85 (141)	..	122	185	B11a	AT8
90	(140)	(95)	123	186	B11b	AT9
91	84	..	124	187	B11c	AT10
92	..	..	125	188 (199)	B11d	AT11
93	86	..	126	189 (243)	B11e	AT12
94	87	(82)	127 (99)	190 (200)	B11f (76)	AT13
95	88	..	128	191	B11g	AT14
96	..	..	129	192	B12a	AT15
97	..	..	130	193	B12b	AT16
98	..	..	131	194	B12c	AT17
99	..	..	132	195	B12d	AT18
100	..	..	133	196 (150)	B12e	AT19
101	..	..	134	197	B12f	AT20
102	..	..	135	198	B12g	AT21
103	..	..	..	181	B31a	AS3
104	..	..	..	..	..	AS4
105	..	..	381	512	B33	PH78
106	..	101	368	484	B60	PH59
107	..	112	366–7	494	B63	PH80
						M.I.N.C.
108	..	..	..	..	C64	ET1
109	93	129	223	317	C49	IS10
110	94	130	225	324	C48	NS25
111	..	..	..	..	..	AT2
112	106	146	..	386	C65	MT9

D.F.A.[2]	D.F.A.[1]	B.D.	B.H.T.[1]	B.H.T.[2]	G.T.P.	(W)
113	113	141	230	338	C66	MT20
114	114	(142)	(241)	(341)	..	MT1
115	115	164	255	343	..	ZT2
116	50	57	207	293	C62	DT17
117	49	56	205	292	C68	MT17
118	..	..	..	..	..	AT4
119	120	144	249	372	C69	MT19
120	119	145	250	374	C12	NT6
121	128	153	234	396	..	MT27
122	121	89b	..	152	..	BT8
123	..	..	..	..	C70	MT4
124	126	..	289	408	..	IT13
125	129	154	235	397	..	MT30
126	53c	166	273	380	C72	ZS2
127	136	..	..	..	..	YT4
128	146	171	275	348	..	UT79
129	..	..	276	350	C2	AT15
130	147	..	278	352	..	ZT10
131	..	156	244	353	C11	NT12
132	..	..	..	..	..	AV12
133	..	..	..	..	..	BT7
134	148	173	282	358	C13	IT29
135	153	174	280	361	..	NS20
136	156	177	284	365	C51	IS40
137	55b	67	..	363	C67b	XT22
138	157	..	..	..	C74	ZT38
139	152	175	281	356	C31	NS13
140	..	..	..	..	..	..
141	207	157	243	..	..	..

INDEXES

(i) MODERN SCHOLARS

(ii) GREEK WORDS AND PHRASES

(iii) GENERAL

SELECT ADDENDA

We have tried to confine ourselves to topics on which new evidence has appeared: there have been fresh discussions of many matters without that advantage.

THE LENAIA

Two substantial new pieces of evidence bear on the relative importance of the Lenaia and the Dionysia.

1. A papyrus commentary on a comic text (P. Oxy. 2737; Austin, *Comicorum Graecorum fragmenta in papyris reperta* no. *56; Luppe, *APF* 21 (1971),93 ff.; *GGA* 227, 1975, 183–5) preserves a new fragment of Eratosthenes: φ[ησὶ δὲ] καὶ Ἐρατοσθένης περὶ Πλάτωνος ὅτι ἔως μὲν [ἄλ]λοις ἐδίδου τὰς κωμωιδίας, εὐδοκίμει, δι' αὐτοῦ δὲ πρῶτον διδάξας τοὺς Ῥαβδούχους καὶ γενόμενος τέταρτος ἀπεώσθη πάλιν εἰς τοὺς Ληναϊκούς. That plays of Plato were produced by others was already known (p. 85), but we had had no evidence that there was ever a category of poets who were or were not entitled to compete at the Dionysia; for a possible parallel for actors see p. 94. It now seems that, at the end of the fifth or the beginning of the fourth century, there was some kind of barrier that competitors at the Dionysia had to cross and that those entitled to compete at the Lenaia were on a lower level. Luppe acutely suggested that an earlier line of the papyrus might be restored τὸ δὲ Ληναϊκ[ὸν οὐχ ὁμ]οίως ἔνδοξο[ν δοκεῖ εἶναι]. The distinction drawn on p. 41 about the prestige of comedy and tragedy at the Lenaia is thus modified.

2. A new fragment of *IG* ii² 2319, the record of tragedies at the Lenaia (p. 109), has been found in the Agora (Camp, *Hesperia* 40 (1971), 302–7); we omit the very slight traces of another column to the left.

$$
\begin{array}{ll}
& [ὑπε:] \; Ἡφαι[στίων] \\
& [Νι]κόμαχος \; [τρί:] \\
& Ἀμυμώνηι \; T \, - \, - \\
& ὑπε \; vacat \\
& ὑπο: \; Ἡφαιστίω[ν \; ἐνίκα] \\
364\text{–}3 \quad & ἐπὶ \; Τιμοκράτου[ς \; poet] \\
& Οἰνοπίωνι \; Ἑκα \, - \, - \\
& ὑπε: \; Ἄρηξις \\
& Θεοδωρίδης \; δεύ: \\
& Μηδείαι \; Φαέθοντ[ι] \\
& ὑπε: \; Ἀνδροσθέ[νης] \\
& Κλεαίνετος \; τ[ρί:] \\
& Ὑψιπύληι \; Φ \, - \, -
\end{array}
$$

$$\underline{\upsilon\pi\epsilon}:\ ^{"}I\pi\pi\alpha\rho[\chi os]$$
$$\underline{\upsilon\pi o}:\ ^{"}A\rho\eta\xi[\iota s\ \dot{\epsilon}\nu\dot{\iota}\kappa\alpha]$$
$$363\text{-}2\quad \dot{\epsilon}\pi\dot{\iota}\ X\alpha\rho\iota\kappa[\lambda\epsilon\dot{\iota}\delta ov\ poet]$$

The first point established seems to be that the Lenaia had three tragic competitors at this period, though the number of plays they produced was still two. The new evidence about plays and poets is perhaps less interesting than that about actors. We had known very little of Kleainetos, nothing of Theodorides, and it seems very unlikely that this is the fifth-century Nikomachos (pp. 99, 258); *Oinopion*, by an unknown, is the only new tragic title. But the discovery of a new actor, Hephaistion, with a dated victory in 365/4, has more far-reaching consequences. The list of tragic actors at the Lenaia (p. 115) should now take the following form:

$$^{"}I\pi\pi\alpha\rho\chi os\ \Gamma\ |$$
$$^{"}A\mu\epsilon\iota\nu\dot{\iota}\alpha s\ |$$
$$[^{'}A\nu]\delta\rho o\sigma\theta\dot{\epsilon}\nu\eta s\ |$$
$$[N\epsilon o]\pi\tau\dot{o}\lambda\epsilon\mu os\ |$$
$$[\Theta\epsilon\tau\tau]\langle a\rangle\lambda\dot{o}s\ ||$$
$$[^{"}A\rho\eta\xi\iota]s\ ||$$
$$[^{'}H\phi\alpha\iota\sigma]\tau\dot{\iota}\omega\nu\ |$$
$$[\,.\,.\,5\,.\,.\,]\dot{a}\delta\eta s\ |$$

With Hephaistion's victory placed in 365/4 and Arexis' second in 364/3, it becomes certain that Neoptolemos' victory was in 368/7 or earlier and likely (we have to assume a missing cross-bar to the alpha) that Thettalos' first victory was not later than 367/6. This is considerably earlier than the bulk of the evidence for these major figures and allows Camp's conclusion that by the 360s the Lenaia was a training ground for young actors who, upon gaining some success, moved on to more attractive fields.

　　More evidence for the Lenaia comes from an early fourth-century herm-base outside the Stoa Basileios among other texts connected with the *basileus* (Shear, *Hesperia* 40, (1971) 256–7; Edmonson, *Hesperia* Suppl. 19 (1982), 48–50; *SEG* XXXII 239; we doubt Edmonson's attempt to date the text precisely to 403/2)

$$^{'}O\nu\dot{\eta}\sigma\iota\pi\pi os\ Ai\tau\dot{\iota}o\ K\eta\phi\iota\sigma\iota\epsilon\dot{v}s\ \beta\alpha\sigma\iota\lambda\epsilon\dot{v}s\ \dot{a}\nu\dot{\epsilon}\theta\eta\kappa\epsilon[\nu]\ \cdot$$
$$o[\dot{\iota}\delta]\epsilon\ ^{'}O\nu\eta\sigma\dot{\iota}\pi\pi o\ \beta\alpha\sigma\iota\lambda\epsilon\dot{v}o\nu\tau os\ \chi o\rho\eta\gamma\dot{o}\nu\tau\epsilon s\ \dot{\epsilon}\nu\dot{\iota}\kappa\omega\nu\ \cdot$$

κωμωιδῶν	τραγωιδῶν
Σωσικράτης ἐχορήγε χαλκοπώλης	Στρατόνικος ἐχορήγε Στράτωνος
Νικοχάρης ἐδίδασκε	Μεγακλείδης ἐδίδασκε

We have a firm date of 388 for one play by Nikochares (Hyp. Ar. *Plut.*); Megakleides was previously unknown. For the choregia of the metic Sosikrates, cf. p. 41; there are now more instances later in the century (*Hesperia* 37 (1968), 376 with 380). That comedy is recorded before tragedy at the Lenaia should modify previous ideas about the rigidity of Athenian practice; we strongly suspect that the Monument of Xenokles (p. 120) should be re-attributed to the Dionysia.

THE RURAL DIONYSIA

IG ii² 3091 (pp. 54–6) is revised and discussed by Luppe, *APF* 19 (1969), 147–51, 22 (1973), 211–12; cf. *TGF* I DID B 5. We should have considered the possibility, perhaps quite strong, that the Telepheia concerned was by the younger Sophokles and the occasion for this dedication. Another rural dedication which may commemorate a city victory is a base for a bronze statue from Varkiza (Anagyrous?) (Mitsos, 'Ἀρχ. 'Εφ. 1965 [1967], 163–7; *TGF* I DID B 2), probably from the 430s: Σωκράτης ἀνέθηκεν· Εὐριπίδης ἐδίδασκεν· τραγωιδοί (14 names follow). If τραγωιδοί means the members of the chorus, it is not clear why there are only fourteen; the alternative might be to attribute the text to the Rural Dionysia and assume a reduced team, including actors.

Evidence for rural theatres has continued to expand; for bibliography, see D. Whitehead, *The Demes of Attica* (1986) 219, in the course of a valuable discussion (212–22) of the evidence for the Rural Dionysia.

THE CITY DIONYSIA

The evidence of P. Oxy. 2737 (above) that, during the career of the comic poet Platon, it was possible to come fourth in comedy at the City Dionysia, is the starting-point for a reconsideration of the evidence for the programme during the Peloponnesian War by Luppe, *Philologus* 116 (1972), 54–75, who argues (contrast pp. 65–6) that there continued to be five comedies during the War and that they had a day to themselves.

The evidence (p. 75 with n. 1) that there were ten choruses of men and ten of boys is supplemented for the second half of the fourth century by lists in *Hesperia* 37 (1968), 375 with 378–9; it is interesting that, for the first time in an official document, the dithyrambic contests are referred to as κυκλίοις (cf. Ar. *Fr.* 156.10 K.–A., Aeschin. III 232).

Changes in the third-century programme are now a little clearer. A decree in honour of Kallias of Sphettos of 270/69 has the earliest known example of the formula καὶ ἀνειπεῖν τὸν στέφανον Διονυσίων τῶν μεγάλων τραγωιδῶν τῶι ἀγῶνι τῶι καινῶι (*SEG* XXVIII 60. 92–4); texts as late as 285/4 and 283/2 (*IG* ii² 654. 41, 657. 61) still simply have Διονυσίων τῶν μεγάλων τραγωιδῶν τῶι ἀγῶνι. The new formula seems to mean 'at the contest of new tragedies' (by the end of the third century, the phrase καινοῖς τραγωιδοῖς replaces it), and the change of formula surely suggests that a contrast is now being made with a newly-introduced contest of old plays. We are now more confident than we were (p. 41 n. 11) that the third-century inscription showing contests of old plays (pp. 123–4) refers to the City Dionysia. A new, very fragmentary, text (*Ath. Mitt.* 93 (1978), 109–18) seems to have given a full record of such a contest in the late third or early second century. For a discussion of this point, see

Peppas-Delmousou, *Proceedings of the Eighth Epigraphical Congress 1982* I (1984) 65–8.

APPENDIX TO CHAPTER II

I G ii² 2323 is re-edited by C. A. P. Ruck, *IG* ii² 2323: *The List of the Victors in Comedies at the Dionysia* (Leiden 1967). Two new fragments, one substantial, of *I G* ii² 2325 are published by D. Peppas-Delmousou, *Ath. Mitt.* 92 (1977), 229–43; they appear to expand the list of known hellenistic comic poets very considerably. The texts from Rome (pp. 120–2) are re-edited by Moretti, *Inscriptiones Graecae Urbis Romae* 215–20; some details are picked out and expanded by Luppe, *ZPE* 8 (1971), 123–8; cf. A. M. Wilson, *CR* n.s. 23 (1973), 126–7, who proposes Ekphantides as an alternative to Kallias in the first lines of *I.G.* xiv. 1097.

THE COSTUMES

Here we must be selective. Not all the discussion has confined itself to representations which pass the fairly rigid criteria of our main text.

Erika Simon, in a full discussion of early representation of satyr-plays (Donna Kurtz and Brian Sparkes edd., *The Eye of Greece* [1982], 123–48), adds a kalpis in Würzburg, probably by the Leningrad Painter, whom we have already seen occupied with satyrs on Fig. 40. Five men, white-haired and bearded, with diadems, sceptres, and ornate cloaks are seated on stools. Before them the Sphinx crouches on a rock. These elders are not all they seem at first sight, since they have identical snub-noses and pointed ears. She has argued (*SB Heidelberg* 1981) that they are really satyrs who have seized the insignia belonging to the true Theban council. The closeness in date to Aeschylus' satyr-play *Sphinx* of 467 (p. 79) is undeniably tempting.

Simon's general conclusion is that the clothing repertory of satyr-play came from comedy. We excluded (p. 210) early representations of comedy from this book on the grounds that they had already been discussed in *Dithyramb, Tragedy and Comedy*, and can hardly return to the matter here. The gap is filled by a listing of the early evidence, much expanded and now possibly extending beyond 480, by J. R. Green, *Greek Vases in the J. Paul Getty Museum* ii (1985), 95–118. But the main purpose of Green's article is to publish the first solid piece of evidence for the costumes of the Aristophanic theatre. An Attic red-figure calyx-crater in Malibu of the late fifth century shows, in the centre of its reverse, a youth facing right, naked but for a short cloak, holding a spear in his left hand and a Corinthian helmet in his right. Facing him is another man, dressed in a himation, with straggly hair and a curly staff. On the left, a woman, dressed in chiton and himation, extends her left hand. Nothing marks this scene as theatrical, but there can be no doubt about the obverse, also illustrated in Sommerstein's edition of *Birds*. Here we have a 'flute-player', frontal, between two dancing men dressed as birds. The flute-player is bearded and wears an elaborately-decorated chiton; unusually, it appears to have only one

sleeve. The dancing men have spherical heads with hooked beaks and pronounced crests; these are not shown as masks, but have 'melted'. They wear
all-over tights, terminating at wrist and ankle, wings, spurs and shoes. But
over the tights, they have short drawers with tails and erect phalloi. Tights and
drawers are ornamented with circles; the drawers have an ornamental circle
on the hip. We have, of course, seen these tights before (Figs. 38, 44, 45, 46,
and, more elaborately, 49) and had assumed them to be native to satyr-play.
Despite Simon's arguments, this must be right; comedy is here adopting an
element from satyr-play (or from something yet older). It further follows that
at least some fifth-century comic choruses were phallic. Identification is more
difficult. There is no chronological obstacle to the obvious hypothesis, that this
is a representation of Aristophanes' *Birds* of 414, and this is the view that Green
proposes. The birds are indeed identically clothed; scholars have on the whole
assumed that the chorus-men of *Birds* and Eupolis, *Poleis*, had distinguishing
features (p. 219; see Sommerstein, op. cit. 6). The reverse can hardly be
brought into *Birds*, in which Peisetaerus and Euelpides are unambiguously old
men (lines 255, 320). Further difficulties are pointed out by Taplin, *Proc.
Camb. Phil. Soc.* n.s. 33 (1987) 93–6, who suggests that the actors are dressed as
fighting cocks, possibly the two Logoi of *Clouds*, whom a scholiast on line 889
says were shown δίκην ὀρνέων διαμαχόμενοι.

New evidence for dithyramb may come from a red-figure column-krater in
Basel of shortly after 480 (Schmidt. *Antike Kunst* 10 [1967], 70–11). On the reverse, two naked satyrs dance round a volute-crater, wreathed in ivy. On the
obverse, three pairs of bare-footed young men dance with raised arms before
an altar, dressed with twigs and ribbons. They are singing, but the letters in
front of their mouths are hardly legible. Over their chitons they wear elaborately decorated and fringed sleeveless jerkins, one of which has a running satyr
on the shoulder; they also have diadems, which reminds us of Demosthenes' dithyrambic chorus (p. 77). Behind the altar stands a bearded and cloaked man
with wreathed hair. He is also singing and may be the *didaskalos*; strictly, it will
only be that or a similar interpretation which will take us into the world of the
theatre. There are those who insist (Schefold ap. Simon, *Ancient Theatre*, 9)
that the altar is not an altar but a tomb, and, if the identical faces of the
dancers imply masks, the possibility of a tragic ghost-raising scene cannot be
excluded. Wherever the truth may lie here, some form of dressed dithyramb is
attested for the Panathenaia (*ARV²* 1172 no. 8; Webster, *Greek Chorus*, (1970),
28, 133 and fig. 9).

It will be seen that, if the evidence is now more copious, it is also more confused. We are even less confident than we were about the truth of the universally held opinion that the Pronomos Vase refers to satyr-play. The stress on
the musicians as opposed to the actors is puzzling for drama, and, even though
there is as yet no clear evidence for masks in dithyramb, the question is perhaps more open than is normally thought.

The οἰκουρὸν γρᾴδιον (p. 227) is at last convincingly represented by a mask
from Knossos (*B.S.A.* 67, (1972) 278 no. 104 with pl. 53*b*).

Pöhlmann, *Museum Helveticum* 38 (1981), 129–46, *Antike und Abendland* 32 (1986), 20–32, has argued from the surviving fragments of the fifth-century *proedria* that the fifth-century theatre was rectangular and that the evidence for chorus-movement needs reconsideration.

The theatre-seats of the imperial period (p. 269) are studied by Maas, *Die Proedrie in dem Dionysos-Theater*.

A serious omission in the book is the absence of any section on political censorship in the Athenian theatre, and at least a collection of the evidence may be helpful. The only contemporary text, [Xen.] *Ath. Pol.* 2. 18, κωμῳδεῖν δ' αὖ καὶ κακῶς λέγειν τὸν μὲν δῆμον οὐκ ἐῶσιν ... need not imply any formal ban. The most explicit passage is the scholion on *Acharnians* 67: ἐπ' Εὐθυμένους .... οὗτος ὁ ἄρχων ἐφ' οὗ κατελύθη τὸ ψήφισμα τὸ περὶ τοῦ μὴ κωμῳδεῖν ⟨......⟩, γραφὲν ἐπὶ Μορυχίδου (440/39). ἴσχυσε δὲ ἐκεῖνόν τε τὸν ἐνιαυτὸν καὶ δύο τοὺς ἑξῆς ἐπὶ Γλαυκίνου τε καὶ Θεοδώρου, μεθ' οὓς ἐπ' Εὐθυμένους (437/6) κατελύθη. The need to assume a lacuna after κωμῳδεῖν and make the ban less than complete arises from *I G* xiv 1097.4 and 13 (p. 121) which listed plays for this period. Other timings for this ban were current in antiquity. Σ Ael. Aristid. or. 3, 8 L.–B. (cf. *Poetae Comici Graeci* V 332, test. iii) κατηγορήσαντος δὲ τοῦ Κλέωνος 'Αριστοφάνους ὕβρεως, ἐτέθη νόμος μηκέτι ἐξεῖναι κωμῳδεῖν ὀνομαστί. ἄλλοι δὲ λέγουσιν ὅτι ἐκωμῴδουν ὀνομαστὶ τοὺς ἄνδρας μέχρις Εὐπόλιδος (cf. Tzetzes, *PCG* ibid. test. iv). περιεῖλε δὲ τοῦτο 'Αλκιβιάδης ὁ στρατηγὸς καὶ ῥήτωρ. Less precise echoes of these statements appear in the anonymous περὶ κωμῳδίας: xviii 38 (cf. xxi 55 ff.) ... οὐ μετὰ πολὺν χρόνον οἱ πλούσιοι καὶ οἱ ἄρχοντες οὐ βουλόμενοι κωμῳδεῖσθαι, ἦρξαντο κωλύειν τοὺς κωμικοὺς τοῦ φανερῶς καὶ ὀνομαστὶ ἐλέγχειν τοὺς ἀδικοῦντας; xix 65 ψήφισμα ἔθετο 'Αλκιβιάδης μηκέτι φανερῶς, ἀλλὰ συμβολικῶς κωμῳδεῖν; xxviii 65 ψηφίσματος γὰρ γενομένου χορηγικοῦ, ὥστε μὴ ὀνομαστὶ κωμῳδεῖν τινα. Σ Ar. *Nub.* 31 ἐπεὶ οὖν τοὺς 'Αθηναίους πρότερον κωμῳδεῖν τὸν ἄρχοντα ὁ νόμος ἐκώλυεν ... is slightly different. As far as we can see, the most certain fact about Cleon's attack on Aristophanes for the *Babylonians* is that Cleon's charges included the words ξένων παρόντων τὴν πόλιν κακῶς λέγει (Ar. *Ach.* 503); that does not tell us under what law the prosecution, if there was a prosecution, was brought. In view of the likelihood that some of this material may simply derive from inferences from comic passages about Aristophanes and Cleon, or Eupolis and Alcibiades, the matter must remain open. We incline to think that there was some kind of formal prescription between 440 and 437; whether there was any reimposition we can hardly know. See also MacDowell, *The Law in Classical Athens*, 128–9.

THE ARTISTS OF DIONYSUS

That *I G* vii 2413–14 (p. 289; Sherk, *Roman Documents from the Greek East* no. 44; Roesch, *Études Béotiennes* pp. 198–202) is a letter from Mummius is confirmed by an unpublished dossier from Argos, which will throw a certain amount of new light on the Isthmian–Nemean guild and their base at Argos in the second half of the second century. Very substantial information about festival-organization in the imperial period will be provided by Michael Wörrle's forthcoming publication of an inscription from Oenoanda. For a complete prosopography of Greek theatre and music, see I. E. Stephanis, Διονυσιακοὶ Τεχνῖται (Heraklion, 1988).

PLATES

Fig. 1

Fig. 2

Fig. 3

Choes. Children at Anthesteria

Fig. 4

Fig. 5

Fig. 6

Choes. Children and youth at Anthesteria

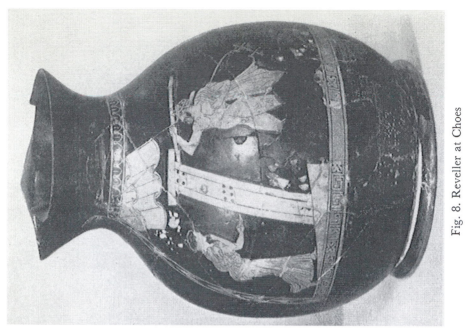

Fig. 8. Reveller at Choes

Fig. 7. Reveller at Choes

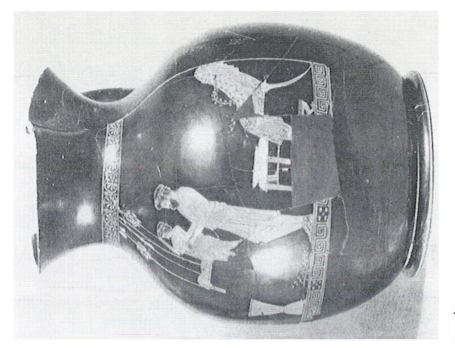

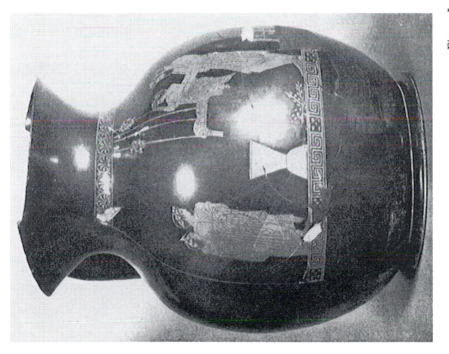

Fig. 9. Infant on swing

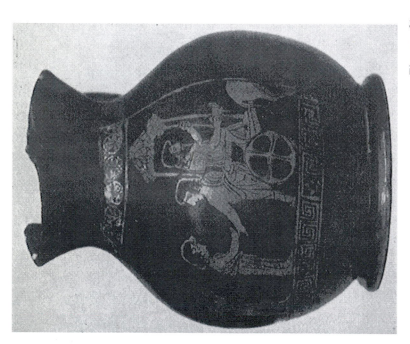

Fig. 10. Chous in New York

Fig. 12

Fig. 13

Dionysiac processions

Fig. 14. Dionysus at sea

Fig. 15. Dithyrambic chorus and flute-player
Bell-krater in Copenhagen

Fig. 17a, b. Kylix from Vulci

Fig. 17c. Kylix from Vulci

a

b

Fig. 18. Stamnos from Gela

Fig. 19. Stamnos in Villa Giulia

Fig. 20a. Stamnos in Warsaw

Fig. 20*b*. Stamnos in Warsaw

Fig. 21. Stamnos in Paris

a

b

Fig. 22. Stamnos from Nuceria

Fig. 24. Chous in Athens

Fig. 23. Stamnos in London

Fig. 25. Monument from Aixone

Fig. 26. View of Theatre at Thorikos

Fig. 28. Theatre at Rhamnous

Fig. 29. Theatre at Ikarion

a

b

Fig. 30. The monument of Lysikrates

Fig. 31. Victory tripod

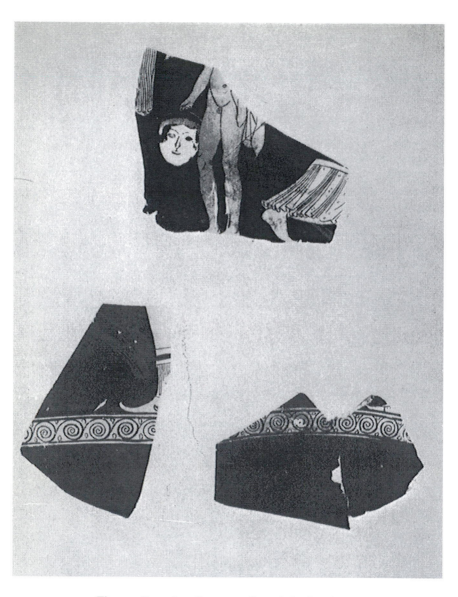

Fig. 32. Oenochoe fragments from Athenian Agora

Fig. 33. Actor (?) and chorus-man
Bell-krater from Valle Pega

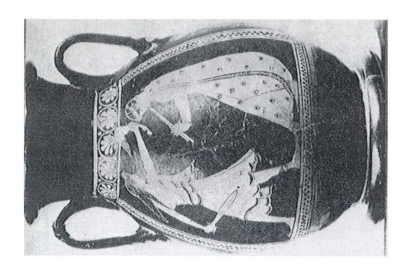

Fig. 35. Maenad and flute-player. Pelike in Berlin

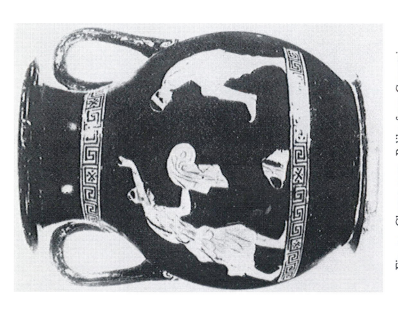

Fig. 34. Chorus-men. Pelike from Cervetri

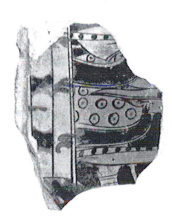

Fig. 36. Hydria fragments in Corinth

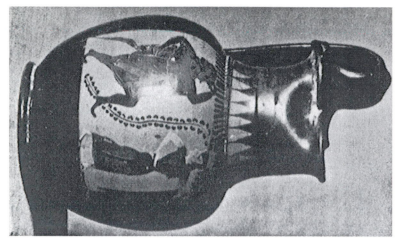

Fig. 37. Oenochoe in London

Fig. 38. Satyr chorus-man. Cup from Vulci

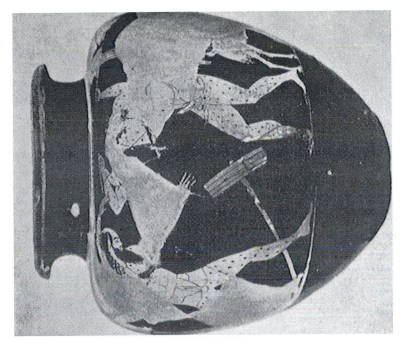

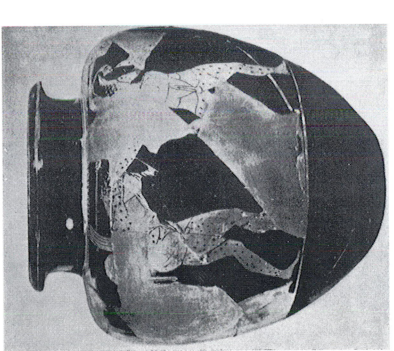

Fig. 39. Stamnos in Paris

Fig. 40. Satyr chorus-men and flute-player
Hydria from Athens

Fig. 41. Hephaistos, Dionysus, satyr chorus-man
Calyx-krater in Vienna

Fig. 42. Calyx-krater from Altamura

Fig. 43. Volute-krater from Spina

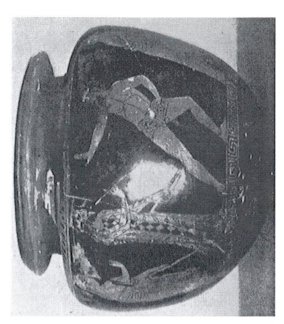

45

44

Fig. 44. Cup fragments in Boston
Fig. 45. Dinos in Athens
Fig. 46. Fragments of bell-krater in Bonn

Fig. 47. Prometheus (?) and satyrs. Krater in Athens

Fig. 48. Orpheus and satyr. Krater in Naples

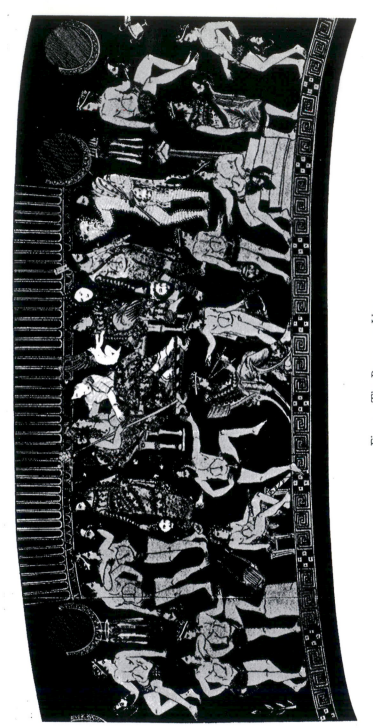

Fig. 49. The Pronomos Vase

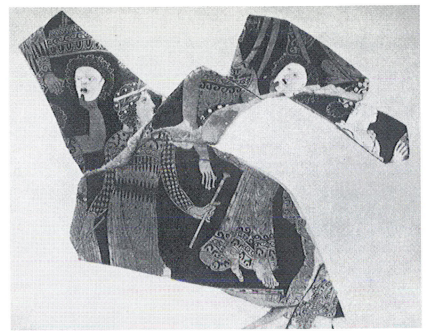

a

b

Fig. 50*a*, *b*. Krater fragments from Taranto

Fig. 50c. Krater fragments from Taranto

Fig. 51. Relief from Peiraeus

Fig. 52 (*left*). Relief in Copenhagen

Fig. 53 (*above*). Fragment from
Athenian Agora

Fig. 54*a*. Actor and mask. Gnathia krater fragment from Taranto

Fig. 54b. Detail of Gnathia fragment from Taranto

Fig. 55. Actor and mask. Painting from Herculaneum

Fig. 56 (*left*). Statue holding mask (Roman copy)

Fig. 58 (*above*). Bronze mask from Peiraeus

Fig. 57. Terracotta mask from Athenian Agora

Fig. 60a. Andromeda (detail)

Fig. 59. Lyssa and Actaeon. Bell-krater from Vico Equense

Fig. 60b. Andromeda

Fig. 62. Dionysus

Fig. 64. Relief by Archelaus of Priene (part)

Fig. 63. Ivory statuette
from Rieti

Fig. 68. Stamnos (Dionysus)

Fig. 67. Lekythos

Fig. 65. Woman putting on boot

Fig. 66. Thamyras

Fig. 69. Bald man

Fig. 70. Amphora (Dionysus)

Fig. 71. Amphora (Dionysus)

Fig. 72. Psykter (Hermes)

Fig. 73. Hydria (Hermes)

Fig. 74. Stamnos (Hermes)

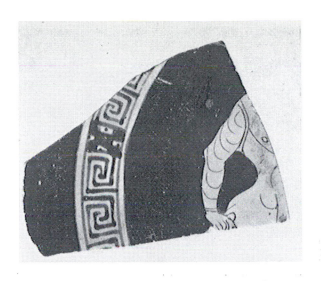

Fig. 75. Cup fragment from Athenian Agora

Fig. 76. Chous from Anavyssos

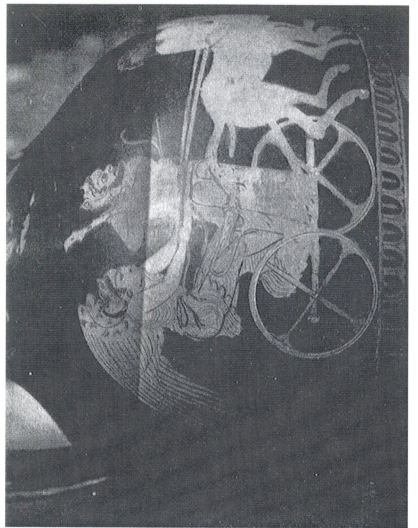

Fig. 77*a*. Chous from Cyrene (Nike, Herakles, and centaur chariot)

b

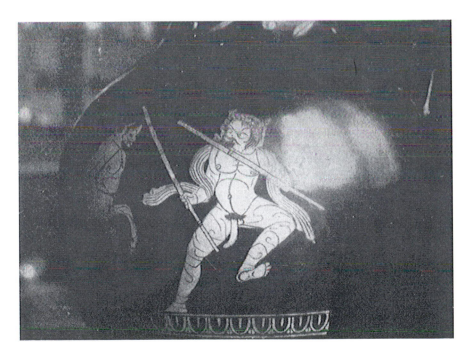

Fig. 77*b, c*. Chous from Cyrene (centaurs and comic dancer)

Fig. 78. Chous in Leningrad

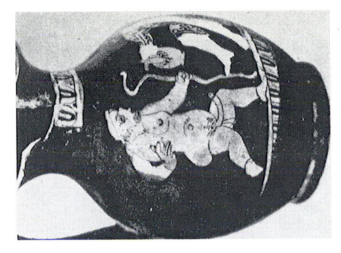

Fig. 81. Chous

Fig. 80. Mask on Amphora

Fig. 79. Chous

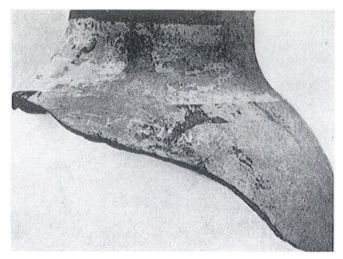

a

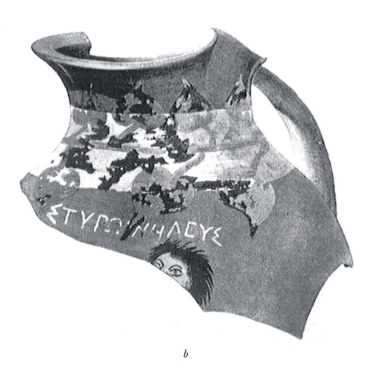

b

Fig. 82. Tyro and Neleus (photograph and water-colour)

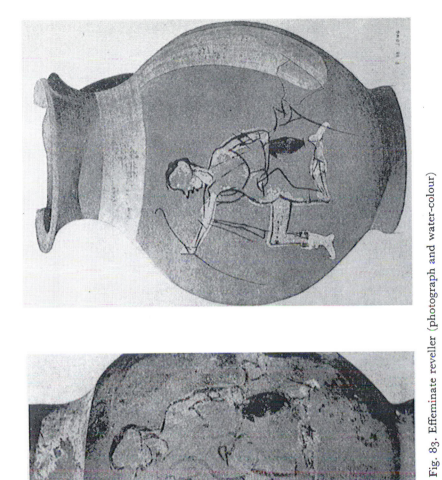

Fig. 83. Effeminate reveller (photograph and water-colour)

Fig. 84*a, b*. Obeliaphoroi (photographs)

Fig. 84c. Obeliaphoroi (water-colour)

Fig. 85. Comic chorus-women

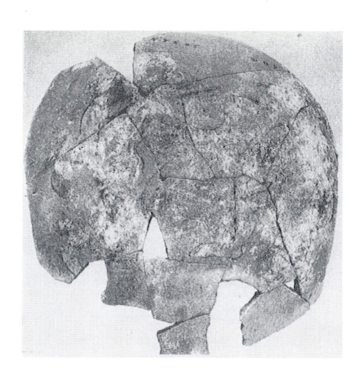

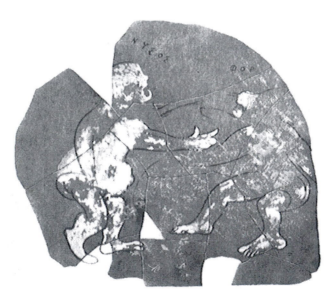

Fig. 86. Dionysus and Phor-
(photograph and water-colour)

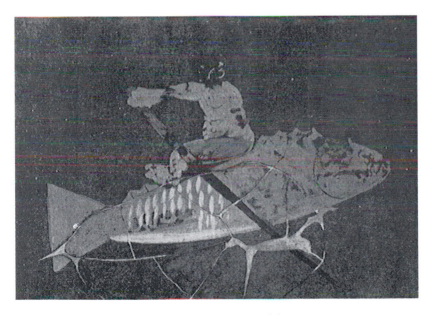

Fig. 87. Oarsman on fish
(photograph and water-colour)

Fig. 88. Marble relief from Lyme Park

Fig. 89. Nurse and baby

Fig. 90. Woman

Fig. 92. Man

Fig. 91. Herakles

Fig. 93. Man carrying
basket

Fig. 94. Water-carrier

Fig. 95. Seated slave

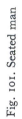

Fig. 99. Fat man

Fig. 98. Man with legs crossed

Fig. 97. Old woman

Fig. 96. Woman raising veil

Fig. 102. Seated man

Fig. 101. Seated man

Fig. 100. Man seated on altar

Fig. 103. Comic cast from Athenian Agora

Fig. 105. Comic scene (South Italian)

Fig. 104. Comic chorus

Fig. 106. Zeus and Hermes
(South Italian)

Fig. 108.
Leading old man (?)

Fig. 107. Kassandra pursues Ajax (South Italian)

Fig. 109. The Menander relief

Fig. 110. Relief in Naples

Fig. 112. Pornoboskos

Fig. 111. Lykomedeios (?)

Fig. 113.
Perfect young man

Fig. 114. Young man

Fig. 115. Young man

Fig. 116. Young man

Fig. 117. Young man

Fig. 118. Kolax

Fig. 119. Parasite

Fig. 120. Sikelikos (?)

Fig. 121. Pappos

Fig. 122. Leading slave
with infant

Fig. 123. Slave

Fig. 124. Slave

Fig. 125. Maison

Fig. 126. Tettix

Fig. 131. Chatterbox (?)

Fig. 128. Old woman

Fig. 129. Old woman

Fig. 127. Slave

Fig. 130. Old woman

Fig. 132. Young woman
(*at top left*)

Fig. 134. Concubine (?)

Fig. 133. Pseudokore

Fig. 135. Hetaira

Fig. 137. Hetaira

Fig. 136. Hetaira

Fig. 138. Girl

Fig. 139. Girl

Fig. 140. Theatre tickets

Fig. 141. The Theatre of Pergamon